The Handbook of MIS Management

Robert E. Umbaugh, Editor

AUERBACH Publishers Inc
Pennsauken NJ

Copyright © 1985 by AUERBACH Publishers Inc

ISBN 0-87769-285-8

All rights reserved. No part of this work covered by the copyright hereon may be reproduced or used in any form or by any means—graphic, electronic, or mechanical, including photocopying, recording, taping, or information storage and retrieval systems—without written permission of the publisher.

Printed in the United States of America

Published in the United States in 1985
by Auerbach Publishers Inc
6560 North Park Drive
Pennsauken, NJ 08109 USA

16 15 14 13 12 11 10 9 8 7 6 5 4 3 2

CONTRIBUTORS

JANET BENSU, *President, Janet Bensu Associates, San Francisco CA*
ALAN BERMAN, *Independent Consultant, Irvington NY*
LAYNE C. BRADLEY, *Vice President, Marketing, Systems Software Division, UCCEL Corp, Dallas TX*
NORMAN H. CARTER, *President, Development Systems International, Studio City CA*
LESLIE S. CHALMERS, *Assistant Vice President for Data Security, Bank of California, San Francisco CA*
RICHARD COTTER, *President, Palantir Systems, Toronto, Ontario*
PHILIP C. CROSS, *Independent Consultant, Tinton Falls NJ*
JOAN DORFMANN, *Managing Editor, Auerbach Publishers, Pennsauken NJ*
KENNETH L. DUNN, *Information Systems Planning Division, General Electric Lighting Business Group, East Cleveland OH*
PAT DURAN, *President, Pat Duran and Associates, La Jolla CA*
WILLIAM R. DURELL, *President, Data Administration Inc, Cypress CA*
LYNDA E. EDWARDS, *Alexandria VA*
THOMAS FLEISHMAN, *Independent Consultant, Van Nuys CA*
FRANCIS A. FRANK, *Vice President of Professional Services, Keane Associates, Boston MA*
LOUIS FRIED, *Director, Advanced Computer Systems Department, SRI International, Palo Alto CA*
THOMAS P. GERRITY, *President and CEO, Index Systems Inc, Cambridge MA*
IAN A. GILHOOLEY, *Manager of Information Services, Pemberton Houston Willoughby Inc, Vancouver, British Columbia*
JERRY GITOMER, *Blue Bell PA*
RANDY J. GOLDFIELD, *Omni Group, New York NY*
WILLIAM A. HANSEN, *President, Hansen Systems Inc, Elk Grove Village IL*
STEVE HEARN, *Manager of Management Support Services, ARCO Petroleum Products Company, Los Angeles CA*
JACK T. HOGUE, *Assistant Professor of MIS, School of Business Administration, University of North Carolina at Charlotte, Charlotte NC*
GERALD I. ISAACSON, *Director of Information Security, Wang Laboratories Inc, Chelmsford MA*
PHILIP N. JAMES, *Chief, Strategic Information Planning, DP Department, Los Angeles County*
ROBERT W. KLENK, JR., *Business Systems Analyst, Computerland, Harrisburg PA*

RICHARD C. KOENIG, *Manager, Computer and Data Security, Union Carbide Corp, Danbury CT*
JOHN A. LACY, *Sales Manager for Business Imaging Systems, Eastman Kodak, Rochester NY*
DAVID P. LEVIN, *President, Netcomm Inc, New York NY*
ROSE LOCKWOOD, *Omni Group, New York NY*
AL MCCREADY, *Manager of Information Systems Consulting, Arthur Young & Co, Salt Lake City UT*
CHUCK MADDOX, *Cincinnati OH*
SANDRA M. MANN, *ADP Security, Security Pacific National Bank, Glendale CA*
ALEXIA MARTIN, *Management Systems Consultant, Information Systems Management Center, Management and Economics Group, SRI International, Menlo Park CA*
JOHN W. MENTZER, *Data Center Director, Peterson, Howell, and Heather Inc, Baltimore MD*
MARTIN E. MODELL, *Information Resource Manager, Merrill Lynch, New York NY*
JAMES H. MORGAN, *J.H. Morgan Consultants, Morristown NJ*
MIKE MUSHET, *Southern California Edison Company, Rosemead CA*
ROGER N. NAGEL, *Professor of Computer Science and Electrical Engineering and Director of Institute for Robotics, Lehigh University, Bethlehem PA*
RICHARD J. NAUER, *Manager of Data Administration, Mobil Corp, New York NY*
JACOB NUSSBAUM, *President of Nussbaum Associates Inc, St Louis MO*
NICHOLAS G. ODREY, *Associate Professor of Industrial Engineering and Director of the Robotics Laboratory at the Institute for Robotics, Lehigh University, Bethlehem PA*
DAVID O. OLSON, *President, The Computer Workshop, Drexel Hill PA*
WILLIAM E. PERRY, *Executive Director, Quality Assurance Institute, Orlando FL*
G. SANDBERG, *IBM Nordic Field Systems Center, Stockholm, Sweden*
WILLIAM E. SANDERS, *Vice President and Director, Information Systems, Gibraltar Savings, Burbank CA*
DENNIS R. SCHUSTER, *Manager of Data Base Administration, General Electric Lighting Business Group, East Cleveland OH*
ERIC STANFORD, *Supervising Auditor, Internal Auditing Department, Atlantic Richfield Company, Los Angeles CA*
FRANK STANLEY, *Technical Services Manager, Computer Task Group, Independence OH*
OTTO SZENTISI, *Vice President and General Manager of Siecor Optical Cable Accessories and Test Equipment, Siecor Corp, Hickory NC*
RICHARD P. TEN DYKE, *Pound Ridge NY*
JOHN M. THOMPSON, *Vice President, Index Systems Inc, Cambridge MA*

DAVID R. TOMMELA, *Assistant Manager, Information Systems, Southern California Edison Company, Rosemead CA*
ROBERT E. UMBAUGH, *Vice President, Southern California Edison Company, Rosemead CA*
RAYMOND WATROUS, *Research Scientist, Siemens Corp, Princeton NJ*
JOHN WHALEN, *MIS Special Projects Administrator, RCA, Camden NJ*
BRYAN WILKINSON, *Manager of EDP Auditing, Teledyne Inc, Los Angeles CA*
BRUCE WINROW, *Wolfe Computer Aptitude Testing, Oradell NJ*
CHARLES M. WISEMAN, *Manager of Corporate Information Systems Planning and Education Services, Greenwich CT*
RAYMOND J. WULF, *Marketing Director for Mass Memory Products, Eastman Kodak, Rochester NY*
MARVIN V. ZELKOWITZ, *Department of Computer Science, University of Maryland, College Park MD*
GARY ZIELKE, *Infotel Systems, Delta, British Columbia*

Contents

Introduction xiii

SECTION I POLICY, PLANNING, AND CONTROL 1

    1 Strategic and Long-Range Planning for MIS 3

    2 Using Information for Competitive Advantage 15

    3 Planning for MIS Resource Usage 23

    4 Corporate Information Processing Policies 41

    5 The MIS Procedures Manual 49

SECTION II MANAGEMENT ISSUES 71

    1 The Leadership Role of the CEO in Information Technology 73

    2 MBO for MIS 79

    3 Steering Committees—Some Thoughts on Pros & Cons 91

    4 How Should Users Pay for MIS Services? 99

SECTION III ORGANIZATION 115

    1 To Centralize or Not to Centralize? 117

    2 Coping with Change: Project Management 131

    3 Integrating Information Technologies 141

SECTION IV SYSTEMS DEVELOPMENT AND PROGRAMMING 149

    1 Application Portfolio Planning 151

    2 Establishing Priorities for Application Systems 161

    3 An Approach to Effective Implementation 173

    4 Structured Methodology 189

    5 Analysis and Design—A Structured Approach 199

Contents

    6 Programming and Testing—A Structured Approach .. 209

    7 Software Engineering Concepts and Techniques 219

    8 Preparing for a System Cost/Benefit Analysis 249

    9 Performing a Cost/Benefit Analysis 257

  10 Controlling Projects: PERT/CPM 271

SECTION V END-USER COMPUTING AND OFFICE SYSTEMS 283

    1 The Information Center—A Powerful Tool 285

    2 Getting the Most from Personal Computers 295

    3 Controlling Personal Computing 303

    4 Guide to Decision Support Systems 311

    5 Managing Office Systems Development 319

    6 Workstation Ergonomics 325

    7 Tying Office Computing to Resource Planning 333

SECTION VI DATA COMMUNICATIONS 345

    1 Data Communications Management 347

    2 Planning for Networks 357

    3 Voice and Data—Putting Them Together 369

    4 Satisfying Data Communications Needs 383

    5 Security for Local Area Networks 399

SECTION VII MANAGING THE DATA CENTER 407

    1 Developing Standards for the Data Center 409

    2 Integrating the Multivendor Environment 415

    3 Career Planning for Data Center Personnel 421

    4 Balancing Data Center Staff and Workload 431

    5 Do You Need a UPS? 437

    6 Designing the Data Center: A Checklist 455

Contents

SECTION VIII DATA BASE MANAGEMENT 469

1. The Manager's Role in Data Bases 471
2. Controlling the DB Environment 481
3. Centralized Versus Decentralized Data Bases 489
4. Improving the Quality of Data 501
5. An Introduction to Relational Data Bases 511

SECTION IX MANAGING THE HUMAN RESOURCE 525

1. Human Resource Management 527
2. Testing MIS Personnel 539
3. Interviewing Techniques 547
4. Succession Planning and MIS—Structure from Chaos 559
5. Personnel Motivation: Benefits & Techniques 575

SECTION X MIS SECURITY 585

1. Protecting Information Resources 587
2. People: The Key to Security 599
3. Physical Security Measures 609
4. Managing Data Security 621
5. Data Security Standards 629
6. Open Network Security 639

SECTION XI EDP AUDITING 649

1. Do You Need an EDP Auditor? 651
2. An Audit Plan for MIS 661
3. Auditing the Security of Your Data Center 669
4. Taking Full Advantage of EDP Auditors 689

Contents

SECTION XII QUALITY ENHANCEMENT 699

   1 Systems Development and Quality Control 701

   2 Software QA 711

   3 Verification and Validation of Software 723

SECTION XIII PRODUCTIVITY IMPROVEMENT 737

   1 Running MIS Like a Business 739

   2 Improving MIS Productivity 745

   3 Office Technology Brings Higher White-Collar Productivity 761

   4 A Path to Improved Productivity—Effective Data Management 767

SECTION XIV NEW DIRECTIONS IN TECHNOLOGY 777

   1 Robotics and Robotics Software 779

   2 Advances in Fiber Optics 791

   3 Optical Disk Technology 801

   4 Graphics Terminal Technology 811

   5 Speech Recognition and Voice Response Technology 819

   6 Expert Systems and Artificial Intelligence 827

Epilogue 837

Index Index-1

Introduction

There is nothing permanent but Change.
Heraclitus, 513 B.C.

The challenges of a rapidly changing technology and an increasingly demanding management responsibility have spurred the information processing industry to take a new look at how the MIS function is managed. Until recently, information processing has been a support, or staff, function, regarded as an overhead cost and rarely as a revenue producer. The common test of value for information processing technology has been, "How much can we save?" Now, however, we are entering a new era, one in which information processing can play a more active role in the mainstream of many businesses—a role that can enhance profit through revenue improvement rather than solely through cost reduction.

Still, many of us work in an environment in which information technology cannot be directly applied to increasing revenue. Or we are involved with government, academic, or nonprofit organizations, where the emphasis is on enhanced quality of service. However, senior management in all types of organizations is beginning to realize that information can have significant strategic importance and that it can now be delivered in a more convenient and easier to use form. New technologies are making the promise of information as a corporate resource a reality.

The application of these new technologies brings with it a new role for the MIS manager; at the same time, the ongoing transaction-based MIS processes must continue to be skillfully managed. We must not only understand, integrate, and optimize digital communications networks, robotics, decision support systems, automated point-of-sale devices, artificial intelligence, and a host of other promising technologies; we must also maintain—and, in many cases, enhance—the baseline systems that support the fundamental processes of our organizations.

This expanded scope means pressure for the MIS manager to play a larger role at the corporate level, increased visibility, and, often, new interfaces previously denied the MIS manager. From this new situation comes the need for this book. Today's MIS manager needs a source of advice, guidance, and workable ideas on how to prosper in such an environment. This book attempts to balance an understanding of technology with the need to *manage* that technology and the people who implement it. We have many sources of information in the technology arena but few sources on managing technology successfully.

Introduction

To put the process of MIS management in perspective, we need a few words on the nature of management and the environment in which we carry out that process.

THE NATURE OF MANAGEMENT

"Management is work, and as such it has its own skills, its own tools, its own techniques."[1] With these words, Peter Drucker introduces his thoughts on management as an occupation. Drucker is perhaps the United States' most gifted thinker on management as a complex process that integrates a diverse collection of related but distinct tasks. An accomplished historian of management processes, Drucker has been able to amalgamate improvements in these processes into management strategies that those of us operating in complex environments can make use of to become better managers.

One of the best definitions of the term *manager* that I know is that a manager is one who is responsible for the work of others as well as for his or her own work. Drucker says that this is not enough. Management responsibility goes beyond work and includes responsibility for contribution; that is, adding something worthwhile both to the process of managing and to the organization as a whole.[2]

I prefer the former definition. Work is traditionally defined as goal-oriented behavior. Given this, the definition of managing can be expanded to state, "management, the work of managers, is the process of being responsible for the goal-oriented behavior of others as well as for the goal-oriented behavior of oneself." Implied in this definition, of course, is responsibility for integration. What we have, then, is management as the process of integrating the behavior of a number of individuals, including oneself, and seeing to it that the behavior is goal-oriented.

This process works quite well as long as we have goals that are predetermined and that contribute positively to the organization. The process of setting these predefined goals is called planning.

One example, of sharp, clean goal setting comes from Lee Iacocca. In his mid-thirties, Iacocca became the head of the Ford Division at Ford Motor Company. By that time, he had perfected a unique management style. Iacocca used this process at Ford, and he uses it today at the company he helped bring back from the ashes, Chrysler. He asks those managers working for him to write down the objectives they plan on achieving in the next three months. He then wants to know their priorities, their plan for reaching these objectives, and, specifically, how they expect to go about successfully meeting these objectives. These objectives then become the standards against which his people are measured.[3] This process has worked well for the man who has become one of the United States' most widely recognized successful managers.

As long as the goals are rather simple and well defined and the workforce is small, the job of management is not all that demanding.

Introduction

When the goals become complex, long range, and ill defined and the workforce becomes large, the job becomes something else indeed. Most MIS managers find themselves in this latter situation. Add to this the environment in which our work takes place, with all of its internal and external influences, and we have a most demanding challenge.

THE ENVIRONMENT

What of the environment in which MIS work takes place today? Let's review a few of the influencing factors that are common to most MIS shops.

Some would say that change is a key influencing factor. Change, however, is the result of internal and external forces and not one itself. Because change is difficult to describe, it can best be understood and addressed if it is approached from the perspective of its causes.

Clearly, technology causes change, often even when we do not adopt it ourselves. This idea is not new to those of us who have been in the computer field for some time. What is new is the speed with which new technology is being introduced and brought to the market. Deciding which technologies apply and in which form and keeping pace with technological developments is both intellectually demanding and time consuming.

Another factor prompting change is the new definition of what constitutes an information system. An information system used to be something that we in MIS built—or, very rarely, bought—and ran on our computers. Now it's something gotten somehow by almost anyone and run on who knows what computer. This is otherwise known as end-user computing: the source of joy for thousands and a challenge for we few MIS managers. This is a healthy development that undoubtedly will make substantial contributions to mankind in the long run but that today is making the MIS manager's job more complex.

Michael Porter of the Harvard Business School frequently speaks out on the potential benefits of this new view of information systems.[4] Porter was among the first to recognize that information, as such, can be used to competitive advantage far beyond the traditional notion that "the more you know the better off you are." His articulation of the idea of using information to erect barriers to entrance to a market has helped many corporate executives take a new look at information as a corporate asset. For many, Information (capitalized here to differentiate it from traditional marketing intelligence) has become a marketing tool for the first time. This strategic use of Information, in addition to the nontraditional uses of information processing hardware (e.g., ATMs), has elevated the importance and visibility of information processing in many organizations.

Yet another external factor is the push of technology. Never before has new technology been conceived, developed, and brought to the market as quickly as has today's information processing technology. It is not uncommon for new microcomputer-based technology to eclipse existing products every 9 to 12 months. In many cases, the push of technology is the

Introduction

cause of change because the technology is developed and commercialized before a *need* exists. The personal computer is a good example of this phenomenon. No groundswell of demand preceded the introduction of personal computers; rather, personal computers were brought to the market and then the demand, or need, for them was created. I doubt that any long-range information systems plan stated the need for such a device before the personal computer was introduced. The same may be true for what is happening in artificial intelligence today. The technology is emerging, and many MIS managers are asking themselves, "What is this stuff good for?"

With each new wave of technology comes better price performance. This trend, which includes communications technology, will continue to the point where, very soon, most needs or wants will be technically and economically feasible. As a result, preoccupation with traditional cost justification will diminish, and value enhancement will rise in its place. This is not to say that the need to measure the wisdom and quality of the investment in information technology will vanish; rather, that the metrics will take on a new dimension.

These forces, and others, are making a demanding job even tougher. Managing MIS organizations has never been easy. There are many examples of failure and, sadly, only a few of success. But we can learn from the successes.

We know that those who survive and, in fact, flourish in the field are quick to adapt to changes in their environment. New and different skills, properly applied, are called for when the environment changes. Some lecture circuit wags like to refer to large existing systems as "dinosaurs," and there is an element of truth in the simile, but *only* an element. These wags predict that the sky will fall on the dinosaurs, crushing them. This need not be the case if we, as MIS managers, are skillful in the way we adopt and adapt new approaches to the way we manage the process and the systems themselves.

Part of this adaptation involves recognition of the forces shaping the changes we are experiencing and an intelligent response. Better planning is a cornerstone of this process. One recent article suggested that any MIS manager who wastes time planning when technology is changing so fast is crazy. Nothing could be further from the truth. In periods of rapid change, systematically assessing the environment, plotting a path, and measuring progress is exactly what *is* needed. Even in periods of rapid change, a good plan provides something from which to intelligently divert. You thus know *why* you correct the course and do not just drift blindly in different directions.

Associated with the need to plan well is the need for better techniques and methods to help in the other responsibilities of MIS management. This handbook provides suggestions for procedures, techniques, practices, and methods that you can adopt outright or modify to meet your needs.

Introduction

The sections of *The Handbook of MIS Management* are organized by topic area and cover such traditional topics as systems development, security, and operations. We have also included sections on current management issues, data communications, emerging technologies, quality improvement, and policies and planning. The objective of the handbook is to balance the two major aspects of our job: technology and management.

HOW TO USE THIS HANDBOOK

In his book presenting a new manifesto for the information processing community, renowned author and lecturer James Martin offers a discourse on the differences between structured information processing, which he calls prespecified, and ad-hoc computing, which he labels user driven.[5] These two types of information processing must, of course, be properly balanced so that they complement not conflict with each other. No truly observant practitioner would advocate the total abdication of computing as we've known it for the past 30 years in order to put full and absolute responsibility on the user. Who, for example, would favor running the corporate payroll in the uncontrolled environment characteristic of personal computer users today? On the other hand, user-directed, user-driven computing is here to stay. In fact, it will continue to flourish as users become more sophisticated and, in particular, as microcomputer-based software becomes even more powerful.

Martin goes on to advocate changes in the way we do both types of computing, and the emphasis *is* on change. Change, in fact, is what has brought Martin and others like him to the forefront of the information processing scene, and, as long as they are skillful observers of that scene, they will remain there. Those of us who are not at the forefront, who are not the industry spokespersons, but who must manage the use of information processing technology to the benefit of our organizations, live these challenges every day. This book is intended to help in this effort. It addresses the real everyday problems that most of us face and offers solutions to them. It is a handbook—meaning that it should be kept close at hand, ready for reference. It isn't intended to be read once and put away.

In compiling this handbook, I have tried to make use of as many examples, checklists, outlines, and sample graphics as practical. Specific recommendations for action are included in every chapter. Not all will apply to every situation, but they should serve as a starting point to develop solutions to the problems you face in your environment. Sometimes we make a point more than once in order to reinforce a particular concept or to allow a section or chapter in a section to stand alone.

In the section on emerging technologies, many topics could not be included because of space considerations. This does not mean that we believe that a specific technology has not evolved to the point of commercial applicability or is not as important as others. It is our intent to cover other emerging technologies in future editions of the handbook.

Introduction

An extensive index is provided that should guide you to the section of the handbook most applicable to your area of concern. Chapter headings can also be scanned to lead you to points of interest.

I encourage you to use the handbook as a reference and as a source of ideas that you can draw on to become a more effective manager of information processing technology and a greater contributor to the success of your organization.

Robert E. Umbaugh
Rosemead, California
November 1985

References

1. P.F. Drucker, *Management: Tasks, Responsibilities, Practices* (New York: Harper and Row, 1974), X.
2. Drucker, 390-395.
3. L. Iacocca and W. Novak, *Iacocca* (New York: Bantam Books, 1984).
4. M.E. Porter and V.E. Millar, "How Information Gives You Competitive Advantage," *Harvard Business Review* 63:4 (July-August 1985): 149–160.
5. J. Martin, *An Information Systems Manifesto* (Englewood Cliffs, NJ: Prentice-Hall Inc. 1984).

Section I
Policy, Planning, and Control

As discussed in the introduction to this handbook, planning is the keystone of effective MIS management. But planning is not easy; if it were, we would all do it and do it well. Easy or not, however, planning is necessary. For proof of this, you need only look at any consultant's report on the review of a failing MIS department; inevitably, the absence of good planning is a major cause of the failure

Information systems management can significantly influence the effectiveness and success of the organizations they support. To do so, however, MIS executives must build a solid working partnership with their colleagues in senior management. One important element that supports this partnership is an excellent strategic and long-range planning process. Chapter I-1, "Strategic and Long-Range Planning for MIS," suggests guidelines for establishing such a process and for producing the necessary plans.

The past 20 years have brought dramatic changes in the way organizations process and use information. At the center of this revolution is MIS management, pressed by technological developments and user demand for information resources. In Chapter I-2, "Using Information for Competitive Advantage," we examine the opportunities that have arisen for MIS management as a result of these changes and suggest a new approach to assessing the value of information systems.

To take full advantage of the power of advanced information processing technologies, resource planning must be carefully done. Unfortunately, resource planning has received little attention in the trade press and in training programs for MIS management. In addition to general planning principles, there are unique requirements involved in planning for complex DP installations. Chapter I-3, "Planning for MIS Resource Usage," describes a method for analyzing present load requirements and projecting future demand. It also presents techniques for managing peak load requirements.

Guiding the planning process, as well as other functions of MIS management, are the policies and procedures of the organization. Data processing is an integral part of most organizations; in too many cases, however, this fact is not reflected in corporate policies. To meet the organization's information needs effectively, MIS management must establish a corporate information policy, an activity that requires an understanding of corporate goals and the role of MIS in achieving them. Chapter I-4, "Corporate Information Processing Policies," explains how the MIS manager can work with senior management to define organizationwide information policies and guidelines.

Many organizations rely on word of mouth or on scattered directives and memoranda to communicate guidelines, set objectives, and teach employees new tasks. This can prove to be a rather haphazard method of operating, however. Word of mouth can go in one ear and out the other, and memos and directives can slip through cracks in desks, never to be seen again. A comprehensive and effectively enforced set of policies and procedures can increase management control, promote consistency in operations, and improve productivity by providing readily available guidelines for employees performing new or unfamiliar tasks. Chapter I-5, "The MIS Procedures Manual," provides an overview of MIS policies and procedures and describes how to coordinate, administer, interpret, and introduce procedures in the DP installation.

I-1

Strategic and Long-Range Planning for MIS

Philip N. James

INTRODUCTION

Despite more than 25 years of experience with computers, management can still face unpleasant surprises from its data processing operations. Frequently, these surprises result from inadequate strategic and long-range planning.

Long-range planning for MIS traditionally has focused on the prioritization of application development or acquisition projects. Necessary as this focus is, it misses the mark by failing to assess the impact of strategic considerations, such as changes in the organization's business, in its culture, or in technology. These considerations may drastically affect both the organization's information requirements and the ways in which they might be met.

Further, most MIS plans fail to identify how the information resource can lead to significant improvements in the organization's competitive posture and success. Today's deregulated financial services industry is a good example of this. Plans should promote change—constructive change—and prepare the organization to take advantage of this change, not merely adapt to it.

THE PLANNING PROCESS

Planning can be categorized in several ways, some of which are described in the following paragraphs. The basic objective of planning, however, is to provide a basis for today's actions and decisions that ensures that the organization's resources are effectively and efficiently acquired and used in support of its mission. Planning is also the rational management of change.

One way of viewing planning is in the context of the organization's mission, as described in the following paragraphs.

Strategic planning is concerned with the mission itself and how it changes in response to the organization and its environment. For the information systems management department, strategic planning means understanding enough about the organization's business and its information requirements to remain effectively supportive.

The results of strategic information resource planning include decisions about direction, often expressed as a "strategic vision" of the future; goals and objectives for achieving the strategic vision; and strategies and action plans for achieving the goals and objectives. The strategic vision should be crisp and motivating for employees at all levels. NASA's strategic vision during the sixties was ". . . to land a man on the moon by the end of the decade . . . ," not ". . . to achieve preeminence in space exploration and travel . . . ."

As Figure 1 shows, planning is a cyclic process, producing actions that cause results and learning from the results. (The key role of environmental analysis is shown in this figure.) Figure 2 shows that the result of planning is action plans for each manager that support the mission and goals of the organization. Figure 3 illustrates this concept differently and also indicates that strategies should be based on the organization's mission and strengths, its competitors' weaknesses, and the opportunities in the environment.

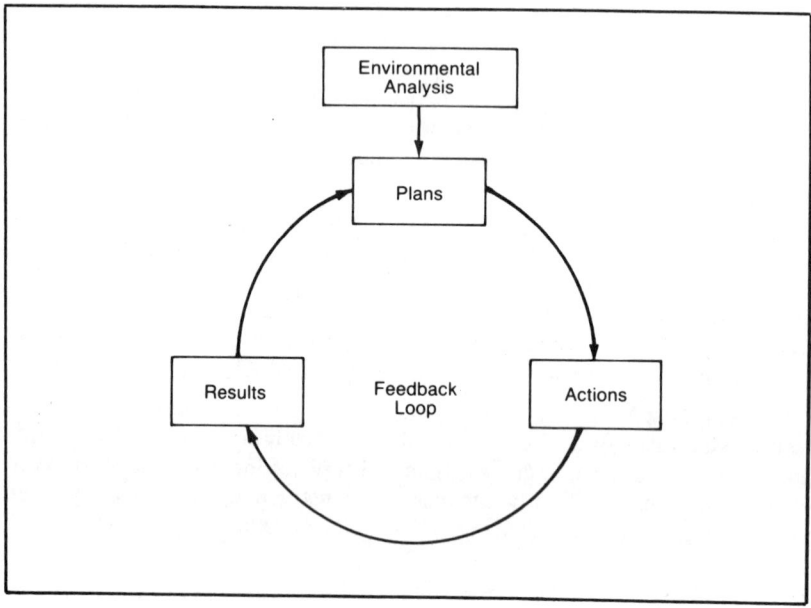

Figure 1. The Planning Process

Tactical planning, given the mission, goals, objectives, and action plans of strategic planning, involves ensuring that the action plans can be carried out. This includes identifying milestones and estimating the resources required for completing them. The one- or two-year budget, the plans for specific projects (e.g., a large application development project), and the master manufacturing plan are examples of tactical plans.

Operational planning is the planning of the daily work required to carry out the action plans, including the management and measurement of the process. Shop floor scheduling in manufacturing and the production schedule of a data center are examples.

Planning can also be characterized by its time frame, as noted in the following paragraphs.

Strategic and Long-Range Planning

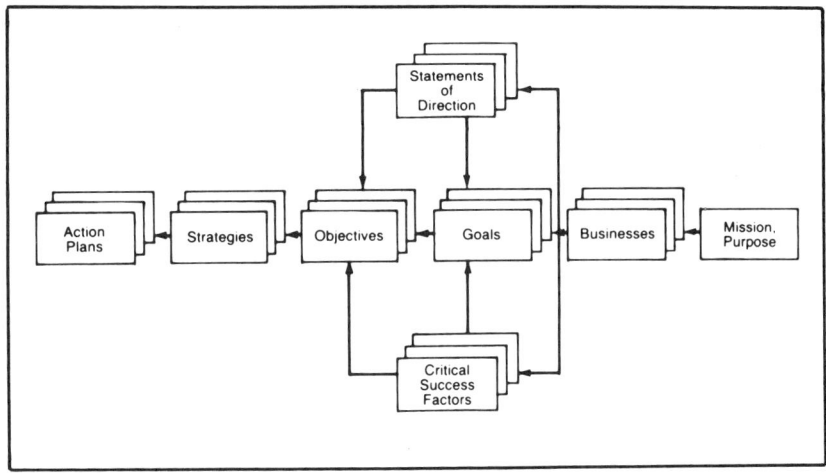

Figure 2. The Objectives of Strategic Planning

Long-range planning usually involves looking at least five years ahead. In some industries (e.g., utilities, forest products), the planning horizon is 20 to 30 years. As a general principle, the planning horizon should reflect the time required to respond to change.

Short-range planning includes one- or two-year financial planning (budgeting), project planning for project management, most operational planning, and other forms of planning for the immediate future.

It is important to maintain a clear distinction between long-range and strategic planning because the two are not synonymous. Long-range planning is

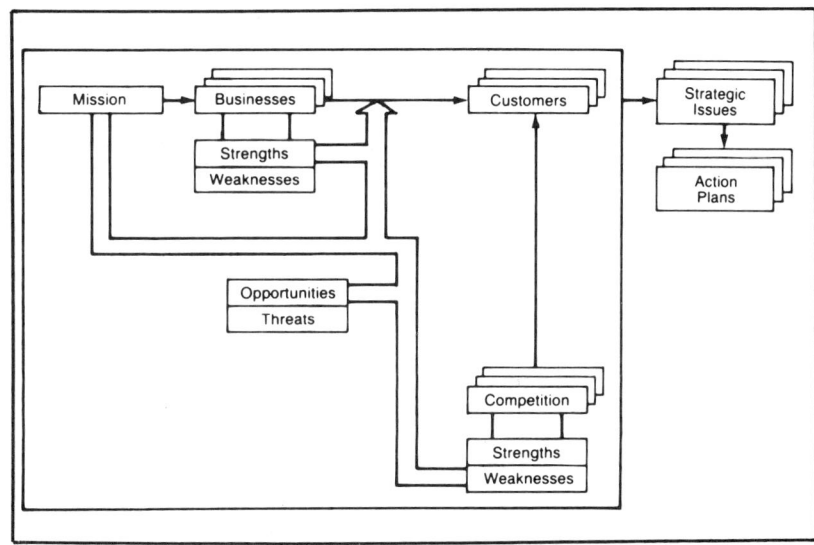

Figure 3. Strategic Business Planning

always long term in nature, whereas strategic planning may be a quick response to an opportunity or threat that requires a fundamental change in the organization's mission or direction. The real distinction is in the emphasis. Strategic planning looks at the few key issues that determine the organization's future course. A strategic plan may be quite short, sometimes only a few paragraphs. Long-range planning follows strategic planning and sets out a chart for navigating the course.

Planning also can be categorized with respect to what is planned. An information resource plan, for example, must address the following elements:
- The information systems requirements of the organization
- The resources needed to meet those requirements, including:
  —Human. Managerial, professional and technical, operational; recruitment, skills/training, career planning
  —Physical. Technology (i.e., hardware, software, systems, and configurations in data processing, telecommunications, and office automation, plus the tools used in the storage and processing of non-machine-readable information), facilities, and miscellaneous equipment and supplies
  —Financial. Operating, capital
  —Information. Has the value of this resource been seriously considered?
- Organizational plans for deploying and controlling the resources.

WHY PLAN?

Frank W. Lynch, president of Northrop Corporation, once said, "If you can't articulate it, you can't do it." A formal planning process forces managers to articulate their objectives, priorities, and action plans. Among the advantages of a formal, documented information resource plan are:
- It expresses management's current understanding of the information resource and how that understanding is expected to evolve during the planning period.
- It identifies and justifies resource requirements during the planning period, helping ensure that the resources will be available. In addition, in a distributed environment it can identify cost-saving and cost-sharing opportunities provided by, for example, surplus equipment, shared software development and acquisition efforts, and the concentration of technical resources.
- It identifies opportunities for effective resource management, including collaboration among departments or divisions within the organization.
- It publicizes the organization's strategic issues and allows them to be addressed by the creative resources of the entire organization.
- It provides a strategic vision as a touchstone to guide current decisions.
- It specifies action plans for achieving objectives.
- The strategic planning process builds commitment to shared objectives and is one element in an effective management team–building-program.
- Properly communicated, it can also provide a powerful stimulus and sense of direction to employees at all levels, focusing their efforts, increasing their productivity, and making them feel that they are a genuine part of the enterprise.

Strategic and Long-Range Planning

- Plans allow more effective responses to unexpected changes in the business environment, often avoiding crisis management.

A key value of documented plans is that they can be improved by taking advantage of insights offered by colleagues.

THE STRATEGIC PLANNING PROCESS

To be effective, the strategic planning process must be driven by the organization's chief executive officer and supported by the significant involvement of the functional executives who report to him or her. It should be a continuous process capable of recognizing and responding to change.

The professional planner catalyzes, facilitates, and supports this process, usually providing a methodology that ensures that the process takes place, involves the right people in the right way, and addresses the right issues. Business planning and information resource planning may be separate processes, but they must be closely coordinated, and the same individuals must be involved in both.

The strategic planning process includes three primary steps: enterprise analysis, environmental analysis, and strategic synthesis.

Enterprise Analysis

The critical first step in strategic information resource planning is to acquire an understanding of the organization being supported. Most organizations consist of a single enterprise—a flow of information and material to deliver a family of products or services sold at a profit. If more than one enterprise is involved, the following comments apply to each.

The basic business processes of most enterprises are remarkably stable. The enterprise's method of organization to carry out the process frequently changes, and the details of the process must change to reflect a changing product mix and marketplace. But the basic structure of information and material flow is surprisingly constant.

It is important to identify the stable elements of an enterprise through a systems approach to enterprise analysis and then to build an information architecture that models the enterprise in terms of those stable elements from the top down in a highly structured way. Among the common approaches to enterprise analysis are IBM's business systems planning, Rockart's critical success factors, James Martin's subject data bases, Chen's entity-relationship models, and systems engineering methodologies. The enterprise model, once complete, must be subjected to rigorous configuration management to ensure that it continues to be a valid model of the business.

This enterprise model becomes the basis for applying information management technologies that support the enterprise. These technologies include the portfolio of data processing applications, the office technologies, and telecommunications. Information resource planning is thus driven by the information needs of the organization, not by information technologies.

Environmental Analysis

The second step in strategic planning is environmental analysis. An organization's information resource is embedded in a complex milieu that includes the organization, the business environment and marketplace in which it operates, the social, political, and economic environment in which it conducts business, and the MIS management profession, including the dynamic world of information technology. Successful management of the information resource depends on having an understanding and awareness of this environment in order to detect change, assess its impact, and trigger changes in the strategic plan.

In addition to the business plan, the evolving environment of information resource planning includes:
- Changing ideas about the nature and use of the information resource and cultural attitudes toward these changes
- Changing technologies for managing the information resource, including changing cost/performance relationships
- Changing attitudes toward technology itself
- Changing characteristics and perceptions as well as the availability of MIS professionals
- Changing characteristics and perceptions of information resource users

Environmental analysis rarely is done systematically as a part of information resource planning. As a result, the MIS organization has often failed to anticipate change. Examples include the pressure for distributed processing and the explosion of personal computers.

The environment can be studied in many ways. Among them are business planning techniques, which focus on customers (users), competitors (vendors and other information services suppliers), strengths and weaknesses, and opportunities and threats. In addition, future research methodologies seek to identify the most probable range of alternative futures in order to identify robust strategies for dealing with them. (Information about futures research techniques, which include Delphi, inferential scanning, and cross-impact analysis, can be obtained from many academic centers for futures research, such as that at the University of Southern California.)

Strategic Synthesis

Once the enterprise and its environment are well understood, a good strategic planning process will address the elements discussed in the following section in some depth. Sometimes this process can be done without documentation. This is often the case with strong centrally managed organizations and was reasonably effective a decade or two ago. In today's world of participatory management, however, a documented plan developed through a group process is preferable because it focuses the energies of the group toward achieving the planned results.

Mission and Market Share. The MIS department's mission may be to satisfy all the information needs of the organization, or management may prefer to segment the market and focus on it selectively. Some common segments are business data processing, technical computing, office automation, data communications, and voice communications. A strategic plan should state explicitly any segmentation planned and should indicate the following:

Strategic and Long-Range Planning

- The share of the total market represented by each segment
- The share of the total market provided by each of the departments serving a segment, plus any outside providers
- The market segments targeted by each competitor and their share of that segment

The elements of strategic planning are discussed in the following paragraphs.

Market. The MIS department's "market" usually is the information needs of the organization it supports. Departments that sell services outside the company will have other markets.

Strategic Vision. A statement of the department's philosophy and of the long-range goals it seeks to achieve make up the strategic vision.

Objectives. Objectives are specific quantifiable results that must occur if the department's goals are to be achieved.

Milestones. For each objective, milestones represent the identifiable events en route to its achievement, with planned dates.

Roadblocks. This element includes anything the department foresees as an obstacle to achieving an objective, together with a strategy for minimizing its impact.

Customers and Stakeholders. Customers actually buy services or products from the department. Stakeholders have an interest in what the department does and can affect its success but do not actually make the purchasing decisions. In a payroll system, for example, there may be customers who bought the system (e.g., the vice-president of finance), customers who buy services provided by the system (e.g., paymasters), and stakeholders who receive the system's products (e.g., all employees). In the best-selling book *In Search of Excellence*,[1] Thomas Peters and Robert Waterman show the importance of knowing the customers and their needs intimately. There is also ample evidence that similar in-depth understanding of key stakeholders is important.

Competitors. Competitors are those who seek to replace the department in providing for its customers' needs. Strategies for competition include better products or services, lower costs, and faster response.

Strengths and Weaknesses. If it is to compete effectively, the department must have a clear understanding of its strengths and weaknesses as well as those of each of its competitors in relation to meeting the needs of its customers.

Opportunities and Threats. A key element in the competitive environment is just that: the environment. This concerns the state of the economy, the state of technology, and anything else that could conceivably affect the department's ability to compete. From this universe, the department must identify opportunities and threats in order to capitalize on the former and avoid the latter.

Action Plans. The planning process is not complete until action plans for each manager are in place that ensure the completion of milestones and the achievement of objectives.

Issues. Many issues surface and are resolved during the planning process. Those important issues that are not resolved become strategic issues that affect success but that, for a host of reasons, cannot be resolved unilaterally.

Critical Success Factors. These are the select things that must go right if the department is to succeed. They are leading indicators, not trailing indicators such as accounting data.

Scenarios. Often the best way to develop an understanding of the department's strategic vision is through the use of scenarios. Although these are most effective when done graphically, narrative descriptions are often effective as well. As backup, any assumptions made should be documented.

STRATEGIC AND LONG-RANGE PLANNING GUIDELINES

The following sections present guidelines for preparing strategic and long-range MIS plans.

Planning Products

The tangible product of the planning process is a hierarchy of documented plans. The *strategic plan* states the organization's mission, strategic vision, goals and objectives, strategies, and issues in the context of its understanding of the enterprise and the environment. The *long-range plan* supports the strategic plan and is a road map for implementing the strategies and achieving the objectives through the effective deployment of resources. It also provides historical information so that the continuity of the program and any discontinuities it contains are visible. The *budget* is a detailed statement of planned actions (including the use of resources) for accomplishing that subset of action plans over a year or two. The *action plans* themselves—including project management plans for specific projects, plans for each functional area, and plans for each organizational unit—are the plans through which work is actually accomplished.

All of these plans are products of a hierarchy of processes. They provide snapshot views of the integrated planning process as well as document it. Among their primary objectives are the documentation of such required resources as financial, material, human, and information.

Documentation of the resources needed is particularly useful because planning is, and must be, a dynamic process. When the environment changes, the planning documents help redeploy resources without damaging sensitive programs.

The following discussion applies to the strategic and long-range plan and should be useful for the general manager and his or her key functional executives as well as for the key executives in MIS.

Strategic and Long-Range Planning

Plan Contents

In addition to an executive summary and introduction, a comprehensive plan should contain the sections described in the following sections.

Philosophy, Mission, and Direction. This section summarizes the organization's current concept of the information resource, its management, and its use in the business; how those concepts are likely to change; and the primary catalysts for change during the planning period.

The Enterprise. This section documents the MIS department's understanding of the enterprise, its information requirements, how these requirements are being met, and how this situation is expected to evolve during the planning period.

The Planning Environment. This section documents the nature of the MIS management environment and how it is expected to change during the planning period.

The Nature and Scope of the Information Resource. This section should discuss the various components of the information resource, explain how they are managed and coordinated in the organization to ensure effective use in support of the enterprise, and describe how they and their relationships are expected to evolve during the planning period. Some areas that, though not now generally included in the information resource, are likely to be by the end of the decade are libraries, file cabinets, record storage warehouses, mail rooms, and people's memories.

The size, structure, and value of the information resource and the use of other resources (e.g., human, financial, physical) to sustain it should be addressed. Quantitative information should be included.

Also appropriate for this section are representations of the organization's current telecommunications network, applications portfolio, hardware and systems software environment, and capacity for information storage and processing. Plans for the evolution of these elements should be included.

Special attention should be given in the narrative to the changing requirements for availability and reliability and the plans for meeting these requirements. The issue of accessibility, or user friendliness, should also be addressed, including training, the general improvement of computer literacy, sociotechnical engineering, and the provision of easier-to-use tools.

Goals, Objectives, Strategies, and Milestones. This section lists the most important items in information resource management that the organization has targeted for each year during the planning period. The objectives, strategies, and milestones should summarize action plans in place; the action plans themselves may be included in the plan as appendixes.

Support of Business Plans. This section summarizes information contained in the plans for each of the organization's business areas, delineating how the information resource will be used to improve competitive advantage,

POLICY, PLANNING, AND CONTROL

increase income, improve productivity or effectiveness, reduce costs, or otherwise achieve business objectives. It supplements the enterprise section by highlighting key elements of that section's comprehensive plan and by showing how they will be supported in terms of the organization's business philosophy.

Benefits. MIS management generally has not been successful in convincing general management as to the value and benefits of DP activities. This section should provide information that improves that situation, in a quantitative form where possible.

Security and Disaster Recovery. The organization should have plans for the physical and logical security of its information and the tools for processing it, including plans for recovery in case of a disaster. The strategic directions and summaries of these plans should be described in this section; the plans themselves can be included as appendixes.

Information Resource Management Issues. This section briefly describes the issues that the MIS department feels stand in the way of achieving—for the department or the organization—the long-term goals or any milestones in the pursuit of them or of pursuing any of the strategies. The impact of each issue (e.g., on goals, competitiveness, revenues, productivity, costs) and a strategy for resolving it should be discussed. Resolution of these issues may require the cooperation of entities outside the organization.

Assumptions. In preparing long-range quantitative data to support plans, it is important to state explicitly the assumptions used. This section gathers the assumptions in a single place.

Figures and Schedules. The quantitative information that supports long-range and strategic planning serves several purposes for the organization. The most effective quantitative information puts the current situation and future plans in a historical perspective so that discontinuities are evident and understood and the validity of strategic directions can be assessed. Past performance, with respect to planning, should also be documented, with targets established for improved planning effectiveness. The information should be displayed in pictorial or graphic form whenever possible, with tables providing specific information as needed. A typical long-range planning horizon is five years; ideally, the historical perspective should cover at least ten years. Organizations should plan their data collection and retention policies with this historical perspective in mind.

It is important to recognize that many of the figures and schedules that form the quantitative part of a long-range and strategic plan are maintained separately as part of the regular management processes of an organization. Occasionally, it may be desirable to modify or combine existing management tools into a form that provides a longer-term perspective—both future and past—and to maintain them in that form. If this is done, a snapshot of them can be included in any planning documents that are produced.

Specific figures and schedules differ from organization to organization.

ACTION PLAN

Putting into practice the preceding principles and ideas is not likely to be easy. The following guidelines may help the MIS manager get started:
1. Assess the current planning process, especially with respect to the following questions:
   —Is it a continuous process that can detect and respond to change?
   —Are the right people involved? Substantively?
   —Have the enterprise and its information requirements been documented effectively? If not, can they be?
   —Have the main forces in the environment likely to affect the enterprise or the organization's support of it been documented? If not, can they be?
2. Where deficiencies occur, develop objectives, strategies, and action plans for repairing them.
3. If the planning process appears too complex or subject to information overload, step back and focus on critical success factors. A thorough understanding of the mission and the expectations of management, customers, and stakeholders is necessary here.
4. Structure planning documents so that the key elements of the plan stand out and are persuasive to senior management.
5. Consider adopting an annual reporting process that sets forth in lay terms the accomplishments versus the plan for the current year, the benefits the organization realized from them, and the plans and their projected benefits for next year.

References

1. Peters, T.J. and Waterman, R.H. Jr., *In Search of Excellence: Lessons from America's Best Run Companies.* Harper and Row, 1982.

Bibliography

"Business Systems Planning." *IBM Information Systems Planning Guide.* 3d ed. GE20-0527-3 (July 1981).

Carlson, W.M. "Business Information Analysis and Integration Technique (BIAIT)—The New Horizon." *Data Base* (ACM SIGBDP quarterly). 10 (1979) 3–9.

Davis, C.G., et al., eds. *Entity-Relationship Approach to Software Engineering.* New York: North-Holland, 1983.

"Enterprise Analysis." *IBM Systems Journal,* 21 (1982).

Kerner, D.V. "Business Information Characterization Study (BICS)." *Data Base.* 10 (1979) 10–17.

———. "Introduction to Business Information Control Study (BICS) Methodology." IBM Technical Report TR 03.113 (September 1980).

MacLean, E.R., and Soden, J.V. *Strategic Planning for MIS.* New York: John Wiley & Sons, 1977.

McKenney, J.L., and McFarlan, F.W. "The Information Archipelago—Maps and Bridges." *Harvard Business Review* (September–October 1982): 109–119; "The Information Archipelago—Plotting a Course." (January–February 1983) 145–156; "The Information Archipelago—Governing the New World." (July–August 1983): 91–99.

POLICY, PLANNING, AND CONTROL

Martin, J. *Strategic Data-Planning Methodologies.* Englewood Cliffs NJ: Prentice-Hall, 1982.

Nolan, R.L. "Managing the Crises in Data Processing." *Harvard Business Review* (March–April 1979): 115–126.

Parker, M.M. "Enterprise Information Analysis: Cost-Benefit Analysis of Information Systems Using PSL/PSA and the Yourdon Methodology." IBM Los Angeles Scientific Center Report G320-2716 (July 1982).

Porter, M.E. *Competitive Strategy.* New York: The Free Press, 1980.

Rockart, J. "Chief Executives Plan Their Own Data Needs." *Harvard Business Review* (January–February 1982): 82–88.

Steiner, G.A. *Top Management Planning.* New York: MacMillan, 1969.

Synott, W.R., and Gruber, W.H. *Information Resource Management: Opportunities and Strategies for the 1980s.* New York: John Wiley & Sons, 1981.

Umbaugh, R.E., "DP Management: A Modern Challenge," *A Practical Guide to Data Processing Management.* New York: Van Nostrand Reinhold Company, 1982, 1–8.

Zuboff, S. "New Worlds of Computer-Mediated Work." *Harvard Business Review* (September–October 1981): 142–152.

I-2

Using Information for Competitive Advantage

John M. Thompson

INTRODUCTION

Although most organizations recognize the importance of their information resource, many are ill-prepared for the role that information technology will play in their operations by 1990. Developments in technology and shifts in attitude regarding the value of information systems are creating major changes within organizations. The MIS manager's function, in particular, is already being transformed. Once a quarterback who was counted on to carry out each play, the MIS manager must now assume the role of organization coach. Before defining this evolving role, however, the MIS manager must recognize and understand the external and internal forces that have prompted the changes now taking place.

Technology Push. One element of change is "technology push." Most experts predict that the annual improvement in hardware capacity will remain at 30 to 50 percent for the rest of the decade. With widespread use of the personal computer, integrated professional workstations may become as common as the telephone by 1990. It is likely that by the end of the decade, many organizations will be dedicating up to 75 percent of their computer resources to applications developed and run by end users. As MIS organizations are decentralized, the MIS manager will be expected to change from managing the supply to managing the demand.

These developments pose a series of problems for MIS management. How will the MIS manager monitor systems that are widely dispersed and outside his or her control? Should MIS managers instead concentrate only on keeping the shop running and replacing aging systems?

The software arena, too, is bursting with new products and ideas. Successful microcomputer software packages, such as those from VisiCorp and Lotus, are being developed and rushed to a waiting marketplace with little or no market research. As a result, many users are turning to the MIS department for help in customizing off-the-shelf software packages.

Likewise, the growth of telecommunications is being spurred by such developments as local area networks and satellite communications. This growth has led James Martin to predict that the 1980s will be remembered as "the decade in which we all became interconnected." As organizations move toward this degree of interconnection, the MIS manager's job will expand in scope from managing applications to encompass the entire information systems environment.

User Pull. In addition to these new and complex directions in technology, the MIS department must contend with "user pull." Organizations have recognized the potentially major contribution of information technology to productivity gains and financial success. To increase productivity, senior management often is willing to invest heavily in improving and updating the information systems function.

Senior managers, excited about the possibilities of fourth-generation systems and integrated professional workstations, are intent on using these new capabilities to meet their needs. Where users once viewed MIS managers as the high priests of technology, increased user understanding of technology and its ready availability may create tension between the MIS manager and an assertive, knowledgeable user.

Aging Systems. Challenged by new technology and user demand, the MIS manager must also confront problems stemming from a 20-year legacy of old systems and outdated technology. Such long-standing problems as two-year applications software development backlogs, high programmer turnover, and obsolete systems command attention. The MIS department's difficulty and slowness in responding to these issues often has created the impression that MIS is not supporting the business, that it is a function without direction.

Exacerbating these organizational problems is the knowledge that many current application systems must be replaced. Replacement systems, however, are often unfunded and difficult to justify. Further, a technology architecture plan is a prerequisite to purchasing in an environment of technology proliferation.

New Strategies. How does the MIS manager create a role that will satisfy the needs of users, keep up with technological advances, and meet his or her own operational requirements? First, new ways of assessing the value of information systems are needed. With a new and informed perspective, the MIS manager can help senior management determine the best business return among the bewildering array of investment options in information technology. Users looking to improve their creativity and productivity can also be given guidance in choosing the best support systems.

Many of the procedures developed in the past 20 years to regulate the development of applications software—for example, the project life cycle and systems development methodologies—are incompatible with the evolutionary prototype development of current management support systems. However, much has been learned about data administration and data security that is applicable. As senior management looks to the MIS department for guidance in using information systems as a strategic resource, MIS managers must have at their disposal the concepts and methodologies that will assist them with this task.

THE VALUE OF INFORMATION

A strategy for information systems must be based on a clear understanding of the potential business value of information technology. Management frequently regards information systems solely from a budgetary or technical viewpoint. This focus must shift to the potential value that information technology represents to the business and to strategies for realizing that potential.

Supporting the Business. Before this shift can occur, management must realize that information systems are intrinsically valueless; that is, their value derives solely from the extent to which they support effective business change. Managers often direct their energies toward the design and construction of a system that addresses a business problem. If, as a result, opportunities for a favorable change in the business itself are ignored, the system will produce little value.

The business environment in which managers seek to add value is one of increasing competitive pressure. It is also marked by the increasing impact of technology and a shifting of computer resources to user departments. MIS managers must recognize the strategic as well as economic value of information systems technology. This value differs according to the nature of the business. Information systems strategy is misdirected in many organizations and cannot support the organization's strategic goals. Such misalignment can prove disastrous. The MIS manager who understands both the technology and the business can knowledgeably advise senior management on the most strategic use of information technology.

Management Effectiveness. As Figure 1 indicates, the third era in the strategic use of information systems has begun. During the first era, information systems were used for economic advantage: automation of financial information improved efficiency and provided by-product control reports for management. The second era ushered in operational automation. With the development of management information systems, management could easily access data concerning the daily operation of the business and its services. These by-product reports, however, were often data rich and information poor.

The advent of the third era and the decentralization of the information systems function has focused attention on systems that provide managerial effectiveness as well as efficiency. Management information systems enabled managers to examine a wealth of data on operational activity. Management support systems (MSS) extend this capability by converting this data into information that can support management decision making. Consequently, information systems have become critical to the earliest stages of strategic planning.

The Changing Value of Information Systems. Figure 1 shows the three advantages of using information technology: economic, product/service, and management. These can be characterized as follows:

POLICY, PLANNING, AND CONTROL

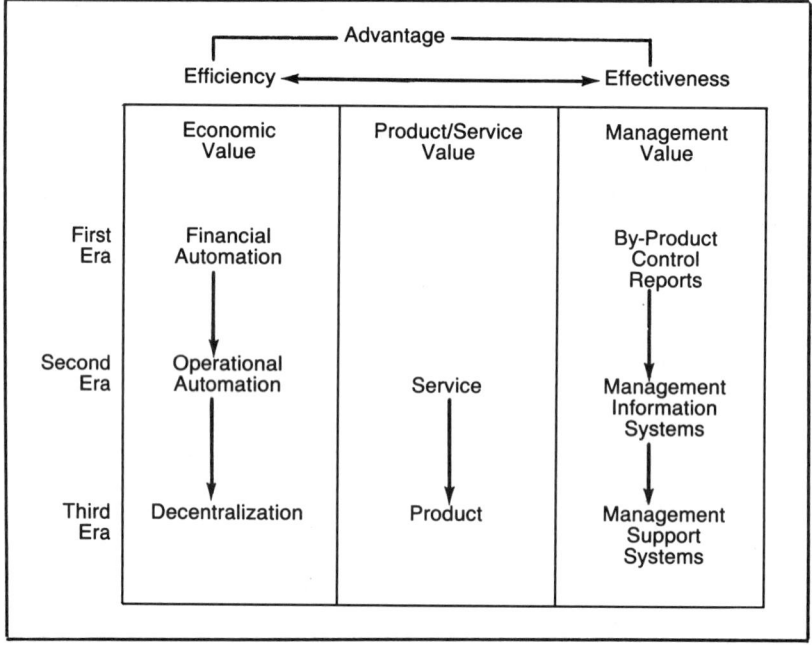

Figure 1. The Changing Value of Information Systems

- Economic—How can information technology achieve cost reduction or avoidance and a return on investment, within a short payback period?
- Product/service—How can information technology become part of the product or enhance it to create a sustainable competitive advantage and improve market share?
- Management—How can information technology improve management effectiveness?

In the third era, managers can use MSS in a creative and strategic way, to assist not only in decision making but in moving the organization into a better market position or even into new markets. In a number of companies, the use of MSS has altered the nature of products and services.

Focusing on the value of information systems both clarifies and simplifies information systems planning. A value-oriented approach provides the MIS manager with the clear criteria—frequently absent in the past—that are needed to make important decisions about the future.

Defining Information Needs. User and MIS managers attempting to define the systems that will support managerial effectiveness must first define the user manager's information needs. Clearly defining these needs before system design and implementation benefits both the user manager and the MIS manager, who may have to support a poorly designed or inadequate system. To support the definition of these needs, a methodology known as critical success factors (CSF) is frequently used.

USING CRITICAL SUCCESS FACTORS

The use of information technology to improve management effectiveness begins with the identification of those factors considered essential to the success of the organization. CSF, which is based primarily on an interview technique, helps managers pinpoint the factors most critical to the achievement of their business objectives. This process helps align the organization's management information systems with its business strategy and objectives so that they support management's achievement of those objectives. Identifying critical factors also helps communicate to the entire organization—and in particular to the MIS department—the information senior management considers important.

The CSF methodology consists of several stages. By questioning key management personnel, an unbiased interviewer helps identify what each considers important to the company as well as to his or her part of the organization. These critical factors, once compiled, form the basis of a management review of the organization's perspective of its business and strategic priorities. Because alignment and consensus are required before further action can be taken, this stage of the process is crucial.

Once the critical success factors have been determined, senior management must work with the MIS manager to develop an information reporting system that can monitor and highlight performance that supports their achievement. Such a system enables management to measure effectiveness in areas essential to the organization. It ensures that senior management will discuss areas of concern to the company and that the entire organization is informed of company goals and objectives.

CSF in Practice. The CSF methodology has proved successful in its use at a large U.S. steel service center. The company, which was growing rapidly, had been small and relatively easy to run for the original owners. Having grown up with the business, the owners held much of its information in their heads; now, however, they turn the company over to the next generation.

The new directors faced problems that had not confronted their predecessors: the business had grown rapidly in size and complexity, requiring quick decision making. For example, the company needed to respond immediately to customer inquiries on the availability and price of steel and within a half-day to steel mill offers to sell secondary steel. Customer orders were accepted for processing on not more than 24-hour notice, and production schedules were revised daily. Clearly, information technology was needed to help manage the business.

To meet these information needs, a data processing system was proposed by an outside firm at an estimated cost of $2.4 million and implementation time of four years. These estimates came as a shock to management. Because there was no guarantee that the functions included were feasible, the risk to the company was high in dollars invested and the company's ability to service its customers if the system failed.

Management began to investigate alternative solutions, among them the CSF methodology. Using CSF, management could pinpoint its information requirements and develop a prototype of the new system. This approach was estimated to take only six to nine months at a cost of less than $250,000, excluding new equipment. Because the risk was within acceptable limits, management agreed to the proposed project.

During the next two months, senior management was interviewed, and the daily activities of senior and middle-level managers were observed. Despite the skepticism of some senior executives, a one-and-a-half-day workshop with senior management culminated in a focused set of business goals and the alignment of the critical success factors with those goals.

Twelve initial critical success factors were narrowed down to four key factors. Specific measures were then formulated that would provide the basis for the development of systems to support these four critical factors. Senior management subsequently reviewed prototype options; within nine months, two prototype systems had been successfully implemented and were supporting daily operations.

Instead of committing more than $2 million and four years on an untried system, this management team used the CSF approach to minimize risk while saving time and money. Within nine months, management was working with a new system that satisfied most of its needs at a cost of less than 10 percent of the system originally proposed.

ACTION PLAN

The MIS manager's role is one of increasing complexity and importance. Faced with the continual evolution of information technology and mounting user demand for information resources, the MIS manager must possess both a command of the technology and an understanding of the business concerns of the organization. The MIS manager can no longer simply monitor and control operations; without an awareness of the wider implications of information systems, he or she will be rapidly overwhelmed by a growing list of problems and demands.

MIS managers can, however, take assertive action to expand their organizational role and become integral to the strategic planning process for information systems. The following steps are recommended:

1. Recognize that information systems value conveys a different meaning to different segments of the organization.
2. Refocus attention from the management of information systems development to the management of change in the business.
3. Emphasize the importance of business value in making decisions about the management of information systems resources.
4. Advocate use of the CSF methodology to help identify the areas of greatest concern to the organization and to ensure that information systems will support these concerns.
5. Encourage the use of prototyping to test new systems. This approach, which is quicker and less expensive than traditional systems development, allows an organization to build a tentative system, test it, make changes based on the tests, and finally arrive at a working system with less risk and investment.

Most important, MIS managers must recognize that their role will not evolve from that of quarterback to coach until the entire organization understands the changes brought about by technology. Knowing this, these managers can act as catalysts for educating the organization. When business managers, technicians, and other employees understand and accept the opportunities and problems created by new information technology, the MIS manager can assume his or her new role with greater ease and effectiveness.

Bibliography

For more information on Critical Success Factors, the reader is referred to the following publications:

Rockart, J.F. "Chief Executives Define Their Own Data Needs." *Harvard Business Review*, March–April 1979.

Rockart, J.F., and Crescenzi, A.D. "A Process for the Rapid Development of Systems in Support of Managerial Decision Making." MIT CISR Working Paper 104 (June 1983), Sloane Working Paper 1447-83.

Waite, T.J., ed. "Critical Success Factors: Improving Management Effectiveness." *Indications*, vol 1 no. 2, Cambridge MA: Index Systems Inc.

I-3
Planning for MIS Resource Usage
Robert E. Umbaugh

INTRODUCTION

Resource planning for data processing is becoming increasingly complex with the growth of online systems, time sharing, communicating office systems, data communication networks, and hardware and software options. Long-range planning is never easy, and it is especially difficult for rapidly evolving technologies. Nevertheless, a comprehensive resource plan is vital for the continued provision of DP service.

Traditional hardware resource planning using trend projections was generally a step function; that is, machine installation was planned and executed in single steps with rather lengthy intervening periods. Batch applications constituted most of the work load and increased as a function of the growth rate of the organization; the estimated impact of new applications was factored into the projections. Because scheduling for use of these resources was completely managed by the data processing department, there were relatively few surprises; because the installation of a major piece of hardware occurred rather infrequently, there was ample time for installation planning.

Although reliability was important in this batch environment, short interruptions were not nearly as disruptive as they are today, where the processing environment is much different. A number of studies report an average 40 percent compounded annual growth in CPU demand and an average 40 to 45 percent compounded annual growth in DASD requirements in major MIS shops. The general impact of such growth on cost, floor space, configuration management, and power and cooling requirements is clear, but how this growth will specifically affect each one of these areas is not clear and requires a good deal of planning. This chapter describes a resource planning methodology specifically designed to meet the needs of a complex DP installation.

CARD PLAYING

Resource planning requirements for hardware and network components can be collected and analyzed using the CARD system:
- Contingency
- Availability
- Reliability
- Demand.

POLICY, PLANNING, AND CONTROL

Contingency. Contingency planning—preparing for the unexpected—is often the last consideration when it should actually be addressed during the early phases of resource planning, so that decisions regarding contingency allotment can be used later as guidelines. Contingency can be addressed by establishing capacity corridors or reserve margin. Reserve margin is unapplied but available resources that are assigned to satisfy unexpected demand. Such resources may be discussed in physical terms (e.g., four DASD devices set aside for contingency) or stated as a percentage or range of percentages (e.g., CPU capacity will be projected load plus 18 percent ± 3 percent). Both capacity corridors and reserve margin are discussed in later sections of this chapter.

Availability and Reliability. Availability, the ability of the system to satisfy the demands placed on it by the user, and reliability, the percentage of uptime of any individual component of a system (including software), should be addressed separately in a resource plan. A redundant configuration could conceivably offer 100 percent availability for a given period, whereas the reliability of an individual component—for example, a CPU—might only be 97 percent.

Demand. Demand systems (online, time sharing, text retrieval, and office systems), which permit users to place demands on resources at will, create a new set of problems. Direct access storage requirements are usually underestimated, networking is complex and costly, and reliability and security become more important. The demand on the system as a whole and on its various components is difficult to project, and the scheduling of MIS resources is no longer under the direct control of the MIS manager. Demand systems are usually most heavily used during the prime shift—that period when most office and line workers are at their jobs—between 7:00 A.M. and 5:00 P.M.. The demand placed on the system during this period typically forms a spike, or peak, on a graph and is referred to as peak load. Identifying and projecting demand and controlling peak load are the primary tasks in MIS resource management.

LOAD DURATION ANALYSIS AND PLANNING

An initial analysis of the processing load imposed on the computer center provides a processing profile that shows the load characteristics for that particular center. The typical processing profile for a center with a number of online systems is a general graph of load and time, where load is calibrated in CPU hours, transactions, or whatever measurement best fits the situation. To be more useful, however, both load and time must be broken down specifically.

Time Zones

One method of capacity planning divides the processing day into time zones and superimposes work-load categories on them (see Figure 1). Use of daily time zones for capacity planning will help the manager avoid the trap of using "average" daily load figures.

MIS Resource Planning

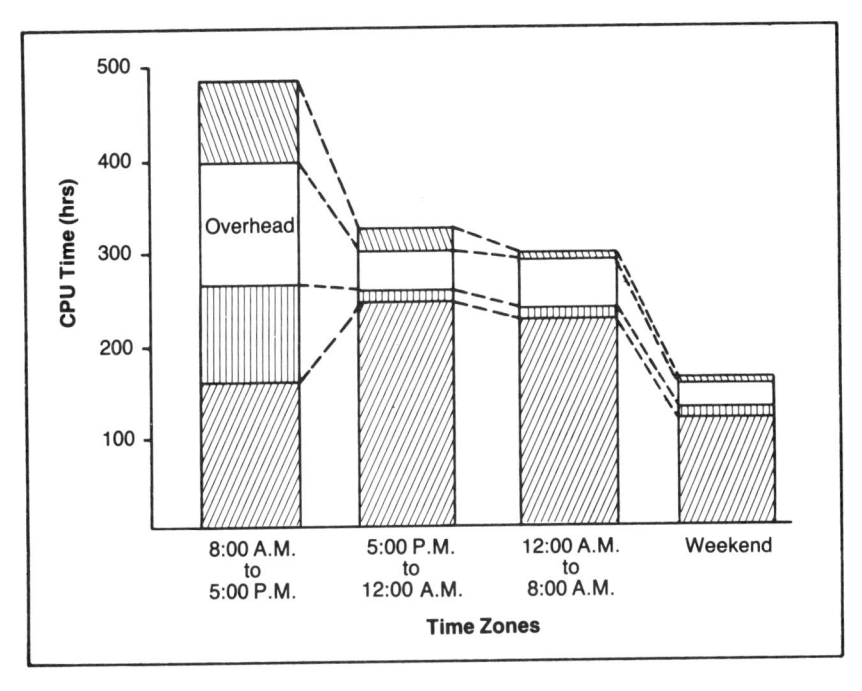

Figure 1. Demand by Time Zones

Viewing the work load in time zones also enables the manager to identify the source and size of peak loads. A more detailed picture of the peak load is shown in Figure 2, which illustrates hourly loading during a typical work day.

Capacity Corridors

Certain assumptions must be made when resource usage is planned. It is impractical to expect 100 percent use of any device's total capacity; therefore, reasonable ranges of performance and capacity corridors need to be determined for each group of devices in order to plan for resource additions. The capacity corridor is established by plotting optimal capacity and a reasonable estimate of practical capacity. For example, for a CPU scheduled to be available 24 hours a day for 22 working days each month, optimal capacity would be 100 percent of the total CPU hours, or 528 CPU hours. A more practical assumption, however, would estimate CPU operation at 85 percent of total capacity for the 22 working days, or 448 CPU hours. The capacity corridor for this CPU is then 448 to 528 CPU hours (see Figure 3).

Whenever projections of work load reach or enter the capacity corridor, the work load is processed "at risk," and some form of response is needed. The response must be decided on before it is actually necessary to take action; for example, projecting the need for a device must precede the real need for the device by the lead time necessary to obtain it. Figure 4 is an example of planning for prime shift work load using capacity corridors; it is somewhat simplified, however, because actual load is shown as a total and does not reflect its components. As increments of capacity are added, the capacity

POLICY, PLANNING, AND CONTROL

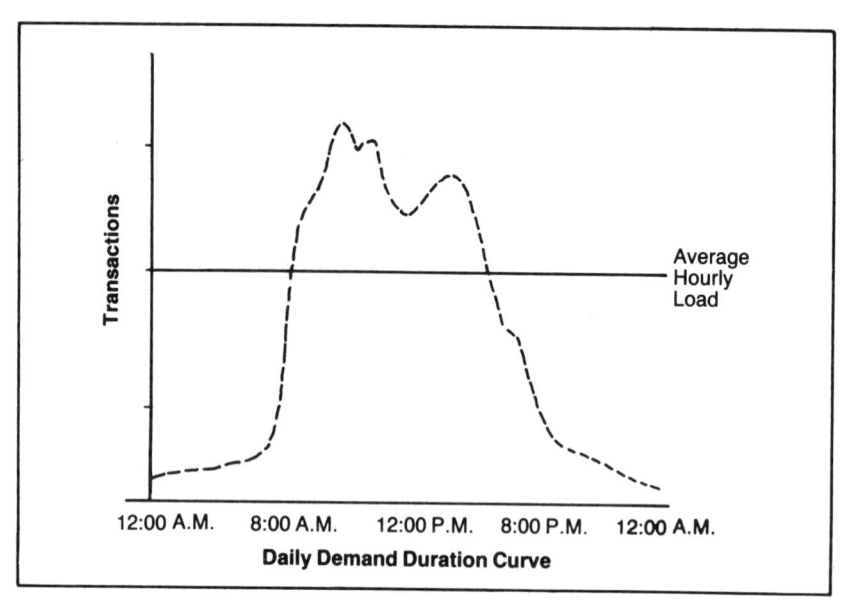

Figure 2. Demand by Hour

corridor rises correspondingly. In June 1984 the installation needed additional capacity; some additional capacity was added in January 1985, but part of the work load continued to be processed at risk within the capacity corridor. As could have been predicted, operating within the corridor resulted in reduced service levels.

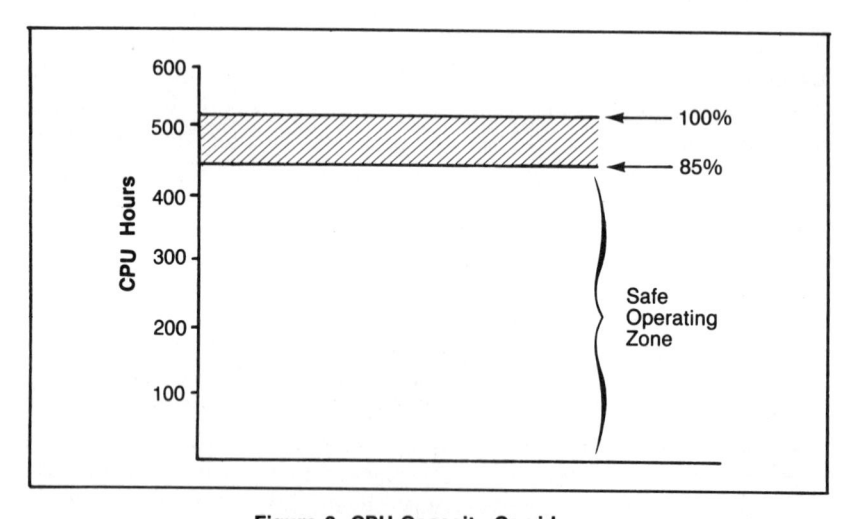

Figure 3. CPU Capacity Corridor

In summary, capacity corridors can help in:
- Establishing reasonable operating levels for various hardware components, especially CPUs

- Forecasting needed increments of processing power
- Determining the point at which part of the work load will be at risk and service levels will deteriorate
- Demonstrating to upper levels of management the need for a reserve margin.

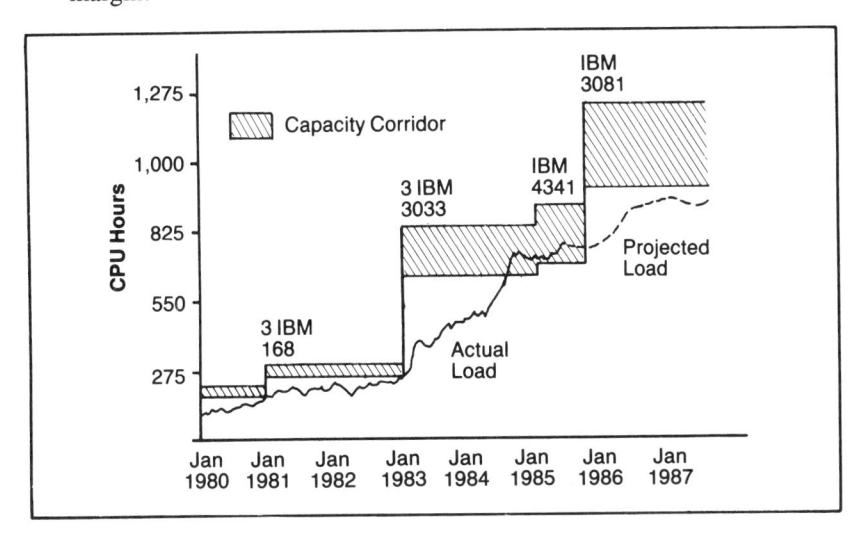

Figure 4. Prime Shift Work Load

Reserve Margin

In order to achieve a reasonable level of reliability, fall-back computing capacity, or reserve margin, is needed. Traditionally, the level of reserve margin was set by rule of thumb. As DP applications increased and the work load grew more complex, however, reserve margin became essential and, for large installations, quite costly. The term reserve margin is probably better than "excess capacity," which implies, quite incorrectly, that the equipment is for the most part unused.

J.F. Chilcott, in a paper presented at the 1981 JUSEC Conference,[1] outlined a method for matching supply with demand using reserve-margin computation. The initial step in establishing and justifying a reserve margin is the design of a load duration curve, which represents the demand expected on every working day in a year, arranged so that the days with the highest demand fall to the left and those with the lowest to the right (see Figure 5).

It is also necessary to know the extent to which the peak hour within a day exceeds the average hourly traffic during the entire working day—in this case, by a factor of about 1.5 to 1.0 (see Figure 2). The load will have a number of different components, depending on the installation, as illustrated in Figure 6.

In addition to different ratios of peak to average demand, the applications have different availability priorities. For a customer service system that supports direct interface with the customer (e.g., an airline reservation system), availability is imperative, whereas it carries a much lower priority for an

POLICY, PLANNING, AND CONTROL

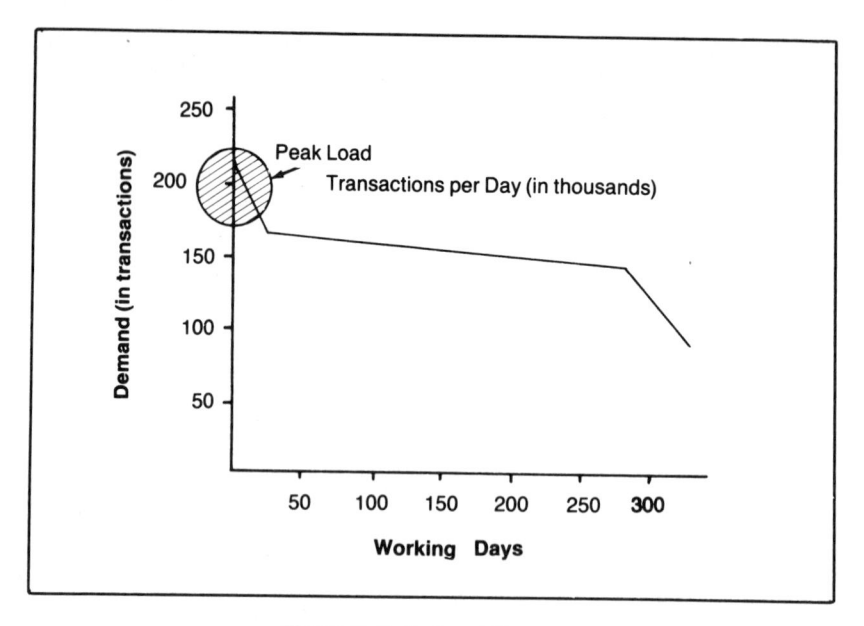

Figure 5. Daily Load Curve

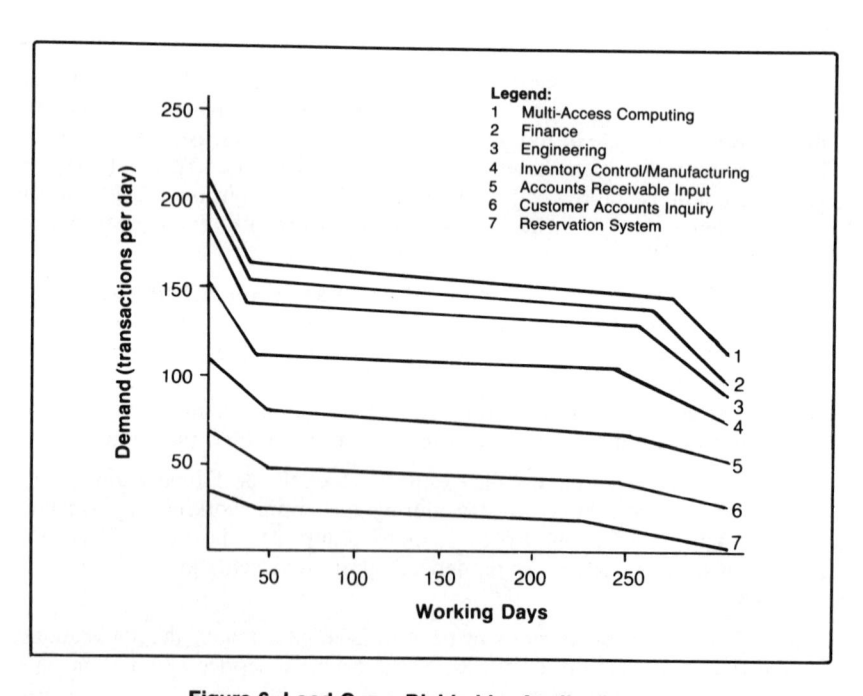

Figure 6. Load Curve Divided by Applications

MIS Resource Planning

online financial planning system that is only used internally. The load duration curve can be arranged with these components ranked as shown in Figure 6, so that the least sensitive to reduction in availability falls at the upper edge of the curve, and the most sensitive forms the base load, which must be available consistently.

The basic criterion for matching computing supply against the demand shown in the curve is that supply must be able to meet the predicted peak hour demand if all computing equipment is working properly and is loaded to a degree that results in a reasonable level of response time (e.g., 70 percent processor loading, resulting in a 3- to 5-second response time). Such assumptions, of course, are not immutable and should be periodically reviewed by senior management. In addition, it may not be essential to plan to meet the entire projected peak hour load every day of the year; a plan might be designed to serve the peak hour traffic on all except three days of the year, as shown in Figure 7.

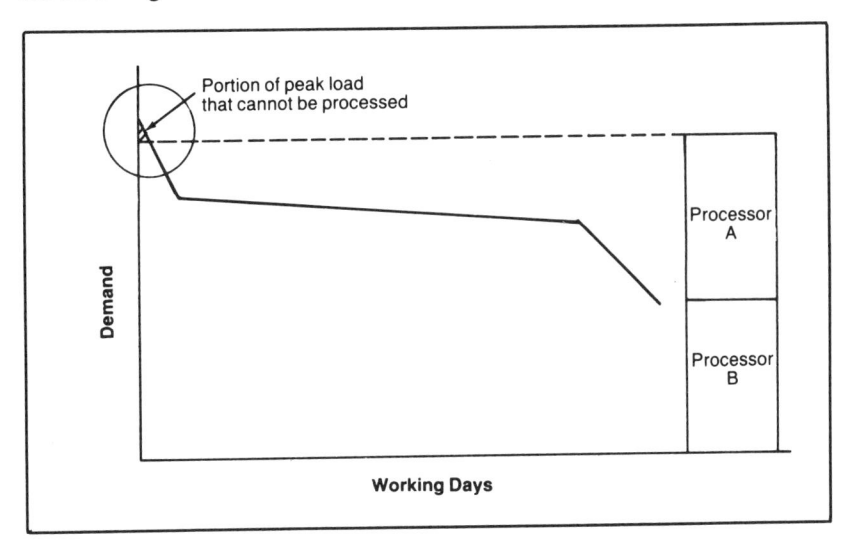

Figure 7. Plan for Meeting All but Three Days' Peak Requirements

Figure 8 illustrates what happens if one of the processors fails. (The example assumes that the total computing power is provided through a multiple-processor installation. For a single-processor shop, there are no fall-back options; the only decision concerns the acceptable length of time for the single processor to be inoperable before other action is taken.) When one processor fails, some loss in processing capacity occurs. The size of the loss depends on machine configuration; the most straightforward case is illustrated here, but the method can be adapted to any other configuration. The shaded area in the illustration represents the transactions that cannot be carried out when one processor fails. A comparison with Figure 6 shows that the essential applications can be serviced, but the less crucial applications are interrupted.

Although breakdown itself is unpredictable, the expected loss or deferral of transaction processing ability can be predicted for a particular configura-

POLICY, PLANNING, AND CONTROL

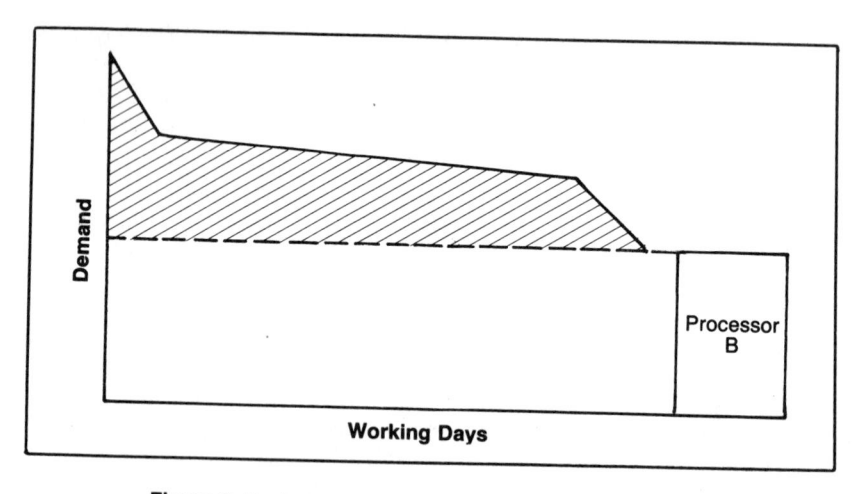

Figure 8. Projected Loss from Failure of One Processor

tion of computing power. What must be determined is whether this is the "right" level of processing loss that should be planned for. One way of determining this is to redraw the plan to reflect a larger, more powerful set of computers, as in Figure 9. The expected loss of transactions is then recalculated as shown in Figure 10, and compared with the expected loss using the smaller processors (see Figure 11). Comparing the difference in lost transactions with the increased cost of the more powerful equipment provides an estimate of the cost per transaction rescued by availability of the greater processing resource.

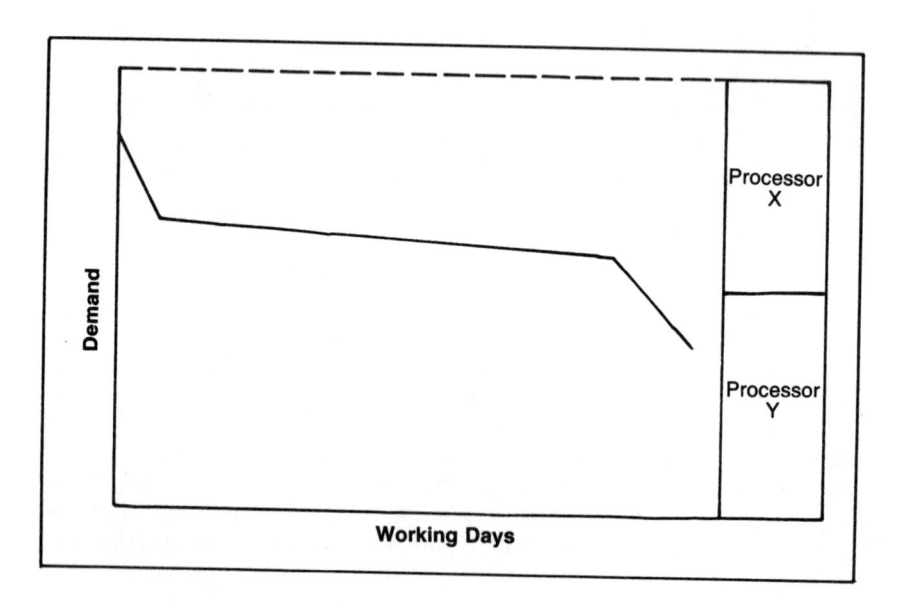

Figure 9. Alternate Plan Using More Powerful Processors

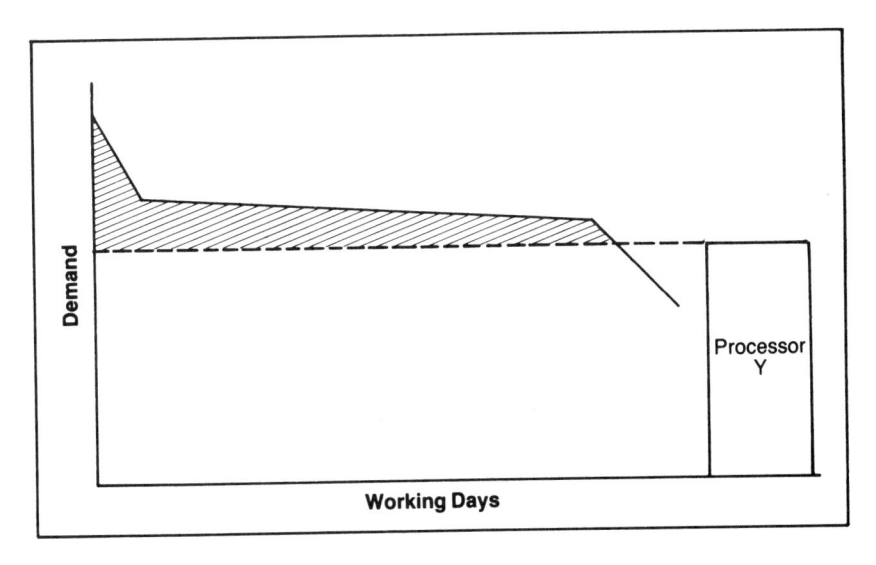

Figure 10. Projected Loss for Alternate Plan

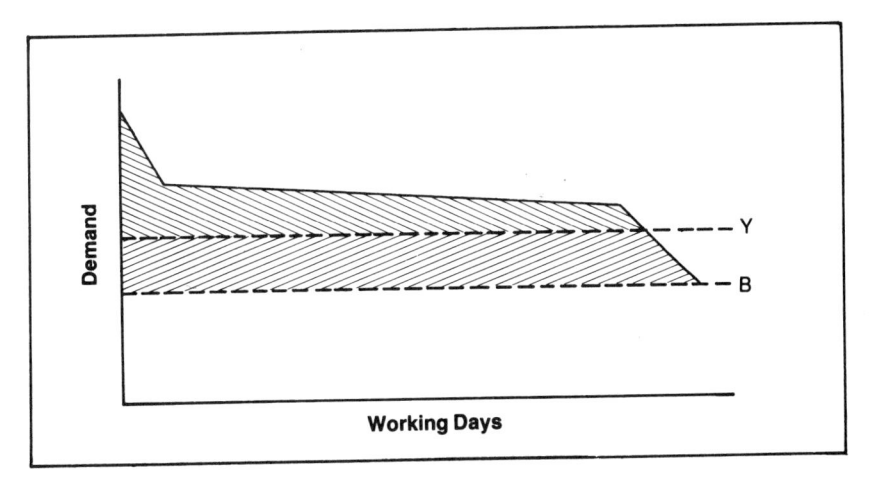

Figure 11. Comparison of Projected Loss

Treating fall-back or reserve margin analysis in this way provides a number of benefits:
- It addresses contingency planning as an integral part of demand/supply planning rather than as an expensive afterthought.
- It allows everyone involved in the investment decision aspect of resource planning—from the computing service user to the financial analyst—to view the processing power available under both normal and contingency conditions in the same way.
- It requires explicit assignment of priorities to the various components of the computing load.

POLICY, PLANNING, AND CONTROL

- It determines the ranking of applications and the ultimate level of computing power by measuring the value placed by users on a lost transaction in each of the applications.

It is important to remember that this planning approach does not make policy; it merely provides a framework for policy decisions. Senior management must define the policy that guides resource planning efforts.

PEAK LOAD MANAGEMENT

In addition to assessing reserve-margin requirements, a number of steps can be taken to address the peak load problem. Five of the more easily implemented techniques are time-of-day pricing, conservation, load shifting, peak shaving, and port closure.

Time-of-Day Pricing. If users are charged directly for computing services, time-of-day pricing—charging more for transactions processed during peak load times than at other times—can be a simple but effective policy. The difference between rates must be substantial, however, to provide a real incentive for off-peak use. It is usually much more palatable to describe the difference in rates to users as a discount for off-peak use rather than as a penalty for peak use. Thus, the MIS department might advertise a normal charge of $400 per hour and $100 per hour for off-peak use.

Conservation. Just as employees are asked to turn out lights that are not necessary, they can be requested to avoid using computing resources they do not need. As with other conservation measures, however, compliance will vary among individuals.

Load Shifting. Outside resources can be used temporarily to delay the installation of an increment of processing power. In highly integrated shops, however, this is sometimes very difficult.

Peak Shaving. Although this technique can take several forms, all revolve around identifying those elements that make up the peak and "shaving" them off. Two methods for doing this are:
- Restricting the use of one or more high-resource-using, lower-priority applications (e.g., a financial modeling package) during peak hours.
- Shifting certain employees' work hours. If application programmers are heavy users of time sharing, their work hours can be changed to off-peak hours. Flexible work hours normally result in lowered peak load.

Port Closure. In a heavy online environment with a large time-sharing load, one method of reducing peak load is to restrict the number of concurrent time-sharing users by restricting the number of ports open to the machine. Of course, this strategy may negatively affect productivity and result in some irate users.

PROJECTING NEED

Projecting need is a critical part of the planning process, and perhaps the most difficult estimation in planning for data processing resources. Projections of future need are based on several sources, primarily the present processing load, which is used as a base and modified according to assumptions dictated by the business environment. An overall strategic plan for the entire organization—a corporate plan, for example—can be helpful when beginning a data processing resource plan, but it is not absolutely essential. Many organizations maintain sets of assumptions that are used for planning in other parts of the business (e.g., financial planning predictions). Such assumptions may be continuous (e.g., a compound growth in sales of 5.3 percent is forecast for the next five years) or discrete (e.g., the company will acquire other companies during 1986 and 1988, adding a total of 200,000 customers to the existing customer base). Use of these assumptions can help the MIS manager to project future work load.

Another source of projected need is the application resource plan, which should be at least as comprehensive as the hardware resource plan. The advantage of this method is that it requires project development personnel to schedule resource requirements for development, production, and maintenance. These schedules must be recognized as educated projections that will change as time passes and user requirements become more clearly established. Based on the projections of need submitted by application development teams, the hardware resource planners can project demand and prepare plans accordingly.

IBM's *Business Systems Planning: Information Systems Planning Guide*[2] describes a more complex, two-phase approach to business system planning. The first phase—identification of requirements—describes the relationships among the various elements of an information system network and is not limited to the computerized information system network. The second phase —definition—documents a long-range application development plan for the design and implementation of decision-oriented management information and control systems that use integrated data bases. The guide is comprehensive, including such elements as methodology descriptions, interview guides, end-product outlines, techniques used to gather requirements in various industries, and examples of the benefits that can result from the use of this technique.

Latent Demand

Latent demand—the work load that would be processed if there were enough resources—is a phenomenon well known to seasoned MIS managers. Latent demand is the basis of two fundamental laws of data processing: "Work load expands to fill existing capacity," and "There is never enough disk space."

Latent demand builds up during periods when MIS resources are saturated and processing needs continue to grow. When new capacity becomes available, this demand is quickly imposed on the system. Taking latent demand into consideration when projecting need is a necessary part of DP resource planning.

A Method for Projecting Resource Requirements

Obtaining reliable forecasts of resource requirements from systems development teams has always been a demanding task. One reason is that they often do not know what the user really needs, when the system will be implemented, how much CPU time will be needed to develop and test the system, or even how much work can be done during a CPU hour. Because the project team may lack such information, wise resource planners will be skeptical of any projections. These projections must be considered, however, because the project team is the only source for forecasts of the impact of future systems. Because of long lead times for delivery of some types of hardware and for all types of facilities, resource planners need all the advance notice they can get.

Several methods can be used to improve the accuracy of application development project team projections. One is to educate the project teams in planning techniques, including assumption preparation and hardware capabilities. Another is to exercise intuitive, "gut feel" planning—many managers can produce excellent strategies using intuitive methods.

Recognizing the inherent problems in making resource projections based on systems development team forecasts, the resource planners can use the following method for gathering data for these forecasts. The process outlined here should be repeated regularly (every six months is a good interval).

Define the Units. Figure 12 depicts a form that can be used to briefly describe the system and its subfunctions. This is useful for checking for redundant systems development efforts and for scheduling application implementation and hardware installation events.

Schedule of Events. Figure 13 illustrates a sample schedule. The solid lines represent the development phase, triangles depict installation and start of production processing, and dotted lines represent regular maintenance during production status for each subfunction.

Resource Requirements. Resource requirements should be stated in terms that are understandable to the development team and the planner. For example, the terms used in Figure 14 are CPU hours translated to percentage of an IBM 3033; gigabytes of DASD, and so on. "Not Currently Available" usually means that the system design has not progressed far enough for the team to even make a guess.

Integration with Hardware Plan. The results of the first three steps are first integrated into a subset of the hardware plan (Figure 15) and later, when all application plans are complete, into the full hardware resource plan.

RESOURCE PLANNING STEPS

Specific resource planning is necessarily more detailed than a long-range data processing plan. Considering each specific event (e.g., the installation of an additional string of disk drives or a major software package) and calculating the impact of that event on the surrounding resources result in better control of resources.

The formal resource plan sometimes omits systems software modifications; however, changes to operating system software and the installation of

MIS Resource Planning

SYSTEM: MMS—MATERIAL MANAGEMENT SYSTEM
Maintains information necessary to support provisions of material and supplies for use in the construction and maintenance of facilities and equipment

SUBFUNCTIONS
1. Identification & Cataloging : Establishes new material codes and maintains information other than standard cost of the material code level.
2. Store Administration : Establishes and maintains parameters that control the replenishment process.
3. Acquisition Analysis : Processes responses to system-generated requests for procurement.
4. Project Planning : Performs bill-of-material processing, maintains schedule, pending movement and material needs.
5. Construction Units : Establishes and maintains construction assemblies.
6. Purchase Order Administration : Establishes and maintains information for all types of purchase orders and releases.
7. Stock Movement : Posts material movement between stores, back stock and open stock, and in-and-out stock.
8. Costing : Establishes and maintains standard costs.
9. Physical Inventory : Posts inventory counts and reconciliation of variances.
10. Monitor for Payment : Performs payment processing, including error recirculation.

Note: Three subfunctions not listed are System Control, Supplier Qualification, and Receiving.

Figure 12. System Description

POLICY, PLANNING, AND CONTROL

SCHEDULE OF EVENTS

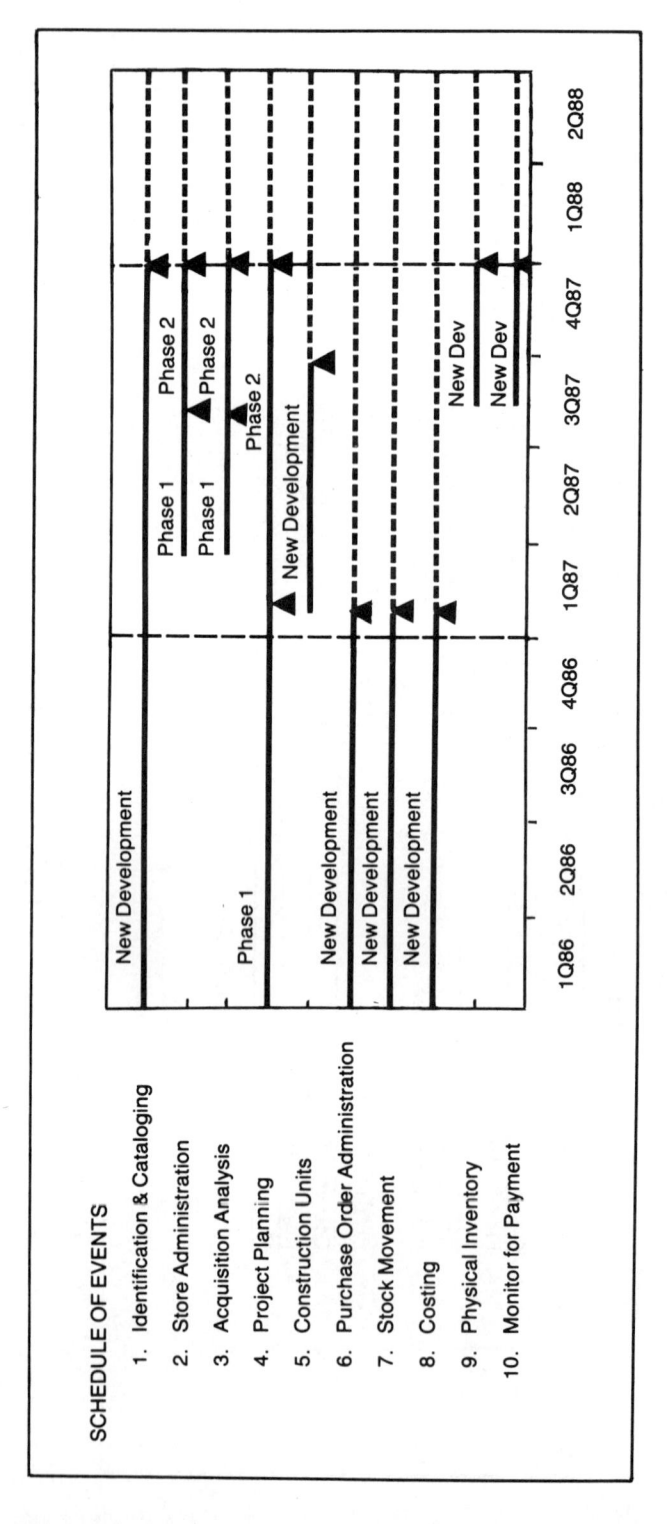

1. Identification & Cataloging
2. Store Administration
3. Acquisition Analysis
4. Project Planning
5. Construction Units
6. Purchase Order Administration
7. Stock Movement
8. Costing
9. Physical Inventory
10. Monitor for Payment

Figure 13. Schedule of Events

MIS Resource Planning

1. CPU (% of 3033)										
TSO	3.8	3.8	3.8	4.0	4.3	5.3	5.5	6.5	7.0	9.0
Online Production	1.2	1.2	1.2	1.5	1.6	2.0	2.5	3.0	3.5	4.0
Batch	5.0	5.0	5.0	5.5	6.0	6.5	7.0	8.0	9.0	10.0
2. DASD (Gigabytes)	5	5.8	6.5	7	7.5	8.5	10	11	12	19
3. Tape (No. of Mounts)	not currently available									
4. 3800 Printer (Lines Printed)	not currently available									
5. COM (Lines Printed)	not currently available									
6. Software (packages)	-- PERT/CPM --	--	--	--	--	--	--	--	--	--
	1Q86	2Q86	3Q86	4Q86	1Q87	2Q87	3Q87	4Q87	1Q88	2Q88

Figure 14. Resource Requirements

CPU — CPU Hours vs Year (1985–1988), showing 50% of an IBM 3033 band, Online and Batch curves.

DASD — Gigabytes vs Year (1985–1988).

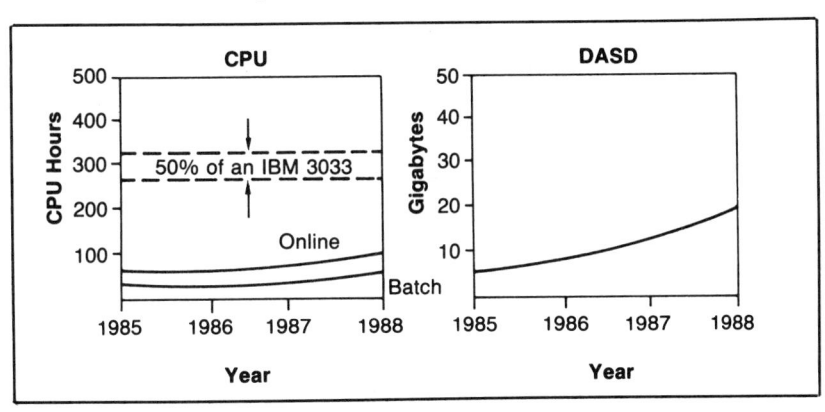

Figure 15. Integration with Hardware Plan

MAJOR DASD EVENTS THROUGH JUNE 1983

Disk.								
IBM 3350-A2F	12	12	12	12				12
3350-A2	4	6	14	19	+2+2	+2	+2	27
3350-B2F	20	20	20	20				20
3350-B2	21	29	48	61	+4+8	+3	+3	79
3380-AA4	0	0	0	0	+1+1	+1	+2+1+1	7
3380-B4	0	0	0	0	+1+3	+3	+4+2+2	15
3330-11	6	6	6	6				6
3330-11	2	2	2	2				2
Controllers.								
IBM 3830-2	14	14	8	3				3
3830-3	0	0	0	0		+2		2
3880-1	0	0	5	12			−2	10
3880-3	0	0	0	0	+1+1		+1 +2	5
Mass Storage.								
IBM 3850	0	0	0	0			+1	1
By Quarters	07/01/82 Two Years Past	3 4	1 2 3 4 1983	1 2 1984	07/01/84 Begin Plan	3 4	1 2 3 4 1 2 1985 1986	06/30/86 End Plan

Figure 16. Sample Event Chart

POLICY, PLANNING, AND CONTROL

```
I.     Executive Summary
       A.   Basic description of MIS activities/purpose of plan
       B.   General assumptions regarding MIS environment
       C.   Financial impact of plan/cost per year/cash flow require-
            ments
       D.   Major hardware/software summary

II.    Strategy
       A.   Milestone events
       B.   Planned activities

III.   Project Analysis
       A.   Summary of each major system (using a form similar to Fig-
            ures 12, 13, 14, and 15)

IV.    Demand System Impact
       A.   Time sharing
       B.   Graphics
       C.   Open shop use

V.     Equipment Plans
       A.   CPU, memory, channels
       B.   DASD
       C.   Tape drives
       D.   Online unit record, data entry
       E.   Offline unit record, data entry
       F.   Communications devices
       G.   Satellite processors

VI.    Software Analysis (operating system)
       A.   Installed software categories (e.g., operating system, com-
            munications software, data base management software, pro-
            grammer productivity aids)
       B.   Forecast software requirements for period of plan
       C.   Major software events (event chart)
       D.   Software configuration chart

VII.   Data Communications Network
       A.   Network configuration
       B.   Network events (event chart)

VIII.  Personnel Plan
       A.   General staffing requirements
       B.   Training requirements
       C.   Recruiting requirements
       D.   Project staffing charts

IX.    Facilities
       A.   Building modifications required
       B.   Space requirements for projects
       C.   Facility event chart

X.     Other
       A.   Word-processing evaluation
       B.   Text-retrieval impact
```

Figure 17. Outline for a Computer Resource Plan

new systems software modules can seriously affect existing applications systems and can alter the processing efficiency of the installed hardware. Changes to the operating system should therefore be integrated with the formal resource plan.

Data communications network planning is also sometimes omitted from the formal resource plan. As the complexity of the network grows and as the relative costs of data communications rise, however, it becomes more critical to include this element in resource planning.

Maintaining an event chart (see Figure 16) for each class of resource will facilitate both planning and scheduling. Event charts should be prepared for the installation of CPUs, DASDs, tape drives, printers, purchased software, and applications software developed in house.

An outline of an MIS resource plan is presented in Figure 17.

CONCLUSION

Far too many DP installations operate without a comprehensive resource plan. If an installation is to prosper, the MIS manager should begin now to improve its resource planning skills. The outline in Figure 17 is a guide to developing a resource plan and should be adapted to the needs of the organization. Application project teams and operating system support teams should be included in the plan development. The plan should be kept current and reviewed regularly. The MIS steering committee can be involved in a higher-level review of the resource plan.

References

1. Much of the material in this section is taken from "Matching Computing Demand and Supply," by J.F. Chilcott, Director of Management Services, British Gas Corporation. This paper was presented at the JUSEC Conference, Rome, Italy, May 1981, and is used with permission of the author.
2. IBM. *Business Systems Planning: Information Systems Planning Guide*. 2nd ed., 1978. GE20-0527-2.

I-4
Corporate Information Processing Policies

Louis Fried
Robert E. Umbaugh

INTRODUCTION

Policies are established by corporations to provide standards for operating in a uniform, predictable manner. They tend to minimize ad hoc decisions and reduce the potential for crisis decision making. Statements of policy are the means by which top management delegates authority and responsibility to subordinate levels of management.

As DP technology continues to grow in complexity, applications become more sophisticated, organizations increasingly depend on MIS, and crises proliferate. What could be a more suitable area for the deliberate planning involved in policy making than the management of information and information processing?

CORPORATE MIS POLICY ISSUES

Like all corporate policies, those relating to MIS reflect the strategy and philosophy of top management. Although this philosophy may seem predetermined by historical practice, it can be changed if an effort is made to identify and rethink those issues relating to information management.

The key issues are identified in the following subsections. In many cases, they are interrelated. Because different organizations have different needs and priorities, the list of issues is not comprehensive nor is a rank ordering of issues implied.

Scope of Information Management

Many senior executives understand that limiting the top MIS manager's responsibility to traditional data processing functions greatly restricts the organization's ability to meet its information needs. These executives recognize that an effective information management system requires the integration of MIS with administrative processing and office-labor productivity programs. Specifically, top management must assign responsibility for review, control, and improvement in such areas as:

POLICY, PLANNING, AND CONTROL

- Office automation—Word processing, dictating systems, interoffice/interpersonnel communications systems, recording devices, copiers, printing services, archival storage, filing systems, and microfilming.
- Communications—Voice and data communications, facsimile transmission, TWX, telex, internal and external mail, and the management problems of vertical and lateral transmission of information.
- Personal computers—The proliferation of low-cost, highly capable small computers must be integrated with an overall corporate strategy on information processing.
- Computer-aided design/manufacturing—Computer-aided drafting, mapping, design modification, testing, and machine control.
- Robotics—Computer-controlled programmable automated devices.

Responsibility for Development Projects

Many studies indicate that the most successful system implementations are those requested and sponsored by users rather than by the MIS function. Because users generally know their needs and requirements, they are in a better position to develop an application system. If a corporation assigns sole responsibility for initiating projects to MIS, it must be fully aware of the risks.

Specific responsibilities in development projects include:
- Project initiation
- Project management
- Successful installation
- Project payback results.

Long-Range Planning

Maintaining consistent support for information management requires a long-range plan. The long-range plan expresses the company's commitment to maintain a stable direction for MIS and also enables the MIS function to plan and develop resources for the future. Top management must also recognize that long-range planning requires the commitment of time and other resources.

Research

Some top executives believe that the MIS function must assume and maintain a leading role in keeping abreast of state-of-the-art developments in data processing. Regardless of top management views on this issue, it is certainly necessary to be aware of the methods, equipment, and technology that could benefit the company. In many companies this issue is ignored; the result is often the implementation of "new" systems based on outmoded technology.

Top management should consider establishing a regular budget (not necessarily a separate staff or department) for applied research in the MIS department. This budget should include appropriate seminars, publications, and educational resources or consulting arrangements.

Centralization versus Decentralization

The centralization/decentralization issue is a complex one that requires extensive investigation and careful deliberation. A decision on this issue should be based on such factors as top management style, diversity of divisional business, economic and technical considerations, and internal politics. It should also be noted that a decision for a centralized or decentralized organization can apply to all MIS functions, systems analysis, hardware, or the independent use of centralized hardware.

Although this issue should be considered an aspect of long-range planning, it can also influence corporate policy.

System Integration

In addition to the centralization issue, management should consider the advantages and disadvantages of system integration (possibly in the form of a centralized corporate data base). System integration has major consequences for information management and processing. Many companies rush to create corporate data bases without fully considering the costs, technical complexity, or potential benefits of such an undertaking.

Impartial Service

Ensuring that the limited MIS resources are allocated equitably throughout the organization is not only a corporate policy issue but also a major user concern. It is widely held, for example, that an MIS manager who reports to the corporate vice president of finance will allot a disproportionate amount of MIS resources to accounting and financial systems. It is advisable, therefore, to establish an organizational method that can prevent both the reality and appearance of favoritism. This may require the implementation of a corporate MIS steering committee or the reassessment of traditional reporting relationships. It is becoming increasingly common to make MIS a separate entity headed by a corporate officer responsible for information processing and reporting at a very high level in the organization.

CORPORATE POLICY STATEMENTS

Corporate information policy cannot be created haphazardly. It must be developed within the context of overall corporate plans and objectives; in fact, if these change, information policy must be adapted accordingly.

Specific corporate policy statements that should precede the development and publication of those relating to information include:
- Statement of corporate purpose—This should expand on those elements of the corporate charter that identify the corporate purpose in terms of business objectives and social responsibilities to employees, stockholders, and customers.
- Strategic business plan—Although not a policy in the formal sense, the strategic or long-range business plan establishes the framework and objectives for company operations. Within these plans, the staff and support functions must consider their ability to meet the needs of operating units.
- Policy publication—This policy should identify the responsibilities for developing, approving, publishing, and distributing corporate policies. Corporate policies may be developed by a "policy and procedures" group or by corporate functional units; approval for policies, however, should be centralized to prevent conflicting policy statements.

POLICY, PLANNING, AND CONTROL

In addition, a corporate tactical or short-range plan can indicate how the strategic plan is to be implemented and identify priorities (but it is not essential to setting policy).

From documents, and with a knowledge of key corporate officials' personalities, further policies can be developed.

Two separate but overlapping policy areas must also be considered. First, policies dealing with the use and distribution of information must be defined. Second, policies covering the responsibilities and operation of information processing must be developed.

INFORMATION POLICIES

The MIS manager should develop and distribute a list of appropriate information policy issues to senior management. He or she should discuss these issues with the management team for information policies. The group's conclusions and suggestions can provide the foundation for developing corporate information policies.

In the following descriptions, where development responsibility is assigned, it may be in conjunction with (or with the support of) a policies and procedures department. Approvals, where indicated, are coordinative approvals and do not eliminate the need for approval by the company president or other assigned executive officers.

Information Processing Policies

The following policies should be developed to enable the implementation of a corporate information processing function.

The MIS Charter. The MIS Charter outlines the MIS manager's authority and responsibilities. The areas of responsibility vary with the organization. Common responsibilities include:
- Developing and maintaining DP systems
- Evaluating and selecting hardware and systems and applications software
- Operating both the corporate and distributed data centers
- Controlling data input and output
- Distributing output reports
- Designing and managing data communications networks or all telecommunications
- Operating the forms control function
- Developing information processing policies and procedures
- Conducting feasibility studies of new manual or automated systems
- Allocating the cost of DP to user departments
- Conducting research into potential systems, methods, or equipment that could improve cost-effectiveness or enhance corporate profit
- Ensuring the security of all DP operations
- Developing and implementing office automation systems
- Reporting on the performance of the preceding areas of responsibility to top management on a specified periodic basis

Corporate Information Processing Policies

If responsibilities are divided between MIS and other groups, the limits of each group's responsibility should be outlined. For example, if both MIS and user groups have systems analysts, the responsibilities for systems analysis, maintenance, and liaison functions should be clearly designated.

The policy should also specify special functions (i.e., functions not generally performed by managers at the same organizational level as the MIS manager) that the MIS manager is empowered to perform. These functions may include:

- Approving certain policies and procedures.
- Reviewing and approving DP equipment acquisitions or external services and contracts throughout the corporation.
- Reviewing and approving systems development proposals.
- Reviewing and approving divisional MIS budgets.
- Reviewing performance of divisional MIS centers (if not directly administered by corporate MIS).
- Approving specific purchase order or expenditure levels for operating supplies. (These are often greater than such levels permitted for other managers to allow for the purchase of large forms orders or magnetic storage media.)
- Approving all forms designs and orders.

The MIS charter should be developed by the MIS manager and approved by the MIS steering committee (if one exists) or by senior management.

The MIS Steering Committee Charter. If a steering committee exists, its charter should establish the steering committee, name its chairman (by title) and members, and designate its responsibilities. Steering committee duties should include:

- Approving the level of MIS expenditure and capability desired
- Approving specific proposals for major equipment acquisitions
- Approving MIS long- and short-range plans
- Determining project priorities

This policy should be developed by the MIS manager and approved by both the manager's immediate superior and the person who has authority to appoint members of the steering committee.

Auditing. The internal auditing function should be clearly outlined in either the auditing department charter or a separate policy. Audit responsibilities may cover:

- Auditing input and output controls
- Reviewing actual report utilization and need
- Ensuring that the MIS function complies with stated policies and procedures
- Evaluating DP operation security
- Reviewing systems design
- Auditing system performance (accuracy and timeliness)
- Auditing archival storage
- Surveying user satisfaction

In organizations with sufficient EDP auditing talent, the internal auditing

POLICY, PLANNING, AND CONTROL

department may also be responsible for periodic tests or code reviews of sensitive programs and annual MIS performance reviews.

This policy should be developed by the internal auditing manager and approved by the MIS manager and senior management.

Cost Allocation. This document establishes corporate policy regarding absorbing or allocating data processing and data communications costs. It designates the responsibility for implementing policy guidelines and indicates whether DP charges will be considered in measuring user performance and profitability. Guidelines are provided to ensure that internal charges do not exceed costs for equivalent service purchased externally. It also states whether the MIS functions will be viewed as a profit or a cost recovery center.

This policy should be developed by the MIS manager and approved by the steering committee or senior management.

Access and Dissemination Policies

The following policies should be developed for accessing and disseminating information in the corporation.

Privacy of Personal Information. A policy that deals with the protection of personal information must be developed. This policy should address responsibility for controlling, accessing, and disclosing (both internally and externally) personal information. The policy should be developed by the employee relations or personnel department and approved by MIS management.

Confidentiality of Information. This policy should address the explicit responsibility of all employees to maintain the confidentiality of corporate information. It should address technical and business information issues separately. It should also identify the individuals whose approvals are required for releasing information to external parties or disclosing information within the company on a "need-to-know" basis. If nondisclosure agreements are required of employees, this policy should be the enabling document. The policy should be developed by the corporate attorney and approved by the engineering, manufacturing, sales/marketing, finance, and MIS managers.

Security of Information. If government work requiring security clearances is involved, this policy should specify the clearances required for various levels, the consequences of breach of security, and the responsibilities for maintaining security. It should be developed in accordance with government guidelines by the corporate security officer and approved by the corporate attorney and all key executives.

Forms Design and Control. Because forms constitute a major vehicle for transmitting, storing, and organizing information, responsibility for their design, development, and control should be assigned. Separate approval mechanisms should be identified for forms used internally and forms used outside the organization. Forms control should provide a means for eliminating redundancy and for developing and maintaining a forms numbering system and

Corporate Information Processing Policies

usage instructions. This policy should be developed by the individual(s) responsible for forms control and approved by the controller and MIS manager.

Reproduction of Information. A policy providing guidelines for, or restrictions on, reproducing information should be developed. This can be done in conjunction with security and confidentiality policies. In some cases, this policy may only be necessary to develop procedures that can help control the use and cost of copying machines. This policy should be developed by the corporate controller with approval by the corporate attorney, security officer, and administration manager.

Information Retention. IRS and other regulations specify the form and content of accounting-related information as well as the length of time that the information must be retained by a corporation. A policy should specifically authorize responsibility for retaining records and for approving their destruction. It should be developed by the corporate attorney and approved by the administration, finance, DP engineering, security, and personnel managers.

CORPORATE PROCEDURES

In most companies, *policies* are documents that assign authority and responsibility. Documented *procedures* explain the methods used to implement policies and specifically assign responsibilities within the organization. Such procedures would include:

- Requesting a project for developing a new system
- Requesting a modification of an existing system
- Canceling or changing a report distribution
- Requesting and using office automation systems and communication services (e.g., mail, telephone, TWX, telex, terminals)
- Using printing services
- Protecting individual employee privacy
- Applying rules for using remote terminal access to computer facilities
- Requesting the acquisition of computer equipment or using external computer resources
- Applying security rules for DP systems

In addition to these procedures, the MIS function requires internal manuals to document such policies, procedures, and standards as:

- MIS policies and procedures—A manual detailing the internal policies and procedures that apply to all MIS personnel or to those activities that cross organizational lines.
- Project control guidelines—A manual describing the entire process of project control for developing and maintaining systems. This manual covers requests for systems, project estimates, systems implementation, documentation standards for systems design and operation, and so on.
- Programming standards and guidelines—A manual detailing the standards for programming and guidelines for improving productivity.
- Controls and operating guidelines—A data center operations manual that indicates standards for input/output controls, auditability, library control, inventory management, computer operations, and so forth.

CONCLUSION

Managing an MIS department without the aid of policy guidance is like taking a trip without a destination. Each MIS manager should accept the responsibility for ensuring that his or her organization has comprehensive, easily understood policies on information management. Once the policies are established, the MIS manager must make a special effort to see that they are understood by subordinates and that each subordinate manager knows what latitude, if any, he or she has in corporate policy implementation. Finally, each manager should establish a process to ensure that existing policies are reviewed periodically so they will not inhibit effective management.

I-5
The MIS Procedures Manual

Robert E. Umbaugh

INTRODUCTION

Policies, procedures, methods, directives, standards—known by different names and found in varying levels of detail, these written guidelines are necessary for the successful direction of any medium- to large-scale organization. They enable management to convey its wishes to large numbers of subordinates over a long period of time. Some managers mistakenly assume that directives contained in various memos, supplemented by effective and frequent oral communication, provide sufficient guidance for the organization. Such communication is essential; however, while the spoken word is occasionally more effective, the written word endures.

This chapter:
- Presents the elements of an effective procedures manual
- Instructs the MIS manager on developing a manual
- Describes how to improve an existing manual
- Offers sample formats
- Suggests roles for various individuals in developing a manual or series of manuals
- Provides a handy checklist for developing and maintaining a procedures manual.

THE DIFFERENCE BETWEEN POLICIES AND PROCEDURES

Policies are established by corporations to provide standards of operating a company in a uniform, predictable manner. Policies perform the following functions:
- Facilitate the exercise of executive leadership
- Establish authorized guidelines to achieve consistency in decision making
- Allow greater delegation of decision making to lower levels of management
- Communicate the principles and rules that will guide management decisions and employee action

Policies are the *what* of executive management; they state the philosophy and strategy of that group and provide an umbrella for all other written guide-

POLICY, PLANNING, AND CONTROL

lines. Figure 1 includes a sample corporate-level policy statement for data processing.

Procedures, on the other hand, describe *how* to implement corporate and departmental policies. They are generally much more detailed than policy statements, often providing step-by-step instructions for specific tasks. They should indicate specifically when, where, why, and by whom tasks should be done. In this chapter, the term *procedures manual* is used generically and includes manuals on such subjects as standards and operating instructions.

PRINCIPLE

The Company provides data processing equipment and services to meet operational, contractual, legal, or managerial requirements.

ACTION RULES

1. **Data Processing Services**
    A. Data processing services shall be provided to meet organizational needs, when approved and authorized by user and MIS management. Such services include:
        1. Systems analysis and program development
        2. System maintenance, including minor system design changes, upgrading of programs and/or documentation, requests for one-time reports or processing, procedure revisions, and report distribution changes
        3. In-house computer equipment or, in emergencies, outside equipment
        4. Computer processing by the batch processing method (either in an open- or closed-shop environment) and by a time-sharing method
        5. End-user computing, office systems, and personal computers
    B. Requests for data processing services shall be submitted on an authorization form to the system sponsor, when designated, for approval and subsequent forwarding to MIS. Assessment of the technical and economic feasibility and determination of priorities between systems is the responsibility of MIS. Review of the functional and economic feasibility and determination of priorities within a major system is the responsibility of the system sponsor or requester.
    C. The manager of MIS shall recommend company-wide systems priorities to the management committee. Such priorities shall be communicated through the distribution of the MIS master plan. The department manager shall prioritize all requests originated within his or her organization.
    D. The use of timesharing shall be limited to computer applications that require interaction between the user and the computer on a real-time basis. Timesharing services shall not be used to provide rapid turnaround for computer applications that can be served by another process at a lesser cost.
    E. Timesharing shall be performed on company-operated computers in preference to supplier-provided services when internal services (equipment and skilled personnel) and supporting computer programs are available.
    F. When company resources are unavailable or when proprietary programs, unique services, or other features are required, supplier-provided services shall be considered.
2. **Supplier or Contract Services**
    A. In addition to the normal prequalification of suppliers provided by the materials services department, suppliers and contract services must be approved as technically qualified by MIS prior to authorizing services.
    B. Discussions with outside suppliers to establish new services or renew existing services or to acquire programs (including acquisition of application program packages) shall be coordinated through the data processing technical support group or, for time-sharing services, through the engineering programming and processing department.

Figure 1. Sample Corporate DP Policy Statement

MIS Procedures Manual

> 3. **Budgeting**
>   A. MIS shall budget manpower, contract, and other associated costs for in-house systems development and maintenance and for computer processing costs for administrative systems.
>   B. The user organization shall budget and control computer usage for open-shop processing and timesharing services (both company and supplier provided) and shall assign accounting distribution for allocation of costs. User departments shall be charged for open-shop utilization of computer systems and for timesharing processes at a rate approximating the cost of the equipment and supplies used.
>   C. User organizations shall budget all supplier and contracted services, including software development and equipment costs, user manpower devoted to the development of open-shop engineering programs, and other manpower not specifically included in A and B.
> 4. **Standards**
>   Standards for systems development, programming, languages, and hardware configurations shall be established by MIS to provide system compatibility among users and suppliers.
> 5. **Exceptions**
>   Any deviations from the provisions set forth in this statement shall require the approval of the responsible user vice president and the manager of MIS.
>
> **DEFINITIONS**
>
> Batch processing: a method in which input to a given program, set of programs, or system is grouped before processing.
> Closed-shop operation: processing systems under the control and scheduling direction of MIS.
> Open-shop operation: processing applications based on user demand, as resources allow, and generally not controlled in terms of validity of input and output by MIS.
> Timesharing: a method in which online interaction occurs between the user at a remote terminal and a central computer.

Figure 1. (Cont)

COORDINATION WITH CORPORATE POLICIES

It must be remembered that MIS policies and procedures cannot be developed in a vacuum; they must not conflict with other existing corporate policies and procedures. Where MIS policies touch on issues covered by general corporate policies, a reference to the appropriate section in the general corporate policy statement should be included. If it is inconvenient for MIS personnel to check the corporate policy statement in such situations, it may be a good idea to include the pertinent passage in the MIS policies (together with a cross-reference).

Most large organizations have groups responsible for the preparation of corporate-level policies and procedures. While such groups are often not of much assistance in developing standards manuals and other technical guidelines for MIS, they can be helpful in the preparation of corporate-level policies for MIS and generalized procedures. At the very least, it is important that the MIS manager and others involved in preparing MIS procedures coordinate their activities with the corporate-level group, if one exists.

ADMINISTERING PROCEDURES

Administering a procedures manual can be a full-time job in a very large

POLICY, PLANNING, AND CONTROL

DP installation. Responsibility for the development and maintenance of procedures manuals should be assigned to one individual, and that person should be accountable for meeting development schedules. This person should also be responsible for setting format requirements for procedures and for providing editorial assistance to those actually writing the procedures.

Since no single person is knowledgeable enough to write every procedure needed in a large data processing installation, it is helpful to assign each procedure to a *sponsor*. The sponsor should be the person most knowledgeable about the subject (not necessarily the manager of that particular function). Management's role in the development of a procedures manual is no different from its role in other MIS functions; management should give direction and review and approve the finished product but should not assume responsibility for developing the details of each procedure.

Updating Procedures

Once the procedures manual is written, it must be kept up to date. An obsolete procedure is sometimes worse than no procedure at all because some people will religiously follow written directives, no matter how out-dated. The IBM ATMS or a similar text management and retrieval system can facilitate the updating process. For installations without such a system, word processing equipment can aid in performing updates.

Some installations have found it helpful to schedule a regular review date for all procedures (e.g., every 18 months). Regular reviews help ensure that all existing procedures are timely and pertinent. If a procedure is not cancelled or drastically rewritten occasionally, the review process is probably not working effectively.

Indexing Procedures

An index must be developed for the procedures manual. A good index will save MIS personnel time in using the manual and provide a handy tool for the MIS manager, who can use it as a checklist during development of the manual, as a tool for ensuring that procedures are reviewed for timeliness and applicability, and as a quick reference for verifying that current issues, regulations, rules, and so on are included in the manual.

If the installation uses a keyword software tool, a keyword index can be used. Such an index is very useful; eventually, more than one procedure will address the same subject from different perspectives, and a keyword index helps to ensure consistency.

INTERPRETING POLICIES AND PROCEDURES

One responsibility often overlooked during the development of a procedures manual is interpretation. Since it is difficult to write every policy and procedure so that only one interpretation is possible, the subject of interpretation should be addressed before conflict arises. One approach is to assign responsibility for interpretation to the appropriate functional manager (i.e., procedures dealing with computer operations are interpreted by the operations manager, and so on). Another approach is to give the sponsor responsibility for interpretation. A word of caution is appropriate here, however, since the interpretation of policies and procedures involves some measure of authority, and the MIS manager may not think it wise to grant this authority to the writer of the procedure. The safest course may be for the MIS manager to reserve the right of interpretation. In practice, interpretation is seldom necessary; however, the MIS manager should decide how to handle the problem should it develop.

INTRODUCING PROCEDURES

Introducing formalized procedures into an organization that has no or few written procedures can be compared with introducing a computerized system into a manually operated user department. The normal work routine will be disrupted somewhat, and orientation and training will be needed. Some employees will welcome the improved control process, and some will be uncomfortable or even hostile about the formalized procedures.

To minimize such problems, the process of developing and implementing an MIS procedures manual should follow all of the steps used in the development of a computerized system:
- Analysis of the "problem"
- Prioritization
- Development
- Implementation phase
- Testing for inconsistencies and omissions
- Maintenance

The introduction of a formalized procedures manual requires discipline and should not be attempted on an ad hoc basis. It should be considered a formal project with all the appropriate attendant controls.

Orienting Employees

It is wise to review each procedure with affected employees as the procedures are developed. The manager involved should give the employees an opportunity to read the procedures and then should cover the highlights and conduct a question and answer period. This may seem a considerable effort; however, managers should not assume that employees have read and understood and will follow written directions. Here again, an analogy can be drawn to the installation of a new computerized system: proper orientation and training are essential for success.

New Employees

It is especially important that new employees be given a complete orientation to departmental procedures and those corporate policies and procedures that are likely to affect them. A new employee handbook especially designed for MIS employees is a good idea. (If the organization already has a handbook for new employees, a supplement for MIS employees will suffice.) A sample table of contents for such a handbook is provided at the end of this chapter. This handbook can be used as the textbook for orientation classes, introduce new employees to installation practices, and help them get settled in their new work environment. A well-designed new employee handbook

POLICY, PLANNING, AND CONTROL

can boost the productivity of newcomers, who will become productive much faster if they can avoid fumbling with housekeeping chores and searching for applicable standards.

PROCEDURES AND ORGANIZATIONAL STRUCTURE

As mentioned previously, policies and procedures should reflect and support the organization's management style. Tightly controlled installations are more likely to develop comprehensive and detailed procedures manuals, while organizations in which subordinate managers have more autonomy may develop fewer procedures.

Policies and Procedures in a Distributed Environment

A decentralized or distributed environment presents special problems when developing policies and procedures. A procedures manual for a decentralized or distributed system should contain the same basic elements as a manual for a centralized environment; however, the unique requirements of the decentralized environment must be taken into consideration. For example, maintaining physical and data security is more difficult in a decentralized environment, and security standards should be emphasized to ensure that the risk of exposure is minimized.

A decentralized operation is less likely to have the same quality of management available to all employees, and the probability of loss of continuity caused by turnover is much greater. In addition, the relatively smaller staffs at local sites usually have less specialized technical talent. These factors necessitate more detailed standards and procedures.

These same factors often lead to inadequate system documentation. If the organization is determined to maintain standard conventions, stringent documentation standards must be installed and enforced. If the organization wants to develop and maintain integrated systems in a distributed environment, measures necessary to integrate data and applications must be addressed in the procedures manual. Different naming conventions can make data and applications incompatible and make integration almost impossible.

Developing standards and procedures in a decentralized or distributed environment can be a problem in itself. If DP is totally decentralized and no central control group exists, it is unlikely that common standards and procedures can be developed. If a central control group does exist, however, this group should be responsible for developing standards. Individual procedures can be written by the various distributed sites; however, responsibility for controlling and reviewing the procedures should be centralized.

Additional guidance concerning the special requirements of decentralized and distributed systems can be found in Chapter III-1.

WRITING THE PROCEDURES MANUAL

For the MIS manager who lacks a formal procedures manual but has many scattered formal and informal standards, gaining control of the operation may seem a formidable task. A structured process for formalizing procedures is the key to success.

MIS Procedures Manual

The first step is to recognize that the installation needs improvement in the procedures area. In some MIS departments, the absence of formal standards and procedures is a major cause of the installation's problems. Taking time to write things down may seem foolhardy when a shop is operating in a "disaster mode"; however, instituting formalized procedures can be of great help in gaining control.

Once the need for procedures has been acknowledged, the MIS manager should resolve to develop them immediately. Postponing the task will only aggravate the situation.

Involving Supervisors and Employees

While the MIS manager may be the first to recognize the need for better overall control of the department, first-line supervisors, project leaders, and other employees often have a better understanding of specific needs. The MIS manager should use these personnel as a resource, asking them to identify all subjects for which procedures are needed. This is the first step in gaining their support for a formal procedures manual. The list developed from their recommendations will contain duplications and omissions; however, such a list provides a good starting point for the development process.

The MIS manager should particularly heed input from supervisors. They receive pressure from subordinates, management, and users and are the key to implementing and enforcing the procedures that are developed. If the organization has existing procedures, supervisors can often identify those that are outdated or incomplete and recommend corrections.

One way to start a formalized procedures process is to have the supervisors prepare a project plan. They can also help identify one individual who will be responsible for implementing the project.

Help From Others

In most organizations significant improvement in procedures is possible. Many large DP installations have a formal set of standards covering the technical side of the operation (i.e., systems development, programming, and, in most cases, operations); however, many installations have not formalized procedures for other parts of the MIS function. Often, many installation procedures are outdated; in some cases the distribution of the procedures to the employees is inadequate. Better organization of the procedures manual can increase its use throughout the organization and improve the productivity of the individuals using it.

Vendors are a good source of ideas for improving a procedures manual. Quite often, they have documentation from other installations that can be made available to customers, and some vendors will provide documentation from their own installations. Professional organizations and other companies in similar industries can also be valuable sources of information on procedures and standards.

In addition, managers should not overlook the possibility of finding help within their own organizations. Frequently, large companies have procedures writing staffs that can help prepare procedures, provide editorial services for

POLICY, PLANNING, AND CONTROL

refining drafts, and help ensure that the format of the MIS procedures is consistent with other corporate procedures.

Procedures Review Board

Using a review board during the development of formalized procedures can provide input from several disciplines, ensure appropriate levels of review and approval, and facilitate acceptance of procedures and standards. The function of the review board is to critically assess the appropriateness and thoroughness of written procedures before they are formally adopted. The review board is not a steering committee—it does not direct the project, and the project development team does not report to the review board. The board need not meet formally during the review process unless there is disagreement among board members concerning the acceptability of a procedure. It is recommended that procedures not be adopted unless unanimously accepted by the review board.

Review Board Members. If an organization has an internal EDP auditing group, the manager of this group should sit on the review board, along with senior members of MIS management and, where appropriate, representatives of major user departments. Including users on the review board can help them understand the important role procedures and standards play in the system development process. In organizations that assign users to project teams, it is appropriate that users also have a chance to review the standards that will guide project development.

Procedures Development Control

As discussed in preceding sections, the development of a procedures manual should be formalized as a project and subjected to the types of project controls used on other MIS projects of similar size. The procedures to be developed should be categorized and assigned priorities. A schedule should be developed and regular progress reports should be submitted to MIS management.

Categorizing Procedures. Some DP installations find it convenient to categorize procedures by organizational segment (i.e., systems and programming, central site computer operations, data entry, distributed operations, etc.). Other organizations find it more convenient to categorize procedures by function (i.e., systems development process, security and contingency planning, production systems, etc.). The categories used should depend on organizational style and the personal preference of management.

Assigning Priorities. The procedures to be written in developing a new manual or updating an existing one should be assigned priorities, with the highest priority given to procedures that have the greatest potential positive impact on the organization. Assigning priorities can be the responsibility of the ad hoc supervisory group that initiates the project or of the review board, if one is established.

Implementation Schedules. MIS management should pay particular at-

MIS Procedures Manual

tention to the implementation schedule for the procedures manual. The schedule should be ambitious; however, it must reflect the fact that time will be required for procedures review by both MIS management and the review board before implementation.

Distribution. Once the procedures manual is developed, the problem of appropriate distribution must be addressed. A quick survey of the DP installation will probably identify some employees who have procedures or standards manuals they no longer need and some who require ready access to manuals they do not have. Many organizations have a central group controlling the distribution of procedures manuals to all departments. In such organizations the MIS manager should work through this group.

EXAMPLES OF PROCEDURES

To further assist the MIS manager in developing procedures, this section includes three sample procedures taken from various areas within the MIS department. In some cases, only part of a procedure is included. The purpose of these samples is to give managers an idea of the level of detail that procedures should include.

Language Standards and Guidelines: COBOL

A. Introduction

The purpose of these standards and guidelines is to encourage a uniform style of COBOL programming that will:
- Improve readability
- Reduce program test time
- Provide programs that are easy to expand, modify, and maintain

These COBOL standards and guidelines are organized according to the divisions required to code a COBOL program. All statements preceded by (S) are mandatory standards. Other statements not so designated are guidelines. Additional techniques for improving efficiency can be obtained from:
- *IBM OS/VS COBOL Compiler and Library Programmer's Guide* (discusses programming, machine considerations, using the sort/merge feature, and fields of the global table)
- Formal training courses
- Technical support department

All COBOL users should have a copy of the *IBM VS COBOL for OS/VS* and *IBM OS/VS COBOL Compiler and Library Programmer's Guide* manuals.

B. General Considerations

(S): Programs are to be compiled under standard LANGLVL (2).

Spacing the Source Module Listing—The EJECT, SKIP1, SKIP2, and SKIP3 statements, when used properly, improve the readability of the source module.

Comments should be used when the information conveyed is essential to the reader.

57

POLICY, PLANNING, AND CONTROL

C. Identification Division
   - (S): Program names (PROGRAM-ID) should conform to the standard program naming conventions (see the Program Naming Convention Procedure).
   - (S): The DATE-COMPILED option must be used. The current date will be inserted in its entirety during compilation.
   - (S): The DATE-WRITTEN option specifying month and year must be used.

The REMARKS area should briefly describe the program's purpose, input/output sources and destinations, general structure, and special problems and should identify all called modules and their purpose, all switches and their function, and all report numbers. A change log should identify production changes.

Job Submission: Submitting Batch Jobs from RJE Facilities

A. General

A dial-up RJE (remote job entry) terminal is located in the engineering programming work space.

The terminal is a Harris 1660 consisting of a 600-card-per-minute card reader; two 1,250-line-per-minute, 132-column line printers; a CRT operator station; keyboard; communications switch; and communications equipment.

The terminal can be linked to the IBM 3090 computer system operating with special communications equipment. By throwing a communications line switch, the RJE terminal can be connected to a Pacific Telephone 4,800-bit-per-second modem that will permit dialing and point-to-point communications linkup with various off-site computer centers. By loading the specific control program for the computer center, the communications link is completed, and processing can take place. The standard control programs now available support:
   - UNIVAC UT 200—in-house, 19.2K bits per second; off-site, 4,800 bits per second
   - UNIVAC HASP workstation—4,800 bits per second
   - IBM 3780 terminal—4,800 bits per second
   - CDC HASP terminal—4,800 bits per second

The dial-up RJE terminal has been cost justified to communicate with various off-site computer centers. Organizations requiring off-site processing can use the terminal during other than normal working hours and will be expected to pay some portion of the equipment cost, depending on the extent of use.

Because of the limited speeds of the equipment, large input and output jobs will be restricted according to a notice posted at the RJE site.

Assistance and/or training related to the operation of the equipment is provided by the engineering programming department.

B. RJE Support

Contact engineering programming personnel for specific information concerning the RJE operation.

MIS Administrative Services: Billing and Adjusting Charges for Computer Usage

A. General
1. User organizations budget for and assign accounting distribution for their use of MIS's computer systems for open-shop batch processing and timesharing services. (See Corporate Policy Statement: *Data Processing Services*.)
2. User organizations are charged for these services (chargeback) at rates approximating the cost of the equipment and supplies used.
3. Chargeback (based on computer operation data) is billed monthly on the computer-prepared report *Computer Chargeback to User Departments* (see sections B and C, following).
4. MIS administrative services prepares and processes the accounting vouchers necessary to set up the charges (see section B, following).
5. If certain conditions adversely affect the usefulness of the computer output, chargeback credits may be applied following investigation of requests from user organizations (see sections D and E, following).

B. Processing—Computer Chargeback to User Departments
1. Computer preparation of the monthly chargeback report is usually completed by the fourth work day preceding the end of the month.
2. Engineering programming receives a complete copy of the chargeback report for use in controlling its time-sharing and open-shop batch processing and plotting services for user departments other than MIS. This copy is used in handling inquiries by user organizations, including requests for chargeback adjustments. Engineering programming also receives a copy of the report on microfilm.
3. MIS administrative services receives a copy of the chargeback report and initially uses it to prepare the following vouchers:
    a. Chargeback: A monthly form 8-3-A (*Miscellaneous Journal Entries*) is prepared, charging the specified accounts of other (user) departments and crediting MIS's account 1023, *Computer Services Chargeback—Credit*. Account 1023 is used to offset expenses for computer equipment and related supplies in MIS accounts 1021 and 1022.

    (Note: Charges for outside services that are input to the system producing the chargeback report are excluded from form 8-3-A because they are charged directly to the user's account on payment.)
    b. Budget Control: A monthly form 8-4-A (*Transfer Voucher*) is prepared to capture data for each of two methods of monitoring and controlling projects and systems.
        (1) Expense Projects: Expense data is entered into this separate system by a charge to account 1021, *Computer Processing Equipment* (identified by a 4-digit expense project number), offset by a credit to account 1021 (no project number). Credit adjustments are entered by reversing the above debits and credits.

POLICY, PLANNING, AND CONTROL

MIS Administrative Services: Billable Services and Rates

The rates and services shown here have been established for billing purposes. Examples for use of these rates are shown in procedure number 41, *Billing and Adjusting Charges for Computer Usage.*

Rates shown for batch, TSO, and mass storage charges are for System/3033 jobs submitted in any job class established in the category of *normal* processing. *Deferred* processing is also available at 50 percent of normal processing rates.

See procedure number 42.19 for specific job class assignment within each of the processing categories.

- Batch Charges
  - CPU Time: $0.08/second
  - Disk I/O: $0.30/1,000 accesses
  - Disk Mount: $2.00 each step
  - Tape I/O: $0.20/1,000 accesses
  - Tape Mount: $1.00 each step
  - Card Reader: $2.00/1,000 cards
  - Card Punch: $6.00/1,000 cards
  - Printer: $0.40/1,000 lines
- Timesharing Charges
  - CPU Time: $0.20/second
  - Disk I/O: $0.30/1,000 accesses
  - Connect Time: $1.00/hour
- Mass Storage Charges
  - Resident Disk Space: $0.15/track
  - Tape Rental: $1.00/month

  Note: One track on a 3350 can contain 190 card images of 80 characters each with a block size of 800 characters (blocking factor 10).
- Miscellaneous Charges
  - Microfilm: $0.10/1,000 lines
  - Plotting: $0.30/minute
  - Terminals, modems, phone lines: various charges

  Note: Contact network control center (NCC) of DP technical support for information on terminal charges/rates.

PROCEDURES MANUAL GUIDELINES

As with most project development efforts, creating a procedures manual is easier if the development team does not have to work from scratch, without models or guidelines based on previous efforts. This chapter includes practical tools and examples to help the MIS manager to develop a procedures manual. The examples included here are intended to provide ideas and to stimulate thinking and are not rigid rules to be followed step by step. Included are a sample procedures manual table of contents, a procedures development control sheet, a complete sample procedure illustrating the general format, and a table of contents for a new employee handbook.

When developing a procedures manual, it is important to ensure that the procedures will facilitate the operation and management of the MIS department and not interfere with day-to-day functions. The procedures must not be so cumbersome that they reduce productivity; it is possible to impose so heavy an administrative burden on the technical staff that form takes precedence over substance.

Table of Contents

The sample table of contents for a procedures manual provided at the end of this chapter is divided into three parts for convenience. This table is only an example and not an ideal list; such an exhaustive list of procedures may be inappropriate for a smaller installation. On the other hand, it may not be broad enough for a very large, highly complex installation. For an installation that is subject to stringent security requirements, a complete security manual could replace the scattered individual procedures on data security, physical security, and so on. A numbering system facilitating location of specific procedures and cross-referencing should be used.

General Format

Figure 2 illustrates the general format for a procedure. The format may vary, depending on the type of procedure; however, the basic structure is the same. The sample procedure, included in its entirety, concerns timesharing facilities.

TIME-SHARING SERVICES

Time-Sharing Facilities

Before you become a company timesharing user, you should become familiar with the administrative controls and procedures as well as the technical facilities (both hardware and software) available to you. These aspects are discussed in the following sections.
  A. Timesharing Support Group (TSS)
  B. Timesharing Option (TSO) Program Development
  C. Timesharing Coordinator (TSC)
  D. Timesharing Terminal Acquisition
  E. User IDs, Passwords, Accounts, LOGON Procedures

A. Timesharing Support Service (TSS)
The timesharing support service is staffed by members of the engineering programming section of MIS. Their function is to provide global support for all in-house and commercial time sharing at the company. TSS provides programming assistance, time-sharing problem resolution, and so on. They should be able to satisfy your technical needs with regard to time sharing at the company.

If at any time when using or attempting to use TSO, you experience hardware difficulties (e.g., if the computer does not answer the telephone), call the network control center (NCC) on 2-2329. TSO programming problems should be referred to TSS on 2-2968.

B. TSO Program Development
If you need to use TSO for an application for which you have no program, contact the TSS group. They will determine if the company has a program that can satisfy your request. If a program must be developed and the request is minor, no further action is required on your part. If the program requires a major effort, however, TSS will request that you submit a form 216 to justify the development of the program. Please reference procedure 01.15.01 for the necessary information to complete a form 216.

Figure 2. Sample Procedure Format

POLICY, PLANNING, AND CONTROL

> Occasionally, a program is cost-justified, but in-house development of the program is not. This may be the case, for example, if a program requires 100 man-hours to develop but will be used only once. In such situations, TSS will determine whether the program is available from a commercial time-sharing service. If it is, they will make arrangements to allow you to use the most cost-effective commercial service.
>
> **C. Timesharing Coordinator (TSC)**
> In order to provide a centralized source of information and control, each user department should have a timesharing coordinator (TSC), selected by department management. The coordinators should control their department's use of both in-house and commercial timesharing. To obtain the name of a particular TSC, contact the TSS group. While technical questions about timesharing should normally be directed to the TSS group, administrative inquiries and problems should be directed to the TSC.
>
> **D. Timesharing Terminal Acquisition**
> The first thing you will need in order to use TSO is access to a terminal. To determine your department's terminal configuration and responsible TSC, please contact the TSS group. If your department does not have a terminal, the simplest means of acquiring access is to share with another department. The TSS group can assist in locating a terminal convenient to your working location and in providing the name of the TSC to be contacted. The TSC should know whether there is any available time on the terminal(s).
>
> If there is no terminal available, or if you expect your use to be too great to be absorbed by existing equipment, you can request a terminal by completing a form 216. You should indicate the requirements for and the benefits to be derived from the installation of a new terminal. Approval depends on compliance with company policy regarding the use of data processing services. If the request is approved, the NCC selects the type of terminal and associated communication equipment that best suits the requirements of your particular application.
>
> **E. User IDs/Passwords/Account Number/LOGON Procedures**
> Access to TSO is secured through use of a user ID and password. Each user ID is a one- to seven-character password that identifies the user to the computer and is always kept secret in order to prevent unauthorized use of user IDs. Associated with this user ID is an account number that includes the account number or work order to which charges for your TSO sessions and disk storage are allocated. Also associated with this user ID is a LOGON procedure that is executed to initiate your TSO session and allocate required data sets.
>
> Submit form 42-100 TSO (*User Identification Request*) to the data processing security administrator (DPSA) to obtain a user ID/password and establish an account number.
>
> User IDs are assigned by MIS and are seldom changed. Passwords are initially assigned by MIS and are changed periodically by the user. It is your responsibility to maintain the confidentiality of your password. Every user has the ability to change his or her password at any time, with an allowable maximum of 89 days between password changes.
>
> If an employee who has access to TSO terminates or transfers, it is the responsibility of the employee's supervisor to:
> - Ensure that the password is changed.
> - Notify the DPSA by telephone of the actions taken.
> - Submit form 42-100 in order to delete the user ID or reestablish it as a valid user ID.
>
> The DPSA can be reached by calling the DP Trouble Desk (2-3600).

Figure 2. (Cont)

This procedure is fairly simple and short; however, it contains all the elements of a generalized procedure. It describes what services are available, how to go about obtaining them, who should be contacted for the various services, and how to use the services according to MIS department guidelines. All acronyms are defined the first time they are used—a very helpful practice for people who only understand English.

Many procedures are longer and more complex than this one; however, a procedure should always cover only one subject.

Control Sheet

Figure 3 is a sample control sheet that can be used when developing a procedures manual and to coordinate the maintenance schedule for all manuals. The control sheet lists the major sections of the manual, the individual responsible for completion or review, and the scheduled completion or review date. In this case, the control sheet is used as a review schedule. For example, the schedule indicates that primary responsibility for the procedure concerning distribution of MIS reports is assigned to the computer operations manager. It also shows that this procedure is scheduled for review each August. If a procedures review board is used, a copy of this schedule should be distributed to all members of the board to inform them of the review dates for procedures under their control.

New Employee Handbook

Figure 4 is a table of contents for a new employee handbook. With high turnover in the data processing field and the resulting need to quickly and efficiently integrate new employees into the organization, it is very important to ensure that new employees have ready access to the information that they need to do their jobs. A manual especially prepared for new employees has proved useful at many installations.

This manual covers items that are useful for a new employee but that are less important as the employee becomes acclimated to the organization; thus it is unnecessary to update copies of the manual once they are issued. It is necessary, however, to review the master copy of the manual periodically to ensure the timeliness of manuals currently being issued. The contents of such a manual can differ greatly, depending on an installation's customs, location, orientation procedures for new employees, and the degree to which other

Review Codes: M-Department Manager C-Computer Operations I-Information Systems	Q-MIS Quality Assurance N-Data Network Operations O-Operating Systems Support	A-MIS Administration D-Planning and Data Management E-Engineering Programming												
Procedure No.	Subject	J	F	M	A	M	J	J	A	S	O	N	D
Section 1													
01.01.01	MIS Policy			M									
01.01.02	MIS Jurisdiction								M				
01.01.03	Organization Chart			A		A			A		A		
Section 3													
01.03.01	Operational Test Procedures			C									
01.03.02	Flowcharts							I					
01.03.03	Runsheets											C	
01.03.04	Sysout Messages—Action	O											
01.03.05	Production Restart Instructions							Q				O	
01.03.06	External Tape Labels									C			
01.03.07	Distribution of DP Reports												

Figure 3. Data Processing Procedure Review Schedule

POLICY, PLANNING, AND CONTROL

Section 1. Welcome to (Organization Name)
MIS Organization Chart (pictures are a nice touch)
MIS Jurisdiction Outline—Organizational Philosophy
MIS Policy Statement

Section 2. Plans and Objectives of MIS
Formal MIS Plans
    Overview
    Where to Find Them

Section 3. Departmental Policies and Procedures
MIS Job Procedures
MIS Standards and Guidelines
Request for MIS Services—Form 216

Section 4. Personnel Matters
New Employee Status
Employee Status Record—Personnel Files
Employment Agreement—Security Agreement
Performance Appraisals—Standards of Performance
Career Development
Employee Benefits—Overview
Charitable Contributions—United Way
Employee Savings Bond Program

Section 5. Office Hours, Timekeeping, and Pay Procedures
Working Hours and Overtime
Holidays
Vacations
Illness and Other Absences
Timekeeping Records and Pay Procedures

Section 6. Security and Emergency Procedures
Security Policies and Procedures
Emergency Procedures
Air Pollution Emergency Procedures

Section 7. Facilities and Services—Data Processing Center and Corporate Headquarters
Data Processing and Corporate Headquarters Locations
Entering the DP Center and Other Locations
Supplies and Forms
Reproduction Service
Mail Services and Addressing Mail
Telephone Services
Transportation—Public, Carpools
Parking Information
Banking Facilities and Automatic Payroll Deposit Service
Medical Services and Pharmacy
Central Systems Library and Other Libraries
Typing and Clerical Services
Conference Rooms—Data Processing Center and Corporate Headquarters

Figure 4. New Employee Handbook Table of Contents

MIS Procedures Manual

> Employee Club Activities
> Tours of the DP Center
> MIS Newsletter
> Suggestions and Questions
> Open Forums with Executives
> DP Training Room and Facilities
>
> **Section 8. New Employee Needs and Responsibilities for Certain Services and Products**
> Supplying Operating Instructions for Computer Operations
> Designing Source Documents for Data Entry
> Obtaining Training in Use of Timesharing Option (TSO)
> Using and Preparing Corporate Procedures
> Understanding Basic Responsibilities of DP Technical Publications
> Handling of Personnel Records and Office Facilities
> Providing Corporate Open-Shop Time-Sharing User Support
> Understanding Basic Responsibilities of Planning and Data Management Support of Application Systems
> Responding to Matters Referred by the Problem Reporting and Tracking System
> Relationships to Other Organizations Working in DP Center
>
> **Section 9. Data Processing Hardware and Software**
> Hardware and Data Communications Network
> Software
> IBM 370 Operating Status Signal Lights
> Peripheral Equipment—Plotters, COM, Scanners

Figure 4. (Cont)

procedures can be used to integrate new employees. This figure lists the contents of a new employee handbook that has been in use for several years.

ACTION PLAN

No large organization can long survive without formal rules and guidelines, and the more complex an organization, the more necessary it is to document those rules. Managers who do not yet have formalized procedures should resolve now to develop them. Managers who already have documented procedures should review them to ensure that they are up to date and still applicable.

Developing a formal procedures manual can be a complex project, requiring the effective organization of many different procedures and the coordination of the many personnel involved in the effort. To manage this project efficiently, the MIS manager should:

- Use project control techniques like those used for other MIS projects
- Use a review board to assess procedures before implementation
- Establish a formal distribution process.

POLICY, PLANNING, AND CONTROL

SAMPLE PROCEDURES MANUAL TABLE OF CONTENTS
PART I—GENERAL MIS PROCEDURES

Section 1. Policy
Statement of Policy for MIS—DP Services Provided	01.01.01
Statement of the Jurisdiction of the MIS Department	01.01.02
High-Level Organization Chart	01.01.03

Section 2. Procedures Relating to DP Administration
Services Provided by Departmental Administration	01.02.01
MIS Budgeting Guidelines	01.02.02
DP Training	01.02.03
Tracking and Resolving MIS Problems	01.02.04
MIS Service Goals	01.02.05
Billable Services and Rates Charged	01.02.06
Control and Payment of Supplier-Provided Timesharing Services	01.02.07
Ordering DP Technical Publications	01.02.08

Section 3. Procedures Relating to Required DP Operating Documentation
DP Operational Test Procedures	01.03.01
Flowcharts	01.03.02
Run Sheets	01.03.03
Sysout Messages and Action to be Taken	01.03.04
Production Restart Instructions	01.03.05
External Tape Labels	01.03.06
Distribution of DP Reports	01.03.07
Off-site Storage of Backup Data Sets	01.03.08
Plotter Use Instructions	01.03.09
Production Rerun Instructions	01.03.10
Production Systems Trouble Call List	01.03.11

Section 4. Procedures Relating to Control and Balancing
Detailed Procedures for Control and Balancing of Each Production Job (as appropriate)	01.04.01
.	.
.	.
.	.

Section 5. Procedures Relating to Hardware Configuration and Capabilities
Hardware Planning and Budgeting Guidelines	01.05.01
Hardware Acquisition Process and Authorization Required	01.05.02
Central System Configuration	01.05.03
Distributed System Configuration—Approved Devices	01.05.04
Data Network Configuration and Standards	01.05.05
Plotter Description, Capability, Limitations	01.05.06
Data Entry Device Configuration	01.05.07
Scanner Device Configuration, Capability, Limitations	01.05.08
Computer Output Microfilm Capability	01.05.09
Report Distribution Equipment Configuration	01.05.10
Timesharing Capabilities, Use, Authorizations	01.05.11
Remote Job Entry	01.05.12

Section 6. Procedures Relating to Data Entry Standards and Guidelines
Data Entry Standards—Source Document Design Requirements	01.06.01

MIS Procedures Manual

Submitting Work to Data Entry ... 01.06.02
Validation Requirements ... 01.06.03

Section 7. Procedures Relating to Job Submission
Submitting Batch Jobs from the DP Center ... 01.07.01
Submitting Batch Jobs from RJE Facilities ... 01.07.02
Submitting Jobs via TSO ... 01.07.03
Jobs Requesting Use of Microfiche ... 01.07.04
Jobs Requesting Use of Plotter ... 01.07.05

Section 8. Procedures Relating to Tapes and Tape Drive Management
Guidelines for Tape Use ... 01.08.01
The Tape Management System ... 01.08.02
Open Shop Use of Closed Shop Tape Data Sets ... 01.08.03

Section 9. Procedures Relating to Disk Space Management
Disk Data Set Classification and Guidelines ... 01.09.01
Data Set Archiving ... 01.09.02
Data Set Management ... 01.09.03
IMS Data Base Space Monitoring ... 01.09.04

Section 10. Procedures Relating to Job Control Language (JCL)
Preparation and Use of JOB Statement ... 01.10.01
Preparation and Use of EXEC Statement ... 01.10.02
Preparation and Use of DD Statement ... 01.10.03
Preparation and Use of the Job Entry Subsystem (JES)
    Control Statement ... 01.10.04
Preparation and Use of the INTERNAL READER ... 01.10.05
Job Classes ... 01.10.06
Sysout Classes ... 01.10.07
Job Entry Subsystem (JES) Form Numbers ... 01.10.08
Forms Control Buffer (FCB) Numbers ... 01.10.09

Section 11. Procedures Relating to Language Standards and Guidelines
COBOL ... 01.11.01
FORTRAN ... 01.11.02
PL/1 ... 01.11.03
VS BASIC ... 01.11.04
Assembly Language ... 01.11.05

Section 12. Procedures Relating to S/370 Libraries
System Library Descriptions ... 01.12.01
Updating Production Libraries ... 01.12.02
Project Development Libraries ... 01.12.03

Section 13. Procedures Relating to Naming Standards
System/Subsystem Names ... 01.13.01
PROC Names ... 01.13.02
JOB Names ... 01.13.03

POLICY, PLANNING, AND CONTROL

Program Names	01.13.04
Data Set Names	01.13.05
Data Element Names	01.13.06
Record Names	01.13.07
IMS Naming Conventions	01.13.08

Section 14. Procedures Relating to Miscellaneous Services

Programming Procedures Used with the Plotter	01.14.01
IBM 3800 Plotting Facility	01.14.02
Guidelines for the Use of Microfilm	01.14.03
Use of the Form Slide	01.14.04
Guidelines for the Use of an Optical Scanner	01.14.05
Use of the IBM 3800 Printer	01.14.06

Section 15. Timesharing Services

Timesharing Services Available	01.15.01
Timesharing Facilities	01.15.02
Programming Language Libraries	01.15.03
Available Software Functions	01.15.04
TSO Equipment	01.15.05
Creating Your Own TSO Commands/CLISTS	01.15.06
Special Commands	01.15.07
Application Programs	01.15.08
LOGON Procedures	01.15.09
TSO Security	01.15.10
TSO Data Set Accessing Conventions	01.15.11
Creating and Modifying Data and Programs	01.15.12
Non-Disk Data for TSO Use	01.15.13
Extended Commands Capability	01.15.14
TSO/Batch Interface	01.15.15
Data Set Conflicts	01.15.16
Error Messages	01.15.17

Section 16. Procedures Relating to Non-MIS Use of Computing Services

Engineering Programming Services	01.16.01
Computer Services Purchased from Outside Suppliers—Administration and Processing	01.16.02
Engineering Application Computer Program Products—Acquisition and Installation	01.16.03
Listing and Punching Card Decks	01.16.04

Section 17. Procedures Relating to the Data Dictionary/Directory

Keywording	01.17.01
Specialized Facilities Under DD/D	01.17.02

Section 18. Procedures Relating to UTILITIES and SUBPROGRAMS

Detailed Procedures for Each UTILITY and SUBPROGRAM Available (as appropriate)	01.18.01

Section 19. Procedures Relating to Debugging and Tuning Aids

Tuning Application Programs	01.19.01

MIS Procedures Manual

    Detailed Procedures for Each Debugging Aid Available (as appropriate)   01.19.02
    .
    .
    .

Section 20. Procedures Relating to Description of DP Systems
    This section should contain abstracts of each production system of major importance to the installation.   01.20.01
    .
    .
    .

PART II—SYSTEMS DEVELOPMENT

Section 1. Procedures Relating to Project Management
MIS Project Management	02.01.01
Project Staffing	02.01.02
Project Schedules	02.01.03
Project Status and Progress Reports—Overview	02.01.04
Project Budgeting Guidelines	02.01.05
Systems Development Standards Enforcement and Deviation	02.01.06
Change Control Boards and Systems Advisory Committees	02.01.07

Section 2. Procedures Relating to Systems Development Cycle
Systems Development Life Cycle—General Definition and Flow	02.02.01
User Responsibilities	02.02.02
Auditor Participation and Responsibilities	02.02.03
Project Initiation	02.02.04
General Specifications	02.02.05
Detailed Design Specifications	02.02.06
Ancillary Systems Design and Interface	02.02.07
Standards and Guidelines for Forms Design	02.02.08

Section 3. Systems Design Specifications
Standards and Guidelines for Phased Plans	02.03.01
Preliminary Systems Design	02.03.02
User Requirements Summary	02.03.03
Major Project Change Control Procedures	02.03.04
Training Plans	02.03.05
Systems Design Acceptance Criteria	02.03.06
Cost/Benefit Analysis and Reports Required	02.03.07

Section 4. Procedures Relating to Structured Methods
    Detailed Procedures for Structured Processes Used (if appropriate)   02.04.01
    .
    .
    .

Section 5. Procedures Relating to System Installation and Evaluation
Systems Installation	02.05.01
Operations Acceptance Criteria	02.05.02
Installation Follow-Up—Problem Resolution	02.05.03
Post-Implementation Audit Activities and Reports Required	02.05.04

POLICY, PLANNING, AND CONTROL

Section 6. Procedures Relating to Project Reports
Project Initiation Report—Standards and Guidelines	02.06.01
General and Detailed Design Phase Reports—Standards and Guidelines	02.06.02
Implementation Report—Standards and Guidelines	02.06.03
Progress Reports—Contents and Standards—Distribution	02.06.04

Section 7. Procedures Relating to Systems Development Documentation Requirements
General Requirements	02.07.01
Indexing, Numbering and Keywording	02.07.02
Flowchart Symbols	02.07.03
Transaction Flow Definition	02.07.04
Data Requirements Definition	02.07.05
Source Input Definition	02.07.06
File Documentation	02.07.07
Program Documentation	02.07.08
Module Definition and Documentation	02.07.09
Supporting Narrative	02.07.10
Supporting Charts	02.07.11
Benefits Matrix	02.07.12
Central Systems Library Documentation Requirements	02.07.13
Off-site Storage of System Documentation	02.07.14
Auditors Review of Systems Documentation	02.07.15

PART III—GENERAL ADMINISTRATIVE PROCEDURES

Section 1. Procedures Relating to Personnel Matters
Manpower Budgeting, Recruiting, Testing and Interviewing	03.01.01
Processing Employee Expense Reports	03.01.02
Maintenance of MIS Personnel Records	03.01.03
Involuntary Termination of Employment	03.01.04
Employee Disciplinary Action	03.01.05
Requests for Wage and Salary Action	03.01.06
Premium (Overtime) Authorization	03.01.07
Employee Training	03.01.08
Processing New Employees	03.01.09
Control of Absenteeism	03.01.10

Section 2. Procedures Relating to Procurement Activities
Signature Authorization Levels	03.02.01
Selection and Acquisition of Data Processing Software—General	03.02.02
Selection and Acquisition of Data Processing Hardware—General	03.02.03
Use of Outside Services for Appropriate Software Analysis and Programming	03.02.04
Proprietary Software—Use and Safeguarding	03.02.05

Section 3. Procedures Relating to Security
Pre-employment Checks	03.03.01
Admission to DP Centers	03.03.02
Building Security/Emergency Procedures	03.03.03
Physical Security Program Audit	03.03.04
Contingency Planning	03.03.05
Data Security	03.03.06

Section II
Management Issues

As information and information processing technology play a more central role in the success of organizations, it becomes more imperative that leadership and direction in this area come from the very top. It is not enough that the CEO blesses the budget each year or receives a copy of the long-range plan. The CEO must take an active interest in the deployment of this critical resource just as he or she does in the deployment of the organization's marketing, research and development, or manufacturing resources. The scope of this new role is examined in the chapter, "The Leadership Role of the CEO in Information Technology."

One way for the CEO and subordinate levels of management, including MIS management, to control information processing resources is to implement a management-by-objective (MBO) program. This process will not be foreign to experienced MIS managers because it entails setting specific goals, assigning responsibility, establishing due dates, and measuring progress and success. This process is exactly what many of us have been using informally to manage data processing for years. Chapter II-2, "MBO for MIS," describes a way to formalize the process and to use it to better control the diverse activities we must manage today.

Another device that many organizations find useful in managing the information resource is the steering committee. Steering committees can serve several purposes: they can improve communication with user management, help set priorities, and help resolve conflict. Properly structured, steering committees can also bring a multidiscipline perspective to the guidance of MIS. Improperly structured, however, they can cause problems, disrupting the operation of the MIS department and driving good management out the door. The chapter titled "Steering Committees—Some Thoughts on Pros and Cons" might help you avoid some of the problems companies have encountered with such committees and perhaps take advantage of these benefits.

One question frequently debated by steering committees is user chargeback. Should users be charged directly for the services they use? In many organizations, data processing services are the only staff service charged back to users. Why should this be? Are DP services so different from other staff services that they need or deserve special treatment? If so, how can a chargeback scheme be structured to fairly reflect services provided? And how much should be charged back? These issues are covered in full in the chapter titled "How Should Users Pay for MIS Services?"

All of these issues are of vital concern to most MIS managers, since they affect the department's functioning at the corporate level. The following pages should stimulate you to respond to the challenges facing you in your environment.

II-1

The Leadership Role of the CEO in Information Technology

Thomas P. Gerrity

INTRODUCTION

Five years ago, most CEOs would have responded to the title of this chapter by saying, "What role? Managing information technology is a job for my staff specialists in that area, not me." Today, the CEO's perspective is rapidly changing as executives find that information technology is fast becoming one of their most powerful tools for improving both their firm's competitive position in the marketplace and its overall internal effectiveness. This chapter examines the reasons for this rapid change and outlines concrete approaches for the CEO to follow in order to capitalize on this formidable new business tool.

INFORMATION TECHNOLOGY: OUT OF THE BACK OFFICE

In the past, business organizations used information technology primarily to automate clerical and "back office" activities. During the early days of information processing, the MIS department played a minor role in helping the business achieve its larger goals. The department improved efficiency in certain operational aspects but had little impact on the business's overall effectiveness or competitive position.

Today, the situation clearly has changed, and the rate of this change is accelerating. We have entered an age in which the effective management of information technology is one of business's primary competitive weapons, and its power is increasing every year. In addition, information technology management affects virtually every function within many businesses. Its influence ranges from day-to-day operations to year-to-year tactics to long-range strategy. Furthermore, the merging of different information technologies—computers, telecommunications, and office automation, for example—offers the potential for even more rapid change across all industries.

Given the emerging importance of information technology, the CEO must become involved in information technology management—not in the day-to-

MANAGEMENT ISSUES

day management role traditionally filled by the senior executive in charge of the technology, but rather in an overall leadership role. The CEO must ensure that the technology is strategically and creatively exploited to its fullest potential. Fortunately for the CEO, he or she can take on this new role without becoming immersed in the technology; strategic information technology management involves issues that already challenge the CEO: developing and implementing business strategy, managing organizational change, and dealing with risk and uncertainty. Information is a critical resource, and its challenges and payoffs are similar to those involved in managing an organization's human and financial resources. In this chapter, we will first explore the major new benefits that information technology offers and then examine the specific steps that enable the CEO to adopt the appropriate leadership role.

THE VALUE OF INFORMATION TECHNOLOGY

Information technology has no value in and of itself. Its value lies not in the technology—sophisticated as it may be—but rather in the effective business change that it facilitates. Information technology can effect change in two ways: by working externally and strategically to enhance a business's competitive position and by significantly improving the organization's internal effectiveness (see Figure 1).

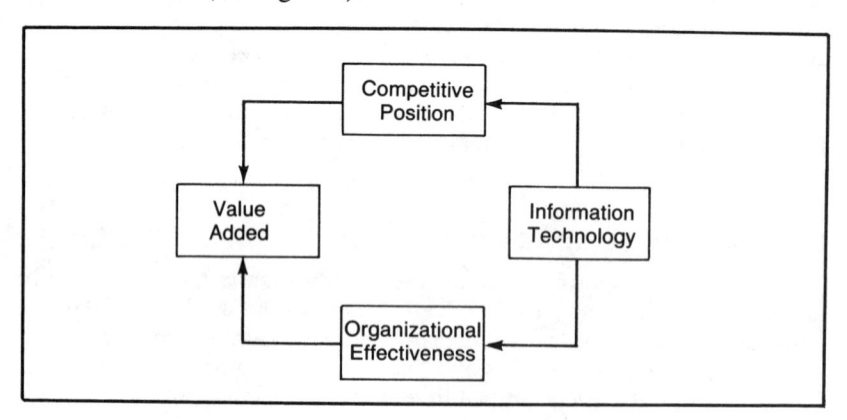

Figure 1. How Information Technology Contributes to Organizational Change

Information Technology as a Competitive Weapon

Many businesses have already determined how critical information technology is to new product development and delivery and to a competitive position in many service industries. This is most notable in financial services, in which a bank or insurance company cannot create new products independent of the information technology necessary to support them; however, recognition of the critical role of information technology is also increasingly true in companies producing "hard" products. In these cases, the information resource is often used as a product extender, which is a method of adding new value through technology-based services to distributors, dealers, and even to the end user. In some cases, these value-added services surrounding

The CEO and MIS

hard products act as strong deterrents to product switching by distributors or end users who become dependent on the product's or service's information component in a way that substantially raises the apparent costs of switching suppliers.

The competitive edge that can be gained with information technology differs according to the type of business and industry in which it is applied. For example, a marketing-oriented business in a volatile market may welcome the use of information technology as a vehicle for rapid introduction of new products or for adding new features to existing products; it may be less interested in technology that offers only cost reductions. In contrast, a relatively stable firm in a stable industry with a control-oriented business may seek value from information technology that can be measured in clear, quantifiable cost reductions that yield a significant competitive advantage. The CEO must evaluate the particular character and strategy of each business segment in the firm and then determine which uses of technology are appropriate to each business segment.

Information Technology for Organizational Effectiveness

The CEO can use technology to improve an organization's effectiveness in two primary ways (see Figure 2). The first is by aligning the information systems throughout the firm to provide consistent "signals" that reinforce and further the CEO's strategic objectives for the business (particularly new strategic thrusts). The second is by using technology to directly support and leverage the effectiveness of managers, professionals, and staff.

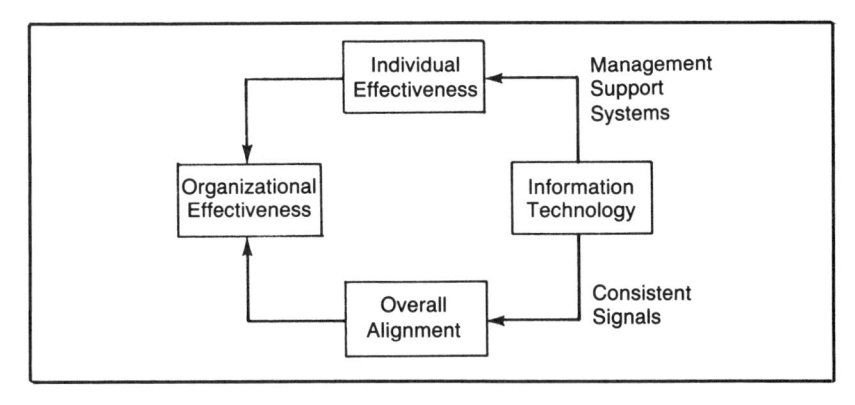

Figure 2. How Information Technology Improves Organizational Effectiveness

Successful CEOs and senior managers recognize the necessary interrelationships and delicate balance between the various critical elements of a successful organization. In their best-selling book, *In Search of Excellence*,[1] Thomas J. Peters and Robert H. Waterman, Jr. narrow these critical elements to seven in the "7-S model": shared values, structure, systems, style, staff, skills, and strategy. According to the authors, companies demonstrating true excellence consistently manage to keep these seven factors in balance and alignment.

Many organizations are discovering the growing power of the systems ele-

MANAGEMENT ISSUES

ment of the 7-S model, particularly in light of recent advances in information technology. One leading practitioner of the 7-S model has suggested that systems are the CEO's greatest point of leverage in affecting internal organizational effectiveness, just as strategy is for the firm's external market position. In this sense, systems can either accelerate a business toward its strategic objectives or encumber an organization, resulting in inferior performance, even if the strategy is sound, the resources sufficient, and the personnel talented.

In a relatively stable business, information technology is used to develop systems that align with and support the strategy, structure, style, staff, skills, and shared values. When all of these elements remain relatively stable, systems will continue to support the business. Today, however, as businesses face increasing change and volatility, systems often reflect past trends and directions rather than the pressing needs of the future. For the CEO managing strategic change, systems can therefore be a potent tool in supporting key objectives. Thus, CEOs increasingly are adopting a leadership role to ensure that information technology resources are aligned with the organization's direction. Otherwise, systems can weigh heavily on an organization, a weight that will certainly hinder the business in the competitive race for survival.

One proven method for achieving such alignment is the Critical Success Factors (CSF) process.[2] Developed by Dr. John F. Rockart of MIT's Sloan School of Management and enhanced and applied extensively in practice by Index Systems, the CSF process enables a company to align its information technology resources with its business objectives. It also enables top management to send consistent signals throughout the organization regarding the issues and directions that it considers most important. The CSF process has become a significant management tool in exploiting information technology.

ENHANCING INDIVIDUAL EFFECTIVENESS

Enormous changes have occurred in the technology that supports enhanced individual effectiveness in organizations. For example, personal computers are proliferating so rapidly within organizations that current estimates predict that by 1990 there will be an intelligent workstation for every two workers in American business.

This trend reflects recent changes in the broader field of Management Support Systems (MSS), which has been around for at least 20 years and includes many techniques for using information technology to support improved managerial and professional effectiveness.[3] The rapid proliferation of personal computers and time-shared terminals has heightened the impact of information technology dramatically. MSS is another area providing the CEO with critical leverage in capitalizing on information technology. As we become increasingly a nation of information handlers and knowledge workers, the influence of information technology on individual effectiveness becomes even greater. The challenge for the CEO is to provide appropriate direction for those employees who must deal with the new technology.

For the CEO, there is an important by-product of this MSS activity: it is producing cadres of computer-literate managers and professionals who are beginning to spot new high-payoff applications for information technology within the firm. Such firms are strategically in a very powerful position as we enter the information age. The CEO's challenge is to exert his or her leadership to ensure that this critical knowledge base is built.

THE ROLE OF THE CEO

The CEO's first step is to recognize that information technology has become a new critical tool for enhancing a firm's competitive position and organizational effectiveness. By taking this stand forcefully and vocally, the CEO will focus the organization's attention and energy on finding and exploiting key business uses of information technology.

The CEO sets the strategic direction for the exploitation of information technology; the actual management of the function within the organization is performed by professional information technology managers. As information technology becomes even more crucial to success, however, the senior information technology executive must become one of the central members of the CEO's senior management team.

As understanding of information technology's potential spreads throughout our society, CEOs must encourage an environment of distributed creativity within their organizations. For example, the best ideas about using information as a product extender are coming from product managers, and the selection of information to improve organizational effectiveness is being chosen by the managers who will use it. Good ideas about how information technology can create business value are no longer the monopoly of the information systems managers.

The CEO and other business managers should avoid getting deeply involved in the technology for its own sake. Nevertheless, CEOs should demand of themselves and their organizations an ever-increasing awareness of the business and management ramifications of information technology. The CEO must view this management evolution as imperative for the effective development and management of the information technology resource.

CONCLUSION

The ubiquitous spread of information technology has added an extra dimension of complexity to the CEO's role. The technology's enormous impact looms over the business, and yet its ultimate form and value are still unclear. But herein lies the opportunity: those firms that today take a leadership role in the strategic management of information technology will be the market and business leaders of tomorrow. Thus, the CEO must understand that the management of information technology profoundly influences the effectiveness of the entire business enterprise as well as its market and competitive positions.

The CEO must become—and remain—an active force in the drive to use information technology strategically and effectively. By unleashing and encouraging the creativity of people within the organization, the CEO can ensure that the new technology is used in ways that add value to the business. This opportunity in today's totally new dimension of business competition must be seized.

MANAGEMENT ISSUES

References

1. Peters, Thomas J. and Waterman, Robert H. Jr., *In Search of Excellence* (New York: Harper & Row, 1982).
2. "Critical Success Factors: Improving Management Effectiveness," *Indications* (Index Systems, Winter 1983).
3. Gulden, Gary, "A Framework for Decisions," *Computerworld OA* (December 6, 1982).

II-2
MBO for MIS
Joan Dorfmann

INTRODUCTION

Effective management of human resources remains one of the most difficult problems for MIS managers, especially those who have risen through the technical ranks. The current focus on increasing knowledge worker productivity makes this problem even more pressing—the corporate budget-watchers want to make sure the organization is getting a fair return on its investment in highly paid MIS experts. Although it is impossible to tune the performance of an MIS staff the way a computer system's performance can be tuned, there are some well-established tools and methods for measuring and improving staff performance. One such method is Management by Objectives (MBO), a management process first given form in 1954 by Peter F. Drucker.[1] This chapter discusses the fundamentals of the MBO process and suggests how they can be applied to the MIS environment.

DEFINING KEY CONCEPTS

In the MBO process, managing is defined as the process of allocating and integrating human, technical, and financial resources toward the accomplishment of specific, clearly defined end results, or objectives. The manager is seen as a "coach" who helps the work unit set long and short term goals and coordinates the efforts of the unit while helping subordinates build the skills they need for increasing self-management.

The overall strategy of MBO is to move superior-subordinate relationships from an inspection level to an exception level (see Figure 1). This strategy is based on the premise that delegating meaningful planning authority to subordinates increases the likelihood that the subordinates will feel satisfaction in achieving personal goals, take the initiative in all phases of planning, prepare for greater responsibility, and develop a cohesive relationship with management, colleagues, and their own subordinates. Because MIS professionals are often highly motivated and project-oriented, the MBO process is well-suited to the DP field.

Statement of Purpose. Each work unit and the people in it have specific, definable roles. To begin the MBO process, the specific contribution of the entire work unit (e.g., the MIS department) to the overall objectives of the organization should be expressed in a general statement of purpose that an-

MANAGEMENT ISSUES

swers such questions as:
- Why does this unit exist?
- Whose needs are being met?
- What resources is the unit managing?
- What are the criteria by which its success can be measured?

This statement should include the economic and functional commitments to be met by the unit and the major types of work to be done. For the MIS department, this information may already exist in a corporate DP policy statement or charter. Using the general statement as a guide, an individual statement must be developed for each person in the unit, describing his or her unique objectives and how they are linked to the functions of subordinates and superiors. If a formal statement of the role of upper managers does not already exist, the unit manager must create such a statement before defining the roles of those within the unit.

Key Result Areas. Within each function there are key result areas that should be defined clearly. These are the critical aspects of every job, in which it is vital to achieve objectives and make a contribution to the overall goals of the organization.

Indicators. Closely linked to each key area are indicators, a group of items that, if monitored, provide a measurement of progress within that area. These indicators also highlight problems as they are encountered and can be thought of as early warning signals notifying managers of the need for corrective action to maintain progress. Indicators should be quantitative and easily observable. Good indicators are dollar costs, units produced, errors produced, hours of uptime, mean time between failures, average error rate, hours or days (e.g., for reports), and so on.

Long-Term Objectives. These objectives define the specific long-range results to be achieved. They need not have a target date, but they must state conditions to be met and maintained on a continuing basis.

Short-Term Objectives. Working backwards from the long-term objectives, the manager must define short-term objectives. These are measurable

Inspection					Exception
Area of Authority Exercised by Superior				Area of Authority Exercised by Subordinate	
Superior plans and announces decision. Superior implements decision.	Superior perceives problem, directs subordinates to gather data. Superior makes decision.	Superior perceives problem, directs subordinates to solve. Subordinate recommends; superior decides.	Mutual discovery of problem. Subordinate solves problem and superior approves plan.	Subordinate discovers problem, proceeds to solve. Superior approves final plan.	Subordinate discovers problem, plans and implements decision. Superior is informed of results.

Figure 1. Superior-Subordinate Relationships

MBO for MIS

end results to be achieved within a given period of time—the objectives around which MBO revolves. In order to be effective, a short-term objective must be stated in a formal manner and include four vital components:
- Accomplishment verb
- Specific end result
- Target date
- Cost (expressed in dollars, man-hours, time, etc.)

A good example of a short-term objective is: Decrease turnaround time (on a given job) from three days to one by July 1, at a cost of two man-months of programming effort.

The main characteristics of a short-term objective are that it must be accomplished within a year or less, and that it is specific regarding the nature of the accomplishment.

Action Plan. The manager, together with each individual in the unit, should develop an action plan that defines the steps, activities, tasks, projects, and so on that are the means of achieving the objectives. A good plan usually includes a time schedule and an assignment of individual responsibility for accomplishing the necessary steps.

Developing Key Areas

The following list of key areas contains items that apply to virtually every professional manager:
- Financial results—MIS management is measured by its ability to operate within budget or to make or save money for the organization through cost reductions and revenue-producing activities.
- Growth—In DP, bigger is not necessarily better; however, increases in the services provided to user departments (often requiring increases in the size and cost of DP resources) are sometimes necessary to meet the organization's goals.
- Organization and business planning—The ability to organize efficiently and operate according to a realistic plan contributes to the effective functioning of any organization.
- Selection, development, and motivation of key personnel—The essence of management is the ability to coordinate other people's talents effectively to accomplish the objectives of the unit.
- Providing management information—While all other managers have some responsibility for providing reports to various levels of management, MIS managers find this to be the most important of the key result areas upon which they are measured.
- Public responsibility—Many organizations, especially very large corporations and government agencies, consider outside activities an important part of a manager's responsibilities.
- Personnel relations—A fundamental measure of success in any business is the ability to get along with other people in the organization.
- Departmental image—Getting along with other departments and other firms (e.g., vendors and customers) is another result area.
- Legal compliance—Meeting the requirements of applicable laws and

MANAGEMENT ISSUES

regulations is especially important for MIS managers, who handle vital financial and managerial information.
- Research and development—For units that have the opportunity to innovate, especially systems groups, R & D is an important result area.
- Operating results—Operating results include a wide range of indicators for quality, timeliness, accuracy, and so on.

In summary, MBO is a technique for managing more effectively by defining roles, key result areas, indicators, long-term and short-term objectives, and action plans. Its purpose is to focus maximum effort on the critical activities that will lead to results in any or all of the key areas identified for the function in question.

MANAGEMENT CONTRACTS

The instrument through which MBO functions best is a written agreement or management contract between a superior and a subordinate. The contract is necessary to ensure clear understanding and agreement between both parties regarding what the key result areas are, which indicators best show progress, and what objectives are to be achieved within the time period specified. While the contract may seem to be an unnecessary formality at the start of the MBO program, it ensures against differences in recollection. This is especially important when problems arise.

The contract should include an introductory statement saying that it is indeed a contract; that it is between the superior and the subordinate; and that it covers a specific time frame. The body of the agreement should define key result areas, indicators, and short-term objectives for the employee. Figure 2 contains guidelines for developing a management contract.

The sample management contract displayed in Figure 3 demonstrates the simplicity of the MBO technique. The key result areas, indicators, and short-term objectives listed are not exhaustive; the depth of a management contract depends on the individual job situation and the personalities of the superior and subordinate entering into the agreement. In general, the contract document should be practical and limited to what is necessary for a clear, meaningful agreement.

Developing the Action Plan

The vehicle for implementing the management contract is the action plan. This is a personal plan, not necessarily subject to agreement between superior and subordinate. After the objectives, indicators, and key results have been agreed upon, it is up to the subordinate to decide how to fulfill his or her end of the contract.

Action steps specify the means of accomplishing the ends defined in the objectives. They should be written down so that the subordinate can keep them in focus and obtain whatever help and guidance is desired from the superior. Some action steps may be delegated, in which case they become part of an objective to be set for another subordinate in the management hierarchy.

MBO for MIS

Key Areas

1. Employees should describe in one to three words four to six of their most important job responsibilities.
2. The key area should be a general area in which employees want to invest their most productive time.
3. The key area should not specify the level of accomplishment to be aimed for.
4. The key area description should not include verbs, specific end results, dates, costs, or indicators.
5. If the number of indicators and short-term objectives for a major job performance category is very large, the category should be divided into two or more key areas for separate consideration.
6. Those areas in which responsibility is shared or delegated should be clearly identified.
7. Since a list of key areas may not cover all aspects of a job, "maintenance areas" or "additional responsibilities" can be listed separately to ensure that the contract is a comprehensive agreement for measuring overall performance.
8. "Relationships inside and outside the organization" and "Self-improvement" should always be key areas for persons in positions of responsibility. However, it may not be necessary to include objectives for these areas within a particular time frame.

Indicators

1. For each key area, specific measurements that highlight progress or problems should be identified.
2. For jobs that are difficult to measure, the employee should develop a brief statement beginning "My job is well done when . . . ," and then list the problems encountered in completing the job. An indicator can be developed for each problem area.
3. For planning and "individual contribution" jobs, the steps in the process can be used as indicators.
4. The most useful indicators highlight problems while there is still time to take corrective action. Indicators that report problems when it is too late to do anything about them are worthless.

Short-Term Objectives

1. Objectives should relate clearly to the key area defined and express a specific result to be attained, within a specific time frame, at an estimated or calculated cost.
2. Cost considerations are necessary to avoid unrealistic objectives that would require resources or time far beyond what is available or justifiable.
3. Objectives should not explain how the results are to be obtained or discuss the feasibility of the goal.

Figure 2. Management Contract Guidelines

The following procedure can be used for developing action steps:
- Define the problem after careful analysis of the situation. Explore as many alternatives as time allows.
- Obtain agreement on the facts, the desired results of the action step, and the methods to be used by involving others in analyzing the situation and by exploring alternative methods.
- Develop details of the steps to be followed (delegating where appropriate), specifying target dates and identifying the individuals with primary and support responsibility.
- Conduct a test of the action steps in as realistic a setting as possible. If a "dry run" is infeasible, obtain a critique from knowledgeable persons not directly involved in the development of the plan.

MANAGEMENT ISSUES

Key Result Areas	Indicators	Short-Term Objectives
Cost Control	Overtime as % of payroll dollars spent for outside machine time	Reduce overtime costs from 6-1/2% payroll to 5% by Dec. 31 without adding to full-time staff at a cost of 15 man-hours
		Reduce monies spent on outside machine time from $800 per month to an average of $400 per month, at a cost of 8 man-weeks in systems time
Planning and Scheduling	Adherence to job schedules	Produce all jobs within 6 hours of schedule by Sept. 1 at a cost of 20 man-hours
	Number of reruns and emergency backup runs	Reduce number of reruns per month from 9 to 3 by Aug. 1 at a cost of $6,000 out of systems and procedures budget
Self-Improvement	Completion of courses	Complete courses in data communications, economics, and accounting by June 30 at a cost of $875 out of the training budget
	Pass test	Qualify for promotion to division administrator by Dec. 1 at a cost of 150 hours of study and classroom attendance time

Figure 3. Sample Management Contract

- Ensure continuing agreement on the facts and on the action steps through reviewing the test results with all who approve resources for or contribute to the implementation of the action steps.
- Implement the plan, establishing provisions for monitoring progress and problems, taking corrective action (e.g., modification of target dates, shifts in responsibility) and, if necessary, revising the original objective.

A realistic, usable action plan is crucial for the success of the MBO process. Figure 4 is a checklist of criteria for evaluating every action plan to ensure that it will be practical and effective.

Controlling the MBO Process

Control is maintained through monitoring the indicators for each key area, which may include time, resources, quantity, and quality. Factors may be specified in dollars (e.g., unit costs, consumption rates, budget allocations), units (e.g., hours, items, reports, test time, requests, complaints, errors), percentages (e.g., overtime, error rates, debugging time, utilization rates), and target points (e.g., milestones, approval dates, delivery dates).

The most effective controls are stated as comparisons to some standard. With this arrangement, progress (or the lack of it) is clearly definable. There also must be agreement on and support for the control measures used and

MBO for MIS

> 1. Does the plan directly relate to a measurable objective?
> 2. Does it have meaningful, measurable indicators?
> 3. Does it provide for interim feedback to enable corrective action?
> 4. Does it specify the criteria for final evaluation?
> 5. Does it include a written activity schedule (e.g., network, critical path, PERT chart, Gantt chart,) to highlight the start date and target date for each significant step, final completion date, and the impact of slippage on any part of the plan?
> 6. Does it list required activities in such a way that employees involved can tell when they are completed?
> 7. Does it identify activities that can proceed simultaneously and those that require partial or full completion of an earlier step?
> 8. Does it detail who is ultimately accountable for accomplishment of the objective and who is directly responsible for specific segments of the planning process?
> 9. Is it developed in significant uninterrupted blocks of time for five separate steps: problem definition, cause analysis, development of alternatives, evaluation of alternatives, and selection of a course of action?
> 10. Does it relate the "ideal" objective to the realities involved in obtaining resources and in performing the necessary interim steps?
> 11. Are contingencies specified that could hinder the accomplishment of objectives?
> 12. Does the plan identify needed communication and collaboration between departments and individuals?
> 13. Does it provide for sufficient involvement of work team members to obtain their full commitment (not just their acquiescence)?
> 14. Are the objectives chosen to encourage team members to strive, while not placing the goals out of their reach?
> 15. Does the plan offer all team members a learning experience that will increase their self-confidence and effectiveness in tackling future problems?
> 16. Is it relevant to many tasks in the organization and not an isolated "laboratory" experiment?

Figure 4. Action Plan Checklist

rapid (if possible, automatic) feedback to key people when corrective action is needed.

APPLYING THE MBO PROCESS

MBO is not a mechanical formula for running a department like a computer system. It is an approach that still requires all the interpersonal skill the MIS manager can muster to be effective. A manager who is sensitive to his or her own strengths and weaknesses and to those of superiors and subordinates is more likely to be successful in getting others to accept MBO and to make the program work.

In the real world MBO is not an addition to the manager's job—it is a way of doing it. MBO is especially pertinent to the problems of managing other managers and supervisors. Most applications have been limited to upper and middle levels of management; however, MBO can extend further down the hierarchy, provided that top management endorses and supports it.

The MBO process can provide help in several problem areas in managing a DP organization. MBO can:

- Provide a framework for defining clear objectives
- Encourage teamwork by identifying common goals
- Aid in scheduling by setting milestones and completion dates for projects and tasks

MANAGEMENT ISSUES

- Facilitate and recognize achievement through mutual agreement on goals and regular monitoring of progress
- Provide clearer criteria for allocating salary increases and promotions

To be successful in the real world, the MBO process should begin at the top levels of management. The MIS manager should clearly define the goals of the organization and develop a management contract with his or her own superior. Only then can the MIS manager apply the process properly within the department.

The MIS manager should work with each immediate subordinate to define key areas, agree on indicators, and develop objectives that:
- Can be measured within a specific time period
- Identify the criteria and performance levels for measuring success
- State conditions for achieving results (e.g., resources needed)
- Have clearly set priorities

It may be useful to identify three levels of performance for each objective: minimum expected (set by the superior), average expected, and maximum expected. This provides some perspective on each objective and counteracts the tendency of participants in a "textbook" management program like MBO to set unrealistic objectives.

Both superior and subordinate should sign and date the contract and retain copies for periodic reviews and discussions. Control and adjustment of performance must be accomplished through continuous evaluation of results and periodic counseling or coaching sessions.

COUNSELING AND COACHING REVIEWS

Once the preliminaries of the MBO process have been accomplished and a network of management contracts has been developed in the DP department, the all-important counseling and coaching phase of management control begins.

Counseling Sessions

Coaching can be defined as teaching skills to subordinates by a direct approach, while counseling is changing a subordinate's attitude (or getting the subordinate to change his or her own attitude) by an indirect approach. The way a superior treats a subordinate who is having a bad day can strongly affect the subordinate's productivity. Therefore, it is important for managers to recognize when a subordinate needs coaching and when he or she needs counseling.

Since periodic reviews should be part of every management contract, counseling or coaching sessions can be scheduled well in advance, in a nonthreatening context. This gives both the superior and subordinate time to prepare.

The counseling session should take place in a business rather than a social environment. This prevents confusion as to whether the discussion is a friendly chat or serious business.

During the session, moral judgments should be avoided, and discussion should be limited to progress on the management contract. It is vital for the superior to listen properly. By this point in the MBO program, the indicators that were agreed upon at the start are telling a story about the subordinate's progress. The superior's function is to determine the background of that story.

Results of Counseling

If the employee is having a problem meeting objectives, the superior should find out why the problem exists, get the subordinate to recognize the problem, and help the employee to develop a plan or corrective action to eliminate the problem. The superior should be careful to criticize performance, not the person. In some cases the problem is due more to overambitious objectives than to poor performance. If this is so, the objectives should be revised to reflect experience.

The function of counseling is to help subordinates meet their objectives— not to tell them how to do their jobs. Above all, the superior must resist the temptation to take over and direct corrective action when problems arise. The MBO process dictates that the subordinate is responsible for plans and performance. While he or she is accountable to the superior, the subordinate is the one responsible for revising objectives and submitting them for management approval. If the subordinate shows no improvement within a reasonable time, then additional sessions should be set up. After each counseling review, the superior should take time to analyze the session and evaluate its success. A checklist to help in this evaluation is included in Figure 5.

1. Did the subordinate have a chance to report his or her views of all the objectives before in-depth discussion of any single objective?
2. Was the MBO process perceived as a management tool (as opposed to an additional clerical burden)?
3. Did the manager's approach result in defensiveness on the part of the subordinate?
4. Did the manager and the subordinate really listen to each other's messages?
5. Was an action plan to deal with existing problems discussed?
6. What aspects of the counseling session should be corrected in order to make the next one better?
7. Did the plans developed in the counseling session include:
   a. Clear understanding of the long- and short-term objectives of the work unit?
   b. Clear understanding of the responsibilities of both parties and their respective priorities?
   c. Concern for factual information rather than assumptions?
   d. A sequence of specific action steps and planned completion dates for each goal?
   e. Firm commitment to the plans spelled out by both parties?
   f. Quantitative and qualitative standards to be used as indicators of progress?
   g. Mutual agreement on which conditions might require revision of plans?
   h. Agreement concerning future review discussions?
   i. Rapid feedback to those who have to take corrective action?
8. Was the atmosphere of the discussion:
   a. Cooperative? Neutral? Polarized?
   b. Mutually trusting? Neutral? Mutually defensive?
9. Did the atmosphere change during the discussion?
10. At the end of the discussion, was the relationship between the superior and subordinate better? Unchanged? Worse?

Figure 5. Counseling Interview Checklist

MANAGEMENT ISSUES

Coaching Guidelines

While the goal of counseling is attitude change, the goal of coaching is teaching the subordinate. The following list of guidelines may prove helpful for coaching.
- Focus on behavior rather than the person.
- Use observations rather than inferences (observations are what we see and hear in the behavior of another person, while inferences are interpretations and conclusions drawn from the behavior).
- Use description rather than judgment. The effort to describe is a reporting process, whereas value judgments focus on "good," "bad," "right," "wrong."
- Describe behavior in terms of more or less rather than either/or, which may exclude the possibility of gradual improvement.
- Focus on behavior related to specific situations rather than behavior in general.
- Share ideas and information rather than give advice.
- Explore alternatives rather than provide answers or solutions.
- Focus on the value of the coaching session to the subordinate rather than the satisfaction it gives the superior.
- Time comments and feedback for maximum effectiveness.
- Carefully evaluate feedback from the subordinate during the coaching session. Listen carefully, and try to interpret accurately the success of the session.

WHY MBO FAILS

Like most management techniques, MBO is sometimes unsuccessful. In such situations, the line manager often complains that the technique was too theoretical and could not meet the demands of the real world. The manager or consultant responsible for starting the program claims that the program was killed through neglect and lack of understanding on the part of the line manager. When failure occurs, assigning blame is not as important as determining why it occurred. Some of the more common causes follow:
- MBO is considered a panacea—MBO is no magic formula; improvements cannot be made simply by repeating the buzzwords. Management effort and commitment are crucial for a successful MBO program.
- Staff management is ignored, and only line managers are included in the MBO program—In many organizations 20 to 40 percent of the management staff is excluded because it is difficult to define their objectives. Therefore, their development is thwarted through the omission of specific responsibilities.
- Responsibility for MBO is delegated—In this situation, the top-level executive assigns responsibility for the MBO program to the personnel manager or some other lower-level person who is expected to report back periodically. Although it is not necessarily fatal for an MBO program to begin within a department, in the long run a successful MBO program must be firmly supported by the chief executive officer.
- Implementation occurs "overnight"—Success is unlikely if the implementation takes place without some necessary training and orientation. A company-wide MBO program may take several years to implement

effectively because of the numerous departments that must be coordinated. As a rule, the larger an organization or department, the more time must be devoted to MBO implementation.
- Managers refuse to delegate—If managers are ignorant about how to delegate or are afraid to do so, then their subordinates will set objectives about purely routine matters and nothing of significance will ever result from the program.
- Subordinates are assigned objectives—This "shortcut" avoids weeks of effort in dialogues between superior and subordinates; however, it also removes the subordinate's motivation and commitment to carry out his or her own objectives. The real value of MBO is the participation of the subordinate in setting the objectives, not the objectives themselves.
- Quantitative objectives are required where inappropriate—Exclusively numeric or dollar-oriented objectives are unrealistic for some areas or positions and can result in failure for otherwise effective managers.
- Objectives are stressed, but the goals and philosophy of the MBO program are not explained—If managers do not understand why they are setting objectives, the benefits of MBO are lost, and the chances of failure are much greater.
- Short-term objectives are isolated from long-term plans—In some cases managers work against long-term goals in setting objectives that make them look good in the short run.
- The objectives of related subordinates are not coordinated—Each subordinate should draw up his or her own list of objectives; however, it is the responsibility of the superior to coordinate the objectives of all subordinates to ensure smooth operation in the department.
- Practical action plans are not required—If objectives are stressed, but action plans are not, the program may die after the initial effort. Conversely, unrealistic requirements for long, detailed action plans can also lead to failure.
- Periodic reviews are omitted—Regular reviews must be used to measure performance, check the validity of the original objectives, and take remedial action while time remains before the target date.
- Feedback is ignored—Managers must have the right kind of information, in the right format, at the right time if the program is to succeed. Achievement-oriented managers require greater feedback to evaluate their performance.
- Success is not recognized and rewarded—Performance should serve as a basis for compensation and other rewards. It should not be used simply as a means of pinning people down.
- The superior does not follow through—MBO contracts must be taken seriously. Priorities must be established and followed and failures corrected.
- Key managers are impatient with initial modest results—As experience is gained each year, the results often become more dramatic. If management has unreasonable expectations, however, the program may not have a chance to mature. This is a frequent problem when managers are not sold on MBO at the start of the program.

Clearly, the MBO program has many drawbacks. Although MBO can and does work, it is a tough, demanding management system that requires highly competent managers to ensure its success.

CONCLUSION

The manager who wants to develop a viable, long-term MBO program must do more than work up a few management contracts, perform periodic reviews, and hope for the best. As mentioned earlier, the approval and support of the chief executive officer is necessary for the long-term success of an MBO program.

A good first step is to design and implement a pilot MBO program within the MIS department (or one part of the department). The MIS manager can involve his or her immediate superior in the program by setting up a management contract with this person. Once this pilot program has produced benefits (e.g., improved performance, tighter control over critical areas of responsibility) other departments in the organization can be added to the program. Throughout the process, the MBO program should always be simple and flexible. The MIS manager should be responsive to new ideas and influences particular to the environment, as well as sensitive to organizational goals and individual needs.

References

1. Drucker, Peter F. *The Practice of Management* New York: Harper & Row, 1954.

Bibliography

Drucker, Peter F. *Managing for Results.* New York: Harper & Row, 1964.

Humble, John. *Management by Objectives in Action.* New York: McGraw-Hill, 1971.

Humble, John, and Humble, John W. *The Effective Computer: A Management by Objectives Approach.* New York: American Management Association, 1974.

Humble, John W. *How to Manage by Objectives.* New York: American Management Association, 1978.

Mali, Paul. *How to Manage by Objectives: A Short Course for Managers.* New York: John Wiley & Sons, 1975.

Managing by Objectives. Cleveland: Association for Systems Management, 1972.

McConkey, Dale D. *How to Manage by Results.* New York: American Management Association, 1976.

McConkey, Dale D. *MBO for Nonprofit Organizations.* New York: American Management Association, 1975

McConkey, Dale D., and Vanderweele, Ray. *Financial Management by Objectives.* Englewood Cliffs NJ: Prentice-Hall, 1976.

McConkie, M. L. "Clarification of the Goal Setting and Appraisal Processes in MBO." *Academic Management Review* (January 4, 1979), 37-40.

II-3
Steering Committees— Some Thoughts on Pros and Cons

John Whalen

INTRODUCTION

An organization's MIS function is somewhat like a company within a company. It is a highly complex, technically oriented function that has counterparts to all the functions of a manufacturing concern (e.g., engineering, production, quality control). MIS operates both a job shop and a continuous production shop, and it often provides services to all segments of the organization.

In many ways MIS is an alien body within the host organization and, if not controlled, can cause serious damage to the host. There have been many instances of runaway MIS costs due to lack of control or to executive "computer fever." In addition, the DP industry is replete with examples of failed projects, dissatisfied users, inappropriate priorities, lack of communication with users, high turnover, and other ills often linked with weak MIS management. Because of these problems, MIS sometimes requires control methods that would not be applied to any other internal function.

Some of the problems faced by MIS managers result from an improper reporting level for MIS, a lack of MIS manager involvement in strategic planning for the organization, and less-than-perfect peer relations with other high-level managers in the corporate structure. Steering committees are usually established to address problems that arise from one or more of these factors and to ensure proper coordination between top management objectives and MIS plans.

THE APPROACH

A steering committee is an advisory group empowered to make top-level decisions for a function for which it is not directly responsible. The committee reports to the top echelon of the organization and is delegated specific executive powers. Each member of the steering committee is partially responsible for the effective use of the resource that the committee oversees.

Essentially, the steering committee operates as a board of directors. While

MANAGEMENT ISSUES

not normally making detailed operating decisions, the committee establishes priorities, controls expenses, and makes economic and policy rulings. One difference between the MIS steering committee and a board of directors is that a board usually contributes to the expansion of an organization, while the steering committee often works to limit and control MIS expansion. When the decision is made to limit DP costs, the committee creates for itself the problems of allocating a limited and expensive resource and resolving the political problems arising from contention for this resource.

There are two types of MIS steering committees. The permanent steering committee is responsible for the overall guidance of the DP function; the temporary or project steering committee is responsible for the successful completion of individual projects.

PERMANENT STEERING COMMITTEE

Because data processing costs run as high as seven percent of the gross revenues of an organization, the permanent steering committee should include the president or chief operating officer of the organization and those executives whose departments use MIS services. Regardless of the MIS manager's reporting relationship, he or she should also be a member.

The duties of the permanent steering committee usually include the following:
- Use the members' knowledge of the organization's strategic and tactical plans to determine appropriate levels of MIS expenditure and capability.
- Approve specific proposals for acquisition of major DP equipment.
- Approve long- and short-range MIS plans.
- Determine whether specific projects are to be undertaken. These decisions are based on expected return on investments, lack of alternative methods, anticipated impact on the organization, and conformity with corporate long-range plans.
- Determine project priorities.
- Review and approve cost allocation methods.
- Review project progress.
- At specific decision points, determine whether projects should be continued or abandoned.
- Resolve territorial and political conflicts arising from the impact of new systems.

Because these duties require ongoing attention, the permanent steering committee should meet regulary—preferably on a monthly basis.

Advantages of Permanent Steering Committees

The permanent steering committee can enhance the MIS function by providing the benefits that follow.

Management Awareness. The steering committee can gradually educate management concerning the factors affecting the cost and efficiency of the MIS function. During one steering committee meeting in which the annual MIS budget was being discussed, the president of the company asked, "Why is money allocated to program maintenance? Can't you get these programs right the first time? I don't see why you should have to touch a program unless a change is requested." The problems of program maintenance were explained to the president as clearly as possible, but he still did not seem convinced. Later, two charts (Figures 1 and 2) were used as an aid in explaining the problems of systems design and programming. The impact on program performance and stability of changes in the operating system, the compiler, the hardware, and the user environment were also explained.

Thus, the permanent steering committee provides a forum for conveying concepts while discussing specific issues or projects. These concepts should be conveyed in noncomputer language whenever possible.

Manufacturing	System Implementation
Customer requirement established	Problem recognized
Customer specifications drawn and request for quotation released	Problem definition, system survey
Applications engineering study	System synthesis
Bid or quotation	System proposal
Product engineering	System specification
Manufacturing engineering	Program definition
Production	Programming, manual writing, etc.
Quality control	Systems testing
Prototype test or first article qualification	Parallel operation
Delivery	Implementation

Figure 1. Comparison of Systems Implementation and Manufacturing Functions

Manufacturing	System Implementation
Production standards available	Production standards often not applicable
Performance a factor of group average effort	Performance a factor of individual aptitude, background, and speed
Operations clearly defined	Operations require creative skills
Specifications known from customer	Specifications to be developed as part of project
Product to meet limited flexibility requirements	System to provide maximum flexibility
Limited coordination needed	Constant coordination and approval required

Figure 2. Dissimilarities Between Systems Implementation and Manufacturing Functions

MIS Coordination with Long-Range Plans. Another benefit is that the steering committee can ensure the continued coordination of the MIS function with the organization's long-range plans. The steering committee provides a vehicle for conveying organizational plans to the MIS manager. In addition, it allows top management to apply its knowledge of the organization's plans directly to the management of the MIS function.

MANAGEMENT ISSUES

Cost Control. While the MIS manager is responsible for maintaining control of MIS budgets and expenditures, the steering committee is responsible for monitoring expenditure levels and for correcting deficiencies in the control mechanisms used by the MIS manager. Annually, the committee should review the MIS budget, which should detail DP expenditures as well as their allocation to the user departments. This review allows committee members to determine how their operations will be affected by DP costs and provides an opportunity to explore alternatives that may reduce costs or permit more effective use of funds.

Establishing and Reviewing Priorities. The committee also establishes and reviews project priorities. Inappropriate priority setting is probably second only to project failure as a cause of high MIS manager turnover. The steering committee has the broad knowledge and authority to assign effective project priorities. As an adjunct to this function, the committee can also approve additional resource acquisitions to meet commitments or to cancel or delay lower priority projects if necessary. It is essential that the steering committee regularly review the priorities of all ongoing projects to prevent inappropriate allocation of the organization's resources.

Project Approval and Review. The steering committee also approves new projects and reviews projects in progress to evaluate their viability and to prevent overcommitment of resources without adequate return. A new project proposal should contain most of the elements illustrated in Figure 3. The detailed proposal is usually prepared by the MIS group, but the MIS manager should *not* present the proposal to the steering committee—this task should be performed by the member of the committee for whom the project will be done.

New System Proposal

1. A statement of the request and a description of the system
2. A statement of the need for the system
3. Analysis of the financial return on the system
   a. Discount rate for cash flow (five-year life suggested)
   b. Return on investment
   c. Payback period
   d. Gross annual savings (personnel, machine use, etc.)
   e. Annual costs (including depreciation and maintenance)
   f. Net savings
   g. Annual cash flow
4. Timing of the installation
5. Alternative approaches examined
6. A work plan or Pert chart for implementation and installation of the system
7. Plans for conversion from existing facilities and methods
8. Any supporting attachments or exhibits
9. Management approvals

Figure 3. Elements of a Project Proposal

Most steering committees require that projects over a minimum dollar cost be submitted for approval (a figure of $40,000 may be appropriate). Any substantial change to the estimated cost of an approved project must be sanctioned by the committee. Monthly reporting of project status can provide the committee with an early warning system to stop potentially unproductive projects. The monthly report can be structured as illustrated in Figure 4.

Resolution of Internal Conflicts. The steering committee is responsible for resolving political and economic conflicts at the highest level. The committee meetings provide a forum for resolving such conflicts by group interaction or by presidential guidance without making the MIS manager the "man in the middle."

Executive-MIS Manager Interaction. The steering committee continually educates the MIS manager concerning the thought processes and operating methods of the top-level executives. Such interaction is a significant benefit for the MIS manager. Of course, there is a corresponding risk involved—the MIS manager is also exposed to the evaluation and judgment of executives.

Status Report
January 1986

1. **Name of Project:** Employee Benefit Statements

2. **Project Leader:** Joyce Bowland

3. **Project Cost ($):** Period ending January 22, 1986

	Labor	Computer	Total
Current Month:	14,088	2,035	16,123
Project-to-Date:	27,715	4,100	31,815
4. Estimated Cost to Complete:	7,800	1,500	9,300
5. Estimated Cost at Completion:	35,500	5,600	41,100
6. Original Estimated Cost:	31,000	6,000	37,000

	Installation	Completion
7. Original Scheduled Completion Date:	1/31/1986	1/28/1986
8. Estimated Completion Date:	2/15/1986	2/28/1986

9. **Purpose:**
The system will provide the capability to produce the annual Employee Benefits Statement ready for mailing during the first week of March every year. An annual $28,000 reduction in operating cost is anticipated.

10. **January Results:**
By January 22, all programs were in the final stages of program testing. The various production runs necessary to create the year-end files were proceeding without problems.

11. **February Schedule:**
Complete testing and verify all programs. If necessary, run special updates to payroll and retirement income files to correct data.

Print Annual Benefits Statement.

Complete documentation of the system and all procedures.

12. **Problems:**
Turnaround time continues to be a problem.

Figure 4. Sample Monthly Project Status Report

MANAGEMENT ISSUES

This exposure is only a danger for the incompetent, however; a well-prepared, effective MIS manager should welcome it.

Disadvantages of Permanent Steering Committees

Perhaps the most common problem with permanent steering committees is poor attendance. The people who should serve on the committee are the executives with the greatest number of pressing responsibilities. Three strategies can help improve attendance:

- The president of the organization should be chairman of the committee and should stress the importance of regular attendance. Without this support the committee is likely to fail.
- Good staff work is required by the MIS manager. Presentations should be precise, clear, pertinent, and should avoid DP jargon at all costs. Visual aids should be developed carefully and in a uniform format. Status reports and proposals for new projects should be distributed in advance.
- Meetings should be brief and businesslike. Top management appreciates subordinates who recognize the value of their time and who act accordingly.

There are other potential disadvantages associated with the steering committee approach. The major problems and recommended corrective actions are discussed in the sections that follow.

Uninformed Action. Occasionally, a steering committee acts precipitously and makes a decision or takes action that is counterproductive. This action can be very difficult to reverse and the effect can be widespread. Good staff work, proper education, and occasional lobbying can help avoid this pitfall.

Squeaky Wheel Syndrome. This is a well-known malady, usually resulting in an inappropriate distribution of "grease." As with most cases of over-lubrication, it usually causes a mess in the long-run. The solution is strong leadership on the part of the chairman. It is his or her responsibility to ensure that the actions taken are in the best interests of the whole organization and not those of a single individual or department.

Insulation. The committee may actually insulate the MIS manager from top management if it is not properly structured or if alternates are permitted to sit in for the principal committee members. The purpose of the committee is to involve top management with the MIS function, not to insulate it. The solution to this problem is proper membership on the committee and stringent attendance requirements supported by the chairman.

The Stall. This problem is also called "analysis paralysis." Committees sometimes avoid difficult decisions by recommending further study. The solution to this common problem is to define a specific goal and a means for achieving it prior to entering the meeting. The member making a presentation should specify the decision or action desired and structure the presentation so that it leads logically to a conclusion or a specific recommendation.

The "Picky, Picky" Syndrome. In this syndrome the committee starts out with noble objectives such as setting high-level priorities and approving major projects and equipment acquisitions; these objectives degrade progressively until the committee is bogged down with choosing modem vendors and interviewing applicants for computer operator positions. This may be helpful if the MIS manager's goal is to keep the committee occupied with trivia while he or she runs the show; however, if effective upper management involvement in MIS is the goal, then this problem must be avoided. This syndrome is more easily prevented than cured—the MIS manager should ensure that the committee has a clearly established charter and should work with the chairman to help the committee stick with it.

Total Usurpation. In this case the steering committee not only steers—it also designs, builds, modifies, maintains, and often wrecks the MIS function by gradually assuming full management responsibility and turning the MIS manager into a highly paid, highly frustrated clerk. The only corrective action is to work to abolish the committee and start over or to find another job.

An Alternative to the Permanent Steering Committee

If the organization already has an executive or management committee whose function is to provide overall policy and planning guidance to the organization, this group may be able to oversee the MIS function. In this case, however, the committee's involvement must be limited to matters of major significance such as setting overall priorities and establishing departmental spending limits. The MIS manager must be an effective and decisive manager to work with this type of committee.

PROJECT STEERING COMMITTEE

As discussed previously, project steering committees can perform some useful functions at the project level. They can be used whether or not the organization has a permanent MIS steering committee. The project steering committee is structured so that the chairman has direct management responsibility for the project's success. (The chairman is usually the executive in charge of the user group that initiated the request.) Committee members should include executives from other groups in the organization that may be affected by the system, managers of the user functions that will be involved with the system, the MIS manager, and the MIS project manager.

The functions of the project steering committee include:
- Review and approve the schedule for project tasks and segments. Segments of the project should be constructed so that the decision to continue the project can be made at several checkpoints.
- Monitor project progress by reviewing periodic reports from the development team.
- Ensure that the resources required for successful completion of the project are available.
- Resolve territorial conflicts among users and among members of the development team.
- Make major systems design and budgetary decisions.
- Provide management direction to the MIS project manager.

MANAGEMENT ISSUES

The success of the project steering committee depends mainly on the clear understanding that the chairman is directly responsible to corporate management for successful completion of the project.

The project steering committee provides a major benefit for the MIS manager. By giving the user executive total responsibility for the successful implementation of the system, the responsibility of the MIS manager is restricted to the proper area—providing the required DP support functions.

The user also receives benefits. Steering committee reviews provide greater assurance that the system design specifications meet his or her requirements, that adequate acceptance testing is performed, that the proper resources are available at the right time, and that a workable conversion schedule is planned. In addition, the costs of the project are more visible, allowing more effective control of project expenses.

CONCLUSION

The MIS steering committee can be a useful tool for organizations experiencing problems in coordinating MIS activities with corporate objectives. Before deciding to use a steering committee, however, top management should consider alternative solutions, such as changing the reporting relationships of the MIS function. If a steering committee is created, the MIS manager will need all his or her managerial skills to work effectively with it. The guidelines presented in this chapter can help the organization to avoid the problems that plague many steering committees, and to ensure that the committee performs the function for which it was created.

II-4

How Should Users Pay for MIS Services?

William E. Sanders

INTRODUCTION

To define MIS chargeback systems, it is necessary to describe the evolution of the DP function and to understand some basic principles of cost accounting. In the classic example, the DP function was originally part of the accounting department. At that time, the primary purpose of the computer was to automate financial recordkeeping. The cost was considered part of the expense of running the accounting department.

As the value and function of the computer became better understood, its use was soon applied to other areas of company business. Consequently, the costs associated with DP were shared among users. Allocating costs was quite simple before the advent of multiprogramming. Logs were kept by hand, and costs were shared by dividing total cost by the number of hours of use, as measured by a wall clock, and charging each user for a prorated share. This was the DP chargeback system in its most elementary form.

The process became more complex as multiprogramming evolved. Multiprogramming provided the means to use previously wasted CPU cycles that were lost when a system awaited the completion of an I/O operation. Usage records could no longer be maintained by manual time recording. More sophisticated methods involving the computer's monitoring and recording its own use were needed and were developed.

Today, a comprehensive and accurate way to measure use of a large group of system resources (e.g., CPU time, disk and tape I/O counts, and print lines) exists for most mainframes and operating systems. Many organizations employ these capabilities to charge in-house users for their share of the costs.

Deciding on the resources for which to charge, determining the rates to be used, and having an appropriate system to handle the recordkeeping are the essential steps in setting up an MIS chargeback system. These items are the subject of this chapter.

MIS AS A CHARGED-OUT COST CENTER

Corporate accounting can view MIS either as an overhead function or as a charged-out cost center. When treated as overhead, the costs of MIS are not

MANAGEMENT ISSUES

charged directly to the user departments. Rather, they become part of corporate overhead, which may or may not be allocated to the various profit centers within the company. The basis for cost allocation is generally indirect and not based on any measurement of use of services.

Occasionally, MIS is treated as a profit center, providing services to its customers at a profit. Customers can be in-house users or outsiders. Although this chapter is written mainly from the perspective of treating MIS as a cost center serving in-house users, many of the ideas discussed here can be applied to profit center situations.

Treating MIS as a charged-out (or absorbed or allocated) cost center involves taking some or all of the MIS department's incurred expenses and directly charging other departments or operations for them, according to some scheme or formula. The costs thus charged then show up directly in the profit and loss statement of the user department and are generally viewed in the same manner as if they were incurred outside the company.

MIS costs can be allocated to achieve either full or partial recovery. In a full recovery approach, the objective is to zero out the costs incurred by the MIS organization through charges to users. With partial recovery, some portion of the incurred MIS expenditure intentionally remains unallocated.

Full Recovery Approach

In a full recovery approach, the objective is to zero out the cost of the MIS cost center; thus, every dollar of expense must somehow be assigned to MIS users. The easiest way to achieve this is to identify the services, units of work, resources, and other items for which a charge is to be made and to treat them as a product line. Cost accounting techniques are applicable in determining the direct and indirect costs associated with each item. Any cost expected to be incurred in running the operation is included in either the direct or indirect category. Rates or unit charges for each item (e.g., resource or service) are determined by dividing the total cost to be recovered for the resource or service (direct and indirect) by the expected use of that resource or service.

In theory, this method of rate setting results in full recovery of costs. In practice, however, this is not the case. Neither the budget/forecast of costs to be incurred nor the estimate of anticipated resource use will ever be exact. The better these estimates are prepared, however, the less the result will vary from a zero balance. There are two methods that can be used to achieve the zero balance desired in the full recovery approach.

Accept a Non-Zero-Balance Condition. The amount unallocated will generally be small relative to the amount charged out. It is equally likely to exceed or undercut the costs. If this approach is adopted, the company should abandon the objective of totally absorbed costs and treat the difference between the amount spent and the amount allocated as corporate overhead. It would then be allocated indirectly, pooled with other overhead, or dealt with according to any other company policy addressing corporate overhead.

Force a Zero Balance Condition. This is accomplished by an after-the-fact adjustment (either a refund or an extra allocation). This can be done monthly if zeroing out each month is important to the company or less often if it is not. It is preferable to make this adjustment less often than monthly since month-to-month fluctuations will occur. If an after-the-fact adjustment is used, there are several ways to determine the amount by which each user's charges will be adjusted. The easiest and most equitable approach is to prorate the amount of refund or extra charge, based on the portion of the total allocation that each user's share represents.

Partial Recovery Approach

Partial recovery is more complicated than full recovery because it is designed to recover only a portion of MIS's costs. While there are two primary reasons for adopting this approach, the effect of both is the same: part of the MIS costs are not charged back.

One reason an organization might adopt this approach is that it feels a charge should be made only for direct costs; overhead or indirect cost is not intended to be recovered. In charging for a programmer's services, for example, only the actual hourly salary of the programmer (probably increased by the cost of direct employee benefits and employer taxes) is charged. Not considered are space costs, utilities, supplies, management expenses, and so on, which would be viewed as departmental overhead expenses not to be recovered through use charges.

The second reason for adopting a partial recovery approach is that the organization feels that some services performed by the MIS department should be charged, while others should not. A large insurance company in the west, for example, charges user departments for computer processing and data entry services but not for systems and programming services. In a nearby aerospace company, a slight variation of this practice is the case. The aerospace company charges for processing services but not for systems development. Programming services associated with the maintenance of a system after it has been completed and accepted by the user are, however, charged. The variations are numerous; however, rarely does a company implement a chargeback system and not charge for production services.

The decision on which functions to charge out will be closely tied to management philosophy and corporate policy. This decision can be brought into focus by examining the reasons for an MIS chargeback scheme.

Reasons for MIS Chargeback

An MIS chargeback system helps to state costs accurately, prevent unjustified services, ensure MIS department cost-effectiveness, and ensure prudent use of resources. The system can thus benefit user departments as well as MIS.

To Accurately State the Total Costs of User Departments. As information processing becomes inextricably interwoven with the operations of most corporate departments and functions, failure to include the costs of processing in user departments' profit and loss statements can be a material distor-

MANAGEMENT ISSUES

tion. Management risks coming to wrong conclusions in making decisions based on cost or net profit levels of an operation that uses central MIS services if the cost of those services is not contained in the total cost of the operation.

To Serve as a Check and Balance against Providing Unnecessary or Unjustified Services. If user departments must pay for services, the organization must help ensure that only necessary and justifiable systems will be developed and operated. Charging for a service is the best way to avoid requests for unnecessary or unjustified work. An MIS chargeback scheme is no guarantee against such requests, however; other devices, such as management review committees and cost/benefit analysis, are also needed.

To Help Ensure that MIS Functions in a Cost-Effective Manner. When MIS costs are charged back to the user departments, some check and balance on MIS expenditures is achieved. Although users generally do not see the details of the MIS budget, they are prone to compare the costs of in-house services with what they would pay outside. If the amounts charged for MIS services fully recover the costs incurred to provide those services, the MIS manager who spends money unwisely will soon receive pressure from users who must bear the expense. This is an important reason for adopting a charge-out approach that recovers all, or nearly all, of the MIS department's operation costs.

To Encourage People to Judiciously Use Certain Resources. The principles of economics can be effectively applied to managing the demand for resource use. By placing a high price on one resource relative to another (e.g., prime shift versus nighttime processing), the organization can alter user demand for a particular resource and create a better balance in the use of available capacity. At times, it may be best for the company to discontinue the availability of a certain resource. A sufficiently high price on a resource often leads users to discover alternatives. This is generally preferable to a unilateral discontinuance of the function by the MIS manager.

CHARGING FOR SYSTEMS AND PROGRAMMING

If a company employs a chargeback system at all, it will generally accept its applicability to data center operations (computer processing, data entry, and so on) but will be uncertain about systems and programming. Some advantages and disadvantages of charging for systems and programming follow.

Advantages

Preventing Unnecessary Systems. Charging for development programming services can be one of the most effective safeguards against the development of systems that are unwarranted from a business standpoint. A department generally will not request a project for which justification is lacking if it must bear the cost. Having a management review committee to approve and set priorities for new development projects can help ensure that only justified projects are undertaken. A department head who is politically adept can, however, push his or her pet projects through, unjustified though they may be. This is less likely to occur when the department bears the development expense.

Enhancing Project Control. The decision to charge for services results in the need for a system to record the data needed for charging (i.e., time utilization by the programming staff). This is a benefit. This information is extremely valuable in controlling projects, thus providing management with information on programmer time use and permitting the maintenance of historical data that is useful in estimating. Generally, an automated project control system is used for this purpose.

Improving Productivity. The discipline required for capturing time use by programmers can actually improve the effectiveness and productivity of the staff. This occurs as programmers, accountable for how they spend their time, become more aware of wasted time and how it affects them, their projects, and their users. A tendency to minimize controllable nonproductive time generally results.

Handling Costs for Outside Services. Most companies use or contemplate using outside services at some time. A chargeback system facilitates handling the costs for these services; costs can be easily passed along to the requesting department, since it is already accustomed to being charged for services of this type. A chargeback system also enables a continuing comparison between the cost of in-house and outside service that is useful to MIS management.

Disadvantages

Increased Overhead. There is overhead involved when maintaining a chargeback system, adding to the administrative cost of running the MIS department. Operating a chargeback system requires software, hardware, and people; depending on the system's scope and complexity, the cost can be significant.

Discouraging Progress. Although discouraging unneeded work is beneficial (as pointed out earlier), desirable activity is sometimes discouraged among users who are too cost conscious and who do not wish to spend money unless absolutely necessary. This problem can be avoided by routinely using an objective cost/benefit analysis procedure for proposed projects.

Interdepartmental Conflict. Some conflicts with user departments are unavoidable in the chargeback environment. Differences of opinion arise on what a given project should cost, and the inevitable cost overrun is certain to cause heated discussion. Both these problems can be overcome through the use of good and consistent estimating and project control techniques.

Loss of Control over Programming Personnel. Users paying for the services of a programming staff may consider programmers "their people."

MANAGEMENT ISSUES

This tendency can make it difficult for MIS to make or control staffing changes. If the manager responsible for programming is not strong and able to resist user interference, chaos can result.

In one case, a manager with a staff of approximately 50 soon found himself in such a predicament. His organization used a full recovery system and charged for all programming. Two user departments were very militant about programmer staff changes and insisted on investigating a new member before accepting him or her into one of their project teams. These departments also would not permit the removal or rotation of a staff member they wished to keep. Because they were paying the bill, they felt they had this right, and the programming manager thus lost an important element of management—control.

A related problem arises when users realize they are paying for the salaries and direct costs of their project team and also contributing to the general upkeep and overhead of the MIS department. User management may decide to put the programmers on their staff in an effort to reduce costs. If this problem is not controlled, the future of the central MIS department is threatened. At this point, senior management may need to reiterate company policy and reestablish equilibrium.

Generally, the benefits of including systems and programming in the chargeback process seem to outweigh the drawbacks. If a chargeback system is adopted, it should include the systems and programming function.

OBJECTIVES OF A CHARGEBACK SYSTEM

Having explored some of the reasons for a chargeback system, the objectives to be achieved in implementing a system will be examined. Meeting these objectives is important in ensuring that the chargeback system will be effective and well accepted.

Fairness. An effective system treats all users equitably. Rates, methods of charging, and so on must be arrived at in an objective manner. One user or group of users must not be subsidized at the expense of another. In a large manufacturing company, for example, all computer-prepared reports were priced according to the number of pages produced—except for the controller's department, which paid a flat $12 per report, far less than the amount charged on a per-page basis. Because the controller had clout, this unfair arrangement continued, to the chagrin of other users.

Stability. Once established, the chargeback system must be permitted to change over time. Changes are necessary, as the environment and the use of MIS change. System evolution should be gradual. Marked changes monthly and yearly in users' costs should result from changes in use rather than from changes in the chargeback system.

Understandability. The system must be comprehensible to those who deal with it. This is the most important characteristic of a good chargeback system. Concepts need to be kept simple, and the user must be able to understand how charges are calculated. For example, some chargeback systems have attempted to convert all resource use to a common unit of measure, sometimes referred to as the System Resource Unit (SRU) or Common Resource Unit (CRU). Under this approach, a user's bill shows only the number of SRUs or CRUs used rather than the actual resource utilization (e.g., CPU hours, print lines, disk I/Os). This approach fails the test of understandability since the user does not know precisely what the charges are for or how they have been calculated.

Flexibility. This is a characteristic more of those managing the system than of the system itself. The system must not be allowed to become a master to be served; rather, it must be seen as a tool of the organization. As such, the system must be flexible and should change as needed to adapt to the needs of the organization.

Perspective. The purpose of the system should be kept in perspective. The amount of time, effort, and cost invested in its operation should be in balance with the size of the company and the importance attributed to the system.

IMPLEMENTATION OF A CHARGEBACK SYSTEM

Certain steps must be taken to implement a chargeback system successfully. These steps represent a comprehensive approach to doing the job. Shortcuts or modifications to the method can be made, however, and will be noted in the following discussion. The steps are:

1. Develop an MIS department budget.
2. Decide which resources will be measured and costed.
3. Estimate maximum and anticipated use levels for each resource.
4. Decompose budget and allocate to cost pools.
5. Calculate resource use rates.
6. Select unit costing or resource method as basis for charging.
7. Develop unit rates for applications using unit costing.

Figure 1 shows functions found in most MIS departments. Neither the structure nor the function within the organization is important nor are they intended to be representative of any particular management philosophy. The chart serves only to illustrate some of the points of this section.

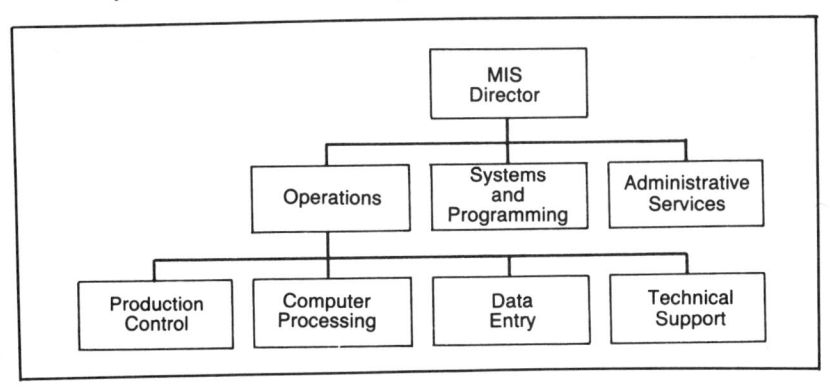

Figure 1. Sample MIS Department Organization Chart

MANAGEMENT ISSUES

Step 1: Develop an MIS Department Budget

Since the objective is cost recovery, the budget or expenditure plan for the year must be prepared so that anticipated costs are identified in advance. The MIS department can prepare a single budget covering all functions, but the chargeback scheme can be more easily developed if a separate budget is prepared for each functional area.

An organization using the partial recovery approach sometimes chooses to set rates on an arbitrary basis (e.g., competitive rates in the area) rather than base charges on actual costs. If this is the case, a budget is not required for the chargeback process, and steps 1 to 4 are unnecessary. Figure 1 shows a sample MIS department; Table 1 is an example of an MIS departmental budget.

Table 1. MIS Department Budget

	A Product Control $	B Computer Processing $	C Data Entry $	D Technical Support $	E Systems and Programming $	F Administrative Services $	Total MIS $
Salaries	150,000	400,000	200,000	100,000	800,000	75,000	1,725,000
Benefit Costs	45,000	120,000	60,000	25,000	200,000	22,500	472,500
Rent	15,000	45,000	15,000	4,500	45,000	6,000	130,500
Utilities	0	10,000	2,000	0	0	0	12,000
Hardware Rental/Depreciation	0	500,000	30,000	0	25,000	2,500	557,500
Hardware Maintenance	0	40,000	2,400	0	2,000	200	44,600
Software License/Rental	0	25,000	0	0	6,000	0	31,000
General Computer Supplies	0	2,000	500	0	0	0	2,500
Tape Purchases	0	15,000	750	0	0	0	15,750
Forms Cost	0	60,000	0	0	0	0	60,000
Travel	0	1,000	0	5,000	20,000	0	26,000
Office Supplies	1,000	2,000	500	500	5,000	2,000	11,000
Services Purchased Outside	0	0	2,400	0	40,000	0	42,400
Total	211,000	1,220,000	313,550	135,000	1,143,000	108,200	3,130,750

Step 2: Decide Which Resources to Measure and Cost

The development of an MIS chargeback system is an evolutionary process; its use also evolves over time. Most users of a system that has been in use for any appreciable period can probably see significant differences between the current system and the original.

One element that often changes is the resources that are charged. Choosing well at the outset can reduce the need for later change, but some change is inevitable.

Although it is not necessarily a good approach to charge for whatever can be measured, sometimes a resource is included in the chargeback scheme for no better reason. It is best to ask what the result would be if the particular item were excluded. If an inequity would result and a fair allocation would be impossible, then the resource most likely belongs in the set of chargeable items. The goal is to develop a scheme that levies charges to each user fairly, based on the cost of providing services. It also should be as simple as possible to administer.

Table 2 contains a list of resources and a likely unit of measurement for each. It is neither an all-inclusive list nor a recommended one but is intended

Paying for MIS Services

Table 2. Representative Resources and Associated Units of Measurement

Resource	Unit of Measure
CPU use	CPU seconds
Disk use	I/O operations (thousands)
Tape use	I/O operations (thousands)
Print volume	Print lines (thousands) or pages
Library or data storage (disk)	Megabytes/month
Library or data storage (tape)	Volume/month
Card reader use	Cards read (thousands)
Card punch use	Cards punched (thousands)
Data transmission facility	Communications line minutes
Main memory use	Kilobytes/second
Data entry services	Operator hours
Systems analysis and programming	Programmer/analyst hours

to show representative resources that can be found in typical chargeback systems.

Step 3: Estimate Resource Use Levels

Estimating resource use levels is a preliminary to Step 6, setting rates. If a chargeback system is based on charging for use of resources at a unit rate, achieving dollar target objectives for the chargeback depends on accurately predicting use. Either of two bases, anticipated actual use or maximum possible use, can be employed to estimate use levels.

The philosophy of setting rates based on anticipated actual use is to have each resource fully recover its costs on the basis of whatever use is made. This means that significant shifts in use require rate adjustments to avoid recovering too much or too little. This approach makes users' costs sensitive to resource utilization by other users. If excess capacity exists in the installation, for example, implementing a major new system will reduce the unit rates and, therefore, current users' costs, since utilization increases while costs to be recovered remain relatively fixed. If a user drops out, however, those remaining must each shoulder a greater share of the total cost.

When setting rates on the basis of maximum possible use, the cost of excess capacity is absorbed internally. Although use levels change, rates remain unchanged since they are based on the theoretical maximum achievable use level for each resource measured. This stability of rates generally is preferred by users over the previous method. If the organization does not object to unallocated costs for excess capacity, this method is the preferable one.

Determining use levels requires access to the statistical data produced by the operating system. Measurement of actual use during periods immediately preceding the implementation of the chargeback system provides the best starting point for estimating future use. Analyzing trends and whatever business planning data the organization has developed to plan for future hardware requirements can also be helpful.

If anticipated actual use is selected as a basis for setting rates, only the one-step process just described is required. If maximum possible use is selected, the further step of determining a maximum for each resource must be

MANAGEMENT ISSUES

taken. It is suggested that, rather than trying to estimate a maximum use level in an analytical manner, current use levels be employed to estimate maximum capacity. For example, if the CPU shows 270 problem program hours per month and it is estimated that the CPU is operating at 75 percent of realized capacity, then 360 problem program hours/month is the maximum (270/0.75 = 360). Approached analytically, the problem could be solved as follows:

$$\frac{24 \text{ hrs/day} \times 365 \text{ days/yr}}{12 \text{ months/yr}} = 730 \text{ hrs/month}$$

Hypothetical annual resource use levels are shown in Table 3. The estimated percentage of maximum capacity on the CPU should be used for other hardware pools, since in most shops, use of these other resources is proportionate to CPU use.

Table 3. Hypothetical Resource Use Levels

CPU Hours	2,100
Tape I/Os	620 x 10
Disk I/Os	800 x 10
Print Lines	500 x 10
Data Entry Hours	35,000
Programmer/Analyst Hours	42,000

Step 4: Decompose Budget and Allocate to Cost Pools

In the discussion of step 4, Table 4 should be used in conjunction with the sample budget in Table 1. In this example, charges are to be made for the following resources:
- CPU time
- Tape I/Os
- Disk I/Os
- Print lines
- Data entry operator hours
- Programmer/analyst hours

There are thus nine cost pools: the six mentioned plus two overhead cost pools and the unallocated pool. Each budget line item in Table 4 is a matrix entry identified by its grid coordinate referenced in Table 1. Table 4 shows the cost pool of each budget line item. In some cases, the dollars were divided among more than one cost pool. These situations are highlighted and explained further in Table 4. For example, line item 1B in the CPU pool represents a $100,000 allocation of the total computer processing salaries listed in Table 1.

Step 5: Calculate Resource Use Rates

This is the process that sets the rate to be charged for each resource. It is a very straightforward step that consists simply of dividing the number of dollars in each cost pool (from Step 4) by the use level for the particular resource (from Step 3).

Paying for MIS Services

Table 4. Cost Pool Allocations

	CPU Pool $		Tape Pool $		Disk Pool $
1B	100,000[1]	5B	75,000[2]	5B	150,000[1]
2B	30,000[1]	6B	6,000[3]	6B	12,000[3]
5B	200,000[2]	9B	15,000		162,000
6B	16,000[3]		96,000	+	54,700[5]
7B	25,000[4]	+	54,700[5]	+	4,328[6]
	371,000	+	4,328[6]		221,028
+	328,200[5]		155,028		
+	25,968[6]				
	725,168				

	Print Pool $		Data Entry Pool $		Programmer/Analyst Pool $
1B	150,000[1]	(1-13)C	313,550	(1-13)A	971,550
2B	45,000[1]	+	21,640[6]	+	43,280[6]
5B	75,000[2]		335,190		1,014,830
6B	6,000[3]				
10B	60,000				
	336,000				
+	109,400[5]				
+	8,656[6]				
	454,056				

	Hardware Overhead Pool $		General Overhead Pool $		Unallocated Pool $
(1-13)F	211,000	(1-13)F	108,200	(1-13)D	54,000
1B	150,000[1]		−108,200[6]	(1-13)D	+171,450
2B	45,000[1]		0		225,450
3B	45,000				
4B	10,000				
8B	2,000				
11B	1,000				
12B	2,000				
(1-13)D	+ 81,000				
	547,000				
	−547,000[5]				
	0				

Final Budget Decomposition $

CPU Pool	725,168
Tape Pool	155,028
Disk Pool	221,028
Print Pool	454,056
Data Entry Pool	335,190
Programmer/Analyst Pool	1,014,830
Unallocated Pool	+ 225,450
Total	3,130,750

Notes:
[1] Computer operations salaries and benefits split between CPU, print, and hardware overhead pools, based on analysis of duties.
[2] Hardware expense allocated to pools based on actual equipment assigned each pool.
[3] Hardware maintenance proportionate to hardware expense.
[4] All software allocated to CPU pool.
[5] Hardware overhead allocated as follows: 60% CPU; 10% tape; 10% disk; 20% print (arbitrary).
[6] General overhead allocated as follows: 40% programmer/analyst; 20% data entry; 24% CPU; 4% tape; 4% disk; 8% print (arbitrary).

MANAGEMENT ISSUES

In this example, the annual resource use levels set in Table 3 are divided by the dollars allocated each cost pool in Table 4. The rate calculations are shown in Table 5.

Step 6: Select Either Resource or Unit Costing as Chargeback Approach

The resource method consists of measuring the resources employed by each user and computing the bill using the rate established for each resource. The user thus receives a bill along the following lines:

1.46 CPU hrs @ $345.32	$504.17
6.81 Mi Disk I/Os @ $0.28	$190.68

To many users, such a bill is meaningless and undesirable. Many prefer units that they themselves can measure (to keep MIS honest) and for which they can predict volume (useful in budgeting for MIS service expenses).

Charging on the basis of item produced or processed (such as number of payroll checks, invoices produced, policies written, or account inquiries) rather than on the basis of resources used is the alternative approach. This approach, called unit costing or standard costing, is described in Step 7.

A combination of the two approaches can be used. For some users or systems, one method may be preferable. As long as the objectives of the chargeback system are met, either approach to calculating a charge for services, if agreed to by user and provider, is acceptable.

Table 5. Rate Calculations

Resource	Calculation	Rate
CPU	$725,168 / 2,100	= $345.32/hr
Tape	$155,028 / (620 x 10)	= $0.25/1,000 I/Os
Disk	$221,028 / (800 x 10)	= $0.28/1,000 I/Os
Print	$454,056 / (500 x 10)	= $0.91/1,000 lines
Data Entry	$335,190 / 35,000	= $9.58/hr
Programmer/Analyst	$1,014,830 / 42,000	= $24.16/hr

Paying for MIS Services

Step 7: Develop Unit Rates for Applications Using Unit Costing

This step is optional and is of interest only if the unit costing approach to recovery, defined in Step 6, is to be used.

The objective of the unit costing approach is to recover the same number of dollars that would be recovered using the resource approach, but to do it using chargeable items other than resources used. The amount of the bill is not at issue but, rather, the manner in which it is calculated. Some creative cost accounting is therefore in order. The following steps will accomplish it.

Decide Which Units to Use. This requires a careful look at the application system to discover units that are meaningful to the user and easily countable and for which change in resource use is somewhat directly proportionate to change in the unit count. In the trust business, for example, a workable unit is the number of accounts being serviced or processed. While the amount of processing performed is to a great degree dependent on the number of transactions processed, the relationship between accounts and transactions proves to be nearly constant over a somewhat stable group of accounts. Therefore, sufficient correlation exists between number of accounts and resource use costs to justify use of number of accounts as the unit of measure. Furthermore, number of accounts is preferable to number of transactions because it is easier to count and simpler for the user to understand and to predict in advance. More than one unit of measurement may be required to sufficiently express processing costs in meaningful application units. For example, the amount of processing for the application might be highly dependent on both transaction count and number of statements produced. In this case, both items should be used as chargeable units.

Establish the Relationship between Number of Units and Resource Cost over a Period of Several Months. Several readings must be taken to set a unit rate. The objective is to recover the same amount by the unit method as would have resulted from the resource method. Table 6 is an example, using just a single unit.

Table 6. Average Units and Resource Costs

Month	No. of Accounts	Resource Cost $
1	5,625	18,721
2	5,700	19,085
3	5,683	18,610
4	5,528	18,302
5	5,632	19,468
Avg	5,634	18,837

Calculate the Unit Rate. Divide the average resource cost by the average number of units. In this example, the average number of units is 5,634, and the average resource cost is $18,837. The average unit cost is therefore $3.34. When using multiple units, establishing the correlation is more difficult, requires more data samples, and is subject to more trial and error.

111

MANAGEMENT ISSUES

Validate the Selection of Unit and Rate Calculation. Taking each of the five months in the sample, the results using the calculated rate are shown in Table 7.

Table 7. Rate Calculations Using Resource Cost and Unit Cost

Month	No. of Accounts	Resource Cost $	Unit Cost (@ $3.34)	% Difference
1	5,625	18,721	18,788	+0.36
2	5,700	19,085	19,038	−0.25
3	5,638	18,610	18,981	+1.99
4	5,528	18,302	18,463	+0.88
5	5,632	19,468	18,811	−3.37
		94,186	94,081	−0.11

In this example, the correlation is excellent. The deviation each month is very small and the total result almost exact. Such precise results will seldom be obtained, and they need not be this good to be workable. A little practice will show whether a proper unit has been chosen.

WHEN TO CHANGE RATES

The decision on how often to change rates is important. Conditions that affect rates change frequently (cost levels, utilization levels, software, and so on). Rates calculated at the beginning of the year to effect the particular recovery philosophy of the installation will probably no longer be adequate by mid-year. Should they be changed at that time?

If the rates being charged are causing excess recovery but are otherwise equitable, they should stand. The excess can be handled at year-end through a refunding procedure, which always pleases users.

If the recovery will fall short of what is needed, there is a choice. Rates may be considered to be a contract with users for the entire year. Having set rates incorrectly, the loss must be absorbed. On the other hand, rates may be seen as subject to change without notice, in which case they should be changed when sufficient justification exists.

"Sufficient justification" is a subjective concept; universal agreement on it may be difficult. Nonetheless, several situations can arise that seem to justify changing rates, provided the installation has adopted an interim rate-changing policy.

If a major change dramatically altering the costs of providing services occurs in the installation, a rate change is warranted. Examples are a CPU change, migration to new disk technology with significantly different price/performance characteristics, or a major software change resulting in changed resource use.

If a material inequity in charging a user who is on the unit cost method of allocation is discovered, a rate change to that user only is justified. This situation can arise through a significant volume change, an application software change, or inaccurate unit cost setting. Unit rates are generally accurate only within a fairly narrow range of volume; once outside the range, a rate change becomes necessary. Application software changes can have a major impact on the efficiency and resulting resource utilization of an application.

Finally, if the installation does not absorb the cost of excess capacity but sets rates based on actual use, a rate change may become necessary when utilization levels exceed a certain limit. A major new application added during the year and not anticipated when rates are set will cause an excess recovery. A new user, for example, is beneficial to existing users since the new application utilizes excess capacity and thus drives down the rates. Conversely, the loss of some processing volume may cause a rate increase to avoid shortfall. Under any circumstances, changing rates more often than quarterly is probably not justified. It is highly desirable to maintain stable rates for the duration of the normal budget period (usually a fiscal year) if at all possible.

CONCLUSION

Designing and implementing an MIS chargeback system requires, initially, setting objectives and deciding the purpose of the system. A 7-step implementation process must then be undertaken in careful detail. The results of such effort can greatly benefit budgeting and productivity in both MIS and user departments.

Section III
Organization

Information systems departments appear to undergo an inevitable cycle of reorganization—from centralization to some level of decentralization and then back to a centralized structure. This cycle may be related to the developmental stages of growth for information systems, or perhaps it is just part of the quest for the right structure for the MIS department. In the chapter titled "To Centralize or Not to Centralize," we find that ways to implement organizational structure, such as distributed processing, should not be confused with the structure itself. Before committing to any one organizational structure, management should carefully analyze the total corporate data processing environment and take steps to ensure that the proposed structure is compatible with the overall organization. History shows that highly centralized organizations usually do well with centralized MIS shops and that decentralization works better when the corporation as a whole is decentralized, as in an organization with many profit centers.

As companies expand and enlarge their scope of activity, efficient management becomes more difficult. Project management is proving to be a successful alternative to traditional management structures, particularly for those organizations in which flexibility and rapid response to an ever-changing environment are important. Chapter III-2, "Coping with Change: Project Management," compares traditional structures with project management and discusses the advantages of using this technique. Guidelines for organizing and staffing as well as for resolving conflict are offered.

Integrating the various technologies that MIS must now manage frequently involves organizational problems. Many organizations have seen a proliferation of word processing and other office systems technologies in the functional areas of the business. This proliferation has posed a problem for MIS management at several levels, since it is usually we who are held responsible for managing information processing technologies that, to some, appear to have run amok. Chapter III-3, "Integrating Information Technologies," offers solutions to integrating these islands of technology while bringing order to chaos.

III-1
To Centralize or Not to Centralize?

Louis Fried
Robert E. Umbaugh

INTRODUCTION

With the advent of improved data communications networks, low-priced small and mid-sized computers with significant processing power and more powerful user-friendly languages, the placement of information processing capability within the organization is of pressing importance to MIS managers. The quest to find the optimum solution to the centralization versus decentralization controversy goes on. Current articles in the trade press provide examples of substantial savings achieved through decentralization. Just as many instances heralding the virtues of centralized organization probably can be found.

As examples proliferate on both sides, concerned managers ask, "What is the answer?" The question should be, "*Is* there an answer?" This chapter explores the latter question. It is most appropriate to start this analysis by examining the objective reasons for both strategies of DP organization.

REASONS FOR CENTRALIZATION

The major reasons for centralization include the following:
- Economy of scale
- Sophistication of applications
- Quality of systems development
- DP expense control

These issues are discussed in the following paragraphs.

Economy of Scale

Economy of scale is the most frequently stated reason for operations centralization. It results from several factors:
- Decentralized small computers may have unused capacity. Centralization on a large computer can eliminate the cost of such capacity.
- Individual small computers may be overloaded, requiring the MIS department to upgrade equipment or purchase expensive service bureau

ORGANIZATION

time. Centralization on a large computer can enable the MIS department to absorb this overload by drawing on unused capacity.
- In terms of floor space, electricity, air conditioning, and other facility costs, a single large installation is more economical than multiple small installations. (Proponents of decentralization are quick to point out, however, that smaller installations do not require expensive chilled water systems and large, costly centralized power hookups.)
- A smaller number of support personnel (e.g., operators, systems programmers) is needed for a large installation than for multiple small installations.
- A single large installation requires fewer management and staff personnel than multiple smaller installations.
- A large computer is more cost effective than a small computer. This statement is derived from "Grosch's Law." H.R. Grosch suggested that the performance of a computer increases as the square of its cost. For example, a computer that costs twice the amount of another should deliver four times the processing power. (Of course, the reverse is also implied. One larger computer could do the work of four smaller machines at half the cost of the four.)

Sophistication of Applications

Large computers offer advantages beyond economy of scale—certain applications not feasible on smaller equipment are made practical by their higher internal speed, greater primary storage, and higher channel capacity. Although in some cases it is technically possible to operate an application on a small computer, doing so absorbs a major part of the computer's capacity.

Examples include scientific computation, data base management systems, and the maintenance of and access to hierarchically structured files for manufacturing systems. In such cases, the application justifies the larger-capacity computer, which, in turn, justifies eliminating smaller computers in the organization to utilize the excess capacity of the large machine.

The trend toward increasing the use of online access to large data base systems further emphasizes the need for a central operation that can provide such access to users throughout the organization. A decentralized operation is inherently incapable of providing this service without expensive network capability and intricate data sharing schemes.

Quality of Systems Development

Centralization permits the design and use of common data bases and common standards for data entry and input validation. It can also enhance the ability to utilize development and project control techniques. Some of these benefits include the ability to:
- Implement a data dictionary, enabling considerable time savings in system modification research.
- Establish and enforce systems documentation standards to ensure future maintainability of systems and programs.
- Regulate standards for user documentation, reinforcing the ability to achieve optimum system benefits.

Centralization vs. Decentralization

- Establish and review proper programming techniques to minimize inefficient computer facilities use.
- Evaluate development projects from an overall organizational perspective, such as establishing priorities and conducting cost/benefit analyses.
- Avoid redundant development of similar systems for different divisions of the organization.
- Apply good project control techniques, ensuring that projects are completed on time and within estimated cost.

In addition, substantial differences exist between the abilities of large and small installations to attract and retain highly qualified technical personnel. Smaller installations frequently suffer a higher turnover rate as talented individuals outgrow the available opportunities. Smaller installations also often suffer from a lack of standards, inadequate documentation, and a lack of professional MIS management.

Retaining highly qualified personnel provides a centralized group with a higher level of expertise. These personnel can provide a greater range of alternative solutions to problems, resulting in a lower cost of development, operation, and system maintenance. Furthermore, a lower turnover rate aids in reducing maintenance costs and risk exposure.

DP Expense Control

Some reasons for centralization do not fit the general areas previously mentioned. Most of these involve controlling the cost of DP on an organization-wide basis and include the following:

- Decentralized installations are difficult to audit for operation or project development efficiency, effectiveness, and conformity to overall organization standards. They may, therefore, be less visible (and perhaps more expensive) than centralized installations.
- Smaller installations usually lack personnel with the skills and experience necessary to perform effective equipment selection. They may simply order from their current or the largest vendor. Frequently, the equipment salesman develops the specifications.
- Smaller installations usually do not have the negotiating power or experience necessary to develop favorable contracts with hardware and software vendors. So-called "national accounts," centrally controlled, can contract at better terms and prices than individual divisions.
- Centralization reduces the cost and improves the quality of personnel training.
- Smaller installations often lack sufficient overview to perform adequate advance planning. This may result in unexpected requirements for equipment or development.
- Decentralization often obscures management's view of total DP cost for the entire organization. Some of the costs of decentralized DP functions may be recorded in other organizational components (e.g., manufacturing, accounting). It is difficult for top management to apply measures of cost (such as DP cost as a percentage of sales) or effectiveness to a decentralized DP function.

ORGANIZATION

REASONS FOR DECENTRALIZATION

In the continuing discussion that is almost as old as the computer industry, there are as many reasons for decentralization as for centralization. In contrast to the arguments for centralization, which involve efficiency, the arguments for decentralization involve effectiveness.

Economies

The economies of DP service do not all favor centralized operation. For example, it is often necessary to practically rebuild facilities (or build new ones) in order to accommodate large-scale computers. The expense associated with such construction can be exorbitant.

In contrast, the use of smaller computers in a decentralized environment can provide significant savings under the proper conditions. A single-purpose minicomputer programmed for a specific application is very inexpensive. Furthermore, if it is used as an office machine, it does not require the operator, programming, and technical support of a general-purpose computer. Some minicomputers can provide online inquiry, saving the cost of data communications for this type of service. The high cost of data communications, the overhead associated with large general-purpose computers, and the potential for under-utilizing the capacity of a large centralized installation combine to mitigate the case against decentralization.

Sophistication of Applications

It is frequently proposed that the applications developed for a centralized operation are far more complex and costly than those required to meet divisional needs. This results from the attempt to meet the needs of all divisions in a single common application. A version of Parkinson's Law often applies in a large installation—applications grow to take advantage of all available capability and capacity.

A major problem that results is that maintenance to the system for one division can potentially affect all divisions. Similarly, if the central computer is disabled, all divisions are adversely affected. Whereas the decentralized installation has only two areas of vulnerability, software and hardware, the centralized installation presents the divisional user with several, including:
- Central computer hardware
- Central computer software
- Communications lines (and/or mail and delivery services)
- Local RJE or terminal hardware

Centralization forces divisions into a common mold that may be inappropriate for their needs. The specific hardware required for one user may differ from that required by another. These different needs could be satisfied with far less complexity and cost by smaller installations.

The centralized installation also creates contention for machine time among users. Several jobs running concurrently on a single machine may delay response time to users and, invariably, create competition for priority of service.

Quality of Systems Development

Proponents of decentralization convincingly argue that local analysts are more attuned to local needs. These analysts acquire an in-depth knowledge of divisional operations, managerial preferences, and organizational strengths and weaknesses. This enables them to establish requirement specifications and design systems that are most suited for the local user. It also helps them to avoid seeking technical solutions to what are fundamentally business problems. The local analyst can also respond more quickly to the emergencies and changes in priorities of local management. In contrast, setting priorities in a centralized environment places the division manager in contention with other users for the central systems development resources. The long lead times required to develop systems in such an environment are out of proportion to business needs.

The close association between the analyst and user also means that the user becomes better educated concerning the benefits and limitations of DP. The user also maintains tighter control of DP personnel and the quality of their work in relation to perceived needs.

Control of DP Expense

Even though most centralized installations allocate their costs to users according to the resources used, the division manager may feel little responsibility for the total cost of DP. The salaries paid to central personnel, the overhead rates, the choice of equipment, the time spent on projects, and the share of resources used all seem beyond the division manager's control. As a result, the allocations are viewed as "paper dollars." The manager's only incentive is to obtain as much service as he or she can from the centralized installation. In contrast, if the DP resource is local, the division manager has direct insight into all the elements of cost and a direct incentive to control those costs.

DP ORGANIZATIONAL DESIGN

The initial organization of the DP function is rarely planned. It begins where the need is first perceived—at corporate accounting headquarters or at a major division headquarters for accounting or manufacturing applications. Even computers installed for scientific purposes have been partially diverted to business applications. From these random beginnings, an organizational form for the DP function grows within a firm.

During the 1950s and early 1960s, the options were limited. If data processing was required at a divisional location, a DP facility was installed. If cost prohibited multiple installations, or if the firm could afford the time necessary to mail or ship data input and reports, the firm established a central DP facility at headquarters.

By the late 1960s, data transmission capabilities began to appear. Innovative DP organizations recognized the potential for either centralization or decentralization inherent in data communications. Given the opportunity to implement alternatives, all that was needed was motivation. This motivation existed in four areas:

ORGANIZATION

- Type of corporate organization
- Economic considerations
- Service considerations
- Political considerations.

Type of Organization

Harvey Poppel points out that the structure of the DP organization is likely to reflect the structure of the organization as a whole.[1] For example, a decentralized manufacturing company probably uses a decentralized mode of data processing while a highly centralized company (e.g., a utility company) probably uses centralized data processing.

As the cost of data processing increases (e.g., as a percent of revenue) and as the push for improved productivity grows stronger, DP is likely to receive more concentrated attention from top management.

An obvious target for management cost control is DP expenditures (often as great as two to three percent of sales). As a result, while many other aspects of company operation remain decentralized, tighter control will be exercised on DP. This may contribute to some emphasis on centralization of DP to achieve better corporate visibility and control. Nevertheless, a significant correlation probably remains between the form of the DP organization, the form of the corporate decision-making structure, and the size of the company and its divisions.

Economic and Service Considerations

While these considerations are addressed separately in the first two sections of this chapter, they are frequently linked to any analysis of the DP organization.

In describing the stages of DP growth, Nolan entitles the third stage "control"—the point at which the initial explosive growth of DP in an organization is over, there is a moratorium on new applications, and the emphasis is on formalized planning and cost control. It is at this point that the issue of centralization versus decentralization often arises.[2]

Part of the rationale for combining the economic and service considerations is the fallacy of isolating DP cost from the other operating costs of the organization. Improvements in the level of service to users may result in cost-saving efficiencies or profit-making effectiveness that far exceeds the DP cost differential achieved by one DP organizational method over another. In other words, the company must accept the principle of suboptimization of certain functions in order to achieve overall optimization of company operations.

Political Considerations

It would be foolish to assume that organizational, economic, and service considerations are always made in an objective, dispassionate manner. This is probably the exception, rather than the rule.

Almost every attempt at reorganization brings forth advocates for each position. Vested interests and territorial imperatives are challenged. Larger di-

Centralization vs. Decentralization

visions making a greater contribution to corporate profits may push for decentralization of DP to extend their autonomy of operation. Smaller divisions may "gang up" to oppose decentralization, viewing it as a threat to their ability to obtain a share of the more sophisticated centralized resources.

The incumbent members of an existing MIS organization may fight reorganization proposals that threaten their positions or reduce their authority. Divisions may claim that they obtain inadequate service. Corporate management may protest that it will lose control and the ability to coordinate efforts and direct priorities based on the greatest return to the overall organization. In fact, almost all of the other considerations may become weapons in the political struggle.

It is essential to remember that any proposal for organizational change will become political; that even if the best decision is reached, it will not be reached in a completely rational and objective manner. Because of political factionalism, the final decision must originate at the highest organizational level (chief operating executive) to ensure the optimum opportunity for success.

THE PROBLEMS OF DP COORDINATION

A critical concern of corporate management is control of DP's cost, use of resources, and effectiveness. Regardless of the form of DP organization, most companies feel that a top MIS executive is required at the corporate level. This executive's minimal responsibilities include coordination of DP activities between divisions and corporate headquarters, overall planning and monitoring of DP costs and resources, ensuring effective use of resources, and providing technical advice to top management. These responsibilities may be examined by viewing the specific functions in terms of planning and control.

Planning

The prerequisite to control is planning. To this end, it is necessary to provide corporate management with overall annual and long-range plans. These involve:

- Maintaining a concise description of the current status of DP systems, hardware, personnel, and costs
- Gathering corporate and divisional systems requirements and priorities
- Developing, in coordination with users, an annual systems plan that is consistent with the resources available to accomplish the desired projects
- Reviewing the systems plan for potential impact on hardware capacity and staffing
- Advising top management of the alternatives available for achieving planned objectives

The plans must be developed with consideration of recent trends in the DP field that impose constraints or add complexity to the system design function. For example, constraints arise through the use of common systems by several divisions, the need for divisional systems to interface with corporate systems, and the use of large standardized data bases.

This is further complicated by the acquisition of equipment from various

ORGANIZATION

vendors and by the rent, lease, or purchase options—an almost bewildering proliferation of alternatives that leads to the need for control.

Control

Tasks relating to control, necessary in either form of organization, include:
- Comparing budgets and performance to budgets for all DP activities
- Reviewing and approving the purchase of equipment, software, and outside services
- Applying management guidelines to the selection of major projects (in terms of cost/benefit analysis and return on investment)
- Establishing and maintaining standards for operating procedures, project development, programming methods, and documentation
- Auditing progress and performance on major projects
- Maintaining a specialized staff to provide services (such as technical advice on hardware, communications, sophisticated systems, or applications software) to the applications development or operating groups throughout the company

The strength of these control functions depends on the management style of the corporation's top executives. A strong top executive who wants centralized control of DP costs and use of resources may impose this type of control through the corporate MIS executive, even if the DP functions are decentralized. Conversely, a centralized MIS function probably will not work well if the top executive wants divisional autonomy in the selection and operation of systems.

ORGANIZATIONAL OPTIONS

The range of options for organizing the DP function can best be analyzed by recognizing that the systems development and operation functions are not constrained to identical organizational paths.

DP Operations

Distributed Input and Control. Remote input and control trace their origins to the beginning of commercial data processing. In its simplest form, distributed input and control means that the user is responsible for controlling input and converting input to machine-readable form. Users may have their own data-entry equipment (keypunches, key-to-magnetic-media, or terminals) or may contract the work to outside vendors. This approach offers several advantages:
- The user feels more responsibility for, and "ownership" of, the system.
- Data entry costs are not a part of the DP organization's budget.
- DP control costs are lowered when users control input and validate output.
- Data entry errors can be corrected by direct user involvement.
- Personnel costs may be reduced by using data entry employees for clerical and control tasks at the user site.

Disadvantages include:
- Equipment costs may be higher due to decentralization and the resultant inability to fully utilize equipment capacity.

- Depending on the size of the installation, additional supervisory employees may be needed.

Some developments during the past few years have made this approach increasingly attractive. Data communications techniques have reduced the time required to transmit data before and after processing. Online and key-to-disk data entry permit extensive editing and validation of data prior to processing. (This not only results in quick correction of data locally, but frequently saves the cost of processing incorrect or incomplete data.) Where central computer capacity is available, online data entry also makes the resultant files immediately ready for processing or can provide for online update of data bases.

Distributed Processing. This has become a buzzword in the DP industry. Very simply, it means that data is processed at separate computer installations that transmit data to each other. There are also permutations of the technique, including classification of distributed systems. These may include partially or completely distributed data bases.

One company maintains its inventory records through the use of minicomputer-based online systems in all locations. Summarized inventory status is periodically transmitted to corporate headquarters for updating central files. All invoicing, order entry, and inventory-related accounting is done locally on the minicomputer. Some of the advantages of distributed processing are:
- "Safety in numbers." The entire operation is not dependent on one main computer. Downtime affects only the immediate local operation.
- Users feel greater system responsibility and believe the system is more responsive to their demands.
- Distributed processing costs may not be substantially greater than remote job entry costs, because the central installation may be able to operate with a less powerful computer.

Disadvantages include:
- Less corporate visibility for local operations.
- Divisions may build up their own DP departments and move to larger equipment.

Remote Job Entry (RJE). This well-established processing method permits use of a central computer (or time on a service bureau computer) by a local station that has tape, floppy disk, or card input/output devices, and a printer. Some advantages are:
- Speed of transmitting input and output.
- Extending the use of existing central computer capability at low cost.
- User feelings of increased system responsiveness.

Disadvantages include:
- Users can create or modify central programs from the RJE terminal. This reduces control over the program library.
- Heavy RJE use can force the central installation into larger equipment. Users are difficult to control, and volume is difficult to forecast.
- Since the RJE terminal provides all the capability of a large computer, users tend to develop their own DP department.

ORGANIZATION

Systems Development Options

Since the extreme ends of the centralization/decentralization spectrum are well known and have been explored earlier in this chapter, this section addresses several variations in use.

User Group Liaison. In almost all MIS organizations, this is a continuing problem that seems to have no solution without additional cost to the company. The solutions that do seem to work are:

Assigning a Person with DP Experience to a Division Staff. Unless the MIS organization is lucky enough to have an analyst familiar with the user division and its problems (and can spare the analyst), it is difficult to find someone with knowledge of both worlds. This leaves two options: transfer an analyst from the MIS group (or hire one) and train that person in the needs of the division, or create an internship program whereby a person is transferred to the MIS organization for 18 months to 2 years, after acquiring a thorough working knowledge of the user area. He or she is then transferred back to the user staff after gaining programming and analysis training and experience.

Assigning Analysts within the MIS Organization as Account Managers. These managers specialize in the needs of, and communication with, a particular division or user function. While this method provides greater control by the MIS group, experience seems to indicate that it does not satisfy users as well.

Decentralized Analysis. This method has been recommended for improving user satisfaction while retaining the benefits associated with centralized design and programming. In this concept, the user maintains a staff of analysts who define system requirements, establish user priorities, participate in acceptance testing, and direct users in implementation.

Several authorities in the DP field indicate that this seems to be a frequently selected organization pattern. Some advantages are:
- User control of the staff permits local direction, flexibility, and assignment of priorities.
- Analysts are more responsive to the user who is their boss.
- Analysts become thoroughly familiar with user problems, personnel, and requirements.
- Analysts protect the interests of the user.
- Acceptance testing prior to implementation may be more rigorous.
- User project managers may enhance visibility and control of DP costs.

Disadvantages include:
- Smaller staffs are more vulnerable to turnover and less likely to have technical expertise in certain areas.
- Corporate documentation and design standards are more difficult to maintain.
- Selection of projects may easily deviate from corporate return-on-investment guidelines.
- Friction between the divisional analysts and central programmers and analysts may result from conflict concerning design criteria.

- Control of applications design as it affects the economic utilization of hardware is difficult to maintain.
- Divisions tend to invent their own solutions to problems rather than use corporate-wide systems. This adds substantially to all DP costs.
- User project managers may not have sufficient technical background to properly manage a complex project.

Decentralized Analysis and Programming. This method emphasizes many of the preceding advantages and disadvantages. Those advantages relating to user responsiveness are enhanced. Acceptance testing and cost control of projects may suffer, however. The disadvantages relating to maintaining standards and system redundancy tend to intensify.

Combinations

Combining features of centralization and decentralization is another alternative once it is realized that the hardware and the systems development function are not necessarily coupled. For example:
- Centralized hardware with decentralized analysis, or analysis and programming
- Centralized analysis and programming of distributed (or mini) computers
- Organization by application, with corporate-wide systems centralized and exclusive division systems decentralized, either with hardware or with hardware and development

The advent of office systems automation and the enhancement of word-processing workstations into full information processing terminals also offers an opportunity to combine centralized computing with local processing unique to the function.

REACHING A DECISION

Change is traumatic, and the average organization is well advised to avoid change unless it is well justified. For this reason, an MIS manager should carefully evaluate the question of organizational change before acting. In fact, one key question should be raised before any detailed analysis is performed: Why is the centralization versus decentralization issue raised at all?

If the answer is that the issue is politically motivated (and it frequently is), the manager should attempt to resolve, by means other than organizational change, those factors that created or influenced the political motivation. This can save the time and cost of performing the studies and may avoid the cost of change.

If the issues are in the realm of service, effectiveness, and cost, they must be addressed as real issues. It is then necessary to balance the requirements of the divisions against those of the overall corporation in terms of these issues and corporate control of standards, resource utilization, and return on investment.

One of the more common rationales for going to decentralized or distributed processing is a desire to give operating units more control over their information processing destinies. Another is the need to improve the quality of

ORGANIZATION

Computer Operations
1. How many installations are too small or too large to enjoy economies of scale in consolidation?
2. Are some installations growing so rapidly that consolidation could avoid continual equipment conversions?
3. What communications costs may occur as a consequence of geographic dispersion and movement to interactive and online systems?
4. How many different kinds and configurations of equipment, languages, and operating systems are in use?
5. Is it possible to level the workload through consolidation—during a day and over longer periods?
6. Can backup be better provided in consolidated centers?
7. Does centralization allow better control over access to confidential files?
8. Will the organization agree on some degree of commonality?
9. What flexibility now exists in modifying configurations?
10. Can currently employed space be used by other parts of the organization?
11. Can the staff be separated?
12. How many programs must be rewritten?
13. How many programs must be redesigned because of such factors as extensive operator intervention?
14. How dispersed are the users of existing decentralized centers?
15. What business risks would be incurred through consolidation?
16. Should centers be organized by application, organizational unit, or along geographic lines?
17. How competent are the current managers?
18. What quality of service are users now receiving?

Systems Development
1. What opportunities exist for developing common systems?
2. Which functions receive strong central guidance now and therefore offer opportunities for commonality?
3. What variation now exists in levels of sophistication?
4. Do we now have adequate quality and quantity of staff?
5. If more than one business exists, how similar or dissimilar are they?
6. Have we grown by acquisition?
7. Do management people typically transfer among divisions?
8. Do we have a strong central philosophy; is ours an operating or a holding company?
9. Do we often add or spin off parts of the business?
10. Are managers familiar with the systems?
11. Is a great deal of missionary and basic educational work needed?
12. Have we purchased duplicate packages?
13. Is there a strong central thrust to management planning, control, and reporting systems?
14. Are users satisfied with their systems?
15. Do the systems meet standards of performance in control and efficiency?
16. Is there an opportunity for one division to learn from another?
17. How much travel would be entailed with any option?
18. Are personnel needs in balance over short periods?
19. Can specialists be efficiently shared?

Planning and Control Functions and Decision Authorities
1. Do centers plan well?
2. Are sound equipment acquisition and financing arrangements employed?
3. Do new projects meet basic ROI and other selection criteria?
4. Are programming, documentation, and control standards in use?
5. Are purchased packages an important component of costs?
6. Do opportunities exist to share or move hardware?
7. Do line managers require external support?
8. How competent are the staffs?
9. Are projects inordinately late or over budget?
10. Are total expenditures well out of line with general industry experience?
11. Does corporate headquarters have a substantial data processing requirement?

Figure 1. DP Organization Checklist

systems development by involving users more and depending less and less upon an overloaded centralized data processing staff. With the advent of user information centers that bring computing power to the users through computerized workstations and user-friendly languages, these needs can be met without full or even partial decentralization. The implementation of the user information center concept overcomes many of the deficiencies of traditional centralized computing without taking on the weaknesses of decentralization.

To resolve these issues, the MIS manager must determine all the appropriate questions or considerations for both the MIS organization and the company and apply weighting factors to a range of positive and negative answers. The resulting matrix will permit an objective evaluation.

In this evaluation, initial attention should be paid only to developing proposed alternative organizational designs and comparative costs, because review of the latter by top management may resolve the question. If, however, the top executive is primarily service rather than cost oriented, this may not accomplish the task. Each MIS manager must determine the organizational and management climate of his or her individual corporation.

The list of questions in Figure 1, developed by Harvey Golub, provides an excellent foundation for the MIS manager evaluating the organization of the DP function.[3]

CONCLUSION

Organizational change should not be undertaken without substantial motivation. The organizational mode of DP must be congruent with the company's management style, organizational design, corporate objectives, and user needs—with the advantages and disadvantages of each mode assessed in light of each. Both experience and research indicate that the following conclusions are applicable to a large majority of DP installations:

- Centralization of computer facilities is usually desirable since it provides greater capacity, permits more sophisticated applications, and usually costs less than other approaches.
- Benefits of centralized programming generally outweigh those of the decentralized approach when considered in the overall corporate context.
- Although systems analysis functions can be performed effectively in either the central or user organization, the user group liaison position becomes extremely important if the centralized approach is used.

In conclusion, there is no easy answer or single best way to organize the DP function. As experience is gained, there may emerge common guidelines for certain industries of given size and geographic distribution. At this point, however, each company must determine the proper solution for itself.

References

1. Poppel, Harvey L. "How to Divide and Conquer the Computer." *Forbes*, May 26, 1980.
2. Nolan, Richard L. "Managing the Crises in Data Processing." *Harvard Business Review* (March–April 1979), p. 117.
3. Golub, Harvey. "Organizing Information System Resources: Centralization vs. Decentralization." In *The Information Systems Handbook*, ed. F. W. McFarlan and R.L. Nolan. Irwin IL: Dow Jones, 1975, p. 70.

III-2
Coping with Change: Project Management

Frank J. Stanley

INTRODUCTION

Project management has evolved to meet the need for an organizational structure that can effectively achieve short-term objectives in a rapidly changing environment. The growth of business in the twentieth century demanded a formal organizational structure, and the hierarchical structures that emerged to meet this need have remained basically the same. However, today's businesses are much larger and must respond to rapidly changing conditions. These organizations face many obstacles in completing projects, including:
- Longer project time frames
- Increased complexity
- Uncertain costs
- Rapidly changing technology
- Unstable economy
- Keener competition
- Changing attitudes in the market and work place

The necessity of functioning efficiently and profitably while contending with these obstacles has created an organizational method that integrates the many activities involved in these efforts—project management.

WHAT IS A PROJECT?

A project is a well-defined effort undertaken by a formally established entity that is expected to produce specified results within a given environment at a predetermined time. Although projects vary in size, duration, and complexity, all have a specific objective; when that objective is met, the effort is complete. The development of a computer system, the introduction of a new product, and the construction of a plant are all projects. Though a computer system can be designed and implemented by a small team in a few months and an oil refinery takes years to complete and commands vast resources, each project can be managed using the same basic concepts.

WHAT IS PROJECT MANAGEMENT?

Project management is the planning, directing, and controlling of company resources to achieve established goals. Originally a method of managing

ORGANIZATION

large-scale military, space, and civilian projects, it has been used successfully by the air force, the navy, and NASA and is currently gaining popularity in private industry where large or complex efforts are undertaken.

With project management, temporary teams of personnel can devote their skills to accomplishing project objectives; they remain together only until those objectives are met. The project is led by a project manager, who ensures its successful completion and supervises all team members. He or she reports directly to upper management or to a director of project management.

Project management is effective in organizations or departments that perform temporary activities. Although a firm whose mainstay is the production and sale of a standard set of products will benefit little from this approach, others (e.g., engineering, research and development, data processing, construction) that produce a continuous stream of projects will thrive.

BUSINESS SYSTEM THEORY

A system is an assemblage of parts forming a complex or unitary whole. Modern businesses are defined as systems because they consist of various subunits that, when combined in an organized manner, perform toward a common goal.

Figure 1 illustrates a simple business system. System input generally consists of raw materials or resources that are processed and then fabricated or reshaped into a system output or product. This simple system is easily visualized in terms of the work of a baker or a carpenter; however, as businesses grow, the organization needed to support these essential activities becomes more complex, obscuring these simple terms.

Modern multilevel businesses perform the same activities but in a more complicated system environment, as depicted in Figure 2. In this environment, the business system functions on three levels:
- Technical—Performing the tasks and technical function directly related to producing and distributing a firm's products.
- Organizational—Coordinating and integrating the various technical activities to achieve organizational goals. This includes planning and directing the use of labor, resources, and production facilities.
- Institutional—Relating the organization and its activities to the environment. This requires the ability to determine which environmental factors are relevant to an organization and to respond accordingly.

Organizations are also subject to environmental influence on other levels. Product demand and the availability of raw materials or qualified personnel

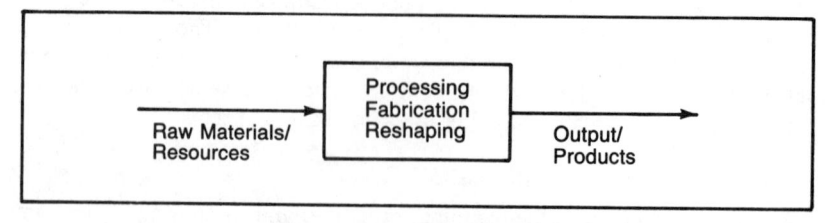

Figure 1. Simple Business System

Project Management

both affect different levels in the organization. For a business system to function well, communications must be effective so that environmental changes can be reacted to swiftly and decisively. Unfortunately, as businesses grow, levels of management increase, communications become more complex, and knowledge of the business becomes fragmented. A business system is further complicated by multiple product lines and schedules, decentralized plant sites, government regulations, and multinational constraints.

To meet such complexities, businesses have adopted many formal organizations over the years. Although the purpose of these organizations is to integrate the functions of the various levels, they have sometimes become so cumbersome that they have added to the confusion.

Traditional Management Structures

Companies and business in general usually expand by adding personnel and positions in the vertical hierarchy of the organization. Most firms adopt a traditional structure, represented by a pyramid-shaped organization chart with vertical lines of authority and communication. It generally falls into one of the following categories:

- Pure functional, or classical, organization—Contains a department or division for each business function performed (e.g., marketing, production, sales, engineering). This structure allows control and functional continuity but responds slowly to a changing environment and emphasizes a functional rather than a project orientation. Figure 3 shows a functional organization chart.
- Line-staff organization—Establishes project managers to solely direct the completion of projects and is therefore an attempt at project manage-

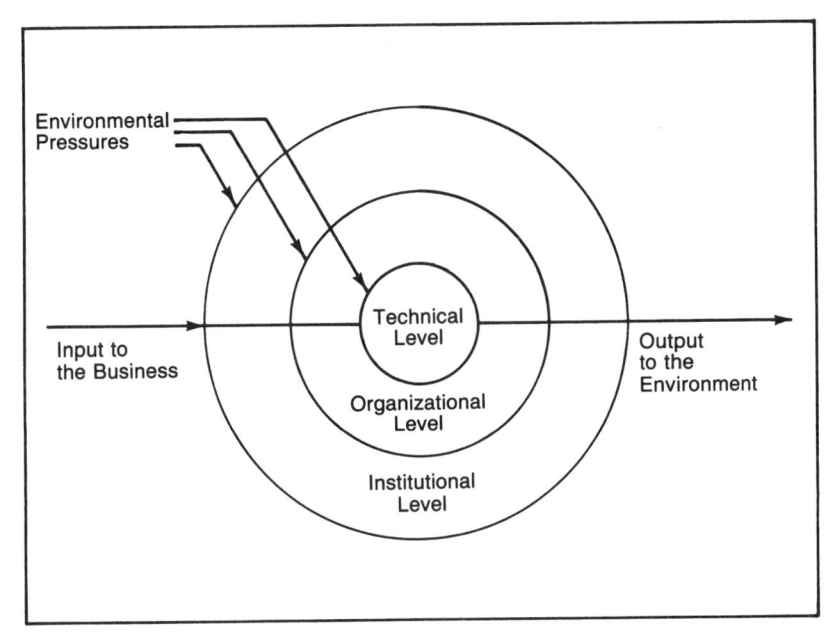

Figure 2. Functional Levels

ORGANIZATION

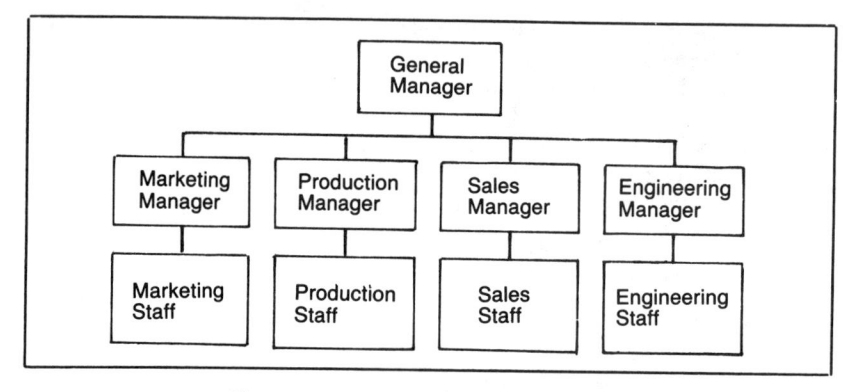

Figure 3. Pure Functional Organization

ment. Because the project manager has limited authority in informal shared-authority situations, this structure is generally unsuccessful. Figure 4 shows a typical line-staff organization chart.
- Pure product organization—Consists of a complete functional organization within each major product area. This organization could have several manufacturing departments, one for each major product. Although this form provides a product or project orientation and reacts quickly, it creates a duplication of effort (e.g., facilities personnel) and inhibits technical growth and exchange of ideas. Figure 5 shows a product organization chart.

Project Management Structure

The project management structure, or matrix organization, combines the features of the functional and product organizations and avoids the problems of the line-staff organization by establishing clear-cut lines of authority. Figure 6 illustrates a matrix organization.

In this organization, project management is considered an accepted and supported management practice. Project managers have clear lines of respon-

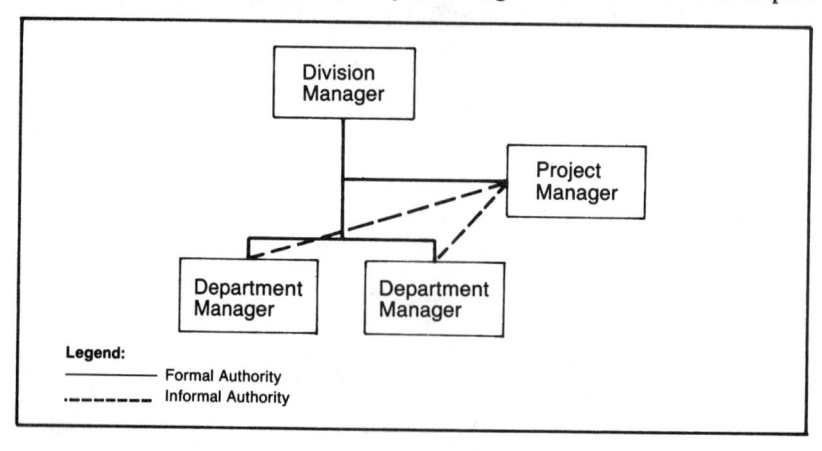

Figure 4. Line-Staff Organization

Project Management

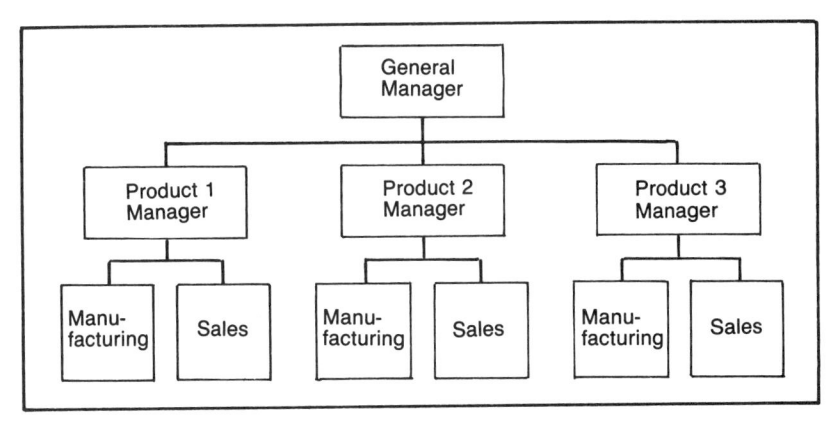

Figure 5. Pure Product Organization

sibility and authority and report to their own director or to upper-level management.

Advantages

The greatest advantage of project management is its unique combination of control and flexibility. While this is especially beneficial to large companies involved in complex, lengthy projects, it is also valuable to more modest efforts and smaller organizations.

Control is achieved when one person or project office is responsible only for managing a project. Free from the routine activities that can dominate a manager's workday, the project manager can focus on the project management task. In addition, because professional project managers generally use fairly sophisticated systems for organizing, estimating, assigning, and track-

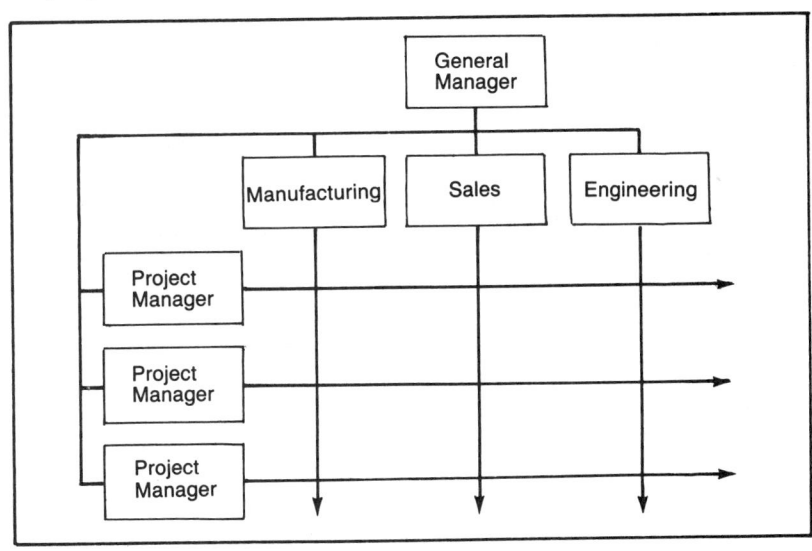

Figure 6. Matrix Organization

135

ORGANIZATION

ing activities, they can detect and respond to changes quickly. Their total control over the project permits significant flexibility. The impact of changes in scheduling, financial support, and resource requirements can be easily determined and adjustments quickly made along the entire project time frame and across functional boundaries. This flexibility and control results in efficient use of company resources. The following are other potential benefits:

- Overall cost is minimized because of more efficient use of people and resources.
- People can be shared and thus contribute to more than one project at a time.
- The projected cost of the project is more accurate and easily obtainable.
- Project team members are more easily motivated because they are working toward a tangible project goal.
- The working environment can be less rigid. Policies and procedures can be tailored to a particular project environment, providing they comply with company rules.
- Conflicts are reduced and, when they occur, can usually be resolved quickly.

Disadvantages

The flexibility and control project managers maintain can be a disadvantage if the project management structure is set up improperly or not monitored regularly. Some disadvantages follow:

- Dedication of resources to one project may draw attention away from other projects or company functions of equal or greater importance.
- The increased cost of administering a project management function may exceed the benefits derived from it.
- The independent operation of each project team may result in duplicated efforts.
- Conflicts between functional and project managers may be difficult to resolve.
- Because most organizations do not function in a project environment, the transition can be costly. The idea must be accepted by all levels in the company, policies and procedures established, personnel hired and reassigned, and pilot projects undertaken to test the new system.
- Staff members may be uncomfortable in reporting to both functional and project managers. This can be especially stressful to some employees during the installation of a project management organization.

Disadvantages should not discourage an organization from considering the technique; project management is not a cure-all, nor is it right for every organization. The concept should be examined for each organization and implemented only if tangible benefits can be derived and management support obtained.

ORGANIZATION AND STAFFING

The success of any project depends on the team assembled to work on it. A typical project is staffed by a project manager—and assistant, if necessary—a project office, and project teams and team leaders.

Not all projects have the same mix of positions. Small projects, for example, may not require a project office staff, or one project team may suffice, without a team leader; in each case, members of the organization would assume project duties.

Project Manager

Because the project manager is probably the most important individual in a project effort, he or she must be selected carefully. Although generally not active in performing project tasks, he or she has responsibility for and control over the total effort. To successfully carry out responsibilities, a project manager must have expertise in three areas: technical considerations, management, and organization.

A project manager should be technically competent in the area of expertise a project entails. For example, an engineering project should be managed by an engineer and a data processing project by a computer specialist. Determining appropriate staffing, dealing with clients and end users, planning activities, and resolving problems are several tasks that require solid technical knowledge. A project manager with the right background more easily gains the respect of the project team and exercises better control through first-hand knowledge of the activities.

Because a project manager's main duty is to ensure that others perform technical tasks in a timely and effective manner, management skills are essential to training, delegating, supervising, mediating, and motivating. The project manager must be able to perform these functions with all levels of personnel as well as with staff members he or she does not know. In addition, the project manager must communicate effectively with upper-level management and with clients and end users.

To achieve more efficient use of resources, the project manager should possess organizational skills to:
- Break down the work into measurable tasks
- Divide the work among available personnel to achieve the most efficient use of skills
- Monitor progress in a timely manner and identify potential problems
- Take corrective action if problems arise and adjust the project schedule as required

Finding an individual with all these skills is not always possible. Sometimes expertise in one area may have to be sacrificed for that in another. Additional support should be provided in any of these areas when necessary.

Assistant Project Manager. This position generally is found only on large-scale projects. The assistant, who must be able to assume the project manager's role in his or her absence, usually coordinates and summarizes project status information, serves as liaison to the project team, and makes minor staffing and scheduling decisions. The assistant also ensures that work is properly carried out and documented. He or she must support the methods, policies, and procedures established by the project manager so that teamwork is evident at all levels.

ORGANIZATION

The Project Office

When large amounts of data must be handled to effectively administer a project, a project office is necessary. It should perform strictly as an administrative function and be kept as small as possible. Project offices are valuable under the following circumstances:
- The project team is large.
- The project scope is wide and cuts across several functional boundaries.
- More than one working or client location is involved.
- The project time frame is long.
- Ongoing communication with customers or users is required.

The Project Team

The project team comprises all staff members who contribute to the project. The project manager sets the staffing requirements for the project team, and both the project and functional managers assign personnel.

Team members' duties include performing tasks according to a published project schedule and reporting their activities regularly. In addition, they must account for lost and unproductive time and anticipate problems and present possible solutions. Team members may work on a project either full or part time for only a short time or for the entire project. Some staff members may work part time on two or more projects simultaneously. Occasionally, specialized skills not found within the organization are required for a limited time. Contracting and consulting firms can then be employed to provide temporary help.

For large teams or teams functioning in more than one area, a team leader may be assigned. The team leader performs the same function as the other team members and is administrative liaison to the project office or manager.

The project manager must gain the support of the functional managers and clarify staffing requirements for them so that they can respond appropriately. Once a project begins, the project manager should keep the functional managers informed of staff extensions and schedule modifications. This enables the functional managers to coordinate the activities of their staff members.

CONFLICTS

Because project teams perform in a highly organized, integrated, and task-oriented environment, any conflict can thwart their success. Because the project environment is temporary, the project manager must work in an environment that is less standardized and predictable than that of a functional manager. Conflicts are inevitable, and the project manager who identifies and resolves them quickly can usually prevent any adverse effects on a project.

In a survey of 150 project managers, Thamhain and Wilemon[1] found that the following seven areas create conflict on most projects:
- Project priorities—Members of the project team or support groups disagree with the sequence of tasks and activities as defined in the project plan.
- Organization—Management personnel disagree with the definition of the

project manager's role, including reporting relationship, scope of authority, plan of execution, and operational requirements.
- Technical opinions and performance trade-offs—In high-technology projects, opinions may differ concerning the best technical approach to the project.
- Personnel resources—Project managers usually want the best personnel on a project. They may disagree among themselves and with functional managers when choosing team members.
- Cost—Because team members and support groups usually work within estimates that they did not develop, they may view the time or funds allocated as insufficient.
- Schedules—The scheduling of project tasks may not coincide with the availability of support groups and team members. In addition, required equipment may not be available for several concurrent projects.
- Personalities—Differences of opinion and problem situations unrelated to technical issues may result from incompatible personalities.

The project manager should be aware of these potential areas of conflict to minimize their impact on the progress of the project.

ACTION PLAN

No rule of thumb can be used to determine whether project management will benefit an organization, nor is there a formula for establishing a project management environment. Each organization must approach the concept after careful research, self-evaluation, and planning and must secure the total support of top management.

A company contemplating project management should consider the following questions:
- Have other companies in the same business attempted to install project management? Why or why not? If they have, how successful have they been?
- What benefits can be gained from a project management structure? Will it improve the current organizational structure?
- Will employees react positively to project management? Will management support elicit their acceptance?
- Will top management support the concept? (This is essential if other levels of management are expected to support it.)

Before proceeding, a company should plan carefully. Project management procedures must be clearly defined, lines of authority established, and methods of conflict resolution determined. Extensive role plays of situations and pilot projects on a limited basis are useful for testing a concept before implementing it on a large scale.

Qualified personnel are a key requirement. The project manager must be able to handle the complexities of the position and must be dedicated to project goals. An experienced project manager should oversee the initial stages of project management to ensure the proper skill level and to provide an excellent example to potential in-house project managers.

Because no two organizations are alike, methods of project management will differ. At the completion of each project, members of the project team

ORGANIZATION

should appraise the project's management. Their critique should effect changes that will make project management more responsive, effective, and beneficial to the company.

Reference

1. Thamhain, H.J., and Wilemon, D.L. "Conflict Management in Project Life Cycles." *Sloan Management Review*, Summer 1975.

Bibliography

Kast, F.E., and Rosenzweig, J.E. *Organization and Management: A Systems Approach*. New York: McGraw-Hill, 1970.

Kerzner, H. *Project Management: A Systems Approach to Planning, Scheduling, and Controlling*. New York: Van Nostrand Reinhold, 1979.

Stanley, F.J. "Establishing a Project Management Methodology." *AUERBACH Information Management Series*. Pennsauken NJ: AUERBACH Publishers Inc, 1983.

III-3
Integrating Information Technologies

Randy J. Goldfield
Rose Lockwood

INTRODUCTION

The development of new technologies for processing, storing, and transferring information has often outstripped the ability of business organizations to assimilate these technologies in the work environment. Beginning with word processing (WP), rapid advances have occurred in many business-oriented technologies, including reprographics, information storage and retrieval, facsimile and other information transfer functions, personal computing, activity management, and teleconferencing. This progress challenged management to find effective ways to use and control these new tools. As the executive with the most technical expertise, the MIS manager often plays a major role in this process.

INTEGRATING AVAILABLE TECHNOLOGIES

The distinction between word and data processing has become nebulous, primarily because of the rapid development of WP software. Some available electronic processing applications—electronic mail, for example—do not fit into either category. As a result of these developments, the MIS manager must address an information network that encompasses the creation of information, its use inside and outside the company, and its transmission through communications facilities.

Any program for integrating DP and WP should take advantage of the numerous opportunities for interfacing existing systems, such as making the corporate data base available to WP operators for text compilation. Conversely, linking WP equipment to existing computer equipment permits the systems staff to generate their own reports or maintain data dictionaries; both applications would be cumbersome or impossible on a mainframe. The cost benefits of such rudimentary interfaces can be enormous. However, an intelligent long-term strategy for integration cannot be confined to DP and/or WP management. The goal is to plan for all the information needs of the organi-

ORGANIZATION

zation, and the first task is to define the range of potential applications.

Listing potential application areas helps to clarify technical questions from the point of view of business operations and pinpoints the intersection of technology and operational needs. The following applications encompass the information needs of most organizations:

- Data processing
- Text processing
- Reprographics
- Information retrieval
- Information transfer
- Personal processing
- Activity management
- Conferencing

Ideally, a program for integrating WP and DP should consider all of these applications.

Data Processing

In most organizations some DP functions will remain centralized and administratively separate from other applications. Such tasks as serving large-volume information needs or providing corporate-wide planning models cannot be decentralized. However, opportunities abound for improving the availability of DP output, and this effort should be the focus of systems planning. MIS managers should be sensitive to user requirements, and MIS personnel should be discouraged from approaching user needs from a hardware point of view.

Decentralized DP. Many organizations find decentralized DP appropriate to their environments. This is most often true in very large organizations or organizations expanding through the acquisition of smaller operating units. In very large organizations (e.g., banks, insurance companies) departmental needs for DP may be large enough to justify dedicated DP facilities on that level. Companies expanding by acquisition may have to contend with incompatible DP facilities. In this case it is usually best to centralize only part of the DP function. Certain management strategies are useful for developing consistency among separate systems; for example, mandatory financial reporting to the corporate controller, consistent systems procedures, and corporate-wide guidelines can all help to ensure proper coordination of disparate operations.

Text Processing

The degree of development of MIS management and its close attachment to technical systems have profoundly affected WP. Initial attempts to manage WP mirrored the experience with DP; WP was isolated in large centers where requests for work were received and processed. Since the centers were not integrated into the functional areas, all the traditional document production protocols (e.g., methods of drafting, turnaround time, access to the typist) were disrupted. This resulted in inefficiency, inconvenience, and dubious cost benefits.

To be effective, text processing applications must be responsive to the functional areas. The current trend is toward a combination of centralized, clustered, and standalone installations. In choosing the best type of installation, a systematic survey should be conducted of document production needs in each functional area. Such a study determines the following:

- Number and size of routine documents produced
- Incidence and size of special documents produced
- Timing of the need for documents
- Incidence of repetitive sections in routine documents
- Protocol for document creation

A realistic assessment of these needs facilitates equipment decisions as well as the configuration of productive work groups.

Standalone WP. Standalone equipment is suitable for small offices that do not need to communicate with other divisions. By choosing WP equipment with sufficient power, memory, and sophisticated software, many small businesses can integrate a wide range of applications on a word processor. One caveat should be mentioned, however: most small businesses have DP needs that exceed the number-crunching capability of even a powerful word processor. Particularly when using programmable WP equipment, many small businesses have been tempted to use the word processor for such DP needs, resulting in slow and cumbersome systems. In such cases it may be preferable to supplement advanced WP applications with time sharing.

Standalone WP can also be used in offices within large companies. In some cases, such as in senior executive offices, routinely produced documents are unique and relatively short. A standalone may be appropriate when a sufficient volume of documents justifies it and immediate input from other offices is not needed when producing documents. Several offices can share a standalone if their needs are similar and volumes are low. In this case a dedicated operator may produce work for several document originators from different offices or departments. This arrangement has many disadvantages, however. Access is not easily related to need, and nondedicated operators are often unproductive.

When considering using standalone WP equipment, an organization should consider its future needs. If there is a chance that a standalone processor may become part of a network or be used as an electronic mail terminal, the ability to upgrade the equipment should be an important consideration.

Work Clusters. The basic principle of the work cluster is that secretarial support and WP are shared but located with the principal functions they support. For example, a marketing manager and four sales representatives might share two administrative secretaries and one WP operator. The senior secretary could act as a clerical supervisor, distributing work in peak-and-valley periods and managing the work flow to the WP operator. Clustered work groups are becoming more common in WP installations. As systems networking grows, clustered work groups will become even more attractive. The work cluster has the advantages of the traditional secretarial support relationship while maintaining the economies of scale of WP. The principal user is located near the WP operator, even though the line of communication

ORGANIZATION

to WP may be through a clerical supervisor. Operators are familiar with their group's work and fully aware of the other functions being performed; thus, the factory atmosphere of isolated WP centers is absent.

Work clusters also provide an opportunity for interface with MIS if communications capabilities exist. With access to the data base, a dedicated operator can use central files for document creation and compilation. More sophisticated networks can link the cluster's word processor with terminals used for other purposes within the group, but the cost-effectiveness of this enhancement depends on the availability of inexpensive compatible hardware.

WP centers may still serve a useful function in applications involving such lengthy, repetitive documents as insurance policies. The most promising opportunity for network applications in WP centers involves interfacing word processors with photocomposition equipment to produce large quantities of lengthy documents. In this case WP may serve as the link between MIS and printing installations. MIS may provide basic lists or statistical information that the WP center inserts into standard texts and then transmits to the print shop.

Reprographics

Planning a reprographics strategy requires the technical expertise of print shop specialists and knowledge of the organization's needs for printed and copied materials. A centralized reprographics facility may be responsible for reprographics input (typed or word processed), print shop operation (including typesetting, paste-up, and finishing), and information distribution. In many cases it may also be useful to assign control of convenience copying, facsimile transmission, and micrographics to the reprographics facility, which is accustomed to handling large volumes of hard-copy documents and equipment.

If the volume of in-house printing is sufficient, careful integration with WP can create substantial cost savings. Computer-output microfilm can provide opportunities for improving the efficiency of record creation and access to stored records.

Information Retrieval

The need to automate access to records varies widely, not only from organization to organization, but among functional areas. Information retrieval capability is closely related to the WP/DP interface desired in any area of the organization. For example, the personnel department may need access to extensive records for such tasks as updating files or meeting reporting requirements. Online retrieval may be useful for updating files but more or less irrelevant for reporting. Access to retrieval capabilities should be based on the user's substantive need.

WP storage media are used for short-term document storage; however, they are unsuitable for long-term electronic storage. Computer output microfilm, on the other hand, is a hard-storage medium that can provide WP users with permanent non-paper storage through DP. Appropriate access to elec-

Integrating Information Technologies

tronic retrieval depends on the frequency of need for reference to current documents and retention policies for inactive information.

Information Transfer

One of the most promising productivity tools in electronic processing is one-way, noninteractive information transfer. This will replace much communication by telephone and paper mail in traditional offices. Electronic mail is possible on any communicating WP system; however, a few systems have software for managing the transfer of information that makes electronic mail a realistic application. Voice messaging systems are already available from several vendors. The huge potential for time and cost savings makes electronic information transfer an important area for planning.

Personal Processing

The personal computer has brought DP into the office through the back door. MIS managers are becoming increasingly familiar with the use and value of personal processors. Standalone processors are used for pure computation and model building, and many such devices have been expanded, using off-the-shelf software, to perform some text processing.

The increasing acceptance of such equipment by managers and its potential applications for technical professionals make the integration of personal computers with centralized MIS functions an attractive option. In the past, the major vendors' equipment strategies have inhibited this development, but the market in professional workstations promises continued growth. MIS/office automation planners must identify the applications that are appropriate for personal processing and the degree to which distributed processing can meet these specialized needs.

Activity Management

The extensive use of distributed processing will unfold possibilities for using electronics in the management process itself. Through automated scheduling, project control, diary systems, and tickler files, management of time and staff can be integrated with information processing. Such systems are justified when the needed access to data and to other personnel warrants them.

Some users may need access to a network of support staff members for project control; others may use the activity management capability independently or with a secretary. Implementation of such systems depends on the availability of suitable software and communications capability.

Conferencing

The telecommunications dimensions of office automation—particularly the potential for teleconferencing and videoconferencing—must be addressed in a long-term strategy. Although most users find it significantly less effective than face-to-face interaction, remote-location videoconferencing has potential for simulating the meeting environment and replacing at least some business travel. To be effective, however, it must be combined with appropriate complementary applications. Transmission and display of data and visual im-

ORGANIZATION

ages will be important ingredients in successful electronic conferencing.

MANAGING INTEGRATION

The integration of WP, DP, and other information technologies is among the most difficult organizational tasks facing business today. Many MIS professionals are ill equipped for managing such a task because they lack experience in areas of the company outside MIS. Although most functional area managers are not technically proficient enough to tackle sophisticated planning strategy, they can help define the ways in which integrated electronic processing can improve business operations. Administrative managers usually understand the management of WP, since it is an administrative function, but lack much knowledge of other technical areas. The operations department may include a communications expert whose knowledge is vital to information management but who is often inexperienced in administration or business operations.

MIS, Administration, and Operations

For small organizations, the integration of WP and DP is relatively simple, since most minicomputers have sufficient processing capabilities, storage capacity, and software flexibility to address many of the building-block applications already described. In larger organizations, where the volume and variety of processing applications require careful management, integration is more difficult. The general trend has been toward developing overall management of information systems through the MIS department.

Many benefits are realized in giving MIS responsibility for overall electronic processing; the most obvious is technical expertise. However, the DP industry is moving steadily toward more user-friendly systems and programming languages. Because technical issues can be monitored by MIS personnel on an in-house consulting basis, some organizations have shifted responsibility for overall information strategy to other areas.

The administrative function encompasses many areas—particularly support activities—where the impact of integration is felt most dramatically. Unfortunately, many sophisticated WP systems compete with systems that can be networked with DP, including statistical, list-processing, or mass-mailing applications. MIS management often finds it difficult to accept administrative control of office automation strategy, since the MIS staff tends to focus on hardware solutions and the administrative staff on human resource implications.

A third, increasingly common solution for automation planning is to assign responsibility to the operations area. The sophisticated purchasing professional often understands the cost-benefit implications of electronic processing and usually monitors operational developments that require changes in equipment. Operations may also have the skills needed to identify optimum applications, justify purchases, and negotiate lease agreements. However, operations specialists are usually not sufficiently familiar with technical trends to be able to plan for the long term. Moreover, the organizational impact of integration may be dramatic, and operations managers may be ill prepared to cope with it.

Office Automation Task Force

Assigning responsibility for company-wide information management strategy is fraught with pitfalls. Many organizations have recognized the difficulties and developed an approach that promises to be the training ground for the next generation of information managers: the office automation task force. By gathering all the expertise at the organization's disposal, the task force gains the following virtues of planning by committee:

- A broad range of administrative and technical experience
- Depth of technical knowledge, encompassing all existing office applications for electronic processing
- Competing points of view
- Dispersed sources of manpower

The intricacy of planning for an integrated information management strategy makes the task force the most promising planning approach available to most organizations. The task force should include members of all the disciplines mentioned previously—MIS, administration, operations, and communications. A vigorous and talented task force often performs best when it is acountable to a manager with considerable experience in the business operations of the organization. The delicate balancing of their interests in pursuit of the best strategy for the organization requires skillful staff management as well as sensitivity to the technical issues.

Of course, this approach has the potential for failure, especially when executive policy does not define clear objectives for the committee or when no one has sufficient authority to ensure that individuals are committed to those objectives. The worst-case scenario for an office automation task force is a committee sharply divided (usually between MIS and administrative members), bickering endlessly over methodology because the disputants can only see their own point of view. A task force that degenerates to this level almost invariably requires a change in the management of the committee, not in its constituents.

This interdisciplinary approach to the integration of all information systems has enormous potential for developing management expertise in what promises to be one of the most important arms of future business organizations. There is no existing body of knowledge for teaching total information management. Not only is the battlefield experience missing, but the technology is changing at such a rate that only very general long-range planning is possible.

ACTION PLAN

The office automation task force approach has the potential to produce unique managerial expertise if the organization works to maximize its benefits and minimize the pitfalls. Company politics will always be with us; however, the manipulation of the task force for political purposes must be discouraged. Among the best ways to do this are to encourage an esprit de corps by stressing the career development potential of the task force to all members and to facilitate cooperative discussion through clear executive policy.

In addition to having publicly understood organizational goals, the task

ORGANIZATION

force should be guided by a solid procedural foundation. This foundation must extend beyond procedures for the work of the task force itself; staff at all levels of the organization must be given guidelines for cooperating with the task force while integrated systems are being developed.

The task force should be responsible for establishing a basis from which future enhancements can be developed. Many procedures will already exist for DP and WP operations in place; however, one of the first tasks of the committee must be to publish guidelines for the duration of the integration effort. This may include limiting equipment purchases to a manageable number of vendors as well as restricting systems applications that may become redundant. If such precautions are taken, the task force can help to ensure that the organization's progress toward the integration of DP, WP, and other information technologies is smooth and successful.

Section IV
Systems Development and Programming

Developing major application systems that meet user needs and that are delivered on schedule and within budget remains one of the most important aspects of MIS management's job. In many MIS organizations, this activity is the largest single consumer of funds. Success or failure for the MIS manager often depends on the proper planning, execution, and control of application systems development. This section is filled with useful advice on carrying out this responsibility.

The activities of the MIS organization can profoundly influence the effectiveness and efficiency of user departments. Through the development and continued use of an application systems plan, MIS management can improve user relations while effectively managing the backlog of user requests. This is accomplished by providing the focus and direction necessary to solve the right problem in the right sequence with the right resources. Selecting applications for development scheduling is not always a straightforward task. Setting priorities is a management decision that must be based on the benefit to the entire organization. Chapters IV-1, "Application Portfolio Planning," and IV-2, "Establishing Priorities for Application Systems," present key considerations for planning, establishing priorities for, and scheduling application development.

Once the applications plan and the appropriate priorities are set, the next step is to develop a strategy for implementing systems. Most organizations cannot afford lengthy application development cycles that delay the realization of promised benefits. Certain development and implementation methods can improve the process. Chapter IV-3, "An Approach to Effective Implementation," presents strategies for attaining benefits rapidly, improving system quality, minimizing the impact on users, and reducing the pressure on the MIS department to deliver the system.

One of the most promising advances in systems development methodology concerns structured techniques. Structured methodology has become increasingly important to the systems development process. It can result in better systems, greater productivity, and more satisfied users. Chapter IV-4, "Structured Methodology," provides an overview of structured techniques, explaining the reasons for their use and outlining their benefits.

Structured techniques for systems analysis, design, programming, and testing represent a major part of the effort to improve MIS productivity. They improve the efficiency of the labor-intensive systems development life cycle and produce more maintainable systems. MIS management should be familiar with these techniques and implement those that best fit the organization. Improving the efficiency of the programming and testing functions—and the quality of the systems produced—is a critical concern of MIS managers. Structured techniques provide proven methods for improving productivity in these systems development functions. Chapter IV-5, "Analysis and Design—A Structured Approach," describes the tools and methods used for structured analysis and design, while Chapter IV-6, "Programming and Testing—A Structured Approach," covers the techniques used for structured programming and testing.

The creation of large DP systems is a complex process. Developing reliable and useful systems on time and within budget involves many activities that, when grouped together, constitute software engineering. Software engineering concepts were first developed for use in defense systems and have since been broadened for application to all areas of systems development. Chapter IV-7, "Software Engineering Concepts and Techniques," discusses a general software engineering approach. The process is outlined, and techniques that apply to management (e.g., project personnel organization and resource estimating) are described. This chapter also describes the techniques that the programmer and analyst can use to better perform their jobs.

Cost analysis and control of systems can sometimes pose as great a challenge as their design and programming. Data processing systems enhance information retrieval and manipulation. Rapid technological advances, however, have increased their potential to create and access more information than is affordable or relevant. Chapter IV-8, "Preparing for a System Cost/Benefit Analysis," provides a method for examining the type and quality of information to be processed by a proposed system before the cost/benefit analysis is undertaken. The analysis itself is described in Chapter IV-9, "Performing a Cost/Benefit Analysis."

The final chapter in this section examines project control. The management of complex development projects and the integration of systems, data base development, data communications networks, office systems, and the many other facets of MIS require effective tools for planning and control. To meet deadlines within budget, the MIS manager should use all available tools. As discussed in Chapter IV-10, "Controlling Projects: PERT/CPM," PERT/CPM techniques are proven tools that can help managers better control all types of projects.

IV-1
Application Portfolio Planning

Mike Mushet

INTRODUCTION

All too often, the MIS organization fails to be perceived by its user community in the manner it expects. From its perspective, MIS attempts to satisfy automation requirements for its user organizations to enable them to meet their entrepreneurial objectives effectively and efficiently. To the user, however, MIS responsiveness often seems sluggish and disorganized. System backlogs are large in most shops, with proportional user dissatisfaction.

User satisfaction is based on more than the development and implementation of a quality systems product. It is influenced as much by the delivery process as by the end product. Consequently, backlog management and user communication are being recognized as critical issues.

This chapter presents an approach to managing the increasing application backlogs and complexities of the MIS environment by addressing the lack of direction and focus of application systems planning that has led to widespread user dissatisfaction. It identifies the essential components of systems planning and notes their relationship to other key MIS and corporate plans.

THE APPLICATION SYSTEMS PLAN

Systems planning is best examined through an in-depth study of the end product—the systems plan itself. The following paragraphs describe the plan's definition, objectives, and limitations.

Definition

The systems plan provides a common structured repository of information concerning the direction, approach, and time frame of the MIS organization's systems development efforts. The systems plan should document elements of the current and future systems portfolio of the enterprise. These elements should be organized to show their intrinsic relationship in a clear and graphic format. Specifically, the plan must define:

- Where the MIS organization is currently
- Where it should be and why
- What steps must be taken to get there
- How much it will cost

SYSTEMS DEVELOPMENT AND PROGRAMMING

The plan should contain information describing the current status and resource capabilities in MIS and in user communities (see the Planning Input section for further detail).

Organizational goals should be expressed through an annotated enterprise model that graphically represents the interrelationships of the various business functions. In addition to a systems perspective, goals for technology positioning, staff growth, and hardware development must be addressed. Goals should be justified by anticipated benefits, which should be stated at a high level.

The steps necessary to achieve organizational goals are defined in terms of systems schedules and ancillary support schedules, such as the installation of a specific development tool. Cost is defined in terms of detail and summary time-phased labor and expense dollars.

A sample systems plan outline is illustrated in Figure 1. In summary, the plan allows MIS management to anticipate future user requirements. Each application request can be assessed as part of overall development rather than individually. By analogy, the reader can imagine the difficulty of trying to solve several jigsaw puzzles simultaneously when given only one piece at a time. The applications plan allows MIS to see where the pieces go even when they are not yet in place.

Objectives

The primary objective of the applications plan is to effectively manage the backlog of both expressed and unexpressed applications while maintaining rapport with the user community. This is done by defining the direction of growth and then communicating this information to all individuals. Each participant will derive his or her own set of objectives and expectations from the plan, with the following advantages:

- MIS Management—MIS management assembles a complete picture of the service it provides and develops guidelines leading to a goal acceptable both to users and MIS. It can provide more accurate and timely input to its support organization (i.e., operations), minimize suboptimal resource allocation, and ensure efficient application of technology.
- MIS Supervisors—Staffing, training, and budget planning are simplified if coordinated with the systems plan.
- MIS Development Staff—The systems plan eases this group's feeling of being caught between MIS and the user while it reduces frustration and turnover and improves morale. This group can also be given the proper training and tools in a timely fashion.
- Operations—This group often feels excluded from decisions that affect it. The systems plan gives operations management a means to more actively participate in systems development efforts.
- User—The systems plan gives the user insight into the relationship between his or her needs and those of other users, enabling more effective planning. The user gains an appreciation for the priority of his or her request and, as part of the planning effort, feels more involved with the development effort.
- Senior Management—The systems plan makes senior management

Application Portfolio Planning

```
    I. Introduction
       A. Audience
       B. Development objectives
       C. Objectives of plan
       D. Use of this document
   II. Resource Assessment
       A. Staff
          1. Description
          2. Strengths
          3. Weaknesses
          4. Desired position
          5. Development action
       B. Hardware Resources
          1. Description
          2. Strengths
          3. Weaknesses
          4. Desired position
          5. Development action
       C. Facilities
          1. Description
          2. Strengths
          3. Weaknesses
          4. Desired position
          5. Development action
       D. Tools
          1. Description
          2. Strengths
          3. Weaknesses
          4. Desired position
          5. Development action
  III. Systems Assessment
       A. System A
          1. Functional description/users
          2. Technical description
             a. Software
             b. Hardware
             c. Resource use
          3. Major problems
          4. Development action
       B. System B
   IV. Schedules
       A. Systems
       B. Hardware
    V. Resources
       A. Cost
       B. Benefit
```

Figure 1. Application Systems Plan Outline

SYSTEMS DEVELOPMENT AND PROGRAMMING

aware of the impact and extent of corporate automation and provides a means of measuring progress.

Limitations

The applications plan serves as a road map, defining the current and planned position and the costs and schedules required to reach the desired destination. The plan's success depends on the assumptions made during preparation, its completeness, and, perhaps most important, the quality of the vehicle used to implement it. If the systems development life cycle is not rigorous, the quality of the systems products is poor, staffing is inadequate, or development tools are lacking, the plan will fail. If these problems are first addressed separately, the planning assumptions may prove close to correct. An applications plan can never be more accurate than its input.

PLANNING INPUT

To project future activities accurately, the applications plan requires various types of input. This input is collected from several areas and includes, but is not limited to, the following (see Figure 2):

- Enterprise model
- Resource assessment
- Systems assessment.

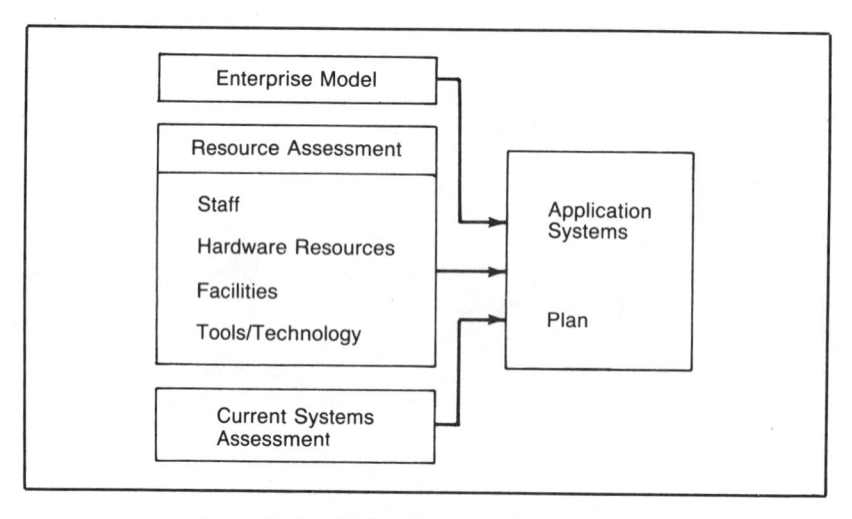

Figure 2. Application Systems Planning Input

Enterprise Model

Enterprise modeling is known by many terms and in its totality is beyond the scope of this chapter. (For further information, the reader may want to refer to the IBM Business System Planning publications.[1]) Briefly, enterprise modeling is a means of identifying and documenting essential business functions. These functions are expressed, usually in graphic and matrix form, in terms of their data interrelationship. Though it refers to the political organizations for which it was derived, the model is devoid of political organiza-

Application Portfolio Planning

tional structure. (The closer a political organization matches the functional organization, the smoother the operation will be.) This separation helps ensure the stability of the model.

As in the in-progress model illustrated in Figure 3, all basic business functions, including those not automated, can be represented. This model also can be represented hierarchically, with each basic function broken down into its essential component functions. Various subject data bases and their logical entities could also be represented. The modeling conventions followed are based on the Yourdon methodology[2]—others can work equally well.

The model is often built by the data administration function in the MIS department with a high degree of user involvement.

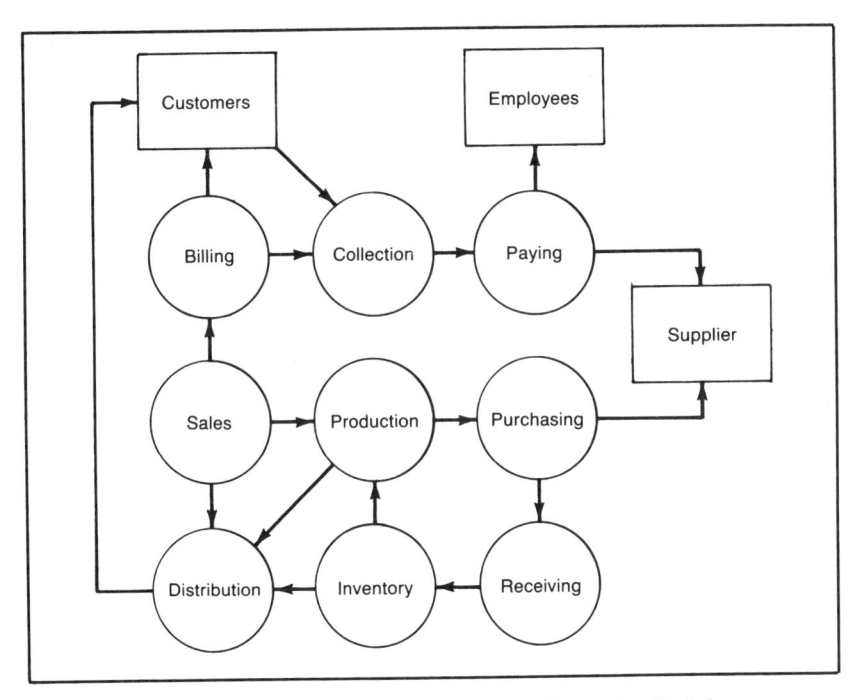

Figure 3. Start of Graphic Component Enterprise Model

Resource Assessment

This planning input contains detailed information on the resources available to implement plan activities. This assessment should cover at least four major areas:
- Staff
- Tools and technology
- Facilities
- Hardware

A critical assessment of staff capabilities is vital. Is the department adequately staffed? Is there the right mix of specialities? What is the potential for growth? How strong is the supervision?

SYSTEMS DEVELOPMENT AND PROGRAMMING

Without the proper tools, even a highly competent staff can be severely handicapped. Is the latest generation of tools available? Are they promoted? Is the staff trained in their use? Is the shop going to be leading-edge? Are there sufficient terminals? Can they be afforded?

Facilities are often overlooked until they become a severe hindrance. What facilities are available? How much growth can be accommodated? Is the work environment conducive to communication and productivity? Are work areas well lit? Seemingly simple things can impede progress and schedules and must therefore be factored into the plan.

Without sufficient hardware, the automation process will stop. How much hardware capacity is left? Is it the right kind at the right time? Increasingly, systems requests are for online systems; what is the shop's ability to support online systems in terms of CPU, memory, disk, and communications lines? Although the development of additional resources is the province of the hardware plan, it derives input from the applications plan.

The preceding assessments should be made critically by knowledgeable MIS staff members.

Systems Assessment

Assessing current systems is essential to informing MIS management of its performance relative to its charter. This assessment should consist of detailed documentation of the existing systems portfolio and should include such information as:
- System name
- Basic functions in terms of the enterprise need
- Development data
- Languages and machines
- Primary input/output/files
- Quantified outstanding backlog of problems and enhancements
- Synopsis of major problems
- Anticipated user direction and priorities

Assessments are derived through combined MIS and user input.

BUILDING THE PLAN

After the planning input has been collected, the formal planning process begins. (Most of the hard work, however, has already been done.) This phase continues to be a joint effort between MIS and its user community. After the planning horizon is established (usually two to five years), the remaining planning effort consists of the following:
- Establishing development goals and objectives
- Identifying activities
- Estimating resources
- Establishing precedence
- Evaluation
- Publication.

Establishing Development Goals and Objectives

A well-executed plan will fail if it does not address the goals and objectives of the enterprise. This is an insidious type of failure because the usual controls give no clue to the impending disaster.

MIS management must clearly define and communicate its charter. If MIS is to manage processes (i.e., technology and automation), one set of objectives will be developed. If its charter is to manage the data, another set of objectives will be developed. Current industry trends are toward the managing data, though most MIS organizations are currently managing processes. The transition is expensive and may be hindered by lack of tools and methodologies. This chapter addresses a process-managed environment but equally applies to one that is data managed.

Identifying Activities

Using the enterprise model and maintaining consistency with the identified objectives and technological factors, the planners should define the missing pieces in the automation jigsaw. Each activity should result in the automation of a new business function or the enhancement of an existing one. The function should be defined from the model so that the resources can be estimated. Identifying activities might take six months to three years; however, the project planning that follows each application plan activity should deliver a product every quarter.

The activity identified in this step should address each known or expected user problem or enhancement. Cost justification is not critical at this stage; if the activity seems justified, it should be planned for. Individual project plans can address cost justification details at a later date.

Estimating Resources

The resources required to complete each planned activity within the prescribed time frame should be defined in their basic units (e.g., worker-hours, office square feet, CPU time) for each basic class of resource. They can then be expressed in dollars.

Two important factors should control the units used in specifying the orders of magnitude. The first is the time frame of the estimate. Estimates for a five-year horizon should be in broader terms than those for the next six months (i.e., worker-months versus worker-days). The second controlling factor is the degree of flexibility of the assumptions. Inexact assumptions require wider estimate tolerances. Activities requiring further analysis should be handled as an unknown quantity and tolerances brought forward in all estimate summaries.

Establishing Precedence

Identified and estimated activities must be placed in logical sequence. This sequence, or priority, will depend on logical relationships, expected return on investment, and politics.

Bills cannot be produced without knowledge of resource consumption. Inventory stock cannot be replenished without knowledge of the quantity to order. These priority-setting relationships are usually easy to understand and may derive directly from the enterprise model.

SYSTEMS DEVELOPMENT AND PROGRAMMING

Some general guidance can also be provided regarding logical relationships. Figure 4 depicts the traditional triangular management model, in which each lower level supports the upper level. An initial difficulty with MIS was that it tried to support upper levels of management without having first firmly established operational systems. Logic requires that operational systems be in place first.

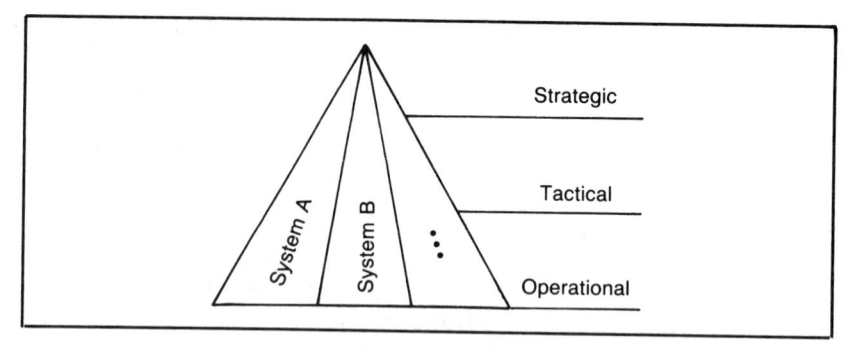

Figure 4. Traditional Management Triangle

At this higher level of detail, a return on investment (ROI) is no more difficult to define than at lower levels, providing the tolerance of estimation is included. The primary purpose is to establish relative priorities among the various activities. Therefore, approximations are usually sufficient, since other priority-setting factors come into play. Having determined the time frame and related cost in the previous steps, a benefit assessment is required to complete the ROI calculation. As with all benefits calculations, it can be expressed as tangibles (i.e., avoidable and displaceable) or intangibles (e.g., smooth operation, good will). The intangibles are influenced by corporate politics.

An MIS manager can effectively match DP resources to user demands when, for example, programmer/analysts are in frequent contact with the hands-on user; programming supervisors communicate often with user management; and senior user management is just a phone call away.

In this environment, MIS develops excellent understanding of true user need, and the user gains an appreciation of MIS's capabilities and limitations. This enhanced atmosphere of communication can often clear the air of political innuendo and sabre rattling.

If this is not the case, MIS management must work quickly to improve communications with users.

Evaluation

The evaluation process comprises several steps. If the plan fails any part of the evaluation, it must be reworked, at least on a conceptual level.

The evaluation determines such things as:
- Do goals and objectives match organizational need?
- Is the overall plan consistent with the goals and objectives?
- Is the plan consistent with those of other organizations?

Application Portfolio Planning

- Are all activities included and clearly stated?
- Is the enterprise model correct?
- Are the resource estimates realistic and stated with the proper tolerance?
- Do the resource requirements exceed those available as identified by the resource assessment?
- Can other support plans satisfy resource deficiencies?
- Can those involved live with the established priorities and precedences?

The overall planning process is shown in Figure 5.

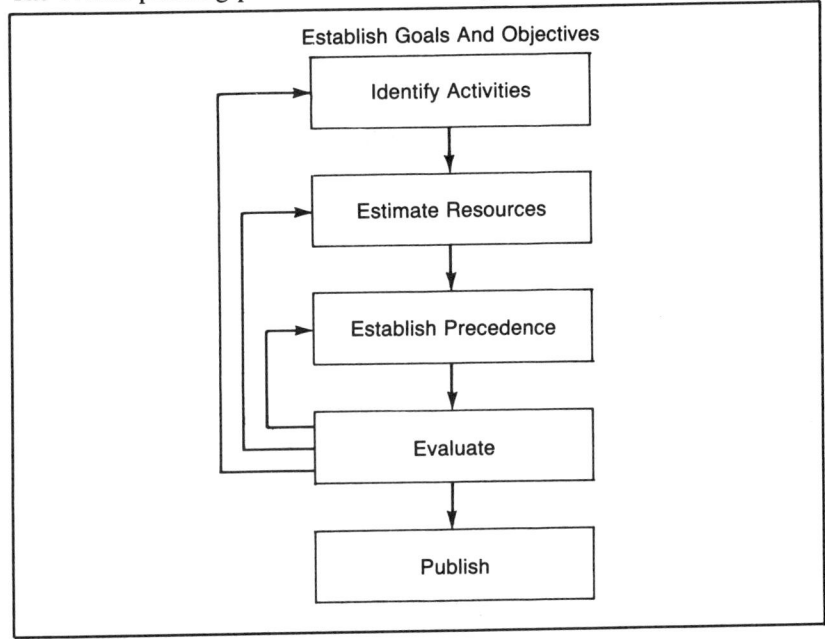

Figure 5. The Applications Planning Process

Publication

The final step in the planning process is to publish the plan. The plan can serve as valuable entree for MIS management to discuss systems planning issues with personnel they may not encounter regularly. The presentation of the plan can be used to demonstrate the concern MIS has for its charter and to foster improved relationships with the user community.

MAINTAINING THE PLAN

Planning is not an exercise to be performed once every few years whether it is needed or not, but an ongoing activity. Not only must the plan itself be kept current but so must the enterprise model, the resource assessments, and the system assessments. Applications planning is an integral part of MIS management, not an addendum, and should be treated as such.

INTEGRATING THE APPLICATION SYSTEMS PLAN

The application systems plan does not exist alone. It is one of many essential nested plans that support the MIS organization. As shown in Figure 6,

SYSTEMS DEVELOPMENT AND PROGRAMMING

the applications plan may derive input from user organization plans as well as factor into it. The applications plan provides primary input to the project staffing, facilities, hardware resource, and financial plans. These in turn feed other plans. Planners should take into account that the update cycle of these other plans may be such that incorrect conclusions can be drawn.

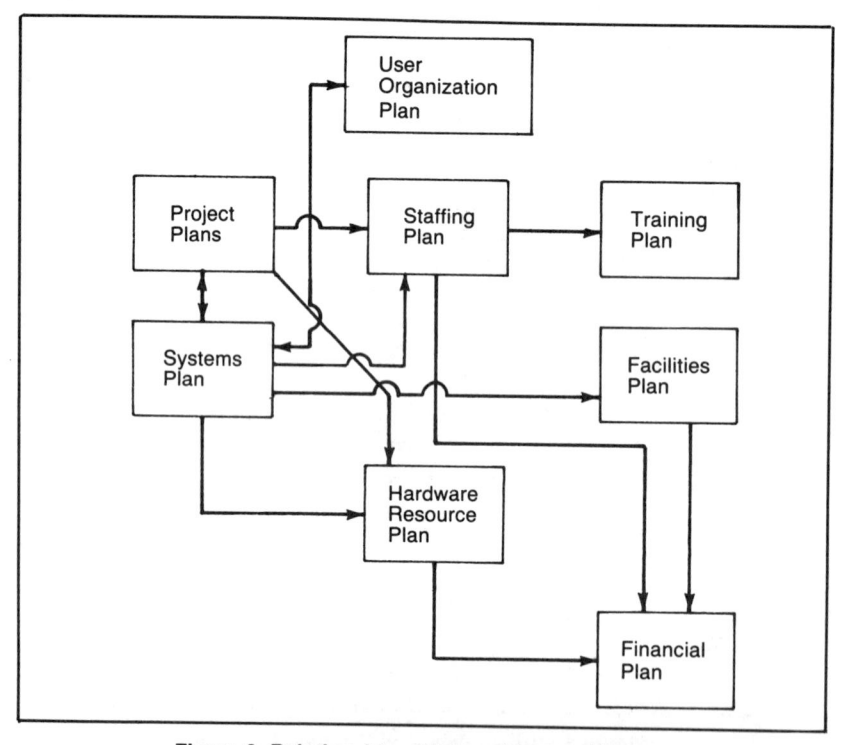

Figure 6. Relationship of MIS and Corporate Plans

CONCLUSION

MIS management is charged with more than the responsibility of managing the people and machine resources under its control. The things it does and the way in which it does them can profoundly affect the productivity and vitality of the enterprise. These efforts must be managed effectively and communicated clearly throughout the user community. The application systems plan provide a vehicle for this. The data collection and model building effort may take three to six months and usually has additional uses. The plan building process may take an additional three to six months, depending on the size and geographic nature of the enterprise. Time invested in this undertaking, however, will prove worthwhile in improved backlog management and user rapport.

References

1. IBM Corporation. *Business Systems Planning: Information Systems Planning Guide.* 2nd ed., 1978, GE20-0527-Z.
2. DeMarco, T. *Structured Systems Analysis.* New York: Yourdon Press, 1978.

IV-2
Establishing Priorities for Application Systems
Louis Fried

INTRODUCTION

The average backlog of development projects for the mature installation is two to four years of work with the current staff size. As a result, a frequently voiced complaint is the slow response of MIS groups to requests for new services or changes to existing ones.

Assuming that staff size is limited by budgetary constraints and that reasonably efficient methods are used for systems development, the only remaining mechanism for improving service is request response based on priority. In other words, it is necessary to establish a commonly understood mechanism for allocating the MIS department's scarce resources.

THE PURPOSE OF BUSINESS SYSTEMS

Computer applications only make sense in the context of the organization for which they were developed. This context establishes the basic need for the system, the criteria management uses to evaluate that need, and the feasibility of successful implementation. Priorities must be established in a manner that satisfies the management-defined needs.

In the past, the purpose of business systems was considered to be the conveyance of information on the status of various organizational aspects—a perception evidenced by the proliferation of accounting-oriented reporting systems. More recently, business systems have been designed instead for participation in the operation of the business itself. For example, online banking systems that process transactions rapidly and maintain the current status of accounts have created an operating environment of total dependency.

Business systems are therefore used not only to enhance the ability to manage and plan for the organization but also to perform the organization's basic functions. These systems support the primary objective of ensuring the organization's survival and growth through adequate profit by providing products or services of sufficient quality on schedule and for a competitive price.

SYSTEMS DEVELOPMENT AND PROGRAMMING

POTENTIAL APPLICATIONS

The priority-setting process involves a broad spectrum of potential applications and users. Many applications are proposed by users on their own initiative; however, the systems analyst must be prepared to examine the feasibility and potential profitability of these proposals and to suggest alternative approaches or prospective applications to the user. For these functions, the following guidelines are reviewed.

Types of Business Information

John Dearden analyzes and classifies different kinds of business information to aid in the understanding of information systems.[1] These classifications are dichotomies of the information function.

- Action versus Nonaction—Action information requires that the recipient take some positive action. For example, inventory shortage reports require the recipient to order the parts on the shortage list. Nonaction information may include notification that some action has taken place (the order has been placed), accounting data that is being accumulated (this may become action information when the accumulation is completed), or information received from books or periodicals.
- Recurring versus Nonrecurring—Recurring information generated at regular intervals (at least annually) includes most accounting, inventory, production, and sales reports. Nonrecurring information includes one-time reports (e.g., special financial analyses or simulations used for business planning).
- Documentary versus Nondocumentary—Documentary information is expressed in permanent form (e.g., written, printed, on magnetic tape). Nondocumentary information is not preserved but transmitted orally.
- Internal versus External—Internal information is generated inside the organization (e.g., accounting reports, production schedules, payroll). External information is generated outside the organization and may include government reports, vendor status information, industry surveys, and competitive analyses.
- Historical versus Future Projection—Historical information includes reports of completed actions (e.g., run payrolls, processed inventory transactions, old accounting reports), which are often the basis for future projections. Future projections include feasibility studies and market analyses.

On the basis of these classifications, Dearden makes the following generalizations about business information:

- Action, recurring, documentary, internal, and historical types of information are prime candidates for automation.
- The timing and accuracy of action information are usually important.
- Precise timing is not important for nonaction information.
- Nonaction information is a prime candidate for elimination.
- Nondocumentary information is almost impossible to control.
- The higher the management decision, the more important external information and future projection become.

Since Dearden wrote the study, nonrecurring information has become increasingly susceptible to automation. His other generalizations, however, remain valid and provide a guide to system selection.

The decision regarding which system to automate may be crucial to the success of the MIS department. A simple application with little payback would delay the implementation of a more important system. On the other hand, a very large, complex application may result in management dissatisfaction because of implementation time involved and because the users of the new system may have not yet acquired the skills needed to implement operational changes.

Some essential considerations in selecting applications are:
- User support of the system is vital to successful implementation.
- Product-related systems are more likely than administrative systems to contribute more to profit.
- The applications selected should be technically feasible and not beyond MIS staff capability.
- Proposed systems should pass some test of economic feasibility.

CRITERIA FOR APPLICATION SELECTION

That selecting applications involves managerial choices and decisions implies a possibility of available alternatives, which include alternative applications for differing purposes (e.g., accounts payable compared to shop floor control or order entry) and alternative approaches to the same system (e.g., batch, online, and manual processing). In this context, choosing to retain the present methods or not selecting a new application also constitutes a managerial decision. Such decisions are also justifiable alternatives and must be presented as such.

The decisions involved in application selection are based on managerial criteria that may be clearly documented, implied from previous selection processes, or known only to the decision makers themselves. To satisfy these criteria, the analyst must first identify them.

Task identification should be approached by directly requesting concerned managers to define their application selection criteria in three areas: qualitative, institutional, and quantitative. The definitions received may be incomplete or ambiguous and require several iterations to obtain a workable set of selection criteria. In addition, the analyst might have to develop a draft of proposed criteria and circulate it for management approval. A final statement should include most of the elements discussed in the following sections.

Qualitative Criteria

Justification for increasingly sophisticated applications cannot be stated in the straightforward economic terms of older systems. For example, clerical savings alone probably could not justify an online airline reservation system. If, however, customer satisfaction, government regulations on flight booking, profitable plane loading factors, and competition are considered, the system may be deemed indispensable.

Such intangible considerations are crucial. Qualitative factors for systems used in the operation of the firm (e.g., production or inventory control) are readily apparent. Successful applications in these areas depend on the speed, quality, and accuracy of transaction input and subsequent processing and reporting. A production control report with a high error rate can severely damage the organization's productive capacity. The same report, if completely correct but issued too late for use by production planners or line foremen, serves no purpose.

Competitive Impact. Another area in which qualitative factors influence application selection is the impact of competition. For example, some hotel chains try to justify the use of online reservation systems on competitive rather than economic grounds. Using competition as the major criterion may be risky, but it is certainly valid. When competition is a factor, management must weigh the potential benefits; an application with a lower quantifiable dollar benefit that provides a competitive edge in that industry may be preferable to one that provides a higher dollar benefit but no competitive advantage.

Prestige. The competitive factor is closely associated with another intangible: prestige. An organization's public relations image is often tied to projecting a modern appearance. A highly visible application, such as computerized billing, may gain points in the selection process because it is expected to benefit the organization's image. Automated billing systems, however, can damage the image of a firm as frequently as they can help.

High Visibility. Service should be a selection criterion for systems with high public visibility. Systems that provide a service to the corporate customer as well as to the organization have a better chance of contributing to its image and competitive stance. For example, a California bank provides checking account customers with a statement listing their checks by number as an aid to checkbook balancing. Another banking example is immediate online verification of account balances—a system that not only helps tellers but also enables a customer to cash a check in any state branch without waiting.

Decision Making. Management decision making may be approached in two ways. Systems that automate the decision-making process show both tangible and intangible benefits (e.g., the use of economic order quantity analysis or min-max routines in inventory systems). Improving the quality of information and the way it is presented to management also improves the quality of decision making—an approach used in cash management. By-products of the accounts receivable and payable systems are used to increase management's ability to make short-term investments, thus adding to the organization's earning power. Complex simulation systems and extremely flexible financial analysis systems are not necessary for decision making. A relatively simple idea, such as producing summary reports in graphic form, can aid management by reducing the time the user needs to analyze report content and assimilate it for decision-making purposes.

Institutional Criteria

Environment imposes constraints on the selection of applications. An organization must maintain equity or balance among its users. Overemphasizing product-oriented applications to the virtual exclusion of financial or administrative applications quickly creates a group of dissatisfied managers. Thus, committing all systems development resources to an application for a single set of users should be avoided. Even if some users are not disturbed by lack of equity, a significant potential for improvement or savings may be missed by ignoring the need for balance.

Systems developed within the firm must be congruent to its policies and objectives; no proposed application that violates them can be successful. The analyst and the MIS manager, however, must be careful to avoid a rigid interpretation of corporate policy. For example, during the fuel shortage of 1973, several organizations formed carpools for their employees. While this policy bore no relationship to an organization's profitability, it was undertaken as a social responsibility. Although a firm's policies and objectives are designated by top management, management's interpretation may change with time, circumstance, and personality. Reasonable applications must be proposed to management in conceptual form to test the boundaries of organizational policies and objectives when changes in the environment indicate changes of interpretation.

An organization's internal political environment may also dictate certain constraints on application selection. Political feasibility, unfortunately, can influence the selection process.

Finally, the human element must be considered. Does the staff have the necessary skills to properly implement the application? If consultants are to be used, do internal personnel possess the skills to monitor their work, implement the product, and maintain the system thereafter? Can the user staff adapt to and operate the system after implementation?

Quantitative Criteria

Quantitative criteria are stated in terms of the explicit cost/earning relationship for a project and measure a proposal's effect on an organization's profit and loss statement. Quantitative factors are therefore presented in terms of dollars estimated with a reasonable degree of confidence.

Such an analysis uses the costs of the existing method as a baseline for comparison. A detailed feasibility study starts with a determination of present costs. In performing a preliminary comparison for project selection, however, emphasis is placed on potential savings without such a detailed study.

A comparison of the present method and one or more alternative approaches should encompass:
- The estimated cost of application development and implementation
- The before-tax earnings or savings expected
- The monthly cash flow of the foregoing factors
- The payback period
- The return on investment

Management may establish criteria in terms of payback period, return on investment, and profit-and-loss impact. Organizations differ in their treat-

SYSTEMS DEVELOPMENT AND PROGRAMMING

ment of application development costs; some may expense these costs, while others capitalize them. The effect on profit and loss will vary. The organization's accounting department should be consulted on the best method of presenting this analysis.

ESTABLISHING PRIORITIES

The decision-making action culminates in the act of setting priorities. Setting application priorities, however, is not merely the final act of decision making but an extensive process requiring the participation of many organizational staff members (see Figure 1). The following sections discuss the responsibilities of those individuals involved in the process.

Planning for Priority Setting

Whether an organization is selecting an alternative for implementing a single application or choosing from among a list of competitive applications, the process of amassing and coordinating documentation and information for final decision making takes time and effort.

The initial responsibility belongs to the director of MIS (or the top DP executive), who must allocate the necessary personnel and budget to the planning and application selection process. The director and a committee of managers and key application analysts should briefly survey potential applications and identify all potential projects for new or replacement systems. The survey includes informal discussions with current and potential users. At this point, no application idea should be discarded as infeasible.

The committee should then establish a budget and proposed plan for accomplishing the steps described in the following section. The budget and plan should be presented to top management for approval. Timing is important; the proposal should be presented immediately before preparation of annual budgets.

Documenting Alternative Applications

Once the necessary effort is approved, the application selection process can begin. Analysts are assigned to each potential application. Background investigation is performed through user interviews and examination of existing documents and reports, accounting records, and other sources that describe each application's current cost and method of operation.

Objectives of the new system should be identified along with a proposed method of achieving these objectives (e.g., through systems development or the purchase of a package). The objectives and proposed method should include the estimated costs of implementation and future operation, the expected benefits, and a rough plan for project implementation with its expected time and cost.

The results of this process should be presented to management as a summary that includes a description of project objectives, an analysis of expected costs and benefits, qualitative and institutional factors, and a rough plan for the use of resources needed to perform the project.

This stage of project selection involves estimates and approximations; it

Establishing Application Priorities

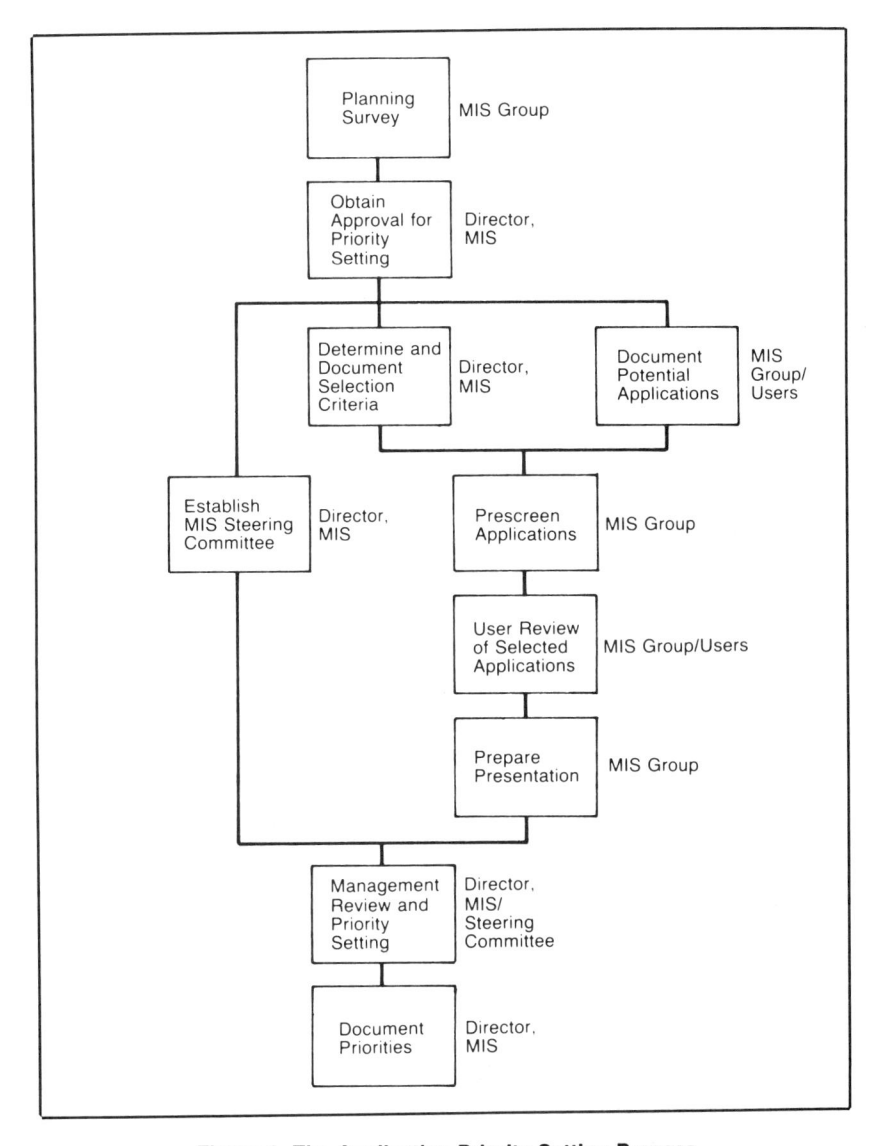

Figure 1. The Application Priority-Setting Process

should be made clear that they do not constitute firm commitments and that detailed feasibility studies will be performed prior to final project approval. Nevertheless, certain key points should be covered in each section of documentation for a proposed application.

The section on objectives should state the following in narrative form:
- The purposes to be served by the application
- The nature of the new system
- The application's technical feasibility
- The estimated overall economic impact

167

SYSTEMS DEVELOPMENT AND PROGRAMMING

- The placement of the application in relation to corporate goals and objectives

The section on costs and benefits should include not only the financial impact (which may be presented in both a tabular and narrative form) but also some description of the qualitative and institutional benefits to be gained by the system's implementation.

Finally, an approximation of a plan for application development and implementation should be made in both narrative and graphic form. This should include development, conversion, and operating plans with some comment on the nature and extent of the user participation required.

For the purposes of presentation, these sections should be summarized into a short statement of conclusions to be placed at the beginning of the presentation.

Establishing Selection Criteria

Concurrent with the investigation of potential applications, the MIS director (or designated representative) must document the selection criteria used by management to evaluate applications. If a steering committee has been formed, the members should be consulted on selection criteria.

Prescreening Potential Applications

When the selection criteria are established and documented, the potential applications are screened for conformance. Prescreening should be done by the MIS director with a committee of managers and key analysts.

Prescreening has two purposes:
- It determines whether any proposed application that cannot pass the test of the criteria should be abandoned; however, upon examination of the proposed application, the criteria may indicate further avenues that should be investigated before an application is finally eliminated.
- It ensures that the proposals are satisfactory for presentation to management and that the survey does not result in too many proposals.

At this stage, no more than six applications should remain for consideration in the priority-setting process. This does not mean that the balance of applications will not be considered in the future; however, at this point, those that offer the greatest benefit and return on investment should be emphasized.

User Reviews

Users involved in the original survey should be informed of the prescreening results. The remaining high-payback proposals should be reviewed with the users and all available detail covered. This review is intended to:
- Gain user comments that might substantially affect the content of the proposal
- Familiarize the user with the proposed application approach
- Verify the expected benefits
- Obtain user commitment to support the proposal to top management

The users should understand that their commitment extends only to obtaining top-management approval for considering the project as a high priority and to obtaining authorization for an appropriate feasibility study. No commitment is made by either party regarding resources, schedule, or benefits until completion of the feasibility study.

On the basis of the user review, the analyst should refine the documentation for presentation.

Preparing the Presentation

A presentation to top management is the next step. This presentation should contain documented proposals for the application projects selected and the proposed implementation plan. The documented proposals should contain a one-page cover summary of the costs and major benefits for each project. The proposed implementation plan (preferably in graphic form) should suggest the sequence in which the high-priority projects should be approached, the DP human and equipment resources anticipated, and a tentative schedule for project development and implementation. Based on this plan, a budget covering the period of the tentative schedule and indicating staff size and costs should be drawn up.

The implementation plan is constructed by the MIS director with the support of the DP managers and analysts after review of the application proposals. Including the DP operations manager is essential to ensuring that operations resources are sufficient to support the selected projects.

Management Review

The complete proposal is now presented to top management. The following are suggested for this presentation:
- Using visual aids (e.g., flip charts, slides) to center the attention of the attendees.
- Rehearsing the presentation and checking the timing; the presentation should be kept brief.
- Alloting time for discussion.
- Designating someone from the MIS staff to act as secretary for the meeting. The secretary records decisions made and notes any questions raised that cannot be answered during the course of the meeting.
- Encouraging the user representative to make the presentation for his or her application. A convinced user is likely to sell a project to management more effectively than someone from the MIS group.

Before the end of the meeting, the decisions should be briefly reviewed with the attendees. If another meeting is required to reach final conclusions, it should be scheduled before the first meeting concludes.

The results of the meeting should be documented, published, and distributed to all concerned parties. This documentation should include the priorities established for each application, responses to any unanswered questions (if a second meeting has not already been scheduled for this purpose), a copy of the schedule project agreed on, and a list of attendees.

SYSTEMS DEVELOPMENT AND PROGRAMMING

Selecting Alternative Approaches to a Single System

The process of setting priorities might initially seem to apply only to contention between different applications. Closer examination of single applications might reveal that they are segmented; it might also reveal priorities established within a project. The analyst's or project manager's task is to determine for each proposed application whether the application can be segmented by partial implementation or by installing successively more sophisticated versions and whether conditions exist that would make such segmentation desirable. (For further information on phased systems development, see Chapter IV-3, "An Approach to Effective Implementation.")

Several conditions that could warrant project segmentation include:
- The possibility of a greater payback on some aspects of the application than on others.
- Users with personal preferences for specific functions.
- Some functions may require faster implementation if any benefit is to be obtained.
- User inability to adapt to a highly sophisticated system without installation of simpler functions first.
- The DP resources budget or capability may prevent implementation of a complete system during the initial project.

If any of these conditions exist, they should be reviewed with the user(s) to determine the best course of action.

The best approach is to establish a project steering committee consisting of representatives from the user groups and the MIS department. A presentation of the alternatives and their costs and benefits should be made to the committee by the analyst or project manager. The project steering committee then establishes priorities and selects the course of action.

When Choice Is Impossible

Some situations do not permit the luxury of choice in setting application priorities. For example, the federal government establishes a withholding tax provision applied to interest-bearing accounts at banks and savings institutions. The provisions are complex and only six months are permitted for their implementation. The institutions involved have no choice but to comply by modifying their computer systems—all other priorities must be set aside. In other cases, either reports are mandated by the government to prove that the organization complies with equal opportunity legislation or the external auditors require a series of special reports to complete their annual audit of the corporation.

These examples indicate that external factors can greatly affect the priority-setting process. When such conditions arise, the only course of action is to inform all affected users of the impact on existing project priorities and to comply with the demands of the emergency.

THE IMPACT OF NEW TECHNOLOGIES

New technologies have been introduced that promise to alter the priority considerations for many applications. The implementation of these technologies in an organization might become a high-priority issue itself. Some examples of these technologies follow.

Office automation systems that share resources enable users to perform certain work functions without depending on the MIS department for assistance. In addition to providing text-editing support and electronic mail, these systems allow users to establish and reference their own files for specific purposes.

Many organizations are witnessing the gradual proliferation of personal computers. These small, independent systems offer a wide range of software for performing such functions as financial analysis, text editing, data entry and retrieval, computation, and graphic display. Furthermore, they often provide languages and tools that can be learned quickly by non-DP professionals. Many problems once requiring MIS assistance can now be solved by the user.

Some organizations provide various approaches to simplify accessing information in the existing data bases of the organization's primary computer system. For example, query systems in both procedural and nonprocedural forms enable a user to construct online queries or special reports directly from a terminal in the user's office. A few organizations are establishing information centers comprising a small group of programmers who use interactive, interpretive languages to quickly construct ad hoc applications for temporary use by users with high-priority requests. If necessary, these temporary application systems can be converted to a more efficient language if found suitable for repeated use.

An opportunity obviously exists to reduce some of the application development backlog, which in turn reduces some of the priority-setting problems by encouraging the use of new technologies in appropriate areas.

CONCLUSION

The most important consideration in setting priorities is that the final decision on application priorities is the responsibility (and right) of the organization's top management. The MIS group is responsible for providing all necessary information and subsequent recommendations to ensure that the management decision is beneficial to the entire organization.

Some key concepts in selecting and establishing priorities for applications are:
- Criteria for project selection must be clearly defined and documented. These criteria should include qualitative, institutional, and quantitative considerations.
- Applications must conform to organizational objectives. These objectives do not remain constant.
- The process of application selection and setting priorities takes time and money, and management must approve the cost.
- The use of steering committees can expedite priority setting and improve the chances for project success.
- Formal documentation throughout the priority-setting process not only simplifies it but also provides groundwork for subsequent feasibility

studies. It also provides a file of future applications from those weeded out in prescreening.
- Presenting too many alternatives to management may result in a suboptimum decision or even no decision.
- User understanding and sponsorship of the proposed applications are essential to success.

Finally, it should be noted that priority setting is not a one-time task. It should be repeated each time resources become available to start a new project. Because most of the documentation already exists, the process becomes simpler once priorities have been established. Only proposed implementation schedules and budgets must be redrawn. In each subsequent review of priorities, projects in progress should be reviewed along with proposed new projects. Management criteria, objectives, and priorities may change in the interim.

Reference

1. Dearden, John. *Computers in Business Management.* Homewood IL: Dow Jones-Irwin, 1966.

IV-3
An Approach to Effective Implementation
David R. Tommela

INTRODUCTION

Many DP installations face a tremendous challenge in fulfilling their users' needs. Aspects of this challenge include:
- Demands for new, large, online systems to meet complex business needs
- Increasing backlogs of systems maintenance work
- Pressures exerted by a turbulent economy
- Increased emphasis on meeting development schedules to cope with a changing business environment

Traditional approaches to large online systems development are proving ineffective as solutions to current DP problems. These approaches typically result in the following difficulties:
- The user is forced to wait until the end of the systems development life cycle before receiving any benefits. In some instances, this delay can be years.
- Because of protracted development cycles, the application specifications to which the system is built do not meet current business needs.
- The user experiences difficulty in adapting to the new system. This difficulty is usually encountered when the "big bang" theory of implementation is employed (i.e., the old system terminates one day and the new one is operational the next).
- The backlogs for DP maintenance and enhancements grow to nearly unmanageable proportions. This problem stems from the difficulties in testing an entire system, premature freezing of requirements, and discovery of needed enhancements after the system is operational.
- The credibility of the MIS department is seriously damaged. The users are rightfully intolerant of long development periods and missed schedules—even if they share responsibility for these events.

This chapter focuses on a group of approaches that mitigates these problems by enabling another strategy for systems implementation. Using one approach by itself makes chances of reaping full benefits remote. Using the recommended approaches in concert and even expanding on them can significantly improve the effectiveness of the MIS department. The topics dis-

SYSTEMS DEVELOPMENT AND PROGRAMMING

cussed in this chapter are:
- Systems development life cycle
- User participation
- Generalized system architecture
- Transition systems
- Prototypes.

SYSTEMS DEVELOPMENT LIFE CYCLE

The systems development life cycle used by an MIS organization helps determine the optional strategies available for implementation. Yet this factor is often overlooked when an organization seeks the causes for lengthy development times. The impact of new techniques (e.g., structured analysis) on the life cycle is also ignored when such techniques are introduced to improve the development process.

Traditional Development Life Cycles

Each MIS organization has some systems development life cycle that defines the steps in developing an information system. The number of steps varies widely but generally fits into the following framework:
- Feasibility study—determining the economic and technological advisability of initiating a new development effort
- Analysis—ascertaining the functions performed by an existing automated or manual system, defining and analyzing new functions required to enhance the process
- Design—determining the software and hardware architecture of the new system, defining the logical structure and specifications of the application functions
- Construction—developing programs and testing, preparing training materials and user procedures
- Implementation—initiating activities for testing, training, and system installation; continuing maintenance and enhancement

The employment of this development life cycle usually follows the forms shown in Figures 1 and 2. These figures show the relationships of phases, not the relative durations of each phase.

Figure 1 depicts the serial approach, where each phase is completed before the next begins. This approach is suited to projects of short duration (less than six months) with limited staffing (approximately three people). Typically, the applications are simple and straightforward in that the number and complexity of functions and their relationships are easily grasped by the developer. Therefore, it is easy to partition the work to be done.

Figure 2 illustrates the overlapping approach, in which some phases begin before the preceding phase is completed. Overlapping phases usually result in earlier delivery of systems. This approach is suited to projects of medium duration (6-12 months) and staffing of approximately eight people. The applications are usually more complex, and the partitioning of work assignments is more difficult because of the interrelationships of application functions.

Effective Implementation

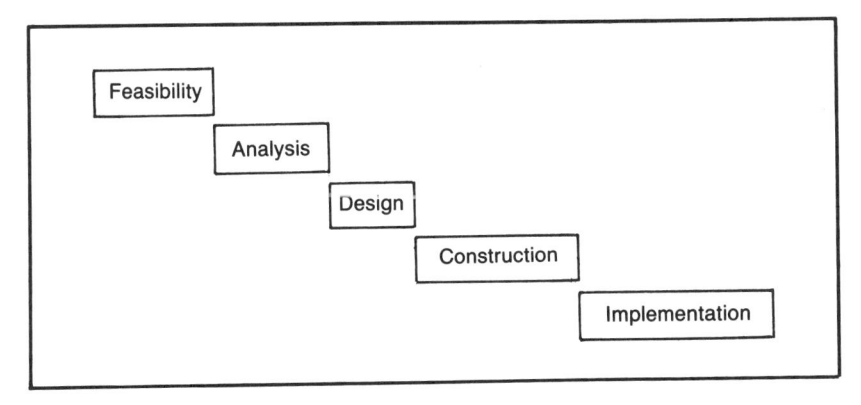

Figure 1. Serial Systems Development Life Cycle

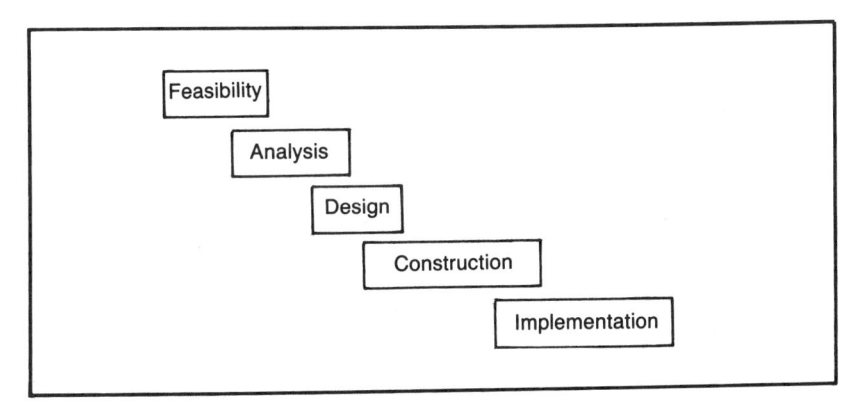

Figure 2. Overlapping Systems Development Life Cycle

Although these two development life cycles work well with short- and medium-length projects, certain problems inherent in both methods make them unsuitable for large, complex projects. The option to select a particular life cycle to match the task at hand is a more effective approach; however, it is usually not condoned by management.

Problems with Traditional Systems Development Life Cycles

Analyzing traditional systems development life cycles reveals the problems of applying them to a large, complex, online application.

Changing User Requirements. Users are expected to state their requirements clearly by the end of the analysis phase. The time between establishing user requirements and delivering the system can be quite lengthy. Changes to the requirements are discouraged and are often the source of dissent between MIS and users. Such changes are in fact valuable because they reflect the user's growing knowledge of the system; however, the traditional development life cycle does not offer a means to manage such changes effectively.

SYSTEMS DEVELOPMENT AND PROGRAMMING

Premature Decisions. This problem is a companion to changing user requirements. The user identifies requirements in a vacuum during the analysis phase. Decisions are made under the weight of a looming target date for the end of the analysis phase. Unfortunately, the user does not know enough about how the whole system will function to make these decisions. In other words, the old adage, "Users don't know what they want until they see it," is true. This serious problem manifests itself in schedule overruns and other calamities when the user sees the system.

The problem of premature decisions is compounded by two serious MIS errors. First, MIS may require the user to sign off or freeze the requirements. Next, MIS decides which functions will be included in the system. Neither party has enough knowledge during this phase to make those decisions. Demands for certainty at the end of a development phase virtually guarantee that the system will not fully meet user needs.

Monolithic View of the System. The traditional systems development life cycle deals with the total application throughout that cycle. A large, complex application poses a formidable problem in performing such development. Even if the application is divided into comprehensible functions, the task of analyzing every function is too great. Again, the traditional systems development life cycle forces an artificial finalizing of the activities of each phase.

Big-Bang Implementation. This is the conclusion of the traditional systems development life cycle (i.e., analyze the whole problem, design a total solution, program the entire system, and implement the system). The big bang occurs when the old system stops one day and the new one starts operating the next. It is almost impossible for a user organization to cope with such an event.

Belated Problem Correction. When the user finally sees the system in operation, a torrent of change requests for enhancements pours in, in addition to the usual problem reports. The gap between user expectations and system capabilities is probably substantial. This gap is largely attributed to matching the wrong life cycle to the project. The changes must be made—often at a very substantial cost—and the lifetime cost of the new system becomes extraordinarily high.

Functional Systems Development Life Cycle

Figure 3 shows a third variation of the systems development life cycle. Although this approach uses the same five phases as traditional development life cycles, deployment of the phases differs significantly. This variation is termed the functional systems development life cycle.

The source of this life cycle is structured techniques. These techniques compel the analyst to define an application hierarchically in terms of its discrete functions. Analysis of these functions then leads to creation of a system design that maintains the functional orientation. Construction and implementation activities also follow this orientation.

Effective Implementation

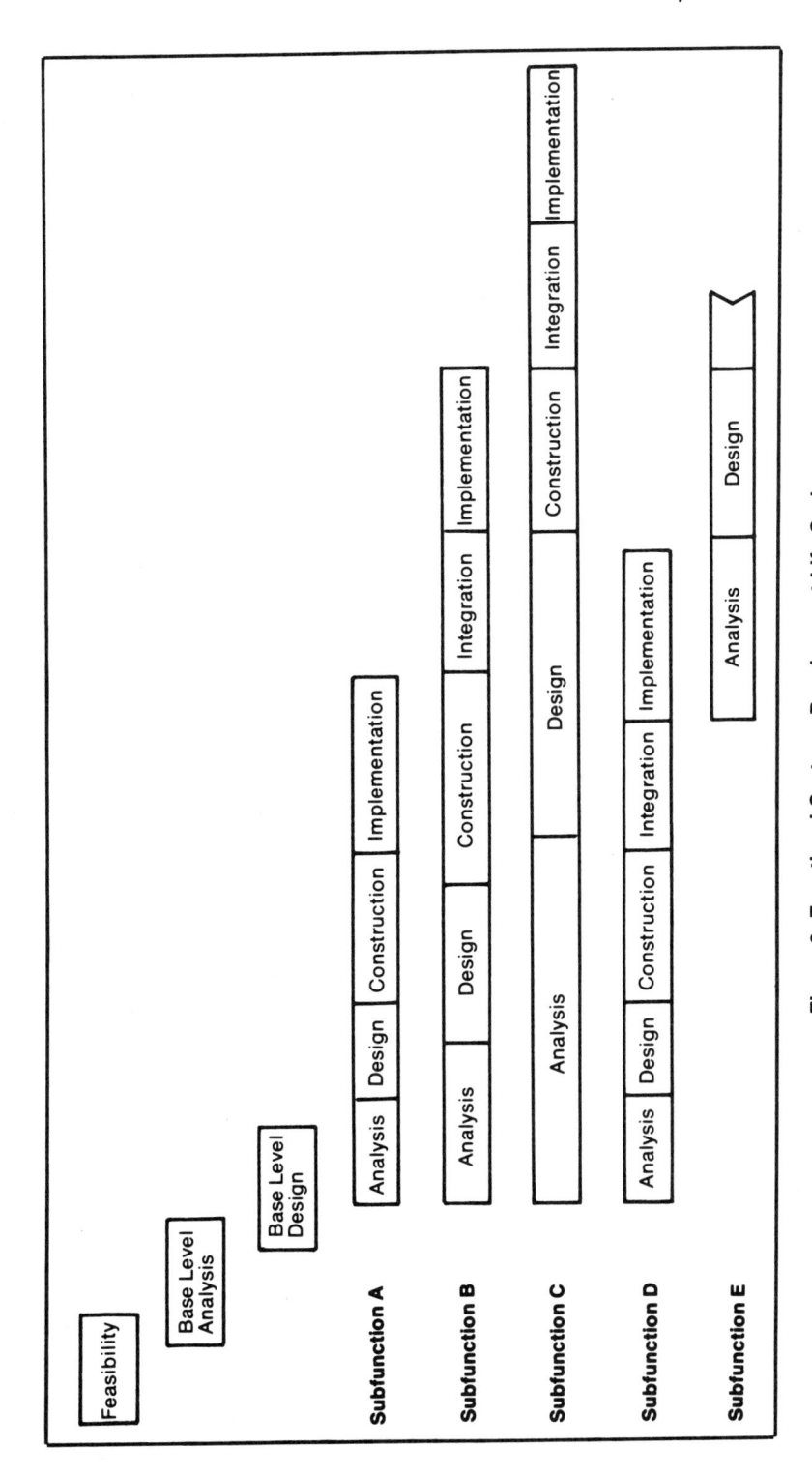

Figure 3. Functional Systems Development Life Cycle

SYSTEMS DEVELOPMENT AND PROGRAMMING

Figure 4 illustrates part of the functional hierarchy of a materials system. The chart shows that the materials system consists of the six major functions identified as level 1. All other system functions are grouped under this umbrella. Level 2 depicts the subfunctions of the major function of procurement. Level 3 is an explosion of the level 2 subfunction of purchase orders. Level 3 components would be further segmented into one or more levels as needed. The number of levels subordinate to each subfunction (level 2) depends upon the complexity of the subfunction.

It is apparent from a cursory glance at Figure 4 that describing the entire materials system in this fashion would result in hundreds of boxes on a chart. The principles of structured techniques, however, ensure that each element is grouped with its companions. Each subfunction can therefore be addressed independently without fear of interference from another subfunction. For the most part, each subfunction can be developed and implemented individually.

Figure 3 shows the life cycle for such a functional development approach. The box entitled "Base Level Analysis" shows that this phase begins during the feasibility study since it contributes to that study. During the base level analysis, enough effort is expended to define the application through approximately level 2 of the hierarchy and to ensure its integrity.

Once it appears that the top of the hierarchy is valid, the base-level design is initiated. This effort defines the basic architecture of the system and continues until the integrity of the top-level design is validated. Once the design is validated, a number of subfunctions can be developed concurrently. The number of concurrent activities depends on the amount of staffing available. Note that each subfunction then follows its own development life cycle, the duration of which depends on its complexity.

In the functional life cycle, each subfunction can be implemented independently. After the first subfunction is implemented, the other subfunctions pass through an additional development phase—integration. The system evolves as each subfunction is integrated with its predecessors.

Benefits of Functional Systems Development Life Cycle

The functional development life cycle alleviates most of the problems of the traditional development life cycle. Extensions to the functional life cycle discussed later in this chapter further diminish these problems. Specific benefits are also associated with this approach.

Early Delivery. Functions are implemented as they are developed, in contrast to the traditional approach that results in waiting until all functions are completed. The user thus has part of the system to use much earlier.

Benefit Definition. It is easier to define the benefits associated with each function of the system. This definition can even be particularized for each user of a function common to multiple users. This approach greatly facilitates validating benefit estimates once the function is implemented.

Priority of Functions. The sequence of function development can be easily established by using benefits and external factors, such as the business

Effective Implementation

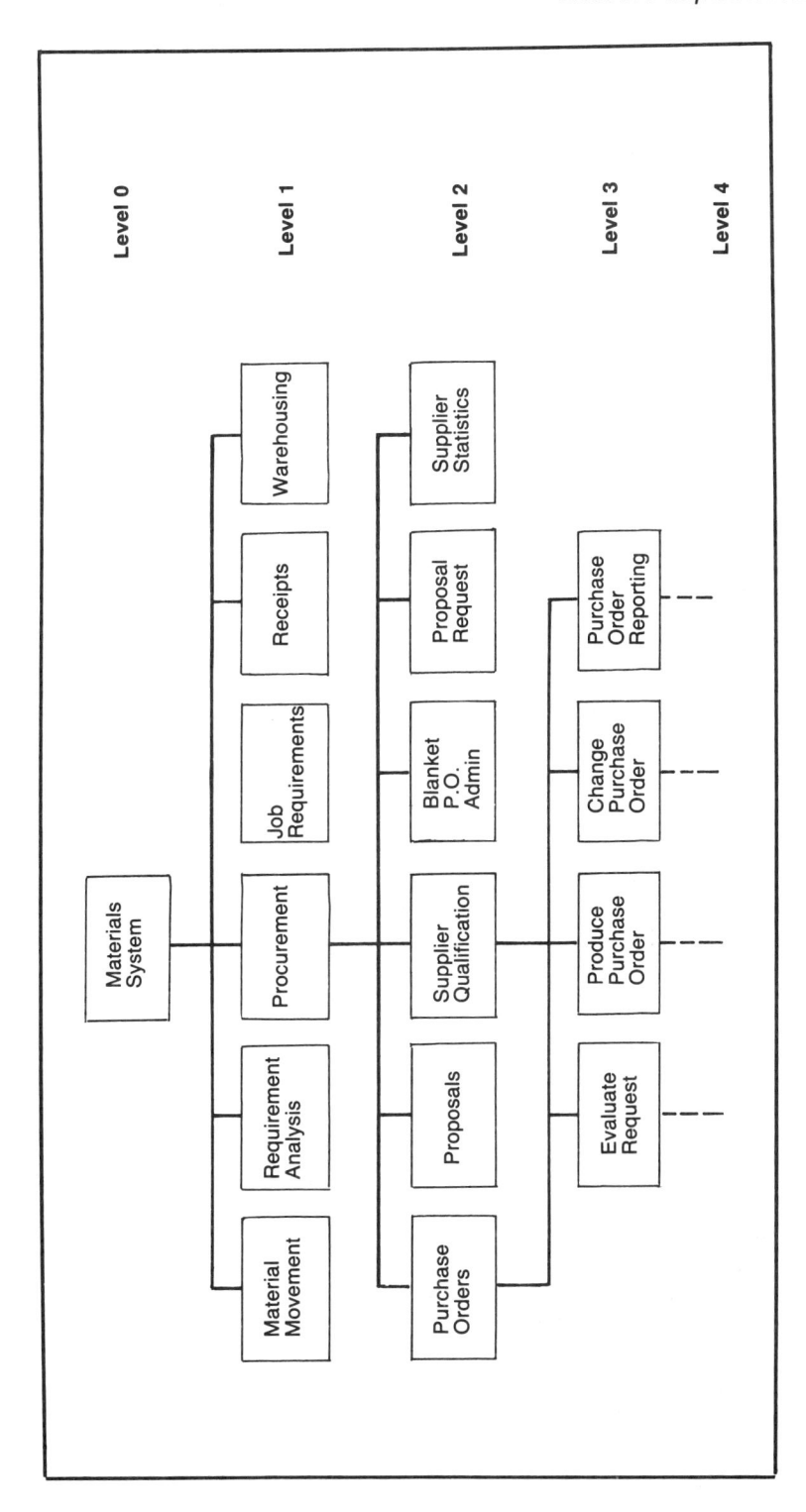

Figure 4. Functional Hierarchy

climate. Obviously, the relationship of functions to one another and DP technical concerns come into play, but not to a large degree. The sequence of priorities can also change readily to meet dynamic business conditions. Setting priorities by functional benefits enables the largest percentage of benefits to be realized long before the entire system is completed.

Impact on Users. The impact on the users caused by introduction of a new system is drastically reduced when only one function is introduced at a time. The tasks of training and procedures development become more manageable. The users are able to adapt to the system more readily and can more easily cope with the change.

Impact on MIS. The pressure to deliver the system is lessened. The users receive functional products rather than waiting for the entire system. Better product quality, time to measure impact on hardware resources, and improved systems developer morale are only a few of the many benefits to MIS. The one negative effect must be emphasized: *It is very difficult to manage a project using the functional life cycle.* The two major sources of difficulty are multiple concurrent activities and the need for extensive communication among all personnel on the project.

System Architecture. The architecture of the system, developed during the design phase, provides a foundation for future development. Essentially, the architecture reflects the functional hierarchy of the application in that functions are isolated from one another. Integration of new functions is easily accomplished. The integrity of the architecture is not violated as each new piece is developed.

In summary, the systems development life cycle plays an important role in determining those options available to improve the systems development process. The life cycle requires alteration to achieve fully the benefits of structured development techniques. It also should be tailored to the project. Significant advantages can be achieved by applying the concept of functional development. The functional life cycle provides a foundation for the other techniques discussed in this chapter.

USER PARTICIPATION

The approaches discussed in this chapter all emphasize early delivery of systems. MIS people often lose sight of this goal in the midst of building a system. This section discusses methods for ensuring that users play a major role in systems development.

The problem usually encountered first during development of a large system is identification of the primary user of an application that spans multiple departments in the corporation. The problem can exist even within one department that has multiple divisions. The solution is to select someone from a user organization as the sponsor of the system. The sponsor's job is to represent the interests of the corporation while working closely with the MIS project manager. In this capacity, the sponsor has:
- Responsibility for obtaining people from user departments to work on the project

Effective Implementation

- The final decision on all application requirements
- Authority for setting development priorities
- Responsibility for representing the project to the corporation

All of these activities are done in cooperation with the project manager. In essence, the sponsor is the MIS project manager's alter ego whose primary focus is on the corporation.

Once the sponsoring organization is identified, the individual (usually a middle manager) who will act as sponsor is selected. The other users who will participate in the project are also chosen. The sponsor and users must be full-time participants, and they must be selected with utmost care. MIS maintains the right to refuse a nominee as well as to replace him or her if the individual does not meet expectations. Absence of this authority seriously reduces prospects for success.

The sponsor should be a person of stature in the user organization, preferably with line, not staff, responsibilities. For the duration of the project, he or she should report to the department head. The sponsor must have authority to make decisions concerning the project. The most important attribute for a sponsor is communications skill. The other users should be selected for their expertise in the application (e.g., purchasing, warehousing, and so on). These individuals also must have authority to speak for their organizations.

The next step is assigning users to particular project teams. The teams should be organized functionally; for example, the user with expertise in purchasing should be assigned to the purchasing team. Some teams require users from several organizations to provide expertise in one function, such as warehousing. The user/MIS teams are assigned to the project until completion; therefore, it is virtually mandatory that user and MIS personnel share the same office space.

User Activities

The user's role is significant once the project is under way. Table 1 is a sample list of user activities during the project life cycle; it is by no means exhaustive.

The sponsor and several key users work with MIS in conducting the feasibility study. Their primary contribution is their knowledge of the application and of its operational environment.

During the analysis phase, users have the most important role since MIS has little knowledge of their jobs. The task is to obtain and document the user's knowledge; thus, the participation of users representing all application areas is critical. An ineffective way to establish user requirements is for a DP analyst to interview users and document the information. A more effective way is to ask the user to document his or her knowledge using whatever tools are employed for the task. If structured analysis techniques are used, the user should be taught how to use such tools as data flow diagrams and structured English. The MIS staff can advise in the use of tools while learning about the application from the user. In this way, the user bears greater responsibility than MIS for the analysis phase of the project.

In the design phase, users advise on how requirements will be met. Users

SYSTEMS DEVELOPMENT AND PROGRAMMING

Table 1. User Responsibilities

Phase	Activities
Feasibility	Identifying requirements Estimating benefits
Analysis	Defining existing functions Defining new functions
Design	Defining document/screen/report formats Guiding design decisions Learning the design
Construction	Developing test data Preparing training materials Writing procedures Preparing facilities
Implementation	Testing Conducting training Monitoring implementation

can have primary responsibility for designing I/O formats. During the analysis phase, MIS learned the application; now the user learns how the system will function. User activities during the construction and implementation phases remain traditional.

In summary, user participation should be proactive throughout the systems development life cycle. This type of involvement substantially reduces many problems usually encountered by MIS on a development project.

GENERALIZED SYSTEM ARCHITECTURE

Many of the concepts in this chapter are based on the use of structured design techniques; one such concept is a generalized system architecture.

There are two components of a generalized system architecture. The first is a logic structure for performing a software function; the second is the generalized software to perform the function in any application environment. Variables to make the software application-specific are provided in tables prepared by a programmer. Program code is not written.

Generalized architecture has proved to be unusually effective for on-line systems. Its advantages include:
- A standard interface image to the terminal user for all applications
- Reductions in development time by 50 percent or more
- A standard system architecture with proven error-free code
- One copy of the executable code
- Improved flexibility of MIS staff assignment by enabling a maintenance programmer to quickly adapt to multiple applications
- Simplified documentation
- Ease of upgrading all applications with improved capabilities

A generalized architecture can be developed by any MIS organization for both online and batch functions. The process consists of:
- Designing a function for a system (e.g., inquiry to a materials file)

Effective Implementation

- Evaluating the design to determine the inquiry activities common to all applications
- Identifying activities unique to each application
- Using tables to describe unique attributes of an application
- Writing the common routines to generate the necessary tables

This approach has been successfully applied to inquiry, order entry, data validation, and order update functions for a variety of applications. Table 2 illustrates the differences between developing an online CICS update transaction the standard way and using a generalized architecture approach.

The example in Table 2 is a hypothetical update transaction containing 25 data elements. The transaction involves presenting a fill-in-the-blanks order display, accepting data, editing and validating data inputs, redisplaying edited and validated inputs, and accepting a completed update. Coding is in CICS command-level COBOL. The left column in Table 2 shows the number of COBOL/CICS statements needed at each stage of the transaction. The right column shows the statements and table entries required for the same transaction when a generalized architecture approach is used. The specific numbers are not important, but the difference between the two columns is significant. The difference in time required for each solution is readily apparent.

In summary, a generalized system architecture developed using the concepts of structured design plays a major role in increasing the number of implementation options. A generalized architecture has great potential for reducing development time while maintaining design integrity.

Table 2. Standard versus Generalized Architecture Systems Development

Standard CICS Programming

Task	COBOL Statements
Map definition with mapping support	75
Main Line coding for new transaction	10
Code update transaction	1,400
Code validations and edits	1,500
Code redisplay of data for update	400
Code transaction completion routine	400
Code I/O	500
Total	4,285

Generalized Architecture Definitions

Task	COBOL Statements	Table Entries
Map definition with mapping support	75	0
Define new transaction		3
Define update attributes		6
Define validations and edits		80
Define screen data		75
Code transaction completion		100
Code I/O	500	
Totals	575	264

SYSTEMS DEVELOPMENT AND PROGRAMMING

TRANSITION SYSTEMS

The preceding sections of this chapter address approaches to the systems development effort. In addition to intrinsic benefits, these approaches can also provide a foundation for implementation strategies that can lead to significant improvements in service to users. One of these strategies is the use of transition systems.

A transition system is a means of easing the conversion to the new application system. It is a temporary system developed to interface with the existing one. Both systems are replaced by the new system at a later date.

Reasons for Transition Systems

The transition system is designed as a stop-gap measure pending implementation of the new system. A transition system substantially reduces pressure on MIS regarding schedules and enhances user/MIS interfaces.

Many development efforts today replace batch with online systems; old system functions are enhanced and new functions added. The greatest opportunity for transition systems is when developing online systems, although the concept can be applied to other areas. Quite simply, a transition system involves building an online front-end to an existing batch system (improving an existing function by replacing its paper input documents). The existing system continues to receive inputs in the same format, but the medium changes. It is important not to add new functions to the existing batch system because that activity conflicts with efforts to build a new system. The greatest advantage of a transition system is that some benefits become available long before the new system is completed.

If structured techniques are used to develop the new system, the appropriate time to begin transition efforts is after completing the analysis of the existing one. The products of these tasks delineate the functions of the old system. It is important to maintain the functional orientation because it simplifies the later process of replacing the transition system with new system functions.

Development Method

The transition system should be developed with a generalized architecture. Processes such as screen presentation, data validation, and data access can be table driven. Such online processes as inquiry can also be generalized. Using a standard architecture reduces development time to a matter of days. Software generators such as IBM's DMS (Development Management System) can also help in this regard.

The most difficult task in building a transition system is obtaining the data validation criteria. Often this information can be obtained only by reading existing program code to ensure identification of nuances not available in documentation. The most time consuming part of development is testing, which is exceptionally rigorous because online facilities are used.

The transition system software is discarded once the new system is developed since it is easier to write new programs than to modify old ones. In fact, industry studies show that it is more effective to rewrite a program if more than 10 percent of the code requires alteration. Maintaining a functional orientation is also important if the code is going to be considered disposable because it facilitates the replacement process.

Transition systems allow rapid development of interim solutions. These efforts need not employ the rigorous development associated with the main project. Minimum documentation and perhaps different development techniques are warranted for software with such a short life.

Benefits of Using a Transition System

The benefits of using transition systems are substantial:
- Time lags in submission and processing of batch documents and error corrections are eliminated. It may also be possible to reduce the data entry staff.
- The online network is established before the arrival of the new system. MIS has time to gain experience with the network, which facilitates the later move to the new system.
- End users become accustomed to using a terminal.
- Benefits are realized early.
- MIS gains experience in building an online system for this application before designing the new system.
- The pressure on MIS to accelerate development is reduced.

PROTOTYPES

The use of prototypes is another implementation strategy that can significantly improve service to users. Ideally, a prototype is used before the final system is developed; however, current software technology is insufficient to accomplish this goal. Nonetheless, a prototype can provide significant benefits even after the final system is developed.

The prototype period begins once a function has been developed and tested for either the transition system or for the new system. The software is installed as operational, but authorization to use it is restricted to one or two user organizations. For example, if an online materials function were being implemented in a retail organization, only one or two stores would use the prototype online receiving function while the others would continue using the existing method. Using a prototype should not be confused with parallel testing. The prototype system is used on a full production basis.

Reasons for Prototypes

Even the best requirements specifications are unlikely to remain unchanged once the system is installed and operating. Unfortunately, what the users agree to on paper is often not what they actually wanted when they see it in real life. Online systems are particularly susceptible to this problem. An earlier section of this chapter discussed a method for assigning users to work on a project to minimize this problem. The basic reason for using a prototype is that it is easier to make changes to a system when it is not fully installed throughout the organization. The duration of a prototype depends on many factors, including application complexity, number of changes identified, and hardware limitations. Usually two to six weeks is sufficient time to evaluate the system thoroughly.

Conducting the Prototype

The project team must participate fully in the prototype, observing the training classes and assisting as needed. Staff members should sit with the terminal operators to gain an understanding of the environment in which the system is functioning. Comments, suggestions, and criticisms should be logged for later evaluation. Meetings with the terminal users should be held at the end of the day to review the items logged.

A flurry of comments is likely to arise during the first few days or weeks. Initial comments tend to be superficial and to necessitate only cosmetic changes to the prototype. Many comments originate from misunderstandings that should have been eliminated in the training classes. As users gain experience, comments become more substantive and may even reveal a need for major redesign efforts. The purpose of prototyping is to bring these questions to the surface.

Making Changes

The cardinal rule of prototyping is to make all needed changes before the system is expanded to include all users. Changes can range from the reformatting of data on a screen to the complete redevelopment of a function. It seldom makes sense to provide the system to all users when it is known to be inadequate. If the concept of installing discrete functions has been followed, a total rewrite of a particular function probably will not require that much time. Adherence to this principle means that full production begins with no maintenance backlog. Furthermore, future change requests will be virtually nonexistent.

MIS's rapid response to requested changes is of the utmost importance. Many minor changes can be implemented for the next day's business for example. Rapid response gains user confidence and respect; if a change is not made promptly, the user may encounter the undesirable item hundreds of times a day while using the system. Thus, a minor problem can quickly become a significant irritant.

Each suggestion or complaint received should be thoroughly assessed from the perspective of the operating environment. Even small items like highlighting data fields can be significant if the lighting conditions of the office environment are considered. The analysis of each suggestion or complaint should be explained in detail to the originator.

Hardware Assessment

Prototyping offers an excellent opportunity to measure the system's impact on network and computer resources. This is often overlooked and results in users who are disgruntled because response time at the terminal is 10 seconds although it was designed to be 5 seconds. The prototype should last long enough to check network management procedures for communication failures, computer failures, requests for vendor assistance, and so on. The user is affected by these matters as well, so it is best to obtain user participation.

Training Assessment

Particular attention should be paid to the adequacy of training programs. The same process used to evaluate the application should be applied to these programs because inadequacies not corrected can cause problems for a long time.

In summary, a prototype offers an exceptional opportunity to implement an error-free system tailored to user needs. Best of all, it results in users who are pleased with the development effort.

CONCLUSION

This chapter has discussed systems development concepts that can provide new strategies for system implementation. These concepts are not theoretical; they are successful in actual practice. In addition to the advantages gained by following the approaches recommended in this chapter, there are some subtle effects on the overall MIS operation that bear brief discussion.

Systems Auditors. Many auditors are accustomed to traditional development practices. Departure from this norm imposes additional educational burdens on MIS.

Changes in User Participation. These approaches require considerable user involvement in ways perhaps unfamiliar to the user from prior MIS projects. A different type of user is needed and probably in greater numbers. Employing key management and operational users on a project can remove them from career opportunities in their organizations and can cause friction between MIS and those organizations.

Ending the Project. The end of a typical development project is usually discernible. This chapter advocates an evolution project life cycle that can be adapted to changing needs. Such projects do not have clearly defined ends; the distinction between maintenance and development is not as clear. This may raise problems in justifying, monitoring, and evaluating projects.

Maintenance. MIS can more easily establish a maintenance team when project completion is easier to identify. With an evolving system, some staff targeted for development have to be retained for maintenance instead of moving to the next function. The size of this staff grows as the system itself evolves.

Hardware Capacity. The need for additional hardware capacity increases as the system evolves. Close monitoring of capacity plans is warranted.

Management. Projects that use the ideas presented in this chapter require managers capable of performing multiple tasks with attention to detail. The difficulties of managing, however, are overshadowed by the potential for early benefits achieved by an MIS/user team.

IV-4
Structured Methodology

Pat Duran
Al McCready

INTRODUCTION

Structured techniques evolved as an attempt to solve specific technical and applications problems. Applications have become increasingly complex, and the tools that were useful for developing a straightforward reporting application, for example, may not be adequate for defining the software to support a nationwide sales and order processing system.

As the proliferation of software packages indicates, most simple software problems have been solved. Many MIS managers today expend more effort controlling the acquisition of software than overseeing its development; they need tools that will help them to understand their own requirements and to evaluate how well different packages satisfy those requirements. MIS managers who still manage software development are tackling applications of increasing complexity, some of which have never successfully been done before; such managers need tools to help control these massive development efforts.

Structured Programming

In the sixties, when structured programming was being discussed and developed in academic circles, the emphasis was on hardware rather than software. This explains the lack of response to the early work on structured programming.[1,2]

The *New York Times* project of 1971 is generally recognized as the first well-documented demonstration that structured programming could pay off in a production environment.[3,4] The project utilized both top-down structured programming and the chief programmer team concept. The results of this project are significant because noticeably improved programmer productivity and greater system reliability were achieved.

In the early seventies structured programming began to receive widespread attention from industry. The rising cost of software prompted managers to investigate ways of reducing software costs, especially the labor cost of software development and maintenance.[5] Most existing programs were difficult to read, understand, and maintain. Programmers developed their own styles so that even those using the same programming language had trouble understanding one another's code.

SYSTEMS DEVELOPMENT AND PROGRAMMING

Structured programming techniques emphasized that code should be readable, understandable, and maintainable. They accomplished this by limiting the ways of stating logic and stressing the use of meaningful names and style guidelines within an organization.

Structured Design

Although structured programming worked well when applied to small programs, the results were less satisfactory on large programs or systems. Some programmers put their code through such contortions to avoid using the GOTO statement that while the resulting program contained only the three basic constructs of structured programming (sequence, selection, and iteration), it was still difficult to read. The problem was that these programs lacked an overall structure. That structure was supplied by structured design.

The seminal article on structured design appeared in 1974, and the ideas were included in IBM's courses on programmer productivity techniques.[6] These ideas were refined by Myers, Page-Jones, and Yourdon and Constantine.[7,8,9] Structured design emphasized improving the maintainability of systems by constructing them of loosely connected components. The idea started to gain acceptance in the mid-1970s and education became readily available from a number of sources.

Structured design and structured programming helped solve many of the technical problems of software development. Systems that were flexible and responsive to user changes were developed within budget and on schedule, with little or no sacrifice in machine costs.

Structured Analysis

Although these technical problems were reduced by structured design and programming techniques, the problem of communications between user and system developer was not addressed. The late seventies saw an increasing interest in structured analysis that emphasized understanding and communicating user requirements for automated support of user business activities.

Similar methods of structured analysis evolved in two ways. Most methods capitalized on certain structured design concepts.[10,11,12] These concepts were enhanced for use in the analysis phase and combined with data analysis and specification tools. Communications heuristics were then applied to the use of all these tools.

The Structured Analysis and Design Technique (SADT from SofTech) was developed in the late sixties and early seventies in response to the problems associated with defining systems requirements.[13] SADT is a tool for solving a variety of complex problems and has been used to analyze software requirements since the early seventies.

REASONS FOR STRUCTURED TECHNIQUES

There are several reasons for employing structured techniques: the cost trends of hardware and software, software maintenance costs, rising labor costs, the ability to solve more difficult problems, and improved software quality.

Cost Trends of Hardware and Software. One reason for using structured techniques is the cost trends for hardware and software. Hardware is now cost-justifiable in a much broader range of situations and applications. This applies in circumstances where significantly increased hardware capacity can be acquired with no increase of cost and in circumstances where a particular hardware capability was not previously cost-justified.

While hardware costs now account for a decreasing percentage of the costs of creating and operating an application system, software costs have increased because the cost of labor in systems development has been rising substantially. A shortage of qualified systems development personnel has raised even further the human resource costs in systems development.

Cost of Software Maintenance. Another important justification for the implementation and development of structured techniques is the cost of software maintenance. For many years, systems were developed and implemented with little or no consideration given to maintenance costs over the life of the system. When it was recognized that systems maintenance represented approximately two-thirds of the programming and analysis resource costs over the useful life of the system, it became clear that designing and implementing a system that is relatively inexpensive to maintain could result in substantial savings. Solving this problem has been a major concern in the development of structured techniques.

Satisfying User Needs. Another concern in the development of structured techniques has been to avoid developing and implementing systems that do not satisfy user requirements. Until users can define their requirements and implement appropriate software application solutions on their own, DP professionals will be required to assist in translating requirements into functioning application systems. Structured systems analysis and design techniques are tools to assist DP professionals and knowledgeable users in creating a product that satisfies user needs.

Solving More Difficult Problems. Most of the straightforward accounting and inventory control problems have now been solved, and the solutions are available as standardized software packages. The industry is now turning toward more complex problems. Users now want MIS to integrate small systems developed in the past and to develop new systems that encompass substantially broader and more complex requirements.

For example, in the past, a public utility company was content with an automated accounting system, an automated inventory system, and perhaps some automated support for the engineering staff. Today this company wants an online construction estimating system that includes materials issue, work order tracking, work order closing, and distribution of labor and materials expense to accounting. This system crosses all traditional departmental and automated system boundaries; the traditional systems analysis and design techniques and approaches, therefore, may be inadequate for producing high-quality work.

Improved Software Quality. One of the significant benefits of the imple-

SYSTEMS DEVELOPMENT AND PROGRAMMING

mentation and use of structured techniques relates directly to the reasons for using them. (Several other benefits of using structured techniques are discussed in a later section of this chapter.) When tools and techniques that are well suited to the organization and the situation are chosen, the quality of the product generated by the analysis, design, and implementation activities is noticeably improved. Producing a better system that is easy to maintain, flexible, more satisfying to users, and better documented is the strongest reason for using structured techniques.

CHANGES IN SOFTWARE LIFE CYCLE

The most significant change in the systems development segment of the software life cycle that results from the use of structured techniques is the increased effort expended in the early phases. This was borne out in the University of Toronto's experience in implementing structured techniques. The system developers there experienced a change in the time devoted to each phase of the life cycle. Structured design reduced the time devoted to coding and testing; structured analysis reduced the time devoted to design.[14] This shift is a natural and important part of the transition to a structured environment, where additional resources are expended in the early phases in the expectation that fewer resources will be required for the total life cycle.

Emphasis on Analysis and Design. The evolution of structured methods in systems development has caused new emphasis to be placed on the analysis and design phases. Projects can go wrong at many different points. Spending a great deal of time, energy, and money on systems maintenance indicates failures in design; extensive debugging suggests problems in module design and in coding and testing methods. Failures in the analysis phase, however, may require much more substantial rework efforts and expenditures, and attempts to recover from analysis failures often prove unsatisfactory.

Proponents of structured techniques, therefore, generally stress the importance of the analysis and design phases. In the past, the output from system testing was often the first tangible product the user could understand and evaluate. This first sample output was offered for user review and approval much too late, since the system had already been designed and coded. Structured systems analysis and design techniques place user review and approval in the early phases of the project. The products of test runs are merely checked for conformance to specifications that were produced and approved much earlier in the development cycle. Changing a mock-up of a proposed report or a description of the proposed logical flow of information is less expensive, less frustrating, faster, and easier than redoing the program code and documentation.

Increased Human Resources. Because of the emphasis on the analysis and design phases of the software life cycle, management must invest more human resources in the development of a system before any program code is produced. The code produced can be expected to be better (and the time in testing shorter) because the code is written from a well-thought-out design specification.

Top-Down Approach. Another aspect of the emphasis on analysis and design is the requirement that the "big picture" be considered before details are developed. This top-down approach is an important part of structured techniques. Often there is a tendency to become immersed too quickly in the details of computer systems design without duly considering the larger structure into which the details fit. The emphasis on a top-down approach in structured techniques requires defining the higher-level system first. Increasing levels of detail can then be placed into this framework.

Constructing a Logical Model. The opportunity to build a logical model of the system before physical design and implementation begins is another advantage of structured techniques. The logical model should be a description of the system that is independent of any current or planned physical implementation. Using tools provided by various structured techniques, the logical design can be laid out in a form easily comprehended by nontechnical users. Flaws in the design that were not apparent to MIS personnel can be pointed out and corrected by users, who have a greater familiarity with the working environment. Logical models enable easier user understanding and evaluation of the system design early in the development process.

Performing Activities Concurrently

The clearer definition of the system that results from structured analysis and design makes it possible to perform more activities concurrently. For example, if system outputs are clearly defined and accepted by the user department in the analysis and design phases, work can begin immediately on the development of user manuals.

Such concurrent activities are not feasible when the programmer who codes the system also makes systems design decisions. When a user manual is written concurrently with the detailed design and coding in a nonstructured environment, some of the programmer's design decisions can cause inaccuracies in the user documentation.

The opportunity for performing concurrent activities in the structured environment includes producing detailed programming specifications and program code. If structured tools and techniques are used to produce complete, accurate, and user-approved analysis and design documents, the project manager has substantially greater freedom and flexibility in subsequent design and implementation activities.

Greater Flexibility

Because concurrent activities are possible, there is greater flexibility in delaying or postponing certain activities. For example, a hierarchical or top-down design may include modules that need not be programmed or implemented until long after certain other modules are operational. In the structured environment, this option can be chosen deliberately, rather than because of fear that problems or design flaws might make the full system too difficult to implement. Because the developers have a clear understanding of the overall system, this flexibility can be exercised, with confidence that the logical interrelationships have been defined and considered.

SYSTEMS DEVELOPMENT AND PROGRAMMING

BENEFITS OF STRUCTURED TECHNIQUES

This section describes those benefits of structured techniques that are frequently cited by practitioners.

Increased Productivity

Structured techniques can result in as much as a 20 percent improvement in overall productivity. (The bank that reported this increase used tested active statements per active person-day as the unit of measure.[15] A university division found itself "producing more procedures at a lower cost."[14] Productivity was measured in number of systems produced and enhanced rather than in lines of code, since fewer statements were used because of minimized redundancy. As these two studies show, it is difficult to compare productivity in different organizations since different measurements are used.

Quality

A number of factors can be used to judge the quality of a system; for example, number of errors found, amount of downtime, and number of user-requested changes that are not the result of business change can be used. Structured techniques are producing a change in the attitude of systems developers who are approaching the attitude of two hardware developers who, when asked to explain the success of their one software product (which had run for two years without an error), replied that they "didn't know bugs were allowed." Structured techniques are bringing people to expect error-free systems.

Testing thus can be seen in a different light. From the time the first diagram is drawn with structured analysis, the analyst's understanding of the user requirements is tested and improved through ongoing iterative review procedures. Testing and quality assurance is built into every step of the process.

Easier Maintenance

Maintainability is one of the primary goals of structured techniques. The quality criteria of structured design are geared to produce a design that is flexible and easy to change, with minimal disruption. Structured programming complements this by increasing the readability and understandability of the code. The postimplementation maintenance that often results from users' increased understanding of their system is minimized through the use of structured analysis, which gives users paper models of their system to experiment with, well before the system is finalized.

Improved documentation is another benefit of using structured techniques that facilitates maintenance. (Often the very existence of documentation is an improvement.) With structured techniques, the development models become the documentation so that documentation is created during development rather than after.

One bank found that structured techniques reduced the ratio of maintenance to development from 80:20 to 40:60 over a three-year period.[15]

Insurance against Turnover

Structured techniques also provide insurance against personnel turnover. The expected improvement in documentation facilitates the introduction of people to a project. Rather than learn about a system by reading code or system flowcharts, they can look at diagrams that present the system in an orderly, top-down fashion. They can see the general outline of the system before analyzing the more detailed levels. The diagrams can easily be followed to focus on particular areas. This smoother orientation process is possible regardless of the stage in which the person is introduced to the project.

A team approach is another safeguard against personnel turnover. There are many variations of the team approach, but all require that several people contribute to systems development and quality assurance. The team approach provides ongoing review (using walkthroughs, the author/reader cycle, or inspections) of the system as it is being developed. Thus, a number of people become familiar with the system and are better equipped to play different roles in the development process, if necessary.

Attracting and Retaining Quality People

The best DP professionals usually want to use state-of-the-art tools and techniques; thus, a company that uses structured techniques often has a better chance of attracting people who are quality oriented. One bank considered the ability to attract and keep good people a major reason for converting to structured techniques. As Page-Jones states:

> A manager owes it to his subordinates to provide them with the most modern and most apt tools for their job. If he doesn't provide such tools, then he should not be surprised if his people become unhappy or tend to move on to other positions.[8]

Attracting and educating good people is not enough to stop turnover, however. People skilled in structured techniques are more attractive to other organizations. To keep these people, opportunities for them to use their skills in a rewarding way should be provided. A progressive environment that stresses personal development will contribute to high staff morale.[14]

Project Management Benefits

Some of the benefits of structured techniques are particularly applicable to the project management process itself. They include easier estimating, better project control, and increased flexibility.

Easier Estimating. Most estimating techniques require dividing the projects into smaller units. Since partitioning into successively smaller units is an essential aspect of the structured techniques, they provide a natural application-related breakdown to serve as the basis for estimating. For example, a structured design depicts a system as a hierarchy of modules with clearly defined interfaces. Programming and integration efforts can be estimated for each module and for the whole system. Similarly, the products of

SYSTEMS DEVELOPMENT AND PROGRAMMING

analysis (which are also partitioned into small units) can be used to estimate the design effort required.

Although this method of estimating projects is not uncommon, estimates done in a structured environment are unusually reliable. This accuracy results primarily from the clarity and completeness of the early stages of the analysis and design.

Attempts are currently underway to develop metrics that will facilitate programming and design estimates. The method is based on the number of components in the products of structured design and structured analysis. Until these metrics are further developed, estimates will still be largely subjective, based on individual experience with similar projects. Structured techniques, however, provide a more concrete framework for these estimates. In addition, tracking actual versus estimated performance on projects and tailoring the next set of estimates accordingly will help to reduce the subjective nature of estimating.

Better Project Control. Because estimates can be based on discrete components, project plans can be developed on the same foundation. This greatly aids project monitoring and control. Rather than monitoring by major milestones, it is possible to monitor by "inch-pebbles".[9] Slippages, therefore, are noticed sooner, when there is a better chance of successful corrective action (or, at the very least, an opportunity to revise estimates accordingly).

Top-down incremental implementation also allows progress to be measured in terms of the number of working modules rather than in number of lines or modules coded. Integration testing starts as soon as there are two modules, and the most important interfaces are tested first. When the programming is 90 percent complete in this environment, it can truly mean that 90 percent of the modules are working rather than that the programmers think they have found 90 percent of the bugs in the code. (The last 10 percent often takes longer to correct than the first 90 percent.)

The review procedures of structured techniques also aid in project monitoring since they increase the visibility of the developing product. For example, the author/reader cycle of SADT is particularly useful in tracking progress and identifying bottlenecks that require management attention. The peer review or walkthrough techniques offered by structured methods provide a quality-assurance function not readily obtainable before.

Increased Flexibility for Managers. Structured techniques increase management flexibility in two main areas:
- The development process itself
- Personnel assignment

The previous section on changes in the software life cycle discussed the flexibility allowed by the overlapping of development activities. A related benefit of structured techniques is the ability to implement systems in several versions of increasing sophistication rather than as a whole. This approach offers the following specific benefits:
- Gives the user a product sooner. The first version should address the

most pressing user needs and also afford user personnel the opportunity to learn new procedures gradually.
- Increases morale because the system can be seen up and running.
- Decreases the cost of user-requested changes that result from using the system, since supplementary versions have not yet been coded.
- May result in reducing the size of the system (and thereby the cost) if a user decides that the details of the last version are unnecessary.

The combination of structured design and top-down implementation techniques enables gradual implementation. The number of versions and the content of each are decided by the user and the system developers.

Another area of increased flexibility for managers is personnel assignment. Since in both structured analysis and structured design the new system is subdivided in such a way that the interfaces among the components are minimized, the design and/or programming of those components can be assigned to different people, with assurance that the pieces will fit together. Analysts can even divide the analysis work once a high-level partitioning is accepted. Of course, structured techniques do not make it possible to assign 100 people to a 100-person-month project and ensure its completion in one month.[16] More work can be done independently and simultaneously, however.

User Satisfaction

It is important to remember that systems are developed to serve some business function. In the final analysis, the user can best assess how well the system meets that goal. Perhaps the single most important benefit of structured techniques is increased user satisfaction. The user has increased confidence in the system because it performs as specified. Bugs can be corrected in a timely fashion. Easier maintenance means that the system keeps pace with the user's changing business needs. Better management control of the development process means that the user can be better informed of project status. Gradual implementation gives the user a system sooner, facilitating training and correction of misunderstandings.

User satisfaction is increased by user involvement in the development process. Structured analysis, in particular, requires almost constant dialogue between user and analyst—the analyst produces a graphic model of the system, and the user reviews it at every step. Misunderstandings are corrected early, and the user can be assured that the project is always directed at the right target. Many users find the structured analysis models themselves very helpful, and some users are now finding it useful to incorporate these models into their training for new employees.

CONCLUSION

Structured techniques work well, but the most important factor in a project's success is still the quality of the people doing the work. Structured techniques will not transform a noncommunicative, detail-oriented person into an analyst capable of seeing the big picture and communicating it to the user and the designer. In the hands of a skilled practitioner—or even a novice with good natural abilities—structured techniques can achieve dramatic improvements in the systems development effort.

SYSTEMS DEVELOPMENT AND PROGRAMMING

References

1. Dijkstra, E.W. "Programming Considered as a Human Activity." *Proceedings of the IFIP Congress,* New York NY, 1965.
2. Bohm, C. and Jacopini, G. "Flow Diagrams, Timing Machines, and Languages with only Two Formation Rules." *Communications of the ACM,* Vol. 9, No. 5 (May 1966), 366–371.
3. Baker, F. Terry. "Chief Programmer Team Management of Production Programming." *IBM Systems Journal,* Vol. 11, No. 1 (1972), 56–73.
4. Baker, F. Terry, "System Quality Through Structured Programming." *AFIPS Proceedings 1972 Fall Joint Computer Conference,* 1972.
5. Boehm, B.W. "Software and its Impact: A Quantitative Assessment." *Datamation,* Vol. 18, No. 5 (May 1973), 48–59.
6. Stevens, W.P., Myers, G.J., and Constantine, L.L. "Structured Design." *IBM Systems Journal,* Vol. 13, No. 2 (1974).
7. Myers, G. *Reliable Software through Composite Design.* New York: Van Nostrand Reinhold Co, 1975.
8. Page-Jones, M. *The Practical Guide to Structured Systems Design.* New York: Yourdon Press, 1980.
9. Yourdon, E. and Constantine, L. *Structured Design.* New York: Yourdon Press, 1975.
10. DeMarco, T. *Structured Analysis and Systems Specification.* New York: Yourdon Press, 1978.
11. Gane, C. and Sarson, T. *Structured Systems Analysis: Tools and Techniques.* Englewood Cliffs NJ: Prentice-Hall, 1978.
12. Weinberg, V. *Structured Analysis.* New York: Yourdon Press, 1978.
13. *An Introduction to SADT.* SofTech Document 9022-78R, 1976.
14. Lippard, M.S. "Structured Methods: The Impossible Dream?" *Computerworld,* Vol. 14, No. 49 (December 1980) In Depth 1–15.
15. Henrotay, M. "Structured Revolution Continues—Large Organization Reports Success." *Futures,* (Fall 1979), 3–5.
16. Brooks, F. *The Mythical Man-Month.* Reading MA: Addison-Wesley, 1975.

IV-5

Analysis and Design—A Structured Approach

Pat Duran
Al McCready

INTRODUCTION

With systems development and maintenance costs taking up an increasingly large percentage of the MIS budget, and with development backlogs threatening to undermine MIS's ability to meet the organization's information needs, the MIS manager should use all applicable methods for reducing these costs and providing effective, maintainable systems more efficiently. Many MIS managers are using packaged software when feasible, or installing online programming tools and higher-level nonprocedural languages to help solve these problems. Structured techniques provide the MIS manager with a group of valuable tools for improving the efficiency and effectiveness of the systems development effort.

Chapter IV-4 provides an overview of structured techniques and discusses their evolution. This chapter discusses the tools and methods used in structured analysis and design, outlining the common characteristics of the various techniques and providing comparisons where significant differences exist. Chapter IV-6 discusses the tools and methods used in structured programming, testing, and reviews.

STRUCTURED ANALYSIS

Structured analysis is used to define and describe the system that best satisfies user requirements, given certain time and budget constraints. Although structured analysis can be implemented in a variety of ways, all versions share important features: use of models, user involvement, iteration, and postponement of implementation details.

Use of Models. All methods use models to describe existing or planned systems. Other industries involved in constructing systems (e.g., buildings, ships, automobiles) have demonstrated that an excellent way to describe a future system is to build a miniature version, or model, of that system. Structured analysis uses paper models (diagrams) that depict the processes in graphic form.

SYSTEMS DEVELOPMENT AND PROGRAMMING

User Involvement. One of the primary reasons for creating models is to facilitate communication with the user; heavy user involvement throughout the analysis phase increases the analyst's understanding of the system, and this understanding can then be fed back to the user for confirmation. In this way, misunderstandings are corrected quickly without affecting final deadlines.

Iteration. As the models are produced and reviewed by users and other analysts, they are revised in response to these reviews. It is not uncommon for a diagram to undergo five or six iterations. By the time any project deliverable is produced, each piece of it has been reviewed and refined, usually a number of times. (User involvement and iteration are discussed further in the section on reviews in Chapter IV-6.)

Postponement of Implementation Details. The models should describe the functions of the system rather than how the system will accomplish these functions. Consideration of design and implementation issues is postponed until agreement is reached on the description of function.

Varieties of Structured Analysis

There are three main types of structured analysis. Two of them were developed by adapting some of the tools and principles of structured design to the analysis phase and complementing them with other analysis tools. The first and perhaps best known was developed by DeMarco[1] and is taught by Yourdon Inc; a similar method was created concurrently by Gane and Sarson[2] of Improved Systems Technologies, now owned by McAuto. The third type, Structured Analysis and Design Technique (SADT from Softech)[3-7] was developed by Doug Ross and his associates to help solve complex problems whether they involved software or not. It is a proprietary technique taught by SofTech Inc. A subset of SADT that is in the public domain is being used in the Air Force's Integrated Computer Aided Manufacturing (ICAM) project and is called $IDEF_0$ (ICAM DEFinition language).

Tools of Structured Analysis

Structured analysis consists of four primary tools:
- Data flow or activity diagrams
- Data dictionary
- Data structure, immediate-access, or entity diagrams
- Transform descriptions or minispecifications.

Data Flow or Activity Diagrams. These tools enable the analyst to partition (decompose) the system into components and show the connections or interfaces among the components (see Figures 1, 2, and 3). Each component can then be partitioned, resulting in a collection of diagrams that present the system in a top-down fashion. The Yourdon data flow diagram and the $SADT/IDEF_0$ activity diagram allow for as many decompositions or levels as the analyst deems necessary. The Gane and Sarson data flow diagram uses two levels, general and detailed. Processes are represented as circles or boxes. Arrows represent data in all three versions, but Yourdon and Gane and

Structured Analysis and Design

Figure 1. Data Flow Diagram

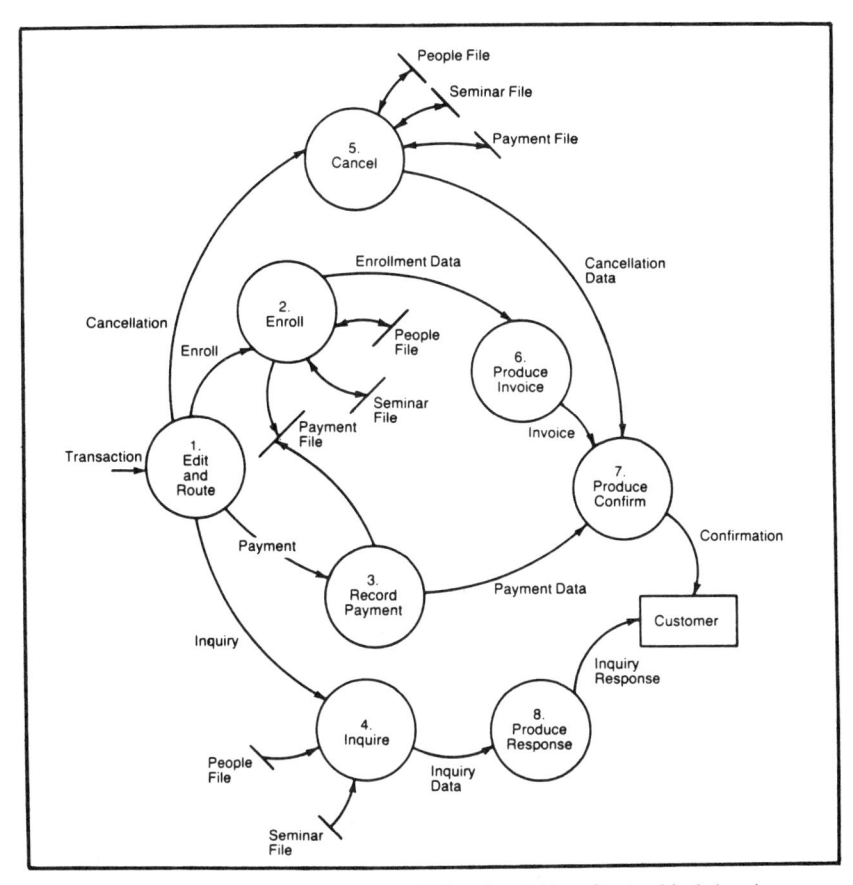

Reprinted by permission of Yourdon Press, New York NY, from Tom DeMarco *Structured Analysis and System Specification*, p. 39. ©1978 by Yourdon Inc.

Sarson have a notation for stored data whereas SADT/IDEF$_0$ does not. SADT/IDEF$_0$ allows for a finer distinction between types of data. The others consider input and output only; SADT/IDEF$_0$ distinguishes among input data (transformed by the process), control data (constrains the process or acts as a catalyst), and output data (produced by the activity). This method also identifies mechanism data (the means by which the activity is accomplished, usually not used in analysis models and therefore not shown in Figure 3).

Data Dictionary. This tool consists of two sections: a glossary that defines the terms used on arrows on the diagram and a description of the components of the arrows. Because components can be described in terms of their subcomponents, the data dictionary provides a top-down decomposition of the data that corresponds to the decomposition of the activities on the diagram. Although the data dictionary is not part of SADT/IDEF$_0$ per se, it has been used with this method successfully. Many analysts consider the data dictionary to be even more important than the data flow diagram.

201

SYSTEMS DEVELOPMENT AND PROGRAMMING

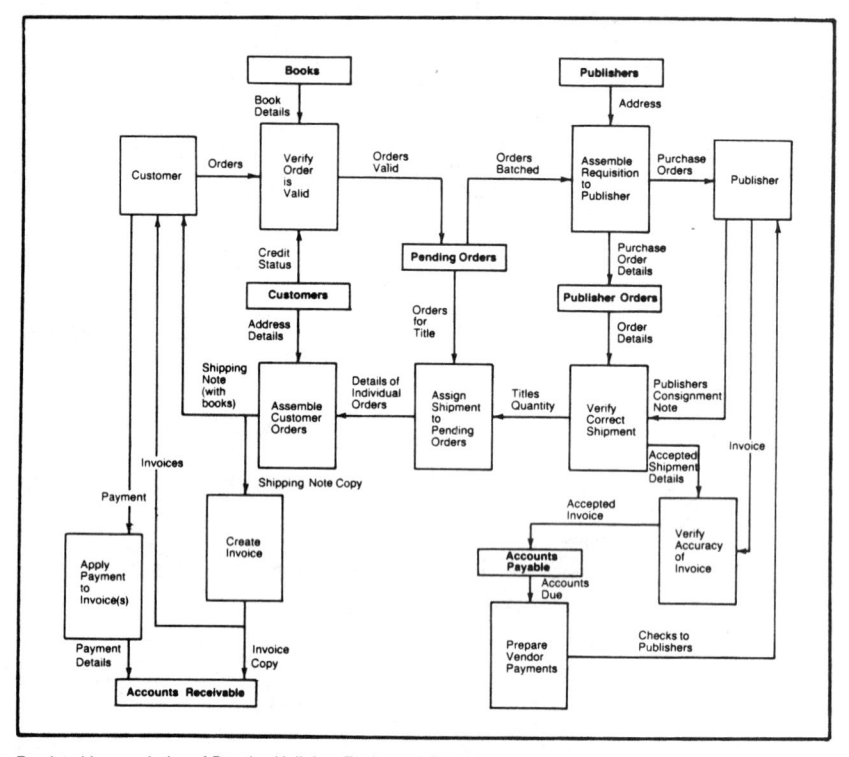

Reprinted by permission of Prentice-Hall, Inc, Englewood Cliffs NJ, from Chris Gane and Trish Sarson, *Structured Systems Analysis: Tools and Techniques*, p. 12. ©1979.

Figure 2. Data Flow Diagram

Data Structure, Immediate Access, or Entity Diagrams. These tools are used to describe static relationships among data and represent the first stage of data base design. All are user-oriented and independent of particular data base management systems.

Transform Descriptions or Minispecifications. Every activity is described either by a lower-level diagram or, for lowest-level activities, by a transform description, which states the policy governing the transformation. A variety of tools are available to express this policy; the tool selected depends on the policy itself and the experience of the personnel involved. Recommended tools include decision tables or trees and Structured English, a version of English with a limited vocabulary and limited ways of expressing logic. The collection of transform descriptions constitutes the specification of the system.

SADT/IDEF$_0$ has no transform description per se. Text usually accompanies every published diagram, although the diagram is reviewed on its own merit without the text. Text is used to supplement the diagram with information pertinent to the model; one legitimate use for text accompanying a model that describes the future system is to provide transform descriptions.

Structured Analysis and Design

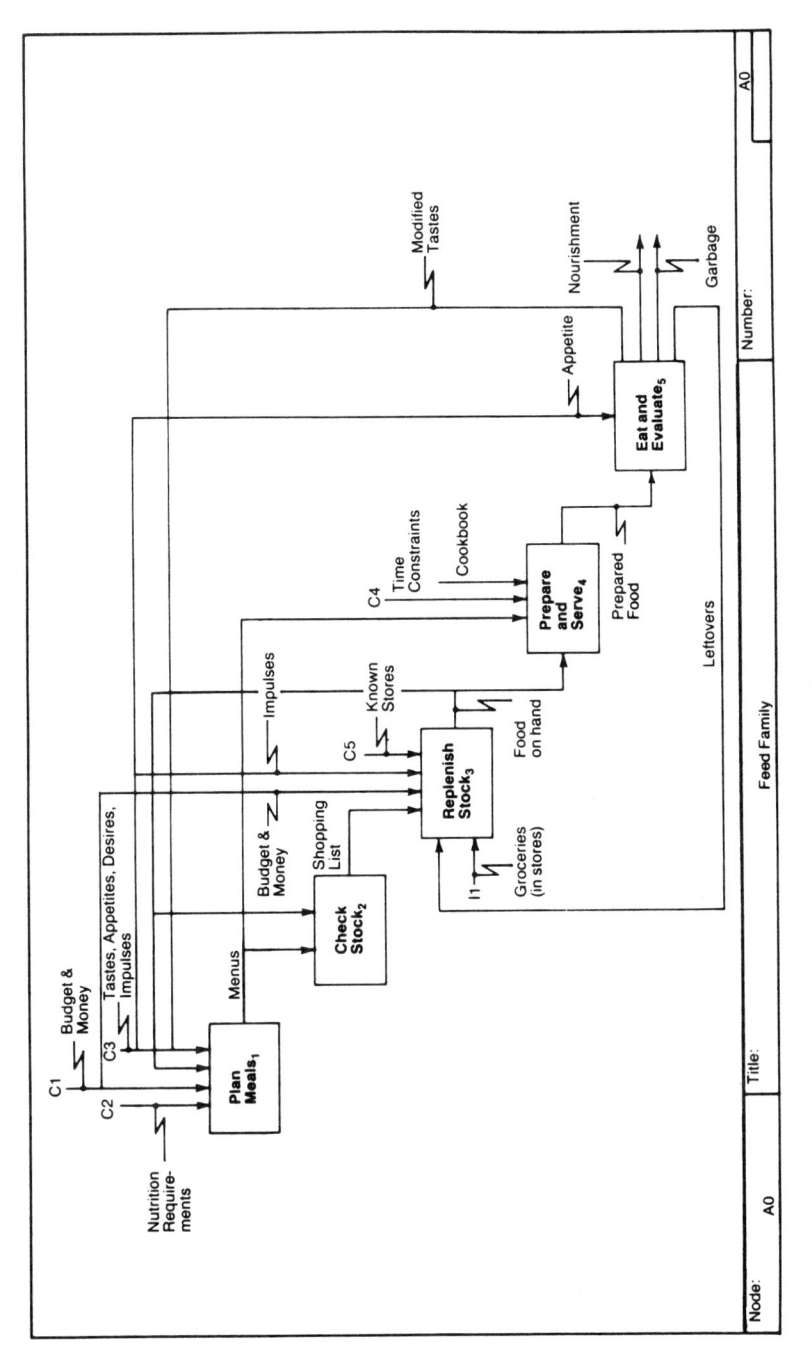

Figure 3. Activity Diagram

SYSTEMS DEVELOPMENT AND PROGRAMMING

Methods

The following paragraphs briefly describe the various methods used in structured analysis.

Approach to Models. Both the Yourdon and the Gane and Sarson techniques involve production of four models:
- Current (or old) physical—A model of how the existing system operates.
- Current (or old) logical—A model of what the present system does, disregarding implementation methods.
- New logical—A model of what the new system must do. This is very similar to the current logical model if the functions of the system are to remain substantially the same while physical aspects are to change (e.g., changing from batch to online or from centralized to distributed processing; altering the scope of the automated system).
- New physical—The new logical model with a minimum of physical characteristics added to it (but including the human/machine boundary).

The rationale for creating these four models is provided in the textbooks.[1,2]

The SADT/IDEF$_0$ approach has no standard set of models (although most practitioners produce a similar set) but rather stresses the importance of identifying the purpose and viewpoint of every model. The purpose—the reason for creating the model—is usually associated with a group of questions the model should be able to answer, and the model can be considered complete when they are answered acceptably. If there is a question regarding whether inclusion of a particular aspect of a system is necessary, a review of the model's purpose usually can resolve the uncertainty. The viewpoint of the model is the perspective from which the subject is analyzed. For example, marketing and engineering typically have very different perspectives, and models from these two viewpoints would differ in terminology and the importance ascribed to different functions. This method may therefore have multiple models that refer to one another.

Approach to Specifications. SADT/IDEF$_0$ diagrams frequently serve as supporting documents for the functional specification and are placed in an appendix. DeMarco emphasizes the creation of a "structured specification" or target document that contains the four basic tools of structured analysis and as little else as possible. The maintainability of the specification itself is important. Both techniques address the importance of traceability (i.e., the design should be traceable to the requirements to ensure that all of these have been met).

STRUCTURED DESIGN

The goal of structured design is to minimize the lifetime cost of a system by emphasizing maintainability, because maintenance has been shown to be the costliest part of a system's life. The basic premise is that the solution should match the problem; components and connections in the solution that do not have a counterpart in the problem should be kept to a minimum.

Some of the features of structured analysis apply to structured design: structured design also uses models for understanding and communicating, and iteration and review are important as well. In addition, structured design includes a collection of evaluative criteria to assist the designers and reviewers. It provides strategies for producing rough designs quickly from the results of analysis. Structured design was developed primarily by Myers[8, 9] and Constantine[10] and has become well known through the work of Yourdon and, more recently, Page-Jones.[11]

Tools of Structured Design

The tools used in structured design include the data flow diagram, structure chart, and evaluation criteria.

Data Flow Diagram. This is the same data flow diagram used in structured analysis, and must be constructed during design only when structured analysis was not used. In design, the leveling is not as important as the collection and interrelation of diagrams at each level.

Structure Chart. This tree-like diagram displays the modules hierarchically and identifies the data that passes between them (see Figure 4). Each box describes that module's function, including all of its subordinate modules. The relationship between supervisor and subordinate is a subroutine call, and the supervisor resumes control when the subordinate finishes its job. The interfaces list the names and the types of data and the direction of data flow. No sequence is implied in the structure chart.

Evaluation Criteria. The main guidelines for evaluating and improving designs are coupling and cohesion. Each is used as follows:
- Coupling is a measure of the independence of modules. Loose, or low, coupling is ideal, as it prevents changes to one module from affecting other modules in the system. The best type of coupling is data coupling (communication by parameters of data elements), and the worst is content coupling (one module refers to the inside of another module).
- Cohesion is a measure of the internal strength of a module. It evaluates how well all the elements work together to accomplish a single function. The goal is functional cohesion—strong modules whose elements contribute to the execution of only one problem-related task. The weakest type is coincidental cohesion, in which a module's elements have no systematic relationship to one another.

Coupling and cohesion are interdependent; modules with strong cohesion tend to be loosely connected to other modules, and weak cohesion tends to result in poor coupling.

Business Analogies

To help in understanding the principles of structured design, some analogies can be drawn between the structure chart and business organization charts. A department should have a clear statement of its responsibilities, and the people in the department should work toward a common goal (cohesion). Departments should be organized so that they can function somewhat independently, and so that the flow of information is mostly vertical rather than horizontal (coupling). This is accomplished in several ways.

SYSTEMS DEVELOPMENT AND PROGRAMMING

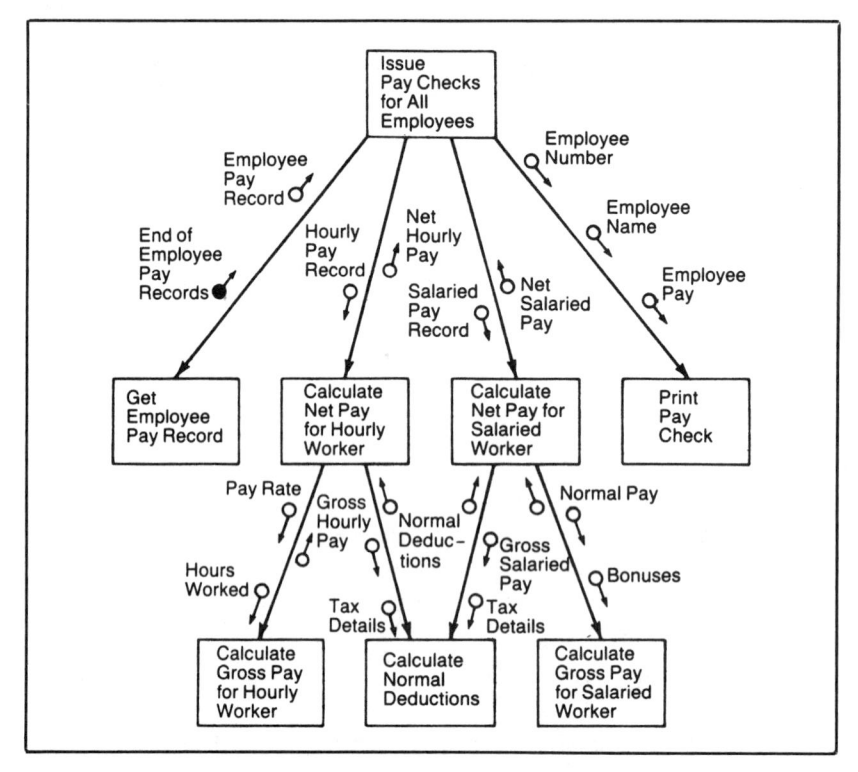

Reprinted by permission of Yourdon Press, New York NY, from Meilir Page-Jones, *The Practical Guide to Structured Systems Design*, p. 42. ©1980 by Yourdon Inc.

Figure 4. Structure Chart

Separating Management and Worker Functions. Most people (modules) in the department do the work; managers control and coordinate that work. The higher a person (module) is in the hierarchy, the more management and the less work he or she does. The modules at the bottom of the structure chart do the calculations and manipulations of data; the higher-level modules are mostly call statements and conditionals that accomplish much of their work by invoking subordinates.

Filtering Information. A company president does not see every piece of information available in the company, only that information needed to conduct presidential business—information that has been filtered and refined. In a structure chart, raw data is usually accessed by the low-level modules and filtered as it passes through the hierarchy; erroneous input can be eliminated. The data seen by the top module is in its most logical state, removed from the physical input/output devices. Thus, the physical aspects of the system, which are subject to change, are separated from the function of the system, which is less likely to change.

Scope of Effect and Control. A department manager makes decisions

Structured Analysis and Design

that affect the people in that department. If, however, one department manager's decisions start affecting other departments, the authority relationships are threatened, and the amount of necessary communication between the departments is increased. In a structure chart, modules that act on a decision should be controlled by the module that makes the decision.

Other heuristics of structured design are discussed in the textbooks.[8-11]

Strategies

Structured design provides two strategies for translating the data flow diagram into a first-draft structure chart: transform analysis and transaction analysis.

Transform analysis is an approach that identifies the major input and output streams, tracks them to their most logical form, and identifies the central transformation. A structure chart is then organized so that the top module deals with the most logical data and the central transformation; this chart is subsequently revised to conform with the guidelines of structured design.

Transaction analysis is a technique for designing maintainable transaction-processing systems that involves separating the transactions by type rather than by common processing requirements. Common modules are invoked by multiple transaction-handling modules.

Most designs use both transform and transaction analysis at different places and times in developing the structure chart; for example, the overall structure may be based on transaction analysis, but within a transaction processor there may be a transform center, or vice versa.

Transition to Programming

Each box in the structure chart represents a logical module. Before programming begins, the physical modules (e.g., compilable programs, load modules, job steps) must be chosen, and module specifications should be written. Module specifications can be delineated by a black-box-oriented description of the module's inputs, outputs, and function; a Warnier/Orr diagram; a decision table or tree; a Nassi-Schneiderman chart; or program design language (pseudocode). The selection of the tool or tools for module specifications depends on company standards, the personnel involved (i.e., their level of expertise and whether the person who did the design will do the coding), the complexity of the module, and whether the module specifications are a programming aid only or will become part of the system documentation.

Other Design Approaches

The versions of structured design developed by Constantine and Myers are based on understanding the flow of data through the system. There are other approaches based on the structure of data. Jackson, Warnier, and Orr are the chief proponents of the data-structure approach.[12-14]

CONCLUSION

This chapter and Chapter IV-6, "Programming and Testing—A Structured

SYSTEMS DEVELOPMENT AND PROGRAMMING

Approach'' provide an analysis of the tools and methods used in structured techniques. The MIS manager can use this analysis to determine which structured techniques can be implemented in his or her organization. Integrating these techniques with the standard systems development life cycle can improve the efficiency of the development process and produce more maintainable systems.

References

1. DeMarco, Tom. *Structured Analysis and System Specification*. New York: Yourdon Press, 1978.
2. Gane, Chris and Sarson, Trish. *Structured Systems Analysis: Tools and Techniques*. Englewood Cliffs NJ: Prentice-Hall, 1979.
3. SofTech Inc. "An Introduction to SADT." SofTech Document 9022-78R. Waltham MA, 1978.
4. Connor, M. "Structured Analysis and Design Technique." *Proceedings of the GUIDE 50 Conference*. GUIDE International Corp, 1978.
5. Ross, Douglas T. "Structured Analysis (SA): A Language for Communicating Ideas." *IEEE Transactions on Software Engineering*, Vol. SE-3, No. 1, January 1977.
6. Ross, Douglas T., and Schoman, Kenneth E., Jr. "Structured Analysis for Requirements Definition." *IEEE Transactions on Software Engineering*, Vol. SE-3, No. 1, January 1977.
7. Duran, Pat. "Communicating Requirements with SADT." *Proceedings of the SHARE 57 Conference*. August 1981.
8. Myers, Glenford J. *Reliable Software through Composite Design*. New York: Van Nostrand Reinhold, 1975.
9. ———. *Composite Structure Design*. New York: Van Nostrand Reinhold, 1978.
10. Yourdon, Edward, and Constantine, Larry L. *Structured Design*, 2nd ed. New York: Yourdon Press, 1978.
11. Page-Jones, Meilir. *The Practical Guide to Structured Systems Design*. New York: Yourdon Press, 1980.
12. Jackson, M.A. *Principles of Program Design*. New York: Academic Press, 1975.
13. Warnier, Jean-Dominique. *Logical Construction of Systems*. New York: Van Nostrand Reinhold, 1981.
14. Orr, Kenneth T. *Structured Systems Development*. New York: Yourdon Press, 1977.

IV-6

Programming and Testing—A Structured Approach

Pat Duran
Al McCready

INTRODUCTION

Two of the major problems facing systems and programming personnel are coping with obscure code that makes corrections and modifications difficult and ensuring adequate testing for systems, despite severe time and budget constraints. Decreases in computer cost/performance and increases in systems development and maintenance costs have made it more important to produce code that is easy to understand and maintain and less important to ensure the machine execution efficiency of the code. Once the code is produced, enormous systems backlogs and increased pressure to get systems up on time and within budget make it difficult to adequately test systems with traditional end-of-cycle methods. Structured techniques for programming, testing, and review provide tools for solving these problems.

STRUCTURED PROGRAMMING

Several similar objectives initiated the development of structured programming. One was to make programming more of a science and less of an art form. Perhaps the primary goal, however, was to produce more readable, understandable, and maintainable code through use of a limited group of logical constructs. The movement toward impersonal, or "public," code in structured programming is often referred to as egoless programming. One of the purposes of such programming is to make the program code easy to understand for someone unfamiliar with the program and the programmer; because a program is read more often than written, it is more important that it be easy to read than easy to write.[1] Another objective has been to produce programming code that is easily proven correct.

Background

Although structured programming eventually might have evolved from an aesthetic desire for better structure and order in computer programs, it was developed in response to an urgent operational need. Prior to its introduction, most well-thought-out computer programs were based on streamlining machine execution because of the relatively high cost of computing power and the smaller capacity of central processing units during the sixties and early seventies.

Because of this orientation, programmers were encouraged to employ obscure logical constructs if such constructs improved the execution efficiency of the application. Readability and maintainability of the program code were not usually considered important; the programmer who could rapidly produce efficient and operational program code was considered the most desirable. Program documentation was usually the only gesture towards transferable or originator-independent code. Narrative program specification, perhaps written in a standard format, and traditional logic flowcharts were generally considered appropriate documentation. Often, the relatively cumbersome charts were constructed only after the program code had been written.

In this situation, it was common for a program to consist of a tangle of internal references with little or no documentation. The problem was exacerbated by the use of unconditional branches (e.g., COBOL GOTOs) in the logic, hence the phrase "spaghetti-string programs." The emphasis on machine efficiency gave programmers artistic license in program design; as a result, program maintenance was a very challenging job, especially in the absence of the program's author.

Varieties of Structured Programming

The terms top-down programming (or design), stepwise refinement, modular programming, and structured programming are often used interchangeably. Occasionally, a programmer will claim to have been writing structured programs years before the term became popular. That programmer may have written modular code, but it probably was not code that could pass the rigorous definitions of structured programming developed during the mid-1970s.

Top-down Programming. Top-down or hierarchical programming (also called stepwise refinement) entails identifying major functions and breaking them down into smaller functional blocks. The highest level of the program is written first, followed by immediately subservient levels in descending order. This process continues until the lowest functional unit is identified. This is not structured programming in the fullest sense.

Modular Programming. The concept of dividing a program into major modules has been usefully employed for some time. The program is organized into functional units, which are coded separately. Unlike top-down programming, modular programming does not restrict the sequence in which the modules are written.

Structured Programming. Structured programming is more restrictive and definitive than the previous approaches. It identifies a limited number of logical constructs that are acceptable to specify the progression of program control. "GOTO-less" programming is somewhat of a misnomer for structured programming. A program can be entirely free of GOTO statements and still not be structured. Conversely, a program with a GOTO statement can be an acceptable structured program. The key feature is the presence of structure rather than the absence of GOTO statements.

Structured Programming Methods

Structured programming uses hierarchical, modular code primarily employing three control structures (see Figure 1), and following guidelines for format and module size. All three basic logical constructs—sequence, selection, and iteration—have only one entrance and one exit.

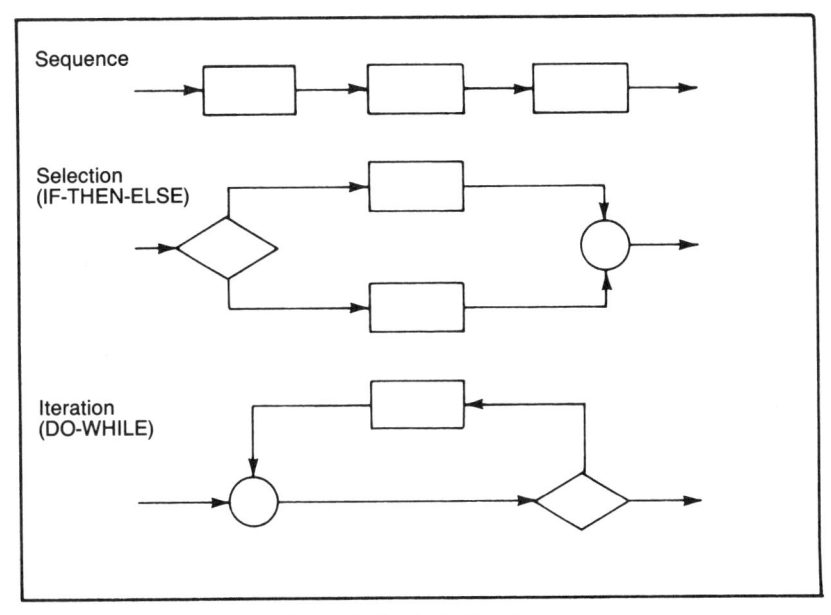

Figure 1. Control Structures

The case construct is sometimes included as a basic logical construct in structured programming (see Figure 2). The case performs one of several processes depending on a value. It is a variation on the selection construct (it involves n-way rather than two-way selection) and can be handled by a nested IF-statement, although enough cases could cause the nested IF to be too deep to be practical.

Figure 2 also illustrates the DO-UNTIL logical construct, an alternate iteration construct (the decision to iterate is made after one performance of the process). Some practitioners use additional variations, especially for iteration; however, these variations should be used in a carefully controlled manner, and only when necessary to clarify the code.

Correctness

Because the goal of structured programming is lasting, useful code, correctness is very important. To a great extent, this depends on the quality of

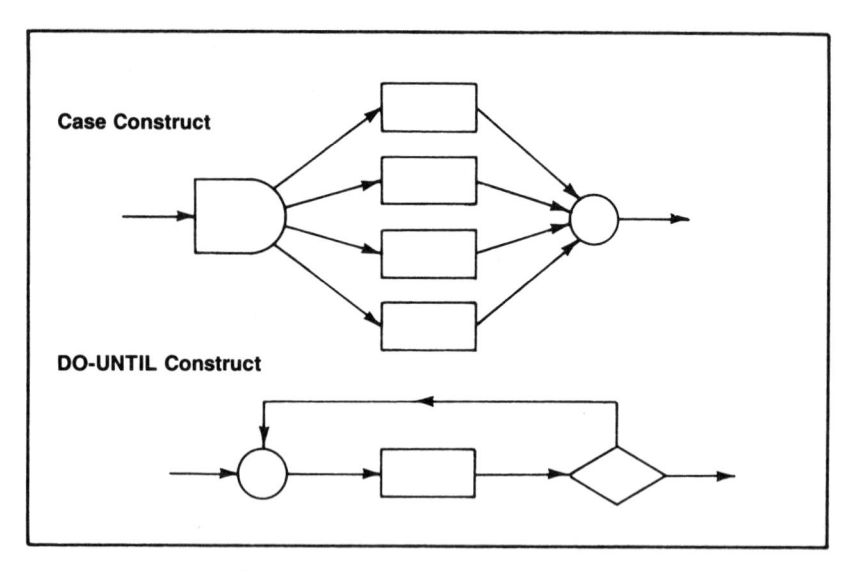

Figure 2. Additional Control Structures

the analysis and design; ideally, structured programming should carry through from structured design and structured analysis. If the analysis and design are executed properly, the structured-programming product is more likely to satisfy the user's needs. A great deal of academic research has been devoted to developing program-correctness proofs and to determining how structured programming facilitates development of correct programs.

Format and Commentary

Most structured-programming guidelines cover the size of code segments, the use of variable and paragraph names, and the layout and indentation of the code. Good paragraph or subroutine names can contribute substantially to the readability of the code, and proper indentation, particularly in nested IFs, can make the code much more understandable.

The guiding principle of structured programming is to write so that another person at another time will easily understand the product. Surprises or misleading or confusing code should never be included. A simple, straightforward approach is the trademark of good structured programming.

Flexibility

Programming to facilitate changes is now recognized as an important consideration. With its emphasis on standardization, readability, and maintainability, structured programming allows a change to be made quickly and correctly by programmers who are not familiar with the program. In addition, improved readability enables a reduction in the level of programming expertise needed to make effective changes.

STRUCTURED TESTING

The goal of structured testing is to identify and correct errors as early as

Structured Programming and Testing

possible in the system development cycle, using incremental testing procedures coordinated with the hierarchical development approach of the other structured techniques. Structured testing utilizes iterative review steps to validate each level of design and development and strives to test the conclusions of the analysis and design phases during each phase.

Background

Traditionally, software testing has been performed late in the system-development cycle, usually after the program code is produced. Such testing is intended only to prove that the system works; simulated data, representing the programmer's concept of the normal expected data structure, is used to test the primary logic paths of the program. Sometimes known or expected error conditions are included to test an error message. An occasional exhaustive test might try to exercise all of the possible logical branches through the program. Retesting the program after correcting an error usually involves reprocessing the data that identifies the error.

Unfortunately, such testing is often funded with the "remaining" project budget in an environment where budget overruns are common. In fact, at the end of a project substantial pressure usually exists to put the system up. Because testing appears to produce few tangible results and can be expensive and time consuming, it is not unusual for this aspect of the implementation to be shortchanged. Structured testing prevents these problems by giving testing an important role in the analysis and design stages.

Types of Testing

In the structured system-development environment, the first test is actually the review of the initial data flow diagrams by the user or subject expert. This type of structured testing, which continues throughout the analysis and design phases, is accomplished by walkthroughs or other review processes.

Structured testing of the programming code requires incremental testing of the modules (i.e., testing the first module, adding modules singly or in small groups, and testing the new combination); this process facilitates error location. Furthermore, because coding and testing can take place concurrently (e.g., coding module 2 while testing module 1), the coding and testing can be scheduled so that a module can be tested immediately after coding.

Incremental testing can be top down or bottom up. In top-down testing, program stubs are used for the called modules that have not been coded. The stub may be a display indicating that the module has been called or a simplified version of the actual module. In bottom-up testing, drivers are used for the uncoded calling modules.

In *Techniques of Program Structure and Design*,[2] Yourdon summarizes the advantages of top-down incremental testing as follows:

1. System testing in its classical sense is virtually eliminated.
2. Major interfaces of the program are tested first. As a result, major bugs are discovered early in the project, while trivial bugs are discovered toward the end of the project.

SYSTEMS DEVELOPMENT AND PROGRAMMING

3. The users can be given a preliminary version of the program at a relatively early stage.
4. If it is not possible to finish the entire program by the time a deadline has arrived, it is likely that a usable subset of the program will have been finished.
5. It is often much easier to find bugs (i.e., debugging as opposed to testing) with a top-down testing approach.
6. Testing time is distributed more evenly throughout the project, thus eliminating the requirements for large amounts of computer time toward the end of the project.
7. The programmers' morale is improved considerably when they can see the results of a successful test of a skeleton of the final program.
8. Top-down testing provides a natural "test harness" for testing lower-level modules.

In *The Art of Software Testing*,[3] Myers concludes that incremental testing is the preferred test procedure and points out that both bottom-up and top-down testing can be done incrementally. Page-Jones[4] explores the possibility of a "sandwich" approach, which uses top-down testing for most of the system but bottom-up testing for certain modules (e.g., I/O modules).

More important than the actual procedure is the point at which the testing is planned. Essential to structured-testing techniques are planning and designing the test method and procedure before the program coding begins. Early design of the test avoids "unconscious" moves toward less rigorous tests because of time or budgetary constraints and helps ensure that the test is working toward the intent or designed objectives.

According to DeMarco,[5] the final acceptance testing should use the target documentation to determine whether the final product meets the original requirements. Acceptance testing in the structured environment is not an iterative process of finding and correcting errors; trivial errors may be corrected, but its intent is a pass-fail decision regarding whether the system successfully meets all requirements.

REVIEWS

The main goal of reviews is quality assurance—the creation of error-free products. Because reviews are an everyday occurrence, misunderstandings and inadequacies can be identified and corrected before they adversely affect the project. Secondary goals include:
- Disseminating knowledge about the system so that more than one person understands the product
- Spreading knowledge about tools and techniques
- Enforcing company or project standards
- Motivating personnel through positive reinforcement and the desire to impress peers.

Features

The different types of reviews share the following features:
- Use of teams—The team, rather than an individual, creates the product; each team member plays a different role at different times. Each member of the team develops a sense of responsibility for the product.

Structured Programming and Testing

- Frequency of occurrence—Depending on the stage of the project and the formality and type of review, reviews may take place several times each day.
- Limitation of information—The material being reviewed should be restricted to an amount that can be reviewed within a reasonable time (an hour or two).

Holding frequent reviews provides quick feedback and helps ensure that each review covers only a small amount of new material. This makes it much easier for those involved in the review to accept and act on criticism.

Types

The two types of reviews are walkthroughs and the author/reader cycle. Walkthroughs have been promoted by a number of companies and individuals; the author/reader cycle is part of SADT/IDEF$_0$. They can be combined with other structured techniques or used independently. Both methods can be used on the same project quite effectively.

Walkthroughs. Structured walkthroughs were developed as part of IBM's "Chief Programmer Team" concept of project organization. Although originally intended as a method for the programming team to review and assist with the production of program specifications, coding, and testing, walkthroughs can be used in all stages of systems development.

In this review method, the programmer, designer, or analyst regularly meets with the other members of the team to perform a group review of the work product. This provides an opportunity to examine it for conformance to the requirements in the target documentation; more important, it provides external confirmation that the logic of the product is correct and that it adheres to project or shop standards. Because of the hierarchical nature of structured systems development, the team is able to concentrate on higher levels of design during early reviews, and subsequent iterations provide increasing amounts of detail for review.

The worker calling for the review collects the documentation and distributes it to the review team. This usually takes place one or two days before the walkthrough, and the bulk of the review is accomplished before the actual meeting. Someone from another part of the project who can inspect the product objectively is often included. The project manager does not attend the walkthrough unless he or she is also an active technician. This encourages a more open exchange of ideas.

The walkthrough is not a group session to redo the design or analysis work. A moderator controls the meeting, the producer describes the product, the reviewers comment, and a recorder documents the findings and recommendations. The team is responsible for identifying problems, and the programmer or analyst is responsible for correcting them. The person whose work was reviewed responds in writing to the items recorded in the minutes of the walkthrough meeting. This guarantees a record of the problem and the action taken to correct it. The team may recommend a subsequent walkthrough. After the review is completed, the entire team becomes responsible for any undetected bugs or problems in the work reviewed.

The Author/Reader Cycle. This type of review is based on written description and response. The author prepares a kit containing the material to be reviewed and sends a copy to the readers, who write comments directly on their kits and return them to the author. The author then responds to the comments, makes notes on a personal copy, and sends the kits back to the readers. Depending on the comments and reactions, a discussion may take place.

The information collected from all the readers is used to revise the model. The next time material concerning that part of the model is distributed, it should reflect the readers' comments. This version is compared to the earlier one, to determine the changes made.

The project files contain all versions of the kits and provide visibility for the project. The cover sheet of the kit includes a list of readers and the times the kit has passed each phase of the author/reader cycle, indicating how much review each kit has had and making it possible to identify bottlenecks easily.

Comparison of Methods. The author/reader cycle differs from the walkthrough in that the dialogue is written and the interaction is on an individual basis. The advantage to this is that there is a written record of both the evolving product and all the comments and that the reader is not influenced by other reviewers. In walkthroughs, the stronger personalities can sometimes dominate, and quiet individuals may not express all their ideas. A major advantage of walkthroughs, however, is that ideas can grow as they are discussed—one person's comment may trigger other new thoughts.

The two review procedures can be combined very effectively on the same project. The author/reader cycle is used for the normal diagram-by-diagram review, and walkthroughs are used after a major accomplishment, a specified time period, or if the author/reader is interrupted by a major problem.

Personnel Qualifications

This type of review of an individual's performance is a strong motivation to produce better quality work. When these review procedures are not optional, quality and productivity can increase significantly. Members of the team, however, must be able to maintain objectivity and impartiality during the review. Authors must be willing to accept criticism of their work, reviewers must provide constructive criticism (it is important to remember that it is the product being reviewed, not the producer), and managers must be willing to step in and resolve issues when necessary.

CONCLUSION

When implementing a structured technique, the principles and benefits of these tools should be considered, and the tools should be adapted to the environment. Some technicians and managers resist the introduction of structured techniques because they disagree with a detail they (sometimes mistakenly) associate with the method. A much more beneficial approach is to understand the techniques, choose the best ones for the organization, adapt them, use them, evaluate their usefulness, and continue to adapt them to meet the needs of a changing environment.

References

1. Brown, Gary D. *Advanced ANS COBOL with Structured Programming*. New York: Wiley-Interscience, 1977.
2. Yourdon, Edward. *Techniques of Program Structure and Design*. Englewood Cliffs NJ: Prentice-Hall, 1975.
3. Myers, Glenford J. *The Art of Software Testing*. New York: Wiley-Interscience, 1979.
4. Page-Jones, Meilir. *The Practical Guide to Structured Systems Design*. New York: Yourdon Press, 1980.
5. DeMarco, Tom. *Structured Analysis and System Specification*. New York: Yourdon Press, 1978.

IV-7
Software Engineering Concepts and Techniques

Marvin V. Zelkowitz

INTRODUCTION

The development of reliable software is a long-standing goal of computer technology. Since the term *software engineering* was first used by Fritz Bauer at a NATO conference in 1968, it has come to encompass all facets of the development cycle of a computer system.[1] Many of the problems present then are still current—low productivity, cost and scheduling overruns, and unreliable products. Nevertheless, several significant developments have occurred, including:

- The recognition of software engineering as a discipline—The Department of Defense language Ada is a significant achievement and has combined many research issues into a production language.
- The proposed Department of Defense Software Technology Initiative—Another attempt at focusing concerted research efforts and funding at the issue of software productivity.
- The emergence of Japanese computer technology—The fifth-generation computer is considered a serious challenge by most U.S. computer manufacturers.
- The proliferation of small systems—The availability of 16- and 32-bit microprocessors, $5,000 business computer systems, and inexpensive home computers is changing the marketplace and altering the rules that have guided software development for the past 30 years.

When construction of the Verrazano Narrows Bridge in New York City started in 1959, officials estimated that it would cost $325 million and be completed by 1965. It is the largest suspension bridge ever built, yet it was completed in November 1964, within budget.[2] No similar pattern has been observed for developing software systems larger than those built previously—for example, the IBM OS project, which involved more than 5,000 worker-years of effort, was exceedingly late.[3]

Part of the reason for this is that a civil engineer can see the added complexity of a larger bridge more easily than a programmer can envision the complexity of a larger program. Much of the current software problem stems from the attempt to apply past experience with smaller projects to large systems programming projects.

SYSTEMS DEVELOPMENT AND PROGRAMMING

Software engineering is interdisciplinary. It uses mathematics to analyze and certify algorithms, engineering to estimate costs and define tradeoffs, and management science to define requirements, assess risks, oversee personnel, and monitor progress. The goal of software engineering is to provide less expensive, more reliable software and to solidify the theoretical basis on which programs are created.

This chapter first outlines the general approach to developing systems and programs, emphasizing aspects that remain poorly understood. Techniques used to solve these problems are then listed. Because all of the relevant topics cannot be fully discussed in this chapter, comprehensive references are included.

STAGES OF SOFTWARE DEVELOPMENT

The complexity of large software systems surpasses the comprehension of any individual. Six separate stages of development, called the software life cycle, have been identified to permit better control of the entire project:
- Requirements analysis
- Specification
- Design
- Coding
- Testing
- Operation and maintenance

Figure 1 illustrates the approximate percentage of development time required by each stage through testing.

Requirements Analysis

The first stage defines the requirements for an acceptable solution to the problem. The computer is a tool for solving the problem—it is not the solution. The requirements analysis focuses on the interface between the tool and the people who use it.

Such factors as processing time, costs, error probability, and chance of fraud or theft must be considered. A requirements analysis can aid in understanding both the problem and trade-offs among conflicting constraints, thereby contributing to the preferred solution.

It is important to distinguish essential requirements from optional features. Are there time or space limitations? What facilities of the system are likely to change? What facilities will be needed to maintain different versions of the system at different locations?

The resources needed to implement the system must be determined. How much money is available for the project? What are the actual required costs? How many computers or computer services are affordable? Can existing software be used? What personnel are available? After these requirements are determined, project schedules must be planned. How will progress be controlled and monitored? What checkpoints will be inserted to measure this progress? What experience acquired from previous efforts is applicable to the current project? After all these questions have been answered, specification of a computer solution to the problem can begin.

Software Engineering Concepts and Techniques

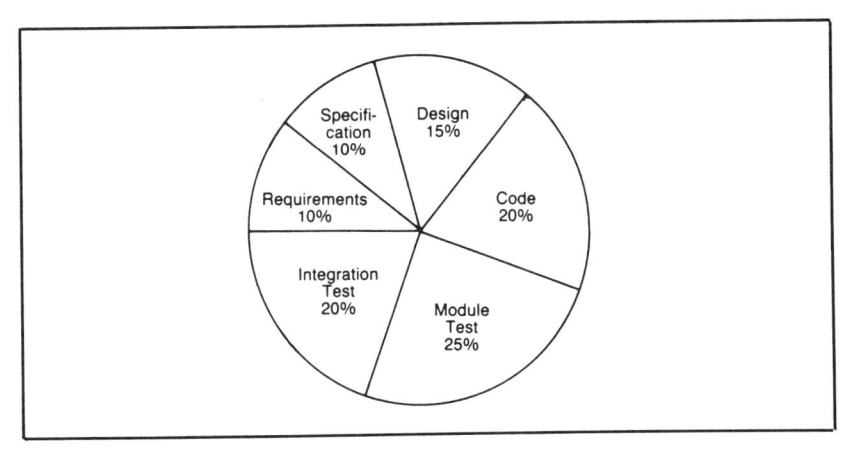

Figure 1. Effort Required on Various Development Activities (Excluding Maintenance)

Pie chart: Specification 10%, Design 15%, Code 20%, Module Test 25%, Integration Test 20%, Requirements 10%.

Specification

Requirements analysis is used to determine whether to use a computer; the specification, or definition, stage defines precisely what the computer is to do.[4] What are the input and ouput to be? For example, a payroll system design must address several questions. Are employee records on a disk file or on tape? How will the output be formatted? Will checks be printed? Is another tape to be written containing information for offline check printing? Will printed reports accompany the checks? What algorithms will be used for computing such deductions as tax, unemployment, health insurance, and pension payments?

Because commercial systems process considerable amounts of data, the data base is a central concern. What files are needed? How will they be formatted, accessed, updated, and deleted?

When a new system supersedes an older one (e.g., when an automatic payroll system replaces a manual system), the conversion of the existing data base to a new format must be part of the design. Conversion may require a special program that is discarded after one use. When the organization is using the older system in its daily operation, bringing the new system online may present a problem. It must be determined beforehand whether the old and new systems should temporarily run side by side.

Answers to these questions are set forth in the functional specification, a document describing the proposed solution. This document is important throughout the project. By defining the project, the specification gives both the user and developer a concrete description. Precise specifications reduce the probability of errors, confusion, or misunderstanding. The specifications allow test data to be developed early; system performance can then be tested objectively, because test data is not influenced by implementation. Because it describes the scope of the solution, this document can be used for initial estimates of time, personnel, and other project requirements.

These specifications define only what the system is to do, not how it will

SYSTEMS DEVELOPMENT AND PROGRAMMING

do it. At this stage, detailed algorithms for implementation are premature and may unduly constrain the designers.

Design

During the design stage, algorithms required by the specifications are developed, and the overall structure of the computer system takes shape. The system must be divided into small modules, each of which is the responsibility of an individual or a small team. Each module has its constraints—its function, size, and speed.

As submodules are specified, they are represented in a tree diagram that shows the nesting of system components. Figure 2 illustrates this for a typical compiler. This illustration, sometimes called a baseline diagram, is not by itself an adequate specification of the system.

A common problem is that the users of a system often do not know exactly what they want, especially in such advanced areas as defense systems. As the project evolves, the user often changes the specifications. If changes are made too frequently it can adversely affect the project. This problem is discussed in later sections of this chapter.

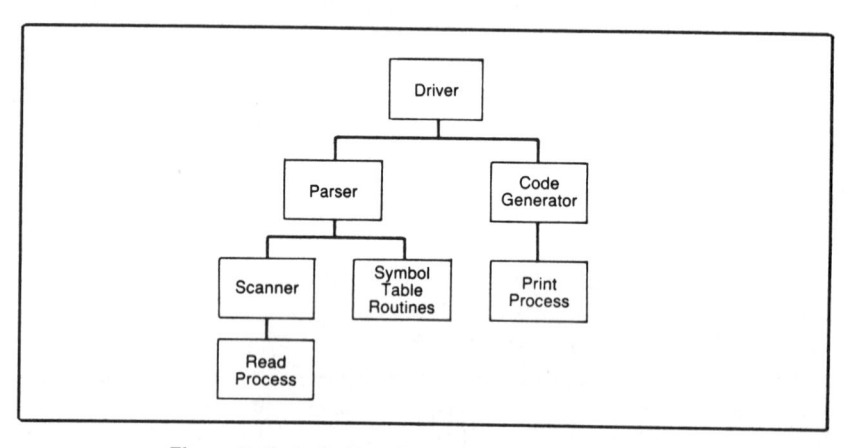

Figure 2. Sample Baseline Diagram for a Compiler

Coding

Coding has been mastered better than any other stage of software development. In one study, it was found that 64 percent of all errors occurred in design; only 36 percent occurred in coding.[5] In the NASA Apollo project, about 73 percent of the errors were design errors.[6]

Coding has been facilitated by the predominance of high-level languages and structured programming. For most applications, complicated assembly language programming has been replaced by such languages as FORTRAN and PL/1 for scientific applications and COBOL for business use. Pascal is making strong inroads, especially for microprocessors.

Embedded applications offer a further challenge. An embedded system is a computer application in a machine whose primary purpose is not to process data. Examples include military applications (e.g., aircraft and radar control) and commercial applications (e.g., automobile emission control or home appliance operation). These applications require real-time response and must analyze data from various external sensors. Although several languages existed for embedded applications (e.g., Jovial for air force applications, CMS/2 and SPL-1 for naval applications), a recent survey concluded that these languages were inadequate for the future; furthermore, 90 percent of the applications studied were written in assembly language. In 1975 the Department of Defense organized the High Order Language Working Group to define a useful embedded systems language. Ada, first published in 1979 and revised in 1982, was issued as a military and ANSI standard in early 1983.[7] At that time, the first production compilers were expected to be available shortly.

Testing

The testing stage may require as much as 50 percent of the total development effort. Inadequately planned testing often results in extremely late deliveries.

During testing, data representative of that to be processed by the finished system should be used; test data cannot be chosen at random. The test plan should be designed early, and most of the test data should be specified during the design stage. Testing is divided into three operations:
- Module, or unit, testing—Subjects each module to the test data supplied by the programmer. A test driver simulates the software environment of the module with dummy routines that replace actual subroutines called by the module. When the module passes these tests it is released for integration testing.
- Integrating testing—Tests groups of components together. Eventually, this procedure produces a completely tested system. Integration testing frequently reveals errors missed in module tests. Correcting them may account for about 25 percent of the total effort.
- Systems testing—Involves the test of the completed system by an outside group. The independence of this group is important.

Buyers may also require their own acceptance test before formally accepting the product. Comparison of the performance of several systems (e.g., of a given software product already available from several sources) is called benchmark testing.

During testing, many criteria are used to determine correct program execution. Basically, however, the program is considered correct if:
- Every statement is executed at least once by test data.
- Every path through the program is executed at least once by the test data.
- For each specification of the program, test data demonstrates that the program performs the particular specification correctly.

These requirements indicate that there is no single criterion that defines a well-tested program. Goodenough and Gerhart proposed a set of consistent definitions for testing and showed that some of these definitions are, in theory, insufficient.[8] (For a survey of testing techniques, see reference 9.)

SYSTEMS DEVELOPMENT AND PROGRAMMING

Verification and validation (V&V) are closely related to testing. A system is validated when testing confirms that it performs according to specifications. A system is verified when it is proved to meet specifications. Current technology is inadequate for achieving both objectives. A validated system may operate incorrectly for cases not included in the test data. A verified system is correct relative only to the initial specifications and assumptions about the operating environment; formal proofs tend to be lengthy, increasing the possibility of error or incredibility.

The term *certification* is sometimes used to refer to the overall process of creating a correct program by validation and verification. Certification uses three distinct definitions:
- Failure—Marks a violation of the system specifications
- Error—An item of information that, when processed by the normal algorithms of the system, produces a failure. Because error recovery may be built into the program (e.g., ON units in PL/1 or exceptions in Ada), not every error will produce a failure.
- Fault—A mechanical or algorithmic defect that generates an error (e.g., a programming bug).[10]

Reliability should not be confused with correctness. A correct program is one that has been proved to meet its specifications. In contrast, a reliable program need only give acceptable answers, even if the data and or environment do not meet assumptions made about them. The system should accept a large class of input data and process it correctly under adverse conditions. A correct system has been described as one that is free from faults and has no errors in its internal data.[11] A program is reliable if failures do not seriously impair its satisfactory operation.

Operating systems with fail-soft procedures illustrate the difference between reliability and correctness. A detected error causes the system to shut down without losing information, possibly restarting after error recovery. Such a system may not be correct because it is subject to errors, but it is reliable because of its consistent operation. A real-time program may be correct as long as a sensor reports correctly. It may be unreliable, however, if bad sensor readings have not been considered.

Operation and Maintenance

The activities noted in Figure 1 represent only one-third of the effort required during the life of the system. Figure 3 illustrates the relationship of maintenance costs to development costs.

No computer system is immutable. Because buyers rarely know what they want, they often request changes to the delivered system. Errors missed during testing will be discovered later. Installations may need special modifications for local conditions.

The division of effort indicated in Figure 3 greatly affects systems development. Techniques that rush development and provide for accelerated implementation may be trading early execution for a much more extensive maintenance operation.

The management of multiple copies of a system is another difficult prob-

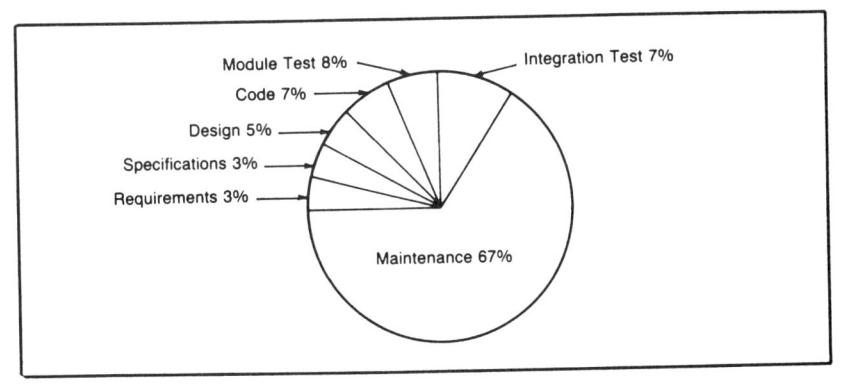

Figure 3. Dispersion of Effort for Large-Scale Software Systems

- Module Test 8%
- Integration Test 7%
- Code 7%
- Design 5%
- Specifications 3%
- Requirements 3%
- Maintenance 67%

lem that must be handled early in development. Once the first line of code is written, the structure of the resulting maintenance operation may already be fixed; it is best to plan for it at that time.

For example, a certain system contains component A. Installation I finds and reports an error. The developer fixes the error and sends a corrected Module A to all installations using the system. Installations II and III ignore the replacement and continue with the original system. Installations I and II discover another error in Module A. The developer must now determine whether both errors are the same, because different versions of Module A are involved. The correction of this error involves correction of both A' (for I) and A (for II), yielding A'' and A'''. There are now three versions of the system.

To avoid this proliferation, systems often receive updates (releases) at fixed intervals. Another useful tool for dealing with myriad maintenance problems is a systems data base started during the specifications stage. This data base records characteristics of the different installations. It includes procedures for reporting, testing, and repairing errors before distributing the corrections.

MANAGEMENT ISSUES

A manager controls two major resources: computer equipment and personnel. Techniques for optimizing the use of these resources are discussed in this section.

Size and Cost Control

A project may fail when management is unaware of developing problems. Faced with catastrophic failure (e.g., hardware delivery is delayed six months), a resourceful manager can usually find alternatives. It is easy, however,to ignore day-to-day problems (e.g., employee absenteeism or many errors during testing).

Most problems occur at the interfaces of modules written by different programmers. Because

$$(\text{the number of interfaces}) = (\text{the number of individuals involved})^2$$

SYSTEMS DEVELOPMENT AND PROGRAMMING

the problem becomes unwieldy when more than three persons are in a development group.

For example, one programmer can write a 5,000-line program in a year. If a system that requires about 50,000 lines of code is to be completed in two years, five programmers would seem sufficient.

The five programmers, however, must communicate with each other. Communication takes time and also causes some loss in productivity, because finding misunderstood aspects of the system requires additional testing. For this simple analysis, each communication path could cost a programmer 250 lines of code per year. Therefore, each of the five programmers (with four communications paths) can produce only 4,000 lines per year; only 40,000 lines are completed within two years.

This means that eight programmers producing 3,250 lines per year are needed to produce the required 50,000 lines. Because a manager is required to direct this large an effort, eight programmers and a manager are actually needed.

Simply counting lines of code is not a good way to estimate productivity; this example is therefore used only to illustrate that a problem exists. There are techniques designed to limit this communications explosion and increase programmer productivity.

Project Personnel. Software can usually be divided into three categories: control programs (e.g., operating systems), systems programs (e.g., compilers), and applications programs (e.g., file management systems). In one year, a programmer can produce about 600 lines of control-program code, 2,000 lines of systems-program code, and about 6,000 lines of application-program code.[12] The type of task affects programmer productivity; the organization of personnel affects performance. For example, with the approach of deadlines, documentation often receives a low priority; however, because 70 percent of the total system cost may occur during maintenance (where documentation is heavily used), this may represent a false economy.

A librarian can avoid this by providing the interface between the programmer and the computer. Programs are coded and given to the librarian for insertion into the online project library. Although the actual debugging of the module is carried out by the programmer, changes to the official module in the library are made by the librarian. The use of a library is further enhanced when an online data management system is used.

Offline information is often filed in the unit development folder. The folder contains specifications, design, source code, and test results. Along with the online data management system, this procedure allows for effective program control and monitoring.

The use of a librarian has another advantage. All changes to modules in the project library are handled by one individual and are easy to monitor; they are often reviewed by the project manager before insertion. This prevents the haphazard incorporation of patches into a system and forces programmers to think carefully about each change. It also gives the manager disciplined product control and helps with audit trails.

Software Engineering Concepts and Techniques

For larger projects, a technical writer may create much of the documentation, freeing programmers for tasks at which they are most skilled.

The culmination of this trend is the chief programmer team concept developed by IBM.[13] The concept takes into account programmers' different levels of capability; the most competent programmer should perform the major work, while others function in supporting roles. As the earlier example shows, communication problems greatly reduce programmer productivity. The chief programmer team is one way of limiting this complexity.

The chief programmer, who usually has excellent programming skills, acts as the head of the team. This individual may be at least five times more productive than the lowest-level team member.[14] The chief programmer functions as the technical manager of the project, designs the system, and writes the top-level interfaces for all major modules.

Large project teams may also have an administrative manager to handle such responsibilities as allocation of time, vacations, office space, and other resources as well as reports of team progress to senior management. The administrative manager is frequently assigned to several programming teams.

The backup programmer works with and performs tasks assigned by the chief programmer. If the chief programmer leaves the project, the backup programmer assumes responsibility; therefore, the backup programmer must also be an excellent programmer. The backup programmer provides the chief programmer with a peer who can competently discuss design concepts and problems.

Two or three junior programmers are also assigned to the team to write the low-level modules defined by the chief programmer. The term junior means less experienced, not less capable. As Boehm states, the best results occur with fewer and better people.

A chief programmer team of five individuals has only seven communications paths as opposed to the 10 paths of a traditional five-member team (see Figure 4). Because the chief programmer can often produce more than the average 5,000-line quota, productivity per programmer could be greater than 5,000 lines per year instead of the original figure of 4,000.

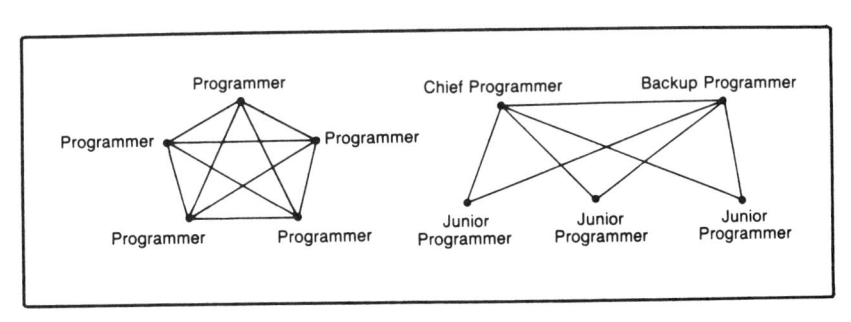

Figure 4. Traditional vs. Chief-Programmer Team Communication Paths

The team may have a librarian to manage the project library—both the on-line module library and the offline project documentation (also called the

SYSTEMS DEVELOPMENT AND PROGRAMMING

project notebook). The project notebook contains records of compilations and test runs of all modules. It is extremely important to the team structure, because all development is now accountable and open for inspection, and code is no longer the private property of any programmer.[15]

The team may include such support personnel as secretaries and technical writers, but team size should not exceed 10 members.

This structure, however, cannot solve all development problems. With fewer individuals involved, competence is crucial. Unlike a larger group situation, it is not possible to work around a nonproductive individual. When a project is extremely large, a group of 10 is simply too small to tackle development, and it should be divided into subprojects that can be handled by groups of 10 members.

Estimation Techniques. One of the most important aspects of engineering is estimating the resources needed to complete a project. Most engineering disciplines have highly developed methods of estimating resource needs. One such technique follows[16]:
1. Develop an outline of the requirements from the Request for Quotation (RFQ).
2. Gather similar information (e.g., data from similar projects).
3. Select the basic relevant data.
4. Develop estimates.
5. Make the final evaluation.

Although this approach has been advocated for software development, most software projects experience difficulty in passing step 1.[17] Because engineers have been building software systems for only 30 years, the prior experience needed to develop the true requirements may not be available. Furthermore, the developer may have little knowledge of similar systems to use in evaluation (step 2).

Developing the estimates (step 4) comprises the following tasks:
4a. Compare the project to similar previous projects.
4b. Divide the project into units and compare each unit with similar units.
4c. Schedule work and estimate resources by month.
4d. Develop standards that can be applied to the work.

It should be noted that the lack of previous experience presents a continuing problem during step 4a. In addition, an adequate set of standards does not yet exist for step 4d.

Experience is the key to accurate estimating. Even civil engineering projects may fail when established techniques are not followed. Although the Verrazano Narrows Bridge was to be the world's largest suspension bridge, its engineers had much experience with similar structures. On the other hand, the Alaskan oil pipeline was estimated to cost $900 million; by the time it went into operation, however, the cost had increased to more than $9 billion.[18] In this case, the design was altered continuously as the federal government imposed new environmental standards (i.e., changed specifications). In addition, new technologies were needed to move large quantities of oil in a cold environment. Previous experience was only minimally helpful.

Software Engineering Concepts and Techniques

Results from computer hardware reliability theory now play a role in software estimation.[19] The cumulative expenditures over time for large-scale projects have been found to agree with the equation:

$$E = K(1 - e^{-at^2})$$

where E is the total amount spent on the project during time period t, K is the total cost of the project, and a is a measure of the maximum expenditures for that time period. This relationship is usually expressed in its differential form, called a Rayleigh curve:

$$E' = 2Kate^{-at^2}$$

where E' is the rate of expenditures, or the amount spent on the project during time period t. The maximum expenditures occur just before the product is released (T_d), a time when it is usually assumed that the effort is winding down (see Figure 5).

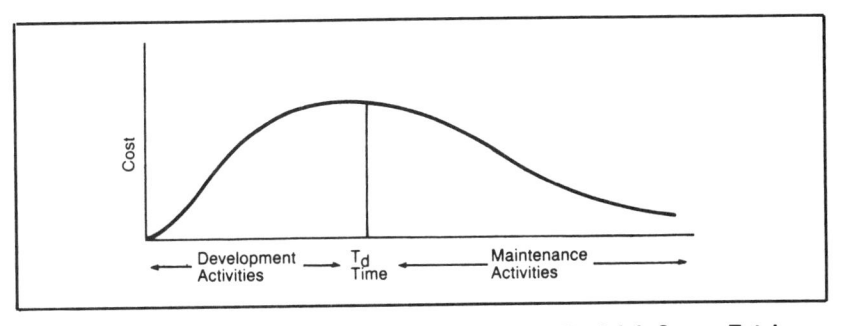

Figure 5. Rate of Expenditures Approximates the Rayleigh Curve. Total Cost (Area under Curve) = K; a = $1/T_d^2$; Rate = $2Kate^{-at^2}$

The Rayleigh curve includes two parameters, K, and a; however, a system can be described by three general characteristics: total cost, rate of expenditure, and completion date. Two of these characteristics are enough to determine the constants K and a. When a project is initiated, the proposed budget is an estimate of K, and the number of available personnel permits a to be calculated. Assuming that requirements analysis determines that these figures represent an accurate assessment of the complexity of the problem, the estimated completion date (the date when expenditures reach a maximum) can be computed and thus cannot be set arbitrarily during the requirements or specifications stage. This method provides the basis for a cost estimation strategy.[20] A mathematical theory of cost estimation that will greatly reduce the need to guess at project costs may be imminent.

Milestones. A milestone is the specification of a demonstrable event in the development of a project. Milestones are scheduled by management to measure progress. The many candidates for milestones include publication of functional specifications, writing of individual module designs, module compiling without errors, and units that have been tested successfully. Milestones should be scheduled frequently so that slippage can be detected early.

SYSTEMS DEVELOPMENT AND PROGRAMMING

PERT charts can be used to estimate the effects of slippage in one stage on later stages.

Report forms can aid in estimating when a future milestone will be reached. A general project summary describing such overall characteristics as system size, cost, completion dates, or complexity can be resubmitted with each milestone. Change reports can be submitted each time a module is altered. (When a librarian is included in the team, this type of form probably already exists.) Weekly personnel and computer reports monitor expenditures. The minor overhead they add to the project is worth the information they provide to management about the rate of progress.[21]

Development Tools. Compilers and certain debugging facilities have been available for some time. Other programming aids are new, and experience with them is less extensive. Cross-referencing, attribute listings, and symbolic storage maps are examples of such aids. Auditors or data base systems can help to control the organization of the developing system. The Problem Statement Language/Problem Statement Analyzer (PSL/PSA) of the ISDOS project of the University of Michigan is one of the first data base systems that provides a module library for storing source code and includes a language for specifying interfaces in system design that can be checked automatically.[22] RSL/SSL is a similar system that specifies requirements and designs interfaces through a data management system.[23]

An alternative approach is the programmer workbench developed by Bell Telephone Laboratories.[24] A PDP-11-based system provides a set of support routines for module development, library maintenance, documentation, and testing. Proper use of these facilities allows accessing information in a more controlled environment.

Reliability

The development of correct programs depends on verifying the correctness of the source program being produced. Formal tools are being developed in this area; meanwhile, management can do much to aid in this effort.

Conceptual Integrity. Uniformity of style and simplicity of structure are usually achieved by minimizing the number of individuals assigned to the project. A chief programmer team greatly enhances conceptual integrity.

A small group minimizes contradictory aspects of a design. In PL/1, for example, the PICTURE attribute declaration may be abbreviated as either PIC or P; in format specifications, however, it must be P.[25] In FORTRAN, the right side of an assignment statement can be an arbitrary arithmetic expression; however, DO loop indexes must be integer constants or variables, and subscripts to arrays are limited to seven basic forms.[26] These are difficult idiosyncracies to remember and illustrate a lack of conceptual integrity that can arise when many people with different objectives become involved in a project. A consistent design is less prone to errors, because the user can follow a simpler set of rules.

Continual System Validation. A walkthrough is a management review of the system under development that confirms that the system is progressing correctly or discovers errors. In one study, it was found that the cost of fixing an error at the coding stage is about twice that of fixing it at the design stage, and correcting it in testing costs about 10 times as much as it does in design.[27]

Periodically, a section of the system is selected for review, and each individual is given information about that section (e.g., a design document for a design walkthrough or code for a coding walkthrough) before the review. In attendance are the project manager (chief programmer), the person responsible for the section being reviewed, and several others knowledgeable about the project. The individual responsible for the module under review then describes it to the others.

The walkthrough is intended to detect errors, not to correct them. In addition, the walkthrough should be brief—no more than two hours. By explaining the design to others, the individual is likely to discover vague specifications or missing conditions.

An important point for management to remember is that the walkthrough is not for personnel evaluation. If the person describing the section perceives it as such, an attempt to cover up problems or present an overoptimistic description may result.

An informal yet effective validation system is code reading, or peer review. A second programmer reviews the code for each module. This technique frequently detects errors when the reader, failing to understand some aspects of the code, asks the author for an explanation.

Independent Verification and Validation (IV&V). The development group usually tests its own product. Because individuals are often reluctant to find errors in their own work, however, it has been proposed that an independent group could perform a more scrupulous review. In addition, the IV&V group would take part in the entire life cycle and could therefore find errors earlier, when correcting them would be less expensive.

In practice, independent verification and validation has indeed achieved higher reliability—at much higher costs. Fifteen to 35 percent of the original estimate must be added to development costs to carry out independent verification. Therefore, one of the intended benefits of IV&V—that of lower costs as a result of earlier error detection—has not been demonstrated in practice. It is a useful technique, however, when reliability is critical.

Measurement. Measurement, crucial to system reliability, is almost ignored by the industry. Software development data is seldom collected, and, when it is, it is rarely evaluated. It is important, however, for management control of a project.

The several areas in which data collection can aid in program development[28] include the Rayleigh curve and other resource models.[29] Program complexity is another aid. The goal is to simplify the software production process, on the assumption that simpler software is the result of a better methodology. It is difficult, however, to measure such production.

SYSTEMS DEVELOPMENT AND PROGRAMMING

To date, this research is not conclusive. The best complexity measure is still lines of code, which is extremely inaccurate. Others include the Halstead Software Science measures, which count operators and operands in the source program[30] and the McCabe cyclomatic complexity measure, which counts the regions produced from the flowchart of a program.[31] A cyclomatic complexity of less than 10 is desirable. Unfortunately, all these measures are generated from the completed source program and therefore are not applicable to predicting results during development.

Because formal certification of large classes of programs is still unattainable, techniques for estimating the validity of programs continue to be considered. One example is the error-day theory. Mills defined an error day as one error remaining undetected in a system for one day.[32] The total number of error days in a system is computed by summing the length of time that each detected error was in the system. A high error-day count may reveal many errors (poor design) or long-lived errors (poor development). Two major problems remain, however, before this measurement can be used. First, it is difficult to discover when a particular error first entered a system. Second, it may be difficult to obtain such information from the system developer.

VERIFICATION AND VALIDATION

Verifying and validating (module and integration testing) a system occupy about 50 percent of a project's development time. Many debugging aids are available to facilitate this effort; most are implemented as programs to test a feature of the system.

Automated Tools

The earliest debugging tools were the dump and the trace. A dump is a listing of the contents of main storage, which can reveal unintelligible data or errors. Unfortunately, a dump may not be taken until long after the fact when the cause of the error is no longer apparent. A trace is a printout showing the values of selected variables after each statement is executed. It also can help a programmer discover errors.

Both techniques are usually ineffective, however, because they supply a great deal of data with little or no interpretation; in addition, more advanced methods are currently available. Flowgraph analyzers, for example, detect references to variables that have not been initialized or are not reused after receiving a value; these conditions usually indicate errors.

Test data generators are also available. Assertion checkers validate that given conditions are true at indicated points of a program. Automatic verification systems have been implemented for simple languages.[33] Symbolic execution has been proposed as a practical means for validating programs written in more complex languages.

The PSL/PSA system is an example of a tool that assists in design and specification. Symbolic dumps and traces are generated with such compilers as PL/C or PLUM.[34] Many of these tools are surveyed by Ramamoorthy and Ho.[35]

Software Engineering Concepts and Techniques

Certification

Programs can be verified at several levels. Conway lists eight verification conditions:[36]

- The program contains no syntactic errors.
- The program contains neither compilation errors nor faults during program execution.
- Test data exists for which the program gives correct answers.
- For typical sets of test data, the program gives correct answers.
- For difficult sets of test data, the program gives correct answers.
- For all possible sets of data that are valid with respect to the problem specification, the program gives correct answers.
- For all possible sets of valid test data and all likely conditions of erroneous input, the program gives correct answers.
- For all possible input, the program gives correct answers.

Complete, automatic program verification may be possible in the future. Current tools operate after the fact, demonstrating that a given program works. Future tools will operate simultaneously with programming as well, helping develop programs that are correct before they are run. Such tools can greatly reduce the amount of testing required.[37]

Verification techniques share the following general structures. A program is represented by a flowchart. Each arc in the flowchart is associated with a predicate, called an assertion. If A_i is the assertion associated with an arc entering statement S, and A_j is the assertion on the arc following the statement, then the statement "If A_i is true, and if statement S is executed, then A_j is true" must be proved (see Figure 6).

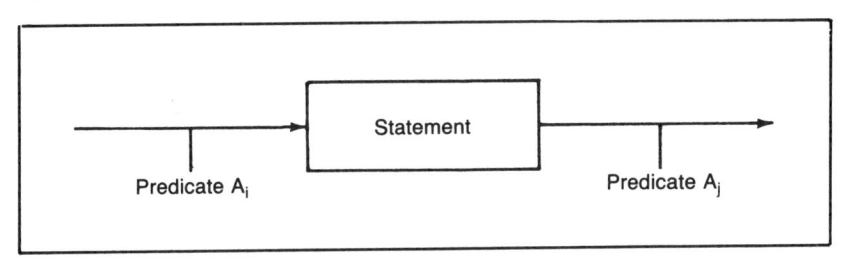

Figure 6. Assertions A_i and A_j Surround Each Statement of a Program

This process can be repeated for each statement in a program (see Figure 7). If A_1 is the assertion immediately preceding the input node to the flowchart (i.e., the initial assertion), and if A_n is the assertion at the exit node (e.g., the final assertion), then the proven statement "If A_1 is true, and the program is executed, then A_n is true" states that the program meets its specifications (A_1 and A_n). This approach was formalized by Hoare, who defined a set of axioms for determining the effects on the assertions (preconditions and postconditions) by each statement type in a language.[38] Verifying program correctness is thus reduced to proving a theorem of the predicate calculus.

Other similar models have been developed. Mills has proposed functional correctness, where the basic theorem of a program is proved as a symbolic

SYSTEMS DEVELOPMENT AND PROGRAMMING

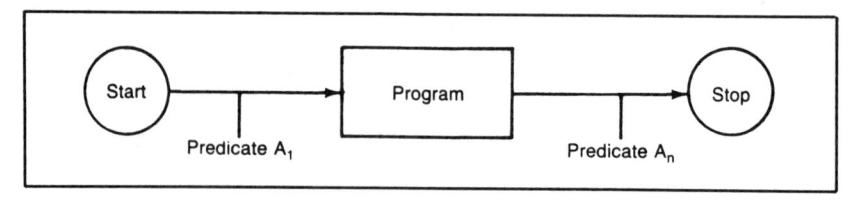

Figure 7. Predicates A$_1$ and A$_n$ Specify Input/Output Behavior of a Program

execution through the program.[39] A program is a function that transforms an input value to an output value. It is only necessary to compute that function. In addition, Dijkstra has proposed the weakest precondition as the basic construct. All of these techniques can formally verify the correctness of the source program.

Certification technique development remains in a preliminary stage and is not fully applicable to large systems. In addition, axiomatic certification is weak in that the output assertion is proved true only if the program terminates. Axiomatic methods are incapable of proving termination, which can often be proved informally by the programmer.

A typical approach to proving that program loops terminate is the following:
- Find some number P that is always nonnegative within the loop.
- Show that for each execution of the loop, P is decremented by at least some fixed amount.

If both conditions are always true, the loop must terminate before P becomes negative. A programmer who uses such rules, even informally, seldom writes nonterminating loops.

The following program fragment can be used as an example:

$$\text{DOWHILE } x < y$$
$$\ldots$$
$$x := x + 1$$
$$\ldots$$
$$\text{ENDDO}$$

Let quantity P be the expression $y-x$, and let $P(i)$ refer to the value of P during the ith execution of the loop. Because $x<y$ must be true for each subsequent iteration, $y-x$ is always nonnegative and the first condition is satisfied for each execution of the loop. The loop contains the statement $x := x + 1$; thus $P(i+1) = P(i)-1$, satisfying the second condition. The loop must therefore terminate.

Although certification will not solve all software problems, it is an important tool. As Gerhart and Yelowitz have shown, however, many published "certified" programs contain errors.[40]

Formal Testing

Goodenough and Gerhart have clarified the concepts of testing.[41] A domain is the set of permissible program input items, and a test is a subset of

Software Engineering Concepts and Techniques

the domain. A testing criterion specifies what is to be tested (e.g., specifications, all statements, all paths).

A test is complete if it meets all the requirements of the testing criterion, and a complete test is successful if the program gives correct results for each input in the test.

These definitions can help define program reliability and validity. A program is reliable if every known error is revealed by every complete test. A program is valid if every error is revealed by some complete test.

With these definitions, several important results can be proved:
- If a program is both reliable and valid, it is correct if and only if a complete test is also successful.
- The criterion "execute every path" is not valid; there exist programs for which all test sets succeed, but the wrong results are produced for some input.

Although this framework is somewhat technical and is not applicable to all programming, it is an important step toward formalizing this process.

Testing Tools

Although tools (mainly compilers) have been used for years to process source programs, they are infrequently used to test programs. Current research is investigating this area.

In general, it is not possible to verify large systems formally, so ad hoc testing is used. A programmer tries a few random tests and then informs management that the module is complete. The manager either accepts the word of the programmer and approves the module or tells the programmer to test some more. Little additional information is available for making informed decisions other than the experience of the manager and programmer. Unfortunately, this technique is predominant.

Stress testing, which is an improvement, pushes the system to its limit. For example, when an operating system is supposed to operate normally with 50 users, 50 to 60 users are put on the system to check its overload characteristics. This situation is more likely to reveal flaws. (Special hardware has been developed to simulate multiple users with predefined job streams.)

Some formal (and implementable) techniques have also been developed. Because it is impossible to test a program with every possible input, some selection criteria must be applied. One such technique is path testing—every unique path through the program is tested. Although this does not guarantee correctness, it is a fairly good sampling technique that is easy to execute. Statement coverage—executing each statement—is another simple but effective technique; frequency counts of statements executed can be made to check completeness. Symbolic execution has also been proposed to check for correctness. The program is interpreted and the symbolic expression of the output is represented as a function of the input variables.

Mean Time Between Failures

Although somewhat useful, analogies with other engineering fields must

SYSTEMS DEVELOPMENT AND PROGRAMMING

be made with care. For example, the concept of mean time between failures (MTBF) for reliability measures does not apply directly to software, although it is sometimes used as if it does.

The physical components of any system, including computer hardware, wear out: transistors fail, motors burn out, and soldered joints break. The logical components of software, however, are durable. A given program always produces the same answer for the same input, as long as the hardware does not fail. A software module "fails" when input reveals an error that was present from the beginning.

MTBF measures the time between identifications of errors; it therefore depends on the kinds of input presented. A compiler used only for short jobs may have a long MTBF; if it is suddenly used for other applications, however, its MTBF may decrease sharply as previously unused logic paths are entered. A long MTBF can therefore be interpreted only as an indication of reliability, not as proof of it.

PROGRAMMING TECHNIQUES

Several authors have mentioned that the number of lines of code produced by a programmer in a given time tends to be independent of the language used, implying that higher-level languages enhance productivity.[42] This is true, because although assembly programs are potentially more efficient, the potential is seldom realized in practice.

The goal in developing early higher-level languages was the ability to express algorithms clearly and translate them into efficient machine-language programs. The efficiency of the resulting code was all-important. This led to some anomalies in FORTRAN, arising from the structure of the IBM 704 for which it was developed (e.g., the three-way branch of the arithmetic IF). ALGOL, which was developed as a machine-independent way of expressing algorithms, contained concepts whose implementation on conventional hardware was inefficient (e.g., recursion, call-by-name); this may explain why ALGOL is not more widely used.

By the late 1960s, it was accepted that a programming language should facilitate writing programs and that the machine should be designed to create an efficient run-time environment. Currently there is a shift toward using the language to make programming and documentation easier and to produce reliable and correct software.

This does not mean, however, that efficiency is being ignored. For example, Pascal was designed to exclude constructs whose machine code is inefficient. Because hardware is less expensive than programmers, reliability has become a major factor—the programmers' tasks are made easier when the computer does more work.

Structured Programming

A major development in facilitating the programming task is structured programming. The premise of structured programming is use of a small set of simple control and data structures that have simple proof rules. A program is then built by nesting these statements. This method restricts the number of

Software Engineering Concepts and Techniques

connections between program parts, improving program comprehensibility and reliability. Although the IF-THEN-ELSE, DO-WHILE, and SEQUENCE statements are a commonly suggested set of control structures for this type of programming, they are not all inclusive.

These simple control structures help programmers certify programs, even informally. For example, a program can be represented as a function from its input data to its output data; in this case, $f(x)$ represents a segment of a program given by the following IF-THEN-ELSE statement:

$$\text{IF } p(x) \text{ THEN } g(x) \text{ ELSE } h(x)$$

Because functions g and h are simpler than function f, their specifications should be simpler. If their specifications are known, the overall function f is defined by:

$$f(x) = (p(x) \wedge g(x)) \vee (\neg p(x) \wedge h(x))$$

where $\wedge$ is read "and," $\vee$ is read "or," and $\neg$ is read "not." The programmer can thus express the formal definition of f in terms of the simpler definitions of g and h. This is the basis for the functional correctness test described previously.

Such languages as ALGOL and Pascal as well as certain subsets of PL/1 contribute to good programming practices by providing these facilities. To repair FORTRAN's lack of structure, more than 50 preprocessors for translating well-structured pseudo-FORTRAN programs into true FORTRAN have been developed.[43] An IF-THEN-ELSE is included in the FORTRAN 77 standard, although a general DO-WHILE is still missing from the language.

System Design

In top-down design, a technique related to structured programming, a programmer formulates a subroutine as a single statement; the single statement is then expanded into one or two of the basic control structures mentioned earlier. At each level the function is expanded in increasingly greater detail until the resulting description becomes the actual source language program in some programming language.

With this approach, also called stepwise refinement, the program is hierarchically structured and is described by successive refinements.[44] Each refinement is interpreted by referring to other refinements of which it is a component. Concerning this method, Wirth states:[45]

> I should like to stress that we should not be led to infer that actual program conception proceeds in such a well organized, straightforward, "topdown" manner. Later refinement steps may often show that earlier decisions are inappropriate and must be reconsidered. But this neat, nested factorization of a program serves admirably well to keep the individual building blocks intellectually manageable, to explain the program to an audience and to oneself, to raise the level of confidence in the program, and to conduct informal, and even formal proofs of correctness. The emerging modularity is particularly welcome if programs have to be adjusted to changed or extended specifications.

SYSTEMS DEVELOPMENT AND PROGRAMMING

Operating systems are often modeled as hierarchies of abstract or virtual machines.[46] At the lowest level of the system is the physical hardware. Each new level provides additional capabilities, or allowable functions on data, and hides some of the details of a lower level. For example, if one level accesses the paging hardware of the computer and provides a large virtual storage for all other processes, abstract machines at higher levels can be implemented as if they had unlimited storage, because this detail is controlled by a lower level.

The concept of a program design language (PDL) to aid in this development has been described.[47] This type of language contains two structures: an outer syntax of basic statement types (e.g., IF-THEN-ELSE, DO-WHILE, and SEQUENCE) for connecting components, and an inner syntax that corresponds to the application being designed. The inner syntax is English-statement-oriented, and is expanded, step by step, until it expresses the algorithm in a programming language.

Figure 8 is an example of a PDL design in which the inner syntax is enclosed in special comment brackets. This technique allows for processing the PDL to check interfaces while permitting a range of design options.

```
max: PROCEDURE( [list to find max from] );
       /* Find maximum element in list */
       DECLARE (maximum, next) integer;
       DECLARE list [array of integers];
       maximum = [first element of list];
       DO WHILE( [more elements in list] );
              next = [next element in list];
              maximum = [max(maximum,next)];
       END;
       RETURN(maximum);
       END max;
```

Figure 8. PDL of a Program to Find the Largest Element in a List

It should be noted that PSL/PSA and PDL complement each other. PSL/PSA is a specification tool that validates correct data use between two modules (interfaces). PDL is useful for describing a given module at any level of detail. Both PSL/PSA and PDL can contribute to the success of a large project.

Although designed from the top down, many systems are implemented from the bottom up. Low-level routines are first coded with drivers to test them; new modules using these low-level routines are then added, and the system is built up.

Top-down development is another technique for implementing hierarchically structured programs. The top-level routines are written first, along with stubs—substitutes for lower-level routines—to interface with them. The stubs return control after printing a simple message and sometimes returning fixed sample test values. The stub is eventually replaced by the full module that includes calls to other stubs; the entire system is gradually developed.

If used carefully, this technique can be valuable; the system's correctness is only assumed, however, not proved, until the last stub has been replaced by the actual module.[48] The documentation specifies the assumptions on each stub. For example:

$$f(x) = \text{IF } p(x) \text{ THEN } g(x) \text{ ELSE } h(x)$$

is a program fragment calling stubs g and h; f is correct only if the modules eventually replacing the stubs g and h are correct.

Top-down development allows users to see the top-level interfaces in the system early, when changes can be made relatively easily. Another approach with the same goal is iterative enhancement.[49] This technique calls for the design and implementation of a subset of the problem first, giving the user a warning system early in the life cycle when changes are easier to make. This process is repeated to develop successively larger subsets until the final product is delivered.

Brooks believes that the first version of a system is always discarded because the concrete specifications for a system are often not defined until the system is completed, and the initial product frequently fails to meet the final specifications.[50] It is often faster and less costly to rebuild a system completely than to try to modify an existing product to meet these specifications. A developer may deliver such a modified system as a prerelease, however, if a deadline is near and the user is demanding results. The user suffers with this version, replete with errors, until it can be discarded or rebuilt. Iterative enhancement can facilitate rebuilding, because the system, although it does not meet all the requirements, is operable early in the development cycle.

PERFORMANCE ISSUES

The chosen algorithms and data structures have a far greater influence on program performance than code optimization or the programming language. Before choosing an algorithm, the programmer faces these questions:
- Can previously written software be used?
- If a new module must be written, what algorithms and data structures will provide an efficient solution?

Many programming languages include mathematical functions (e.g., sine, logarithm, and square root) in their standard software package subroutine libraries. Such modules are usually written for general functions. For efficient programs, more specific algorithms are often required. Working from the more general code, the programmer can easily develop these algorithms. The more specific algorithms can then be evaluated and installed in the subroutine library if they are considered generally useful.

Difficulties with this procedure include:
- Identifying which standard algorithms to package—This is easier in such mathematical areas as statistical testing, integration, differentiation, and matrix computations than in such nonnumerical areas as business applications.
- Transporting and interfacing with packaged software—Some progress has been made with programs stored in read-only memories that plug into microprocessors and with interface processors on computer net-

SYSTEMS DEVELOPMENT AND PROGRAMMING

works. A major problem area is interfacing software directly to other software; no conventions yet exist for constricting such an interface. Some help is afforded by such concepts as the pipe in UNIX, which provides a general communications channel between programs.[51]

Algorithm Analysis

The evaluation of a particular algorithm's efficiency usually includes the following type of analysis. A formula is calculated that describes the cost of executing that algorithm relative to the number of input items. For example, an algorithm to add n numbers is $O(N)$ [read: on the order of N], that is, directly proportional to n. A linear search for an unsorted array is $O(N/2)$; a binary search is $O(\log N)$.

Many practical problems (e.g., job scheduling) involve several combinations of alternative possibilities and selection of the optimum solution. In these cases, it may be better to restrict the search to finding an acceptable—as opposed to the best—solution. (For a discussion of these issues and a survey of algorithm analysis, see reference 20.)

Efficiency

In many cases, the results of algorithmic analysis are not extensive enough to help the programmer, and several other techniques are needed to assist in location and removal of sources of inefficiency. One such tool is an optimizing compiler, which, for some languages, can yield significant improvements.[52] The value of such tools, however, is limited[53] and can be realized only for programs that are used often enough to justify the investment in optimization.

One of the most powerful aids is the frequency histogram, which reveals how often each statement of a program is executed. It is not unusual to find that 10 percent of the statements account for 80 percent of the execution time.[54] A programmer who concentrates on these bottlenecks in the algorithms can realize significant performance improvements with minimum investment. This technique has been used in some interactive operating systems (e.g., UNIX and MULTICS), which began as high-level-language operating systems. Bottlenecks have been replaced by assembly language routines in less than 20 percent of these systems.

THEORY OF SPECIFICATIONS

The objective of system specifications, an area of software engineering now under study, is to describe specifications early in the life cycle with a metalanguage. This places restrictions on the design and may later help establish whether the specifications have been met.

An example of such a specification is structured programming, which restricts the form of statements a programmer may use; this restriction contributes to comprehensibility and allows proof of program correctness.[55]

Formal theories are also being developed in the area of data abstraction, which uses concepts of levels of abstraction, information hiding, and module interfacing to restrict access to the internal structure of data. Parnas formalized these ideas, which were already being used by expert programmers.[56] He defines data as a collection of logical objects, each with a set of allowable states. With this definition, procedures can be written to hide the representation of these objects inside separate modules. The user manipulates the objects by calling the special procedures.

Several languages that incorporate these concepts have been developed (e.g, Euclid[57], CLU[58], and Alphard[59]). These languages permit programmers to define abstract data types that are able to encapsulate the representation of logical objects.[60] When concurrency is an issue, the use of abstract objects must be controlled by synchronization (e.g., locks or signals); in this case the abstract type managers are called monitors.

Ada is the first commercial language to include data abstraction concepts, called packages.[61] Each package comprises a specification part, consisting of the data objects and function names known outside the package, and a body part, consisting of the details of the source programs. Other packages know only of the package's specification part.

A programmer first defines the package's specification part and places it in the system library. Other programmers can refer to this specification to build other packages. The programmer later can build the body of the package. As long as the specification does not change, the body of the package can be altered. Reliability is enhanced, because the programmer cannot inadvertently use the details of another package.

Another kind of specification consists of higher-order software axioms, six axioms that specify allowable interactions among processes in a real-time system.[62] One axiom prohibits a process from controlling its own execution, thus eliminating recursion in a design. Another axiom states that no module should control its own input data space, making it impossible for a module to alter its input variables. Although these axioms are not complete, they represent an important first step in formalizing specifications for system design.

HARDWARE TRENDS

The development of the powerful microprocessor is rapidly changing the software development world. A personal workstation—a 16-bit microprocessor with an instruction time of less than $1\mu sec$, 1M bytes of main storage, almost 100M bytes of disk storage, a high-resolution-graphics terminal, a high-speed communications network interface, and such software as the UNIX operating system with Pascal—can be purchased for about $25,000. Previous surveys have estimated that mainframe hardware expenses per programmer are also about $25,000. The cost of workstations is therefore comparable to traditional mainframe systems.

A personal workstation, however, offers many advantages, including:
- Reliability is much higher when 40 programmers have their own machines rather than sharing a single $1 million processor.
- Response time is not degraded by the load.
- Programmers no longer need physical proximity to the mainframe to avoid high communications costs.

Applying this technology is a new research area. The integrated environ-

SYSTEMS DEVELOPMENT AND PROGRAMMING

ment is one such application. The programmer builds and debugs a program using a tabletop system. It is estimated that a 1M-byte machine can be used to build and interpretively execute a 20,000-line Pascal program. The need to build compilers rather than interpreters may be obsolete except for the most complex calculations requiring the utmost speed of execution.

Syntax-directed editors are an example of how the speed and capability of the computer can be used to aid the programmer. Instead of a standard text editor, the programmer uses a special editor that knows the system. When an IF statement is to be added to a program, typing "IF" causes the following to be displayed:

```
        IF <expression> THEN
            <statement>
        ELSE
            <statement>
```

Source code can thus be developed much more rapidly. This concept is the design basis of such systems as CPS.[63]

High-resolution graphics and artificial intelligence techniques are used for such systems as the Xerox Palo Alto Research Center Smalltalk. This system is an attempt to merge operating system, language, and testing features into one integrated system using the power of the microprocessor. These systems, however, are still in their infancy.

Japanese engineers are using this technology for their fifth-generation architecture.[64] Because the Japanese written language consists of several thousand characters, translation of a requirements document from Japanese into a computer design using Roman letters poses additional software design considerations.

It is not surprising, therefore, that artificial intelligence techniques are critical to fifth-generation architecture. The goal is to build a Prolog engine with advanced hardware and VLSI technology and then work on such issues as character and voice recognition and automatic translation.

The project is of significant interest to U.S. computer manufacturers, considering the impact of Japanese competition on the domestic automobile and electronics industries. Although the fifth-generation computer is unlikely to be built by its 1990 target, the concerted effort and funding should generate interesting research.

In the United States, the Software Technology Initiative, a Department of Defense project with similar goals, is scheduled to start at the end of 1983.[65] This project, which will provide several hundred million dollars to improve software productivity by an order of magnitude within the next decade, should spur research of practical value to the industry.

ACTION PLAN

Many techniques have been proposed to aid in software development; however, a recent survey of U.S. and Japanese industry revealed that the level of tool use was uniformly low. Organizations still do not value tools as a productivity aid.[66] Although compilers are generally used, program design languages are the only new developments that have been incorporated as standard tools, and they are often used without a processor to format and analyze the text. Design reviews and walkthroughs are common; in one location, however, 13 of the 33 subjects discussed during the walkthrough were items that could have been processed easily by a computer tool.

Accepting the change in hardware configuration (from large centralized mainframes to distributed workstations) will be a major test of management in the near future. The other critical factor is the management of people. As Boehm recommended several years ago, the computer programming manager should perform the following steps.[67]

Use a Sequential Life-cycle Plan. A software life cycle like that outlined in earlier sections of this chapter should be followed. This allows for feedback that updates previous life-cycle phases as the consequences of previous decisions become known. It also encourages milestones to measure progress.

Perform Continuous Validation. Each new refinement of a module should be certified. Walkthroughs and code reading should be used. The hierarchical structure of the system should be clear in all documentation.

Maintain Disciplined Product Control. All output of a project—design documents, source code, and user documentation—should be formally approved. Changes to documents and program libraries must be strictly monitored and audited. Code reading, project reporting forms, a staffed development library, and a project notebook all contribute to this goal.

Use Enhanced Top-Down Structured Programming. PL/1 and Pascal offer suitable control and data structures. Preprocessors exist that augment FORTRAN for these structures. In Ada, packages should be used. Description techniques (e.g., stepwise refinement, nested data abstractions, and data flow networks) should be utilized.

Maintain Clear Accountability. Milestones should be used to measure progress; a project notebook can aid in monitoring each individual's efforts.

Use Better and Fewer People. The chief programmer team, in which individuals are accountable for their own actions, aids in this effort.

Maintain Commitment to Improve the Process. Although progress has been made in understanding how large-scale software systems are built, the process is far from perfected. Costly mistakes are no longer tolerable when systems are so large and so much depends on them. Management aids must be improved and project control techniques developed. Software management will become even more like that of other engineering disciplines if its practitioners exercise the patience necessary to gain the experience on which future theories can rely.

SYSTEMS DEVELOPMENT AND PROGRAMMING

References
1. Nauer, P., and Randall, D. "Software Engineering." NATO Scientific Conference. Brussels: 1968.
2. "Everything About the Narrows Bridge is Big, Bigger, or Biggest." *Engineering News Record.* Vol. 166, (June 1961), pp. 24–28; "Narrows Bridge Opens to Traffic." *Engineering News Record*, Vol. 173, (November 1964), p. 33.
3. Brooks, F.P. *The Mythical Man-Month.* Reading MA: Addison-Wesley Publishing Co, 1975.
4. Fife, D. *Computer Software Management: A Primer for Project Management and Quality Control.* National Bureau of Standards, Institute of Computer Sciences and Technology, Special Publications, April 1977.
5. Boehm, B., McClean, R., and Urfrig, D. "Some Experience with Automated Aids to the Design of Large Scale Reliable Software." *Proceedings of the 1975 ACM International Conference on Reliable Software*, New York, 1975.
6. Hamilton, M., and Zeldin, S. "Higher Order Software—A Methodology for Defining Software." *IEEE Transactions on Software Engineering.* Vol. 2, No. 1 (March 1976), pp. 9–32.
7. Carlson, W.E. "Ada: A Promising Beginning." *IEEE Computer.* Vol. 14, No. 6 (June 1981), pp. 13–16.
8. Gerhart, S., and Yelowitz, L. "Observations of Fallibility in Applications of Modern Programming Methodologies." *IEEE Transactions on Software Engineering.* Vol. 2, No. 3 (September 1976), pp. 195–207.
9. Huang, J.C. "An Approach to Program Testing." *Computing Surveys*, Vol. 7, No. 3 (September 1975), pp. 113–128.
10. Denning, P.J. "A Hard Look at Structured Programming." *Infotech State of the Art Report on Structured Programming.* Maidenhead UK: Infotech International Ltd, 1976.
11. Parnas, D.L. "The Influence of Software Structure on Reliability." *Proceedings of 1975, International Reliable Software,* 1975, (ACM SIF-PLAN Notices, Vol. 10, No. 6 June 1975).
12. Wolverton, R.W. "The Cost of Developing Large Scale Software." *IEEE Transactions on Computers*, Vol. 23, No. 6 (1974), pp. 615–636.
13. Baker, F.T. "Chief Programmer Team Management of Production Programming." *IBM Systems Journal*, Vol. 11, No. 1 (1972), pp. 56–73.
14. Boehm, B. "Seven Basic Principles of Software Engineering." *Infotech State of the Art Report on Software Engineering Techniques.* Maidenhead UK: Infotech International Ltd, 1977.
15. Weinberg, G.M. *The Psychology of Computer Programming.* New York: Van Nostrand Reinhold, 1971.
16. Gallagher, P.F. *Project Estimating by Engineering Methods.* New York: Hayden Book Co, 1965.
17. Wolverton, pp. 615–636.
18. "Alaskan Pipe Cost Probe Hits Snag." *Engineering News Record*, Vol. 198 (April 1977), p. 14.
19. Putnam, L., and Wolverton, R. *Quantitative Management: Software Cost Estimating.* New York: IEEE Computer Society, 1977.
20. Basili, V., and Zelkowitz, M. "Analyzing Medium Scale Software Development." *Proceedings of the Third International Conference on Software Engineering,* 1978.
21. Basili, V., and Zelkowitz, M. "Analyzing Medium Scale Software Development"; Walston, C.E., and Felix, C.P. "A Method of Programming Measurements and Estimation." *IBM Systems Journal*, Vol. 16, No. 1 (1977), pp. 54–73.
22. Teichroew, D., and Hershey, E.A. "PSL/PSA: A Computer Aided Technique for Structured Documentation and Analysis of Information Processing Systems." *IEEE Transactions on Software Engineering*, Vol. 3, No. 1 (1977), pp. 41–48.
23. Davis, C.G., and Vick, C.R. "The Software Development System." *IEEE Transactions on Software Engineering*, Vol. 3, No. 1 (January 1977), pp. 69–84.
24. Dolotta, T.A., and Mashey, J.R. "An Introduction to the Programmer's Workbench." *Proceedings of the Second International Conference on Software Engineering,* 1976.
25. *American Standard PL/1.* American National Standards Institute, x.53-1976, August 1976.
26. *American Standard FORTRAN.* American National Standards Institute, x3.9-1966, March 1966.
27. Boehm, B. "Seven Basic Principles of Software Engineering."
28. *Collected Software Engineering Papers: Volume I.* NASA GSFC Software Engineering Laboratory (July 1982).
29. Boehm, B. *Software Engineering Economics.* Englewood Cliffs NJ: Prentice-Hall Inc, 1981.
30. Halstead, M. *Elements of Software Science.* New York: Elsevier North Holland Inc, 1977.
31. McCabe, T.J. *New Approach to Structured Testing.* IEEE Computer Society, 1983.
32. Mills, H.D. "Software Development." *IEEE Transactions on Software Engineering,* Vol. 2, No. 4 (1976), pp. 265–273.
33. King, J.C. "A Program Verifier," PhD Dissertation, Computer Science Dept, Pittsburgh PA: Carnegie-Mellon University, 1969.
34. Conway, R., and Wilcox, T. "Design and Implementation of a Diagnositc Compiler for PL/1." *Communications of the ACM*, Vol. 16, No. 3 (March 1973), pp. 169–179; Zelkowitz, M.V. "Third Generation Compiler Design." *ACM National Computer Conference.* New York, 1975, pp. 253–258.

35. Ramamoorthy, C.V., and Ho, S.F. "Testing Large Software with Automated Software Evaluation Systems." *IEEE Transactions on Software Engineering*. Vol. 1, No. 1 (1975), pp. 46–58.
36. Conway, R. *A Primer on Disciplined Programming*. Cambridge MA: Winthrop Publishers, 1978.
37. Dijkstra, E. *A Discipline of Programming*. Englewood Cliffs NJ: Prentice Hall Inc, 1976.
38. Hoare, C.A.R. "An Axiomatic Basis for Computer Programming." *Communications of the ACM*, Vol. 12, No. 10 (October 1969), pp. 576–580, 583.
39. Dunlop, D.D., and Basili, V.R. "A Comparative Analysis of Functional Correctness." *ACM Computing Surveys*, Vol. 14, No. 2, (June 1982), pp. 229–244.
40. Gerhart, S., and Yelowitz, L. "Observations of Fallibility in Applications of Modern Programming Methodologies." *IEEE Transactions on Software Engineering*, Vol. 2, No. 3 (September 1976), pp. 195–207.
41. Goodenough, J.B., and Gerhart, S. "Toward a Theory of Test Data Selection." *IEEE Transactions on Software Engineering*. Vol. 1, No. 2 (June 1975), pp. 156–173.
42. Brooks, F.P. *The Mythical Man-Month*. Reading MA: Addison-Wesley, 1975; Halstead, M. *Elements of Software Science*. New York: Elsevier North Holland Inc, 1977.
43. Reifer, D.J. "The Structured FORTRAN Dilemma." *SIGPLAN Notices*, Vol. 11, No. 2 (1976), pp. 30–32.
44. Wirth, N. "Program Development by Stepwise Refinement." *Communications of the ACM*, Vol. 14, No. 4 (April 1971), pp. 221–227; Wirth, N. "On the Composition of Well-Structured Programs." *Computing Surveys*, Vol. 6, No. 4 (December 1974), pp. 247–259.
45. Wirth, pp. 247–259.
46. Hansen, P. Brinch. *Architectures of Concurrent Programs*. Englewood Cliffs NJ: Prentice Hall Inc, 1977.
47. Caine, S.H., and Gordon, E.K. "PDL—A Tool for Software Design." *Proceedings 1975 AFIPS National Computer Conference*, Vol. 44, Montvale NJ: AFIPS Press, pp. 271–276.
48. Denning, P.J. "A Hard Look at Structured Programming." *Infotech State-of-the-Art Report on Structured Programming*. Maidenhead, UK: Infotech International Ltd, (1976), pp. 183–202.
49. Basili, V., and Turner, A.J. "Interative Enhancement: A Practical Technique for Software Development." Pennsauken NJ: AUERBACH Publishers Inc, 1978.
50. Brooks, *The Mythical Man-Month*.
51. Ritchie, D.M., and Thompson, K. "The UNIX Time-Sharing System." *Communications of the ACM*, Vol. 17, No. 7 (July 1974), pp. 365–375.
52. Weide, B. "A Survey of Analysis Techniques for Discrete Algorithms." *Computing Surveys*, Vol. 9, No. 4 (December 1977), pp. 291–313.
53. Lowry, E.S., and Medlock, C.W. "Object Code Optimization." *Communications of the ACM*, Vol. 12, No. 1 (January 1969), pp. 13–22.
54. Knuth, D. "An Empirical Study of FORTRAN Programs." *Software Practice and Experience*, Vol. 1, No. 2, (1971), pp. 105–133.
55. Dijkstra, E. "GOTO Statement Considered Harmful." *Communications of the ACM*, Vol. 11, No. 3 (March 1968), pp. 147–148; Knuth, D. "Structured Programming with Statements." *Computing Surveys*, Vol. 6, No. 4, (December 1974), pp. 261–301.
56. Parnas, D.L. "On the Criteria for Decomposing Systems into Modules." *Communications of the ACM*, Vol. 15, No. 12 (December 1972), pp. 1,053–1,058.
57. Popek, G.J., Horning, J.J., Lampson, B.W., Mitchell, J.G., and London, R.L. "Notes on the Design of EUCLID." *Proceedings of the ACM Conference on Language Design for Reliable Software*, New York, 1977, pp. 11–18.
58. Liskov, B., et al. "Abstraction Mechanisms in CLU." *Communications of the ACM*, Vol. 20, No. 8 (August 1977), pp. 564–576.
59. Wulf, W., London, R., and Shaw, M. "An Introduction to the Construction and Verification of ALPHARD Programs." *IEEE Transactions on Software Engineering*, Vol. 2, No. 4 (1976), pp. 253–264.
60. Liskov, B., and Zilles, S. "Specification Techniques for Data Abstractions." *IEEE Transactions on Software Engineering*, Vol. 1, No. 1 (1975), pp. 9–19.
61. LeBlanc, and Goda, J.J. "Ada and Software Development: A New Concept in Language Design." *IEEE Computer*, Vol. 15, No. 5, (May 1982), pp. 75–82.
62. Hamilton, M., and Zeldin, S. "Higher Order Software—A Methodology for Defining Software." *IEEE Transactions on Software Engineering*, Vol. 2, No. 1 (March 1976), pp. 9–32.
63. Teitelbaum, T., and Reps, T. "The Cornell Program Synthesizer—A Syntax-Directed Programming Environment. *Communications of the ACM*, Vol. 24, No. 9, (September 1981), pp. 563–573.
64. Moto-oka, T. *Fifth-Generation Computer Systems*. North Holland Publishing Co, 1982.
65. Martin, E. "Strategy for DoD Software Initiative." *IEEE Computer*, Vol. 16, No. 3, (March 1983), pp. 52–59.
66. Zelkowitz, M.V., et al. *Software Productivity Survey of Industry* (in press).
67. Boehm, B., et al. "Seven Basic Principles of Software Engineering." *Infotech State of the Art Report on Software Engineering Techniques*. Maidenhead U.K.: Infotech International Ltd, 1977.

SYSTEMS DEVELOPMENT AND PROGRAMMING

Bibliography

Aho, A., and Ullman, J. *Theory of Parsing, Translation, and Compiling.* Englewood Cliffs NJ: Prentice Hall Inc, 1972.

Basili, V., and Turner, A.J. "Iterative Enhancement: A Practical Technique for Software Development." *IEEE Transactions on Software Engineering,* Vol. 1, No. 4 (1975), pp. 390–396.

Caine, S.H., and Gordon, E.K. "PDL—A Tool for Software Design." *Proceedings of 1975 AFIPS National Conference.* Montvale NJ: AFIPS Press, 1975.

Conway, R. *A Primer on Disciplined Programming.* Cambridge MA: Winthrop Publishers, 1978.

Conway, R., and Wilcox, T. "Design and Implementation of a Diagnostic Compiler for PL/1." *Communications of the ACM,* Vol. 16, No. 3 (March 1973), pp.169–179.

Cooley, J.M., and Tukey, J.W. "An Algorithm for the Machine Calculation of Complex Fourier Series." *Mathematics Computation,* Vol. 19, No. 90 (1965), pp. 299-301.

Denning, P.J. "Fault Tolerant Operating Systems." *Computing Surveys,* Vol. 8, No. 4 (December 1976), pp. 359-389.

Dijkstra, E. "GOTO Statement Considered Harmful." *Communications of the ACM,* Vol. 11, No. 3 (March 1968), pp. 147–148.

Dijkstra, E. *Discipline of Programming.* Englewood Cliffs NJ: Prentice-Hall Inc, 1976.

Goodenough, S., and Gerhart, S. "Toward a Theory of Test Data Selection." *IEEE Transactions on Software Engineering,* Vol. 1, No. 2 (June 1975), pp. 156–173.

Hansen, P. Brinch. *Architecture on Concurrent Programs.* Englewood Cliffs NJ: Prentice-Hall Inc. 1977.

Hoare, C.A.R. "An Axiomatic Basis for Computer Programming." *Communications of the ACM,* Vol. 12, No. 10 (October 1969), pp. 576–580, 583.

Jeffery, S., and Linden, T. "Software Engineering is Engineering." *IEEE Computer Science and Engineering Curricula Workshop.* New York: IEEE, 1977.

King, J.C. "A Program Verifier." PhD Dissertation. Pittsburgh PA: Computer Science Department, Carnegie-Mellon University, 1969.

Knuth, D. "An Empirical Study of FORTRAN Programs." *Software: Practice & Experience,* Vol. 1, No. 2 (1971), pp. 105–133.

Knuth, D. "Structured Programming with Statements." *Computing Surveys,* Vol. 6, No. 4 (December 1974), pp. 261–301.

Liskov, B., and Zilles, S. "Specification Techniques for Data Abstractions." *IEEE Transactions on Software Engineering,* Vol. 1, No. 1 (1975), pp. 9–19.

Liskov, B., Snyder, A., Atkinson, R., and Schaffert, C. "Abstraction Mechanisms in CLU." *Communications of the ACM,* Vol. 20, No. 8 (August 1977), pp. 564–576.

Lowry, E.S., and Medlock, C.W. "Object Code Optimization." *Communications of the ACM,* Vol 12, No. 1 (January 1969), pp. 13–22.

Mills, H.D. "Software Development." *IEEE Transactions on Software Engineering,* Vol. 2, No. 4 (1976), pp. 265-273.

Parnas, D.L. "On the Criteria for Decomposing Systems Into Modules." *Communications of the ACM,* Vol. 15, No. 12 (December 1972), pp. 1,053–1,058.

Popek, G.J., Horning, J.J., Lampson, B.W., Mitchell, J.G., and London, R.L. "Notes on the Design of EUCLID." *Proceedings of 1977 ACM Conference on Language Design for Reliable Software.* New York, 1977.

Ramamoorthy, C.V., and Ho, S.F. "Testing Large Software with Automated Software Evaluation Systems." *IEEE Transactions on Software Engineering,* Vol. 1, No. 1 (1975), pp. 46–58.

Reifer, D.J. "The Structured FORTRAN Dilemma." *SIGPLAN Notices,* Vol. 11, No. 2 (1976), pp. 30–32.

Ritchie, D.M., and Thompson, K. "The UNIX Time-Sharing System." *Communications of the ACM,* Vol. 17, No. 7 (July 1974), pp. 365–375.

Weide, B. "A Survey of Analysis Techniques for Discrete Algorithms." *Computing Surveys,* Vol. 9, No. 4 (December 1977), pp. 291–313.

Wirth, N. "Program Development by Stepwise Refinement." *Communications of the ACM,* Vol. 14, No. 4 (April 1971), pp. 221–227.

Wirth, N. "On the Composition of Well-Structured Programs." *Computing Surveys,* Vol. 6, No. 4 (December 1974) pp. 247–259.

Wulf, W., London, R., and Shaw, M. "An Introduction to the Construction and Verification of ALPHARD Programs." *IEEE Transactions on Software Engineering,* Vol. 2, No. 4 (1976), pp. 253–264.

Younger, D., "Recognition and Parsing of Context-Free Languages in time n**3." *Information Control,* Vol. 10, No.2 (1967), pp. 189–208.

Zelkowitz, M.V. "Third Generation Compiler Design." *Proceedings of 1975 ACM National Computer Conference.* New York, 1975.

IV-8
Preparing for a System Cost/Benefit Analysis
Louis Fried

INTRODUCTION

The value of information is determined by accuracy, quantity, timeliness, and effect; quality information can be conceptualized as the balance between its value and cost. Each aspect, however, is difficult to assess objectively. This chapter defines information aspects and provides a method of evaluating their requirements in light of a proposed system. (Chapter IV-9 outlines how to perform a cost/benefit analysis of a system design for this information.)

DETERMINING INFORMATION VALUE

Cost and Quality

The value and quality of information do not always increase proportionally. For example, information quality may be improved by a faster processing speed; however, implementing an online fixed assets depreciation system with inquiry capability, would not increase the value of such information when depreciation is reported monthly. Beyond a certain point, the value of information becomes less responsive to increases in quality (see Figure 1).

Similarly, the relationship of quality and cost is not constant. At the lower level, relatively small investments can gain substantial improvements in information quality. In complex, highly sophisticated systems, large sums spent on further improvements can gain relatively small increases in quality.

Each level of quality represents a different set of specifications. Given an available technology, the most efficient set of specifications would produce a curve like that in Figure 2. The efficiency frontier represents the set of systems that provide each level of quality at the lowest cost. For any level of efficiency, cost rises with increased quality.

Although the curves comparing value to quality and cost to quality are generalizations (it would be difficult to guarantee their validity based on estimates for a proposed application), they can be superimposed to determine the range of optimum quality (see Figure 3). Within this range, the point at which the slope of the value curve matches that of the cost curve identifies the design configuration for a system that maximizes net benefits. The opti-

SYSTEMS DEVELOPMENT AND PROGRAMMING

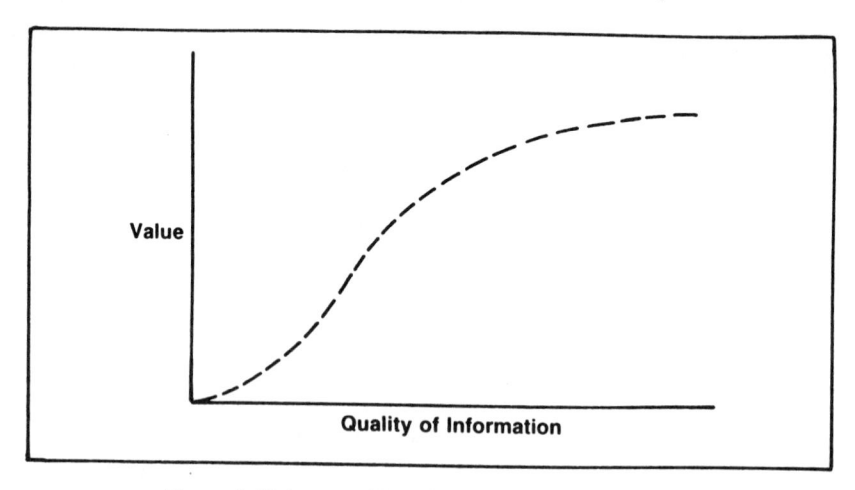

Figure 1. Value as a Function of Information Quality

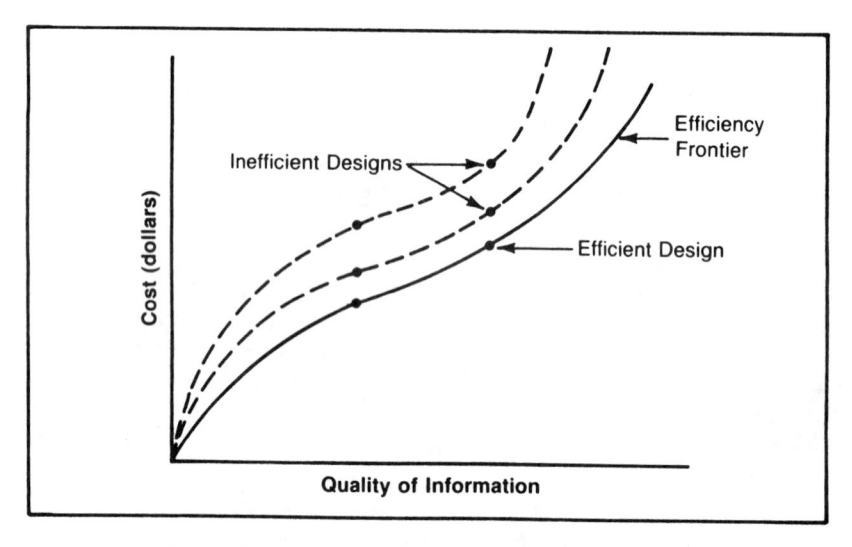

Figure 2. Cost as a Function of Information Quality

mum system does not provide every piece of useful information; unfulfilled information requirements—those that cost more to satisfy than they contribute in benefits—are inevitable.

Cost and Technological Advances

Consideration should also be given to the fact that costs respond to technological advances. During the past 30 years of information processing, each generation of computers has reduced the cost per element of processed data. Both hardware and software advances have not only lowered processing costs but have provided new levels of capability and capacity.

Preparing for Cost/Benefit Analysis

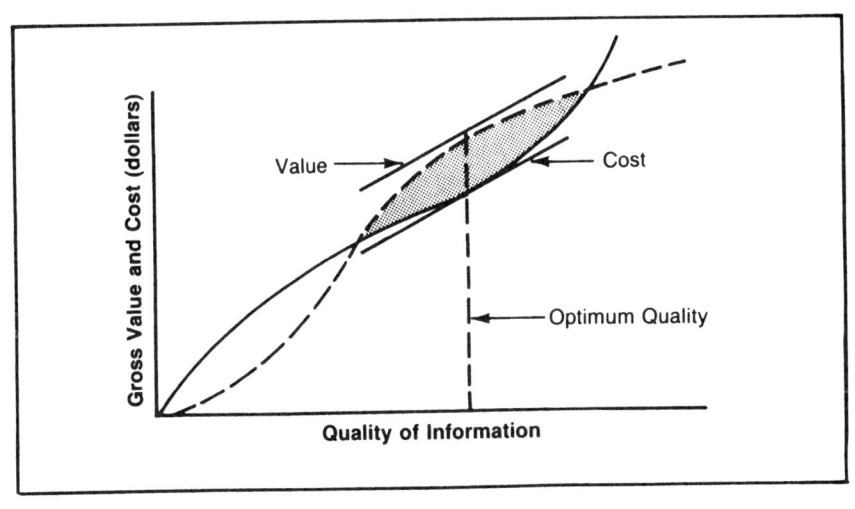

Figure 3. Determining the Optimum System

Responses to technological advances vary. In the simplest approach, an organization lowers the cost of processing only by converting the present system to the new technology. In terms of the cost/value concept, this method would simply shift the cost curve to the right, leaving the value curve unchanged (assuming the information value remains constant, since the system was not modified).

The system could also be redesigned to include the capabilities provided by the new technology. Because this approach can enhance the information value as well as reduce the processing cost, the resulting optimum system design (the point at which net benefits are maximized) would be at a higher level of quality.

Accuracy of Information

One common justification of DP systems has been information accuracy. There are various degrees of accuracy, however. In addition, improved accuracy implies increased costs for such operational areas as:
- Error detection routines in programs
- Collection and maintenance of redundant information for error detection and correction
- Externally maintained controls
- Hardware devices for increasing input accuracy
- Internal program-to-program run controls
- Redundant processing
- Extensive program testing and validation
- Rigid and extensive program-change control procedures

Because the value of accuracy differs according to purpose, the amount spent on each of these activities should be consistent with the level of accuracy required by the system.

Establishing a program for computing results to three decimal places is futile if the input is reliable only to one decimal place; in addition, the user

SYSTEMS DEVELOPMENT AND PROGRAMMING

could be misled to assume the validity of the apparent level of accuracy. The reliability of available input should dictate the level of accuracy designed into processing functions; reports should never imply an accuracy that does not exist. Accuracy, therefore, should be the closest representation of fact. The quality of decisions based on information presented to a user depend on how closely that information parallels reality.

Operating activities (e.g., payroll, check reconciliation, purchasing, invoicing) generally require higher levels of accuracy than administrative activities. In comparison, a lower accuracy level is expected in inventory and shop floor control systems, in systems that include periodic verification (e.g., replanning of the work flow) as part of the ongoing system, and in those resulting in regular file replacement or validation. Because they are often summarized and rounded to the nearest thousand dollars, monthly reports to top management can include another level of accuracy. Still another level should be anticipated for such demographic studies as market surveys, opinion polls, and censuses. Thus, the rule for determining the degree of accuracy required is: The cost of operating a system is unnecessarily increased by specifying levels of accuracy beyond those actually valid or usable.

Quantity of Information

The value and content of information are directly proportional. Information that is already known is redundant and worthless. Information that confirms expectations increases in value. Relevant information, which illuminates the unexpected or previously unknown is the most valuable.

Timeliness of Information

The elements of speed in data processing are the frequency of updating the information and the frequency of reporting, or responding to user needs. It would be costly to assume that these two elements are automatically linked. Applications may require quick updating and retrieval, quick retrieval only, or neither. For example, the need for online updating and response is readily justifiable in such applications as airline reservation and process control systems. Some inventory and production-control applications that process high volumes may require online updating and response to avoid stock-outs while minimizing inventory size. In many such applications, it is sufficient to provide overnight updating with online inquiry or overnight updating and reporting.

Response speed dictates that the processing method chosen may vary in cost. Although sequential batch processing may be inexpensive, a demand for faster response time and an increased frequency of processing can make this method burdensome and costly. The next steps would be indexed sequential processing and, if response time is reduced to the minimum (online inquiry), a random processing approach. A comparison of the costs of these methods is illustrated in Figure 4.

Extent of Automation

A final consideration in the cost/value trade-off is the amount of an application that should be automated. Generally, 80 percent of the benefit can be

Preparing for Cost/Benefit Analysis

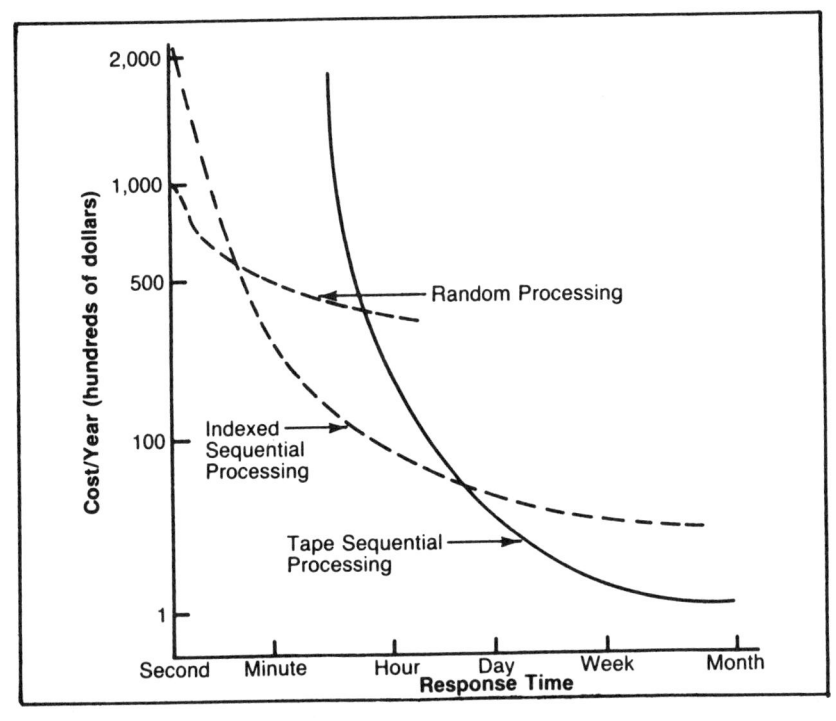

Figure 4. Cost as a Function of Response Time

gained from spending 20 percent of the cost. The remaining 20 percent of the benefit requires 80 percent of the project cost. Although the proportions may differ in practice, this rule implies that automation should stop within the areas of actual payoff.

Simple decision making that follows clearly defined and fairly constant parameters usually can be automated; however, complex decision making involving flexible and ill-defined goals should continue to be handled by people. Each process in the proposed application should be examined for allocation to machine or manual processing. The only reason for automating a task that could be done more efficiently manually is if the results of that task are integral to the further processing of information by the total application.

GENERAL APPLICATION CONSIDERATIONS

Advances in information system technology have produced system designs with capabilities that increase the value of information by improving its form. Although these features add to the cost of application implementation, they also substantially extend system benefits. Some of these facilities shift both the cost and value curves of information through techniques that initially seem to be more technical than information oriented.

Proving information through multifunction terminals or workstations that include integrated office support systems can provide the user with an array of tools—instead of a single function. For example, the user can receive in-

SYSTEMS DEVELOPMENT AND PROGRAMMING

formation at the terminal or on paper, can coordinate information with other users through electronic mail, and can modify or extend information being coordinated. A new dimension is added to information value by enforcing the communication of information among users and by providing office support tools.

Adding end-user-query and report-writer facilities to standard data base applications enables the user to obtain specialized information rapidly, thereby avoiding the delays implicit in requesting programmer assistance. The speed of response to new problems dramatically increases the information.

As the number of online applications increases, system failure can not only become more costly in terms of lost worker-hours but can discourage effective system use. Consequently, the value of quick response time for which the online application was designed may be lost. The reliability of the environment in which the application is installed must therefore be addressed during system implementation. Designers should consider the value of fault-tolerant systems that support continuous operation during component failure or that provide rapid recovery from failure. Designers should also determine how much user data could be lost during system recovery.

Response time must be considered in two ways. First, the system load must not be so heavy that poor terminal response time inhibits system use. Second, responses to requests for new information or extensions to existing information must be handled promptly to maintain information value. One method of supporting quick response time is through query and report writer systems. Another approach is to consider the potential for change when designing new applications and thereby ensure rapid response to changing conditions. Although additional effort is needed to design the application, information value is increased through application flexibility, and the cost of future application enhancements is reduced.

During the past few years, substantial effort has been devoted to improving terminal use and user productivity through ergonomic design. Several recent research and design projects have concentrated on developing application design standards that improve the user's ability to learn and use the applications, increasing system use and information and application quality.

CONCLUSION

The cost/benefit analysis identifies the system design that can produce quality information at the lowest cost. The cost analysis addresses three major elements:
- Present operating costs and their projections
- Operating costs of proposed alternatives
- Implementation costs of the alternative system selected

The remainder of the analysis concerns three types of benefits:
- Tangible—Reduced operating costs and increased profits produce these benefits.
- Intangible—These benefits include improved decision making and information accuracy.
- Borderline—Certain intangible benefits have tangible value.

Preparing for Cost/Benefit Analysis

Before the cost/benefit analysis can be performed, however, two final decisions must be made. First, the cost/benefit analysis for a proposed system must be projected over a long enough time period to allow amortization of the initial investment. Corporate guidelines usually clarify management's expectations regarding payback on investment, and these guidelines should be adhered to in the cost/benefit analysis. In addition, the cost/benefit analysis should not be projected beyond the expected life of the new system, although minor modifications can be included.

Second, whether to use fixed costs (e.g., overhead) or marginal costs (e.g., labor) for the analysis must be decided. Because the purpose of implementing a new system or application is often to affect fixed-cost levels, the usual definitions (i.e., costs that remain constant) do not apply, and the analyst must carefully examine all areas that the new system may affect.

Chapter IV-9 provides further information on these final considerations and outlines how to perform the cost/benefit analysis.

IV-9
Performing a Cost/Benefit Analysis

Louis Fried

INTRODUCTION

Several cautionary statements should be made about cost/benefit analyses. First, the more money and time spent, the more refined the analysis and the more accurate the conclusions. As with any investment, however, neither time nor money should be spent out of proportion to the expected return. For example, performing a comprehensive analysis for a small project or for one with a fairly obvious payoff would be wasteful.

In addition, the cost/benefit analysis is based partly on the expected costs of application development, implementation, and operation, which are based on a conceptual application design. Because the conceptual design may indicate costs that exceed the potential benefits, a brief preliminary study of potential benefits should be performed before the conceptual design is prepared.

Finally, the cost/benefit analysis should be updated at the completion of each major phase of the development life cycle before programming that needs requestor approval—for example, requirements specification, system design, and program specifications. The updated cost/benefit analysis should be included in the package to be approved at established control points to prevent continuation of a fiscally unsound effort.

COST/BENEFIT CONSIDERATIONS

Management must address two considerations regarding the cost/benefit analysis. First, because the decision to develop and implement a new system involves a one-time investment, the analysis must be projected over a period sufficient to amortize the initial investment. An investment payback is usually expected within one to five years (in some cases even longer). This corporate guideline should be followed: the analysis projection should not exceed the stated payback objective because any proposal that does not meet the payback criteria within that period would be economically infeasible.

The expected life of the system should also limit projections. For example, an expected life of three years (after which replacement or major modification would be required) should limit the projection regardless of payback cri-

SYSTEMS DEVELOPMENT AND PROGRAMMING

teria. Minor modifications expected during the system's life may simply appear as costs within the projection.

The second consideration concerns the type of cost to be used: fixed and/or marginal. Generally, fixed costs do not vary with volume, marginal costs do. Examples of fixed costs are building rent, property tax, and business license payments. Expenditures for power supplies, telephones, purchasing, inventory control, payroll operation, and management that remain fairly constant, despite volume changes, can also be fixed costs. Marginal costs include expenditures for raw materials, labor, supplies, and tools. If a fixed level of personnel is required, regardless of volume, only the expenses that vary with the work load can be considered marginal costs. An analysis that uses both fixed and marginal costs creates an unnecessary amount of work and should only be performed when required by management.

Because the objective of a new or modified application is often to adjust the level of fixed cost, the organization's usual cost definitions cannot be used in the analysis. Instead, the analyst must carefully identify cost elements that will be affected by the new application to define all others as fixed costs. To ensure that fixed costs are excluded from consideration, a statement of these elements should be included in the analysis.

COST ANALYSIS

A cost analysis addresses four major elements:
- Present operating costs
- Present operating cost projection
- Operating costs of proposed systems
- Implementation costs of proposed systems.

Present Operating Costs

The cost elements described in the following sections are treated as marginal costs unless noted otherwise. Restricting fixed-cost elements to those positively identified as such provides the widest latitude for exploring costs and benefits.

Operating Personnel Costs. Staff costs are frequently the major expense of an existing system. The documented analysis of the existing system, which should be completed before this phase of the study, can be used to identify the activities of personnel in the user area. Staff members participating in activities relating to a proposed application form the operating personnel base. Analysts should also consider administrative personnel directly involved in the application and should account for the number of workers affected by the change. Similarly, the cost of all part-time work on the application should be included.

If possible, actual salaries or hourly rates (rather than average rates) should be used. In the benefit analysis, the user is asked to identify personnel savings, which should be consistent with the costs in the cost analysis.

At a detailed level, it may be wise to identify personnel costs by function within the application since the new system may affect each functional area differently.

Overhead Costs. Floor space, utility, telephone, and other overhead expenses should be included only if they may change with the introduction of the new system; otherwise, such expenditures should be classed as fixed costs. Employee benefits, however, should always be considered a marginal cost. A rate for application to base salaries is used by most organizations in budgeting employee benefits.

Computer Costs. If the existing system is automated, computer costs must be estimated, a task complicated by several factors. First, if the new application will not create a need for additional computer hardware or operating personnel, management must decide whether to consider automation a marginal cost or whether supplies should be the only computer-related marginal cost. Second, although the new application may not necessitate the acquisition of new equipment, it may hasten the time when the total work load exceeds capacity. As a result, an unrelated application may require an unwarranted amount of justification.

The elements of MIS department cost that will be changed by the application should also be identified and included as a marginal cost. These costs can include supplies, data entry personnel and equipment, data storage media, and possibly an extra shift of computer operators.

The cost of computer capacity should be recognized in a section separate from the assessment of marginal cost. An internal rate for computer time can be multiplied by the time used for the application; if no such rate exists, the time needed for the application should be noted and later compared with the time use expected by the proposed alternative methods. This approach enables management to judge the alternative methods of allocating existing computer time.

The section addressing computer capacity should also include a measure of system limitation. The computer is responsive to volume changes in fixed increments. Exceeding computer capacity by a small amount may trigger a cost increase sufficient to obtain the next incremental level of capacity. Therefore, management support for the system recommendation can only be obtained by comparing the present level of computer use (either as a percentage of total available computer time or as a number of hours per month or day compared with the hours available for the same period) with the level anticipated by the proposed application.

Maintenance Costs. The maintenance of office equipment or facilities adds to existing system costs. Maintenance costs can also involve the systems and programming effort in maintaining the effectiveness of the existing system. Computer time for maintenance activity should be calculated on the same basis as run time.

Supply Costs. These costs include special forms, cards, magnetic tape, and similar computer or general office supplies. If available accounting records do not permit supply analysis for the particular application, estimates of use can be obtained from user personnel, verified by user management, and priced by determining average costs (in consultation with the organization's purchasing department) or by referring to the internal supplies catalog.

SYSTEMS DEVELOPMENT AND PROGRAMMING

Amortization Costs. If the existing system is automated and the organization has a policy of capitalizing system development, the current system must be amortized or a portion of the capitalized cost written off as expense when the new system is implemented. Even without a policy of capitalizing such expenses, management may want to know how effective this application area has been in achieving its previous goals.

Because office equipment and other capitalized items can add amortization charges to the application area, these costs should be considered if equipment can be eliminated or changed. These charges cannot be excluded if the equipment is stored for an indefinite period but can be eliminated if the equipment is sold or used within a reasonable time to avoid the purchase of such equipment in another area.

Present Operating Cost Projection

As mentioned, costs of the current system should be projected to cover the life expectancy of the new system or the payback period, whichever is shorter.

Occasionally, the expected cost increase in continuing to use the present system (as compared to implementing its replacement) would be most effectively demonstrated over a longer time period. Similarly, when the benefits obtained from a replacement system would be most significant near the end of the payback period, it may be appropriate to extend the time covered by the analysis.

The following factors should be considered when projecting the costs of the existing system:
- Operating personnel costs
  - —Impact of business fluctuations on the number and type of personnel.
  - —Regular salary increases and inflation.
  - —Labor market and salary ranges for the type of personnel required.
- Overhead costs
  - —Potential increases in employee benefits resulting from inflation and existing or pending legislation.
  - —Changes in floor space, utility use, and telephone availability resulting from increases or decreases in business volumes.
- Computer costs
  - —Inflation
  - —Impact of increased transaction volumes on computer use and equipment requirements.
  - —Increases or decreases in marginal cost, as affected by changes in business volumes.
- Maintenance costs
  - —Increasing cost of maintaining application currency and satisfying changing requirements (potential major modifications).
  - —Increasing cost of equipment maintenance caused by aging hardware and inflation.
  - —Purchase of additional equipment to expand the application and remain compatible with existing hardware.
  - —Cost of replacing obsolete equipment.

- Supply costs
  —Inflation
- Amortization costs
  —Amortization costs generally do not change unless equipment must be replaced, added, or sold as a result of obsolescence or fluctuations in business volumes.
- Other considerations
  —Business volumes can be constrained by continuing to operate the present system. This may be shown as either a cost of the old system or a benefit of the proposed system.

A key factor in making projections is recognizing that business volumes can increase or decrease and that conversion to a system with a higher fixed-cost base can be quite costly if business declines. By projecting costs for likely increases and decreases in business volume, analysts can avoid this potential trap.

Operating Costs of Proposed Systems

Projecting costs on the basis of proposed functional specifications for a system is, to a great extent, a guessing game. The analyst must arrive at the best estimate for expected operating costs while reducing the unknowns and the risk in management's decision-making process.

The operating cost elements to be estimated are substantially the same as those determined for the existing system; differences are:
- Operating personnel costs
  —The number of personnel whose employment will be terminated or who will be transferred from the application area should be taken into account.
  —Changes in the type of skills or the job classifications of personnel needed to operate the new system should be anticipated.
- Computer costs
  —Additional peripherals and special equipment dedicated to the new system should be included. For example, if average growth requires two additional disk drives during the next year, but four are required as a result of implementing the new system, then the cost of two drives is reasonably attributed to the new system.
  —The capitalizing of items over the defined dollar value should be guided by organizational policy. The amortization of these purchased items is shown as an operating cost.
  —Expense items acquired during the implementation period can be charged to development and implementation. Those acquired later should be shown as operating costs.
  —Capital expenditures include the cost of terminal equipment dedicated to the application, communications network connections or local area networks, and changes to the office layout caused by the application design.
  —Communications costs for the application must be considered part of the operating cost.
- Maintenance costs
  —User management must understand that new systems also require

maintenance. During the first six months, maintenance can be considered an operating cost or part of the implementation cost. Thereafter, expected maintenance costs should be treated as an operating cost.
- Amortization costs
  —Although corporate policy may not require capitalization of the system implementation cost, a valid cost/benefit study demands such figures in the comparison. The system implementation cost should be amortized over its expected life and shown as an operating cost.
- Other considerations
  —The value of additional capabilities can be estimated by user management in terms of contribution to net profit (before taxes) and shown as earnings resulting from the new system.

Management must be provided with an understanding of the proposed alternatives and of the risk of the estimating process. A comprehensive evaluation can be used to develop a structure of operating costs for each proposed alternative (see Figure 1). Each alternative (including the existing system) is assigned optimistic, most likely, and pessimistic estimates of operating costs for the range of possible business volumes (i.e., lowest possible, expected, and highest possible volumes). This approach determines the fixed-cost base, the maximum costs, and the costs expected for each alternative and provides insight into the risks of each estimate. When benefits are matched, the resulting charts indicate the expected feasibility of the system at various business levels.

The estimates and charts should serve only as working documentation; such detail should not be presented to management. Estimates can be summarized for presentation to management by:
- Averaging optimistic, most likely, and pessimistic estimates.
- Using weighted averaging.
- Expressing confidence factors or ranges (in terms of plus and minus percentages) to the most likely estimate or to an average.

Business Volume Estimates		
Lowest Possible	Expected*	Highest Possible
Estimated Operating Costs	Estimated Operating Costs	Estimated Operating Costs
Optimistic	Optimistic	Optimistic
Most Likely	Most Likely	Most Likely
Pessimistic	Pessimistic	Pessimistic

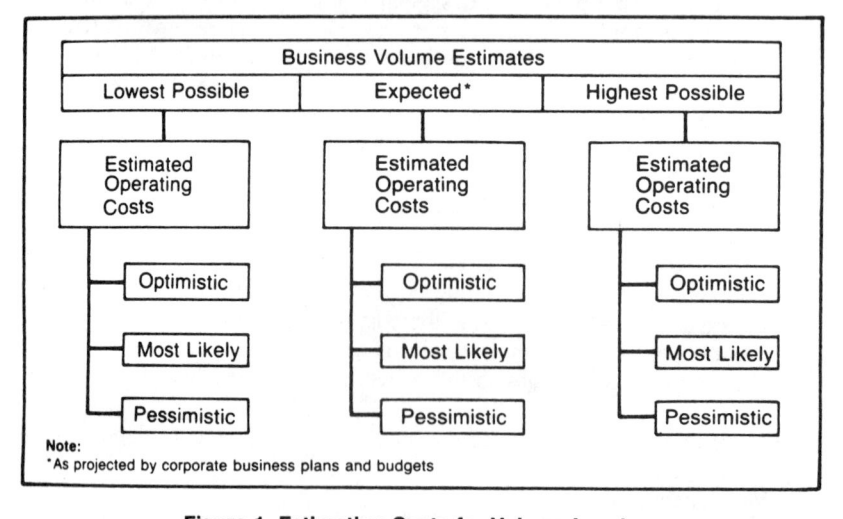

Note:
*As projected by corporate business plans and budgets

Figure 1. Estimating Costs for Volume Levels

Performing Cost/Benefit Analysis

- Applying probability theory calculations during the estimating process to obtain one estimate with an expressed level of probability. The accuracy of the resulting estimates through other methods is inconclusive.

An analysis is incomplete if estimates are not projected over time. Unless all implementation costs can be recovered within the new system's first year of operation, estimates should span several years. Again, the estimates should be guided by the expected life of the system or the time necessary for payback of the implementation cost, whichever is shorter.

Figure 2 illustrates an operating cost worksheet format that can be used for compiling estimates; Figure 3 shows a summary of operating cost estimates over five years.

Implementation Costs of Proposed Systems

The following must be considered in implementation costs for alternative systems:
- System design and programming effort (through final system test). It may be desirable for this cost to include the maintenance effort required for the first few months of operation, since this is the debugging phase of the project.
- System modifications. These are treated as a separate item when the alternative is to purchase a software package.
- Preparation for conversion, including the review and cleanup of existing files (manual and automated) as well as planning for organizational change or acquisition of temporary help for the conversion period.
- Development and publication of new and revised policies, job descriptions, and operations manuals for user personnel.
- Conversion of manual files to machine-readable form or conversion and reformatting of existing computerized files.
- Training of personnel who will use the system. Special training of analysts or programmers can be included with design and development costs.
- Pilot operation of the new system or parallel operation of the new and old systems.
- Miscellaneous project tasks.
- Cost of hardware and peripherals, installation, software, office modifications, and specialized forms for conversion. When completely or partially dedicated to the application, these costs must be considered capital expenditures in the cost/benefit analysis, unless the application uses existing facilities without significantly affecting capacity.

Figure 4 presents a sample worksheet for a project using a software package to implement a new application. These costs may be summarized and spread over the life of the project to provide management with a view of how the project will be budgeted.

Figure 5 shows two ways of summarizing project costs. The summary of total costs includes computer time charges at the in-house rate and approximately half of the project management costs (which are reallocated if the project is not done). This chart enhances the comparison between the alternative uses of the available resources.

SYSTEMS DEVELOPMENT AND PROGRAMMING

Elements of Annual Cost	Present System		Alternative System					
			Optimistic		Most Likely		Pessimistic	
	Employees	Amount ($)	Employees	Amount ($)	Employees	Amount ($)	Employees	Amount ($)
Data Processing	14.5	254,600	2.5	30,000	3	36,000	4	48,000
Supplies and Forms		13,300		10,700		11,900		12,800
Operating Personnel	94	583,425	76	482,175	85	527,550	90	561,825
Overhead		252,817		208,942		228,602		243,547
Maintenance Cost								
Personnel	0.2	4,800	0.3	7,200	0.3	7,200	0.3	7,200
Computer Time		17,000		10,000		11,700		12,300
Other								
Amortization of Special Equipment or Software				7,600		7,600		7,600
Subtotal	108.7	1,125,942	78.8	756,617	88.3	830,552	94.3	893,682
Amortization of Implementation Cost				26,638		23,034		35,229
Final Total	108.7	1,125,942	78.8	783,255	88.3	853,586	94.3	928,911

Figure 2. Operating Cost Worksheet

Performing Cost/Benefit Analysis

	Present System		Alternative System					
			Optimistic		Most Likely		Pessimistic	
Year	Employees	Amount ($)	Employees	Amount ($)	Employees	Amount ($)	Employees	Amount ($)
1	108.7	1,125,942	78.8	783,255	88.3	853,586	94.3	928,911
2	119.5	1,238,536	81.9	822,418	91.8	904,801	99.9	1,003,244
3	131.4	1,363,389	85.2	863,539	95.5	959,089	105.9	1,083,482
4	144.5	1,498,628	88.6	906,715	99.3	1,016,635	112.3	1,170,160
5	158.9	1,648,491	92.2	1,045,336	103.3	1,077,633	119.1	1,263,773
Total	158.9	6,873,986	92.2	4,421,263	103.3	4,811,744	119.1	5,449,550

Capital Expenditure $88,000

Figure 3. Operating Cost Summary

SYSTEMS DEVELOPMENT AND PROGRAMMING

Cost Elements ($)

Project Tasks	Systems Analysis	Program-ming	Key-punch	Computer	Forms and Supplies	Outside Contract Services	User Adminis-tration	User Personnel	Project Manage-ment	Total
Systems Design and Programming										
Systems Modifications	13,500	16,000		5,200			80			34,780
Preparation for Conversion			1,600	1,250		8,200		11,860		22,910
Clerical and Operating Procedures	9,750	750			1,000			840		12,340
File Conversion	2,675	2,050	9,660	16,075			200	3,350		34,010
Training	1,875						240	1,560		3,675
Pilot and Parallel Operation			900	5,250			540	1,400		8,190
Other Project Tasks									14,800	14,800
Subtotal	27,800	18,800	12,160	27,775	1,000	8,200	1,060	19,010	14,800	130,605
Capital Expenditures		38,000								38,000
Final Total	27,800	56,800	12,160	27,775	1,000	8,200	1,060	19,010	14,800	168,605

Figure 4. Implementation Cost Worksheet

Performing Cost/Benefit Analysis

Summary of Total Costs ($)						
	First Quarter	Second Quarter	Third Quarter	Fourth Quarter	Fifth Quarter	Total
Optimistic	39,921	33,682	31,346	36,346	27,410	168,705
Most Likely	45,909	38,734	36,044	43,897	30,120	194,704
Pessimistic	52,795	44,544	41,450	52,582	34,050	225,421

Summary of Out-of-Pocket Costs ($)						
	First Quarter	Second Quarter	Third Quarter	Fourth Quarter	Fifth Quarter	Total
Optimistic	31,545	27,670	19,865	32,945	21,165	133,190
Most Likely	36,281	31,820	22,844	37,887	24,340	153,172
Pessimistic	41,723	36,593	26,270	43,570	27,991	176,147

Figure 5. Implementation Costs

The summary of marginal costs, excluding allocated expenses, is used to determine the economic feasibility of the project. The implementation costs in this chart are used to generate summary figures (e.g., by averaging) for project cost amortization on the operating cost worksheet as well as cash flow and payback analyses.

BENEFIT ANALYSIS

Benefits are usually classified as tangible, intangible, and borderline. Borderline benefits are intangible but have a tangible value. The following sections describe how these benefits can be determined and presented.

Tangible Benefits

Tangible benefits derive from two sources: cost reductions in operations and profit improvements. Cost reductions in operations are readily identifiable when projecting the cost of alternative application systems. Profit improvements can result from new sources of revenue, such as:
- Additional processing capacity for increased business volumes
- Marketable by-products of information generated by the system (e.g., name and address listings, property transactions)
- Marketable software produced during system development
- A program of short-term investment that improves cash management by increasing cash flow (as in a new invoicing system) or conserving cash (as in a new inventory control system that improves inventory turnover)

These benefits are tangible enough to warrant inclusion in the previous operating cost analyses as earnings.

On this basis, the tangible benefits of proposed alternatives can be determined by comparing the projected costs of the present system with those of implementing and operating the alternative system over a specific time period. As illustrated in Figure 6, these figures may be used to construct a cash flow analysis comparing the alternatives. (The cost of continuing present system operation is part of the cash flow of the alternative until the new system has been implemented.)

SYSTEMS DEVELOPMENT AND PROGRAMMING

When the benefit clearly exceeds the investment, a cash flow analysis may suffice. If, however, the projected benefits are so small that an adequate return on the investment is questionable or the pattern of cash flow between alternatives differs but the resulting benefits are nearly equal, a present-value analysis should be conducted. This technique, which uses an internal rate of return to convert future cash flows to present dollars, can indicate substantial differences between alternatives.

The payback analysis is valuable when alternative approaches are being considered (see Figure 7). The payback period is determined by the point at which the cumulative savings (loss) amount becomes a positive figure. By clearly illustrating the value of one approach over another, this analysis can show that a somewhat simple design alternative with an immediate payback is more economical and effective than a complex one or that substantial benefits can be gained from an increased investment and longer implementation time. (The delayed implementation of even the best-designed system, however, can be too late to meet user needs.)

Intangible Benefits

Truly intangible benefits, which can include such items as stronger decision making, increased information accuracy, improved report production, and higher employee morale, should be presented to management in a separate section of the cost/benefit analysis. This section should also address such concerns as the potential risks to project success, the impact of personnel turnover on the project, and the management guidance needed for project personnel.

Year	Present System	Alternative System			
		Implementation	Operation	Earnings	Total
1	1,125,942	164,584	1,125,942	—	1,290,526
2	1,128,536	30,120	921,676	(6,000)	945,796
3	1,362,389	—	891,998	(28,000)	863,998
4	1,498,628	—	945,517	(33,000)	912,517
5	1,648,491	—	1,002,248	(37,000)	965,248
Total	6,763,986	194,704	4,887,381	(104,000)	4,978,085

Figure 6. Cash Flow Analysis (in dollars)

Year	Present System	Alternative System		
		Total Cost	Saving (loss)	Cumulative Saving (loss)
1	1,125,942	1,290,526	(164,584)	(164,584)
2	1,238,536	945,796	292,740	128,156

Figure 7. Payback Analysis (in dollars)

Borderline Benefits

Although seemingly intangible, borderline benefits have a tangible value with some level of reliability. Evaluating these benefits may be as simple as identifying areas of potential cost avoidance or as complex as requiring operations research techniques.

Bayesian analysis is one effective and easy-to-use operations research method. This approach entails the following:
- Considering the parameter's possible values for the period(s) in question.
- Assigning a subjective probability weight to each possible value of the parameter. (The sum of the probabilities of all possible events in a set [universe] is 1.)
- Calculating the expected value of the parameter and using this value as the estimate.

This process can be illustrated by deriving an estimate of how profit will be affected by improved information used in decision making. For example, the user may decide that three values are possible: no improvement in profit (a probability of 0.05); $30,000 of improvement (a probability of 0.80); or $50,000 of improvement (a probability of 0.15). The estimate can be calculated by adding the products of each value multiplied by its assigned probability:

Expected Increase in Profit ($)		Probability of Occurrence		Expected Return ($)
0	×	0.05	=	0
30,000		0.80		24,000
50,000	×	0.15	=	7,500
		1.00		31,500 (estimate)

If several users are consulted on the same estimate and if the report clearly explains the process used to construct the estimate, the results from the Bayesian analysis can be averaged.

Individual estimates can be further refined (as part of a group of estimates) by using the Delphi technique, which consists of an iterative series of responses from members of the group being interviewed. The first estimates should be collated, and the extremes and mean determined. In the second series of interviews, each group member is separately informed of the first collated results and then asked for a new estimate. Three or four such iterations result in an increasingly congruent set of responses with a high degree of probability based on the varied knowledge and viewpoints of the participants.

When their source and content are properly noted, these estimates can be included as earnings or cost in the operating cost projections.

COST/BENEFIT ANALYSIS REPORT

The cost/benefit analysis should be presented in a concise format oriented toward decision making. A suggested structure is discussed in the following paragraphs.

Summary. The report should begin with a one- to three-page summary that includes a cash flow analysis for all desirable alternatives as well as for continuation of the present system. It should also include computation of the payback period and return on investment (savings plus earnings divided by implementation cost for each year of the projected period) for the proposed system alternatives.

Cost/Benefit Analysis. This section should contain supporting details for:
- Present system operating cost projection
- Alternative systems operating cost projections
- Implementation cost for alternative systems
- Projected earnings for tangible and borderline benefits
- Projected savings
- Sources of information.

Intangible Benefits. The intangible benefits determined for the alternatives and the sources of such information should be noted separately for each alternative. If some of the intangible benefits are integral to the proposal, they can be mentioned in the summary and then detailed in this section.

CONCLUSION

The cost/benefit analysis is usually the most important determining factor in the project selection and priority-setting process. A comprehensive approach to cost/benefit analysis can influence design considerations, the selection of realistic alternatives, and the final management decision making process.

Although the technical feasibility and design of the alternatives are usually determined by the systems analyst and the MIS department, upper management should prepare the cost/benefit analysis because this group is most familiar with corporate goals and objectives and most accustomed to making decisions that benefit the entire organization.

Bibliography

Emery, J. "Cost/Benefit Analysis of Information Systems." *The Society for Management Information Systems*, 1971.

IV-10
Controlling Projects: PERT/CPM

Jerry Gitomer
Robert E. Umbaugh

INTRODUCTION

The duties of the MIS manager are especially difficult because DP functions have the characteristics of both factory and research laboratory functions. On one hand, data entry, computer operations, and quality control are comparable to factory fabrication, assembly, and inspection. In a DP installation, production problems are solved through the addition of equipment and operators or the use of an automating technique. On the other hand, systems analysis, design, and implementation are comparable to laboratory study, hypothesis, and experimentation. The management of development projects presents more complex problems. The addition of personnel or computer test time does not always solve—and may even compound—scheduling problems. Even the best-managed installations occasionally miss a deadline or exceed a development budget.

This chapter discusses the use of the Program Evaluation and Review Technique (PERT) and the Critical Path Method (CPM) as aids in the control of development projects. Although they do not replace good management techniques, PERT/CPM can be combined to provide a graphic, disciplined approach.

PERT/CPM OVERVIEW

PERT and CPM are network analysis techniques that were developed in the late 1950s. Prior to the advent of PERT/CPM, complex projects were scheduled through the use of Gantt charts (see Figure 1). On these charts, one line is designated for each activity, and a second, cross-hatched line shows actual progress. Although easy to prepare and understand, Gantt charts do not show interrelationships, dependencies, or realistic activity progress.

Network analysis charts such as PERT/CPM specify particular tasks and show the sequence in which they must be performed. Although a PERT chart (see Figure 2) is the more difficult of the two to prepare, it provides a more explicit basis for evaluating progress during project execution.

SYSTEMS DEVELOPMENT AND PROGRAMMING

The PERT analysis technique is oriented toward events (the attainment of goals); CPM is oriented toward activity (the activities necessary to attain goals). Although several differences initially distinguished the two techniques, these have diminished. Figure 3 shows a PERT/CPM chart for the project illustrated in Figures 1 and 2. In Figure 3, however, the time schedule for each activity is shown to scale.

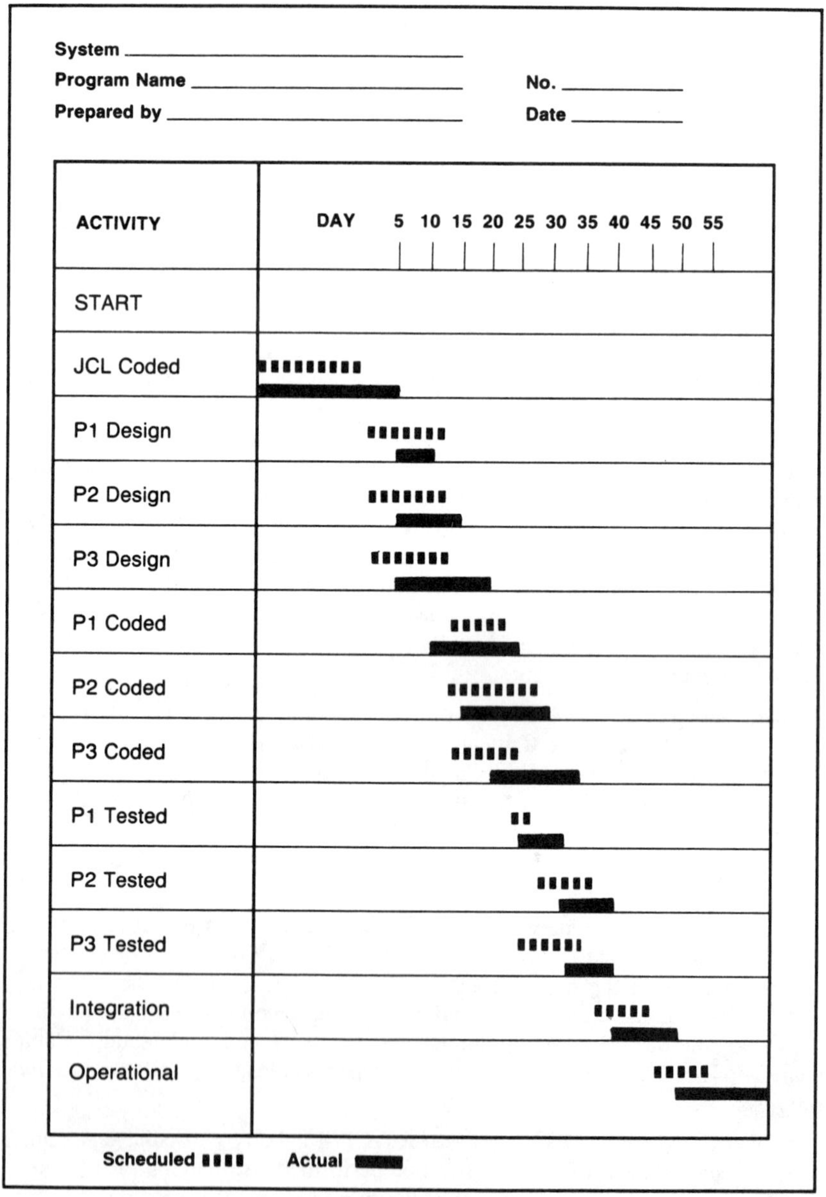

Figure 1. Gantt Chart

PERT/CPM

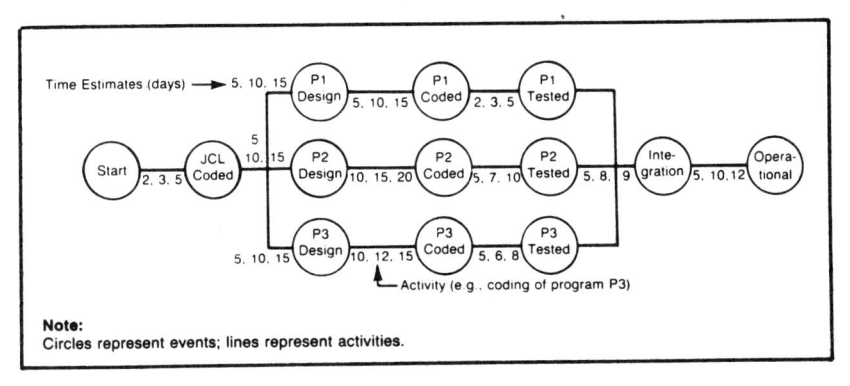

Figure 2. PERT Chart

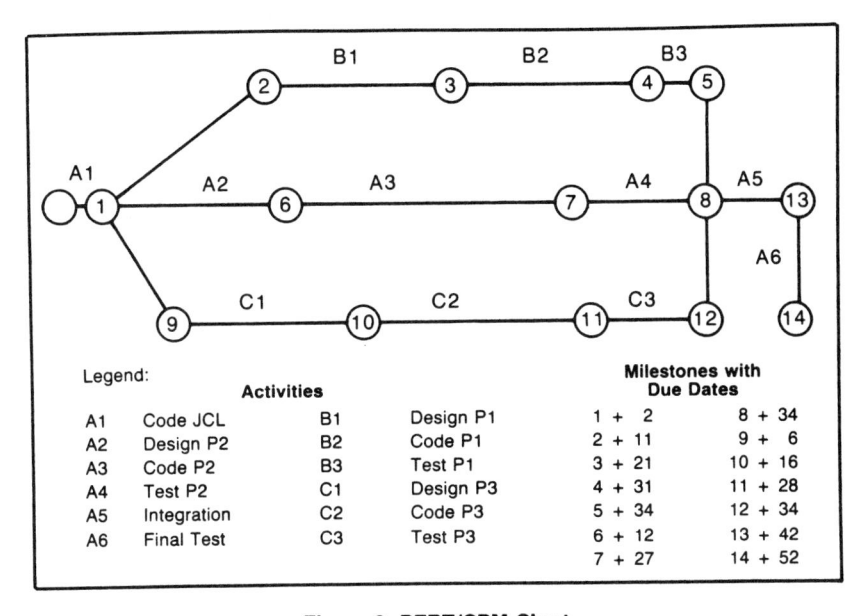

Figure 3. PERT/CPM Chart

Figures 2 and 3 show the differences between an event (the end of a task) and activities. Figure 3 also shows milestone and due dates. Event 10, for instance, must be attained by the 16th day of the project if that leg of the project is to remain on schedule. The end of the project, event 14, is scheduled 52 days from the project start.

PERT/CPM forces the analyst to establish milestones (PERT events) and to prepare schedules for each activity, dictating such determinants as when the milestone should be reached and when the next set of activities can begin. The resulting schedule forces the project to become more detailed and promotes more accurate scheduling. Because problems are identified earlier, corrective action can be taken sooner.

A PERT/CPM system divides the project into activities, following a mod-

SYSTEMS DEVELOPMENT AND PROGRAMMING

ular scheduling approach that generally parallels top-down implementation design concepts.

Establishing PERT/CPM

PERT/CPM control systems require more work than some other scheduling techniques but can be of greater value to the manager. The manager must take the following five steps to establish PERT/CPM systems:
- Identify all activities that must be performed
- Determine the sequence of activities
- Estimate the time required to perform each activity
- Prepare a time-scaled chart of activities
- Determine the critical path (i.e., the longest sequence of events, which dictates total project time)

In a data processing development project, activities are similar for each function at the design level and for each program module at the implementation level. The easiest way to identify the activities is to prepare a form for each function (see Figure 4). The advantage of using a form is that only the function or program module and an identifying code must be entered, if an online or personal computer–based system is not used.

Project Name: _____ ID: _____
Segment Name: _____

DESIGN ACTIVITIES

Activity	Code	Calendar	Worker	Responsible
Define User Requirement	.10			
Prepare High-Level Functional Spec	.15			
User Review	.20			
Detail Functional Spec	.25			
User Final Review	.30			
User Sign-Off	.35			
Design Specification	.40			
Design Review	.45			

(Days: Calendar / Worker)

Figure 4. Design Activities

The design and implementation phases of a project should be scheduled separately because the completed design determines the implementation plan. PERT/CPM helps managers arrive at realistic schedules that can be used to monitor and control the project design and implementation plan. Thus, the premature preparation of an implementation plan defeats the purpose of PERT/CPM.

The sequence of activities is standardized within an installation. Because testing before the code is written is difficult, a sequence should be specified that assures that certain activities are scheduled before others in the project (see Figure 5).

PERT/CPM

```
Project Name: _____  ID: _____
Program/Module Name: _____
              IMPLEMENTATION ACTIVITIES
                              Days
   Activity         Code   Calendar  Worker   Responsible
Detail Design
Design Review
Program/Module Design
Design Review
Code and Test
Final Test
```

Figure 5. Implementation Activities

The method used to estimate the time required for each activity is the chief difference between PERT and CPM. With CPM, the manager usually prepares only one estimate of the time required. With PERT, however, the manager prepares estimates for best-case, average-case, and worst-case possibilities and then computes a standard estimate as follows:

$$\frac{\text{worst-case estimate} + 4(\text{average-case estimate}) + \text{best-case estimate}}{6}$$

Because PERT estimates generally allow more time than CPM estimates do and more than is actually required to complete the activities, the PERT three-estimate technique should be used for activities in which personnel have little or no experience. The CPM single-estimate technique should be used for familiar activities because greater accuracy is attainable for activities with known characteristics.

Estimates should specify both calendar days and worker-days and, when possible, the personnel assigned to each activity. This final recommendation is important because the information shows the variation in performance among systems analysts and programmers working in the installation. For example, less performance time for completing a given task should be estimated for an experienced employee than for a trainee.

After the preliminary chart is constructed, the critical path is determined. Often, the initial critical path estimate must be revised because it exceeds the deadline. Reducing critical path time means reducing individual activity time. Managers can do this by adding personnel, reassigning senior personnel, or reestimating the tasks.

Several task reevaluations, including personnel reassignment, are usually necessary to develop a shorter schedule. If the manager cannot adhere to a realistic schedule to meet the required deadline, additional personnel or outside assistance may be needed.

Maintaining the Charts

After reevaluations, the charts must be revised. In theory, PERT/CPM charts can be manually prepared and maintained; considering their instability, however, this is usually inadvisable except for small projects, which can

SYSTEMS DEVELOPMENT AND PROGRAMMING

be charted manually on magnetic or cork boards. Each task is recorded on a slip of paper and tacked to the proper place on the time grid.

Many PERT/CPM scheduling tools are available as software packages for personal computers. These are inexpensive and easy to use.

Some critical areas must be considered when using PERT/CPM. Greater time and effort may be required. Accurate estimates are crucial to an effective schedule. A poor estimate cannot be corrected by using PERT/CPM.

A MODEL FOR PERT/CPM

The following step-by-step procedure can be used as a model for applying PERT/CPM. The example given illustrates the scheduling of a batch application, consisting of three application programs and three utility programs. The chief programmer team consists of the chief programmer, the assistant chief programmer, two senior programmers, and six junior programmers.

Activity Identification. The first step is to identify each required activity. Only major activities are included in this example. In practice, the level of detail that is charted should relate to the scope of the project, as indicated by the following list:

1. Design job control
2. Test job control
3. Specify file copy utility
4. Specify sort (invoice within vendor sequence)
5. Design proof list
6. Review proof list design
7. Code and test proof list
8. Design check print
9. Review check print design
10. Code and test check print
11. Specify sort (voucher within department sequence)
12. Design distribution report
13. Review distribution report design
14. Code and test distribution report
15. Train user personnel
16. Train operations personnel
17. Perform acceptance test

Sequential Activities List. The second step is to prepare a sequential list of the required activities. Figure 6 shows the sequence in which the activities will be performed. The sequence codes are based on a hierarchical notation scheme used to emphasize which activities can be performed at the same time—for example, activities 3.1 through 3.6, if sufficient qualified personnel are available.

Activity Time Estimation. The third step is to estimate the time required to perform the activities listed. Sample time estimates, expressed in worker-days, are listed in Figure 7. Some activities require as little as one worker-day. (Many MIS managers believe that no identifiable activity can be performed in less than one worker-week and, therefore, schedule accordingly.)

Preliminary PERT/CPM Chart. The fourth step is to prepare a preliminary PERT/CPM chart (see Figure 8). Each circle on the chart is an event and represents the completion of an activity (a strictly constructed PERT chart would label all activities and events). Each line represents an activity. The numbers above the line indicate the sequence code; the number of personnel

PERT/CPM

Sequence Code	Activity
1.1	Design Job Control
2.1	Test Job Control
3.1	Specify File Copy
3.2	Specify Sort (Invoice within Voucher)
3.3	Design Proof List
3.4	Design Check Print
3.5	Specify Sort (Voucher within Department)
3.6	Design Distribution Report
4.1	Review Proof List Design
4.2	Review Check Print Design
4.3	Review Distribution Report Design
5.1	Code and Test Proof List
5.2	Code and Test Check Print
5.3	Code and Test Distribution Report
6.1	Train User Personnel
6.2	Train Operations Personnel
7.1	Perform Acceptance Test

Figure 6. Sequence of Activities

Sequence Code	Activity	Worker-days
1.1	Design Job Control	3
2.1	Test Job Control	2
3.1	Specify File Copy	1
3.2	Specify Sort (Invoice within Voucher)	1
3.3	Design Proof List	36
3.4	Design Check Print	30
3.5	Specify Sort (Voucher within Department)	1
3.6	Design Distribution Report	36
4.1	Review Proof List Design	9
4.2	Review Check Print Design	9
4.3	Review Distribution Report Design	12
5.1	Code and Test Proof List	45
5.2	Code and Test Check Print	30
5.3	Code and Test Distribution Report	45
6.1	Train User Personnel	2
6.2	Train Operations Personnel	2
7.1	Perform Acceptance Test	3

Figure 7. Estimated Time for Activities

assigned to the activity is noted in parentheses. Vertical lines show when an activity must start or end, and diagonal lines indicate slack time (i.e., the number of excess days available for completing the activity as compared to the scheduled completion time).

The chart shows the critical path as a single horizontal line extending from the project's beginning to the completion of activity 7.1. The time estimated for the critical path is 38 days. Because this chart is based on the assumption that unlimited labor is available, it must be modified.

SYSTEMS DEVELOPMENT AND PROGRAMMING

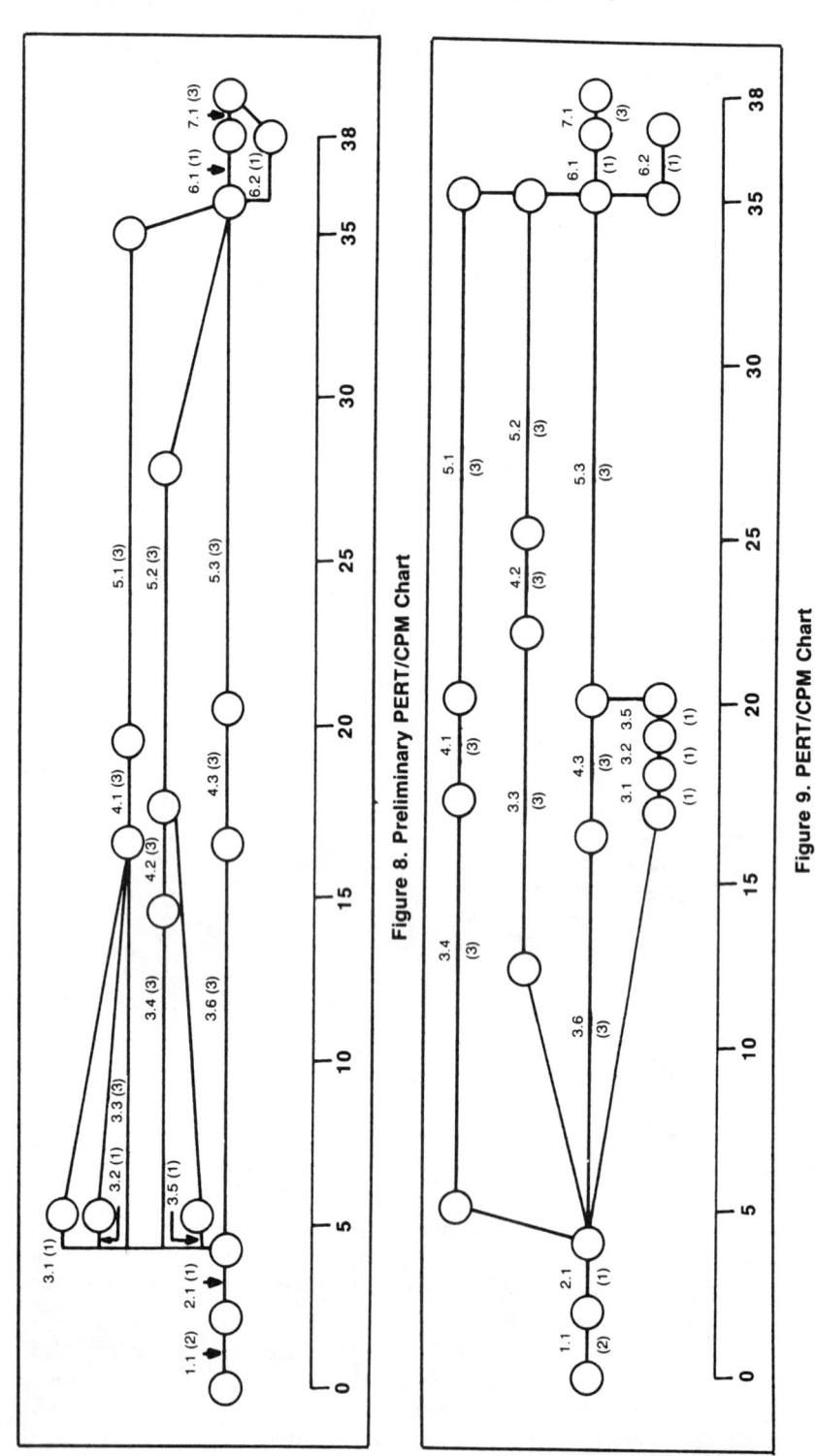

Figure 8. Preliminary PERT/CPM Chart

Figure 9. PERT/CPM Chart

PERT/CPM

Example of a PERT/CPM Chart

Figure 9 is based on the assumption that each activity should be started as late in the project as possible. The chart should reflect the labor available. In this example, the critical path is not affected. In most cases, a final PERT/CPM chart reflecting actual labor availability would differ considerably from a preliminary PERT/CPM chart. In Figure 9, the team assigned to activity 3.3 and the person assigned to activities 3.1, 3.2, and 3.5 appear available to work on activities 3.4 and 3.6 for several days. This is represented by diagonal lines that show slack time on a PERT/CPM chart.

Figure 10 shows the impact of reassigning personnel from activity 3.3 to activities 3.4 and 3.6 during the slack time. The individual assigned to activities 3.1, 3.2, and 3.5 is not reassigned, based on the assumption that he or she is the chief programmer who should be supervising and managing the project rather than working on it directly. Reassigning personnel results in a saving of four days. In this example, four days is a 12.5 percent reduction in the time required to complete the project.

Crisis Revision Chart

If plans change, a revised PERT/CPM chart should be prepared. If, for example, an emergency arises on day 11 and the project team loses one senior programmer and two junior programmers, no time would be lost in transition because other members of the chief programmer team are available. The project would thus be on schedule at the end of the 10th day. A new estimate of time required to complete activities is prepared. Already completed activities show no time and activities in progress show only remaining time. A new schedule should be prepared starting from the morning of the eleventh day. Figure 11 shows the crisis revision of the PERT/CPM chart, which is based on the revised time estimates in Figure 12.

The revised chart (Figure 10) implies that a satisfactory chart already exists for the project. Because the existing chart places all three major activities on parallel critical paths, further revision can be achieved by adding the remaining time estimates for each critical path and then maneuvering labor to maintain relative completion dates. In the example, the Proof List path shows 66 worker-days, the Check Print 61 worker-days, and the Distribution Report 64 worker-days—a total of 191 worker-days. With six people assigned to these tasks, the work can be completed in 32 calendar days by shifting one person from Check Print to Proof List for two days and one person from Check Print to Distribution for one day. The objective is to assign the workers among the various critical paths so that all tasks are completed simultaneously.

With the chief programmer team and top-down implementation used in this example, personnel can be more easily interchanged and temporarily reassigned. If the installation uses other types of project organizations, time must be allotted for familiarizing personnel with new assignments.

In addition to crisis revision, a chart should be revised when activities are not completed according to the schedule. (This is required only when the activity is on the critical path.)

SYSTEMS DEVELOPMENT AND PROGRAMMING

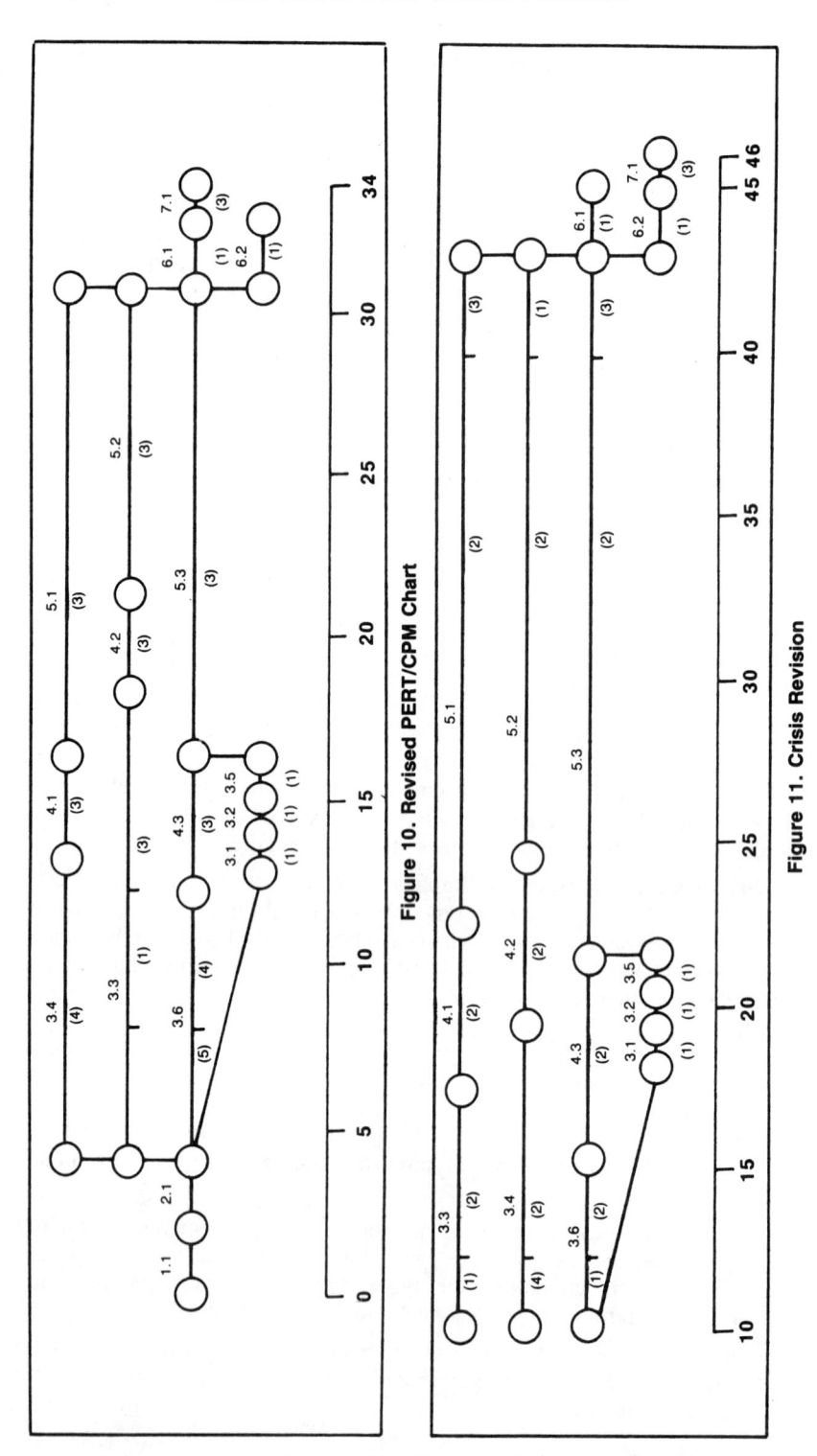

Figure 10. Revised PERT/CPM Chart

Figure 11. Crisis Revision

PERT/CPM

Sequence Code	Activity	Worker-days
1.1	Design Job Control	0
2.1	Test Job Control	0
3.1	Specify File Copy	1
3.2	Specify Sort (Invoice within Voucher)	1
3.3	Design Proof List	12
3.4	Design Check Print	22
3.5	Specify Sort (Voucher within Department)	1
3.6	Design Distribution Report	8
4.1	Review Proof List	10
4.2	Review Check Print	10
4.3	Review Report Distribution	12
5.1	Code and Test Proof List	44
5.2	Code and Test Check Print	30
5.3	Code and Test Report Distribution	44
6.1	Train User Personnel	2
6.2	Train Operations Personnel	2
7.1	Perform Acceptance Test	3

Figure 12. Revised Time Estimates

CONCLUSION

Although PERT/CPM is not a substitute for good management, it may improve present methods. Systems analysts and programmers are scarce, expensive resources; thus, their time should be used efficiently.

Because PERT/CPM scheduling systems are available for almost all personal computers, the MIS manager should use this powerful tool to improve control of and gain high productivity in systems development activities.

Section V
End-User Computing and Office Systems

"Let MIS put you in the driver's seat" might serve as a good motto for those of us who have embraced the concept of end-user computing. Giving the end user—who is really the *only* user—more and more control over his or her use of computing resources has proved to be a powerful lever for many MIS managers.

One way to accomplish this shift in control is through an information center (IC). To meet ever-increasing user demand for information, many MIS managers are implementing, or at least investigating, the information center concept. Chapter V-1, "The Information Center—A Powerful Tool," discusses the benefits and risks inherent in establishing an IC.

Another approach to end-user computing, one that often complements the IC, is personal computing. For the first time in the history of computing, users are selecting and buying personal computers (PCs) for their departments. MIS professionals no longer need to review existing computing systems before users purchase PCs; however, users do require assistance in implementing their new systems. Chapter V-2, "Getting the Most from Personal Computers," discusses skills that new users of PCs should possess and examines how these skills can best be taught. The five components of computer literacy are defined and discussed, and a methodology is presented for establishing a computer-literacy program to help implement personal computers in user departments.

With the implementation of personal computers come several issues of concern to the MIS manager. Among these issues are data security and integrity, systems auditing, compatibility, backup, and the economic life of a system. Chapter V-3, "Controlling Personal Computing," is written for the MIS manager who is concerned with controlling the use of personal computers in the organization.

Yet another way to give more computer power to decision makers is through decision support systems (DSSs). A DSS is a practical, achievable information system for assisting upper management with difficult decisions. A DSS can be developed and implemented in a matter of weeks or months at a relatively low cost. Given the low development cost and the potential for even small improvements in top management decisions, a DSS can often result in substantial returns on investment. The basic methodology for development, utilization, and management of the DSS often differs significantly from that of traditional information systems applications, however. This methodology, which is described in Chapter V-4, "Guide to Decision Support Systems," requires the attention and understanding of both functional and MIS management.

Chapter V-5, "Managing Office Systems Development," offers guidelines for the successful and productive implementation of office automation. The MIS manager should encourage all users to read this chapter and put its ideas into practice. It describes the basic systems development processes we apply to large projects, scaled down for these less complex systems.

Workstation ergonomics has gotten a lot of attention lately, not only in the trade press but among labor activists and in some state legislative offices. Several states now have related laws either enacted or pending; consequently, it is an area of rapid change. The MIS manager should be aware of what is required as well as of what is needed. Chapter V-6, "Workstation Ergonomics," offers a comprehensive discussion of the more pertinent issues and includes many steps you can take now to improve the working environment of computer-assisted workstations.

The final chapter in this section, "Tying Office Computing to Resource Planning," concerns integrating office computing and traditional computing through information resource planning. By using application portfolio modeling and considering the full spectrum of information processing—from large-scale management information systems to individual word processing applications—the MIS manager can better manage and control the information processing resources of the entire enterprise.

V-1
The Information Center — A Powerful Tool

Steve Hearn

INTRODUCTION

End-user computing. Decision support systems. Fourth-generation languages. Application backlogs. Software bottlenecks. Outside time sharing. Scarce DP talent. Improved price/performance. Growing user demand and sophistication.

These and many other challenges confront today's MIS managers as they attempt to meet their organizations' demands for information. For some managers, the goal is simple: survival. For others, it is more ambitious: assuming technological leadership in order to help determine the success and direction of their companies. In each case, the alert manager is always searching for better ways to satisfy user demand and improve user relations, thereby demonstrating the value of the MIS department.

The concept of the information center (IC) emerged from this search. In summary, an IC is an organization whose objective is to provide the tools and support that allow end users to deal directly with some subset of their DP needs. As such, the IC facilitates end-user computing, providing tools rather than solutions. The IC is independent of any particular tool or technology and typically encompasses several. It usually is part of the MIS department, although a user department can set up its own IC if MIS is reluctant or unable to provide that support. Large organizations may establish multiple ICs as part of their DP services strategy. While the information center concept may have appeared threatening to the MIS manager of the 1970s, it may prove indispensable to the MIS manager of the 1980s.

Redefining the MIS/User Relationship

What distinguishes an information center from other support structures? The key is the change in the basic responsibilities that have traditionally defined the relationship between the MIS group and its users. In providing end users with tools and support, the IC group is removing obstacles rather than imposing them, and the MIS group ceases to be a bottleneck and instead becomes a proponent. An area of conflict can be transformed into a cooperative team venture. Given this altered set of responsibilities, the IC provides the following services:

END-USER COMPUTING AND OFFICE SYSTEMS

- User-friendly tools—Powerful, flexible, and easy to learn and use, these tools are nonprocedural (i.e., they specify what, not how) and are usually interactive.
- Guidelines in use of tools—The IC staff should provide guidelines specifying the appropriate tools for each application and those applications or parts of applications that should be developed by MIS.
- User training—The IC staff should develop and administer the appropriate training for each tool. Self-instructional texts, computer-assisted instruction, tailored reference material, and stand-up training may all play a role.
- DP resources (including data)—In addition to tools, users require terminals, CPU cycles, storage, and other resources to develop and run applications. Many applications also require access to data (or copies of data) already stored in a computer system. Some ICs assume responsibility for providing all aspects of service. Others provide a walk-in center with a few terminals and leave other aspects of the service to other groups in MIS. In the latter case, the IC should be involved in coordinating other aspects of the service and representing the users' best interests.
- Consulting and technical assistance—Together with training, these activities are the most visible to users. They are absolutely necessary for users to avoid frustration and achieve full productivity.
- Evaluation and installation of new tools—Since a newly established IC cannot provide effective support for a complete range of tools, it must evolve to fill holes in its "product line." Even when no holes exist, a new tool may come along that is better than one already supported; such an innovation deserves evaluation.

Given this set of responsibilities for the IC, users assume their own set of responsibilities in return:

- Justification—The IC should neither act as a watchdog, determining if a given application is worthwhile, nor have to sign off on each application. User management should decide what justification, if any, it requires and leave enforcement to the user. The IC is simply providing a service that users are justifying to their own management.
- Development resource—Users supply the labor necessary to develop the application. The IC staff should not do any programming for users, except perhaps to make data available. Unless a firm stance is taken on this issue, the IC cannot achieve the leverage it requires to operate effectively.
- Application knowledge—No one knows the user's business better than the user. This fact alone is a powerful force determining the success of the IC.
- Documentation—The users should determine what documentation is required and then assume responsibility for developing it. Documentation is typically not necessary for ad hoc applications. For repetitive applications the cost of the documentation must be weighed against the ease of recreating the whole application if necessary. Often a fairly basic set of run-time documentation is sufficient, especially since the mechanism itself probably goes a long way toward formalizing an undocumented manual process.

- Application execution—The demand processing aspect of an IC requires users to execute the application and verify the results. Although users may elect to have certain periodic jobs scheduled by operations, they should take responsibility for solving most problems.
- Maintenance—Since the users developed the application, they are also responsible for maintaining it.

In addition to altering the traditional relationship between users and MIS, an IC should also differentiate itself from current internal and external services in areas such as service level, tools, applications, required documentation, approval level, controls, and cost. This distinction is the key to carving out an IC niche and delivering the full benefits the information center promises.

WHY ESTABLISH AN INFORMATION CENTER?

Forces for Change

Why have so many organizations recently shown interest in establishing information centers? One need look no further than the problems faced by a typical MIS shop to understand one important force for change. Such a shop typically has an application backlog of more than a year. And this is the known backlog—the invisible backlog of unvoiced needs may be several times larger. Skilled MIS professionals are scarce, and turnover is a continuous threat to project continuity, budgets, and schedules. The maintenance load is heavy and consumes resources that would otherwise be devoted to application development. Users are restless: Some have turned to outside time-sharing services; others have purchased micros or minicomputers and embarked on their own paths. The cost of technology is plummeting, resulting in new applications. The MIS staff is generally slow to implement new productivity-boosting tools and techniques. And the outlook for improvement is slim: users outnumber the MIS staff and are increasingly demanding and vocal.

While these programs have always existed, two recent events have combined to set the stage for implementing an IC: the evolution of user-friendly tools and the renewed willingness of users to undertake certain DP applications.

A new generation of hardware and software tools exists today. Designed specifically for the non-DP person, these tools incorporate human factors that contribute to ease of learning and use. The new software tools are oriented toward results rather than developing the results. Although this nonprocedurality is achieved at the expense of the full capabilities of a procedural language like COBOL, it makes supported applications easier to develop by at least an order of magnitude. The charges sometimes leveled about expected inefficiencies in execution need to be tempered by the realization that the cost of technology is falling at 20 to 30 percent a year and that application development consumes a large part of the MIS resource, both staff and machine. Taking everything into account, most companies find that the high-level tools available today are underused.

The other part of the picture is the user's willingness to undertake certain DP applications. This attitude is spawned in part by frustration with the MIS group and by the prevalence of articles and vendor ads touting the availability of technology and its ease of use. Users are coming to believe that they too can directly participate in the computer revolution. Any success that fellow users may have had in a DP do-it-yourself endeavor strengthens this view, especially if any problems encountered are downplayed. Another reason for the growing user willingness to undertake DP applications is that an increasing number of entrants into the work force have had some educational exposure to DP technology that they can apply on the job.

Economic Justification

Despite the changing conditions that have created an opportune setting for the information center to proliferate, no IC should be established without a sound economic basis. Pilot efforts may require a leap of faith, but eventually management must be convinced that the center and its associated costs are worth the expense.

It is worth noting that on the average an established IC returns two dollars for every dollar expended, significantly higher than most DP application areas. The specific tools and applications, together with their management, will determine the actual cost/benefit.

A sampling of IC applications supports the argument that a solid business case exists for their implementation. At one company, ad hoc applications showed a productivity improvement factor—defined as the effort without the IC compared to that with the IC—ranging from threefold to more than a hundredfold. At the same time, return rates of repetitive applications ranged from 50 to several thousand percent. For some of these applications, a one-time use of an application more than paid for its development.

Because of the do-it-yourself nature of an IC, these benefits are achieved with very little MIS investment relative to other application development. While most DP applications require extended use to recoup the development expense, IC applications, which are generally smaller in scope, may pay for themselves immediately. The fact that an entire application may take minutes to develop opens up a new vista of applications that have been buried in the invisible backlog. Applications of interest to an individual or single work group suddenly take on new significance since the benefits can be substantial.

The potential saving on outside timesharing expenses also offers an incentive for many companies investigating ICs.

Other Benefits

In addition to economic benefits, several other benefits make an IC attractive. Users can assume more control over their data, applications, and costs. Since users need not go through the MIS programming group, the end product may better meet their needs and be delivered in a timely fashion. Certain applications can be developed quickly and inexpensively compared to non-IC alternatives. This permits both the emergence of a new type of application as well as the possible implementation of projects to which MIS has assigned low priority. The result: increased user productivity and effectiveness.

MIS also receives additional benefits. Perhaps the most significant of these is that user relations should improve once users understand that the IC offers an effective way of helping them get their jobs done. An IC group that successfully supports users can reduce much of the conflict between MIS and its users. Ad hoc requests or maintenance changes, which otherwise distract the MIS group, may very well decline, freeing time for major applications unsuitable in an IC. Finally, users will learn firsthand the problems associated with application development, giving them an understanding of the problems MIS faces. Such users are likely to be more forbearing in future negotiations with MIS.

ELEMENTS OF SUCCESS

Despite the several benefits, some ICs fail. Several keys to success follow.

A Service and Entrepreneurial Orientation. MIS groups usually view themselves as service organizations. This orientation is critical in an IC, which must present itself as part of MIS and yet be more responsive and willing to work toward common goals. The IC must overcome any inertia toward the status quo as well as any distrust users may harbor toward MIS.

The best way to achieve this service orientation is for the IC manager to direct the IC as an entrepreneurial organization that must actively market its services and be responsive to client demands in order to attract and retain clients. This philosophy should permeate the organization and be reflected in both attitudes and decisions. Newsletters, subscription drives, open houses, marketing strategies and plans, and brochures all become part of an organized effort in support of this attitude. The effectiveness of such effort should not be underestimated.

Right Tools. Regardless of the service orientation, the IC must market and support a set of tools that its clients will find easy to learn and use and valuable to their jobs. These tools should be carefully selected with a goal of minimizing both the number of tools and gaps in the IC product line. A typical center may support from 3 to 15 tools, depending on its maturity and available resources.

Right People. If a center is to be successful, its staff must have a strong service orientation and excellent communications and interpersonal skills. Technical and application skills, although important, play a less significant role because they can be learned relatively quickly.

Supportive Climate. For the IC to flourish it must have the support of users and other DP groups. This support is not a given, and often users will prove more supportive than MIS, a problem that poses significant challenges to the IC manager. Support can be won if the IC works hard for a few success stories and is aware of the threat it may pose to others.

Justification by End User. MIS cannot and should not justify an IC; that justification must come from users. This is especially important considering that computer use will increase substantially if the IC is successful. This

END-USER COMPUTING AND OFFICE SYSTEMS

change must be portrayed as user-driven demand having associated benefits to which users can attest. A company with a chargeout scheme will find justification much easier, since the user's willingness to bear the charge, coupled with the tenets of sound management, implies that the offsetting benefits are achieved. Benefit surveys, in both companies with and without chargeout, provide additional justification.

Data Availability and Integrity. The data needed by users must be available as well as accurate, timely, dependable, and understandable. In some cases users key in the data; in other cases some version of production data must be made available without jeopardizing production operations.

RISKS

The risks associated with an information center fall into four major categories as discussed in the following sections.

Proliferation of User Contact Points. If the IC is part of the MIS group, the latter probably has several points of contact with users. How will this new service be blended into the existing organization so that confusion is minimized and conflicts avoided? To whom should users talk, and under what conditions? Who should speak for MIS?

Application Inappropriateness. As mentioned, some types of applications are inappropriate for an IC. What mechanism, if any, ensures that only appropriate applications are created? What are the implications if an inappropriate one is set up? Are bootleg systems going to be created, and what are the risks of this? Will any of the IC applications tie in to other DP applications, and if so, how? When will a given tool prove inadequate to the application, and what are the alternatives?

Runaway Demand. If the IC is successful, will demand for computing cycles, storage, and other resources prove insatiable? How can growth be managed? Should growth be dampened, and if so, how?

Political Issues. Given the current relationship with the user community, is establishing an IC the best option at this time? How dependent is the success of the IC on the support of other DP groups? What are the likely battles over roles and responsibilities of user support? What threats does the IC pose to certain people and organizations?

Evaluating whether to establish an IC based on the importance of these risks is a management responsibility. The risks may prove too severe for some organizations. For those willing to assume these risks, however, the rewards can be substantial.

ESTABLISHING AN INFORMATION CENTER

The approaches to establishing an IC vary widely. Some companies simply decide to rename an existing organization and hope for the best. Others plunge ahead and live to regret their overzealousness. The recommended approach is to plan carefully and execute a pilot of the concept. This minimizes the risk and maximizes the chance of success. Based on the results, an informed decision can be made before any long-term commitment is made.

Stating Goals and Strategies

The overall plan begins with a statement of general goals, such as determining if an IC is applicable in the current environment and, if so, establishing such a group on a firm footing.

The purpose of these goals is to gain consensus on the general direction and to serve as landmarks as the work progresses. Careful thought should be given to the wording of the goals and to their implications.

After development of the goals, the next step is to develop the strategies to attain those goals. These strategies might entail acquiring management support for a study, conducting the study, conducting a pilot if called for by the study, and evaluating the results of the pilot. Like the goals, the strategies must be carefully developed and analyzed.

Conducting the Study

A pilot should never be launched without a preliminary study to determine such matters as whether a pilot is desirable, what its scope should be, what its objectives are, what its work product should be, and what resources it requires. Failure to devote the proper time and attention to the study impedes the overall effort.

Study details vary by organization, but several items are keys to success of the pilot. If the effort is considered important, as any IC study should be, time must be made available for it. This often means committing full-time resources to its completion. Management support is critical, and agreement on the study objectives is essential. The specific questions to be answered should be identified before beginning; these include the feasibility of the concept and projections of demand. The detailed design of the center should also be addressed, including:

- Activities and functions
- Classes of applications within the company and the initial hardware and software needed to support these applications
- The internal organization of the IC and associated job descriptions
- The financial and administrative requirements of the center
- The strategy to be employed in making data available to the users and the permitted interfaces to production systems
- The criteria to be employed in determining the appropriateness of applications
- The service and product marketing strategies

The study should also evaluate performance measurement criteria, both for the IC and for its staff ("on schedule and within budget" does not apply to an IC!). The organizational placement of the IC must be resolved, as should development of the business case for establishing an IC. The risks must be identified, not only of the IC concept itself, but of the pilot and even the consequences of forgoing a pilot once a study has been completed. A pilot implementation plan must be produced as well as a longer-term plan based on the success of the pilot.

A study work plan and a commitment to stick to it help ensure timely completion. Despite the volume of work involved, if the proper planning is done the study can probably be completed in 8 to 10 weeks of team effort.

The last key item the study should address is identifying the pilot users and their requirements. It is recommended that the first question be resolved, with user concurrence, before the study begins. A good choice would be political allies outside MIS with a record of supporting technology and innovation. Potential applications should be plentiful, and the user group should contain many bright, adaptive people willing to try something new and unfazed by a few problems. Identifying the user requirements for those applications requires discussions with the pilot users during the course of the study.

Defining the Pilot Service

Although the actual tools supported by ICs vary widely, the basic service is typically online and interactive, although personal computers and other technologies may also be supported. The IC should be viewed as a utility, with users electing whether to use the service and controlling how much is used. The pilot should be compatible with this basic view and should capitalize on the advantages of an internal time-sharing organization over external ones. The service should be defined as different from existing services in such aspects as responsibilities, organization, responsiveness to user needs, required documentation, controls, necessary authorization, and tools. This attracts user attention and encourages trying something new and, it is hoped, better.

Whatever software is selected for the pilot should be user friendly and easy to use. It should suit client applications identified during the study and should have a quick learning curve. In keeping with the tentative nature of all pilots, it should be inexpensive or already available.

A similar decision must be made regarding what system the applications software should run on. Most companies simply use the existing in-house system, although an alternative is to rent time outside until the pilot is completed. Several companies bring in a new, small-scale processor dedicated to supporting the pilot work load. This approach avoids disruption of the existing system, reinforces the differential nature of the service, and recognizes that a multiple-processor strategy may be desirable in the long run to deliver the best availability and response time. Whatever approach is used, the system should be reliable, and the cost should be appropriate to a pilot project setting.

Approaching the Pilot

The length of the pilot varies, depending on the preparation needed to begin support of the first user. Once the first user is trained, approximately three months should be sufficient to assess whether a long-term commitment should be made to the IC concept.

It is important going into the pilot that everyone understand and agree to its goals, which typically pertain to validating the following conditions:
- The risks are manageable.
- The proposed design and operation are appropriate.

The Information Center

- A satisfied user base can be established.
- A training program can be set up.
- Detailed operating procedures are developed and usable.
- The operation falls within the expected cost.
- The anticipated benefits are achieved.
- User demand exists beyond the pilot group.

A strong staff should be assembled to support the pilot, with communications and interpersonal skills being key considerations. Ideally, the IC pilot project leader should have participated in the study. The project leader should report to a politically influential person, since the problems that arise must be resolved quickly.

Finally, the pilot project leader should temper the entrepreneurial thrust with an understanding of the dangers of overextending oneself in the pilot. This can be accomplished by limiting the pilot to a small but credible client group and supporting only a few products.

Conducting the Pilot

Given the relatively short pilot period, it is important that everyone work hard, work smart, and be personally committed to success. The pilot project leader should try to formalize implementation and support responsibilities with the other parts of MIS. This serves to ensure a smooth implementation, prepare for postpilot expansion, and validate procedures associated with actual user support. As much work as possible should be done before actually beginning client support. This might include such matters as setting up equipment, developing extracts of production data, training the staff, and developing training materials. Once client support begins, the pace can be expected to pick up substantially, and it will be difficult to go back and regroup.

As the pilot progresses, care must be taken to meet the key issues head on. These issues usually pertain to application appropriateness, data integrity, and economics. Failure to resolve these issues means the pilot is less than a success.

It is recommended that the IC group establish a beachhead at the client location so that problems can be quickly discovered and resolved. Many problems cannot be adequately handled by phone, and much rests on the success of the pilot.

Finally, the major pilot activity involves keeping everyone informed. Presentations, meetings, and status reports keep both users and MIS informed, interested, and able to step in as problems arise.

Presenting the Results

The amount of effort necessary to prepare the pilot results depends on three factors: management's initial inclinations toward ICs, how well management has been kept up-to-date, and what management expects as a work product. A well-polished, organized presentation or report takes longer to develop but stands the best chance of influencing decisions. A crisp, professional approach reflects favorably on the effort and accurately indicates the planning and work that have preceded it.

END-USER COMPUTING AND OFFICE SYSTEMS

Adjusting to the Postpilot Environment

Assuming the pilot was successful and management has given approval for expanded service, it is important to recognize that the postpilot period is not simply more of the same. Instead, it marks a period when new expenditures can be profitably made to streamline the service, enhance its capabilities, improve ease of use, and leverage the staff. Operational responsibility may shift in the case of a separate processor. A walk-in center might be opened. Additional products could be investigated.

At any rate, the objective after the pilot should be to shift operations toward some long-term optimal approach and to plan and prepare for the future while meeting current needs.

IMPLICATIONS FOR THE DP ORGANIZATION

An information center has an impact on the MIS organization as well as the client community. DP groups that have been wrestling with personal computers and office systems suddenly find a new force with which to contend. The IC must be blended into the existing organization, and yet new organization structures are suddenly possible and begin to fall into place. For example, a substantial number of organizations transfer responsibility for personal computers to the IC. Office systems functions and data management/administration functions are also seen to be closely related to the IC. The challenge is to build a responsive, strong organization that can best serve the user. There is no one right answer to addressing the organizational implications, and yet decisions must be made.

The IC also has an impact on the systems development life cycle. For the first time, users have a practical way to meet their data requirements directly if they are given the right data to manipulate. Consequently, over time the role of the systems and programming groups might well shift to become that of data collectors, "sanitizers," and presenters, with the user doing the actual formatting of output. If this occurs, the implications are far-reaching.

Finally, the IC affects data base and file design, since these are rarely developed with direct user access in mind. The problem is not so much one of efficiency as the unlikelihood that the end user will relate well to the internal intricacies of current applications. For example, users will not know that code 04 refers to the Midwest Sales Office. These problems are often addressed by creating some kind of data extract from production files and restructuring it for user access. As a long-term solution, however, this is far from optimal.

CONCLUSION

An information center may very well be the key to forging a successful relationship with users during the 1980s. The concept has experienced good acceptance and success in many companies and in many industries.

The key to successfully establishing a center lies in a carefully planned study, followed by a pilot with well-defined objectives and deliverables. Under this approach, the risks are minimized and the chances for success are greatest.

V-2
Getting the Most from Personal Computers
David O. Olson

INTRODUCTION

Although most MIS departments have little experience with implementing personal computers, users of personal computers request their assistance. Broadly stated, these requests are requests for computer literacy, a frequently used but seldom defined term that can have a different meaning for each user. This chapter presents the five components of personal computer literacy, recommendations regarding the degree of literacy required, and questions that should be asked when determining whether to use in-house staff or external vendors for computer-literacy training.

COMPUTER LITERACY

The term *computer literacy* refers to the basics that people who are not computer oriented need to know. While the term is commonly associated with personal computers, its application can extend to minicomputer and mainframe computing systems. The arrival of personal computers has made users more aware of the need to better understand all computer systems affecting them. This chapter, however, focuses on computer literacy as it applies to the implementation of personal computers in business and in industry.

Computer literacy is a comparative term whose definition consists of at least five components:
- Knowledge of computers
- Knowledge of computer applications
- Experience in computer use
- Skills in computer programming
- Awareness of the issues involved when personal computer technology is implemented in an organization

These components are discussed in the following sections.

Knowledge of Computers

Novices are confused by "computerese." Bits, bytes, kilobytes, ROMs, RAMs, operating systems, 6502 microprocessors, floppy and hard disks, tracks, sectors, control keys—all are words in a seemingly foreign language,

END-USER COMPUTING AND OFFICE SYSTEMS

but are eventually necessary for new users to know and to understand if they are to function successfully in the world of computing.

Courses in data processing for non-DP professionals represent the traditional method for teaching the terms and concepts of computers. This approach is obsolete for new personal computer users, since they do not need to be inundated with terms and definitions that are beyond the scope of their immediate question, "What can a personal computer do for me?"

Furthermore, individuals in business and industry need to understand the basics of computer theory. They do not, however, need to know how to design, build, or program a computer. The beauty of the personal computer is in its software. Thousands of off-the-shelf software packages are available for personal computers. Almost any kind of program available for a minicomputer or mainframe is also available for a personal computer. Thus, the skill required of personal computer users is not programming but translation. Users must learn to translate highly technical instruction manuals into a context that is meaningful to them. One student, examining a manual for a user-friendly software program exclaimed, "If this is a friendly program, I'd certainly hate to meet one that's unfriendly!" Too often, jargon and acronyms that DP professionals casually toss about are incomprehensible to new users. Thus, computer-literacy training should follow the "need to know" rule and teach only information that is absolutely basic to running off-the-shelf software.

The traditional approach to computing calls for specialists from MIS departments to meet with end users, determine their needs, examine system capabilities, provide cost and time estimates, get approvals, and return several months later with a system proposal for the client to review. In personal computing, this process is shortened: a need exists, an off-the-shelf program is loaded, an application is created. Instead of months, this process takes only minutes, hours, or at most, days.

End user questions are basic: What is a terminal, a monitor, a disk drive, a program disk, and a storage disk? Users want to know how to modify software for their applications, how to store data on a disk, and how to retrieve data from a disk. These are needs that are most obvious and most often articulated by first-time users.

Knowledge of Computer Applications

Users of personal computers are interested in at least five software applications:
- Spreadsheets
- Data management systems
- Charting and graphing
- Word processing
- Communications

In a business setting, the first two applications are needed by 90 percent of all users. Interest in charting and graphing seems to come mostly from senior managers. Word processing on a personal computer is used primarily in small businesses. Currently, communications between personal computers is unpopular, probably because of the difficulty of interfacing with timesharing systems and the high cost of commercial data bases.

New users first need to learn what their software applications can do. Second, they must know the fundamentals of how the software works. In spreadsheets, for example, the concepts of columns and rows, variable column widths, and matrix cells that can be addressed as individual variables, should be explained. In data management systems, new users must understand the concepts of files, records, fields, sort indexes, and print formats. Third, new users must be able to determine whether a need can best be met by a spreadsheet, data management system, or other application. Finally, new users must be able to examine an existing report, modify a software package to handle that report, and enter data to compile future reports.

Therefore, this approach for personal computers takes new users from knowing to doing by describing the program to them, showing them what it does, teaching them how to use it, and then helping them to create their own applications. This transition takes many hours of support for each new user.

As stated earlier, the most important skill to teach new users is not programming but rather translating—that is learning—the terminology used in a particular software program. Instruction manuals for spreadsheets and data management systems frequently use such terms as cells, inserting, deleting, cursors, replicating, values, labels, saving, loading, fields, alphas, numerics, indexes, print formats, files, and file definition. These are terms and concepts whose definitions are specific to an application; users need to know them to interpret instruction manuals for off-the-shelf software. In this context, then, computer-literacy training is analogous to reading, writing, and arithmetic. Just as no school teacher would use James Joyce's works to teach reading to primary students, no computer-literacy instructor should use JCL to teach users of personal computers.

Experience in Computer Use

Another aspect of teaching new users, one that is usually unspoken but should be addressed as part of computer-literacy training, is fear of computers. There are two kinds of potential computer users: voluntary and forced. Voluntary users approach the MIS department for assistance; forced users do not. Forced users, however, are the ones who really need the help.

Many advertisements suggest that anyone can quickly learn to use a personal computer. Some potential users believe this but will give a multitude of reasons why they cannot take the time to learn. Some do not fear computers themselves; rather, their fear is of accidentally breaking the computer. The teaching approach called for in this situation may be compared to behavior modification in that users must touch and use a computer to learn how it works, realizing that it is sturdy and cannot be broken by normal mistakes. New users should also realize that there are no stupid questions. In other words, training by manuals alone is insufficient; hands-on exploratory sessions and individual supervision are required.

The most important facet of teaching managers and professionals to use personal computers is to provide them with an opportunity for hands-on experience in a highly supervised setting. The student:teacher ratio should be no more than four students for every instructor. There should never be more than two people per computer or more than sixteen people per seminar.

At least two levels of seminars can be conducted on a formal basis: literacy and business applications. A literacy seminar can be a one-day program. Content should focus on an overview of the most frequently used application packages (e.g., electronic filing, word processing, spreadsheets). If two people share a computer, less pressure is placed on participants to perform since another student is there to help, and twice as many employees can participate in the course. The audience may contain those who are interested but unsure of how the personal computer can be used and those who are doubtful of their ability to operate one.

A two-day business applications seminar is ideal for those who currently have underused or unused personal computers sitting in their offices. Each participant should have his or her own computer. The content of this seminar should include a brief orientation to electronic keyboards, an elementary presentation of DP concepts as they relate to the personal computer, and extensive training in developing spreadsheets and data management systems; any additional information may be confusing. At least four hours should be provided for participants to work on their own applications. Participants should arrive with blank disks and leave with working applications.

A key ingredient in these courses is the instructor, who must therefore be chosen carefully. The instructor must possess a deep understanding of DP concepts; however, it is just as important that he or she understands the fears and apprehensions of new users. In addition to prior teaching experience, instructors should have extensive experience with both the personal computer and the software that they are teaching. Furthermore, instructors should have broad business experience. If they are to teach spreadsheets, they should understand the development and use of the financial reporting systems that their students want to implement. Simply stated, instructors must understand the needs of and develop a rapport with their audience.

The one or two days spent in a classroom should be just the beginning of support to be given to personal computer users. It is one thing for new users to "know"; on-the-job performance is something else. Organizations most successful in using personal computers are those that provide ongoing support systems. Some of that support should come from the MIS department. Follow-up sessions with seminar participants should be scheduled to help users with the development of specific applications. This kind of follow-up may take from 2 to 40 hours; such support can rapidly deplete MIS department resources. Thus, other means must be developed to provide ongoing support. Several ways to reduce the amount of time MIS personnel must spend with each user are discussed in the following paragraphs.

Start-up effort, teaching the initial group in the organization to use personal computers, requires the most time. During this time, the MIS department should develop lists of key departmental contacts who can be called upon to provide support to new users. It should also begin to develop such user organizations as IBM's GUIDE organization. The MIS manager should consider assigning one staff member the responsibility for writing and editing a personal computer newsletter. Other user activities that should be considered include software sharing, circulating a list of applications that users have developed, and asking other users to review new software packages, equipment, and peripherals. By developing activities in which new users can help themselves, the MIS department can reduce the time necessary for user support.

Skills in Computer Programming

Although new users do not need to know how to program, they must eventually perform such tasks as making backup disks, revising file names, and deleting files. Skills needed to perform these elementary maintenance tasks are beyond the scope of a literacy or business applications course. Rather, the MIS department should develop such procedures and teach them on an individual "need to know" basis during support sessions.

Issues Involved in Implementing Personal Computers

First, an organizational policy and guidelines for purchase of personal computers must be established. Without them, one could expect to find anything from a Timex-Sinclair 1000 to a Heathkit appearing on desktops. The ultimate result would be chaos since nothing would be compatible with anything else.

When considering the purchase of personal computers, some managers believe the MIS department to be reactionary when it responds, "Personal computers are inappropriate." Such managers might say, "Others are using them, why shouldn't I? MIS is simply trying to control our lives."

In one sense, this assessment is correct; however, some control is necessary. The task, then, is to realistically assess user needs for personal computers while remembering that the option of stamping "request denied" onto a purchase requisition is probably no longer feasible. Current prices of personal computers are such that almost any first-level manager is given authority to make the purchase decision. Thus, MIS managers must not develop "David and Goliath" adversary roles. Instead, they should develop a needs-analysis form. Questions to ask include "What do you want to do?" and "When and how often do you want to do it?" By determining the scope of user needs, MIS managers can use the information to develop meaningful, realistic recommendations.

The second issue involves two types of problems that arise when personal computers are implemented in user departments: machine problems and people problems. Machine, or computer, problems include data lost because of improper backup, confusion regarding computer use, and lost disks. In other words, the problems that managers are accustomed to facing and handling whenever new systems are implemented must also be faced when implementing personal computers. The major difference is one of scope, that is, since more users will have access to personal computers, more users must be trained.

The interpersonal problems are mainly problems in attitudes. While many people are eager to learn about personal computers, not everyone is eager to

END-USER COMPUTING AND OFFICE SYSTEMS

integrate them into their daily lives. Since there are no textbook answers, the best approach for dealing with these problems is to use common sense, based on a careful examination of each problem as it arises.

Two audiences must be addressed when implementing personal computers: decision makers and decision implementers. Decision makers are those who, for whatever reason, have decided that their department or division now needs to have personal computers. Decision implementers are those who must learn how to use the personal computers that the decision makers have bestowed upon them.

The decision makers should be told the disadvantages of personal computers. They are probably already aware of the advantages, which include reduced DP costs, immediate processing turnaround, and the ability to quickly develop custom applications. However, decision makers, usually middle- and senior-level managers, need to understand that personal computers are not a panacea for departmental problems. Work loads do not decrease, problems do not lessen, and, most certainly, paper does not disappear. If anything, the opposite may occur. While staff members learn to use the new computers, they may fall behind in their work. Problems may increase because every new user will be at a different level of understanding. Paper is certainly not eliminated; in fact, as new reports are generated from the personal computer, there may be more paper than before.

Unfortunately, decision makers often expect decision implementers to have their staff functioning at 100 percent efficiency in approximately three days. The decision makers, however, may not understand that spreadsheets do not magically appear on a storage disk; someone must create them. In addition, data management systems are not created; they evolve, sometimes over a period of weeks. Helping these managers to understand how long it takes a staff to complete personal computing projects is a major project in itself. The decision makers probably do not use personal computers themselves; thus, their understanding of the problems their staff is facing may evolve slowly, because such understanding is not attained vicariously—it must be experienced personally.

IMPLEMENTING A COMPUTER-LITERACY PROGRAM

Computer literacy can be taught by in-house staff or by external consultants. There are advantages and disadvantages to each approach. The two major considerations when using in-house staff members are whether they have the expertise to design and deliver a computer-literacy program and whether they can contribute the time necessary to develop the program. Approximately 30 to 60 days of full-time effort is required to design a computer-literacy curriculum.

In addition to the curriculum, student materials must be developed. Paper handouts can simplify the off-the-shelf software program and can be used as references after the seminar. Disks are required to provide examples of how software can be used. Both are critical.

At least four, possibly as many as eight, personal computers are required for the seminars. Although it is possible to conduct a literacy seminar using computers from two vendors (e.g., IBM and Apple), such an approach is not recommended until the teaching staff has had some experience with the seminars. Instead, it is best to focus on one personal computer, with all students working at the same keyboard design on the same software program.

The following three questions should be asked in determining whether to use in-house or external consultants to conduct computer-literacy training:
- Does the staff have the needed expertise?
- Can these individuals afford 30 to 60 days to work on this project, and can they conduct computer-literacy seminars on an ongoing basis?
- Is the necessary equipment available for the seminars?

If the answer to any of these three questions is no, then the use of external consultants to conduct the computer-literacy training should be considered.

Several questions should be asked when selecting outside consultants to conduct literacy training:
- What is their experience with personal computers?
- What is their experience in training novices to use personal computers?
- What is their business background?
- What is their approach to teaching personal computers (i.e., lecture versus hands-on training)?
- What equipment and software do they use to teach?
- How many students participate in each class and how many instructors are there for each class?

After these questions are answered, the MIS manager can put the consultants to the test by enrolling in one of their classes and taking along one or two potential personal computer users to help in evaluating the seminar. The MIS manager may then assess the effectiveness of the seminar content by observing the users as they operate personal computers in their jobs.

ACTION PLAN

Previously, those needing data processing did their work according to the mainframe computer schedule. With the advent of the small computer, an increasing percentage of those needs can be fulfilled by the user's personal computer, in a schedule convenient to the user. This change calls for MIS managers to take a proactive rather than reactive role, that is, to become involved and stay involved in planning for and implementing personal computers.

The MIS manager should follow these steps when implementing personal computers:
1. Develop an assessment form to review and determine systematically the best personal computer for the job.
2. Let potential users know that the MIS staff is interested in personal computers and is willing to help in selecting the best computer for the job.
3. Talk with users of personal computers in the organization to obtain their input regarding the kinds of problems that they are experiencing. Help to develop solutions to those problems.
4. Establish a computer-literacy training program and determine how it should be conducted.

END-USER COMPUTING AND OFFICE SYSTEMS

5. Develop user support functions (e.g., personal computer organizations, newsletters, lists of available application packages, reviews of hardware and peripherals) to reduce the dependence of personal computer users on the MIS department.
6. Listen to the users. As their needs change, so must the MIS department's support.

V-3
Controlling Personal Computing
Eric Stanford

INTRODUCTION

Personal computing, or end-user computing, is the use of computing systems in which the end user plays a dominant role in defining, developing, and creating automated processing and output. Personal computing is not limited to personal computers (desktop computers or microcomputers)—it can involve computers ranging from mainframes to word processors.

Among the advantages of personal computing is the end user's improved ability to identify needs and determine when those needs have been met. Because end users can exist in any organization and at any level therein, a broad population can access computing services. In addition, personal computing allows the implementation of many valid applications previously delayed because they were considered too small to receive priority from information services organizations. The disadvantages of personal computing include distribution and duplication of DP resources and reduced control and security for data and equipment.

PERSONAL COMPUTING CONTROL ISSUES

Many applications that use personal computing technology do not pose control threats. Concern should be limited to those areas at risk—that is, areas in which company business, data, or operations can be affected. Many of the control threats discussed in this chapter are difficult to counter because of the limitations of current technology. Because vendors have progressed slowly in addressing and solving these issues, management must take the initiative to remedy some problems directly.

Although personal computing holds considerable promise for improving productivity, competitiveness, and cost-effectiveness, it requires the implementation of additional controls. To take full advantage of this technology, management must recommend controls whose overall goal is to promote rather than discourage the use of this technology. The most effective approach is to develop management awareness of the technology's usefulness and to provide education about the controls needed to promote its effective use.

END-USER COMPUTING AND OFFICE SYSTEMS

The issues affecting personal computing are similar to those encountered in traditional DP operations. However, management is often minimally aware of personal computing control problems. Managers should review each of the issues discussed in this chapter to determine current practice, needed controls, how to implement controls, who should be responsible, and whether a corporate policy is required to enforce these determinations.

Data Security

During the past 20 years, the more traditional MIS environment—in which control of data and data access is centralized—has experienced a reliable and sophisticated level of security control. Data security controls for personal computing using either mainframes or microcomputers are less effective, especially with the accelerated distribution of data outside data centers. Both data and computers are moving into our offices. Data communications is playing an increasingly prominent role in personal computing, improving information access but reducing data security. With the distribution of the computing resource to the end user, these control responsibilities are also distributed. Most user managers fail to understand control responsibilities and to implement the procedures needed to protect their data. Many user managers are unaware that data can "walk out" of their facilities on diskettes and through telecommunications. Employees who use personal computing technology to work at home are enhancing their productivity but creating additional threats to data security as well as availability.

Data Integrity

Data integrity, or the reliability and availability of data, depends primarily on the guarantee that data will be properly input and maintained. Office supervisors have always faced the problem of reviewing and verifying the accuracy of their employees' work. Management must also understand how their employees are using the new technology, an assessment often difficult to make when a part of the process has been automated using a personal computing system. Furthermore, use of personal computing may make it more difficult to retain a distinct separation of duties (e.g., when one employee is responsible for programming, running, and reviewing the results of an automated process).

During the past 20 years, integrity controls have been developed in traditional DP facilities and systems to ensure that data is correct and complete. Other controls have been developed to ensure compatibility with business and processing cycles. However, very few of these controls are readily transferable to the new personal computing systems.

The lack of controls is further complicated by the fact that data can be uploaded or downloaded between the personal computing system and the host computer. Downloading refers to the movement of corporate data created in one of the organization's central computer systems to a microcomputer or another mainframe personal computing system, using the software available at that location. Central system controls over input, editing, accuracy, and completeness, however, often are not transferable. The upload capability enables movement of data created on the distributed personal computing system to one of the organization's central business data bases.

Uploading significantly increases risk, since integrity controls are often unavailable on personal computing systems. Uploaded data may taint the corporate data bases on which business decisions depend.

Environmental and Ergonomic Design

Environmental and ergonomic issues concern the design of the work place so that it facilitates efficiency, health, and safety for the type of work being performed. Insufficient attention has been paid to the environmental and ergonomic problems associated with installing personal computing systems in existing offices (e.g., desks at the wrong height, inadequate air conditioning). Such problems could cause increases in employee absences, worker compensation claims, and damaged equipment. In addition, existing security systems are probably inadequate to protect the added capital expense of a portable computing system (averaging $10,000) as well as valuable stored data.

Efficiency

Various syndromes can lead to inefficient use of personal computing systems.

The "We Must Become Programmers" Syndrome. When personal computing systems are installed, the temptation is to develop original software to meet user requirements. Unfortunately, this approach can lead to attempts by unskilled or unqualified persons to program complex systems. Instead of writing new applications software, organizations with personal computing installations should maximize use of off-the-shelf software packages to solve DP problems.

The "Reinvent the Wheel" Syndrome. Many problems encountered by personal computing users may already have been solved by others in the company. Employees should be encouraged to consult other users before attempting to research and identify solutions.

The "Buy Now, Decide How to Use Later" Syndrome. During the years, practitioners of traditional DP approaches have learned some very expensive lessons about designing and developing new computer systems. One of the main lessons has been that system development must begin with the identification of requirements, followed by identification and development of a hardware and software system to meet those requirements. Inefficiencies will result when companies buy personal computing systems without first determining user requirements.

The "New Toy" Syndrome. Many corporations seem to have acquired personal computing systems because it is fashionable to do so. This approach, as well as the "buy now, decide how to use later" syndrome, can lead to considerable inefficiency and frustration when a system fails to meet user expectations.

Many U.S. corporations insist on rapid payback of personal computing investments. This is supportable because of several factors: the equipment is usually relatively inexpensive, applications are limited in scope, and the

END-USER COMPUTING AND OFFICE SYSTEMS

technology is changing rapidly and should be able to be upgraded or replaced frequently.

An important consideration regarding efficiency involves organizational dependence on personal computing. Generally, once an organization adapts to the use of computer technology, its commitment to that technology increases as its ability to survive without that technology decreases. The availability of system time and computer terminals then becomes critical. (The related need for backup and recovery is discussed later in this chapter.)

Productivity suffers during the initial learning period after systems are first installed. This problem is aggravated by the misapprehension that any user should be able to understand any package running on a personal computing system—and with a minimum of instruction. Most new users are forced to train themselves, which frequently prolongs the learning process.

SYSTEM AND DATA AVAILABILITY

As the organization becomes committed to the use of computer systems and integrates them into its daily operations and procedures, data availability becomes critical. Deficiencies frequently exist in the support of data availability. Rather than depend on one or two experts, management should encourage consistent cross-training of employees so that more than one employee is aware of the systems and their use, developing brief but concise procedures explaining system use and implementing naming standards for programs, files, and procedures.

Backup and Recovery

Another important aspect of data availability is backup and recovery. Many new personal computing users seem to learn the importance of backup only after experiencing some catastrophic failure. In other words, when a system fails and data or programs are lost, the users then begin to think about how to prevent future data loss. When systems are distributed throughout different locations, corporate disaster recovery plans may overlook the need to identify critical personal computing functions and coordinate a program for their backup.

System Compatibility

Increased use of personal computing systems leads to increased sharing of data and programs. As personal computing systems mature, their users soon begin to demand the ability to upload and download host computer data. At the same time, demand also grows for the ability to transfer data and programs from one personal computing system to another; however, little consideration has been given to how this data can be exchanged. Most manufacturers do not build devices that are readily compatible with one another, and therefore different devices cannot readily exchange data or programs. Failure to plan for future integration needs will limit access and exchange of needed data. Thus, many corporations favor the acquisition of compatible devices. Adopting a policy of rapid payback of personal computing investments may help preserve flexibility for later changes in approach.

MANAGEMENT AND DIRECTION

Most initial users of personal computing technology are newcomers to DP. Lack of experience often causes new users to encounter costly delays and mistakes. Existing MIS organizations have the experience to provide the necessary coordination and focus; however, some MIS organizations may not be participating at an appropriate level, and in some cases they may not be prepared to take on this new role. New skills are needed in order to train and advise users regarding the new technologies. In addition, MIS may be tied to the more traditional services that it currently provides and may be constrained by budgets or unwilling to consider the benefits of providing both types of services to the user community. In some cases, user organizations have been unwilling to seek help from MIS. This urge to go it alone is often costly and counterproductive.

CHANGING AUDIT NEEDS

As users automate tasks and functions, they will integrate previously manual (and auditable) tasks into DP systems. Automation thus has several implications for internal auditors. For example, automation of these tasks should include consideration of the control issues discussed in this chapter. Because most personnel involved in automation are not DP professionals, they require education and guidance, which is the responsibility of the MIS organization. The auditor may have to play a role early on in educating DP personnel about control issues. In addition, if the current trend toward user-managed DP continues, the functions being audited are likely to be increasingly automated. To be effective, all auditors—not just EDP auditors—must become increasingly computer literate.

Some U.S. corporations have approached this problem by assembling an inventory of all their microcomputers and annually auditing the microcomputers and all applications supported. Audits, however, should continue to be scheduled on the basis of the risk associated with the function or process being performed. Therefore, audits of the process, not the machine, should be performed. Internal auditors should prepare guidelines to use when they encounter user-developed applications within processes being audited. Considerable education will be needed to help auditors become consistently computer literate.

CONCLUSION

Senior management involvement is essential to ensure effective, controlled use of personal computing technology. Issuing a statement encouraging the prudent use of this technology is a good first step. Because of the benefits and competitive advantage gained from personal computing, control of its use should ultimately promote rather than discourage its acceptance. Another management action is the implementation of a corporate policy that addresses the impact of personal computing on data security, integrity, availability, backup, and recovery. Implementation of effective control policies satisfies the requirements for support and protection of user-managed data and systems.

Return on investment should be targeted at one year. Because personal computers have been used for a relatively short time, their economic life span remains unknown. Industry concensus seems to be that technological developments are moving very rapidly in this field, and systems could quickly become obsolete. Further, improvements in communications between systems are also developing quickly. Because of these developments and the relatively low cost of personal computing, organizations should retain maximum flexibility to allow for system upgrading or replacement. Therefore, return-on-investment decisions should be attained in one year. In addition, projects undertaken following this philosophy tend to be kept to manageable size.

Responsibility for controls should reside with user management and the MIS department. Moving systems into user-managed areas shifts control responsibility from traditional MIS departments to the system users, who may prove ill prepared for this new responsibility. Because the MIS department is experienced in system design, control, and implementation, an MIS-user partnership must be formed to assist new users. However, users cannot escape ultimate responsibility for controls within their operations. User managers must understand the nature of the control function and perform necessary review and analysis. Areas in which significant control problems exist and for which managers must take responsibility are data security and integrity, efficiency, data availability, and system documentation.

To assist users most effectively, some MIS departments may have to keep an open mind about the benefits of these systems as opposed to the more traditional systems. This requires a willingness to recommend the best (not necessarily the traditional) choice for problem resolution; providing the necessary consulting, training, and assistance to users in application requirements development; and providing guidance to potential users considering the purchase of hardware to promote standardization as well as to obtain the cost reductions available with quantity discounts.

User departments have a responsibility to do their part to make the partnership work. Managers should encourage their employees to seek help and accept advice from the most competent, experienced source in the company—their MIS department.

Environmental and ergonomic problems must be resolved. Management must survey the facility thoroughly before installation to avoid ergonomic and environmental problems. To provide corporate guidance and identify the size of this problem, a review at the corporate level is required. Standards and guidelines should be established to assist personal computer users in this area. Once recommended solutions are available, they should be disseminated throughout the organization.

Data base access and sharing must be controlled to prevent data loss. When data is used by more than one person, integrity and security are more difficult to ensure. Guidelines are needed to ensure that both users and the MIS department understand their joint responsibility for data integrity and security. MIS has responsibility for the security and integrity of shared data; users must maintain security for their own data in unshared situations.

Education and controls are required to overcome risks introduced by data communications. The growing use of data communications has introduced new risks to personal computing; potential problems are exacerbated by the substantial growth associated with personal computing communications and the use of local storage and improved transportability of data (i.e., on diskettes). The trend toward using personal computers for business purposes in the home and in other non-work place locations further increases the risk of data exposure and security breaches through dial-up and other types of access. These breaches may result from employee carelessness, industrial sabotage, or hobbyists who violate security for entertainment.

Professional sources should provide training and education to improve productivity. New users of personal computing often fail to realize that others in their organization have already experienced the installation and implementation of these systems. This can result in multiple and even concurrent acquisition and training efforts. In addition, inefficiencies result when users train themselves in the use of personal computing systems and their software products. Personal computing users must identify sources for professionally designed training on the packages they intend to use. Users should avoid experimenting with systems as a method for learning to use them. Home or off-hours study should be encouraged as a way to improve productivity and reduce time lost at the work place.

Internal auditors must become computer literate. As the trend toward user-managed computing continues, audited functions increasingly will become automated. Adequate review of audited functions and processes requires that internal auditors be trained in EDP auditing techniques.

A multiple-device strategy should be considered. In addition to the many devices and personal computing approaches available, mainframe and minicomputer systems can provide effective personal computing. Any potentially beneficial application or technology should be explored. Given what appears to be an ever-changing market, an early decision in favor of a single strategy may prevent a company from taking advantage of future technological developments.

A strategy and direction for the use of personal computing must be established. Effective and controlled use of personal computing resources depends largely on effective planning. Companies should establish:

- A strategy for developing and implementing personal computing systems, including equipment migration paths, security plans, and communications approaches
- Objectives and policies identifying responsibility for control
- Responsibility for user support, including education, control consulting assistance, and hardware selection
- Management approaches to obtaining maximum benefits from personal computing system investments

Adequate control of personal computing resources depends on action by both corporate management and the MIS department. Careful consideration of the issues discussed here will help an organization establish this type of control.

V-4
Guide to Decision Support Systems
Jack T. Hogue

INTRODUCTION

Upper-management decision makers deal with problems that are difficult to solve. This difficulty stems from the complexity of the problems (i.e., hundreds of variables) and the changing structure of the problems (e.g., the elimination of variables no longer relevant and the introduction of new relevant variables). Upper management's dissatisfaction with the effectiveness of applying the computer at their level is well known. This ineffectiveness can be traced to many factors. One major factor is the significant difference between the well-structured processes supported by traditional computer applications and the highly unstructured or semistructured process of upper-management decision making. The same approach simply does not work in both situations.

The time required to develop computer applications is often an issue. An application backlog of one to three years typically is intolerable to a senior manager who needed an answer yesterday. Many upper-management decisions are unique and thus require ad hoc information. There is no time to pass through the application backlog.

Application development that bypasses the traditional information system backlog can generally be referred to as end-user computing. Decision support system (DSS) applications can be considered a subset of end-user computing. A significant issue in this area is the control of computing outside of MIS. End-user computing must eventually be brought under the umbrella of MIS control in order to centralize control of these resources. Among the benefits of centralization is the ability to avoid data and program redundancy. Documentation standards and data integrity are also key advantages. This control issue has received only superficial examination.

DSS CHARACTERISTICS

Although no consensus has been reached as to what constitutes a DSS, a typical definition might state that a DSS is an interactive, computer-based information system developed specifically for the purpose of assisting with unstructured and semistructured upper-management decisions. While this

definition is helpful, identification of the criteria that tend to distinguish a DSS from other forms of computer support is perhaps more useful. These criteria indicate that a DSS:
- Supports but does not replace management decision making
- Is directed at the semistructured decisions of middle and upper management
- Is interactive (it must operate in real time)
- Has data and models organized around, and dedicated to, a specific decision or group of closely related decisions
- Is very user friendly

The fourth item in the preceding list is worth specific examination. With a DSS, both data and models (i.e., logic routines and mathematical and statistical analysis programs) are accessed through commands or keystrokes from a single user interface. All elements are combined into one "package," or DSS. This DSS is used to address a single decision (e.g., a corporate merger) or a group of closely related decisions (e.g., financial planning).

Decision support systems can be further characterized by their utilization by management. They tend to support management throughout the decision-making process, which includes the following:
- The collection and assimilation of information on current conditions and situations through a current data base
- The design, development, and evaluation of alternative scenarios
- The selection or recommendation of a course of action

A final—and primary—characteristic of the DSS is the decision(s) for which it it utilized. Because the DSS is built around, and dedicated to, a single decision, the decision is one of considerable importance to the organization. The applications that have a high priority for DSS support are those that are critical to the success of the organization.

DSS APPLICATIONS

Decision support systems have been developed for a large number of applications, most of which are in those areas traditionally associated with corporate-level strategic planning: finance and marketing. Other DSS applications are specific to an industry or utilized on a nonrecursive basis (e.g., merger analysis). The following paragraphs describe some of the most common DSS applications.

Corporate Financial Planning. Financial planning is probably the most common DSS application. This may be due to the availability of excellent software (e.g., IFPS, or interactive financial planning system, from Execucom Inc, Austin TX) to aid in system development. One-, five-, and ten-year planning cycles typically are supported by the DSS. Two major characteristics of these DSSs are the large number of variables they can incorporate and their ability to examine an array of scenarios (i.e., what-if simulations).

Pricing and Promotion. These applications allow the decision maker to explore the implications and repercussions of various price and promotion strategies. Drawing on a financial model of the organization (perhaps developed from the financial planning DSS), the decision maker can alter price, advertising, commission, or any other variable of interest.

Mineralogical Exploration. These applications, common in large petroleum firms and utilities, present the current state of drill sites, potential drill sites, and in-production sites. The decision maker can examine the impact of varying levels of success at the sites. Drilling progress can be monitored and results incorporated into the corporate financial plan.

Transportation Routing. Decision support systems in this category are used by both staff and top management. At one extreme are dispatchers at a large railway examining different routes in terms of alternative optimization criteria (e.g., to minimize lateness or maximize payload). Air traffic controllers use similar systems. At the other extreme is the vice-president of marketing for a major airline examining alternative air routes to decide which routes to offer. Relevant variables might include potential market size, local labor rates, local fuel costs, and competition.

Portfolio Analysis. This was perhaps the first formal DSS application, and it is common today. With this type of DSS, brokers can continually monitor the market, examining alternative investments for a potential increase in return.

DSS DEVELOPMENT

Development of a DSS typically differs in one or more ways from that of traditional information systems applications. The factors of greatest interest include the basic methodological approach, personnel involved, length of time required, and system flexibility.

Methodological Approach

The basic approach to the development of a DSS is evolutionary and iterative. Although a DSS passes through the traditional systems development life cycle (SDLC) stages of analysis, design, implementation, and operation, the frequency of these phases is considerably higher, and their duration is typically shorter. In fact, while developers of traditional systems may attempt to minimize the number of iterations, developers of a DSS will put a premium on modification of the system.

Although most DSSs are developed in this iterative fashion, the approach for a particular DSS will depend on certain factors. The more structured the DSS application, the more likely a traditional SDLC approach will be used. This approach typically involves the use of what are termed DSS tools—basic system components, such as traditional programming languages, statistical packages, and mathematical models.[1] More appropriate for less structured applications is a DSS generator, a software "package" that facilitates evolutionary development of a DSS, typically in a specific functional area (e.g., finance).

Other factors that may affect the development approach to a DSS are the cost of the system, the personnel who develop it, and the scope of the DSS (e.g., departmental versus corporate). The evolutionary strategy is more common with less-expensive systems developed by the end user for use at an individual or departmental level. The evolutionary approach should be strongly encouraged whenever feasible because it often leads to a system more satisfactory to the user.

Development Personnel

Historically, the developers of a DSS are usually the end users. With very few exceptions, MIS personnel take only a supportive role, primarily in the areas of hardware and operating system functions and in providing data extracts from corporate data bases. The user typically assumes responsibility for the specification and programming of logic and data input. Again, this depends on certain factors, primarily the type of technology utilized (i.e., a DSS generator versus DSS tools); DSS generators greatly facilitate end-user development. When MIS personnel take the lead in developing the DSS, they must work in partnership with the user rather than as leaders.

Development Time

The time required to develop a DSS is the most varied of the development factors. Time frames range from a few days to one or even two years. The primary factors affecting development time are the scope of the application and the availability and use of a DSS generator. Probably the most effective step that can be taken to shorten development time is the acquisition of a DSS generator.

System Flexibility

The purpose of a DSS is to provide support for a decision or closely related group of decisions. Regardless of the scope of the decision(s), most DSSs are utilized by more than one individual. These individuals use the DSS either separately, in support of multiple decisions, or jointly (either all at once or individually), in addressing a group decision. Of critical importance to DSS design, therefore, is the system's ability to appear user friendly to whomever operates it. This means that the DSS must be flexible not only to the variations in style of one individual but also to several individuals. Typical components that enable the DSS to meet this requirement include the availability of the output in a variety of formats (e.g., different levels of detail and graphical and tabular representations), different levels of interaction menus (e.g., beginner to expert), and variable questioning sequences.

DSS ACQUISITION

The acquisition of DSS capability should be evaluated within the organization similarly to other corporate acquisitions. The bottom line should be profitability; in order for a DSS to be considered successful it must contribute positively to corporate profit. Costs of the DSS can be determined through traditional means, but benefits present a major difficulty: almost all DSS benefits are intangible and hence extremely difficult to measure. To assist in this area, Peter Keen recommends the use of the value analysis concept.[2] In this approach, if the costs of development are relatively low (as in the case of a limited-scope DSS developed from an existing DSS generator), the benefits need not be quantified. In this case, returns will most likely heavily outweigh costs. If the costs are normal or high, Keen notes that an in-depth quantification of benefits is needed. Most DSSs fit easily within the first, or low-cost category.

Most organizations that have developed DSSs have not, thus far, formulated an organization-wide policy regarding their development. DSS acquisitions can be approached from three perspectives. First, each DSS application can be considered in isolation from others and the needed capabilities acquired just for that specific DSS. Second, a general-purpose DSS generator can be acquired that will support a variety of different but related specific DSSs. Third, an organization-wide DSS group (similar to the organization-wide MIS group) can be organized to establish DSS policies. Most organizations have taken the first approach, primarily because DSSs traditionally have been developed for a single decision or decision category by the decision maker and his or her staff, whose concerns do not extend beyond those of the decision maker. With considerable attention being focused on end-user computing, information centers, and DSSs, however, there is currently greater awareness of the need to improve the coordination of end-user (e.g., DSS) applications.

The recommended approach is something of a "middle-out" methodology. First, the most critical category of decision to be supported (e.g., strategic planning) should be selected. Development of the first DSS for this category will include the acquisition of a DSS generator. This cost will most likely require a detailed cost/benefit analysis and lead to what appears to be a traditional SDLC. Subsequent specific DSSs (developed from the DSS generator) may then be created without great concern for ensuing profitability. The initial purchase of the DSS generator will allow for rapid, inexpensive development of the subsequent DSSs. After the organization has had some experience with DSS development, it should establish an organizational policy for the coordination of DSS activity.

DSS ADMINISTRATION

The management and control of decision support systems is not a simple issue. Traditional information systems applications typically fall under the direct control of MIS. Unlike MIS-developed applications, the DSS typically is developed by end-user personnel within the decision maker's department. Further, the user typically specifies and programs the logic of the application. It is not surprising, then, that the end user maintains administrative control over the DSS. This works fine during the period when specific DSSs begin to appear; as DSSs proliferate, however, central coordination becomes necessary.

Users and MIS personnel should expect to assume defined roles with regard to specific DSSs. The decision maker and his or her staff should assume primary responsibility for all aspects of the DSS throughout its development, including approval, analysis, design, implementation, and operation. MIS must be prepared to assume a supportive role and provide consultation and expertise as needed. This will typically include selecting hardware and DSS generators, interfacing DSSs and operating systems, and establishing computer communications links. Central coordination of specific DSSs is discussed in a later section.

FOCUS OF THE FUTURE

Several DSS-related topics need specific attention. That they have not yet been considered in any detail is not surprising, given the relative infancy of the DSS field. First and most important is the relationship between the DSS and MIS. Considerable attention should be directed at establishing the responsibilities of the user and MIS, primarily concerning overall control of corporate DSS applications. Practical experience has not yet led to the establishment of reliable guidelines.

Two closely related topics of concern are documentation and data integrity. Although not peculiar to DSSs, problems in these areas are even more pronounced in DSS applications than in more traditional applications. With the user in control of the DSS, with frequent revisions of DSS content, and with multiple users of the DSS, a lack of documentation and data integrity standards could lead to the eventual downfall of decision support systems. This returns attention to the need for a central controlling mechanism as the most important factor in the growth of DSSs.

One emerging category of DSS that is expected to provide a major input into group decision making is the group DSS.[3] This DSS operates in a meeting room in which each participant has a CRT and input capability. Each individual views information, comments orally, and contributes personal opinion to the DSS. The group's information is then consolidated through a delphi technique. Revisions in projections and expectations are made using the individual inputs until a consensus is reached. Currently uncommon, such systems are expected to be used with increasing frequency.

ACTION PLAN

When beginning to confront the development of DSSs, an organization should adopt a three-phase process. First, an initial group of specific DSSs should be developed for a category of decision-making tasks. This should proceed as previously discussed in the sections describing DSS acquisition and administration.

Once the organization has this experience to its credit, the second phase, coordination, should begin. The first step in this phase should be to organize an MIS function (individual or group) to act as a liaison to existing specific DSSs. The most important aspect of this function should be its visible support. The users of the specific DSS must be able to sense a genuinely open and positive attitude. A logical position in the organization for this function would be the information center, if one exists. For each specific DSS, the newly created DSS group should conduct an inventory of and document the existing DSS applications. This inventory should include the source and use of DSS resources, the mutual responsibilities of MIS and the users with regard to each specific DSS, and the actual programs and procedures for use of the DSS.

The third and final phase in the process is consolidation and control. The organization should begin this phase by increasing the size and membership of the DSS group to include MIS representation and functional area DSS users. It would be this group's mandate to establish goals and procedures for the central administration of specific DSSs. Of particular interest should be the responsibility and authority of MIS and the user in DSS development, operation, modification, and data base update. Specific organizational policy and procedure should be established jointly by the DSS group and its superior, the corporate computer steering committee.

References

1. R.H. Sprague, "A Framework for the Development of Decision Support Systems," *MIS Quarterly* 4, no. 4 (December 1980): 1-26.
2. P.G. Keen, "Value Analysis: Justifying Decision Support Systems," *MIS Quarterly* 5, no. 1 (March 1981): 1-16.
3. G.P. Huber, "Issues in the Design of Group Decision Support Systems," *MIS Quarterly* 8, no. 3 (September 1984): 195-204.

Bibliography

Alter, S.L. "Development Patterns for Decisions Support Systems." *MIS Quarterly* 2, no. 3 (September 1978): 33-42.

Hogue, J.T., and Watson, H.J. "Management's Role in the Approval and Administration of Decision Support Systems." *MIS Quarterly* 7, no. 2 (June 1983): 15-26.

Keen, P.G., and Scott Morton, M.S. *Decision Support Systems: An Organizational Perspective.* Reading MA: Addison-Wesley, 1978.

King, W.F., and Rodriquez, J.I. "Participative Design of Strategic Decision Support Systems: An Empirical Assessment." *Management Science* 27, no. 6 (June 1981): 717-726.

Naumann, J.D., and Jenkins, M.A. "Prototyping: The New Paradigm for Systems Development." *MIS Quarterly* 6, no. 3 (September 1982): 29-44.

Sprague, R.H. "A Framework for the Development of Decision Support Systems." *MIS Quarterly* 4, no. 4 (December 1980): 1-26.

Wagner, G.R. "Decision Support Systems: The Real Substance." *Interfaces* 11, no. 2 (April 1981): 77-86.

V-5
Managing Office Systems Development

Francis A. Frank

INTRODUCTION

The office automation industry is inundated with control techniques, methodologies, guidelines, standards, and step-by-step procedures for designing and implementing office systems. Most project control techniques, however, are ineffective because they concentrate on controlling the effort and fail to manage the environment. That is, these methods measure and monitor only two project elements—time and effort—and overlook the third and most important aspect—people. Office automation managers admit that project objectives are not met because of this mismanagement. Managers must therefore question why they continue to emphasize project control and fail to manage people.

One reason may be that management is confused with control. Control does not imply management; in fact, overcontrolling the effort results in projects managing people rather than people managing projects. Before a project can be controlled, the people involved in the project must be effectively managed.

The Project Manager. A project manager should be responsible for project, people, and therefore productivity management. The project manager must survive in an environment constrained by schedules, budgets, hardware and software requirements, priorities, and, most important, people. This manager depends on people who are not under his or her direct authority and whose priorities may conflict with the project's goals and objectives; project testing, for example, is a secondary concern to a word processing manager responsible for document production.

Primary Development Areas. The largest challenge facing the project manager is identifying, isolating, and concentrating on those areas of development that ensure project success. The office systems development process involves hundreds of tasks and phases. Six of these areas, however, directly affect productivity management:
- Defining the project
- Involving applicable employees

END-USER COMPUTING AND OFFICE SYSTEMS

- Estimating time and cost
- Breaking down the project
- Establishing procedures for change
- Establishing acceptance criteria

If these fundamental principles are neglected during project development, the office environment is at best difficult and at worst disastrous. This chapter explains how to use these principles to develop an effective office system environment.

PRODUCTIVITY MANAGEMENT PRINCIPLES

Project Definition

Project managers agree that a project should be defined before it is implemented; however, time constraints often cause projects to be implemented without being defined. These constraints occur because time that should be allotted to project definition is either allocated to the design team or eliminated by the users, who want the office system to be implemented as soon as possible.

Definition Objective. A project definition has two primary objectives: for developers, it determines how much definition is needed; for users, it ensures that the design will work. Because the definition often includes only technical parameters and aspects, it generally can be used only for development. To satisfy both objectives, the project must be defined according to the system's use—not its development. These requirements can best be determined by talking with those who will eventually use the system. The design definition, therefore, ensures that authorization from the appropriate user personnel is secured before the project proceeds from the definition to the implementation.

System Test Plan. Defining a system's use requires user and project personnel to communicate across the development and implementation phases. A system test plan, for example, confirms the office functions, identifies the conclusion of the definition phase, and initiates the acceptance criteria. If the design team cannot predict how the system will be used, the definition phase is not complete. Because the plan is in business language, it highlights whether any major functions have been omitted. Omissions identified at the start of the project can be easily resolved.

Employee Involvement

A project environment must be structured and sustained so that all the people involved understand what is expected of them. This environment can be easily accomplished if the project is viewed according to the roles, goals, and responsibilities of each individual directly, indirectly, or informally associated with the project.

Office automation managers are usually preoccupied with organizing the development process; they are not yet concerned with the system's eventual use. A systems development project that emphasizes the system's use, however, encourages user involvement. Depending on the level of user involvement, a system can be developed in one of three ways: with the users, for the users, or to the users.

A work environment that ensures that the roles and goals of the project will be realized on time and within budget fosters and supports team motivation. Project teams should first be grouped by function; their roles and responsibilities should support systems development and, more important, end use. The project should then be broken down by people—not by activity—to reinforce individual contributions and understanding. Although many motivational factors can contribute to project success, the key element is recognizing and rewarding individual efforts throughout the project.

Time and Cost Estimates

The difficult task of estimating project time and cost is often compounded by management pressure to be prematurely precise, compelling the project manager to make time and cost estimates before all the details are known. The objective of estimates is to establish a project schedule and budget. A reasonable and reliable estimate is the project team's most useful vehicle for recognizing and achieving project goals. Ill-conceived estimates, however, can hinder the team throughout the project.

When an estimate is requested, two questions should be addressed:
- How will the estimate be used?
- What level of precision is required?

The type of estimate dictates its level of precision. For example, in a feasibility study, where the project estimate is only one of many factors considered in the final decision, extreme precision is not required. In project implementation, the estimate is both a measurement and a control and should therefore be more precise. The level of precision is in direct proportion to the project's activities and purpose.

In addition, if there is no method for predicting, measuring, and managing them, project changes can negate well-conceived estimates and schedules. The project manager can manage change (and not be managed by it) by budgeting for change. (This is discussed in a later section of this chapter.)

Project Breakdown

The first three principles of productivity management—project definition, employee involvement, and time and cost estimates—establish the rules and environment for project implementation. Ideally, all office systems should be implemented on time, within budget, and to the satisfaction of users. Because estimates are not precise, they should be confirmed by the project manager early in the project, when discrepancies can be easily resolved. This fourth principle of productivity management—project breakdown—addresses the problem of confirming estimates.

A project can be broken down by such techniques as short-interval scheduling, decomposition, and top-down and bottom-up development. Although all techniques have significant advantages, for the most part they concentrate more on the effort required rather than on the results obtained.

END-USER COMPUTING AND OFFICE SYSTEMS

The 80-Hour Rule. The 80-hour rule (developed by Keane Associates Inc) is a results-oriented methodology. The rule states that no one will work for more than two weeks (80 hours) without a deliverable product. The rule is used to manage people, who are responsible for the effort; monitor elapsed time, which is a criterion of progress; and measure products, which are the result of people's effort over elapsed time. In other words, the 80-hour rule ensures that a project estimate will produce a deliverable product in two weeks.

The primary benefit of the 80-hour rule is that effort is translated into results by the individuals who actually apply the effort and deliver the results. If estimates and results are not identical, project discrepancies can be caught early in the project. The 80-hour rule also benefits both the project members and manager. Project members control how, when, and in what sequence products will be delivered. The project manager monitors the project's progress more easily because each product is delivered within the two-week period. Although it is not difficult to break a project down into two-week segments, this process does require thought, discipline, and the ability to think in terms of results and not merely effort.

Procedures for Change

Changes have traditionally affected project schedules and budgets, degraded system integrity, and precipitated animosity among systems personnel, users, and management. The problem is not with changes—which are often crucial—but rather with poor change management. Carefully controlled changes can improve the system; the project manager, therefore, must develop an approach for handling system changes effectively.

Just as projects are managed to stay within budget, changes can be controlled by allocating a budget for them. When a change is deemed necessary, the project manager must obtain management approval to use the budget. Since only the system user can truly assess the value of the change, the decision to include the change, reject it, or implement it later must reside with management.

Budgeting for change is the first step toward managing change; the next steps are preparing a request for using that budget effectively and gaining management's acceptance. As the project progresses, the project manager must evaluate changes more rigorously, because their impact on schedule, budget, and system integrity increases exponentially over time: a change made early in the development cycle has a significantly smaller impact than the same change made during later stages.

Acceptance Criteria

The final principle of productivity management addresses the long-standing problem of system acceptance. If acceptance criteria are agreed on before project implementation, system acceptance is a well-defined task. The system test plan, which concentrates on how the system will be used, concludes the design phase and begins the acceptance phase.

Acceptance that occurs only once, at the end of development, usually creates user misgivings and anxiety; acceptance should therefore be a series of agreements and authorizations to proceed. Requests for authorization to proceed should be formally submitted to management. Formal acceptance of the requests ensures that the project proceeds without any risks, that critical decisions are supported, and that the developers fully understand the reasons for management's decision.

The project definition is the basis for acceptance criteria. If the system's use cannot be predicted, the definition is incomplete and requires revision before the project team proceeds to the next task. The acceptance document concentrates on the system's usability and operational soundness; it is the blueprint on which all subsequent technical engineering is based. Casual treatment of the acceptance criteria is self-defeating and is the most frequent cause of project failure. Formal acceptance should become a routine part of project development.

CONCLUSION

Each of the six principles of productivity management is vital to project success. The project definition is the basis for the acceptance criteria. If the project has been accurately defined, the system functions as planned. Employees involved in the project must understand their responsibilities and authorities in designing the system for effective use. Time and cost estimates result in a schedule and budget for the project with provisions for managing change. Using the 80-hour rule for project breakdown ensures that the estimate is measured against the products delivered. Procedures for change provide a method of incorporating and managing changes to improve the system.

The office systems development process occurs in a complex and demanding environment that consists of hundreds of sequentially dependent tasks and activities. The project team depends on many people to identify, isolate, and implement these activities within this environment. Productivity management that concentrates on the human aspects of office systems development ensures that projects begin and end on time and within budget.

Bibliography

Umbaugh, R.E. and Juliff, R.J., "Office Technology, Paperwork, and Productivity," *National Productivity Review* (Summer 1982) 250–169.

V-6
Workstation Ergonomics
Alexia Martin

INTRODUCTION

The era of information technology—the electronic creation, manipulation, and distribution of information—has produced such organizational benefits as increased output, maintenance of a competitive business edge, and survival in difficult economic times. As office automation continues to evolve, it will become increasingly important that it achieve another goal—improved quality of the work environment. Truly successful office automation is contingent on the attention given to ergonomic factors both during and after the implementation of automated office systems.

Ergonomics is the science of adapting equipment and environments to human skills and physiological requirements. Although this chapter describes the word processing ergonomic recommendations and guidelines developed by one company, these principles are adaptable to any organization.

BACKGROUND

In 1980 the secretaries—current and prospective users of word processing—in a large service organization presented management with a list of questions concerning the potential impact of office automation on the secretarial/clerical staff. Several questions were:

- Will the NIOSH (National Institute of Occupational Safety and Health) guidelines for health protection of CRT operators be followed?
- Can all employees (not just managers) receive understandable, nontechnical information regarding potential health threats created by office technology (e.g., word processors, laser-based copiers, terminals)?
- How will promotional opportunities and salaries be affected by office automation?
- What types of training will be available?

In response to these questions, management recommended a review of the organization's use of automated office systems, primarily word processing.

First, it was decided that an individual's direct manager (with assistance, if necessary, from corporate management—personnel or information resources) was responsible for answering questions concerning salary, training, and promotions; corporate management alone was responsible for answering questions regarding ergonomics. A survey team, consisting of the vice president of information resources, a research psychologist, and an office automation consultant, was then formed. The team visited each of the organization's word processing operations. Such factors as physical environment, equipment, vendor support, activity profiles, and methods and procedures were discussed with word processing operators, supervisors, and, in several cases, line managers.

The team prepared a checklist for conducting interviews and measuring physiological aspects of office automation. The checklist addressed eight areas that ergonomics literature has judged as potentially troublesome for CRT users and included a section for comments on the attitudes, preferences, and general observations of the operators and supervisors.

The review team also measured the size of display characters; display character crowding; the operators' viewing distances to hard-copy materials and CRTs; noise levels; glare; ambient temperature, work space arrangement and lighting; and storage space. These measurements were subsequently compared with established ergonomic design criteria.

Table 1 describes the problems and requests encountered at one or more of the word processing sites and discusses, where appropriate, their significance in the organizational context.

As a result of this review, measures were implemented to improve inadequate word processing conditions and practices and to maintain acceptable ones. Recommendations based on the review were incorporated into guidelines for subsequent word processing equipment acquisition and implementation. The guidelines, many of which were based on NIOSH recommendations, were distributed at management meetings and published in a company newsletter. Some guidelines were deliberately broad; they indicated desirable actions or characteristics and did not stipulate how they were to be achieved by department managers. Others were specific and integrated with corporate policies, with only justified deviations permissible. (For example, senior management's approval of system acquisition is contingent on whether the request includes costs for any alterations to the work space and specification of the preferred system.)

RECOMMENDATIONS AND GUIDELINES

The discussion of ergonomic recommendations and guidelines is divided into two parts: corporate practices and a user implementation checklist.

Corporate Practices

An organization should take the following specific steps to ensure that an automated system is responsive to user needs.

Communication. Both management and staff must completely understand their roles in the following aspects of office automation:
- Cost/benefit justification—Facilitates the approval of ergonomic measures. For example, the hidden potential costs of indirect lighting, air conditioning, or printer sound enclosures should be identified.
- Implementation guidelines—Include a site survey to identify potential work space modifications, training requirements, and facility design alternatives.

Workstation Ergonomics

Table 1. Ergonomic Issues

Adjustable Screen and Keyboard
Employees requested adjustable components to optimize work areas and reduce operator stress and fatigue.

Standardized Text
The entry of standardized contract, proposal, and report text on word processing systems was suggested as a means of reducing document production time. (Although a considerable amount of such text existed, the staff was unaware of its location or, because of telecommunications inadequacies, could not access it.)

Communications
The communications links for transferring text between two word processing systems or between these systems and computers were not always available.

Crowded Work Space
Work space was crowded because inadequate storage or work space necessitated added shelving near word processing terminals.

Diverse Procedures Used
Employees who transferred from one department to another noted that WP procedures differed.

Eye Complaints
Supervisors reported that many operators complained of eyestrain and requested eye exams. Without further study, the cause of the reported eyestrain could not be determined, although display quality (which varies among word processing systems in terms of character size, crowding, and full/half-page screens), glare, and sloppy author input are all possibilities.

Footrests
Some staff members requested footrests for added working comfort.

Glare
Overhead lights, sunlight, white walls, or light-colored clothing caused screen glare—a contributing factor to eyestrain.

Heat Problems
Word processing equipment (e.g., CPUs, disk drives) existing in offices without local air-conditioning control raised temperatures to uncomfortable levels.

Inadequate Electrical Outlets and Wiring
Some offices had an insufficient number of electrical outlets or inadequate wiring to add equipment such as lamps or word processing units.

Increased Stress
Unreasonable author and management expectations and conflicting priorities contributed to operator stress.

Unadjustable Light
Unadjustable light levels caused eyestrain.

Inadequate Equipment
A lack of funds prevented the acquisition of an adequate number of terminals (or other equipment).

Office Layout
Terminals, printers, CPUs, and disk drives were positioned without regard to comfort or convenience.

Inadequate Vendor Support/Maintenance
The support and maintenance of some word processing vendors deteriorated because they could not keep pace with their sales growth.

Printer Feed Problem
Printers in confined areas created paper loading or feeding problems.

Printer Noise
Printers located near operators were distracting and noisy. (Sound enclosures can reduce noise.)

Scheduling Problems
Heavy work loads occasionally caused scheduling conflicts and operator frustration. (Under such circumstances, typewriters may be an alternative to word processing keyboard entry.)

Sloppy Author Input
The quality of drafts seemed to have deteriorated with the advent of word processing. Sloppy drafts can increase WP problems because a word processing operator must glance back and forth between the paper and screen display, which require different lighting. Some operators find it difficult to read drafts written in black lead on yellow paper.

Standard Acquisition Process
A standardized plan for word processing system acquisition was suggested as a means of accelerating the cost-justification process. (Few operators and managers knew that such a plan already existed.)

END-USER SYSTEMS

Table 1 (Cont)

Static Problem
Static electrical charges caused word processing equipment to malfunction, particularly at installation. Power fluctuations also caused occasional equipment failures.
Technical Training
Vendor-supplied technical training was inadequate.
Telephone Handling
Word processor users were frustrated by having to answer telephones while at the terminals.
Terminal Height
The height of terminals placed on temporary roll-away tables or stationary tables and desks was not adjustable for operator comfort.
Terminal Noise
Some word processing terminals emitted nerve-wracking, high-frequency noise (this differs from printer noise).

- Shared versus exclusive operation—Employees must understand the advantages and disadvantages of shared and exclusive word processing or other variations that may affect business operations.
- Author guidelines—Regulate the use of word processing support services. Such guidelines should emphasize the need for legible writing and clear instructions and explain scheduling and priority criteria.
- Breaks—These periods should be established according to a formal or informal departmental policy. NIOSH recommends a 15-minute break (i.e., time to work on non-CRT tasks) every two hours for moderate ocular demands and a 10-minute one every hour for extreme ocular demands. These breaks are not mandatory, however, and their length should be based on the individual, task, environment, and/or equipment. Ideally, users should be able to determine their own needs.
- Corporate resources—It is important to communicate the availability of corporate resources, for example, training on preferred systems and telecommunications-based services, which include the development of protocol and format conversion facilities between preferred systems and other computer resources.
- Standard text—Employees must know which standard text has possible multiple uses and how to access it.

Selection of Preferred Systems. Many organizations have identified a few preferred systems to provide compatibility in, for example, formats, training, and procedures and obtain the best discounts. In addition, a few vendors can be controlled more easily than many; such leverage may be needed to improve service or maintenance.

Ideally, preferred systems meet all ergonomic criteria. Although they are not government mandates, these criteria enable users to adapt the system to their needs and justify system selection. The preferred systems and the rationale for their selection should be available to management and staff.

Ergonomic criteria for CRT screens include a tilt/rotate base; operators can then change the position of the screen to accommodate their needs and minimize glare. CRTs should also have a nonreflective screen.

Workstation Ergonomics

Keyboards should be detachable—connected by coiled cables—to allow greater freedom in their placement. This is particularly important when terminals are placed on desks rather than on special tables. Keys should have a dull finish to reduce potential glare. In addition, keyboards should have a maximum pitch of 11 degrees to minimize the operator fatigue that often results when hands are constantly elevated. Ideally, keyboards should also have a height adjustment facility.

Display height is a function of the operator's eye position. An operator's line of sight is usually 10 degrees below the horizontal. The display area should be within a 30-degree cone from this position, based on the NIOSH recommendation that screens should be 18 to 28 inches away from the operator. (It is important to note that because reading glasses are designed for a 10- to 12-inch viewing distance, operators with such glasses may have difficulty unless lenses specially designed for the terminal viewing distance are used.)

Characters should be legible at the appropriate viewing distance. Orange phosphor characters on an amber background have proved to be the most readable and easiest on the eyes. Although nonglare screens are preferable, a glare filter may be added if these are not used.

Radiation levels from CRTs are not hazardous to operators, but excessive voltage from faulty flyback transformers are. Periodic preventive maintenance by the vendor should be mandatory to minimize potential problems. Trained in-house personnel can eventually provide this service for preferred systems.

Printers should be purchased with, or adaptable to, sound enclosure hoods.

For each preferred system, an organizational representative should be selected to convey complaints and requests to the vendor and monitor responses. Management's establishment of user groups for the preferred systems facilitates the sharing of procedures and resources.

User Implementation Checklist

A user implementation checklist eases the office-automation process and ensures that it results in a safe, comfortable, and efficient work environment, which will enhance the quality of worklife.

General Considerations. The implementation plans for automated systems should be discussed with all staff members; formal and informal communication should be promoted throughout the implementation. Corporate guidelines can be helpful in determining what the staff should be told. Employees tend to resist automation if they do not feel free to participate or are unaware of changes.

Because their involvement in the selection process promotes system acceptance, users should test various offerings or define benefits for the cost/benefit justification required by management.

Facility Design. A well-designed facility is vital in an environment in which people and computers work together.

END-USER SYSTEMS

Indirect lighting of 200 to 300 lux should be used for background lighting. Direct light of 500 to 1,000 lux should be added for concentrated viewing (e.g., source documents) and screened from other CRT operators.

Light requirements for the majority of conventional office work are 500 lux; individuals older than 40 require one and a half to two times as much light. CRT luminance contrast, however, should be one-third of normal light. Since the CRT emits 50 to 100 lux, less lighting is required to achieve the 3:1 balance.

To avoid glare, terminals should be placed away from windows, unless the windows can be shaded. In addition, terminals should be positioned to avoid the reflection of overhead light; a hood can be used to reduce glare if such luminance is unavoidable. Walls should be painted a matte-finished dark color; if walls are white, a picture should be hung behind the operator to avoid reflected light. Glare filters can be added to CRTs with reflective screens to prevent eyestrain caused by artificial and natural light falling on the CRT.

The heat generated by some systems and components may necessitate additional air conditioning. Rooms housing numerous pieces of equipment require a separate heat adjustment.

Most systems include a multitude of wire connections. If it is not possible to run wires off the floor, they should be fastened down with brightly colored tape to alert personnel. A more expensive alternative is to purchase workstations that conceal wiring.

The operation of some system components (primarily printers and occasionally disk drives) can be quite noisy. Hoods, sound-absorbent materials, white noise, and a carefully planned office layout can reduce noise.

The space requirements for people and equipment vary. Vendors can assist in defining the requirements for their products. An office layout should be planned to accommodate equipment, files and supplies, reference material shelves, plants, and other "comfort" items such as extra chairs.

Workstation Design. A workstation should be comfortable and flexible enough to meet the changing needs of the office and users.

The terminal stand should be adjustable within a range of 23 to 31 inches from the floor. If only a fixed height is available, the stand should be approximately 27 inches high. Although the 30-inch height of a regular desk is adequate for writing or viewing material, it is too high for the terminal keyboard. Excessive keyboard height can tire operators, who must keep their hands constantly elevated.

Terminals occasionally include a stand for source material, although the use of stands should be optional. A well-placed stand reduces eye fatigue by eliminating the need to refocus from the screen to the source document.

A screen monitor that does not tilt or rotate can be placed on a device or stand that enables operators to adjust the screen's position to their needs. Ideally, the top of the screen should be within the operator's horizon and between 18 and 28 inches from the operator's eyes.

Chairs should be adjustable from the user's sitting position and include self-locking castors, cloth-padded seats, detachable armrests, pneumatic height adjustments, and movable backrests. The chair must provide comfortable and adequate back support, especially during lengthy periods of CRT use.

Some operators request footrests, since elevation of the feet usually readjusts posture and relieves stress from the lower back. Before a footrest is installed, however, the seating arrangement should be reviewed to determine whether the chair and terminal heights are appropriate for the operator; adjustments should be made as necessary.

Other work space requirements depend on specific tasks and are determined by the development of work flows or a task analysis.

Training. Formal or informal training can be provided by either the vendor or a co-worker; both methods have proven strengths and weaknesses. Adequate time should be allocated for the actual training as well as the valuable review sessions that follow. The trainee should have no other responsibilities during the training period.

System Management. Only one person should be responsible for managing the system, that is, scheduling work, interacting with the vendor or in-house vendor contact, and acting as a liaison between the system operators and authors.

CONCLUSION

Ergonomics is critical to successful office automation. With foresight and planning, automated office systems can be used to achieve not only the organizational benefits of improved productivity and an increased competitive edge but also the personal benefit of enhanced quality of work life.

V-7
Tying Office Computing to Resource Planning
N. Dean Meyer

INTRODUCTION

Many organizations are currently exploring the application of electronic information tools in the office. In the process, company personnel are learning to manage a new staff function. Managers who assume responsibility for office automation are, however, often bewildered by the variety of information available about technologies, business benefits and their measurement, organizational issues, and implementation techniques. The range of opportunities is as vast as the range of approaches, but established facts are scarce. Common concerns among office automation managers include:
- Gaining a charter and management support for the office automation function
- Understanding the role of the office automation manager as an entrepreneur initiating a new staff service
- Staffing an office automation team with the right mix of skills
- Building relationships with other staff and user groups
- Planning the diffusion of innovations throughout a complex organization
- Implementing projects that improve the way other people work

Although management strategy must be tailored to each organization, there are patterns that have been successful in establishing office automation programs. Examining these experiences can help all managers chart a course that is organizationally and technically sound.

This chapter reports the results of an in-depth study of a diverse cross section of office automation programs. It examines patterns of success and suggests a basic game plan that can guide a manager in initiating an approach to office automation. The scope of office automation and some relevant terminology are defined. The chapter then describes the exploratory research method. Finally, the research results are reported and distilled into a management strategy to introduce office automation into the organization.

SCOPE OF OFFICE AUTOMATION

As indicated in Table 1, office automation includes various tools designed to support office work.[1] These tools can be applied in two ways. First, they can be used to improve the efficiency of routine, well-structured administra-

END-USER SYSTEMS

Table 1. Office Automation Tools

Tools	Examples
Text Handling Tools	Word processing; typesetting; professional authorship
Decision Support Systems	Calculators; statistical packages; forecasting models; ad hoc modeling languages
Graphics Tools	Charts & graphs; line drawings; computer-aided design tools
Time Management Tools	Calendar & project management systems
Telecommunications Tools	Teleconferencing; facsimile; terminal-oriented message switches; computer-based message systems; voice message systems
Information Sources	Internal MIS data bases; large public data bases; local office data base management systems

tive processes. These applications focus on cost displacement (i.e., either reducing costs or precluding cost increases). Cost displacement can be realized through mechanization or automation.[2]

Second, office automation tools can be used for value-added applications (termed "augmentation") that increase the effectiveness of managers and professionals.[3] The benefits of value-added applications are very contextual and as difficult to measure as the value of professional work. By increasing managerial productivity, these applications have the greatest potential for improving organizational performance.[4] Just as word processing was an innovation of the past decade, value-added applications represent the challenge of the 1980s.

Before presenting the research method used for this study, two important concepts must be clarified. First, office automation is defined in this chapter as the direct use of information tools by managers and professionals. Second, given that organizations change slowly, successful practitioners begin with small-scale, value-added applications for a limited group of users. In this study, these carefully managed initial applications are termed "pilots." A pilot need not, however, be limited to an organization's first application of office automation. From the user's perspective, each application of new tools to solve a problem is a pilot in itself.

THE STUDY

The research study sampled senior managers who are responsible for office automation in 35 companies throughout the United States and Canada. Respondents are users (not vendors) and represent a cross section of manufacturing, service, and government organizations. The sample is skewed toward large organizations (median annual revenue of $2 billion—approximately three-fourths of the firms gross more than $1 billion annually*). The organizations studied provide a rich base of experience. The sample size is sufficient to identify several indications—and on some issues, clear statistical evidence—of what does and does not work.

Each respondent was asked to participate in a semistructured interview

conducted over the telephone. The questions explored were:
- Where did the idea of office automation come from?
- What is the organizational climate?
- How was the concept sold?
- What is the role of the office automation manager?
- What are the charter and organizational considerations, staffing, management tactics, and accomplishments to date?

A Yardstick for Progress in Office Automation

Stage of growth is a proven measure of an organization's progress in the diffusion of innovation.[5] Table 2 lists four important stages of office automation growth and their salient characteristics. These stages range from early conception—in which organizations begin to use such simple tools as word processors—to consolidation—which is characterized by the widespread use of advanced office automation systems.

Table 2. Stages in Office Automation Growth*

Stage	Characteristics
Conception	
Early	Cost-displacement applications (e.g., WP, administrative telecommunications, & records management)
Advanced	Cost-displacement applications; plans to build first pilot of managerial & professional information tools
Initiation	
Early	Use of pilots by information professionals
Advanced	Use of pilots by managers & professionals
Contagion	
Early	Use of limited set of office automation tools by multiple end user groups
Advanced	Widespread use of limited set of office automation tools; pilots of advanced integrated systems
Consolidation	Widespread use of integrated office automation systems

Note:
* The particular stage theory used here is L.H. Day. "Stages of Growth in Office Automation" (paper presented at the Diebold Automated Office Program. Fourth Plenary Meeting, Boca Raton, FL, October 25, 1979).

Figure 1 shows the distribution of responding organizations across these growth stages in the spring of 1980, when this research was first conducted. At that time, more than one-third of the organizations had reached the initiation stage and constructed their first pilot. Nearly one-fourth had reached the advanced initiation stage and introduced managerial and professional tools to a user group.

Figure 2 illustrates office automation activities in a similar sample of organizations one year later.[6] Comparison of the two figures suggests a rapid diffusion of office automation within the sample organizations. By 1981, 62 percent of the respondents had constructed their first pilot and nearly one-

END-USER SYSTEMS

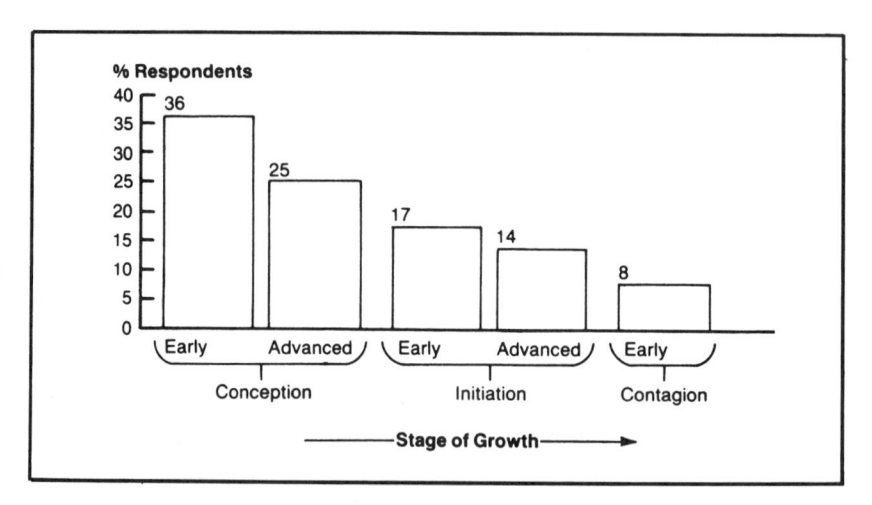

Figure 1. Respondents by Stage of Growth—1980

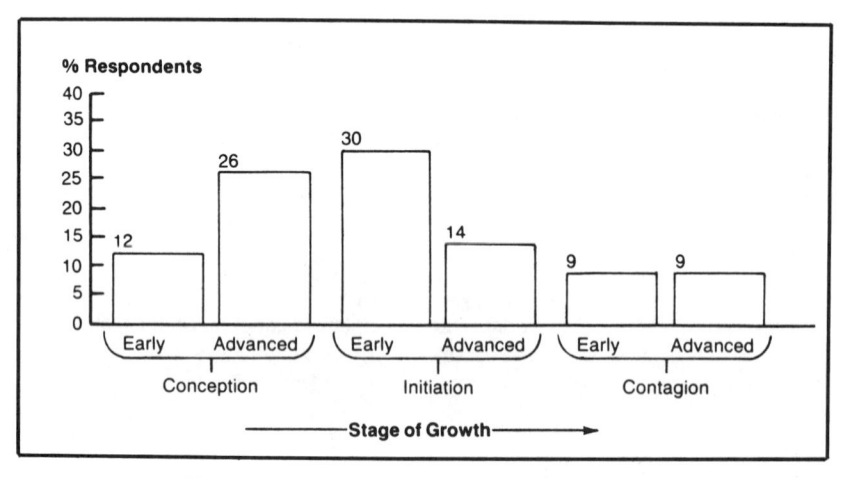

Figure 2. Respondents by Stage of Growth—1981

third had introduced tools to a user group. Nine percent in this sample had progressed to the advanced contagion stage—experimenting with pilots of advanced integrated office automation systems.

After sorting organizations by stage of growth, researchers compared strategies used by the most advanced companies with those of less advanced organizations.* Those in the more advanced stages offer a history of growth and an image of the future of office automation. Such characteristics as industry, size, and geographic area had no correlation with the growth stages of these organizations. The variables that were the most significant predictors of growth stage are discussed in the following sections. These findings are then used to develop management strategies for encouraging office automation.

Organizational Environment

The interest and endorsement of top management appears to be helpful in gaining a formal charter and funding for the first pilot. (The median level of endorsement among the organizations surveyed was presidential.) Although it is helpful to gain acceptance of the concept of value-added benefits, management support alone is not sufficient. In fact, management support had no correlation with the stage of growth, staff size, and rate of progress reported by respondents.

In the more advanced organizations surveyed, interest in office automation was related to a recognized organizational need. Moreover, organizational acceptance of value-added applications clearly facilitated progress in office automation. Value-added benefits were accepted as legitimate in 70 percent of those organizations in the advanced initiation stage as compared with only 30 percent of organizations in a less advanced stage. Of the 30 percent who built these pilots without considering value-added benefits, half justified them on a cost-displacement basis. Organizations in the least advanced stage justified office automation as the next step in office technology.

Charter

Two-thirds of the study respondents showed office automation on their official organization charts. The likelihood of a formally recognized charter appears to increase as organizations progress through the stages of office automation growth. It is unclear, however, whether a charter aids growth or vice versa. Clearly, top management interest, established management objectives, and high-level endorsement help in gaining a charter. A formal charter, however, does not guarantee protection from organizational challenges. (Seventeen percent of the respondents believed that their charters could be challenged.)

The charters of most respondents included (either formal or informal) responsibility for planning office automation and for implementation (at least of pilot projects). Responsibility for actual budgeting and operation of equipment was, however, typically delegated to users and/or technical support groups. This finding is consistent with other research on the differing responsibilities of operating groups and in-house consultancies focused on innovation.[7]

Half the respondents indicated some control over user choice of vendors. This control was exercised to guarantee that new equipment could be integrated with existing units without purchasing expensive interface processors. No correlation existed, however, between vendor control and the stage of growth. This finding implies that such control contributes little to the establishment of the office automation function.

In 48 percent of the responding organizations, the office automation group reports to the MIS or data processing department; 42 percent of the office automation groups report to a corporate administrative department, and 10 percent report to other departments of the organization. Comparison of the 1980 and 1981 studies shows a shift toward reporting to data processing. Roughly 60 percent of the office automation groups in the latter study report-

END-USER SYSTEMS

ed to the information systems executive. There was, however, no relationship between location of the office automation group in the organization and its stage of growth. MIS and administration each contribute different and equally necessary skills—successful implementation of the office automation function requires the cooperation of both.

Personnel

In the study, the personal, active interest of the current manager or superior usually provided the impetus for exploring office automation. Thus, at least initially, the office automation manager in responding organizations tended to be self selected.

Most organizations in advanced stages of growth had a full-time manager devoted to office automation, while only half the organizations in less advanced stages did. The median level of these office automation managers was three steps down from the chief operating officer and was typically known as director. The position of the office automation manager within the organization could not, however, be correlated with stage of growth.

The managerial role was an independent variable, having no correlation with level, location in the organization, or type of industry. The personality of the office automation manager was more significant than the location of the function within the organization. When asked how they perceived their role in the organization, 40 percent of the respondents chose the term "entrepreneur" (i.e., one who ferrets out new opportunities). These respondents were from organizations in above-average stages of growth.[8] The next most popular category was termed "researcher" (i.e., one who contributes new ideas and information to the organization). These respondents tended to come from organizations in an average growth stage. Such passive roles as consulting staff, service bureau, and the purely technical role of designer were cited by respondents from organizations in less advanced stages.

The median staff size of responding office automation groups in the 1980 study was three full-time employees. Most of the groups with advanced pilots had a minimum of three full-time people and a median staff size of six. An increase in staff size seemed to presage a change in stage.

All the groups that succeeded in building pilots for office automation users had a mix of data processing, administrative, and business skills. In contrast, those in the conceptual stage were lacking one or the other. Subsequently, the frequent addition of a behavioral science professional as organizations move into the contagion stage has been noted. These observations provide a clear map of staffing and professional development.

Tactics

By far the most powerful approach to building user awareness is a showcase pilot project to automate all or part of the office automation staff group itself. This tactic was used by all those in the sample who had implemented office automation tools for users.

Those organizations that did not initially have the appropriate funds often began by doing studies to highlight the potential benefits of office automa-

Office Computing

tion. Internal management presentations were common, and a few organizations also distributed outside reading material and arranged for speakers (e.g., vendors, consultants) to speak about office automation.

Several organizations spent money prior to gaining management support for office automation. Thirty-six percent of the organizations that have office automation applications, and two out of three of those in the early contagion stage, incurred expenses before receiving a formal charter. In many of these cases, the pilot itself was the action. While this kind of fait accompli may be risky, it is clearly a powerful tactic. (Unfortunately, those organizations that tried a fait accompli and failed were not studied.)

There was a clear relationship in the organizations surveyed between the stage of growth and level of user involvement. Office automation professionals were characterized either as facilitators who help users solve user-perceived problems or as experts who recommend solutions to staff-defined problems. Those organizations with pilot projects in their own office automation groups were more likely to be facilitators, and 96 percent of those who have built advanced pilots for users have taken the facilitative approach.

Two-thirds of the respondents formed user councils to structure some of the user management involvement. The more successful organizations did not form a council until their staffs were prepared to deliver pilots. (Here they tended to use the council to focus on business rather than on technical issues.) The user council can be an effective way to get user managers thinking about the potential of office automation. In addition, the council was used to solicit aid in identifying high-payoff business opportunities.

Use of Office Automation Tools

At the time of these surveys, the majority of respondents were using word processing, data processing, and administrative telecommunications networks of some sort. Less than 20 percent, however, reported using records management programs. Organizations whose office automation groups were responsible for the operation of all these administrative systems were below average in their stage of growth.

Among advanced organizations, the single most popular pilot approach involved the user of computer-based message systems for professional-to-professional telecommunications.[9] These systems were found in 70 percent of advanced groups. Most of the remaining organizations in the advanced stage used other forms of asynchronous electronic mail to support communications between departments.

Eighty percent of the advanced groups also used some form of local data base management systems for administrative support, including forms data bases, calendar management, correspondence tracking, to-do lists, project plans and status files, and group bibliographies. Both local data bases and telecommunications tools were typically present when office automation was introduced into the organization. Seventy-five percent of the advanced pilots began by integrating tools, typically combining telecommunications with local administrative data bases. In many cases, users acquired advanced multifunction systems that exceeded their needs and later grew into them. A less

END-USER SYSTEMS

common pilot approach focused on professional writing tools—high-level text editors that allow professionals to sketch, structure, and edit their thoughts directly at the computer terminal.

It should be noted that personal computers have spread rapidly since the time of this study. Simple decision support systems (e.g., automatic spreadsheet systems) may now be more common management and professional information tools.

The organizations surveyed became interested in office automation tools from one to twenty years ago. Organizational interest in managerial and professional applications represented a median of two and one-half years. It took these organizations an average of six months to gain management approval, one year to build the first pilot for use by the office automation group, and two years to build the first pilot for a user group. While this was the most typical pattern for introducing office automation tools, one-third of the groups in more advanced stages built a pilot for users before (or at the same time as) building a pilot for their own use.

MANAGEMENT STRATEGIES FOR OFFICE AUTOMATION

Having examined a cross section of organizations that are actively exploring office automation, patterns of successful evolution can be observed. Management actions can be described in terms of three major efforts:
- Building a capability to deliver various office automation tools
- Building organizational momentum by successfully implementing office automation tools
- Planning for the future of office automation within the organization.

Building a Delivery Capability

The capability to deliver office automation services must include an awareness of available tools and their applicability as well as the ability to manage their implementation. Before this delivery capability can be established, however, a single point of responsibility for office automation must be identified within the organization. It is relatively unimportant to whom in the organization this new function reports. Rather, the central issue is identifying the right individual to manage office automation.

The activities of this key individual are crucial in establishing office automation as a staff function. This manager must assume an active role as pioneer, create a collaborative environment that melds a balanced mix of skills on the office automation team, and be respected by both users and staff groups. Typically, the first office automation manager is self selected. A conscious top management selection might occur later, in the contagion stage.

Careful staffing of the office automation team is equally important. It should combine data processing, administrative, and general business talent. Behavioral skills are a valuable asset when available. In general, a business orientation and good interpersonal skills are at least as important as technical knowledge, which can be more easily taught or subcontracted.[10]

The office automation team must also establish a leadership position within

Office Computing

the organization. A formal charter helps, but it might be difficult to acquire prior to some objectives have been accomplished. Control over vendor selection is also helpful and ensures that the team is aware of activities throughout the organization; however, it is generally not essential. In fact, this type of control can be counterproductive if it jeopardizes the implementors' image as helpers who are on the user's side.[11]

Implementors aware of only a single tool tend to become almost technology salespeople representing a solution in search of a problem. Conversely, awareness of the broad range of information tools available allows implementors to respond flexibly to unique business needs. This awareness can be developed through various means, including conferences and workshops, on-site seminars and training, reading, and vendor demonstrations. The most advanced users agree, however, that direct experience is needed to understand what the advanced tools are, what they can do, and what is required to make them work. Thus, a key step in building a delivery capability is the creation of a pilot for the internal use of the office automation group. This pilot can be used as a testing ground and a showcase to demonstrate possibilities to users. Furthermore, a staff pilot can increase team credibility by showing that the staff group practices what it preaches.

Tools to support the office automation team itself should not require cost justification as a specific application, but rather the cost should be justified as research to explore the potential organizational benefits of office automation. To maximize learning, the pilot should combine the most powerful set of tools available. (These pilots typically cost from $1,000 to $2,000 per month.)

Delivery capability is further built by training members of the office automation team in implementation skills. As agents of change, they must be aware of the impact of technology on individuals, work groups, and organizational politics. Furthermore, these agents must develop listening, group facilitation, negotiation, and mediation skills. Numerous participative project management techniques are applicable to office automation implementation. This kind of explicit training in the role of consultant is an important form of professional development.

Finally, delivery capability is enhanced by collaboration with other relevant staff functions, including the data processing, administrative, operations research/management science, finance, and personnel departments. Implementing the variety of office automation technologies requires this range of skills. The office automation group should cast itself as the integrating focal point of the organization rather than as a competing technology group.

Building Organizational Momentum

While building a delivery capability, the office automation team must establish momentum in the organization by building applications for various users. Initially, its primary objective should be to establish a reputation for being useful to other groups throughout the organization.

User awareness can be enhanced in the pilot stage through management presentations, studies of the current information environment, and the show-

END-USER SYSTEMS

case pilot itself. Bids for top management support should focus on obtaining acceptance of the concept of value-added benefits.

The most important step in building organizational momentum is the success of the first few pilots. Early small successes build a reputation for the implementor and create a climate conducive to change. These initial pilots should address business problems that are considered important. Further, the pilots should be tested in areas of the organization that are visible and whose users are committed to project success.[12] Conversations with leading office automation managers suggest three key questions in choosing a pilot application:
1. What functional area is most important and central to the organization (i.e., who has the power)?
2. Who in that functional area is a well-respected, progressive opinion leader who will make an effort to apply office automation to daily work?
3. What are the opinion leader's major business problems? What tools can be acquired to quickly meet a perceived need?

This kind of analysis can identify high-leverage pilots. The training of managers in office automation applications can be a very powerful way to involve users in the pilot identification process.[5] For an initial pilot, a project of limited scope is advisable. The project should be useful within nine months or less—before the problem fades and user staff changes.

Careful management of change is essential to pilot success. Particularly in early pilots, serious thought should be devoted to involving users and monitoring potential sources of resistance to change.[13] Once an initial pilot is successful, the office automation team can use its credibility to spread enthusiasm in the organization. At the same time, the team can plan more advanced capabilities in pilots for other opinion-leading user groups.

Planning

The first level of planning for office automation—to gain management attention—can be simply a rough statement of the potential benefits of office automation in the organization. This statement can be based on financial and labor cost statistics and the experience of others in the field.

A more detailed plan permits short-term pilot actions that are consistent with longer-term integrated design goals. Too much technical detail can, however, be counterproductive, limiting the office automation team's ability to be flexible and responsive to user needs. Furthermore, technical detail can distract the office automation manager from the more important task of building organizational momentum. Thus, the office automation manager must walk a fine line between top-down planning and bottom-up implementation.[14]

Comprehensive plans are more than technological forecasts. In addition to technical trends, these plans are used to research organizational and environmental trends (e.g., new business directions, economic and demographic trends, evolution in the use of new tools). In more advanced stages of growth, office automation planning may become an integral part of business planning.

Once credibility is established, user councils may become involved in identifying pressing business needs that require good information tools. Users often are in a better position to identify ideal pilot locations. Moreover, the involvement of a user council can minimize competition between users and office automation managers for resources. When properly managed, user councils focus on user needs before giving attention to technical considerations. By including users in the planning process in this way, the office automation team can increase its organizational effectiveness.

CONCLUSIONS

This chapter summarizes the experience of a cross section of current office automation users and highlights important issues for managers who are attempting to form a new office automation function. The recommendations presented are not intended to be off-the-shelf answers to problems encountered by office automation management because every organization is unique and must develop its own approach.

This article also presents an exploratory research study. Its results validate the intuition of many practitioners and are consistent with previous work on the diffusion of innovation in other disciplines.[15] More formal research, however, is needed on the diffusion of office automation.

This research focuses primarily on the initiation stage—where managerial and professional pilots are started. During this stage, the concerns of office automation managers are similar to those of operations research managers in the 1950s and data processing managers in the 1960s. Management issues change, however, as organizations move through stages of growth. The contagion stage involves management concern for rapid and widespread delivery. The subsequent consolidation stage emphasizes the efficient, widespread delivery of common support services and the integration of tools. These issues will be of growing importance to office automation managers in the mid-1980s.

The primary challenge today in most organizations is getting an evolutionary process started—a process that has the potential of leading to significant improvements in the way business is conducted. Continued exchange of experiences among office automation managers will be useful to those organizations getting started on this exciting management discipline.

References

1. Meyer, N.D. "Office Automation: A Progress Report." *Office: Technology and People*, April 1982.
2. Diebold, J. "Automation: The Advent of the Automatic Factory." Master's thesis, Harvard University, 1952.
3. Englebart, D.C. "A Conceptual Framework for the Augmentation of Man's Intellect." *Vistas in Information Handling*. Edited by P.W. Howerton and D.C. Weeks. Washington, DC: Spartan Books, 1963.
4. Meyer, N.D. "The Relationship between Office Automation and Productivity." *National Productivity Review*, Winter 1983.
5. Rogers, E.M. *Diffusion of Innovations*. New York: Free Press of Glencoe, 1962.
6. Meyer, N.D. "Research Report: Human Resource Issues in Office Automation." Paper presented at the Diebold Automated Office Program, Plenary Meeting, San Diego, CA, March 1981.

END-USER SYSTEMS

7. Beer, S. *Platform for Change*. Chichester, England: John Wiley and Sons, 1975.
8. This is consistent with research in other fields. See, for example, Maidique, M.A. "Entrepreneurs, Champions, and Technological Innovation." *Sloan Management Review*, (Winter 1980), pp. 59–76.
9. For more complete description of computer-based message systems, see Meyer, N.D. "Computer-based Message Systems: A Taxonomy." *Telecommunications Policy*, December 1979.
10. A further discussion of staff selection criteria is offered in Meyer, N.D. "Consciously Staffing an Office Automation Group." *Computer Decisions*, December 1982.
11. Attributes of a charter statement are discussed in detail in Meyer, N.D. "Organizing an OA Support Group." *Computer Decisions*, October 1982.
12. Meyer, N.D. and T.M. Lodahl. "Pilot Projects." *Administrative Management*, February–March 1980.
13. Meyer, N.D. "The People Issues of Office Automation." *IMPACT: Information Technology*. Administrative Management Society, (four-part series, September–December 1982).
14. Meyer, N.D. "Planning for Integration in Office Automation." *Systems, Objectives, Solutions*, November 1981.
15. Bean, A.S., R.D. Neal, M. Radnor, and D.A. Tansik. "Structural and Behavioral Correlates of Implementation in U.S. Business Organizations." *Implementing Operations Research/Management Science*. Edited by R.L. Schultz and D.P. Slevin. New York: American Elsevier, 1975.

Section VI
Data Communications

In most medium-sized and large organizations, data communications is already part of the overall information systems strategy, and it is rapidly being adapted by smaller organizations. As a result, communications planning is becoming a critical responsibility of the MIS manager. Understanding communications technology, however, is not easy. This section is designed to help MIS management take advantage of the power of data communications technology and of the options available to exploit this potential.

Chapter VI-1, "Data Communications Management," serves as a primer on data communications, describing transmission modes, line types, terminal/modem interfaces, and line-sharing devices. Readers with a good grasp of data communications fundamentals may wish to skip this chapter and go directly to Chapter VI-2 for a detailed discussion of communications network planning.

Planning and implementing a data communications network is a complex task involving organizational as well as technical issues. The network design process must be integrated with the organization's business goals and strategies. Because network planning, implementation, and maintenance require skills not usually found in a batch-oriented DP environment, training is critical. Chapter VI-2, "Planning for Networks," advises the MIS manager on how to avoid the common mistakes in planning and operating a data communications network. Staffing and implementation guidelines are presented to help ensure a successful network strategy.

Integrating voice and data communications is a topic of considerable interest today. Current technological advances in data and voice communications make the integration of these functions seem inevitable. Integration can be total—incorporating voice, text, and data processing—or it can be as limited as grouping data and voice under a single manager. To help MIS managers understand the benefits of integration, Chapter VI-3, "Voice and Data—Putting Them Together," discusses such advantages as cost savings and improved operations and goes on to describe effective implementation procedures.

In most cases, the design and integration of a data communications network requires a thorough needs assessment. As noted in Chapter VI-4, "Satisfying Data Communications Needs," this planning methodology involves the identification of workable alternatives for the delivery of communications capability and ultimately guides hardware and software selection. The planning effort must continue through pilot testing, training, and resource optimization. Based on the recent implementation of a data communications network, this chapter describes a typical needs assessment exercise.

Another topic of considerable interest today is local area networks (LANs). A key issue here is the security and control of data on the LAN. Chapter VI-5, "Security for Local Area Networks," describes measures that MIS management can take to provide effective data security in LANs. Among these measures are terminal control, access control, identification methods, and environmental control.

VI-1
Data Communications Management
Gary Zielke

INTRODUCTION

Data communications now plays a major role in meeting the information needs of most organizations. Online systems and distributed processing are now common, and the importance of data communications will only increase as local area networks and office automation become cost-effective strategies for more firms. Therefore, MIS management must include network requirements in systems development and MIS resource plans. This chapter provides a management-level overview of the basic components of a data communications network, including transmission modes, communications lines, line-sharing methods, and front-end processors.

LINE CONFIGURATIONS

Whether a network is centralized or distributed, three basic types of lines are used to support the processors:

- Point-to-point—This is the simplest and most common type of support. It is frequently the most costly, however, since it requires a one-to-one terminal-to-port ratio.
- Multipoint—Multipoint (or multidrop) support allows several terminals to share a single communications line, thus saving costs. Polling is used to prevent line contention; the host CPU gives each terminal, in turn, permission to transmit. This implies more sophisticated communications support; as a result, many minicomputers do not support multipoint operations.
- Loops—Loops are a form of multipoint operation in which the line connecting the terminal forms a loop that starts and ends at the CPU or controller. Loop systems are generally used only for local networks.

TRANSMISSION MODES

Several modes exist for transmitting data over these communications lines; some of the more common techniques are described in the following paragraphs.

Character Mode. Single characters or bytes of data are transmitted as they occur. A character-mode terminal, for example, transmits each character as it is typed. This is one of the simplest forms of transmission and requires very little terminal or computer sophistication.

Block Mode. All data generated is buffered for transmission in block form. Each block of data is framed by appropriate start and stop characters so that the receiving device can detect the beginning and end of each message. Most systems using block mode provide an error-checking sequence at the end of each block so that data damaged during transmission can be detected and retransmitted.

Asynchronous Transmission. This technique is used with character-mode transmission to indicate to the receiving terminal the beginning and end of each character. A single bit is added to the front of each character, and one or more bits, depending on the speed and code, are added to the end. This delimits the characters and allows the receiver to synchronize with the transmitter at the start of each new character.

Synchronous Transmission. If block mode is used, it is unnecessary to delimit each character. Because characters are all of equal length and immediately follow one another, delimiting is reduced to a counting function in the receiving terminal. The start and stop bits used in asynchronous transmission can therefore be eliminated and considerable overhead can be saved. The beginning of a block, however, must still be identified; this is done with a special sequence (a sync character). Although synchronous transmission is normally used with block mode, asynchronous transmission may also be used—but with higher overhead.

Simplex, Half-Duplex, and Full-Duplex Transmission. Simplex transmission is transmission in one direction only; however, few systems are pure simplex. Half-duplex is transmission in either direction, but such transmission cannot be simultaneous. Most interactive applications are half-duplex: an inquiry is made into the system and a response is returned.

Full-duplex is simultaneous transmission in both directions. Individual users generally do not communicate in full-duplex mode. A concentrator or multiplexor supporting several terminals, however, would function in a full-duplex mode; at any given time, some terminals would transmit while others received.

COMMUNICATIONS LINES

Communications lines are available in analog and digital formats. Analog lines were originally designed for voice communications; data terminals are connected to them through modems, which convert digital signals to analog. Digital lines (e.g., AT&T's Digital Dataphone Service) were designed specifically for data transmission, and do not require digital-to-analog conversion. Analog lines are now slowly being converted to digital since such transmission is advantageous to both user and carrier.

Consequently, modems will eventually become obsolete, and analog voice signals will have to be digitized before transmission. Ultimately, voice and data transmission requirements will be served by the same network.

Data Communications Management

Dedicated Lines. Communications lines can be designated as either dedicated or switched as well as being analog or digital. Dedicated lines, often called leased or private lines, provide a permanent connection between two or more points and are available in either a two-wire or four-wire format. In a two-wire line, the same path is used for both transmitting and receiving; a four-wire line has two paths: one for transmitting and one for receiving. A fixed monthly fee, based on distance and speed category, is charged for dedicated analog lines, which are grouped according to data speed capability:

- Narrowband—maximum speed of 150 bits per second
- Voiceband—maximum speed of 9,600 bits per second (recent modem developments have increased this to 14,400 bits per second)
- Wideband—speed capability of 56K bits per second and beyond

Digital dedicated lines (e.g., DDS service) are available at specific speeds: 2,400, 4,800, 9,600 and 19,200 bits per second, at a monthly fee based on distance. Such lines are usually available in a four-wire format and require no modems, since the interface to the terminal is through a data service unit (DSU).

Switched or Dial-Up Lines. Switched, or dial-up, lines require dialing or addressing to establish a connection; the most common example is AT&T's telephone network. This network offers a number of advantages. It is available in many places, and the cost of accessing it is low. Network design is simplified, and responsibility for the network's reliability and availability is placed on the carrier. The network, however, is based on a two-wire format and is limited to a maximum speed of 4,800 bits per second. In addition, errors are typically more frequent on switched lines.

No general rule exists for choosing between dedicated or switched lines; each application must be evaluated independently to determine the more suitable approach.

MODEMS

Modems, also called data sets, convert digital signals generated by the data terminal equipment into a form suitable for transmission over analog lines. Traditional modems (the word modem is derived from a contraction of the words modulate and demodulate) use a technique called modulation. An electrical signal, called a carrier, is varied in proportion to an input signal (the output from the terminal). This process is done at the sending end of the communications line, while the reverse process, demodulation, occurs at the receiving end and allows the terminal signal to be reclaimed from the transmitted signal. A more complete description of modulation is available in *Auerbach Data Communications Management.*[1] Modems are typically classified by three characteristics: speed, synchronization, and distance.

Speed. Modem speed is measured in bits per second. Most modems with speeds of 1,800 bits per second and below can operate at any speed up to and including the rated speed. For example, a 300-bit-per-second modem could operate at 110, 150, or 300 bits per second without any adjustment. This is generally not true for modems operating at speeds of 2,000 bits per second or greater. A 4,800-bit-per-second modem, for example, generally operates at

DATA COMMUNICATIONS

only 4,800 bits per second; however, operation at a lower speed may be possible with the proper switch setting or an internal wiring change.

Synchronization. Modem synchronization (either asynchronous or synchronous) precludes a continuum of speeds between 0 and 4,800 bits per second. This synchronization must be compatible with terminal synchronization; that is, if a terminal is operating in an asynchronous mode the modem must also be asynchronous. Most low-speed modems (0 to 1,800 bits per second) are asynchronous, while most higher-speed modems (2,000 bits per second and up) are synchronous. Synchronous modems generate a clocking signal that is used by the terminal to transmit or receive binary data signals. This internal clock typically operates at a fixed speed, allowing most higher-speed modems to operate only at the rated speed.

Distance. A more recent modem classification is based on distance. At very short distances (most terminal vendors recommend 50 feet), no modem is required. Short-haul modems, sometimes called linedrivers or limited-distance modems, can often be used at distances of less than 10 miles. These modems can provide significant cost savings over the conventional or long-haul modems required for transmission distances greater than 10 miles.

Half- and Full-Duplex Operation. Most modems can operate in either half- or full-duplex mode. Table 1 illustrates the relationship between half- and full-duplex operations and the type of communications line (two-wire or four-wire) required. Although there are exceptions, this table applies to the majority of modems.

Compatibility. Modems must have compatible characteristics if they are to communicate with each other. Even though the characteristics may appear to be compatible, the user should not simply assume that similar modems from different vendors are compatible. If it is necessary to mix modems from several vendors, compatibility should be the first item questioned. Vendor statements regarding compatibility should be supported by tests or by referrals to other users.

TERMINALS

Users interface with the system through terminals, which are a very important part of any data communications network. Services exist for classifying the endless variety of terminals available on the basis of intelligence, input/output media, or application. Because they provide a convenient summary of what is available, such services are very helpful to users during the initial selection process.

Table 1. Type of Facility as a Function of Speed and Duplex Operation

Speed	Half-Duplex	Full-Duplex
1,200 bits per second or less	2-wire	2-wire
1,200 bits per second or greater	2-wire	4-wire

Data Communications Management

A potential user should prepare a checklist of features and requirements for evaluating various products. This checklist should include:
- User characteristics—Does the terminal match the characteristics of the users and the application?
- Compatibility—Are the product's speed, code, and protocol compatible with the host computer?
- Availability—Is the product built yet?
- Reliability—Will the product withstand the rigors of the planned environment?
- Vendor track record—What type of support can be expected? Will there be a guarantee—and a vendor to honor it?

Before the final selection is made, the terminal should be installed on a trial basis and tested under actual operating conditions. The information gained from this trial and the reactions of the users can greatly minimize potential problems.

Terminal-Modem Interfaces

The common physical and electrical interface between a terminal and a modem or computer port is the Electronic Industries Association (EIA) standard, RS-232C. Its salient characteristics are a 25-pin connector, a distance limitation of 50 feet, and a speed limitation of 20 bits per second.

The 25 pins can be grouped into four functional groups: grounds, data transfer, timing, and control. Most systems, however, do not operate with all 25 leads active, but with some subset of from 3 to 16 pins. (The number of interface leads required to operate a specific terminal or modem should be described in the equipment's operations literature.) A thorough knowledge of the interface's operation is essential for effective trouble shooting. Most diagnostic equipment is of little help if the user is not familiar with interface operation.

In recent years, RS-232C has become inadequate for new systems. The new RS-449 interface (already introduced) offers the following characteristics:
- 37 + 9-pin connector
- Distance limitation of 4,000 feet
- Speed limitation of 10M bits per second

The RS-449 provides more functions as well as greater distance and speed capabilities; many products already include the RS-449 capability.

Another interface standard, the X.21 (from the Consultative Committee for International Telephone and Telegraph [CCITT]), replaces the RS-232C when terminals interface to digital networks. Support for this interface has already been announced by some computer vendors and, as North American digital networks grow, the X.21 could become the primary interface standard.

LINE-SHARING DEVICES

Line-sharing devices reduce communications line costs by allowing several terminal devices to share a single communications line. Comparing the cost of individual lines against the cost of a shared line and the line-sharing hardware will justify the line-sharing approach. Aside from this economic benefit, there is no inherent advantage to line sharing.

Line sharing is possible because most terminal applications that require human operator input use a communications line inefficiently. Surveys indicate that character-mode terminals typically transmit characters only 5 to 15 percent of the time, with the remaining time given to operator thinking or waiting. In addition, many terminals do not operate at the communications line's maximum speed. A dedicated voicegrade line can operate at 9,600 bits per second, for example, but the terminal may only be running at 1,200 bits per second. These factors clearly provide sharing opportunities. Although both multiplexors and concentrators (two types of line-sharing devices) perform the same function, their implementations are sufficiently different to warrant separate descriptions.

Multiplexors

Multiplexors are available as:
- Frequency division multiplexors (FDMs)
- Time division multiplexors (TDMs)
- Statistical time division multiplexors (STATDMs)

Users must be knowledgeable about the advantages, disadvantages, and differences of each to select the right device for an application.

Frequency Division Multiplexors. FDMs divide a communications line electrically into a number of smaller channels, much like dividing a large freeway into a number of smaller lanes. Each terminal operates on its own distinct channel, but all terminals share the same physical communications line. No modems are required because the multiplexor itself provides this function. FDMs also provide multidrop capability without requiring multidrop protocols, but do so at a lower maximum speed. To share a line, the speed per channel cannot exceed 600 bits per second. Even at 300 bits per second, however, only six terminals can share a single four-wire line, making FDMs rather inefficient compared with other multiplexors.

Time Division Multiplexors. TDMs perform the sharing function by interleaving and increasing character speed on the communications line. To continue the highway analogy, a TDM is like a single high-speed lane into which all traffic merges. Provided that the output speed of the multiplexor is at least equal to the sum of the input speeds, all information can be transmitted without congestion. TDM line efficiency is greater than that of FDMs. A voicegrade line operating at 9,600 bits per second, for example, can support more than thirty 300-bit-per-second terminals, a five-fold improvement over FDMs.

Statistical Time Division Mutiplexor. TDMs function by assigning fixed time slots on the high-speed line to each terminal; if the terminals transmit only 15 percent of the time, the time slots are mostly empty, and overall line efficiency is reduced. STATDMs assign these idle time slots dynamically to terminals on a first-come, first-served basis. A STATDM thus supports two to four times as many terminals as a TDM with no increase in the output line speed. Because of their increased efficiency and such features as automatic retransmission of errors between multiplexors, STATDMs are replacing FDMs and TDMs in many applications.

Concentrators

Although they perform the same function, concentrators differ from multiplexors in the following ways:
- Concentrators are typically single ended. Deconcentrating is done in the host computer, and host compatibility is required.
- Concentrators use packet or message interleaving, while TDMs use bit or byte interleaving.
- Concentrators have a minicomputer architecture.
- Concentrators often perform other preprocessing functions in conjunction with concentrating.

If the host computer supports concentrators, the amount of port hardware required is reduced.

FRONT ENDS AND COMMUNICATIONS SOFTWARE

Communications processing might be defined as the manipulation of information for its transport or presentation. Unlike data processing, communications processing does not affect the content of the information. In general, front ends might be described as devices that remove some or most of the communications processing load from the host computer, leaving it with more resources for data processing. Functions often performed in a front end include:
- Serial-to-parallel conversion
- Channel multiplexing
- Message assembly and buffering
- Line-protocol handling
- Addition and deletion of start and stop bits and sync and other special control characters
- Modem control
- Code conversion

Systems that do not use front ends perform these functions in the host computer. This can limit the communications capability of the system; it can also place a heavy nonproductive processing load on the host computer. When users select a computer system for medium to heavy teleprocessing use, they should investigate what provisions have been made to lessen the CPU's communications processing workload. A system may otherwise give a rather disappointing performance because of high communications processing overhead.

Front ends can range in size from relatively large computers to microprocessor-based systems that, although not normally called front ends, perform many of the same functions. Some front-end functions are performed in hardware or firmware, while others, such as protocol support and message buffering, are performed in software. Depending on the size and complexity of the system, the software can be as simple as a device driver or as complex as a full-function access method. Software can reside entirely in

DATA COMMUNICATIONS

the host or partially in the host and partially in the front end, or it can be distributed throughout the network in concentrators and distributed processors.

Complexity and capability in general increase with system size. For this reason, communications support is rather limited for most minicomputers but is quite comprehensive for large mainframes. Potential purchasers must understand at least the capabilities of communications software before making commitments. This understanding should preclude the unwelcome discovery that a function is either impossible or very cumbersome after the system is installed.

NETWORK PLANNING AND IMPLEMENTATION

Planning and implementing a data communications network can be summarized in the following five steps:
- Determine network/system objectives
- Gather relevant design information
- Develop alternatives
- Implement selected alternatives
- Measure and follow up.

Setting Network Objectives

This is the most important part of network planning because it determines the network's direction. The corporate data processing plan as well as the business plan should be reviewed when establishing these objectives, so that future developments with data communications implications can be allowed for in the network architecture.

Gathering Design Information

If setting objectives is the most important step, this one is often the most difficult. The appropriate information and detail needed for designing a network are often hard to obtain because users themselves frequently do not know their precise needs. Lack of detail at this stage could make decisions between alternatives more difficult during the next stage. Design information should therefore include:
- Terminal and processor locations
- Transaction volumes and types
- Performance criteria
- Reliability requirements
- Growth projections
- Cost guidelines.

Developing Alternatives

With simple networks, developing alternatives may be nothing more than a paper and pencil exercise. As size and complexity increase, however, the designer may need assistance, such as outside consultants or packaged design aids. There are two important rules to follow when using such services:
- An external service should not be used as a substitute for understanding the problem. Invariably, the recipient of the service has the ultimate responsibility for the final product.
- Questions should always be asked. If an outside service does not provide satisfactory answers, this may be an indication of future problems.

Implementation

Implementation coordinates all the previously independent activities, and speaking with someone who has first-hand implementation experience can provide valuable assistance in avoiding mistakes. Implementation is an important time because it is during this period that users generally form their initial impressions of the system. False starts should be avoided; a thorough checklist and progress chart to flag any deviations from the plan will help eliminate such possibilities.

Measuring and Follow-Up

Once a network is in and working, it should be reviewed and compared with the design objectives. This is a very important but frequently overlooked step; the results of this comparison provide feedback that will make succeeding design exercises easier. A system for regularly measuring and recording volume and performance data should be part of the procedures; it will provide invaluable information for the network's future modification or expansion.

CONCLUSION

Once a network has been implemented and accepted by the user community, the job of maintaining and managing it begins. Many tools exist to ease this task. Hardware and software aids available from modem, terminal, and computer vendors as well as independent suppliers provide a great deal of useful diagnostic information. Real-time monitoring of the modem/terminal interface at remote sites, for example, is now routine. Data line monitors allow technicians to view the transmitted data as it appears on the communications line; patching and switching hardware allow a rapid change of faulty equipment and automatic switchover to backup systems.

Hardware, however, does not provide the management structure or operational procedures required to pull all this together. Network management should be recognized within the corporate structure as a necessary and important function. Good procedures are essential at the operational level and should be developed for:

- Network performance measurement and evaluation
- Network availability measurement with vendor feedback
- Preventive maintenance
- Trouble reporting
- System backup and restoration
- Disaster plans
- Network changes and additions
- Vendor negotiations

This stress on network management should not be misconstrued as a recommendation either to build empires or to develop reams of documentation; however, it is important and should not be ignored. Corporations that manage their communications well will be the most successful organizations in the years to come.

References

1. *Auerbach Data Communications Management,* published bimonthly by Auerbach Publishers Inc, 6560 N. Park Drive, Pennsauken NJ 08109.

VI-2
Planning for Networks
Layne C. Bradley

INTRODUCTION

From a technical viewpoint, the concept of processing data by means of a network of processors (i.e., hardware and software configurations) is not new. Remote job entry and, more recently, network job entry are proven applications. Because new technology generally develops faster than the ability to apply it appropriately on a wide scale, it is often designed and first used by a relatively small group of pioneers who recognize its potential value. If the new technology proves successful, other users soon rush to take advantage of it. The tremendous growth in online systems well illustrates this tendency, as does network processing.

Several factors other than technical innovations have contributed to today's rapidly growing interest in computer networks, including the following:
- The continuing concern over such productivity issues as processing costs, effective resource management (e.g., sharing work loads among multiple computing sites), and personnel costs associated with developing and running computer systems
- The growth of personal computers and their integration into processing networks
- The trend toward unattended operations (i.e., networks of large host processors connected to smaller remote processors that can operate almost automatically, with little or no intervention by operations personnel)
- The need for an effective disaster recovery plan to ensure that processing will continue even if one or more processing centers becomes inoperable

Although network organization and architecture vary depending on such factors as corporate structure, hardware and software availability, and business objectives, there are five basic reasons for their implementation:
- To achieve load leveling across resources, or balance the work load among several processing centers (see Figure 1). The desire to optimize resources is a major force behind this trend.
- To provide remote support, or use computer networks to support additional processing capacity at remote sites that are not necessarily major standalone processing centers (see Figure 2). Remote unattended operations are associated with this category.

357

DATA COMMUNICATIONS

- To integrate personal computers into mainframe networks as opposed to merely linking personal computers (see Figure 3).
- To provide realistic disaster recovery capabilities (see Figure 4).
- To establish local area networks (see Figure 5).

In summary, the concept of building large networks of computers is becoming a reality. This move is being driven by technological innovation, productivity and cost issues, and increasing computer literacy and involvement on the part of corporate management.

```
                    CPU A
                   /     \
                  /       \
               CPU B ---- CPU C
```

In this configuration, distributed computer networks are used to balance work loads among multiple CPUs.

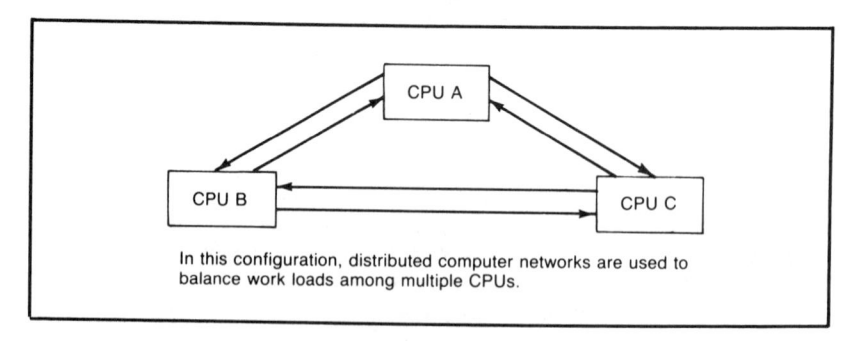

Figure 1. Load Sharing

```
              Local Host
             /    |    \
            /     |     \
         CPU A  CPU B  CPU C
```

In this configuration, distributed computer networks are used to support additional processing capacity to and from remote sites as required. In some cases, CPUs A, B, and C could represent unattended processing sites.

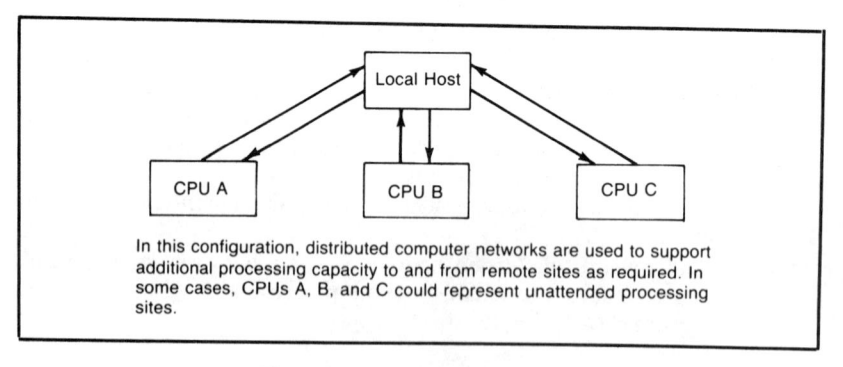

Figure 2. Remote Support

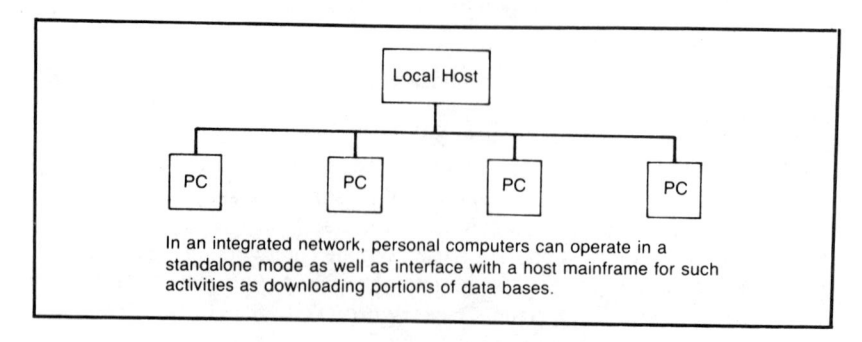

```
              Local Host
           /    |    |    \
          PC   PC   PC   PC
```

In an integrated network, personal computers can operate in a standalone mode as well as interface with a host mainframe for such activities as downloading portions of data bases.

Figure 3. Personal Computer Integration

Planning for Networks

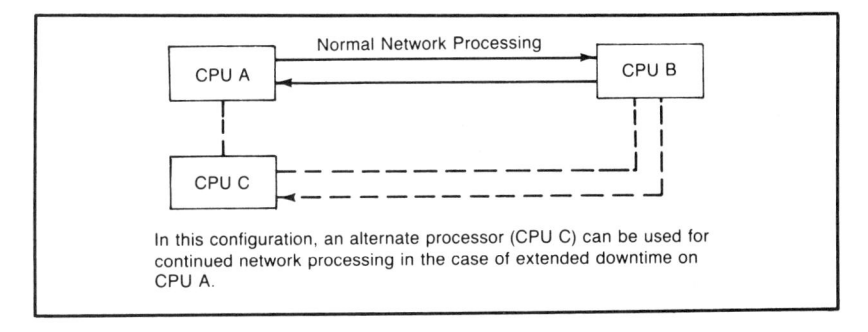

Figure 4. Disaster Recovery

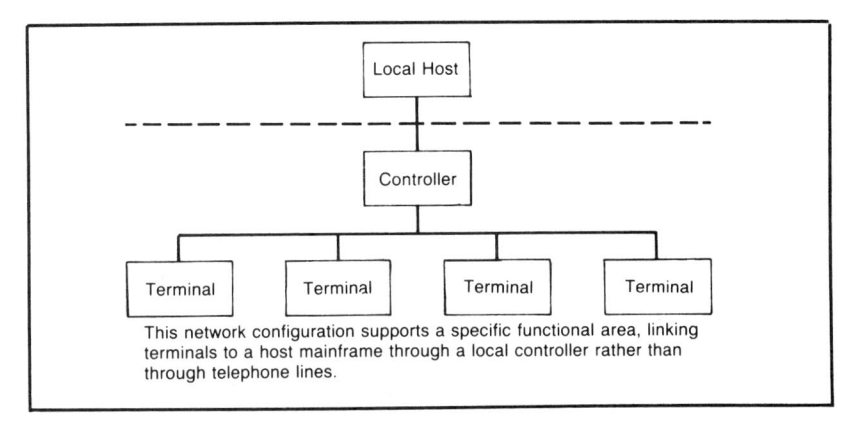

(In this configuration, an alternate processor (CPU C) can be used for continued network processing in the case of extended downtime on CPU A.)

Figure 5. Local Area Network

(This network configuration supports a specific functional area, linking terminals to a host mainframe through a local controller rather than through telephone lines.)

The Management Perspective

Network processing has a major impact on any organization that implements it as part of its MIS strategy. The success of a network processing strategy is based on sound planning by corporate management as well as MIS management. Because network processing usually involves a large capital expenditure, the commitment of both levels of management is necessary. However, corporate management generally has not been deeply involved in activities related to the MIS function. The increasing use of online systems has begun to change this situation. Functional line managers usually have a large portion of their budgets tied up in using online systems and thus must become more involved to help ensure a high degree of productivity for the costs.

Because distributed computer networks further complicate the issues of productivity, cost, and user involvement that accompanied online systems, management input in this area is mandatory.

Business Considerations

Although the MIS manager is responsible for planning and implementing a distributed network, senior corporate management must offer coordination

DATA COMMUNICATIONS

and input. Because of the significant impact distributed computer networks have on a business organization, they must be established in response to sound business needs.

Online systems have moved information processing capabilities directly to the user level. As a result, decisions critical to the success and profitability of a business now rely on immediate availability of information. Distributed computer networks extend information processing and communication from local corporate headquarters to the entire corporation, whether it is dispersed around the country or around the world. Because an abundance of information will flow through this network and be used to make critical business decisions, the use, availability, control, and security of this data must be carefully planned.

When developing a network plan, the MIS manager should consider the following business concerns:
- The corporation's strategic business objectives
- Return on investment goals
- Corporate organizational structure
- Centralized versus decentralized operations
- Management styles and philosophy

Once these concerns have been analyzed, the MIS manager can determine why a distributed computer network should be established and what structural and functional management guidelines should be followed in implementing it.

Before the MIS manager develops a detailed implementation plan with his or her staff, the following technologies must be evaluated to determine how they might fit into the corporate MIS strategy as well as the distributed network plan:
- Personal computers
- Information centers
- Distributed data bases
- Unattended computer operations
- Office automation systems.

PLANNING FOR THE NETWORK

Setting Goals and Objectives

As with any major plan, the first step is setting goals and objectives. This can be a complicated process when a company is establishing a distributed computer network because the decisions involve so many elements. Business goals and functional levels must be considered. As discussed, the business goals and objectives form the guidelines for the entire project. Unless they are established, the project runs the risk of producing a technical success but a business failure.

Some considerations in setting the business objectives are:
- What is the long-term corporate business strategy (e.g., diversifying by acquiring businesses)? Will the distributed computer network support this strategy?

Planning for Networks

- Does the long-term MIS plan meet corporate strategic goals? Does the distributed computer network clearly support the MIS plan?
- Should the network produce a true, definable return on investment? If not, is its cost justified for other than financial reasons? If so, what are they?
- Is corporate management aware of the true cost/return situation?

Functional objectives concern the performance of the network and thus involve considerable technical consideration. Service-level agreements for the network are derived from this process. The objectives are basically to determine what the network is designed to do and what levels of computer performance are required to do it.

Determining the Scope of the Network

This phase of the planning cycle is actually a part of the objectives-setting process. Both short- and long-term planning are required. For example, the initial short-term objective of the network may be to link two of a corporation's data centers to allow for load sharing. However, the long-term corporate strategy may include acquiring several companies in the following three to five years.

In the case of the long-term strategy, the primary question would be how to handle the information processing needs of these companies. Since such specific knowledge about companies usually is not known far in advance, MIS management should develop a broad plan that addresses the possible information needs of new companies. The plan should consider two basic situations: a company with its own computer system that must be integrated into the network and a company without a computer system.

If this approach is taken and contingency plans are developed when the corporate business strategies are set in motion, the future impact on the MIS department can be significantly reduced.

The following information should be obtained before defining the scope of the network:

- The corporate objectives regarding network use
- The type of distributed computer network to be established initially (e.g., a local area network rather than a large host-to-host remote processing network)
- The type and volume of work expected to be processed on the network
- Whether the network should initially be limited to specified users or applications
- The short- and long-term impact of the network on the organization and staffing of the MIS department.

Defining Management Requirements and Constraints

In this step, the management parameters of the network are identified. Budgets are established (both start-up and ongoing for at least three years), and time frames for successful network implementation are identified. Control over the project must be established within the organization. For exam-

DATA COMMUNICATIONS

ple, will the corporate steering committee or MIS management have complete control over network implementation?

Risk analysis from a managerial perspective is another important aspect. Two sides to this process must be considered. First, what risks might arise as the project progresses (e.g., excessive costs, turnover of key personnel, technical limitations, organizational constraints)? Second, what are the risks of not implementing the network? These might include loss of competitive edge, inability to pursue corporate acquisitions effectively, and inability to expand markets rapidly as a result of slow distribution of information to geographically dispersed divisions.

A simple three-step plan is:
1. Identifying the risks
2. Identifying the worst-case results relating to the risk
3. Determining a set of management guidelines to follow in each case.

Determining Organizational Capabilities

In addition to considering the general impact of a network on the MIS organization, the corporation must address its detailed effects. This is done to establish whether the organization is in a position to initiate such a complex project. If not, the organization must explore measures that will allow it to initiate the project as well as implement and manage the network over the long term.

The following questions must be answered:
- Is the current MIS structured to accommodate a distributed computer network? If not, what kind of reorganization is required?
- Should a new group be established for network support, or should the functions be distributed across the current organization?
- Is the number of personnel sufficient to get started? How many additional personnel will be required?
- Who should have overall responsibility for developing and implementing the network?
- What additional training is required for MIS personnel? How soon will it be available? What does it cost?
- Are the current physical facilities adequate? If not, what type of expansion or rework is necessary?

Making the Final Decision

Higher levels of general management may be tempted to approve the implementation of a distributed computer network. They may be swayed especially by the publicity on this topic in the trade and business media. However, the MIS manager must ensure that corporate general management understands the implications of implementing a network.

Once all the information is presented to corporate management and the decision is made to proceed, the MIS manager is responsible for implementing the network.

Planning for Networks

IMPLEMENTING THE NETWORK

Establishing a Project Team

The first step of implementation is to establish a project team. If the planning process as described has been followed, several staff members were probably involved in the decision to implement the network. This group would serve as part of the project team.

The most important decision is whether the project team should be permanent or temporary. That is, should the task be considered basically as any other new development task and use the standard organizations, or should a special team be established? This decision will be based primarily on the planning analysis done earlier. However, because the implementation of a distributed computer network is not a typical task for the organization, a special team consisting of the most skilled personnel is usually preferable.

If a special team is established, its primary tasks will include developing the required procedures and policies and, if necessary, recommending organizational changes to support the network on an ongoing basis.

Since the idea of distributed computer networks may be new to the project team, training must be included in the overall planning effort. This training will affect the expected schedule for implementing the network.

Once the project team has been established, standard project management controls and procedures can be followed. However, some revision may be necessary as the project progresses because network planning will be a new area for the organization.

Managing the project will be even more difficult if the network involves geographically dispersed data centers and the project team comprises representatives of all of these centers. Effective coordination of activities and centralization of authority in a single project leader instead of a committee are critical to success in such an environment.

Defining Technical Considerations

The project team must develop the technical requirements for successful network operation. Although these depend on the type of network to be established, certain technical elements must be considered:
- What are the hardware and software requirements?
- What are the lead times for acquiring the appropriate hardware or software?
- What kinds of network test equipment and software are available?
- What types of communications lines are involved?
- What will be the backup and recovery capabilities of the proposed network?
- Are there special facility requirements (e.g., space for telecommunications devices)? Is electrical power sufficient?
- If the network will use telephone or leased lines, what is the history of support from the local communications company? What kinds of transmission error rates can be expected from the communications company?

DATA COMMUNICATIONS

The ability to simulate the activities of the network, traffic volumes, and what-if situations should be considered. Several software systems are available for this purpose, and one should be incorporated in the network development project as early as possible.

Establishing Network Control

Two major areas to consider are change control and problem tracking and resolution.

Change control is not new in MIS. Production applications are usually protected from new or revised processing changes through a formal change control mechanism. Although similar, change control for a distributed computer network becomes critical. Depending on the use of the network (e.g., distributed point-of-sale operations in a retail environment), network failure caused by unplanned or uncontrolled changes could be disastrous from a business point of view. The criticality of the network to the actual business of the corporation may demand a change control mechanism separate from others used in the organization.

Effective tracking of problems and their timely resolution are also mandatory. Procedures must be implemented to identify problems quickly, track them through to resolution, and provide follow-up capabilities (e.g., reports) to determine what happened and why, what action was taken, and what preventive measures to adopt. Several vendor-supplied systems address this area and should be investigated by the project team and implemented if not already in use.

Training MIS and User Personnel

Effective training of all personnel is essential to the overall success of the project. Determining the type and level of training to offer is difficult because of the varied levels of expertise required by MIS and user personnel.

For MIS personnel, three levels of training must be accomplished: managerial, functional, and technical. Managerial training involves familiarizing all appropriate managers with the basic concepts, capabilities, limitations, objectives, controls, and procedures necessary for the successful operation of the network.

Functional training, which is much more detailed, is given to those MIS personnel who will be directly involved in the ongoing operation of the network. The network communications control group and some computer operations personnel usually receive this training.

Finally, detailed technical training is required for the personnel supporting the network (e.g., the technical software support group and any in-house hardware maintenance personnel).

As with any project, the depth of training required depends on the expertise required of assigned personnel. Training requirements can be assessed through a skills analysis effort, in which required skills are matched against the expertise of personnel. Gaps indicate where training must be developed and applied.

Planning for Networks

On the user side, training is primarily at the management and functional levels. Management training teaches user managers the basic concepts, reporting procedures, problem tracking and resolution, and service-level agreements as they apply to the network. Functional training teaches the user how to use the network on an operational basis and how to report problems with network facilities.

Establishing Ongoing Support

The final step in implementing a distributed computer network is to establish a support and maintenance system for the network. If the project team comprises personnel from several departments in the MIS organization, they may return to their previous responsibilities when the project is completed. As a result, a permanent support organization must be established.

This unit must be planned and staffed early in the project so that its personnel can be trained and assigned. The support group must be in contact with the network users. This can be done through a network control center that the user can contact for quick resolution of any problems. The support group must be adequately staffed and trained to ensure successful operation of the network.

ACTION PLAN

Implementing a distributed computer network involves a complex interaction of hardware, software, security, personnel, and procedures. This complexity is compounded by the need for MIS personnel and users at remote locations to interact.

From the MIS manager's viewpoint, a few points should be noted to help ensure the success of a distributed computer network:

- An extensive analysis and planning effort must precede the decision to implement the network.
- The decision to implement a network must be based on sound business reasoning. The network should not be implemented simply because it is technically feasible and appealing.
- The structure of the network must complement the corporate business strategy.
- The complexity of the task should not be underestimated.
- Understaffing must be avoided. Lack of appropriate expertise can lead to failure.
- Corporate general management must understand the magnitude of the task, short- and long-term costs, and the risks. Its commitment must be obtained at the outset.
- The structure of both the project team and the ongoing support organization must be carefully considered.
- Training shortcuts must be avoided. Learning through mistakes can be disastrous in such a project.

Although this is not a comprehensive list, it highlights major management considerations. Failure to address them properly will threaten the outcome of the project. Figure 6 summarizes by category the types of questions to be asked.

DATA COMMUNICATIONS

Business Planning Considerations

1. What are the corporation's strategic business objectives?
2. What are the goals for return on investment?
3. What is the corporate organizational structure?
4. What do centralized versus decentralized operations entail?
5. What management styles and philosophy are held?
6. What is the long-term corporate business strategy (e.g., diversifying by acquiring businesses)? Will the distributed computer network support this strategy?
7. Does the long-term MIS plan meet corporate strategic goals? Does the distributed computer network clearly support the overall MIS plan?
8. Should the network produce a true, definable return on investment? If not, is its cost justified for other than financial reasons? If so, what are they? Is corporate management aware of the true cost/return situation?
9. What are the corporate objectives regarding network use?
10. What type of distributed network will initially be established (e.g., a local area network rather than a large host-to-host remote processing network)?
11. What type and volume of work are expected to be processed on the network?
12. Should the network initially be limited to specified users and applications?
13. What is the network's short- and long-term impact on the organization and staffing of the MIS department?

Organizational Considerations

1. Is the current MIS organization structured to handle the implementation of a distributed network? If not, what kind of a reorganization is required?
2. Should a new group be established for network support, or should the functions be distributed across the current organization?
3. Is the number of personnel sufficient to get started? How many additional personnel will be required?
4. Who should have overall responsibility for developing and implementing the network?
5. What additional training is required for MIS personnel? How soon is it available? What does it cost?
6. Are the current physical facilities adequate? If not, what type of expansion or rework is necessary?

Technical Considerations

1. What are the hardware and software requirements?
2. What are the lead times for acquiring the appropriate hardware or software?
3. What kinds of network test equipment and software are required or available?
4. What types of communications lines are involved?
5. What are the backup recovery capabilities for the network?
6. Are there special facility requirements (e.g., space for telecommunications devices)? Is electrical power sufficient?
7. If the network will use telephone or leased lines, what is the history of support from the local communications company? What kinds of transmission error rates can be expected from the communications company?

Figure 6. Distributed Network Issues

In a project of such magnitude, the tendency is to focus on the short-term objective—getting the network implemented and running—and to allow the future to work itself out. This reaction is normal and is usually caused by pressure from corporate management to see a quick return on investment.

Network planning, however, must become an ongoing, critical part of the MIS manager's responsibilities. Although all the details for the following five years cannot be projected, the MIS manager must have some understanding of the future information needs of the corporation, how the network will support those needs, and what actions must be taken to ensure that the network continues to provide the required service.

VI-3
Voice and Data—Putting Them Together

James H. Morgan

INTRODUCTION

Three major factors have influenced the rapidly growing interest in integrating data and voice communications:

- Technology—Speech-digitizing technologies permit data and voice to be carried simultaneously in a communications channel.
- Vendor product lines—Many vendors offer both data and voice communications products, because a number of users prefer to deal with a single communications vendor. Vendors traditionally marketing only one of the technologies are expanding into the other in an effort to retain and expand their customer bases.
- Equipment location—Users are finding advantages in locating data and voice communications equipment together: for example, reduced space requirements, shared staffs, and improved operations, with resultant cost savings.

There is thus strong incentive to integrate the previously separate functions of data communications management and voice communications management into a single data/voice management function.

Integration of data and voice is not 10 or 20 years in the future; it is already in progress at a number of organizations and will increase during the next five years. Organizational five- or ten-year plans must therefore address such integration, recognizing the advances in data and voice communications technology. This is an ideal time for management to take advantage of the continuing rapid growth of technology by investigating vendor offerings and preparing for any organizational restructuring. This is wise even if there are no plans during the next few years for much actual data/voice integration.

Although a number of organizations may wish to integrate data and voice communications completely, this may not be practical or desirable for others. Large, separate networks with heavy capital investment and large staffs, for example, would make immediate integration difficult.

Total integration of data and voice signals can be considered the high end of the scale; the low end of the scale is a situation in which only the management of the data and voice communications functions is integrated.

DATA COMMUNICATIONS

PLANNING THE NEW FUNCTION

Integrated or combined data/voice communications will generally be a new function for a company. In some companies, data communications may have started under voice communications and evolved later into a separate department. In most cases, however, data communications spun off from an area such as DP/MIS, office administration, or finance. Whatever its genesis, data/voice communications must now be treated as a new function, and thought must be given to establishing its position within the organization. It is essential that upper management devote sufficient time and study to planning for and implementing this function.

The Data/Voice Communications Manager

The manager of this new function will be responsible for all communications, including data, voice, facsimile, and electronic mail.

Data Communications. This includes the data communications network with its modems, multiplexors, computer front ends, software, message switching, packet switching, facsimile, technical control center/network control center, and test equipment.

Voice Communications. This includes the telephone network with PBXs, tandem switches, leased lines, and such ancillary systems as automatic call distributor (ACD), least-cost routing (LCR), station message detail recording (SMDR), centralized attendant service (CAS), common carrier interface equipment, and test equipment.

Data/Voice Communications. The manager must also assume responsibility for such integrated digital data/voice products as PBX/tandem switches, microwave, satellite, T carrier and data/voice channel banks; digitized voice, such as pulse code modulation (PCM), delta modulation (DM), and linear predictive coding (LPC); voice response units; local networks; and packetized voice.

It should be noted that these new products do not fit easily with the traditional functions of either the data or the voice communications manager, and it would be difficult to decide which products to assign to each manager. Dividing them in any proportion is an unrealistic solution; the most obvious and appropriate answer is to group the equipment under the umbrella of a combined data and voice communications management function.

Digital Technology

Digital technology is the common denominator in integrating data and voice communications. Data has, of course, always been transmitted in digital form, and the availability of inexpensive LSI chips to convert analog to digital voice has made voice digitizing more practical. Once digitized, the voice bit stream can be interleaved with other digital signals.

Other analog devices such as facsimile and video are becoming digitized; digital microwave, satellites, packet switching, fiber optics, and coaxial cable continue the movement to digital technology. Telephone switching is also moving in this direction, with digital PBXs, tandem, and central office; even the local loop is being digitized.

This increasing movement toward a world in which virtually every signal will be digital is even being acknowledged by the telephone companies with their vast analog investments. The only area of disagreement seems to be how soon this world will arrive; some observers predict it will be 25 to 35 percent digital in five years and 90 percent in ten years. This accelerating pace is another reason for upper management to seriously consider the immediate designation of a combined data/voice communications management function.

Another driving force is the trend toward office automation and the acceptance of the workstation concept. The workstation, a multifunction terminal, provides access to voice, data processing, data entry/retrieval, word processing, electronic mail, facsimile, video, and other functions. This multiple functioning can most easily be accomplished with electronically integrated communications links, combining data and voice. It would be almost impossible in this situation to separate data and voice management.

ADVANTAGES AND DISADVANTAGES

Whether an organization chooses to integrate its data and voice communications into a single network or to combine them with a single management function, a substantial number of benefits can result.

Advantages of Full Integration

At the higher level of integration, advantages would include those described in the following paragraphs.

Direct Cost Savings. Almost all benefits can be converted to cost savings, some more easily than others. The communications department can enjoy direct cost savings, for example, by cross-training and sharing staffs and by integrating separate data and voice shift operations, analysts, and project leaders. This would free personnel for other duties and could potentially decrease the number of new hires. Direct cost savings could also accrue through integration of the data, voice, facsimile, message, and other networks; elimination of modems; use of wideband facilities; and optimization of expensive trunks and leased facilities.

Indirect Cost Savings. Upper management will also derive substantial ongoing cost benefits from communications. Communications is now being viewed as an area for investment that will provide an attractive return on investment elsewhere (e.g., in other departments and divisions).

Ongoing System Improvements. A single data/voice communications manager who has a broad outlook on communications can optimize improvements to the system. (A broad outlook tends to reduce the risks involved in making any management decision.) Upgrading existing systems and planning, specifying, and evaluating new systems can be performed more efficiently by such a person, especially in light of the increasing integration of data and voice communications. The impact of a new digital PBX with data

DATA COMMUNICATIONS

capabilities, for example, is better evaluated by a manager with responsibility in both voice and data than by a more limited telephone-only manager.

The cost/benefit analyses that accompany or precede system improvements should be performed by a person who can look beyond the restricted data and voice domains. The benefits, again, extend past the communications department into other user departments and beyond the immediate future.

Single Corporate Contact. Another advantage of designating a communications manager is that it provides a single, responsible corporate contact for communications suppliers. Having one, knowledgeable contact enables suppliers to demonstrate capabilities, cost savings, and other product benefits more easily. This also allows users to learn promptly about new technologies and products (users sometimes forget that there are real benefits in cultivating vendor contacts).

Other benefits, both tangible and intangible, must be considered. Integrating data and voice communications under a single manager can improve company operations; this ultimately converts into cost savings. There are also the concomitant factors of a decrease in crisis management and reduced staff tension. A modern communications operation may also encourage corporate expansion into new and lucrative marketing areas.

Advantages of Minimal Integration

Corporate management will find benefits even when only the management of data and voice communications is integrated (the low end), and there is little or no functional integration. Organizations with full-time separate data and voice communications managers may be able to combine the positions under one data/voice communications manager. Smaller companies, for example, that could not afford separate managers and hence assigned the functions as extra, usually unwelcome, duties to purchasing agents and finance officers may be able to justify a new full-time post.

Combining management of the data and voice communications functions may enable a small company to hire a professional communications manager whose primary concern will be full-time dedication to the communications function. It should be noted that some of the advantages of low-end integration discussed in the following paragraphs are also applicable to higher-end integration.

Cost Savings. A lack of time and/or interest may have prevented an in-depth investigation of potential areas of savings; the new manager, however, will find this among his or her responsibilities. The new manager will be able to perform ongoing analyses of communications costs—in particular, telephone line charges. Savings of 10 to 40 percent are possible, based on the use of such aids as the following:
- Least-Cost Routing—Sometimes called Alternate Route Selection (ARS), this device can be used as a standalone unit or integrated into the PBX. It automatically selects the least-cost way to complete a call (e.g., FX, WATS, DDD). Typical toll call savings are about 20 percent.
- Station Message Detail Recording—As a standalone system or integrated into the PBX, SMDR provides such information as number called,

calling extension, length of call, time of day, and so on. Each extension receives a monthly statement that is effective in reducing personal calls and lengthy business calls. SMDR can also ensure that all trunks are working and can provide management reports for optimizing trunks (numbers and types). A 10 percent saving is not uncommon.
- Centralized Attendant Service—Built into a telephone system, this switching mechanism routes calls for a dispersed group (such as a retail store chain) to a central facility. Calls to outlying stores are answered by attendants at a central location and are routed back to the appropriate person. This eliminates the need for attendants at the remote locations and provides more control of the telephone operations.
- Automatic Call Distributor—As a standalone or integrated system, ACD can effectively route incoming calls to personnel on an order-of-arrival basis. This can be extremely helpful in such service-oriented areas as order taking, reservations, and the like.

Management Reports. A variety of useful management reports are provided by these aids as well as by PBX output. SMDR, for example, can identify the originators of unnecessary calls and inoperative (yet paid for) trunks, and the basic PBX reports can predict some pending system failures. These reports can help optimize operations and can provide significant cost savings. First, however, the reports must be read—and interpreted properly— to derive their maximum benefits. A manager with responsibility for both data and voice communications can read and interpret these reports in terms of the overall communications function.

Other Cost Savings. Additional savings can derive from judicious selection of communications equipment. The selection of an interconnect (non-telephone company) system, for example, should be considered only if a skilled, dedicated communications manager is available to perform a solid cost/benefit analysis. Time and skill are required to evaluate the numerous vendor offerings, to deal with sales presentations, to write a detailed, protective contract, and to implement the system properly. The payoff, with a three- to five-year break-even point and a number of special functions, can be most attractive to upper management. Such a payoff, of course, depends on a successful project (which may in turn depend on having a full-time data/voice communications manager).

As technology advances rapidly and more vendors enter the communications field, the potential for cost savings increases. Attaining these savings, however, depends heavily on the availability of a person with the right skills and the time to exercise them. The only options for a company without a dedicated communications manager are to rely on telephone company representatives, to use an outside consultant for cost-saving suggestions, and to accept a passive approach in which the company initiates no action but merely responds to random visits by vendor personnel.

Disadvantages of Integration

Although there are substantial advantages to both high- and low-end integration of data and voice communications, management must also recognize the disadvantages.

One basic disadvantage is the greater difficulty in finding a good data/voice communications manager. The data/voice communications manager must possess broader, wider-ranging talent than a data or voice communications manager. Among other qualities, he or she must be somewhat of a visionary, people oriented, management oriented, and broadly attuned to the company's business. Although people of this caliber are always hard to find, they are available. Usually, however, the data/voice manager-designate does not completely meet the new job requirements and requires some guidance from and development by upper management.

The requirement for upper management's time and support in establishing the new function must not be underestimated or the implementation may be costly and less than successful. Although these and other disadvantages must be considered, they are considerably outweighed by the advantages.

Pitfalls. There are a number of pitfalls, or temporary disadvantages, involved in implementing any level of data and voice communications integration. This is essentially no different from any other implementation. Most of the pitfalls seem to be political rather than technical in nature, again pointing to the necessity for a well-rounded manager who can deal with the politics of business.

Long-established working relationships are shaken; empires are threatened. Communications people who are very comfortable in their positions are asked to give up some of that security to move into a different environment. They may be required to learn different skills; some people will be very enthusiastic, others will feel nervous and threatened, a few may resign. Personnel attitudes depend greatly on how upper management presents the new concept and environment to the staff. If the situation is handled correctly, many staff members will see the positive aspects of integration and accept it. The introduction of the subject must therefore be carefully planned and properly presented.

Technical pitfalls must also be recognized. The physical integration of communications systems, possibly into one room, and the electronic integration of data and voice signals (to the degree desired) must be carried out successfully. User departments and other observers watching from the sidelines will be encouraged or discouraged by the success or failure of the move. A half-day communications outage, for example, will have an adverse effect; a smooth integration, on the other hand, will encourage support.

There will, of course, be other technical and nontechnical problems; management can minimize them through awareness and appropriate preventive measures.

ESTABLISHING THE NEW FUNCTION

The Role of Upper Management

In many large organizations, the data and voice communications functions are so separate that the current common point is an executive vice president or even president of the company. The role of upper management in establishing this new function is therefore critical. Upper management must either provide the initial idea and impetus or must strongly support the idea, regardless of its source. This support must be visible; it is essential in defusing the potentially explosive political situations that always occur when separate groups are broken down and reformed.

To be convinced of the need for and the rapid coming of an integrated data/voice communications function, upper management must have some knowledge of the driving forces previously described as well as their implications for the organization's future operations.

Because the data/voice communications manager will be working closely with other departments, such as MIS and office administration as well as sales, accounting, engineering, and other support departments (e.g., building management), upper management should request the help of these departments in defining the communications manager's functions.

A meeting with representatives of all departments may be doubly helpful. Such a meeting provides the opportunity to apprise the departments of the intention to combine data and voice communications on at least the management level and to explain the reasons for the move. The benefits to the departments should be pointed out at this time and comments should be solicited from department representatives; the dynamics of the group generally elicits better responses than does a written request for input.

The Need for a Five-Year Communications Plan

Fifteen years ago, most user companies had no formal communications plan. The local telephone company representative visited periodically and suggested new ideas and products that were currently available. It was indeed a monopoly situation—one that served very well for many decades.

After the 1968 Carterfone decision introduced interconnect competition to telephone companies, many users formed distinct voice communications groups to take advantage of the competitive situation. A data communications group rose up separately (often as an offshoot of data processing) to handle the data network with its growing number of teleprocessing links. Although both groups may have had some kind of five-year plan, few plans addressed the integration of voice and data realistically. Most practitioners considered the concept too distant for immediate consideration.

Communications technology is advancing so quickly at this time, however, that such a communications plan must be given far greater importance, and the integration of voice and data must be considered. At one time, a communications system, such as an analog telephone PBX, might have been expected to last 12 to 20 years. Now, however, it is conceivable that the lifetime of newer systems—first-generation digital PBXs, for example—may be only 5 to 7 years. This short life cycle is due not to inferior systems but to the rapid acceleration of technology and the concomitant obsolescence of systems.

It is no longer feasible for most users to develop a limited communications plan; the individual data and voice plans should be combined into a single integrated communications plan. In fact, today's five-year plan must consider issues broader than transmission media. Such areas as word processing, image processing, electronic mail, teleconferencing, video, security, environmental control, emergency power sources, local loops, and multifunction workstations must be addressed.

The question arises, of course, of actual preparation of the plan. Should this important five-year plan be drawn up before selecting the new manager, to aid upper management in understanding the organization's particular situation and to better define and plan the data/voice communications management function? Who should draw up the plan: a committee, the voice or data communications manager, or an independent consultant? The choice may be none of these; it may be to select the new manager first and to assign him or her an initial task of drawing up a good five-year communications plan. Another possibility might be to outline the plan in just enough detail to enable the selection of the new manager, who could then flesh it out. There is no single best answer. Each situation is different, and both approaches can be used successfully. (It should be noted that this integrated five-year communications plan may itself become part of a larger plan as organizations move further into office automation.)

The implications of office automation must be considered when an integrated data and voice communications management function is implemented. Today, most organizations have prepared for office automation by establishing a major new department, typically called Information Services and including communications, MIS, and office administration. The manager of this department is usually designated Director/VP of Information Services. Sometimes the three original groups remain essentially intact and merely report to the new director; in other instances, the three groups are broken down and rebuilt with people from all three former groups. Neither of these approaches is best for all companies, and solutions vary accordingly. Because such reorganization has serious implications for company operations, the move toward full office automation should be preceded by at least low-end integration of data and voice.

IMPLEMENTING THE DATA/VOICE COMMUNICATIONS MANAGEMENT FUNCTION

The data/voice communications manager should be chosen before heavy implementation is begun. (The sample job description in Figure 1 is intended only as an example, to aid in the selection of a new manager. It should be modified as appropriate.) Although this stricture may appear obvious, one should remember that the implementation will, to some extent, reflect the new manager's background and personality. It is also essential that the intention to implement be publicized throughout the company; there is hardly a department that will not ultimately be affected. Such publicity can be verbal (at a general managers' meeting, for example) or written—preferably, it will be both. A positive, forward-looking image of the new function should also be projected. Reasons for the integrated function should be given, explaining the benefits to various departments (e.g., direct cost savings, increased staff productivity, simpler operations, and encouragement to develop new company products).

Integrating Voice and Data

> The data/voice communications manager shall have responsibility for all communications in the company: data, voice, image processing (fax), electronic mail/message systems (including the communications area of word processing), video, and teleconferencing. The manager will continuously evaluate:
> - A variety of communications media, public and private, analog and digital:
>   Copper pair, coaxial cable, fiber optics, microwave, satellite, packet switching, carrier, and wideband
> - Common carrier vendors:
>   Traditional and other common carriers, including specialized common carriers and value-added networks
> - New communications systems (both hardware and software):
>   Modems, multiplexors, controllers, telecommunications access methods, switches and accessories (e.g., LCR, SMDR, CAS, ACD), terminals, and local loops
>
> The data/voice communications manager will establish a program to expand his or her area of interest beyond telephone and data communications to cover potential communications areas. To achieve this, the manager will establish and/or strengthen working relationships with MIS, office administration, building maintenance, finance, legal, user departments, and outside parties such as other common carriers, interconnects, and consultants. The data/voice communications manager must also possess verbal and written communication skills (these are at least as important as technical skills).
>
> If data and voice communications have not yet been integrated, the manager will make preparations for such integration and work toward its implementation.
>
> The data/voice communications manager will prepare and maintain a fairly detailed, realistic, five-year communications plan that incorporates integration, digital technology, office automation, and so forth. A one- or two-year plan scheduling system implementation should also be prepared.
>
> The manager will organize and develop a staff to carry out these goals in a timely, cost-effective manner. An ongoing training program will be established for both staff and manager. Appropriate management techniques will be used to maintain a high level of productivity, morale, job satisfaction, and to minimize employee turnover.
>
> The manager will establish a communications budget, viewing communications as an area of investment for cost savings in other departments. A business-like approach will be taken at all times regarding communications costs. For example, the latest tools will be used for optimizing lines and calling patterns, for keeping track of costs, and for minimizing staff.
>
> The manager will also attempt to address broader communications issues as they relate to his or her department and to the organization.

Figure 1. Data/Voice Communications Manager Job Description

The Schedule

An aggressive, yet realistic, schedule showing the implementation phases should be drawn up jointly by the responsible upper manager and the communications manager. These phases vary according to the desired level of integration and the background of the new manager. If the new manager comes from the voice side, for example, he or she may wish to leave operations unchanged for a month or longer while learning about data communications. This will enable him or her to plan the fine details, in terms of equipment and organization, that are crucial to smooth integration.

Although the upper manager should not be involved in the minute details

DATA COMMUNICATIONS

of integration, he or she should monitor the progress of the implementation schedule because of the critical nature of this function.

Organizational Structure

The organizational structure for the new data/voice communications function will vary according to such factors as a company's size, sophistication, dependence on communications, present organization and manner of operation, personnel, and short- and long-term plans. Regardless of size, however, certain positions and duties must be covered, including communications analyst, project leader, ordering and bill payment, operations technician, maintenance technician, console attendant, and so forth. In smaller companies, one person may handle several of these functions; larger companies may require several people.

Figure 2 shows sample data/voice communications organizational charts for medium and large companies. At the lowest level of integration (simply merging the management functions), the structure remains essentially unchanged—except, of course, for the managers.

The Staff

Generally, the communications staff remains intact during implementation of a combined data/voice communications function, although some new personnel may be hired. Management should avoid any layoffs as part of the implementation—such a move tends to destroy any spirit of enthusiasm and cooperation.

Staff job descriptions, however, will have to be changed to reflect the requirements for broader knowledge. Matching the new job descriptions with the existing staff must be handled very carefully by the new data/voice communications manager. The majority of cases should present no problems; however, voice and data people might compete for a favored job. The guidelines for making a decision in this case are similar to those for selecting a data/voice manager. Such nontechnical factors as the candidate's willingness and ability to learn about (or gain experience in) the other communications area should be considered. Seniority may also be a factor, though a less important one.

In general, combining data and voice does not significantly raise the job requirements in terms of education and experience. Qualifications for communications analysts involved in planning and network analysis, however, might be slightly increased to accommodate more theory; an additional year or two of education and/or experience is desirable. These increased requirements should be of consequence only when the company goes outside for additional staff; currently employed analysts should not be penalized by being denied a desirable position. It is wiser to provide them with an opportunity to learn.

When hiring a new data/voice analyst, a rough guideline on education would be several years of post-high school communications-oriented training, such as two years of college or technical school. Three to five years of strong experience are desirable. The exact amount of education and experi-

Integrating Voice and Data

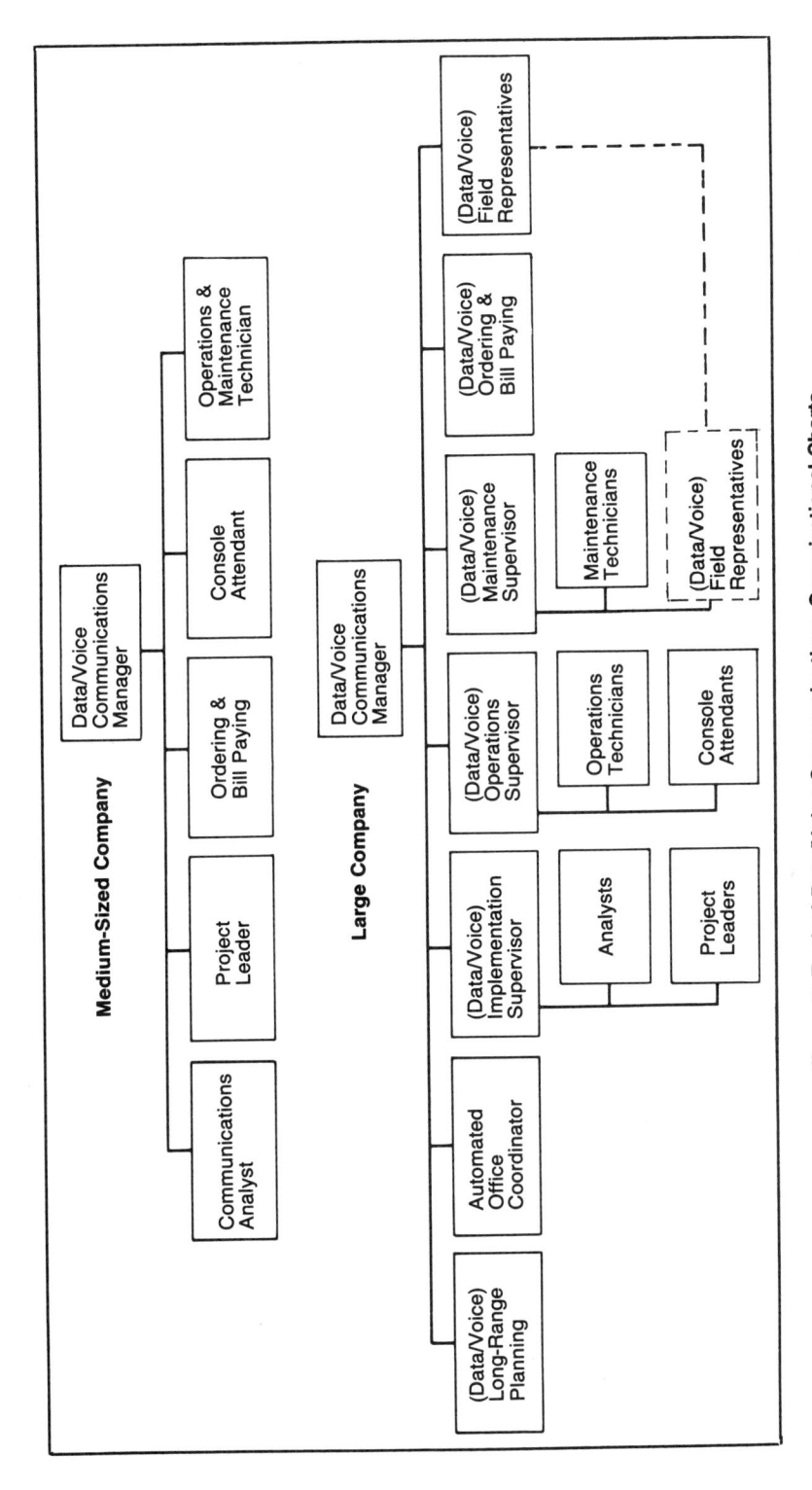

Figure 2. Typical Data/Voice Communications Organizational Charts

ence required depend on the company size and its sophistication in communications.

Unfortunately, good communications analysts, project leaders, and technicians are hard to find in many parts of the country, especially when they offer combined data and voice skills. Increasingly critical factors in luring rare talent are the organization's location and its image. Management may not be able to improve the location, but it should foster the company's reputation as a good, reliable, fair employer. A reputation such as this will certainly prove a staffing advantage.

Training

The new communications manager must establish a good cross-training program for him- or herself as well as for both the voice and data staffs. An organizational chart for the new communications department can be helpful in determining the cross-training required for each staff member, according to the new or modified job. This can be on-site training performed by the new manager (if qualified), an appropriate senior staff member, a specialized training company, or an outside consultant. Although on-site training with equipment on hand is generally preferred, off-site training provided by vendors might be considered for operations and maintenance technicians. Communications analysts can benefit from industry seminars as well as from the one- or two-week off-premise courses offered by telephone companies.

A period of intensive training should precede the actual changeover to integrated operations to permit the manager and staff to feel comfortable with the change. Training should thereafter be an ongoing part of the group's activities; the rapid advances in technology make it both essential and cost-justified.

INTEGRATING DATA AND VOICE SIGNALS AND EQUIPMENT

In the following discussion of the integration of data and voice signals and equipment, it is assumed that the organization has separate data and voice networks, as most currently do. Many of the points discussed are germane, even with low-end integration that combines only the management function.

Although an organization may be eager to integrate data and voice communications, it is not an overnight process. There is generally a substantial amount of money invested in equipment (which must be amortized), the selection of integrated data/voice equipment takes time, careers are affected, and the integration of separate departments and operations must be planned carefully and implemented gradually.

Another factor limiting the speed of data/voice integration is the availability of equipment from vendors, although the concept is well proven and some equipment is already in use. An increasing array of integrated data/voice equipment is now becoming available from vendors, however, and this equipment is being purchased by users.

Master Equipment Plan

It will be helpful for the new data/voice communications manager to develop a master plan for the gradual acquisition of equipment to enable the integration of the separate data and voice networks (which may take several years). Some equipment and operations integration can begin immediately: for example, centralizing lines and test equipment and combining staffs.

The master equipment plan must consider the equipment currently on hand, the company's direction, and the financial needs and restrictions. This plan, including an equipment acquisition schedule, should become part of the five-year communications plan. The manager must, of course, recognize technological trends in communications and take advantage of them. The following descriptions will provide upper management with an overview of the kinds of data/voice equipment the new manager may acquire:

- Digital PBX—Digital PBX telephone switching systems, which have been replacing Centrex and other analog switches for the past several years (8,000 were installed between 1974 and 1980), have the potential for directly switching both voice and data digitally, eliminating the need for modems. Several vendors have already added integrated data/voice switching enhancements to the earlier voice-only capability. Voice has already been digitized and switched in digital form in these PBXs, and many users have been waiting for vendors to offer digital data switching through the same paths. This requires vendor development of interface plug-in modules for direct switching of data traffic.
- T-1 Carrier—This is a wideband digital transmission system only recently available to users, although the telephone companies have been using it successfully since 1962. T-1 carrier provides a 1.544-megabit-per-second stream capable of carrying digitized data and voice channels at various speeds.

Other data/voice equipment should be considered; some is available now, and some will be available in the near future. Such equipment includes adaptive multiplexors, data/voice modems, linear predictive coding, digitized voice channel terminals, local networks (wideband coaxial, ring, and bus), alternate data/voice lines, satellite and microwave channels, and so forth. The manager must also seek out common carriers providing integrated voice and data services.

It seems obvious that the acquisition of such integrated communications equipment will cause problems for organizations with separate data and voice communications managers. How, for example, would the projects be assigned? How would a coherent equipment acquisition program be implemented? Who, indeed, would get what? Establishing an integrated data/voice communications management function appears to be the only rational way to answer such questions and resolve the attendant problems.

Integrating Present Equipment

Before acquiring new equipment, and to build up some momentum toward integration, the data/voice communications manager should consider physically relocating some separate data and voice equipment into one area. Data and voice test and control equipment might, for example, be joined in one main control center.

There are other possibilities. If a company were acquiring a new analog or digital PBX at this time, the PBX switch could be placed in the data commu-

DATA COMMUNICATIONS

nications operations room. It could then be integrated into the already existing network control center operation and placed under the care of data communications technicians cross-trained in PBX operations.

CONCLUSION

This chapter discusses many cogent reasons for integrating the data and voice communications management function. Justifications, cost savings, timetables, and levels of integration will, of course, vary from company to company.

The intent of this chapter is to educate upper management concerning the numerous benefits (especially in the area of cost savings), the potential pitfalls, and the techniques of integrating voice and data communications, and to encourage prompt implementation of the integrated management of these important functions.

VI-4
Satisfying Data Communications Needs

David P. Levin

INTRODUCTION

The Bell System divestiture is causing significant restructuring in the telecommunications industry. In addition to the numerous competing organizations from within the Bell System that will result from the breakup, many new companies will be contesting for a place in the communications market.

In addition, the Federal Communications Commission recently repealed tariff filing requirements as a prerequisite for reselling telecommunications services, thereby enabling any company to sell data communications equipment and services. Selecting communications products and designing effective networks is therefore becoming increasingly difficult. Products from many vendors overlap, so users must carefully evaluate their requirements when building a data communications network.

Today, a user may choose from several major value-added networks (VANs), including GTE Telenet, TYMNET, Uninet, Autonet, and Cylix, all of which offer many types of services. Each has different ways of pricing, making comparisons difficult. Knowing when to use VANs is also often difficult. It is even more difficult to plan a communications network for a new information processing system. For example, projecting traffic patterns and bandwidth requirements is subjective. Careful planning becomes especially valuable as communications requirements change over time. This chapter details the steps to use in building a data communications network based on a network installed recently at a broadcasting sales representation firm.

DATA COMMUNICATIONS NETWORK PLANNING STEPS

The following list suggests steps for planning a data communications network. The MIS manager should:
1. Perform a needs assessment to define design criteria
2. Survey available data communications technology in terms of generic solutions
3. Perform a preliminary analysis of viable generic solutions with approximate costs
4. Request information on specific vendor offerings

DATA COMMUNICATIONS

5. Specify communications delivery requirements and proposed alternative solutions
6. Develop requests for proposals for specific hardware and software components
7. Evaluate vendor responses and refine alternative ranking with costs, using a ranking matrix to show strengths and weaknesses
8. Based on the results of the ranking matrix, request best and final vendor bids
9. Select network components and negotiate final business terms
10. Plan installation, testing, support, and operational management
11. Arrange pilot installation and preliminary acceptance testing as hardware arrives
12. If acceptance testing is successful, begin training and volume installation
13. Tune system and plan for future growth once system is fully installed and operational.

CONSIDERATIONS IN THE NEEDS ASSESSMENT PROCESS

A good network plan begins with a thorough assessment of needs. Although this step is often overlooked, it is the single most important factor in ensuring a cost-effective network design. Its major requirements are common sense and determination: there are no right or wrong answers, only good and bad assumptions.

Compiling Profiles

Five profiles are needed to help define network design criteria:
- User profile—Compiled by listing users by job function, surveying potential users, and determining personality traits of major user groups
- Usage profile—Compiled by determining online availability hours, typical peak periods, and average number of hours per day of terminal interaction and printing
- Geographic profile—Compiled by determining total audience, areas of concentration, and user population density and relating usage to geographic areas
- Applications profile—Compiled by determining the importance of the application to the organization, revenue impact, and flexibility of response time
- Hardware profile—Compiled by determining types of devices necessary and their locations

A national television and radio sales representation firm recently installed a national data communications network to support an online sales proposal and analysis system. This project will serve as an example throughout this chapter.

The system enables local sales staffs to use the same sales proposal formats, including audience projections, as those used by their national representative when selling spot advertising. The new network replaced one that could not support the anticipated growth in station subscribers.

User Profile. This profile should include a list of potential system users

Data Communications Needs

and their job functions. If detailed information is required, a formal written survey of potential users may be conducted. It is also important to determine the general personality traits for each major user group.

A feature of the representative's system was an administrative messaging (i.e., electronic mail) system intended to replace the TWX machine. The national sales department of a television station commonly uses its TWX to confirm orders placed by its national representative. This confirmation process was incorporated into the total sales system. This network also replaced a current IBM 3270-type network with terminals and printers located within each of the national representative's 15 sales offices. The functions in the representative's regional sales offices are also in television station sales offices. The user profile for this network includes the following information:

User by Job Function	Frequency of Usage
National sales manager	Very occasional
National salesperson	Very occasional
National sales assistant	Moderate
Local sales manager	Occasional
Local salesperson	Occasional
Local sales assistant	Frequent
Person responsible for TWX traffic	Frequent

Closer examination reveals that only sales assistants and the individual responsible for TWX traffic are potentially frequent system users; everyone else is an occasional user at most.

The TWX operator's personality traits include an aptitude for office machines as well as computer and communications equipment and a potential for learning new systems. This would probably also apply to the typical sales assistant, although possibly on a less sophisticated level.

Usage Profile. The usage profile includes such information as the requirements for online availability and typical peak traffic periods. In this example, users of the sales proposal system required online service during weekdays from 8:00 AM to 8:00 PM local time. Saturday was a critical day only for online operation at some stations. Thus, Saturday hours from 9:00 AM to 5:00 PM were requested. Much of this information was collected informally by talking with various station and office personnel. A written survey is a more formal method for obtaining such information in greater detail.

The average number of hours per day of remote terminal interaction and printing is an important part of the usage profile. The broadcast sales system usage was projected as follows:

Size of User	Projected Terminal Usage (hr/day)	Projected Printing (pages/day)
Small television station	1	10–15
Large television station	2–3	20–50
Small sales office	2–4	20–40
Medium sales office	10–15	50–100
Large sales office	20–25	100–200

DATA COMMUNICATIONS

Typical peak periods were projected to be late morning and late afternoon, and Friday was projected as the probable peak during the week. Seasonally, the peak period is late summer and early fall, corresponding to the new television season.

Figure 1 shows the typical growth pattern of an online network system. The first stage of system introduction is characterized by very slow growth. There is constant growth during the second stage of system acceptance. Heavy growth occurs during the third stage with volume cutovers and increased marketing efforts. Growth slows in the final stage as user saturation occurs.

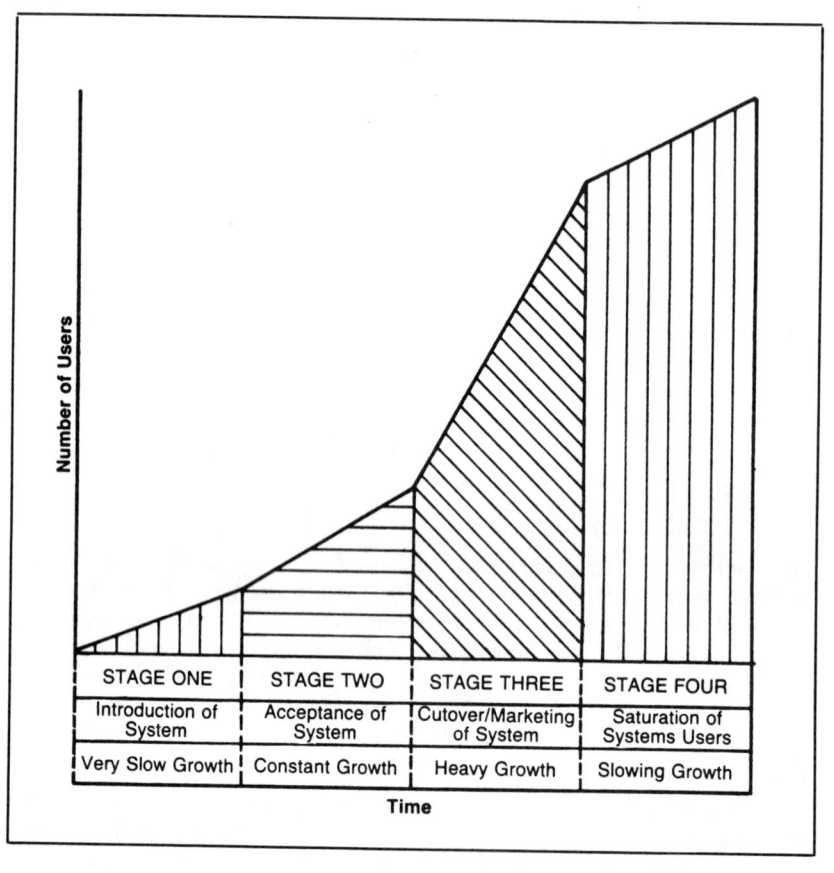

Figure 1. Typical Growth Pattern of Users for Data Communications Network System

Geographic Profile. This simple network has a potential user base of more than 100 stations throughout the contiguous United States. The national representative described in this example is notably strong in the Southeast and Midwest. Areas of lesser concentration include the Northeast, California, and the Middle Atlantic states. The representative's 15 offices closely correspond to the 13 most populated cities in the U.S. with two sales offices located in both Chicago and Los Angeles. All terminals within the representative's New York offices are attached locally to the host.

It appeared that usage in each geographic area was related to advertising dollars spent in those areas. Thus, New York is first, followed by Chicago and Los Angeles. The representative has small local concentrations of users in such cities as Chicago and Los Angeles where the representative maintains two separate offices in addition to one station. A more dispersed pattern occurs in California where Los Angeles and San Francisco share three offices, and five stations are scattered throughout the state.

Applications Profile. Understanding the importance of the application to the user organization is fundamental to designing an effective communications network. For example, it costs airlines thousands of dollars in lost revenues when their reservation networks are down for even a few minutes. The financial consequences of system downtime and poor response time in the proposed network design should be examined. In the broadcast sales system, the impact of system downtime for 10 or 15 minutes was more inconvenient than costly.

The same is true of response time in this network. The first significant effect of poor response time is interference with efficient keyboarding, which occurs once response time degrades beyond three to five seconds for most interactive applications. Greater inconvenience results if response time falls to 15 or 20 seconds. In this example, response time requirements can be flexible.

Hardware Profile. The largest remote user is the representative's Chicago office, whose projected need was for four terminals and three high-speed dot-matrix printers. Several of the larger offices needed three terminals and three printers, but the majority of the rep offices required only two of each.

Because the sales proposal system is used by the stations' national and local sales departments, it was thought that some might want two terminals with one shared printer. Conceivably, a station could want both a terminal and printer in each department for a total of two terminals and two printers. However, less than 10 percent of the stations indicated a desire for more than a terminal and a printer.

The number of terminals in the representative's major sales offices will increase by one or two terminals per year. The number of devices in the stations will increase minimally and not immediately.

Special Requirements

Most MIS and data communications operations perform various tasks at different times to meet all organizational needs. Each information processing system has special needs, such as a high volume of printing or simultaneous printing on different paper forms. The television sales representative had both requirements. The majority of reports needed by the representative's sales offices were printed in the evening when no terminal traffic occurred.

DATA COMMUNICATIONS

This unattended printing strategy played a major role in the overall resource management effort and system design.

The sales offices wanted three printers to enable them to print contracts, proposals, and electronic messages simultaneously, thus greatly reducing paper handling and changing. Therefore, the system design provides cost-effective high-speed dot-matrix printers instead of the more costly line printers. The price of three dot-matrix printers is approximately the same as two medium-speed line printers, and they are far more convenient and productive.

Traffic Flow

An estimate of traffic flow can be useful if certain underlying assumptions are remembered. Generally, the user can estimate the average transaction lengths in and out of the computer. The intent of traffic analysis is to estimate the average traffic per unit of time as well as the peak traffic load. Various traffic analyses exist for modeling data communications networks, but these simulation techniques are beyond the scope of this chapter.

Proper estimation of the line speed necessary to support the network is as important for economic justification as it is for traffic requirements. Line speed choices should be considered as follows:

Type of Service	Typical Line Speed (bps)
Low-volume dial-up terminal	1,200
High-volume dial-up terminal	2,400 or 4,800
Low- to medium-volume dedicated terminal controller	2,400 or 4,800
High-volume dedicated controller	4,800 or 9,600
Host-to-host links	56K or 1.544M

Modem prices continue to decline as does the cost per unit of bandwidth. Analog dial-up and leased lines continue to be the most popular method of data communications transmission. Therefore, analog modems determine the economics of line speed. Approximate analog modem costs (depending on features) are as follows:

Analog Modem Speed (bps)	Approximate End-User Purchase Price ($)
1,200	700–1,000
2,400	900–1,200
4,800	1,800–2,400
9,600	2,600–5,600

Again, bandwidth requirements are generally less important than economic and host resource issues when line speeds are being considered. For example, 12 terminals, each processing 30 transactions per hour (1,000 characters in and 2,000 characters out per transaction), would create a total of 2,400 bits per second of actual data message traffic.

Future Growth

Recognizing sources of future network growth is the best defense against installing an obsolete network. In the broadcast sales system example, sources of growth are television stations, radio stations, and new sales offices. Obviously, the television stations represent the greatest growth potential; they are located throughout the country with some areas of concentration in the Southeast and Midwest. Radio stations represent a completely untapped market, and connecting these stations was not an immediate requirement. The number of new representative sales offices would be very limited, and any new office would probably be located in a major city where a station subscriber is also located.

NETWORK ISSUES

Most networks have specific areas of user concentration that may be served cost-effectively by numerous networking techniques, including local area networking, communications concentration, multiplexing, and multidropping. Because users of the broadcast sales system are located throughout the U.S., use of a single local area network is precluded. A combination of multidropping with concentration or multiplexing is more suitable. Multidropping is attractive because of the small number of terminals per location, the distance between locations is hundreds of miles, and because of the need for dedicated service. Concentration or multiplexing is desirable because there are several small concentrations of users scattered throughout the country, and the relatively low level of data traffic and line usage lends itself well to statistical time-division multiplexing (STDM). Hub sites were then initially planned for New York (the host site), Chicago, Atlanta, and San Francisco or Los Angeles.

Networking Alternatives

Networking alternatives can be roughly divided between public and private transmission facilities. Private facilities include Bell voicegrade leased lines, GTE Telenet private packet network facilities, and AT&T Dataphone Digital Service circuits. Public transmission facilities include the AT&T Direct Distance Dialing, the GTE Telenet and TYMNET 300/1,200 bits per second dial-up network, and the Source.

The Bell 3002 unconditioned voicegrade four-wire analog line is the most popular data line for dedicated data communications networks. In many instances, the challenge is to squeeze every last bit from the data line rather than investigate alternative transmission facilities. Most VANs offer dedicated connections into their network, which appears as a dedicated channel to the user (see Figure 2).

Networking Techniques

Certain networking techniques—specifically, multidropping, multiplexing, and concentration—use dedicated leased lines to realize certain economies of scale. Multidropping is the technique of connecting a small number of different locations on bridged data lines (see Figure 3), with each station or con-

DATA COMMUNICATIONS

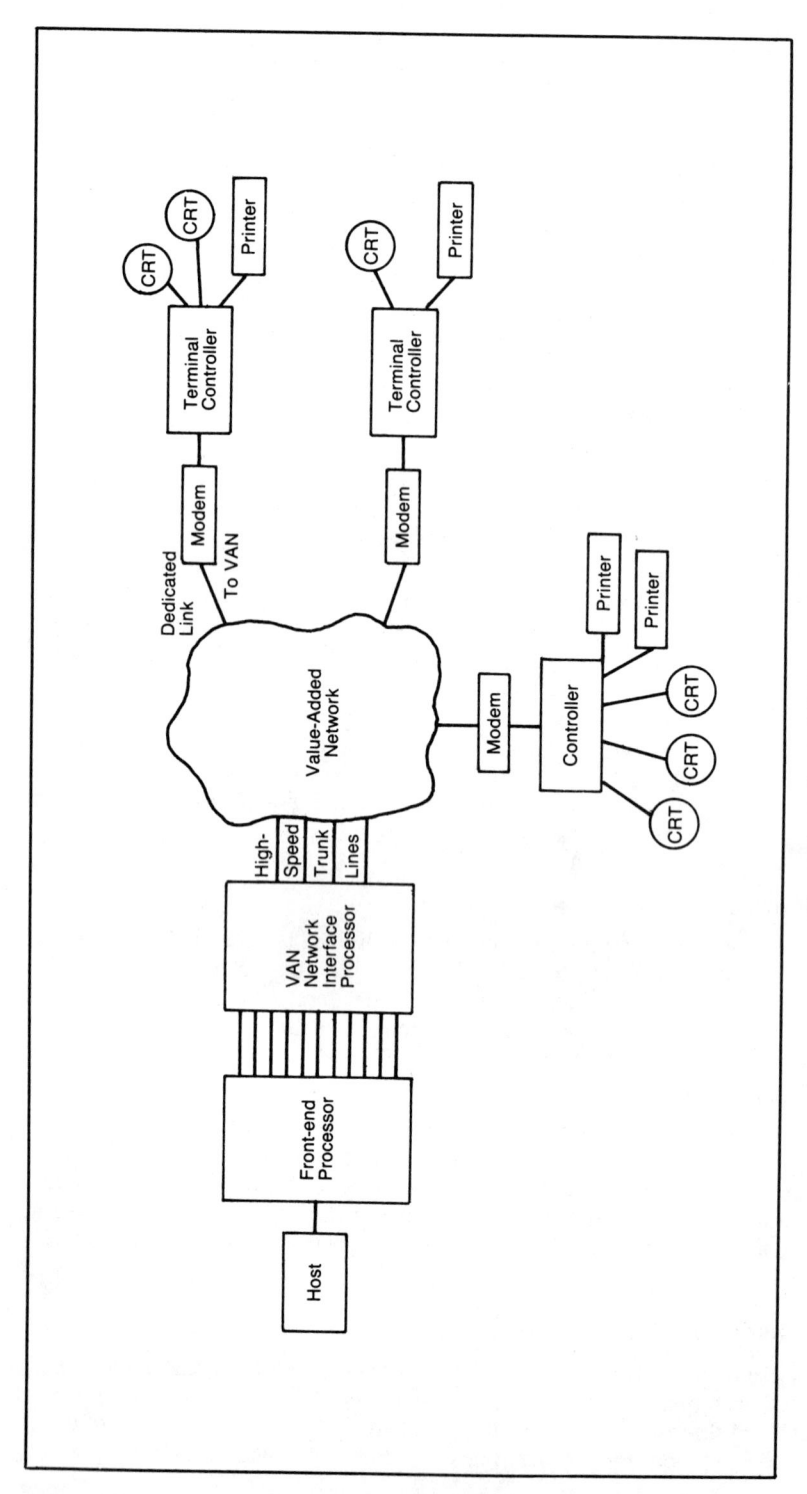

Figure 2. Dedicated VAN Links

Data Communications Needs

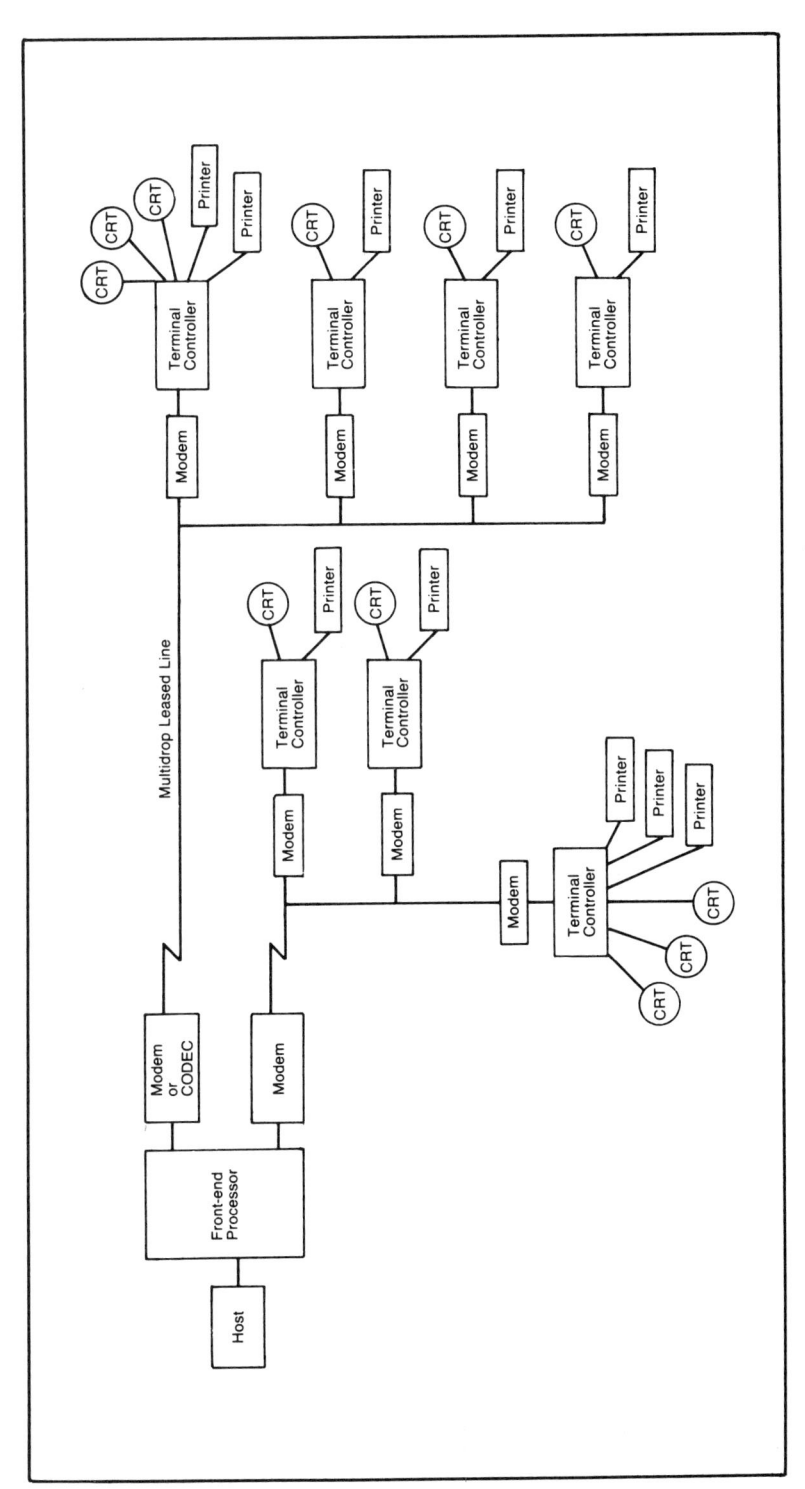

Figure 3. Multidrop Leased Line Configuration

DATA COMMUNICATIONS

troller on the line polled for traffic. Disadvantages of multidropping include:
- Line turnaround and protocol polling severely limit the amount of traffic and number of stations that can share a line.
- The bridged data line is extremely difficult to maintain and long periods of downtime are common.
- One defective station can affect the entire line totally preventing communications on that line.

Multiplexing is the technique of using regional hub locations throughout the network. In the sales support system example, the offices and stations are located in cities throughout the U.S. (see Figure 4). Hub cities would probably include Chicago, Los Angeles, and Atlanta. San Francisco, Minneapolis, Detroit, Charlotte, and St. Louis are other possible smaller hubs.

Multiplexing is convenient because multiplexor hardware is relatively transparent to the network. Statistical time-division multiplexing is particularly effective because it dynamically allocates its time whenever users need it. Most multiplexors have sophisticated diagnostic and control capabilities, which greatly assist in network problem determination and reconfiguration.

Multiplexing has some inherent limitations. For example, data transparency means a significant amount of communications overhead, which also means time delays that can radically change traffic patterns. In a polled, binary synchronous 3270-type network, the tail circuits from the multiplexor to the user locations may be multidropped. A maximum of three drops are advisable, depending on data speed, traffic patterns, and central processing resources.

Concentration is similar to multiplexing, except a more intelligent communications controller is used (see Figure 5). Typical remote concentrators include an IBM 3705 or 3725; an NCR Comten 3650, 3670, or 3690; an Amdahl 4705; and an IBM Series 1 or other minicomputer with custom telecommunications software. Concentrators are more expensive than medium-sized multiplexors but are comparably priced with front-end processors and large-sized multiplexors. Concentrators generally accommodate multiple protocols and use higher-speed (56K bits per second and up) trunk lines to the host. Concentrators strip off all unnecessary communications control blocks and efficiently repackage the data for transmission to the host.

Estimating Network Costs

Table 1 shows the estimated costs for four different networking alternatives for connecting the sales offices and stations:
- Using dedicated VAN connections to user locations as well as to the host.
- Using multipoint leased lines to connect six to eight users per line to the host.
- Connecting up to three users per line to multiplexor hub sites in Atlanta, Chicago, and Los Angeles. Each hub site is in turn connected to a multiplexor at the host location through one or two high-speed trunk lines.
- Connecting up to five users per line to a concentrator hub site in Chicago or directly to the host site in New York.

Data Communications Needs

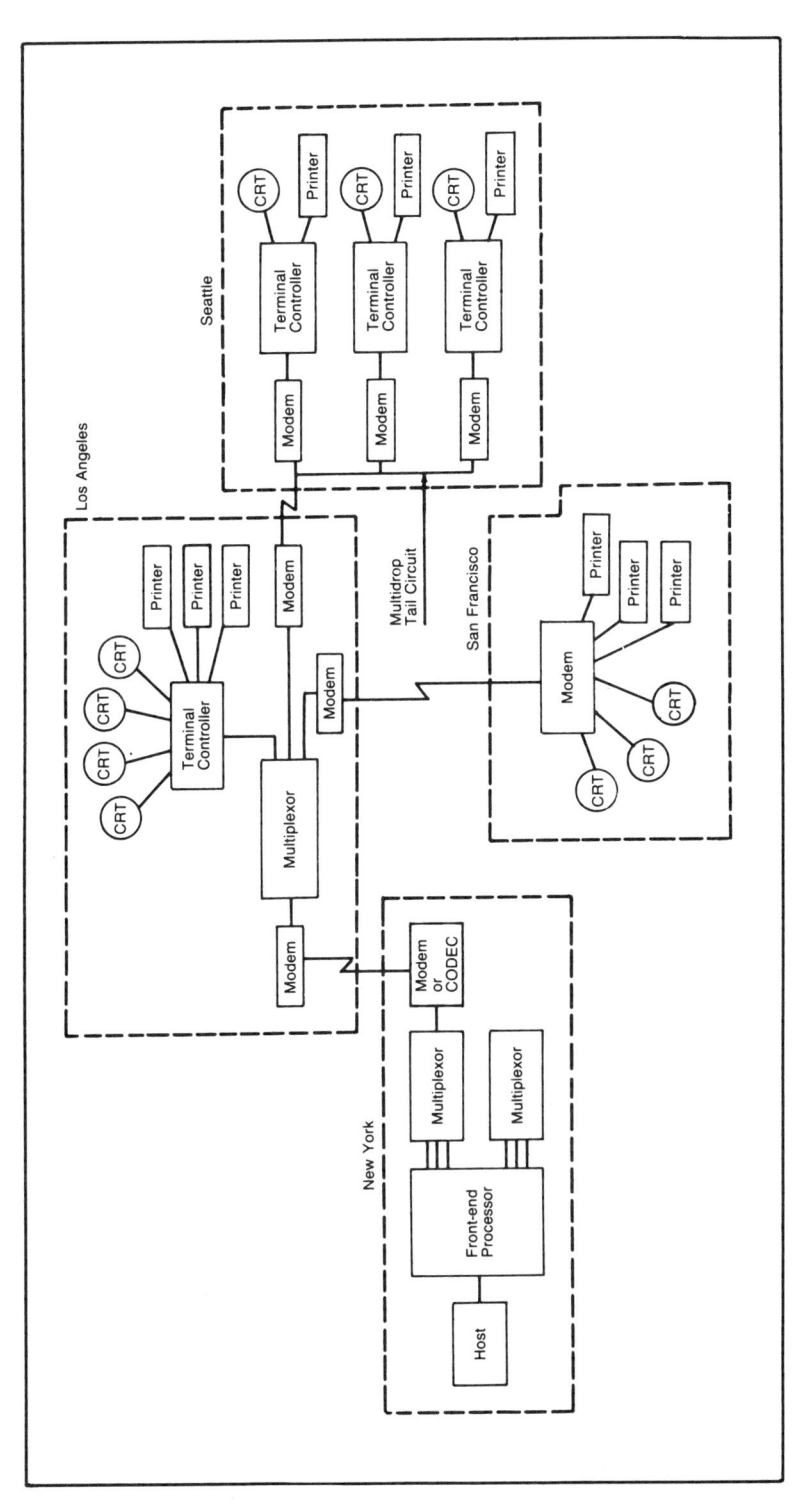

Figure 4. Multidrop Tail Circuits

DATA COMMUNICATIONS

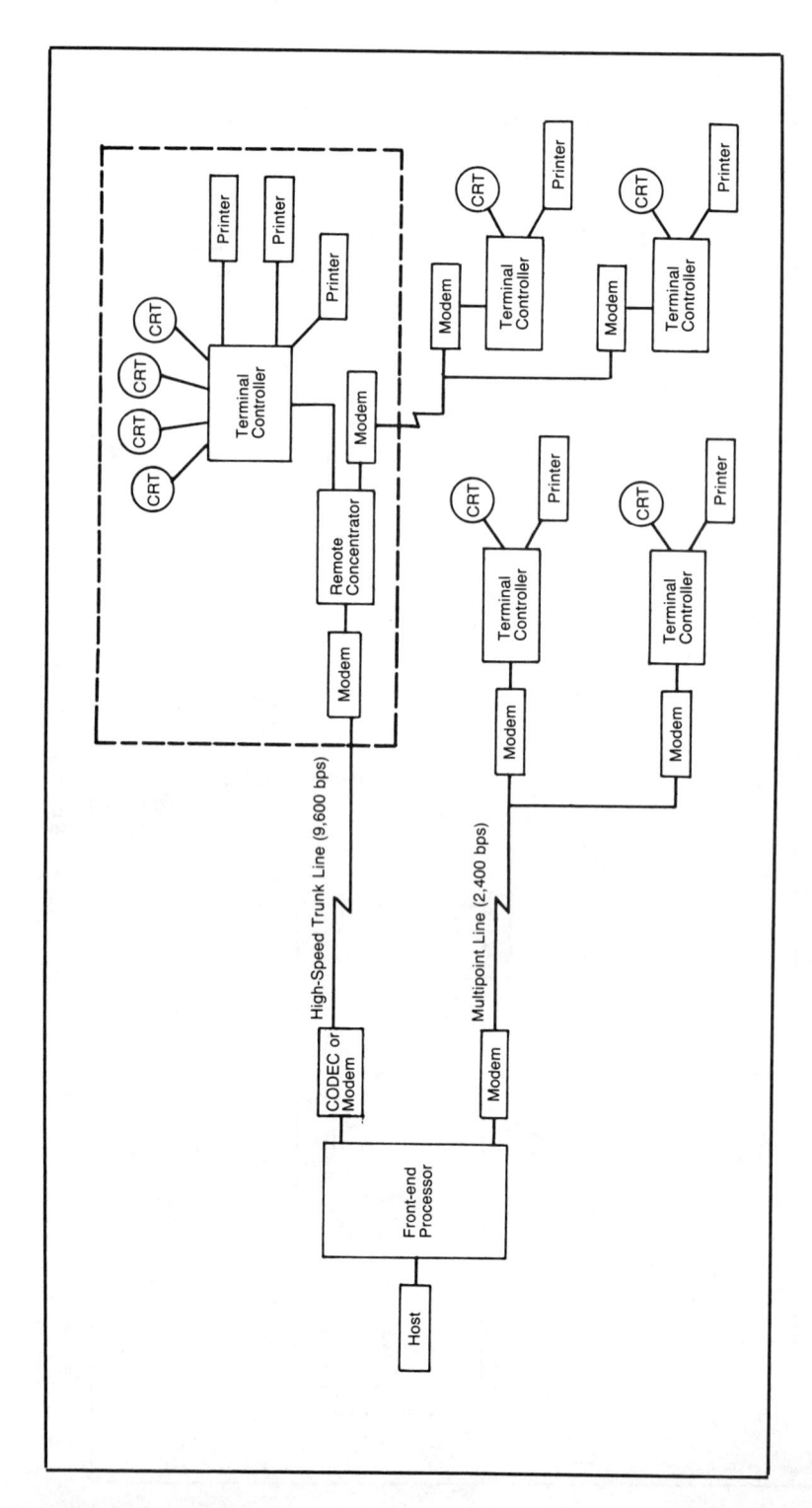

Figure 5. Concentration with Multidrop Tail Circuits

Data Communications Needs

Table 1. Estimated Alternative Network Costs

	Dedicated VAN ($/mo)	Multipoint Leased Lines ($/mo)	Multiplexing w/Multidrop ($/mo)	Concentration w/Multidrop ($/mo)
Front-end Processor	2,500	2,500	2,500	3,500
Front-end Processor Ports	1,100	1,100	1,100	500
Remote Communications Controllers	—	—	—	5,000
Multiplexors	—	—	2,400	—
Data Lines	14,300	42,000	35,000	30,000
VAN Dedicated Remote Lines	27,000	—	—	—
VAN Host Interface	3,000	—	—	—
Host Communications Software	1,000	1,000	1,000	2,000
Total	48,900	46,600	42,000	41,000

Assumptions:
Comten 3670 M85 or IBM 3705 M80 front-end processor
Remote communications controller is similar to front-end processor
Multiplexors lease for $400 per month each
Dedicated 2,400-bps VAN connection is $600 per month
VAN 9,600-bps dedicated data line to host is $1,300 per month

---

An examination of the dedicated value-added networking alternative reveals a requirement for a front-end processor (e.g., an IBM 3705 Model 80 or an NCR Comten 3670 Model 85). The basic lease cost for this front-end processor is estimated at $2,500 per month. Front-end processor ports typically cost $100 per month; 11 ports are required to support all offices and stations.

No remote communications controllers or multiplexors are required in this alternative, because the VAN provides these services as part of its basic network. Eleven 9,600-bit-per-second data lines are required from the VAN central office to the user's host at a cost of $1,300 per month per line. All 45 locations require a 2,400-bit-per-second dedicated link into the VAN at an estimated cost of $600 per month per location. This cost should include any charges for data traffic (e.g., kilopacket or kilocharacter charges).

A network interface processor is required to handle packet assembly/disassembly (PAD) and traffic management activities. The cost of the interface processor is an estimated $3,000 per month. As an alternative, a software program residing in the proper front-end processor would offset the need for the interface processor.

Finally, host communications software is required, including an access method and teleprocessing monitor at a cost of $1,000 per month. Total cost for the dedicated value-added networking alternative is estimated at just less than $49,000 per month. This does not include host processor resources or terminal equipment costs.

An effective alternative to value-added networking is to use dedicated multipoint leased lines. The same front-end processor is required with approximately the same port requirements: no remote communications controllers or multiplexors are used in this configuration. Leased-line costs are estimated at $42,000 per month. No VAN lines or host interfaces are used, and host communications software is $1,000 per month. Cost for the multipoint line alternative totals $46,000 per month.

DATA COMMUNICATIONS

Multiplexing is currently the most popular networking scheme. In the example, the same front-end processor is used with 11 ports. Multiplexor hub sites are located in the Chicago, Atlanta, and Los Angeles sales offices. Six multiplexors are required at an estimated cost of $400 per multiplexor per month.

A significant line savings is possible when a multipoint line configuration is changed to a multiplexor-based configuration, which also includes multipoint tail circuits. Data line costs are estimated at $35,000 per month for the multiplexing network configuration. No VAN services are required, and the host communications software requirements are the same as for the previous alternatives. Cost for the multiplexor networking alternative are about $42,000 per month.

The concentration configuration is somewhat less expensive with data line costs of $30,000 per month. A larger front-end processor with additional main memory is required, as is additional software to support remote concentration. The required number of front-end processor ports is cut in half. Two remote concentrators in Chicago and Los Angeles cost an estimated $2,500 per concentrator per month. Total cost for the concentration configuration would be approximately $41,000 per month.

Comparing Networking Alternatives

In this example, the dedicated VAN proved most costly. The VAN, however, does provide problem determination and resource management services, which are an additional cost with other leased-line networking alternatives.

Although more cost-effective, the multipoint leased-line configuration is severely limited in design. Serious problems include stringent limitation of data traffic volume with adequate response time, difficulty in network diagnostics and maintenance, and the high cost of adding users.

The point-to-point and multipoint lease-line network configurations were most popular during the past decade. Concentration became popular during the late seventies and continues to grow at a slow but steady pace. Multiplexing has recently become very popular as the price of microprocessor-based STDMs drop. Virtually every major data communications equipment vendor currently offers a family of multiplexor products.

The state of the art in statistical multiplexing is a microprocessor-based box that accepts 4 to 24 asynchronous or synchronous inputs for combined transmission over one or two 9,600 bit-per-second trunk lines. When two trunk lines are used, load sharing enables the multiplexor to dynamically allocate traffic across both trunks, thus compensating for changes in line conditions. If one trunk fails, all traffic is automatically routed through the remaining operational trunk. The network stays up, but with somewhat slower response time, depending on the load.

When used with asynchronous inputs, the STDM can realize economies of scale from a ratio of 5 to 1 and 10 to 1. An overbooking ratio of 2.5 to 1 is commonly used for polled 3270-type bisynchronous devices. Even with synchronous data link control (SDLC) or other packet protocols as inputs, an economy of scale between a ratio of 1.5 to 1 and 2 to 1 is common. This overbooking ratio compares the maximum input bandwidth to the required trunk link bandwidth.

Multiplexors are becoming so cost-effective that concentration in the near future may be feasible only for very large networks. Multiplexors are reliable and easily maintained by hardware vendors, whereas concentrators generally require sophisticated systems programming support personnel, a costly resource.

ACTION PLAN

A needs assessment should begin with a compilation of profiles that describe the scope of the design problem. The nature of the user community should be evaluated and the application and usage pattern examined to guide the total network design. Geographic and hardware profiles suggest the type of transmission facility best suited to the design requirements, and special requirements must be considered.

The average network currently grows between 20 and 30 percent per year in number of locations and traffic volume. Therefore, projected traffic patterns should be examined and related analyses performed. The implications of different growth rates should be understood so that alternative network topologies that permit significant growth may be developed.

An evaluation of networking alternatives must include cost considerations. Within the cost and service context, the many networking schemes available should be considered, including multidropping, multiplexing, concentration, and VAN facilities. A network design should be chosen that is cost-effective in the long run without the initial purchase of excess capacity.

VI-5
Security for Local Area Networks
Alan Berman

INTRODUCTION

Local area networks (LANs) have, in a short time, become an important part of data processing technology. They evolved from the dumb terminals connected to centralized computers, prevalent in the 1960s. Although these early networks used low-speed transmission lines, they did provide interactive facilities directly with the host computer.

During the 1970s minicomputers came into use. They were inexpensive compared to mainframes and adaptable to particular application needs; however, they could not handle the increasing number of users who required access to the same information (i.e., shared data files). The need for shared data files, common use of storage and peripheral devices, and interdepartmental data sharing and transmission mandated the development of the computer technology and communications links that allowed computer-to-computer data transfer.

The distributed minicomputer phase led to the design of networks that would satisfy individual job needs. The dumb terminal gained intelligence as a result of microchip technology. Privately owned computer-to-computer networks were developed to optimize the use of shared resources over high-speed communications links, and these evolved into local area networks.

Any new technology demands new security measures and a protected environment in which to operate. LAN security must start with the device that provides entry into the network—the terminal.

The two primary areas of concern when dealing with terminal security are identification/authentication control and environmental control.

IDENTIFICATION/AUTHENTICATION CONTROL

Identification/authentication deals with identifying a user or terminal and authenticating that the user is allowed to access the system. Essentially the identification/authentication process ensures that a user is who he or she claims to be. This can be demonstrated by the user through four methods:
- Unique knowledge (something only one person knows)
- Unique possession (something only one person has)

DATA COMMUNICATIONS

- Unique performance (something only one person can do)
- Unique attribute (something only one person is)

The first of the above methods deals with passwords; the other three relate to physical methods of identification and authentication. (For simplicity, the term ''identification'' will be used hereafter for ''identification/authentication.'') The categories of identification differ in approach, installation and maintenance costs, and degree of security provided, but all aim to provide an identification mechanism that uniquely defines each terminal user.

THE PASSWORD

The password has been used by every type of system that provides the rudiments of security in an automated environment. Because many LAN terminals identify only the source of the transmission, a method must be established to identify individuals who attempt to access sensitive files and data elements within files. A password methodology identifies each user's access capabilities.

This method works well in a hierarchical data base environment because the password can serve as a control mechanism for acquiring information in the data base schema. For example, one group of password holders may only be allowed to access summary departmental information; detailed information may be restricted to holders of another group of passwords.

Files that do not have a hierarchical data base structure can use passwords only to restrict access to the entire file. Any other security measures must be coded within the application modules.

For password security to be effective, the password must be entered with each request, thus identifying the terminal user. Although this procedure is somewhat cumbersome, it can be an effective and inexpensive means of providing user identification.

KEYS AND OTHER POSSESSIONS

In the possession category (something only one person has) are portable identification devices introduced into a device permanently attached to the terminal. When the two items are mated, the result is either recognition and entry to the next phase of identification or rejection and exclusion from the system. As with all the physical identification equipment types examined, these devices have various forms, degrees of sophistication, and costs.

Lock and Key

The most common device is the terminal lock and key system. One of the oldest security identification devices, its strength lies in its simplicity: the user inserts the key into the lock and turns it to the proper position, and the terminal is ready to communicate. Installation is usually an option provided by the manufacturer at relatively low cost. Maintenance cost is almost nonexistent; the only maintenance is replacement of the lock for security reasons (e.g., a key is lost or stolen) or because of a physical malfunction caused by improper use of a key (e.g., forcing it into the lock or breaking it off in the lock). Because the lock is built into the terminal cabinet, no external cabling is needed. Replacement is simple and inexpensive; it is done by changing the lock cylinder and issuing new keys.

There are three major drawbacks to this physical security measure: user behavior, ease of penetration, and lack of flexibility.

User Behavior. Removing the key when the terminal is not in use seems bothersome to many employees. Workers often put the key in the terminal in the morning and remove it only when ready to leave for the day. Few employees remove the key before leaving the terminal for breaks or lunch. In many cases, the key is in the lock whenever users are in the office, and it is not unusual to find keys in place 24 hours a day, seven days a week. This carelessness and complacency can be remedied by periodic inspections during regular working hours. Building security staff should conduct inspections during evenings and weekends. All security violations should be reported, and personnel evaluations should reflect employees' security awareness and compliance.

Ease of Penetration. The second drawback to key and lock security is the relative ease with which the system can be penetrated. Any lock can be forced open, picked, or opened by an unauthorized key. Forced entry—inserting a device (e.g., a screwdriver or nail file) into the lock and damaging the lock cylinder to the extent that it can be opened—is detected as soon as someone tries to use the terminal with an authorized key. This method is seldom used, because it is easy to detect and it allows the invader only a very short time to perpetrate illegal transactions.

A more common method of illegal entry is picking the lock using a lockpick, which, when used skillfully, turns the lock without a key. The advantages of this method are obvious: repeated access and no signs of forced entry. This form of illegal access can continue for quite some time. Even if there are suspicions that an unauthorized person is using the system, the most probable action is to change the lock. This does not protect the system, however, because the new lock can also be picked if it is similar in structure to the old lock.

Although forced entry and lock picking threaten terminal security, the probability of penetration through the use of an unauthorized key is far greater. These keys are copied, privately or commercially, from authorized keys that are stolen and then returned. The criminal must copy and return a key before anyone realizes or reports that the key is missing. On realizing that the key is missing, an employee is more likely to cover up its disappearance than report it to the authorities and reveal carelessness in guarding the key. When the key is found, the employee is relieved, and the brief disappearance is never reported.

To protect against illegal access, companies purchase cylindrical, "pickproof," or magnetic locks and keys that are more difficult to duplicate. Stamping "Illegal to duplicate, violators will be prosecuted" on keys lessens the likelihood of entry through illegal means. The more sophisticated the locks and keys, the more talented and inventive the terminal invader must be.

DATA COMMUNICATIONS

Most computer crimes occur because opportunities present themselves to persons who work at terminals; therefore, making penetration more difficult may provide a sufficient deterrent to these crimes.

Inflexibility. The greatest drawback to lock and key security is its inflexibility. It allows only a few persons access to a terminal. Issuing more than three or four keys to a terminal would result in lost keys, operators waiting to use a particular terminal, and an unhealthy environment for both security and operator productivity. Conversely, it would be unmanageable for an employee to have keys to more than two terminals. This inflexibility, more than any security consideration, makes lock and key security impractical in most operating environments.

The Magnetic Card

The magnetically encoded card system overcomes the difficulties of lock and key security. About the size of a credit card, the magnetic card is equipped with an identification strip magnetically encoded with a machine-readable identifier. The card is inserted in a specially designed magnetic card reader, which is connected to the terminal by a cable. When the card is properly inserted into the reader, the magnetically encoded identification number is transmitted to the system host to be verified against a control file of authorized users. Restrictions can limit the types of input, specify the hours of eligibility, and prohibit the use of certain terminals. The system is more expensive than key and lock because additional equipment (card reader and cable) is required. Although the card reader can malfunction and need adjustments to correct alignment problems, maintenance is typically minimal, and incidences of malfunction are infrequent. Cards can be replaced quickly and at reasonable cost. When a card is reported lost or stolen, it is made ineligible for terminal access on the central verification file. This invalidation is done through a specially equipped and secured terminal. If the card is found, it can be made eligible using the same terminal. This eliminates the cumbersome and time-consuming task of replacing all locks and keys when a breach of security is suspected.

The magnetic card system avoids the three basic inadequacies associated with lock and key security. Strengthening physical security requires extra effort to change employee behavior commonly associated with lock and key systems; however, the problems of penetrability and flexibility are resolved easily.

Stopping Careless Behavior. To ameliorate careless behavior, all magnetically encoded cards should also be used as identification cards throughout the organization. Each card should have the employee's picture, employee number, and signature, and it should be required to enter the building, enter the company cafeteria, and cash payroll checks. Because the card must be carried at all times and has personal significance to the employee, it is less likely to be left unprotected. The chance of theft or misappropriation is therefore reduced.

Lower Risks of Penetration. The risk of penetration is reduced because there is no physical area (such as a lock cylinder) to pry open to gain access. Since the device is driven by electronic impulses rather than mechanics, penetrating the device requires specific knowledge of security systems.

Enhanced Flexibility. The magnetically encoded card is more flexible in its applications than the lock and key. It can fit into any reader and allow the operator to use any terminal in the system. The use of certain terminals can be limited to certain operators, but this is done in the verification file software, not in the card reader. If a card is lost or stolen, no hardware changes are required; the verification file is simply updated to make the card invalid for terminal operation. This is simpler, more efficient, and more responsive to the time constraints involved in invalidating user authorization than changing keys and locks.

The Token

Another device that falls into the possession category is the token. Unlike the magnetic card and the key, the token is not inserted into a receptacle. Instead it transmits a radio signal to a receiver attached to the terminal. When the user is in close proximity to the receiver, the transmitted signal is received and the terminal status is set to "on." When the user moves out of terminal receiver range, the terminal status is changed to "off," rendering the terminal inoperable.

Ending Careless Behavior. This type of device deals best with the behavioral aspects of physical device security. If the user leaves the immediate terminal area, the terminal shuts off. No data entry or key removal is necessary. The token is easily attached to a belt or carried in a pocket, reducing the chance of loss or misplacement.

Difficult to Penetrate. The transmission signal is very difficult to duplicate without the use of highly specialized equipment, substantially reducing the likelihood of system penetration. Tokens cost about as much as magnetic cards and require very little maintenance because they have few moving parts.

A Flexible System. The system is flexible; the transmission signal can be adjusted so that a single token activates one or several selected terminals.

ANATOMICAL AND PERFORMANCE DEVICES

For user-carried devices, loss, theft, and temporary compromise of the device present the greatest security risks. Greater control of device distribution can abate these risks. For example, devices can be held in a safeguarded distribution point when they are not being used. This effort is effective in a centralized user environment, but where users are dispersed throughout a wide area, this method is difficult, if not impossible, to implement and enforce. The solution is to make the device one that cannot be lost, left in a terminal or reader, or stolen. The device has to be a physical part of the user. As noted earlier these identifiers fall into two categories:
- Anatomical identification devices (what a user is)
- Performance identification devices (what a user can do).

Fingerprints and Palm Prints

Anatomical identification devices are parts of the anatomy that uniquely identify an individual. Two common methods are the fingerprint and the palm print. For both, a hand-shaped device is attached to the terminal; when the user places his or her hand in the appropriate slot or groove, sensors in the device transmit an electronic translation to the host computer. The host searches its files for a match and identifies the user. Fingerprints and palm prints are invalidated in the same manner as magnetic cards.

Experimental Anatomical Devices

Although the hand is the primary source of anatomical identification, experiments have been made with other parts of the anatomy. Lip prints and the size and shape of the head have unique identification qualities, but both are in very early experimental stages as identification devices. However, beta tests are being performed in facial identification. The terminal is equipped with a closed-circuit camera that transmits the user's image to a centralized site for verification. The drawback to this method is matching faces against an electronically coded file. The operator could insert a photo-engraved identification card into a reader, allowing the system to match the camera image to the card image, but this has all the problems associated with a possession device.

Voice Prints

Performance identification devices are concerned with actions that uniquely identify a user. Two methods have met with some success: voice prints and signature analysis.

For voice prints, a speaker attached to the terminal relays a predetermined spoken message from the user to the host computer. The electronic equivalent of the vocal message is compared to one previously recorded and encoded. If the two match, the user is allowed to access the system.

Signature Devices

The use of signatures as identifiers is very common. Two methodologies are used: the more traditional one compares the signature submitted to the verified one on file; the other measures the impulse time required to initiate the signature. Since the signature is written more often than anything else, the amount of time necessary for the brain to recognize this request and initiate the mechanical act is shorter than for any other written task. By measuring this impulse time, signature authenticity can be confirmed. Because the mechanism that performs this measurement is more complex than the one that simply compares signatures, this newer method has only been used experimentally; however. it has been shown to reduce the risk associated with signature forgeries.

Other Security Precautions

In addition to other security measures, the user is usually required to enter his or her name, employee number, and other information, plus a password, into a terminal. Such input is necessary so that the name or employee number can be used as a search argument against the verification file to find the user's fingerprints, voice print, or signature. This combination of password plus physical identifier provides the best measure of security.

ENVIRONMENTAL CONTROL

Environmental control is all but ignored in most organizations, but the potential for breaches of security should be sufficient cause to take preventive measures. These measures are often inexpensive, and many simply require some concern for security while the terminal installation is being planned.

A U-shaped arrangement of terminals tends to provide the greatest operator privacy, particularly when many terminals are required in a relatively small area. With this arrangement an operator is never looking directly at the screen of the person seated directly next to him or her. Operators face the backs of terminals, providing a private environment. Supervisory personnel should be positioned at the open end of the U. From this position, they can inspect cabling switches and have a full view of operator performance.

Every video screen should be equipped with a polarized screen filter. The filer serves two purposes: it removes glare and allows the operator to work longer without eye strain, and it permits information on the screen to be viewed only from directly in front of the screen. No operator can see the information the next operator is working on. These filters are available for all standard-sized screens at minimal cost, and they are good investments in maintaining a private and secure environment.

CONCLUSION

Unauthorized system users can do serious damage. Their aim can be to steal confidential information (for private use or for resale to a competing company), tamper with vital records, or satisfy curiosity about coworkers' personnel files. Once data integrity is breached, every file becomes suspect.

Preventing such incursions is of paramount importance. The MIS manager should carefully consider security devices, selecting one (or several) by weighing cost, administrative controls, and stringency requirements. In addition, examining the terminal environment can lead to tighter security at minimal cost.

Section VII
Managing the Data Center

In many organizations, the importance of the data center to the daily functioning and overall success of the enterprise is increasing. Frequently, the data center runs seven days a week, 24 hours a day in response to the growing dependence on computers. Although managing the data center requires the same care and attention that managing any other complex function demands, it imposes additional considerations because of the technical nature of computer operations. This section of the handbook addresses some of these special needs.

Some data centers rely on word of mouth or on scattered directives to establish operational guidelines and to train new employees. This method of operation, however, can lead to confusion, inconsistency, and reduced productivity. A comprehensive and effective set of data center standards can establish the guidelines needed to ensure consistent and productive performance. Chapter VII-1, "Developing Standards for the Data Center," describes how to create and maintain a standards manual and includes both an outline for a manual and sample standards.

Dealing with more than one vendor when buying or servicing DP equipment can lead to problems. However, this approach also has its advantages, not the least of which is motivating competing vendors to provide better service. The problems of such an environment can be managed successfully when management approaches them systematically. Chapter VII-2, "Integrating the Multivendor Environment," discusses these problems and suggests practical solutions.

Recognizing the importance of the job done by operations personnel is an important aspect of managing the data center. We sometimes pay more attention to the people working in what some consider the more glamorous areas of information processing—for example, end-user computing and systems development. We should not, however, overlook the need to properly plan for the careers of our operations personnel. In the chapter titled "Career Planning for Data Center Personnel," we examine career charts, job families, changing job conditions, and career projections for operators.

Another aspect of staff management in computer operations is scheduling personnel to cover the operational needs of the data center. Various options for defining the data center workweek are described in Chapter VII-4, "Balancing Data Center Staff and Work Load."

With the need to operate for long periods without interruption comes the need to understand the power requirements of the data center. This inevitably leads to discussion and, often, to the consideration of an uninterruptible power supply (UPS). Processing problems caused by variations in commercial electrical power can be extremely frustrating and hard to identify. These problems are often serious enough to justify the installation of a UPS. Chapter VII-5, "Do You Need a UPS?", discusses the functions of a UPS, the characteristics that should be considered when selecting a UPS system, and the procedures for installing such a system.

Designing a new data center or undertaking a major remodeling of an existing center requires many talents. Site suitability, space requirements, logistics, physical construction, and many other factors must be considered. Chapter VII-6, "Designing the Data Center—A Checklist," assists in defining the activities required in this effort. The checklist can also be used to assess the adequacy of existing facilities.

VII-1
Developing Standards for the Data Center

Bryan Wilkinson

INTRODUCTION

In order to meet users' needs and production schedules and ensure continuity of data center operation, MIS must establish, and enforce compliance to, a set of standards. The most effective way to accomplish this goal is to develop a data center standards manual, which not only covers all operating contingencies but is accessible to and followed by all data center personnel. Because the data center operations group interacts with many other departments within an organization, the MIS manager must also ensure that the other groups can contribute to the development of the manual and that the manual does not conflict with standards developed for other departments within the organization. This chapter discusses two types of standards that should be covered in a data center standards manual, provides a sample outline of manual contents, and explains how the standards manual should be developed.

TWO TYPES OF STANDARDS

Two types of standards should be included in a data center standards manual: procedural and performance standards. Procedural standards explain how to do something; performance standards measure how well a task is done. Procedural standards are usually based on experience and company policies; they are developed to increase efficiency, accountability, control, and uniformity of practice (which results in continuity of operation). Performance standards are usually stated in terms of performance goals (e.g., no more than one unscheduled downtime per month) and minimum acceptable performance (e.g., 600 keystrokes per hour for data input). Both types of standards should be documented in the data center standards manual. The MIS manager must oversee the development not only of these standards but of the manual that documents them.

DEVELOPING A STANDARDS MANUAL

The DCOM should make a senior staff member responsible for gathering data for and developing the standards manual for two reasons: first, the task of developing the manual requires a data center staff member with broad operations experience; and second, by assigning the task to a senior staff member, the MIS manager emphasizes its importance to all personnel in the data center. In addition, the development of a data center standards manual requires the participation of management and staff in other departments. The data center staff member chosen should be familiar with departments and personnel throughout the organization. The MIS manager may need to provide direction for this liaison function, particularly if inconsistencies in organizational operating procedures are discovered.

Many organizations have a documentation group responsible for writing standards. This group can help MIS determine the best format for a manual, help gather data, and even write the standards to be included in the manual. However, technical standards should be written (at least in draft form) by a staff member with practical operations experience. If organizational policy dictates that the final manual be written by the documentation group, the staff member responsible for development of the standards manual and the MIS manager must review and approve the standards written by the documentation group. Whether or not MIS personnel actually write the standards manual procedures, responsibility for development of the manual resides with MIS.

Data Gathering

Before a data center standards manual is written, the following information should be collected:
- Written procedures and practices for the entire organization
- Written procedures and practices for other departments
- Vendor manuals for data center equipment and software
- Standards manuals from other organizations
- Books or other reference materials on standards and procedures

At this stage, the person responsible for developing the standards manual should interview managers or senior staff members in other departments whose procedures might affect data center standards. For example, procedures in the personnel, EDP auditing, and security departments would certainly influence data center standards.

Preparing an Outline

The ideas and materials obtained in the data gathering stage should then be organized in outline form. The outline should list the topics to be covered in the standards manual and, ideally, should provide brief descriptions of how each topic will be covered. For example:

> C. MAINTENANCE
>
> This section will describe the frequency of maintenance and actual maintenance procedures for all data center equipment. A list of the equipment follows . . . .

A complete and carefully organized outline clarifies what topics should be covered in the standards manual. A good outline also provides enough information for reviewers to understand the scope of each topic. The outline can greatly influence the quality and relevance of the final standards manual.

As discussed previously, a data center standards manual should include both procedural and performance standards. Figure 1 provides a sample outline of topics that might be covered in the procedures sections of a data center standards manual. Performance standards (e.g., data entry speed) may be more difficult to define and document, particularly in terms of quantitative measures. Data entry speed depends on the type and quality of source documents as well as the skill of the data entry operator. MIS should carefully evaluate—at the outline stage—any performance standard that is being considered for inclusion in the standards manual.

Once developed, the outline should be reviewed by the MIS manager as well as by all departments involved in the manual's development. MIS should resolve any problems resulting from the review and give final approval to the outline.

Format

When MIS has approved an outline for the standards manual, the person responsible for the manual's development must then choose a format. This decision is usually made in conjunction with MIS and the documentation group, if appropriate. The manual developer may also want to survey other data center staffers (the end users, in this instance). Various formats can be used for a data center standards manual. Two of the most common are the paragraph form and the play-scripting form. The paragraph form is a straightforward extension of the outline. Each topic heading is followed by paragraphs that explain a particular standard. The second format, play-scripting, consists of two columns, headed Responsibility and Action. (The columns might also be headed Problem and Resolution, depending upon the standard or procedure described.) Whatever format is chosen, each major section of the standards manual should explain the standards covered in that section and the reasons (if appropriate) for the standards; each section should also reference related materials (e.g., other sections of the manual, other organizational standards manuals, and forms).

Writing Effective Standards

When writing the standards manual, the writer should:
- Plainly state whether the rule or actions are rigid (must, shall or will), advisory (should), or permissive (may).
- Spell out exceptions—If none are stated, none should be permitted.
- Specify authority and responsibility—Any conditions that modify this authority or responsibility should be included.
- Be consistent—A standard should not contradict other standards in the manual or other organizational or departmental standards.
- Avoid double-talk—If a procedure or policy is not stated clearly in the manual draft, the unclear entry should be rewritten, or the policy or procedure reexamined to determine whether it is valid.

Figure 2 provides a sample standard and illustrates the clear writing that is crucial to readers' understanding of the standards documented.

OUTLINE—DATA CENTER STANDARDS MANUAL
(PROCEDURAL SECTIONS)

I. **Glossary of Terms**
   This section will define terms used in the standards manual, including terms specific to data processing that might be unfamiliar to new employees, outside auditors, and consultants. A list of terms to be defined will be developed and circulated for review at a later date.

II. **Organizational Chart**
   This section will include organization job titles and corresponding responsibilities, but not employee names. The personnel department will provide actual job descriptions.

III. **Personnel Policies**
   This section will include policies established specifically for the data center as well as organizational policies supplied by the personnel department. Subsections will cover:
   A. Sick time, excused absence, lateness
   B. Leave
   C. Time sheets and pay period policies
   D. Overtime
   E. Review and promotion
   F. Dismissal
   G. Nondisclosure agreement
   H. Classified material and confidentiality issues

IV. **Hardware, Software, and Systems—Operation and Maintenance**
   This section will cover all data center equipment and software. It will be organized into subsections, each devoted to a specific piece of equipment, software package, unusual hardware configuration, operating system, or application. Relevant standards, including operation and maintenance procedures, will be described where appropriate. A list of the subsections follows:

V. **Data Center Practices**
   This section will explain standard operating procedures related to the following:
   A. Shift-to-shift communications
   B. Logs and reports
   C. Numbering and naming conventions
   D. File labeling and maintenance
   E. Record retention and storage
   F. Input/output control
   G. Inventory control
   H. Housekeeping
   I. Purchasing/leasing policies
   J. Copyright laws—This subsection will be developed in conjunction with the legal and personnel departments

VI. **Safety**
   This section will cover safety procedures designed to prevent accidents and damage to resources as well as the procedures to follow if an accident or damage occurs. Appropriate references will be made to sections VIII and IX.

VII. **Security**
   This section will cover both physical and data security procedures. Penalties for violation of security procedures will also be described. The security and legal departments will participate in the writing of this section.

VIII. **Emergency Procedures**
   This section will describe the step-by-step procedures to take in response to catastrophic events. The list of topics to be covered is currently under development by the Emergency/Disaster Recovery Committee and will be circulated separately for review.

IX. **Disaster Recovery**
   See section VIII.

Figure 1. Sample Outline—Data Center Standards Manual (Procedures)

Data Center Standards

SECTION 5. OPERATING PRACTICES

A. Shift-to-Shift Communications

Purpose
Shift-to-shift communications are essential for efficient data center operation. Operations personnel coming on duty must know not only what problems occurred during prior shifts but what corrective actions, if any, have been attempted or accomplished. This eliminates wasted effort and frustration for your coworkers.

Standard
The lead operator will give a verbal report of all activities that occurred during his or her shift to the succeeding shift lead operator and turn over all appropriate documentation, including logs and trouble reports, when the succeeding shift lead operator reports for duty. In the absence of the lead operator, the designated lead operator for the shift will perform this reporting duty.

Figure 2. A Sample Standard

MAINTENANCE

The standards manual must be updated as data center or organizational procedures change. The MIS manager must ensure that the person responsible for maintaining the data center standards manual is informed of any changes that might render sections of the standards manual obsolete. MIS should then establish a periodic revision schedule for the standards manual and should implement the following practices, which apply to the original manual as well as to revisions:

- Each standard should include an effective date and, once revised, a revision date (or number).
- The standards manual should include an index that lists the latest date for each standard.
- Revised standards should be issued when major events, such as new equipment installations, occur.
- A cover memorandum describing the scope of the revision should be issued with each revision.
- When a revision is issued, changed information should be identified; a vertical bar in the margin next to changed material is often used for this purpose.
- Whether or not major events have occurred, MIS should periodically review the standards manual to ensure that it is up to date, accurate, and clear to the readers.
- MIS should maintain a directory of manual locations and individuals who have personal copies. This directory should be reviewed periodically to determine whether manual distribution is still appropriate.
- For ease of update, the data center standards manual should be prepared on word processing equipment. A backup copy of the manual should be maintained.

ACCESS TO THE STANDARDS

All data center personnel must have access to the standards manual. MIS can provide a copy of the manual to each data center staff member or place copies of the manual at convenient locations in the data center. MIS should also distribute copies of the data center standards manual to other departments in the organization. Alternatively, MIS may want to put the standards manual online so that data center staffers and other personnel can access the standards through a terminal.

CONCLUSION

MIS must not only establish data center operating standards but ensure that they are documented clearly so that data center personnel understand and comply with them. The first step in this process is to assign an experienced staff member the responsibility for developing a standards manual. The process of developing and maintaining a standards manual includes the following actions:
- Data gathering
- Outline development
- Outline review and approval
- Writing of the standards manual
- Manual review and approval
- Distribution of the standards manual
- Periodic review of the manual distribution list
- Periodic revision of standards.

VII-2
Integrating the Multivendor Environment

Thomas Fleishman

INTRODUCTION

One of the most challenging tasks facing the MIS manager is hardware selection. Selection can be complicated by the numerous vendors who supply hardware components that are compatible with the CPU manufacturer's hardware. The price of equipment from these vendors is generally attractive, and the performance statistics may indicate that the equipment is at least equivalent to, if not better than, hardware available from the CPU manufacturer. In some cases, such claims are valid and can be verified by performance history (i.e., availability, reliability, serviceability). In other instances, price is the only indisputable factor upon which the MIS manager can base a decision.

Because each data center has a unique environment affecting hardware decisions, either a single- or a multivendor approach can be appropriate. The MIS manager must recognize, however, that the decision to use multivendor equipment produces new responsibilities to deal effectively with any conflicts that may arise. From the beginning, the MIS manager must communicate with the vendors, administer and control them, and develop clear, acceptable guidelines within which the multivendor installation must function. This chapter addresses the problems inherent in multivendor installations.

SELECTION FACTORS

Several factors determine whether selecting equipment from a new vendor is desirable or even necessary. Some more common factors are:

- Availability—If a CPU supplier does not have a particular component required for an application, equipment from another vendor may be the only alternative.
- Performance—If the MIS manager is faced with specific performance criteria for the installation, only one vendor may be able to supply the hardware needed to meet the requirements.
- Reliability—With the proliferation of equipment and vendors, the MIS manager has a wide range of alternatives. If one requirement is reliability (e.g., a defined, allowable mean time between component failures), equipment from a different vendor may meet the reliability specifications.

- Cost Reduction—As noted, equipment from one vendor may cost less than the same item offered by another. This factor is the most difficult for the MIS manager to address because he or she must determine whether quality will be traded for cost. In general, however, cost is the most common reason for installing a new vendor's equipment.
- Equipment Usage and Location—With the proliferation of distributed and online processing, the MIS manager must consider the environment in which the components will be installed. Often the physical surroundings and use of equipment are much harsher than in the traditional computer center.
- Ergonomics—The growth of online systems has brought with it the issue of person/machine relationships (ergonomics). This is particularly of issue in the wide use of CRTs. The size, screen, keyboard, and other physical attributes of the equipment should be considered in any acquisition decision.

TRADE-OFFS

The MIS manager may become disconcerted when talking with other managers who have made the multivendor/single-vendor decision because he or she will find a wide range of views. Some data centers will provide testimonials for a given component while others will be in the process of replacing the same equipment. Although checking references is advised, MIS must still make the final decision based on various trade-offs.

Presumably, a level of performance has been established for the existing equipment. Will equipment from a different vendor meet the established level of performance? If not, the MIS manager must determine the risks. Replacing disk drives in an online environment entails a significantly higher risk than exchanging tape drives or a printer. Is MIS willing or even in a position to accept the risk exposure if the new vendor's equipment does not perform? Is any cost-saving factor significant enough to offset the risk level and the potential cost of any backup (or backout) measures that may be necessary?

Fitting the Existing Configuration

New vendor equipment must function in the installation's configuration. In one center that acquired a new printer, preinstallation testing was inadequate. Consequently, the printer could not handle all the special and multipart forms required by the users. It worked well on some forms but not on others. In another instance, certain disk drives were outstanding in installations that had minimal pack mounting requirements but failed frequently in a data center that had a great deal of disk mounting activity. Such situations stress the need for MIS to recognize the unique characteristics and configuration of the installation when assessing equipment from new vendors.

Quality of Service

MIS must investigate prospective vendor's service levels. Some internal tracking procedures are recommended before making such an assessment. These procedures should contain quantitative measures that are shared with the vendors and are based on the requirements of that installation.

Intergrating the Multivendor Environment

Specific measures may include:
- Responsiveness—What is the average time a vendor requires to respond to a service call?
- Repair time—What is the average repair time for a given component?
- Resource availability—Does the vendor provide resources, such as technical specialists, in a timely manner?
- Incidence recurrence—If a specific component develops problems, is it fixed on the first service call or is it necessary to recall the customer engineer (CE)?
- Management attention—In cases of serious or recurring problems, do vendor managers volunteer assistance or must they be contacted?

These measures enable MIS to develop a formal means of tracking service in a multivendor environment. This is an important consideration in controlling and administering vendors. MIS needs a comparative measure of service to manage the facility and the vendors represented.

Customer Engineering

The manager of a multivendor installation will find that the level and quality of CE support from the manufacturer largely determines the success or failure of the installation in terms of equipment performance. The manager should initially establish whether the manufacturer can provide:
- On-site support—Will CEs reside in the installation, or will they be dispatched from a central call desk?
- Continuity—Will the same CEs provide support on all the installation's service calls, or will CEs be randomly assigned from a branch or regional pool?
- Experience—Do the supporting CEs have experience with the type of installation and configuration in the organization's data center?
- CE support organization—Are the CEs part of the equipment manufacturer's organization, or do they belong to a third-part maintenance organization contracted to provide service support?
- Local parts depot—Are parts stored in a nearby warehouse in case of hardware failures that require part exchanges, or will there be major shipping delays in procuring the necessary parts?

Each of these questions must be seriously considered by the MIS manager who expects an effective multivendor environment.

The unavailability of a CE or a particular part can cause severe and unnecessary problems in an installation. If these problems are addressed when the hardware is acquired, certain provisions and contractual guarantees can be established with the vendor to minimize further problems or enable MIS to withdraw from the acquisition agreement without financial penalties.

For example, one vendor openly acknowledged that CE support was minimal and that he could not ensure timely response. The vendor did, however, offer another service contract at a significantly higher cost, guaranteeing CE availability at an installation within four hours. In this case, the data center manager was sufficiently impressed with the vendor's equipment to pay this higher maintenance cost.

MANAGING THE DATA CENTER

In another instance, a data center manager found that a third-party service organization had been contracted to support a piece of hardware. Although the vendor agreed to certain service requirements, the service organization was not committed to provide the necessary support. After lengthy negotiations and at considerable expense, the manager was able to reach the agreements he sought.

Financial Status of the Vendor. The MIS manager can often avoid problems by evaluating the financial status of a potential vendor. The MIS manager can then decide whether the prospective vendor has the proper resources to continue as a viable business organization, capable of providing the necessary long-term support and service.

Contractual Considerations. Depending on the MIS manager's level of confidence in the prospective vendor, certain performance and service criteria may be itemized in the acquisition contract. These can range from CE response time to specified availability information. Specifically, financial penalties or component replacement may be defined for failure to meet any contractual requirements. All contractual demands should be negotiated between legal representatives for the vendor and MIS. The degree of cooperation shown by the vendor during negotiations may indicate what MIS can expect after the vendor installs the hardware.

MONITORING THE VENDOR

Even in a single-vendor environment, the MIS manager must recognize that it is imperative to establish some objectives for equipment performance and service support to evaluate a vendor. Such measures are even more critical in a multivendor installation. Benchmarks and component performance tracking are two methods of evaluation.

Benchmarks

Before acquiring equipment, the organization should become familiar with the vendor's hardware and its specifications in order to establish performance benchmarks. This is important for assessing whether the equipment is meeting its advertised capabilities and whether the vendor is complying with the requirements included in the installation agreement. The continuing failure of the equipment to meet a benchmark may be grounds for replacing the equipment.

Component Performance Tracking

MIS managers are increasingly recognizing the need for establishing a specific function responsible for tracking the performance of individual hardware components. Studies in large installations indicate a significant payoff on component tracking. Because a specific drive or channel often causes many outages or system degradation in a center, the ability to quickly detect a faulty device is valuable.

In a multivendor environment, component tracking can have the additional benefit of establishing a rating system to help the manager determine which vendors provide satisfactory performance. Tracking may be performed manually; operations personnel complete incident or trouble reports that are transmitted to someone who compiles the data and issues a periodic report. Although better than none at all, this method is cumbersome and inefficient, especially in larger installations.

A preferable alternative is an automated tracking and reporting system. Such packages can be developed in-house or purchased, depending on the capabilities of the staff, the CPUs, and the operating systems involved.

One effective tracking system provides a daily report on all hard and soft failures on each component in the shop. The person assigned to the tracking function must contact vendors whose components fail and ensure that corrective action is taken.

An additional feature of this tracking system is particularly helpful in controlling a multivendor environment. Each month the organization that markets the tracking package provides a comprehensive data base compiled from data supplied by installations subscribing to the system. The data base indicates a given installation's performance relative to that of other centers using the same configuration and brand of equipment.

For example, if a center has CPU "A" with disk drives "B" installed and 12 other centers use the same CPU/disk configuration, the monthly report will show a performance ranking based on an algorithm of soft and hard failures for all 13 centers. For the MIS manager to effectively control a multivendor environment, such a system is almost mandatory, especially in large, multi-CPU installations.

Communication among Vendors

The manager of a multivendor installation may discover that, in order to maintain a smoothly operating center, he or she (or a member of the data center operations staff) must coordinate communication among vendors. This is necessary if MIS expects to resolve problems that are vague and/or involve more than one vendor. These problems occur quite frequently because the vendors are competing on an active market that does not encourage communication among them.

Several data center managers have dealt with this communication problem by holding frequent meetings of all vendor representatives with equipment installed in the center. Even when there are no specific problems, these meetings are held to maintain open communication among the vendors.

CASE STUDY

The following case study illustrates the problems that were faced by a data center manager in a multivendor installation. For the sake of brevity, only the major aspects are outlined.

The data center manager was under considerable pressure to further reduce equipment costs. After assessing the installation, he decided that meaningful savings could only be realized by replacing the set of 24 disk spindles that had been leased from the manufacturer of the facility's major CPU.

MANAGING THE DATA CENTER

The manager contacted several manufacturers and, after a period of evaluation, decided to replace all 24 spindles at one time for an approximate annual savings of $73,000. The spindles were on a three-year lease. From the time of installation it became evident that the acquisition of the new disks was a mistake. Although the disk manufacturer had an impressive facility and was supplying thousands of units worldwide, the product was relatively new to a large-scale, 24-hour-a-day online business environment. Because the support organization was untrained, with no prior exposure to the CPU manufacturer's equipment, troubleshooting was time-consuming. Since the interfaces were not well understood, communication between the disk and CPU vendors was nearly impossible. No CE was permanently assigned to the account, and trouble calls became futile as an army of CEs tried to solve the problem while major online data base systems remained unavailable to users.

After several months, the equipment appeared to stablize, but then the center began to experience serious channel interface problems. Much of the manager's time was spent mediating recriminations and disagreements between the CPU and disk vendors.

Finally, as the interface problems were resolved, the incidence of head crashes increased dramatically. It took approximately four months to trace the problem to the foam-rubber-seal stripping insulating the spindle door. Apparently, the frequent mounting and demounting of packs hastened the deterioration and disintegration of the stripping, eventually contaminating the packs and causing the head crashes. After assessing the overall situation, the manager decided to absorb the $27,000 penalty to replace the disks. (This had been contractually accepted as a potential backout arrangement during the lease negotiations.)

The disk manufacturer was only partially at fault. It introduced a device that was not fully tested, without an adequate support organization or the trained personnel required to back up the product. The data center manager was equally at fault for failing to perform an in-depth evaluation of a new product that was being introduced into a critical online business environment. With a project plan outlining specific, clearly defined milestones and performance objectives, the manager could have deferred a decision on the product in question. This became evident after the fact; upon contacting other installations, the manager learned that his problems were not unique and were experienced in varying degrees by other users.

CONCLUSION

The use of equipment from multiple vendors is often justified by cost and performance. As plug-compatible equipment continues to proliferate, the selection process becomes more complex.

The MIS manager should approach the multivendor installation as he or she would approach any other business decision by considering the risk/benefit trade-offs in the context of the data center environment. Establishing a project plan that details equipment performance and support should be mandatory. If possible, contractual backout arrangements should be specified and accepted by all parties concerned.

VII-3
Career Planning for Data Center Personnel

William A. Hansen

INTRODUCTION

Anyone who has been in the DP industry more than a few years has witnessed substantial changes. Many people remember when the operations department was a huge room filled with electrical accounting machines. The author of this chapter entered the data processing field in time to see the last of the IBM 1401s and the first System/360s. The System/370 generation has now reached maturity, and the DP industry is awaiting its successor. Card systems have given way to tape, and tape has given way to disk. Mass storage, online systems, teleprocessing networks, and data bases have expanded the capabilities of new systems and broadened users' perceptions of DP systems.

These innovations have affected not only the capabilities of systems but also the personnel in the systems and programming departments. Specialized positions, such as those held by data base administrators and teleprocessing analysts, have been created. In the past, only one systems programmer was required. In most medium-sized shops today, the control program, access methods, job entry subsystem, telecommunications software, and data base software are each handled by a different programmer; several more staff members must handle the other pieces of software that constitute a complete operating system. In larger shops, a team is required for each of these functions.

Although career opportunities in systems and programming have grown tremendously, little has changed for operations personnel except the equipment they handle. Many, if not most, operations departments use job descriptions and organizational structures that were developed in the early 1970s. The lack of organizational change has both institutionalized old problems and introduced new ones. This chapter describes these problems and offers MIS management several suggestions for facilitating the future growth of data center operations personnel.

JOB STATUS IN OPERATIONS

Job requirements for programmers and operators have always differed substantially. Although most early programmers were former users, it soon became evident that programming required special training. Today, most companies require applicants for programming positions to have either a college degree or previous experience in data processing. Companies with internal training departments will accept a degree in such related fields as mathematics or business.

Programmers have received considerable attention in recent years, with numerous articles and books covering their education, career paths, organization, management, certification, and psychology. The growing need for skilled programmers has resulted in increased salaries and job opportunities; specialization has created jobs that did not exist several years ago. The programmer/analyst has been replaced in many cases by a coder, librarian, programmer, technical designer, team leader, analyst, data base administrator, and several other personnel. Although the search for greater productivity may have caused this diversification, the result has been more jobs, more money, and greater opportunities for advancement.

Accompanying this trend is the controversy over whether programmers should be considered professionals, with the same status as physicians, lawyers, or certified public accountants. No one, however, has seriously asserted professional status for operators. The following sections offer reasons for this difference.

A Problem of Challenge

Twenty years ago, when programming had already been recognized as an intellectual activity, computer operators performed a series of manual procedures: placing cards in a reader, mounting the correct forms in the printer, hanging tapes, and pressing buttons. Operators were also required to type commands to keep jobs running.

Because changes occurred gradually in operations, operators adapted without difficulty. However, few people outside operations and few managers within operations noticed these changes, and they continued to view operators as glorified button-pushers.

Although some operators still load cards, change paper, and hang tapes, these tasks are now minor aspects of their jobs. Online systems, less expensive direct-access devices, teleprocessing, micrographics, mass storage devices, and other innovations are reducing the amount of time the operator must devote to hardware. Approximately 90 percent of the operator's time is now involved with software, including entering commands, responding to messages, and, most important, checking the status of each system component in order to maximize the overall efficiency of the system.

Antiquated perceptions of the operator's job are thus a major factor in the lack of change in the staffing of operations positions. Operations personnel are still hired from vocational ranks. Many new operators are former data entry operators or clerks in user departments. Some are graduates of technical schools or junior colleges, where they were trained on secondhand equipment. Most are hired with little or no experience and are expected to learn on the job.

Salaries for operators have not increased at a rate equal to that enjoyed by programmers, despite a much higher turnover rate in operations and an equally critical need for skilled people. Good operators are hard to keep. The most qualified operators seek employment in large, innovative companies that offer salaries comparable to those for programmers.

Many operators are dissatisified because of the lack of opportunities for advancement. While a programmer can expect promotion to project leader, analyst, or systems designer, most operators cannot advance beyond the positions they reach after a few years of experience. Career planning addresses only the traditional path from Operator C to Operator B to Operator A.

Some operators consider seeking programming jobs as an escape, because programming is seen as a path toward advancement in salary, opportunity, and respect. However, although programming and operations may both be highly technical, they require different skills.

Evaluating Operations Work

A survey by J. Daniel Couger and Robert A. Zawacki indicates that "the people in operations consider themselves on the bottom of the totem pole."[1] This situation has been acknowledged for some time, and the survey suggests the underlying reasons. Computer operators, data entry personnel, and data control personnel rated their jobs significantly below other occupations in four of five key characteristics and two of three job motivators. In general, operations personnel believe that their jobs lack variety, that they receive little feedback on their performance, that they have little responsibility, and that they lack a sense of task identity because they rarely see more than a small part of a complete application. The only areas in which operations personnel rated their jobs near the normal ratings for other jobs were task significance and job meaningfulness. Although these ratings were still lower than those of people in other jobs, the responses indicate that operations personnel do believe their jobs have value to the company. An operator once confided that the message an operator usually receives is that "your job is important; you are not."

Couger and Zawacki calculated the motivating potential of an operator's job. In this category, operations personnel and their supervisors ranked significantly lower than other white-collar and blue-collar workers and especially lower than other MIS personnel. Surprisingly, however, operations personnel are relatively satisfied with their jobs. Couger and Zawacki believe that most operators "are not unhappy 'biding their time' in present jobs—in anticipation of promotion to better jobs." Organizations can satisfy their employees "by paying them well, keeping bosses off their backs, and arranging things so the days pass without undue stress or strain." Jobs must be restructured to increase motivating potential and thus improve productivity. Couger and Zawacki recommend job enrichment and job enlargement. Although they offer a procedure for soliciting suggestions and following through on them, they do not offer specific suggestions for restructuring jobs. This decision is left to individual installations.

Thomas Zillner reaches the same conclusions.[2] He considers computer operations "boring and rarely [offering] enough challenge to attract and/or retain fully qualified people from other jobs, leaving operations to less imaginative individuals." He recommends involving operations personnel in the

MANAGING THE DATA CENTER

early phases of systems design to improve documentation, job run characteristics, and error-handling procedures. He also offers suggestions to operators interested in career advancement within the field of operations. These include taking advantage of educational opportunities, volunteering to improve system documentation, learning more about the installation's major applications, and joining professional organizations.

Such recommendations, however, do not change the basic nature of the job from which good operators are fleeing. Again, a restructuring of the job is the essential requirement.

CHANGING JOB CONDITIONS

An MIS manager has several options for easing the shortage of skilled operations personnel. Many organizations are trying to create more specialization and identify new job functions in operations. The few experienced personnel are designated master console operators; the rest of the system is run by unit record operators, tape pool operators, and disk pool operators.

This type of organizational structure suffers from some of the same problems discussed in the previous section. Unless a serious effort is made to cross-train personnel, the lower-level operators become bored quickly. In addition, no one has been trained to fill the position of master console operator.

Although such an arrangement may appear to improve conditions for the master console operator, this usually is not the case. If lower-level operators perform the easy tasks, the job tasks of the master console operator become even more repetitious. Increased specialization also reduces the operator's sense of task identity, since he or she sees an even smaller part of the whole job. In addition, few installations increase the responsibilities of the senior operator when the lower-level tasks are removed.

The senior operator's job is also being limited by technological advances. Modern operating systems are making many decisions formerly made by the senior operator. In cases where the operating system still allows flexibility, many installations have transferred some responsibility from the operator to the systems programmer. For example, many installations now restrict the operator from altering the number of active partitions or initiators.

Recognizing Job Importance

The importance of the operator's job must be recognized. Although operators may require less training than other MIS personnel, they are in a critical position. It is not uncommon for two or three operators to control equipment worth $3 million to $10 million. One mistake can cost thousands of dollars in rental costs and reruns, aside from the impact of a down computer on a nationwide network. While a careless programmer can cost the installation in test time and debugging, a careless operator can bring the entire corporation to a halt with a misplaced elbow.

In addition, no other MIS group (except possibly a few systems programmers) has such unrestricted access to an organization's files and records. Security software packages (e.g., RACF, Secure, ACF_2) are adequate for protecting data sets from unauthorized access by means of a terminal; however, these security measures cannot prevent an operator from taking a company's most valuable data.

The following paragraphs describe some necessary steps for improving the operator's job.

Job Conditions. The organization should ensure that salary levels for operations personnel are equivalent to those offered by other corporations. The operators should also be questioned to determine if they face any unnecessary job hassles. Eliminating employee dissatisfaction is an easy step and one that most installations have already taken, according to the Couger-Zawacki survey.

Training and Advancement. The next step is a commitment to training and career advancement. Employees must be aware of all jobs available within operations and the skills needed for promotion to those positions. Salary ranges should be publicized, provided that a higher salary can be offered for greater skill and responsibility.

Employees who want to improve their skills should receive some financial support. Most companies offer a tuition refund program so that employees can enroll in college classes in a job-related field. The MIS department's policies regarding attendance at conferences and seminars and membership in professional organizations should be made known. If personnel are routinely sent to special events, everyone should know how to apply and how delegates are chosen.

In-house training facilities are another approach to improving employee skills. Self-study and multimedia courses can help employees attain skills that they can then demonstrate. The demonstration of skills rather than the completion of courses should be used as the criterion for advancement. This approach eliminates the need to make exceptions for new employees with previous experience and precludes the possibility of promoting employees who merely pass time in a class. Training materials that teach specific job skills should be selected rather than those that address a particular subject. The most motivated students are those who can see a clear relationship between mastering course objectives and achieving success on the job.

If an organization has a full-time training manager, his or her assistance should be sought in creating a formal skills inventory to determine what skills are required for each job function and what skills staff personnel already possess. Such information can assist in the development of a cost-effective approach to staff training that permits staff to participate only in those courses that address immediate skill requirements.

Each organization has its own training policy. Some require a mandatory number of training days per year for each job function; others train on a more sporadic basis. Whatever the policy, it is very difficult to prevent a motivated employee from learning. If in-house training is unavailable, the operator may elect to read manuals at the console or enroll in courses after working hours. Thus, it is important that the employer provide materials to employees who want them. However, paying employees to take classes is always less successful than establishing a target (e.g., a required skill), offering training opportunities, and rewarding those who succeed with a better job.

MANAGING THE DATA CENTER

Management should not be discouraged if some employees do not seek additional training. These people might be sufficiently challenged by their current jobs and should not be forced into positions of greater responsibility if they show no desire to advance. Operators have resigned rather than give up easy (albeit low-paying) jobs that they have mastered.

Publicizing career paths and making training available solve the career advancement problem until the employee reaches the senior positions within operations.

Application Identification

The lack of task identification is a major problem with most current operations jobs, according to Couger and Zawacki. Generally, operators see only a portion of an application and do not understand how their contribution fits into the whole. Zillner recommends that operators seeking advancement should make an effort to learn how each job they run actually works. For example, an operator should study the documentation to learn what happens as an input tape is processed to produce an output tape. The ability to knowledgeably discuss the applications being run is one way of building user and programmer confidence in the operator's abilities. Furthermore, a broader knowledge of applications among operators can reduce errors and false starts and improve overall motivation while stressing the organization's general business goals.

As soon as operators are asked to learn about the jobs they are running, a formal procedure is needed to identify and follow up on their suggestions. One easy way to develop a procedure is to modify the traditional trouble report to accommodate suggestions and recommendations from the operations staff. If such a procedure is not implemented, numerous problems can develop.

One reported case involves an installation that used a traditional suggestion box but had no follow-up procedures. An operator modified the production JCL for a job by moving the temporary data sets passed between steps from tape to disk. The job execution time dropped from 55 minutes to less than 5, primarily because of the removal of 24 tape mounts. After going through proper channels, the operator was able to demonstrate his changes to management. The managers, however, concluded that there must be some reason for the way the job was designed because analysts know more than operators. (In fact, the job was a carry-over from before disks were invented.) The operator continued to use his version of the JCL whenever he ran that job. He was soon fired for "exceeding his job description." Not only did the company lose a valuable employee, but the episode had even more costly consequences. The operators who remained stopped making suggestions and started performing only the minimum work required. In addition, the more skilled operators quietly looked for other jobs or applied for transfers to programming. The application existed in the same form for a couple more years and was even converted when the company switched hardware vendors. Considerable computer time and operator effort were lost. Years later, a maintenance programmer happened to find the job and make the recommended changes.

Data Center Careers

As illustrated by this example, operators must be provided with a means for making suggestions (and having their suggestions implemented), or the organization risks continued inefficiency, the loss of talented employees, and a lack of motivation on the part of the remaining operators.

Improving Group Interaction

The installation in the preceding example also illustrates productive relations between operations and systems programming. Initially, MIS personnel's disregard of the operations department was such that operations personnel had little input in matters that directly affected them. For example, during a major conversion, the programming department decided what run documentation it would provide to operations. This decision produced numerous abends that could not be fixed by the operations staff. The reluctance of the programmers to respond to telephone calls at 3:00 A.M. led to the creation of a technical support group within operations to diagnose and correct JCL problems, approve all run documentation, and write all production JCL.

This installation required a major shakeup to correct all these problems. A new operations manager and a new systems programming manager guided operations through the conversion according to schedule. They were unaware that their predecessors had never communicated about their tasks. The previous failure of the systems and programming departments to meet conversion dates convinced senior management to give operations a free hand. A new systems programming staff wrote a new user manual, disregarding standards written previously by the programming department.

The change was substantial. Operators helped set standards that systems programmers enforced through operating system parameters. Operators requested and quickly received such job aids as console commands for listing catalogs and data set labels. Operator morale as well as productivity increased significantly. The technical support group started working directly with users to improve scheduling and response time to problems.

Much of the improvement at this installation was a direct result of giving operators a greater voice in operational functions and establishing communication between operators and systems programmers. When operators noticed a problem and asked for help or recommended a solution, the systems programmers responded. The decrease in problems encountered, coupled with the increase in throughput, conveyed to senior management the capabilities of both groups.

A PROPOSED CAREER PATH

Most installations now have a job known as technical support specialist, operations analyst, or scheduler. These personnel within operations are the first to be contacted when a production job terminates abnormally. Technical support specialists are allowed to correct JCL errors but must contact the appropriate programming personnel when a problem results from a programming error. At many installations, this group is also responsible for maintaining the production program library and the JCL procedure library. They often write or approve the JCL and run documentation for all production jobs. In some cases, technical support specialists are the liaison between operations and the user departments, filling a function similar to that of customer representatives in a service bureau. The position of technical support specialist is a logical step up for operators, especially for those who have made an effort to learn about the applications they are running.

Another logical growth path for the operator is to advance to the position of junior systems programmer. Many systems programmers have four-year degrees in computer science. Although this is a reasonable prerequisite for senior positions, it is not required for the tasks performed during the first few years on the job. In addition, at the junior level there is little need for extensive programming experience. Most junior systems programmers use utility programs or other parameter-driven systems. While the senior systems programmers make long-term plans (selecting equipment and software packages) or are involved with highly technical work (performing system generations or modifying and tuning the operating system), the junior staff performs more routine daily responsibilities such as monitoring utilization and error reports, performing routine maintenance, and helping the master console operator diagnose system-related problems. Senior operators could move easily into these positions. This approach would allow the more technically trained specialists to move into jobs requiring their skills.

Figure 1 illustrates a suggested career path for operations personnel. The planned path from senior operations positions leads to systems programming. The distinction made between professional and paraprofessional jobs is noteworthy. Like entry-level operations positions, entry-level programming positions are often filled by people with two-year degrees from junior colleges or technical schools and little or no DP experience. Senior master console operators, like senior programmers, require years of experience to master their jobs.

To perform their jobs, junior systems programmers, technical support specialists, and master console operators do not need to know any programming languages. However, for advancement to senior systems programming positions, they must know an assembler programming language for the computers used in their environment. All three jobs involve extensive interfacing with the operating system by means of operator commands, JCL, and utility control statements. Experience in any of these positions is advantageous for either of the other two. The skills acquired in these positions should be prerequisites for senior systems programming positions.

These three positions should be placed at an equal level on organizational charts. Employees should be able to reach them by following several career paths. Once there, they should be given the opportunity to rotate among the three positions.

By encouraging lateral job changes, managers can solve several problems simultaneously. Valuable employees who would otherwise leave because of the lack of advancement opportunity may remain. Cross-training can also increase overall productivity by increasing communication and decreasing the number of mistakes caused by ignorance. In addition, cross-training can protect the installation against the loss of a key employee by providing backup. The skill level in these jobs can be raised if cross-training in all three

Data Center Careers

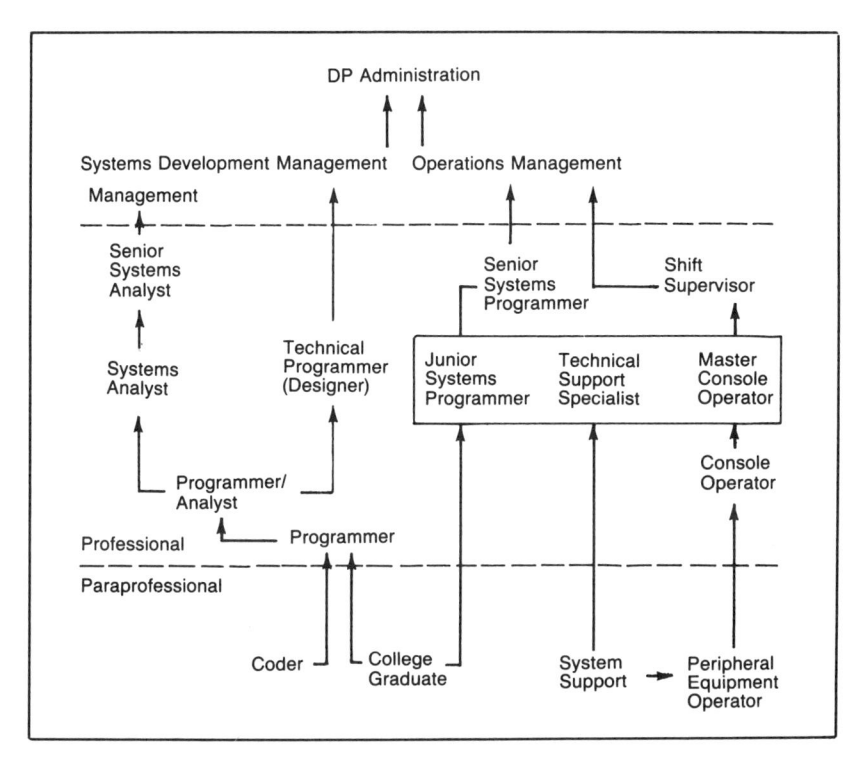

Figure 1. A Suggested Career Path Chart

positions is mandatory for promotion to senior systems programming positions.

An installation may encounter problems in implementing such a plan, however. For example, an organization's definition of a professional employee may introduce problems for operators who must work overtime. The proposed career path, however, offers the opportunity for everyone to progress according to his or her ability. Very few people climb from the bottom to the top of an organization; most reach their limit somewhere in the middle. Those who reach senior programming positions will do so only by demonstrating that they can assume the responsibility capably.

An option that is not obvious from the chart is implementing the career path plan by hiring only college graduates on the way to systems programming for all master console operator vacancies. This approach can bring the needed technical expertise to this job. Personnel who succeed in this position demonstrate that they are competent individuals who should be given an opportunity to move into more technical positions within the organization.

ACTION PLAN

The following steps are suggested for improving the operator's job:
- Address basic job conditions first. Pay competitive salaries and eliminate unnecessary job hassles.

- Define the skills that must be demonstrated for promotion to a particular position and offer the necessary training.
- Encourage attendance at conferences, seminars, and professional meetings. Publicize tuition refund and internal training programs.
- Encourage operators to learn more about the jobs they are running and to suggest methods of improving performance. Develop a procedure to follow through on their suggestions.
- Give operations personnel a greater voice in matters that directly affect them.
- Redesign jobs and career paths to provide greater opportunities for staff to advance within operations and to enter systems programming.

Implementing these suggestions should reduce turnover, increase productivity, and help develop any corporation's most valuable resource—people.

References

1. J. Couger, and R.A. Zawacki, "Something's Very Wrong with DP Operations Jobs," *Datamation* (March 1979).
2. T. Zillner, "Operator's Job Can Be Creative, Satisfying," *Computerworld* (June 4, 1979).

Bibliography

Recommendations and Guidelines for Vocational-Technical Career Programs for Computer Personnel in Operations, Association for Computing Machinery, 1981.

VII-4
Balancing Data Center Staff and Workload
John W. Mentzer

INTRODUCTION

One problem that MIS often faces is the question of which workweek the data center should adopt. Unfortunately, no one clear answer has been found. Some organizations have studied the problem and decided to adopt the three-day workweek, while others have decided against it. Some have tried it and then returned to a five-day or modified five-day workweek schedule. Why? What are the views of people who have tried it? This chapter presents the experiences of two data center managers who have taken different approaches to the problem.

THE THREE-DAY WORKWEEK

For two years, the operators at "Company A" had been putting in excessive overtime because the data center was working a three-shift, five-day workweek and scheduling overtime for Saturday and Sunday. With an ever-increasing work load, the installation of new systems, and hardware/software instability during the installation of a new multiprocessor came the increased need for overtime. A shift manager was asked to develop a work schedule that would reduce or eliminate overtime and maximize the company's use of its computer resources.

The company chose the three-day workweek after considering other alternatives, including swing shifts (i.e., rotating shifts with staggered days off), four-day workweeks, and several variations of the five-day workweek with staggered days off. Although other organizations had successfully implemented variations of the five-day approach, related administration problems were thought to be too serious at this site for the five-day workweek to be considered.

The three-day week seemed to address all of Company A's problems. Its only drawback was the need to hire personnel for the fourth shift. Considering the drop in overtime and improved employee morale, management felt that this was not a significant disadvantage.

The shifts selected were 9:00 A.M. to 9:30 P.M. and 9:00 P.M. to 9:30 A.M. This selection was based on the assumption that nightly production would be completed by 9:00 A.M. and that user departments would start work by 9:00

A.M., thus providing overlap time for problem consultation. The first night shift began Sunday at 9:00 P.M. (logical Monday), and the second night shift began at 9:00 P.M. Wednesday (logical Thursday). Sunday requirements were covered by overtime or by staff members working every third Sunday. The shifts rotated from the beginning to the end of the week every four to six weeks to avoid anyone having constant weekend and holiday work. There was no night- to day-shift rotation.

When staffing requirements for each shift were initially determined, all operators were given the opportunity to state their shift preference; all but a few got their first selection. As new employees were hired and trained, all employees eventually received their first choice.

Before implementing the three-day workweek, the company made every effort to ensure that all questions regarding work hours, vacation and holiday pay, benefits, and other company personnel issues were answered fully. This meant that the administration and maintenance of the program schedule and the logging of hours was a major task.

Since implementing the three-day workweek, the company has noted two indications of productivity stability and improvement: operator errors have remained at acceptable standards, and employees on the three-day schedule have a better attendance record than the corporate average.

Company A has found that the three-day workweek offers many work and personal benefits, including the following:
- Overtime is reduced and employee morale improved.
- Because of the shift turnaround, employees do not always have to work the same days. Thus, they are exposed to all jobs under different conditions (e.g., weekly jobs, monthly jobs).
- Shift turnarounds per week are reduced (12 versus 15), thus improving shift-to-shift communication.
- Employees have more leisure time to enjoy.
- Employee recruitment is easier because the three-day week attracts many prospective employees.
- Many employees can extend their time off by scheduling vacations around the shift turnaround.

However, some problems with the three-day workweek have occurred at Company A. For example, an employee must work six days straight in conjunction with the shift turnaround. Fatigue can be a factor, though it may be no greater than the end-of-week tiredness experienced by employees on the five-day workweek. It is also difficult for employees to attend school, particularly if they work the day shift. In addition, technical training must be done on an overtime basis or on the day shift, which adds to the work hours for night-shift personnel.

The three-day workweek has been in effect for several years at Company A and, in the management's opinion, has been very successful despite its problems.

THE FIVE-DAY WORKWEEK

The data center at "Company B" had significant problems providing ser-

Balancing Staff and Workload

vice to its users. A high rate of growth had outpaced the data center's ability to maintain a current set of standards and procedures, and the constant upgrading of hardware and software created an unstable environment. The operations department worked a three-day schedule with four shifts, rotating both from beginning to end of week and from night to day.

Many of the company's MIS personnel as well as its users had trouble communicating with computer operators and felt that operations personnel did not have a sense of urgency or priority about important jobs. Most jobs ran daily; when problems occurred, the midweek shift change often meant that a different operator came on duty with no knowledge of any problems or resolution attempts that had occurred earlier in the week. When this occurred, someone from systems or production control had to provide continuity of problem resolution. Depending on the shift rotation, it could take the company up to 10 days to communicate changes or information to all employees. Information was often overlooked because of this lengthy delay as well as the burden placed on five-day employees to communicate information to all shift personnel involved. In addition, the 12-hour workdays made training difficult to schedule.

THE MODIFIED FIVE-DAY WORKWEEK

To try to improve the situation, the company chose to adopt a workweek that more closely met business needs while still providing some staffing flexibility. A five-day workweek with some staggered start times was adopted. Figure 1 shows the staffing schedule used at Company B for the modified five-day workweek.

With the modified five-day week, Company B realized the following benefits:

- Reduced personnel rotation—Assigned to permanent shifts, employees could plan their time better. The new schedule also required less administration of schedules, vacations, and holidays than the three-day schedule did.
- Improved communication across shifts—Information was given to the first shift with a request to forward it to the second shift, which then forwarded it to the third shift. In the morning, a supervisor checked to see whether the information had been related as directed. If not, the communication responsibility could be clarified immediately. Related questions could be resolved within 24 hours. The morale of shift personnel improved because they felt they were now part of the communications loop.
- Increased continuity—Problem resolution had maximum continuity because the same people ran a job every night and personnel knew of past problems and resolution attempts. Staggered days ensured continuity on weekends.
- Facilitation of training—Training sessions could be scheduled more easily. Off-shift employees could come early or stay late for training classes, which was much more feasible after an eight-hour workday than after a twelve-hour one. In addition, miniclasses were often scheduled for the half-hour shift overlaps.

MANAGING THE DATA CENTER

- Reduced fatigue—When the shifts were rotating and personnel worked six 12-hour days, the company noticed a pronounced decline in operator attention and motivation as the week progressed. This was alleviated with the five-day week.
- Simplified overtime scheduling—For example, if another operator was needed for a shift, an employee could be asked to work an extra four hours. With the three-day week, this would have meant a 16-hour shift in addition to any required training time.
- Improved performance evaluation—It became easier to recognize top performers and reward them under the modified five-day week.
- Better shift coverage—The five-day week allowed increased staffing per shift. Staff was added for peak days and time periods and decreased on the weekends when software testing and hardware installations take place. No increase in overtime was necessary.
- Improved user relations—Users felt they had better communications with the operations staff when the midweek shift change was eliminated.

The only disadvantage that Company B found with the five-day workweek was that several employees preferred the three-day schedule. A few employees even left the company to find the three-day workweek elsewhere. Nevertheless, the company has not experienced significant turnover problems. Internal job posting also helps find candidates for openings.

In summary, Company B found that moving from a three-day to a five-day workweek helped stabilize its data center operations and maintain a more cohesive team in the data center.

First Shift

Position	Sunday	Monday	Tuesday	Wednesday	Thursday	Friday	Saturday
Shift supervisor		X	X	X	X	X	
PCA		X	X	X	X	X	
PCA	X	X	X	X			X
Operator	X	X			X	X	X
Operator		X	X	X	X	X	
Operator		X	X	X	X		
Operator	X	X	X			X	X
I/O clerk			X	X	X	X	X
Tape librarian		X	X	X	X	X	
	4	8	8	7	7	7	4

Second Shift

Position	Sunday	Monday	Tuesday	Wednesday	Thursday	Friday	Saturday
Shift supervisor		X	X	X	X	X	
PCA		X	X	X	X	X	
Operator		X	X	X	X	X	
Operator		X	X	X	X	X	
Operator	X	X	X	X	X		
Operator	X	X			X	X	X
Operator			X	X	X	X	
Tape librarian		X	X	X	X	X	
	2	7	7	7	8	7	2

Third Shift

Position	Sunday	Monday	Tuesday	Wednesday	Thursday	Friday	Saturday
Shift supervisor		X	X	X	X	X	
PCA		X	X	X	X	X	
Operator		X	X	X	X	X	
Operator		X	X	X	X	X	
Operator			X	X	X	X	
Operator	X	X	X			X	X
I/O clerk		X	X			X	
I/O clerk	X	X	X	X	X		
	2	7	8	7	7	7	2

Figure 1. Modified Five-Day Workweek Schedule

CONCLUSION

The experiences of data center managers who have used or evaluated various shift staffing plans (other than the standard Monday-Friday with three shifts) indicate the following guidelines:
- A three-day workweek may work best in a stable environment. Well-defined procedures and processes along with minimal change requirements are prerequisites to successful implementation.
- Use shift hours to provide significant overlap with the prime shift. For example, one successful data center works midnight to noon.
- Resolve all salary and benefits issues in advance. The administration of a three-day workweek requires extra effort regarding all personnel questions.
- Do not consider a change in workweek lightly. It is a major undertaking, and all possible ramifications should be carefully thought out.
- Examine such issues as company commitment, and be certain you are willing to live with the results of the new shift plan.
- Talk with other data center managers before adopting the plan you are considering. At least one of the managers polled may have tried and abandoned the plan you are considering. Find out why and determine whether his or her company's problems apply to your site.

VII-5
Do You Need a UPS?
Chuck Maddox

INTRODUCTION

An uninterruptible power supply (UPS) is an electrical power conversion unit that provides high-quality "conditioned" AC power despite variations in a normal or emergency power source. This conditioned power protects DP and related equipment from problems frequently encountered with normal commercial power sources:
- Voltage transients
- Voltage sags/surges
- Voltage brownouts
- Momentary outages (flickers)
- Long-term commercial power outages (if the UPS is coupled with a standby generator)

An understanding of the basic functions of a UPS is needed to determine whether such a system is actually required. The acquisition of a UPS should be justified based on an economic comparison of the cost providing the UPS and the cost of downtime and restart time caused by normal power source problems. (Consideration should also be given to downtime and restart time resulting from delayed equipment failures that can occur when components are damaged by a power deviation but do not fail immediately.)

This chapter discusses the functions of a UPS and describes the basic characteristics that should be considered when selecting a UPS system and planning for its installation. A glossary of technical terms associated with UPS systems is provided at the end of this chapter.

FUNCTIONS OF A UPS

A UPS accepts various input power supplies within specified parameters and converts them to output power within the parameters needed for DP equipment. Acceptable input power sources include local utility power, standby generators, or battery power. This chapter discusses the static-type UPS, which contains a solid state rectifier and inverter. Most UPS units sold today are of this type.

In this type of UPS, AC power from either the commercial utility or standby generators is rectified—converted to DC power—and fed to the inverter and battery. The battery "floats," drawing a small amount of current from the rectifier to maintain a full charge. When AC power is interrupted, the

MANAGING THE DATA CENTER

battery instantaneously begins to discharge, maintaining continuous power to the inverter. The inverter converts the DC power from the rectifier or battery to AC power of the proper voltage and frequency for the DP equipment. The UPS is equipped with a static bypass switch and static disconnect switch(es) to disengage the UPS and transfer the critical loads to raw utility or standby generator power in the event of a UPS malfunction. This transfer occurs so quickly (in approximately 0.040 second) that it is completely invisible to a computer. UPS lockout circuits prevent the static switch(es) from operating unless the input AC sine wave and the UPS output sine wave are synchronized. The UPS has built-in timing to ensure that this synchronization occurs when the UPS is receiving commercial utility power.

Figure 1 illustrates the basic components of a typical UPS system.

UPS CHARACTERISTICS

The first step in selecting a UPS system is to compare the characteristics of different manufacturers' systems. The following paragraphs discuss some of the major characteristics that should be considered.

System Efficiency

One of the most important characteristics of a UPS is system efficiency. The more efficient the unit, the less it will cost to operate. To warrant consideration, a UPS system should operate with 90 percent efficiency at full load with the battery fully charged.

Overload Protection

To protect UPS systems against dangerous overload, the UPS inverter current output is limited when that output begins to exceed the unit's kVA rating. Typical current limit values are 1.5 times the rated level for 10 seconds and 1.25 times the rated level for 20 minutes.[1] Current limitations can be exceeded when equipment that draws high amounts of current is suddenly placed on a UPS system. To protect itself from damage in these instances, the UPS bypass circuit (see Figure 1) is activated, and the computer equip-

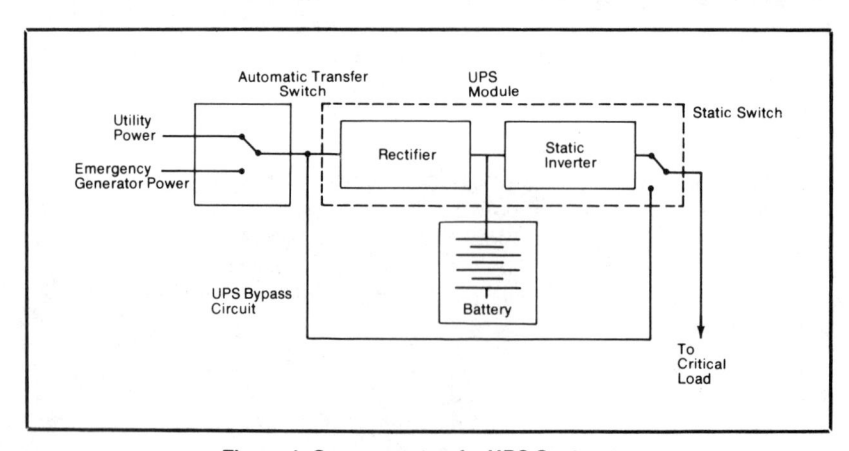

Figure 1. Components of a UPS System

ment is powered by unconditioned public utility power with its high available current capacity.

Unbalanced Load Operation

On three-phase electrical systems, as much as 80 percent of the typical load may be single phase. Even when the systems are well designed, load imbalances can occur as a result of normal operating conditions. Some UPS systems offer 100 percent load imbalance operational capability while others are more limited. The more limited a system is, the greater the risk in encountering problems in this area.

Post-Installation Shakedown Period

UPS failures may occur within a short period after bringing a unit on-line. This "burn-in" period should last no more than 30 to 45 days, with failures progressively decreasing during this period. In order to plan for a burn-in period failure, the user should ask the vendor how much operational testing and burn-in time a unit receives before leaving the factory. The more testing performed by the vendor, the less the user must be concerned about early failure.

Warranties and Maintenance

UPS warranties generally cover parts and service for a specific amount of time—usually one year. After the warranty period, the unit can be maintained through a full- or limited-service maintenance agreement or on a time and materials basis. In either case, replacement parts are nearly always an expense to the owner.

Survey of Users

To obtain unbiased information on the performance of UPS systems, the prospective buyer should ask each manufacturer's sales representative for a list of companies that have UPS systems installed. When contacting companies for information on installed UPS systems, questions should be as specific as possible and should cover the following items:
- Average number of failures per year
- Average amount of time needed for repair
- The manufacturer's replacement parts policy
- The manufacturer's commitment to repairing defective UPS systems quickly
- The manufacturer's policy on repairable parts
- Names of other companies that use similar UPS systems

This information will help in evaluating UPS systems in the following areas.

Mean Time Between Failures. Mean time between failures (MTBF) is the average amount of time between failures of a piece of equipment. To be relevant, this figure should be based on the past operation of the equipment in question rather than on that of a similar unit. MTBF serves as an indication of operational problems and (to a degree) maintenance expenses that can be expected.

Mean Time to Repair. Mean time to repair (MTTR) is the average amount of time required to repair a failed unit. This figure represents the average length of time required to diagnose and repair a typical failure on a specific piece of equipment. It does not include lag time between equipment failure and notification of the proper repair facility, lag time while awaiting a repair specialist, or lag time while awaiting parts. These items should also be considered before choosing a unit.

Notification and Repair Procedures. Notifying the proper repair agency of a unit failure is an in-house function; however, specific notification procedures should be established by the vendor. Lag time while awaiting a repair specialist is related directly to the availability of the specialist. The availability of repair specialists and the manufacturers' repair procedures should be investigated before the purchase decision is made. For example, some manufacturers maintain repair specialists in most major U.S. cities; other manufacturers must send a specialist from the manufacturing plant to service a defective unit.

Spare Parts Policy. Lag time while awaiting parts is related to three factors. First, it depends on the quantity of spare parts maintained on location by the owner. Most UPS manufacturers will provide a list of recommended spare parts to a prospective purchaser. This list should be evaluated very critically to ensure that a sufficient number of high-failure items are recommended and that a large number of superfluous items are not included.

Second, lag time while awaiting parts can be directly affected by the quantity of spare stock items maintained by the manufacturer. Manufacturers attempt to keep as little capital as possible tied up in spare parts.

Third, the manufacturer's commitment to repairing a defective unit quickly can also affect the lag time. Regardless of the system's size or use, a UPS system failure should be considered an emergency situation by the manufacturer and acted upon accordingly.

SIZING A UPS SYSTEM

Because sizing a UPS system involves electrical power conversion equations and requirements, it should be done by an electrical engineer. The equipment loads to be included on the UPS should be critically reviewed by the data center manager, however. UPS capacity is quite expensive. This review should include present loads, planned additions, and long-range expansion. Additionally, the effect of interruptions and costs that will result from the addition of UPS capacity in the future should be addressed.

Present Loads. In determining present loads, all critical equipment must be considered. For example, processors and peripherals used for online processing must be connected to the UPS. To avoid the cost for additional UPS capacity, however, noncritical equipment (e.g., equipment used for batch processing that can be delayed in case of a power outage) may be connected directly to utility power. If this arrangement requires the installation of a separate distribution system, however, the cost of this effort should be com-

UPS Systems

pared to the cost of adding enough UPS capacity to support the noncritical equipment.

Planned Additions. Because of the operational interruptions and major expense required to add UPS capacity, the UPS initially installed should provide adequate capacity for planned additions to the equipment load. The cost per kVA of UPS capacity may decrease as the kVA rating increases; if so, this should be considered when determining initial capacity.

Long-Range Expansion. Plans for long-range expansion should also be considered when sizing a UPS system. If it is probable that additional long-term UPS capacity will be needed, specific provisions should be made during the initial UPS installation. These provisions include planning for or providing the physical space needed for expansion and installation as well as planning for increased electrical distribution system capacity. These provisions will reduce the impact of adding UPS capacity in the future.

Adding Capacity. If additional UPS capacity is required, an electrical and mechanical engineer should be consulted to determine possible ways to reduce the impact of the changes. One procedure is to install a temporary power circuit around the existing UPS system until the system is modified and tested.

Electrical distribution systems are normally designed with a specific amount of current-carrying capacity, expressed in amperes (amps). Starting at the power supply point, the electrical distribution system components (e.g., main feeders, interruptor devices, fuses) limit the distribution system capacity. As the current continues through the entire electrical system, power panels, and circuit breaker panels, current-carrying capacity decreases at each successive distribution point. The result is a system design balanced to accomplish a certain function through a certain distribution of electrical power at a certain cost. Thus, any attempt to modify an electrical distribution system should be reviewed by an electrical engineer.

A UPS system installed on an existing electrical distribution system is limited by the capacity of the distribution system and the power loss of the UPS itself. If the sum of the operational power requirements and the power consumed by the UPS exceeds the limits of the distribution system, then the distribution system must be upgraded or replaced. Either alternative can be very expensive.

REDUNDANCY

Because UPS operation is continuous, reliability is crucial. The configuration of electrical components in the typical UPS enables redundancy to be built into the unit. As illustrated in Figure 1, equipment for the three UPS functions (rectifier, DC bus, and inverter) is housed in a single cabinet, comprising one UPS "module." The capacity of a single module varies depending on the manufacturer and model. If the user's critical capacity exceeds the capacity of a single UPS module, additional modules can be connected in parallel to the critical bus.

MANAGING THE DATA CENTER

Using this arrangement, redundancy can be achieved by adding one more module than is required to provide enough capacity for the critical load. Thus, if one module fails, it can be automatically disconnected without affecting performance. In addition to an extra module, redundant UPS systems require static output isolation and effective monitoring to ensure that a failed module is promptly disconnected from the critical bus.[1]

UPS BATTERY CONSIDERATIONS

The UPS battery provides continuous power flow to the critical bus in the event of an interruption in AC power to the UPS. Since the battery is a storage unit for DC power, the size or capacity of the battery in relation to the inverter output/load rating determines how long the battery can support the installation's power requirements. Generally, provisions can be made for 5 to 60 minutes of operation. If standby generators are used, battery capacity (battery support time) can be reduced, because the battery must support the critical loads only during generator start up and transfer. To protect against standby generator failure, however, sufficient battery support time is needed to permit completion of an orderly computer system shutdown with or without standby generators.

Battery Configurations. Two different battery configurations are available for supplying DC power to the UPS. One configuration involves a dedicated battery for each UPS module—this method eliminates the chance that a single battery failure will disable the UPS. The second configuration involves a common battery with battery breakers for each module. This configuration is generally used in UPS systems due to the low failure rate of lead acid battery systems and the lower initial investment for a common battery system[1].

Types of Batteries. Various types of lead acid or nickel cadmium batteries are used in UPS systems. No single type is best for all applications. The choice of battery type is based on such factors as environmental temperatures, desired life, cycling capabilities, maintenance requirements, deep discharge capabilities, warranty, and available capacity throughout battery life.[2] Suggested minimum requirements are:
- 20 year life span
- 100 percent full replacement warranty during first five years
- Additional 15 year pro rated replacement warranty
- The capability to be discharged and charged more than 500 times
- Good high current, short term load capacity

Suggested minimum environmental requirements include:
- Temperature of 77° to 86°F
- Relative humidity of 40 to 80 percent
- Three or more air changes per hour (depending on type of battery).

Recharge Time. An important battery characteristic is the time required to recharge the battery after use. This time period is often given as the ratio of recharge time to discharge time. A 5:1 ratio indicates that five hours of recharge time are necessary to recharge a battery to 90 percent of the initial charge level after one hour of use. UPS batteries with 8:1, 12:1, or longer recharge times are available at a somewhat reduced expense; however, the savings does not compensate adequately for the greatly reduced battery service.

Battery Installation. When installing a UPS battery, special attention must be given to installing the battery bus. All connections should be torqued to the manufacturer's recommended value, and then each connection should be checked again. Failure to tighten all connections to the recommended values could result in an electrical fire when the battery is load tested.

STANDBY GENERATOR

A UPS system provides protection against a multitude of commercial utility power problems; however, the one problem a UPS cannot protect against is a long-term power outage. To provide this protection an emergency standby generator is required. The most practical type of standby generator is a fully automated system.

Automatic Transfer Switch

A transfer switch is required in any standby power generator system. In an automated system, this transfer switch determines when the standby generators should be started, when to transfer to standby power, and when to transfer back to utility power. The switch does this by sensing voltage and sometimes frequency values to ensure that the values are within specified parameters. The decision concerning whether to use only voltage or both voltage and frequency parameter limits is normally made by the consulting electrical engineer.

Problems have been encountered in attempting to sense frequency on either utility or emergency generator power when supplying power to a 300 kW or larger UPS system. Most frequency sensing devices used today operate on an AC sine wave zero-crossing timing principle. If an AC power source is connected to a static control rectifier (SCR) such as is found in a UPS, a "glitch" is created in the AC sine wave when the SCR fires. The depth of this glitch is directly related to the load placed on the power source by the SCR. At about 300 kW, the glitch crosses the zero point of the AC sine wave (see Figure 2).

The frequency sensing device in the automatic transfer switch sees this glitch as a defective frequency signal and transfers to the standby generators. The effect of the rectifier on the standby generator is even more drastic than on utility power; thus the automatic transfer switch will flip flop from utility power to standby generator and back until the load is reduced or the frequency sensors are bypassed.

Other problems that may result from this SCR disturbance are:
- Disturbance to connected loads
- Generation of RF frequencies
- Adverse effects on metering devices such as frequency meters

If these effects are not severe, it is possible to use only voltage detection for the automatic transfer switch and to use reed-type frequency meters. If asso-

MANAGING THE DATA CENTER

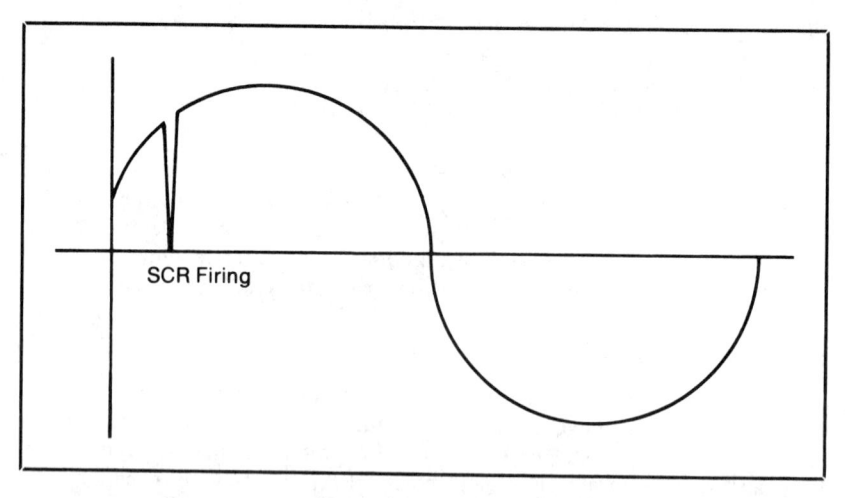

Figure 2. AC Sine Wave Disturbance Resulting from SCR Firing Loaded to 300 kW

ciated disturbance problems are severe, it may be necessary to install an isolation transformer.

Fuel Storage

The fuel storage capacity of the standby generator engine determines the amount of time an installation can operate on standby power without refueling. Refueling requirements of less than 24 hours should be avoided if possible; the generator should be able to run for two to three days under full load conditions before refueling.

Refueling capability may require some careful planning. For example, if the DP installation is located far above street level in a multistory building, access to fuel delivery trucks may be limited.

If the fuel storage tank is not directly accessible for the fuel delivery truck, a refuel line will be needed. Installing a refuel line involves ensuring proper fuel line slope to allow an adequate flow rate and ensuring drainage so that no fuel remains in the line after refueling operations. In addition, if the fuel storage tank is isolated from the refueling point, a detection and warning system is needed to indicate when the fuel tank is full. If the fuel tank is located in an enclosed area, other fuel storage arrangements are required:
- Continuous forced ventilation
- A specially sealed pit area to contain the fuel in the event of a tank leak
- Explosion-proof lighting.

Sequence Start Capability

When an installation is equipped with a standby generator, high electrical load units should have sequence start capability. Only units that can tolerate a short power outage and have automatic restart capability can be considered. However, sequence start capability reduces the required generator rating and thereby reduces the initial purchase expense.

UPS Systems

Increased UPS Reliability Requirements

When using a standby generator in conjunction with a UPS, the increased reliability of a redundant UPS is crucial. This is because the UPS bypass circuits that connect the critical load directly to utility power in the event of a UPS failure are locked out when the UPS is powered by an emergency generator. As discussed previously, providing bypass capability without power interruption to the critical bus requires synchronization of the UPS output AC sine wave with the UPS input AC sine wave. UPS systems have built-in timing and synchronization circuits to accomplish this while using utility power; however, because emergency generator frequency is unstable, these synchronization circuits cannot function when the UPS is connected to the generator. Thus, if the UPS fails during a utility power failure while being powered by a standby generator, the power to the critical load will be interrupted even though the generator is functioning properly.

INSTALLATION CONSIDERATIONS

In planning for the installation of a UPS system, long equipment lead time should be expected. Although the lead time will vary depending on the manufacturer and the size of the UPS, lead times of eight months to a year are common for some large systems. Thus, the UPS should be ordered as soon as possible during the planning stage and the lead time used to prepare the site and meet all support requirements.

Electrical Distribution System

A UPS typically requires an increase of 30 to 33 percent in distribution capacity. Two features of UPS systems can reduce the effect of the UPS on the building's electrical distribution system, thus reducing initial installation expenses.

Current-Limiting Feature. In addition to supporting both the DP equipment load and the UPS system, the electrical distribution system must have enough capacity to meet the battery charging requirements of the UPS. Most UPS systems have a mechanism to limit the amount of power supplied for battery charging while maintaining the critical load. This current-limiting feature reduces the required rating for a standby generator (if one is used) and reduces the capacity needed in the building's electrical distribution system.

Walk-In Feature. Another UPS feature that reduces the unit's effect on the distribution system is a walk-in or ramp-in mechanism. This mechanism prevents sudden surges when utility power is first connected to the UPS.

Other Efficiency Measures. Two measures that can also help to reduce installation expenses are keeping heavy feeders as short as possible and locating service entrances, switch equipment, standby generators, UPS, batteries, and loads in close proximity.

Space

Before installing a UPS, the data center manager should plan to provide

MANAGING THE DATA CENTER

ample space for the equipment and its operation. Space considerations include the following:
- Electrical and mechanical equipment
- Ease of maintenance
- Electrical clearance
- Safety
- Parts and test equipment storage
- Future growth needs

Like any other piece of mechanical or electrical equipment, a UPS system will require scheduled and unscheduled maintenance. To perform this maintenance, passageway clearance is required around opened doors and removed panels. There must be room around the UPS for test equipment and drawings. In addition, personal injury is most likely to occur when panels and doors are open, exposing "hot" wiring. Providing sufficient room for maintenance reduces safety hazards. Considering the potential for personal injury, sufficient space for maintenance cannot be overemphasized.

Specific UPS support equipment such as drawings, manuals, test equipment, and spare parts should be maintained in the general area of the UPS. Cabinets with lockable doors provide adequate storage for these items. Of course, space for future UPS expansion should be considered at the time of UPS installation in order to prevent costly redesign.

Cooling Considerations

A UPS system must be operated within a specific temperature range. The required operating environment should be documented in the manufacturer's operating specifications. The heat produced by a UPS is related directly to kVA size, with a slight variation among manufacturers. The larger the UPS, the more heat it produces. Refrigeration cooling can be considered for small units; however, as UPS systems increase in size, it becomes more economical to simply remove the hot air and supply fresh outside air. This procedure can be used as long as the outside ambient air temperature does not exceed the maximum acceptable input cooling air temperature of the UPS (normally 100° to 104°F). In geographical areas where the ambient air exceeds this temperature, the air must be conditioned by water chillers or other methods.

UPS systems are typically rated for operational temperature limitations of 0° to 40°C or 0° to 50°C. The maximum operating temperature can be very meaningful to a prospective purchaser. First, the higher ambient operating temperature limitation indicates that the electronic components of the system are of high quality. This results in extended component life during operation in normal ambient temperatures and provides an extra margin of safety when it is most needed.

Floor Loading

UPS systems and related equipment such as batteries, switch gear, and standby generators are very heavy in relation to their physical size. As a result, in-depth consideration must be given to how the equipment is placed on the floor.

Modern multistory office buildings usually have a floor loading capacity of

75 pounds per square foot. While this is sufficient to support small UPS units, additional support is required for medium-sized to large units. The structural support needed may range from a simple housekeeping pad to major structural reinforcements. Plans to install a UPS system in this type of structure should be analyzed by a structural engineer.

Installation of a UPS on an on-grade floor presents fewer problems. Again, however, deterioration, different types of support, and so on dictate that the support structure should be analyzed by a structural engineer.

Rigging

Receiving and installing the UPS system also requires planning. Most manufacturers have a preinstallation checklist. If a manufacturer does not have one, the data center manager should prepare such a list before the unit is delivered. This list should include, but not be limited to, the following items:
- Receiving facilities
- Entranceway
- Hallways less than five feet wide
- Turns
- Stairways
- Doorways less than seven feet high
- Computer room raised floor
- Special handling equipment (if necessary)
  - Forklifts
  - Pallets
  - Cranes

Developing and using such a checklist can prevent many aggravations when the UPS arrives.

Maintenance

An in-depth maintenance program should be established to maintain the unit in peak operating condition. Although some types of electronic equipment operate almost indefinitely with very little attention, a UPS is not among them. UPS and battery manufacturers provide recommended preventive maintenance requirements. Preventive maintenance can be completed either by in-house personnel or by a vendor. In most cases, a combination of in-house and vendor-contracted maintenance is most appropriate. Battery maintenance should be performed monthly and can become rather expensive if done by a vendor. UPS preventive maintenance may be required quarterly or semiannually and may require detailed technical knowledge. Preventive maintenance records should be completed and maintained—in almost every battery cell or UPS failure, past performance data is needed to correct the problem.

Lighting and Utility Plugs. Lighting and utility plug wiring for the UPS area is often connected to the UPS bus. This causes problems when the UPS is totally shut down and input power is disconnected for scheduled or unscheduled maintenance. In these instances, drop-cord lighting and extension cords are required to perform the maintenance. A better system is to connect half the lighting and utility plugs to the utility power and half to the UPS bus.

MANAGING THE DATA CENTER

Remote Annunciation. In the event of a UPS malfunction, immediate action should be taken to repair the UPS. Therefore, if the UPS is not located in the general vicinity of operations personnel, remote audible and/or visual UPS status annunciation is required. Installing a remote annunciation circuit is not difficult, but problems have been encountered in this area when low voltage annunciation signals are used. The most common problem is false malfunction annunciation, which often occurs when these low-voltage circuits are installed in conduits with high-voltage circuits (208 volts or more). To avoid this problem, low voltage circuits should be installed in dedicated conduits or shielded cables. Because circuit and system designs vary, specific recommendations should be obtained from the UPS supplier.

Safety and Security Considerations

Shower and Eye Wash. A UPS installation is not complete until emergency safety provisions are provided to comply with OSHA requirements. A safety shower and eye wash must be installed in the vicinity of the battery room. The unit should not be located where it will be a hazard in itself, but it should be easily accessible to a person blinded by battery acid.

Telephone. For safety purposes and to facilitate UPS system maintenance, a telephone should be located in the UPS area. The two-man system is normally used by technicians when working in and around a "hot" bus. In the event of an accident, a means of immediate communication is necessary. A telephone in the UPS area also saves time when technicians must contact local supply houses for parts.

Fire Detection. For safety, insurance, and economic reasons, fire detection in a UPS area is a necessity. One of the most common systems used is ionization detection, sometimes called smoke detection. These devices sound an alarm when they detect a specific product of combustion. Unfortunately, polyvinyl chloride (PVC) is now used extensively as electric wire insulation. When PVC burns, it produces large amounts of water vapor and chlorine gas but very little ionization. Thus, electrical fires in today's equipment are difficult to detect with ionization detectors. One solution is to combine ionization detection with photoelectric detection. It should be noted, however, that photoelectric detectors are more expensive than ionization detectors.

To determine what actions are necessary in case of fire, the data center manager should consult with an electrical engineer, a local fire department representative, and an insurance representative. The fire detection system can be designed to trigger a local and/or remote alarm, to shut down the air circulation system, and to activate electrical power disruptor devices.

Lightning Protection. Installation of lightning protection devices should be considered when the building housing the UPS is taller than surrounding buildings or is isolated on high ground.

Security Measures. The UPS physical area should have at least the same degree of security as the rest of the DP installation. Since very little technical

knowledge is required to extensively damage "hot" bus work, very tight security measures should be considered. Some security systems to consider are:
- A dedicated door lock
- Card key access
- Door monitors
- Closed circuit television.

Testing and Training

Factory Acceptance Testing. After a UPS unit is assembled, but before it is delivered to the user, complete operational and load testing should be performed at the factory. Since this testing is normally done without a battery, it cannot be substituted for user acceptance testing; however, documented final results of these tests should be made available to the user.

Load Testing. Before connection to the critical bus at the user site, the UPS and the UPS battery should be load tested to ensure that there are no installation defects. In this test, a dummy load is connected to the UPS, and three separate tests are performed:
- A full load test on the UPS using utility power
- A full battery capacity test with the UPS powered by batteries
- A full load test on the UPS using standby generators (if used in the installation)

If these tests are successful, installation can be completed and the critical bus connected to the UPS.

User Acceptance Testing and Personnel Training. After installation, user acceptance testing should be performed. During this testing user representatives should be trained in the operation of the UPS. Some UPS systems must be sequenced up and down in specific steps to prevent damage; these procedures should be explained. In addition, the impact of UPS failure should be fully explained to operations personnel, and the necessary emergency procedures should be documented.

CONCLUSION

Selecting and installing a UPS system requires careful planning. Various vendors' systems should be evaluated to determine which unit possesses the characteristics needed; the unit should be sized to meet the power capacity requirements of the installation; and proper preparation should be carried out regarding space, floor loading, electrical system, cooling, rigging, maintenance, safety, security, testing, and training. The guidelines in this chapter can help MIS in this effort. Because of the complex electrical and structural issues involved, an electrical and a structural engineer should participate in the planning and installation process.

GLOSSARY OF UPS TERMS

alarms Printed messages describing an off-limit condition or failure that also rings the alarm buzzer.

MANAGING THE DATA CENTER

annunciation The printed circuit card control monitoring alarms and status information for sequential message printing.

auto-retransfer The completely automatic transfer/retransfer cycle. Retransfer is only accomplished if the reason for transfer was a power module overload. An optional bypass function.

auxiliary commutated An inverter bridge circuit that uses another set of smaller thyristors and commutation capacitors to turn off the main power thyristors.

bat save An automatic circuit preventing unnecessary battery discharge. If the module output breaker is open and the module goes to battery power, a shutdown is initiated after 10 seconds. If a module is on battery and has loading, and the bypass utility is within specification, that module is shut down and a transfer is made to utility power (unless sufficient modules not on battery remain).

battery A string of 187 cells connected in series, continuously floated across the DC link of the power module.

bridge current limit One of two inverter output current limit controls. Each individual bridge is separately monitored, and its maximum commutation limit is protected by this instantaneous current limit. Each bridge current limit acts independently for the first 6 cycles of the overload or fault, providing maximum inverter output capacity.

brownout Utility input voltage to the rectifier 10 percent below nominal. The rectifier continuous rating range is from +10 percent to −15 percent.

center point ground A resistor ground connection to the center point of the battery string. Permits a first accidental ground and detection.

common battery A single battery bank that simultaneously serves all power modules. May consist of series strings of 187 cells.

commutation Turning off a conducting thyristor, generally using a capacitor charged opposite to the conducting polarity.

complementary commutated An inverter bridge circuit that uses the basic power thyristors in conjunction with a spanning reactor and commutation capacitors for each bridge leg to turn each other off.

critical load Those devices that are to be protected from abnormalities on the utility mains; typically, a DP system.

current limit The maximum current set point of the rectifier regardless of loading. Normally sufficient to supply the full load rating of the inverter and recharge current to the battery.

datalink The redundant pairs of wires between modules that cause the entire system to operate in unison. Results in load sharing, equal voltage and frequency, and in-phase operation. Two different circuit configurations are employed for improved redundancy.

DC link The two-wire connection between the rectifier and the inverter. The battery is floated across the DC link.

DC window The input operating range of the inverter, 421v DC to 290v DC. A wide window is required due to the wide terminal voltage swing of the battery (float 2.25, open circuit 2.06, initial 1.8 and final 1.55 volts per cell).

electronic interlock A circuit matrix between printed circuit cards that detects a loose card and also prevents start-up or logic power being applied if a card is missing or in the wrong card slot.

UPS Systems

equalization Required monthly boost charge for antimony type lead acid batteries.

expandable UPS A UPS to which power modules can be added for increased rating or redundancy. Normally the bypass is sized for this future expansion. The single module form with integral bypass is nonexpandable.

final voltage The voltage of the battery at which discharge should be terminated. A function of the discharge rate and the inverter DC window capacity.

float voltage The well regulated voltage of the DC link and of the battery string to maintain full charge capacity. Typically 2.25 volts per cell.

individual battery A dedicated battery bank for each power module.

individual control Each power module and the bypass have their own logicenter and no common or master control.

initial voltage The voltage of the battery at the beginning of a discharge. The value depends on the discharge rate and ranges from 1.8 to 1.7 volts per cell.

instant detection The UPS control has fast-response monitors for automatic operation that detect out-of-tolerance parameters within the control before the output wave form is disturbed.

instant stop The use of the six inverter bridges as a static disconnect. A very fast (about one millisecond) method for isolation and shutdown of a power module.

interphase transformer A combination of an instantaneous load sharing device for the two rectifier bridges and a DC filter inductance for smoothing the 12-phase bridge DC ripple.

inverter The portion of a UPS containing the equipment and controls to convert DC power to the precise AC power for a load.

inverter bridge Four thyristors and associated components that periodically turn on and off to impose a square wave voltage of alternating polarity to an output transformer primary winding.

inv reg Inverter regulator and associated inverter control printed circuit cards.

lead antimony alloy, lead acid A battery requiring a monthly equalization boost charge; requires increasing water additions and charge current with age and has a one year warranty with 15 to 18 years expected life. Normally not used for UPS in the U.S.

lead calcium alloy, lead acid A battery that does not require monthly equalization boost charges, reduces water consumption by 80 percent, and is warranted for 20 years.

logicenter The central enclosure within the module containing the printed circuit card controls.

metering The solid state instrumentation of the module contained on printed circuit cards for display on the digital readout.

neutral transformer A separate output transformer that forms the fourth wire as neutral when required by the customer.

nonredundant UPS A UPS with exactly enough power modules to supply the rated load.

optional current limit A reduced normal current limit setting of the rectifier for redundant systems with utility or diesel generator capacity limitations.

MANAGING THE DATA CENTER

overload The capacity of the rectifier to supply power to the inverter when the inverter is overloaded to 125 percent or 150 percent of its rating. This rectifier rating does not require any power from the batteries, and is available even when the incoming voltage is at -15 percent. The rectifier has two current limit set points in addition to the normal current limit set point that is automatically adjusted by the actual load being supplied by the inverter.

phase lock The matching and tracking of the power module frequency with the utility input source to the bypass. Tracking is within the limits of plus or minus 0.5 Hertz from nominal and a slew rate no faster than one Hertz per second. Automatic disconnection occurs when these limits are exceeded.

power module The basic rectifier-charger and inverter unit. The modules may be paralleled to provide the rated UPS capacity.

power supply A DC to DC power supply for the logicenter. Power source is the utility (suitably rectified to DC) and the Battery.

power walk-in The turn-on sequence of the rectifier upon return of the utility input. The DC output voltage ramps on to equal the battery voltage and then the current limit setting ramps on to provide a minimum inrush to the rectifier.

pulse width modulation (PWM) Many small duration square wave pulses, forming an approximate sine wave.

rectifier-charger The portion of a UPS containing the equipment and controls to convert the input AC power to regulated DC power for the inverter and batteries.

rec reg Rectifier regulator and associated rectifier control printed circuit cards.

redundant UPS A UPS having one more power module than is required to supply the rated load—an on-line spare. Requires static disconnect in each output to protect the critical bus upon failure of one module.

redundant fans An extra operating fan for each ventilated compartment. Louvers on the top of each fan prevent reverse air flow through a failed fan.

remote annunciation An operator's panel remote from the UPS.

retransfer The automatic solid state switching of the load from the bypass to the power modules. Pushbutton initiated.

reverse power The excessive flow of power from the system critical bus to a failing power module that results in the critical bus going outside specification limits.

safe final discharge voltage The voltage at which a battery should be terminated to avoid overdischarge. The voltage varies with discharge rate. The battery can remain in an open circuit condition for up to one week without recharge, requires no special boost charge to recover, and results in no loss of future battery capacity.

step wave The use of inverter bridge square wave voltage pulses into an output summing transformer to form an approximate sine wave.

seq. logic Sequence logic and associated automatic operation controls and monitors for the most advanced UPS on the market.

sequential message printing All printed messages are preceded by the time-of-day stamp and then are printed in the order or time sequence in which they actually occur. A powerful diagnostic tool.

static bypass switch The portion of a UPS containing the equipment and controls for high-speed switching of the load from the UPS inverter output to the utility mains without any abnormalities.

static disconnect A continuously rated thyristor switch in series with the output of each power module. Required for redundant systems only.

status messages Printed messages describing the present state of significant aspects of the equipment (e.g., Inverter Breaker Closed, Inverter Ready, Ramp on Rectifier Volts.)

symmetrical current limit One of two inverter output current limit controls. Each output line current is monitored to cause a phase-back of inverter output voltage symmetrically on all three phases to limit current flow to rated values. Operates subsequent to the first six cycles of the overload or fault, which is controlled by the bridge current limit.

system critical bus output The combined output of the power modules and bypass that powers the critical customer load.

transfer The automatic solid state switching of the load from the power modules to the bypass. Can also be pushbutton initiated.

T1, T2 Inverter output transformers, each with three primaries connected to an inverter bridge. The secondaries are connected in series to form a zig-zag wye three phase output.

UPS Uninterruptible power supply; a "buffer" between the utility mains (or other power source) and a load that requires uninterrupted, precise power.

utility input Power source into the bypass and rectifier. May be separate, and include diesel generator auxiliary supply.

12-phase bridge Two three-phase full-wave rectifier bridges, each consisting of six thyristors, one with wye input transformer, one with delta input transformer.

References

1. *Battery Performance Comparison: Switchgear—UPS—Emergency Power.* Vol. ALC, Issue 901. Columbus OH: Arthur N. Ulrich Co.
2. Ibsen, Ole N. "Uninterruptible Power Supplies for Larger Computers." *WESCON Fall '78,* IEEE Computer Society Conference, September 12-14, 1978, Los Angeles CA.

VII-6
Designing the Data Center: A Checklist

Philip C. Cross

INTRODUCTION

Selecting, planning, and designing a modern computer center is a complex and difficult undertaking. It not only requires a large capital investment but also establishes an operating environment that directly affects data center reliability and flexibility in accommodating change and expansion.

Electrical filtering, water cooling, and stringent temperature controls are necessary if today's more sensitive (yet more powerful) computer components are to be safeguarded. Up-to-date data communications centers are needed to monitor and support information network operations.

As business reliance on MIS continues to increase, companies must maintain their own uninterruptible power sources to mitigate the effects of brownouts or blackouts. In addition, physical security precautions to safeguard confidential data and to protect personnel and equipment have become critical.

This chapter discusses a phased project approach using a site selection team. It also discusses building requirements and provides a checklist for data center site selections.

PHASED PROJECT APPROACH

The phased project approach is ideal for a major task such as data center site selection because it is well suited to the sequential (though sometimes overlapping) stages of feasibility study, design, and implementation. In this approach, each stage is incorporated into the appropriate project phase and is assigned milestones and time schedules. The phased project approach provides a disciplined methodology for coordinating the individuals and groups that provide the expertise required for successful execution of project tasks.

If given sufficient time and information, a project team of qualified and experienced members should be able to design a data center that will accommodate future needs for space, utilities, ancillary areas, and environmental conditions. To ensure successful selection, design, and implementation, the team should include the following members.

MANAGING THE DATA CENTER

Data Center Operations Manager. The data center manager must live with—and take responsibility for—the new or expanded data center. Therefore, the MIS manager should assign to the data center manager responsibility for ensuring that:
- All requirements are accurately defined.
- The scope of the project includes all necessary tasks.
- Team member responsibilities (both direct and supporting) for performing tasks are unquestionably clear.
- Rules for reporting and controlling progress are followed.
- The project is well managed at all times.

If unanticipated problems occur, the data center manager must immediately identify them and assign them to the responsible team member(s) for resolution. The data center manager must follow up these problems and, if necessary, revise the project task schedule. Senior management must be kept apprised of the project's status and informed of actions that require their level of authority. To ensure that these needs are met, the data center manager should serve as project leader.

Engineering Specialists. These members are responsible for advising on such areas as air conditioning, fire suppression and warning, physical security, building construction, electrical power, and water chilling requirements.

Architect. The chosen architect must have previous first-hand experience in designing data centers. He or she should be able to take advantage of the best materials, equipment, and construction techniques yet work within practical schedules. The architect can provide further assurance that the proposed data center will satisfy physical operating requirements.

Physical Plant Construction and Maintenance Personnel. These members must ensure that all environmental, mechanical, and electrical equipment and structural plant facilities are installed and maintained within prescribed performance standards and according to schedule.

Internal Auditing Staff. Because the internal auditing staff will periodically check the completed facility, they should be involved early in the project to obtain their advice on areas of physical and data security. This precaution helps to ensure that due consideration is given not only to the physical selection and design of the data center but also to the methods and procedures of its operation.

Equipment Vendors. Equipment vendors must participate throughout physical planning and implementation. They can then be held accountable for providing guidance and assistance to guarantee that their equipment is located and installed properly. They must at least provide written environmental specifications necessary for optimal equipment operation and maintenance.

Vendor involvement should not be difficult to obtain. Most vendors have technical specialists who can define requirements and offer valuable advice as plans are developed and during implementation.

SITE SELECTION

When selecting a new site, MIS should consider the following factors.

Security. The neighborhood location and the plans for safeguarding valuable assets are prime considerations. Restricting entry to the site may require such measures as guards, fencing, perimeter lighting, alarms, and TV monitors.

Accessibility. Ease of access for delivering equipment and supplies is important. If elevators will be used for delivery, their capacity and dimensions must be adequate for large computer equipment. In addition, the work flow between access points and work areas should facilitate easy transport and movement.

Power. A reliable electrical power source is critical for uninterrupted service. MIS should avoid electrical power services that depend on a single source of fuel and should investigate an uninterruptible power supply (UPS) or other independent alternate power source.

Data Communications. Online networks are necessities in most data centers. Therefore, the ability to obtain reliable, expandable, and serviceable data communications is a prime requirement in site selection.

BUILDING REQUIREMENTS

Basic requirements must be accommodated in a new building design. These requirements must also be incorporated at reasonable cost when refurbishing and preparing an existing building for data center occupancy. MIS should evaluate the following design considerations when selecting a data center site.

Floor Space

Floor space must satisfy immediate as well as projected needs. When selecting space to house the computer equipment, the following should be considered:
- Function—How will the space be used? Functions such as processing, I/O, office, and storage influence the desired shape of the floor space. For example, a long, narrow computer room should be avoided.
- Area—Will the space accommodate the devices to be housed and provide ample room for movement of personnel, equipment, and supplies?
- Partitioning and expandability—Can areas be subdivided? Can walls or partitions be removed? Columns that decrease the flexibility of the space should be avoided.
- Functional relationships—Are related departments on the same floor? If not, can related activities be located near stairways on consecutive floors?

When evaluating existing potential sites, a floor plan of each site must be developed to show its dimensions and the locations of columns, doors and windows, permanent and temporary walls, and other factors affecting the usability of the space. Although a particular site might provide sufficient floor space, the arrangement may prevent the space from being used efficiently.

Physical Construction

The building's physical construction is important whether the building is to be purchased or leased because of the expensive equipment it will contain and the organization's dependence on the data center. Floor loading capacity and wall construction must be sufficient to support heavy equipment and to isolate one area from another in case of natural or man-made disasters. Consideration must be given to other subtle requirements that can easily be overlooked, including drainage, hallway maneuverability, ceiling heights, plumbing, and electrical line raceways.

Physical Security

To some degree, automated security measures and security-minded employees can protect against willful destruction, but usually at considerable expense. Such costs can be reduced, however, if the basic building structure provides a reasonably secure physical framework. If it does not, later measures may never provide adequate protection.

Fire Protection

Fire protection is best achieved through proper building construction. However, there will always be combustible equipment and furnishings within the building, so it is necessary to ensure that fire extinguishing equipment is immediately available and that local fire-fighting services can handle fires and other disasters with reasonable facility.

Power

If sufficient electrical power is not available within an existing building, MIS should determine whether it is possible to bring sufficient power into the building and into the areas where it will be needed.

ACTION PLAN

Since it is highly unlikely that an existing site will be satisfactory in all respects (particularly if it was not originally intended to serve as a data center), many companies elect to build new centers. In addition, the time, effort, and expense required for conversion often far exceed those needed to build a new data center. For this reason, the project team should ensure that all possible site alternatives are thoroughly analyzed and compared regarding:
- Current and future requirements
- Cost (initial and ongoing)
- Implementation time
- Professional expertise required

After completing the analysis, the project team should prepare a position paper (along with a graphic presentation if necessary) that identifies and describes each site and indicates the best alternative. All factors substantiating the recommendation should be included in the paper.

Designing the Data Center

Often, selection is a simple process of elimination because many sites under consideration will not satisfy basic criteria (e.g., space or security). When key criteria are met but less essential criteria are not, trade-offs must be made to select a site.

Any site recommendation to senior management should include a complete and detailed implementation plan. Such a plan helps management understand the scope and impact of the project, thus minimizing later "surprises."

Because of the high degree of dedicated effort required, the project design phase cannot begin until full approval is granted for the site. A presentation to senior management can help alter their thinking on key issues and provide wider latitude in site selection.

The following checklist will help MIS to consider the many factors involved in selecting a data center site.

HOW TO USE THE CHECKLIST

The data center manager should check off the appropriate column(s) for each item as follows:

YES— Does conform.
NA— Not applicable.
PAR— Partial. (This column should be checked if there is partial conformity, and a number should be entered in the NOTE column keyed to an explanation on a separate page describing what is meant by partial.) If action is to be taken, the ACT column as well as the PAR column should be checked and a number entered in the NOTE column, keyed to an explanation of what is planned. If action will not be taken, the NO column as well as the PAR column should be checked.
NO— Does not conform. (If no action is to be taken, no other column should be checked. If action is to be taken, the ACT column should also be checked, and a number keyed to an explanation on a separate page should be entered in the NOTE column.
ACT— Action is to be taken. Either the PAR or NO columns should be checked, and a number explained on a separate page should be entered in the NOTE column.
NOTE— A number keyed to an explanation found on a separate page.

BUILDING SITE SELECTION CHECKLIST

1. City _____
2. Address _____
3. Location type: Urban _____ Suburban _____ Industrial complex _____
4. Existing building _____ New building _____ Which floor _____
5. Owned _____ Leased _____ Lease rate _____ Lease term _____
6. Floor space (sq. ft.) _____

MANAGING THE DATA CENTER

	YES	NA	PAR	NO	ACT	NOTE
7. Low risk from environmental threats: (a) Aircraft traffic						
(b) Earthquakes						
(c) Flood						
(d) Hurricane/tornado (flying debris)						
(e) Heavy ice/snow						
(f) Nearby hazardous industry						
(g) High crime rate						
8. Secure utility service entries						
9. Ability to limit/restrict physical access to the data center						
10. Water hardness is not a potential problem						
11. Available multiple-grid commercial power service						
12. Proximity to a telephone company office capable of supporting the required teleprocessing load						
13. Available public transportation						
14. Available parking spaces						
15. Proximity to an adequate labor market to staff the site						
16. EEOC ramifications taken into consideration (if relocating to another site)						

Building Construction

	YES	NA	PAR	NO	ACT	NOTE
17. Compliance with codes and references: (a) OSHA requirements						
(b) Fire Protection (CO_2)						

Designing the Data Center

	YES	NA	PAR	NO	ACT	NOTE
(c) Fire Protection (halon)						
(d) Electronic Computer/DP Equipment						
(e) National Electrical Code						
(f) Air Conditioning						
(g) Steel and concrete construction						
18. Local codes: (a) Structural # _____						
(b) Electrical # _____						
(c) Lighting # _____						
(d) Heating # _____						
(e) Cooling # _____						
(f) Plumbing # _____						
(g) Fire Protection # _____						
(h) Elevators # _____						
19. Special considerations: (a) Loading dock truck-bed height						
(b) Adjustable ramp for loading dock						
(c) Tractor-trailer truck deliveries						
(d) Local ordinances restricting deliveries to building						
(e) Hallways between loading docks and computer room or form and supply storage areas wide enough for a forklift to negotiate corners						
(f) Hallway surface protected from damage when moving supplies and equipment						
(g) Elevators, ramps, doors, and other passageways can accommodate large, heavy equipment						

MANAGING THE DATA CENTER

	YES	NA	PAR	NO	ACT	NOTE
(h) Motor generator (MG) site isolated or acoustically treated to protect personnel against the high-pitched whine produced by MG						
(i) MG and controls located as close to the computer room as practical to eliminate long runs of 400 Hz output power loads						
(j) UPS generators located on the rooftop or in a specially prepared, ventilated area						
(k) Well-ventilated UPS battery area						
(l) Special floor loading for UPS system, water tower, and other heavy equipment						
(m) Airtight computer room or vault if a gas fire-extinguishing agent will be used						

Space Requirements

                                                                         Sq Ft   Sq Ft
                                                                         Present   Future

20. Operations:
    (a) Supervisory and administration
    (b) Computer room*
    (c) Media library (tape and disk)
    (d) Unit record
    (e) Input/Output
    (f) Offline facilities (printers, plotters, COM)
    (g) Data preparation (keying)
    (h) Forms, data, and supplies storage
    (i) Bursting and decollating
    (j) Booking, binding, and distribution
    (k) Customer engineering
    (l) Communications room (modems, test equipment)
    (m) Operator break area
    (n) On/near-site program/data backup storage
    (o) Other _____

    Total operations

*Use total service area when calculating component space. Add space for aisles and input-output carts, and provide a minimum clearance of 42 inches between separated units to permit other equipment to be brought in or removed.

Designing the Data Center

21. Service areas:
    (a) MG area (as required)
    (b) UPS system (batteries and equipment)
    (c) Trash storage/elevator set-off area
    (d) Electrical service room
    (e) Telephone service room
    (f) Halon/CO_2 bottle storage and weighing space
    (g) Other _____
    Total service areas
22. Systems programming:
    (a) Supervisory
    (b) Clerical
    (c) Programmers, no. ____ × ____ sq. ft.
    (d) Analysts, no. ____ × ____ sq. ft.
    (e) On-site documentation files
    (f) System reference library (SRL) manuals
    (g) Other _____
    _____
    Total systems programming
    Grand total space requirements

	YES	NA	PAR	NO	ACT	NOTE
23. Location of computer room: (a) Positive drainage of area under raised floor						
(b) Positive check valve to prevent sewer or other drain backup						
(c) External windows in computer room south, east, and west walls covered with glare-reducing materials to reduce solar heating effect						
(d) External windows can be or are covered with shatter-resistant material						
(e) Watertight structural walls and ceiling of computer room and tape library to prevent damage from water entering from above						
(f) Sunken floor installed to avoid use of ramps leading to computer room						
(g) Form and supply storage areas readily accessible from the printer area						
(h) Water lines under floor for use by computers or related equipment only						

463

MANAGING THE DATA CENTER

	YES	NA	PAR	NO	ACT	NOTE
24. Freight elevators: (a) Door opening width minimum 48 inches						
(b) Door opening height minimum 90 inches						
(c) Portion of elevator ceiling is removable to accommodate extra-long items (e.g., pipes, conduits)						
(d) Weight capacity can handle heaviest unit plus safety factor (e.g., 4,500-lb. tape vault)						
(e) Floor area accommodates items 72 inches by 48 inches						
(f) Floor surface withstands marring by steel rollers on freight-handling equipment						
(g) If designing a new building, elevator manufacturers are involved early in planning						
(h) Adequate space for loading, unloading, and temporary storage						

Power

                                          kVA Requirements
                                      Present   Future

25. Capacities required:
    (a) Computer (kVA)
    (b) System MG
    (c) Ancillary equipment
        (1) Air conditioning
        (2) Lights
        (3) Data sets
        (4) Pumps
        (5) Water conditioning
    (d) Future expansion
    (e) Source equipment
        (1) Separate transformer
        (2) MG
        (3) UPS
        (4) Engine generator
        (5) Gas turbine
    (f) Total power requirements

Designing the Data Center

	YES	NA	PAR	NO	ACT	NOTE
26. Regulation: (a) Outages (1) Duration (time)						
(2) Frequency						
(b) Disturbances (1) Light flicker						
(2) Other (e.g., motors, welders)						
(c) Brownout/low voltage						
(d) Lightning						
(e) Electrical utility's performance data (interruptions) checked						
(f) Power monitor						
(g) Starting motors (dip in power)						
27. Distribution: (a) Voltage (208/230)						
(b) Separate feeder (1) Sized for expansion						
(c) Adequate number of circuit breakers						
(d) Receptacles ordered						
(e) Isolated equipment ground						
(f) Emergency power-off						
(g) Computer system MG wiring						
(h) Computer system MG backup						
(i) Lightning arrestor						
(j) Labeled circuit breakers and power cables/cord						
(k) Fuel supply for engine generators						
(l) Monitor for all three phases						

MANAGING THE DATA CENTER

	YES	NA	PAR	NO	ACT	NOTE
(m) Cable raceways						
(n) Ground fault breakers						
(o) Labeled signal cables						
28. Water services: (a) Hot and cold water for washrooms, maintenance sinks, and drinking fountains						
(b) Hot water approximately 140° available for humidifiers serving the data center (domestic hot water can serve this purpose)						
(c) Trapped floor drains under raised floor (preferred locations are under water-using CPUs or CDUs as well as under room conditioner)						

Process Cooling

	YES	NA	PAR	NO	ACT	NOTE
29. Equipment location and security: (a) Outside heat exchanger (dry coolers or cooling towers) on roof or within building						
(b) Locked quarters for chillers, pumps, and related equipment						
(c) Process cooling units within computer room						
(d) Disconnect emergency shutoff accessible to authorized personnel						
30. Design criteria and load calculations: (a) Recommended temperature and humidity in installation planning manual checked						
(b) 80 percent maximum relative humidity under floor						
(c) Outside heat exchanger selected for worst possible operating conditions						

Designing the Data Center

	YES	NA	PAR	NO	ACT	NOTE
(d) Maximum outside air quantity of 15 cubic feet per minute per person						
(e) 30 percent added to total load to accommodate expansion						
(f) Minimum chilled water temperature of 48°						
(g) Comfortable design conditions in the keypunch area						
(h) Tape library, card storage same design conditions as computer room						
(i) Under-floor air distribution						
(j) Glycol heat recovery						
31. System and equipment selection: (a) Equipment selected to accommodate future cooling load						
(b) Redundancy to avoid downtime						
(c) Evaporate pad or steam humidifiers						
(d) Year-round operation for all equipment						
(e) Glycol for reliability and energy conservation						
(f) Equipment failure alarm warning						
(g) In-room water chillers for CDUs and CPUs						

Section VIII
Data Base Management

Although the concept of data base management was developed more than 20 years ago, only recently have most organizations learned how to begin to manage data. The realization that data is a corporate asset likewise goes back about 15 years, and still not all of us treat this asset with the same respect and control that we give to, say, the corporate physical inventory.

Planning for the data base environment involves many complex management issues. Although energy is usually focused on technical considerations, management and organizational issues also require planning and coordination. These issues frequently are given little more than cursory attention, but the strategy for their identification, definition, and implementation forms the framework for any data base planning effort. Chapter VIII-1, "The Manager's Role in Data Bases," discusses the management, planning, and organizational issues related to establishing a data base environment within an organization.

Corporations that invest huge sums to gather data should insist that the investment be properly managed. Data bases must provide accessible, timely, and accurate data that decision makers can translate into useful information. Chapter VIII-2, "Controlling the DB Environment," presents basic data resource management principles and recommends specific activities for managing information resources more effectively.

Data bases are often designed as all-encompassing files for one group of related applications. What might represent the optimum use of the data base environment—to store and control an organization's operational and managerial data in its entirety—is often ignored. The decision to centralize or decentralize the data base environment demands serious consideration. Each form offers advantages and disadvantages, and the reasons for choosing one over another are numerous and complex. Chapter VIII-3, "Centralized Versus Decentralized Data Bases," presents the advantages and disadvantages of each form; it also discusses the role of the data dictionary and the data administrator.

As today's business shifts from an environment dominated by manufacturing to one dominated by information, corporate executives must concentrate on the quality of their information as well as on the quality of their products. Because information is a valuable corporate asset, businesses must manage their information resources with the same rigor as more tangible assets, such as personnel, inventory, and equipment. Chapter VIII-4, "Improving the Quality of Data," examines the causes of erroneous corporate information and discusses the software tools that can improve data accuracy.

A second shift in business today is one from tightly controlled information processing resources to open use of most resources by the user community. Supporting this new environment are powerful software tools and new concepts. One group of tools and concepts concerns relational data bases. Relational data base systems offer the user simple, high-level data base processing. These systems incorporate features that complement network and hierarchical systems, providing data structures that are easy to understand and that offer increased data independence. Chapter VIII-5, "An Introduction to Relational Data Bases," examines the relational data base concept and presents a comprehensive evaluation of the relational approach.

VIII-1

The Manager's Role in Data Bases

Martin E. Modell

INTRODUCTION

Briefly stated, the strategy for establishing a data base environment within an organization must address the following areas:
- The conceptual difference between data and information
- The different kinds of data usage and the requirements of their various environments
- The people and organizational problems and issues arising when one or more DBMS packages are installed in a firm
- The costs and benefits of a data base environment
- The place of a data base in the evolution of the corporate MIS function
- The impact of data base technology and facilities on the existing development and user environment
- The criteria for DBMS selection.

DATA VERSUS INFORMATION

The orderly compilation, cataloging, and storage of transactions (data) generated as a result of doing business form the basis of a firm's files. In its broadest sense, this compilation of data, comprising the records of the firm, can be called the company data base. In other words, it represents the company memory, and only data properly stored, processed, indexed, and cross-referenced can be remembered.

Organizations are slowly learning to think of their data as a valuable resource; some companies could hardly function effectively—if they could function at all—without access to their data files. Also, there is a growing recognition that rapid and complete access to timely, accurate data can facilitate corporate growth and prosperity.

With the preceding discussion in mind, some formal definitions will now be presented:

Data, the plural form of the Latin word *datum,* meaning fact, implies multiple facts.

A data base, then, is a base of facts—an ordered, validated, edited, and

DATA BASE MANAGEMENT

indexed file of the firm. A data base brings together identical, similar, and related data, storing it for future use.

A data base management system is a package of computer programs for the automated definition, creation, manipulation, and maintenance of a firm's files. In addition, a DBMS provides the ability to structure the data and define, create, and maintain the interrelationships among the various data aggregates.

Information is data that has been processed, analyzed, or derived. Therefore, information can be generated from a data base, but a data base does not contain information per se.

An information base is an organized, stored base of information.

An information management system is a facility that allows users to derive information from data or from wherever information is stored. Succinctly, then, data is fact; information is usually opinion. Data is objective; information is subjective. Data is input; information is output. Data is permanent; information is transitory.

DATA ENVIRONMENT

An environment in which users share common data implies centralized control or coordination, and this can cause many organizational problems. "Who is the custodian of the data?" is an old, but still valid, question illustrating these problems. Typically, one organizational function originates data, one maintains it, another relies on it for day-to-day operations, and yet another determines its deletion from company files. These functions may be part of, and may possibly be shared by, many different corporate departments, which prompts other questions: Who may authorize access to the data? Who may authorize a change or modification?

Thus, the new organizational relationships and requirements, as well as the new management approaches, that develop when building a data base environment must be addressed within the context of the existing corporate culture.

Data as a Resource

The value of data to corporate management is determined partially by the ease with which it can be retrieved, processed, and presented as a decision-making tool. The value of data also depends heavily on the accuracy and currency of its content and on the user's ability to assemble it into meaningful categories and to relate those categories to one another.

Because a firm's data is a business resource, it must be managed as one. Traditional resource management techniques and organizational units only partially address this task; new methodologies, procedures, and organizational structures must be developed. To harness this resource, a firm must understand the current environment, identify the proposed environment, and define the steps to reach the desired end. Most important, management must decide on the desired environment and how it should differ from current operations. In addition, management must commit the necessary corporate resources and attention to achieving a smooth migration.

OPERATIONAL VERSUS INFORMATIONAL DATA

One of the primary data management issues facing corporate decision makers is the use of data within the organization. Two distinctly different kinds of data support two distinctly different functional roles. These functions can be identified as operational and informational, and management must view and treat the two classes of data differently.

When the levels of data are illustrated on the classical organizational structure pyramid (see Figure 1), the distinction becomes clear. The operational units are at the lowest level, with informational units at the next level, and decision support at the highest level. In operational units, the functions are vertical and the focus of data is limited to a specific organizational segment. Systems at this level are developed by vendors on a client-specific basis, and the data is used to facilitate and control the firm's daily business transactions. Most corporate systems are developed at this level because these systems, customized to the user's needs, are usually controlled by that user.

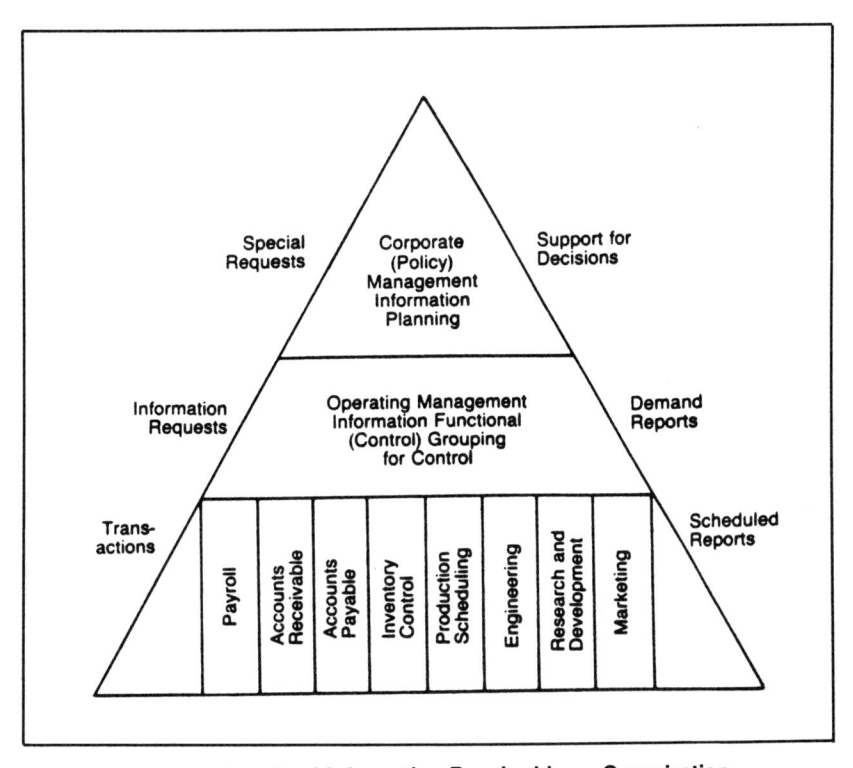

Figure 1. Levels of Information Required in an Organization

Organizational Differences

In an organization in which the systems are well developed but the organization is in the expansion phase of its growth,[1] management's information needs are usually satisfied by summaries of reports developed originally for

DATA BASE MANAGEMENT

use by operational personnel, containing data extracted from operational files.

Operational systems support the lowest level of the pyramid and are transaction based, cyclically processed, usually batch oriented, and operated in a current time frame—transactions are accumulated and processed on a periodic basis. The files created from those transactions represent the data accumulated during the period and are designed for processing expediency rather than for the production of information. Operational systems are vertical in nature and are built to support a particular function; each function is traditionally called an application.

Informational systems are more broadly based, more horizontal in nature, and usually derived from the firm's operational files. Although applications exist within informational systems, they are geared toward report generation rather than processing of data. Informational systems arrange existing data to provide the organization's control, coordination, and planning functions with business information. These systems are retrospective because they are concerned with past occurrences and predictive because they extrapolate past events into future trends. Informational systems data tends to be less precision dependent and more statistically oriented—the focus is on the entire data population, samples, or specific segments rather than individual occurrences in the data population.

A third category of systems, both horizontal (informational) and vertical (operational) in nature, can be classified as administrative systems. These include systems, usually categorized as overhead, that support the organization as a functioning unit. The most common examples of these administrative systems are personnel (human resources), financial (budgeting), and accounting systems (general ledger). These systems support planning, management, and control, rather than a specific business aspect of the firm.

Differences in Data Usage

Operational systems support processing needs. Transactions resulting from business operations must be verified, validated, and processed. These transactions, or inputs, should be aggregated and organized to obtain a consolidated view of the data. Management also considers all customer data (the sum of all customer transactions) and all order data (the sum of all order transactions) as units. Files are built as convenient places to segregate and record the business data. No single transaction or transaction type shows the entire customer profile or order history; the aggregate is necessary.

Processing is oriented toward identification, validation, application, and storage of those transactions, much the same as though no automation were applied. Reporting is accomplished by collecting related transactions and presenting them in a meaningful form depicting their status, trend, and condition. Other operational reports are referential in nature—trial balances, log sheets, error reports, exception reports, and control reports. Because of their origin in the firm's transactions and the periodic nature of their processing, the data bases or files in operational systems are usually consistent within the boundaries of an application system, but not necessarily with other application systems.

Informational systems, arising in part from operational systems files, are not part of the process support mechanism; all data within these systems has been processed elsewhere. Extractive and derivative in nature, informational systems attempt to match and integrate data from a variety of sources. They are query driven, structured around logical business and data models of the firm (or firm segments) and depict and capture data relationships rather than transaction status. They are statistically organized to provide trend, status, and condition views of multiple functions and their interactions. Unlike operational systems that count widgets, informational systems provide information about the relationship between the number of widgets counted and the amount of raw material to make them.

Although data accuracy is never unimportant in any environment, it is less important in informational environments because they represent ex post facto information and focus on groups, classes, or categories of units rather than on single units. This distinction is noteworthy because informational systems data is usually read-only, and thus not changeable.

Now that the distinctions among operational, informational, and administrative systems are more clearly defined, it becomes evident that an organization needs perhaps three distinct systems: an operational system to serve the transactional data and processing needs of the users, an administrative system to support the staff, and an informational system to serve management.

MANAGEMENT INFORMATION SYSTEMS

A management information system (MIS) is created to provide management with the information it needs, on time and in the proper format. The greatest problem in the creation of an MIS stems from the traditional functional approach to DP. The systems create specialized files, but no single file is sufficient to answer more than simple queries. Answering complex questions requires retrieving multiple files, extracting information, and creating another file, which then must be processed as required.

An MIS or decision support system (DSS) implies that although individual functional areas may have their separate systems and files, corporate needs require a certain level of data aggregation and integration. This allows upper management to view the corporate functional system from an organizational level. Thus, the unifying thread of an MIS is not the fact that it is a single system serving all, but rather that the data, which acts as the base for all parts, is common to all who need information.

The integration is really a consolidation of all like elements of data—those related to the same subject. For example, an organization with files of purchase orders, invoices, payments, inventory, receiving, and vendor information could consolidate these files into a material management data base in which all data related to that function would reside as an integrated whole, with data segregated and organized according to a logical model, reflecting the natural aggregates of data and the relationships that exist among them. Thus, MIS can be transformed into corporate information systems (CIS) founded on the data base approach (see Figure 2). The key to understanding the design criteria for a CIS is to recognize that it is data driven and not process or function driven—it is based on a data model, not a process model.

DATA BASE MANAGEMENT

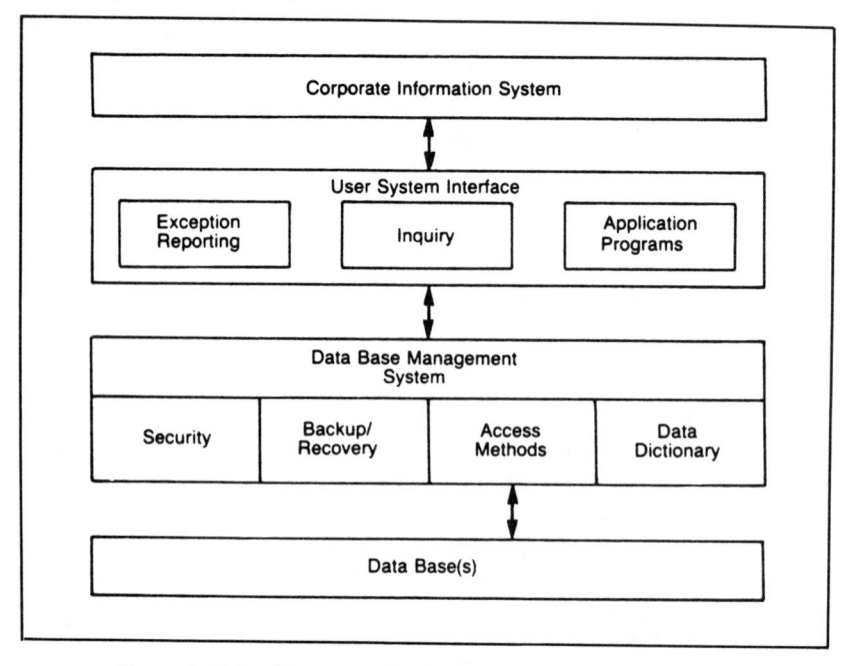

Figure 2. Major Elements of a Corporate Information System

MULTIPLE MANAGEMENT LEVELS

All managers must understand the purpose of their organization—its policies, programs, plans, and goals. Managers differ, however, in their individual informational requirements, the ways they view information, their analytical approaches to using it, and their conceptual organization of relevant facts.

Another factor complicating the management of information is the organizational level of the individual manager (see Figure 1). A manager at the lower operating levels needs data to make daily operating decisions. At the upper levels of management, however, both data and information are needed to support long-range planning and policy decisions. Managers at other organizational levels also require information in varying degrees of detail. In addition, they must be able to probe the corporate data base to answer questions, especially ones that are vague or poorly defined when first posed. The success of management information systems thus depends on methodologies that produce:
- A common data base
- A consistent set of data definitions that are acceptable throughout the organization
- A flexible data organization able to support both structured and unstructured queries.

Organizational Impact

As the organization evolves technically, the people constituting the organization—and their interactions that define the organizational structure—change to adapt and function effectively in the new environments. New techniques, methodologies, and modes of thinking also develop. The firm's employees need to be trained, not only in the mechanics of the new program packages but also in the concepts behind its design. The centralization of data and the centralized generation and dissemination of information require new organizations for control and support.

The evolving concept of separate data resource management (DRM) functions for operational systems and information resource management (IRM) functions for informational systems dictates that these units, within their respective spheres, manage the data and information resources. Each unit is responsible for its own architectural and administrative functions—data administration, information administration, data base administration, and information center administration. The technical and administrative specialists constituting the DRM and IRM functions are also charged with developing and propagating the new methodologies and techniques of data and information management.

The responsibilities of these groups (in firms with more than one control point), vary from firm to firm. If management commitment and direction are present, and the lower organizational levels are receptive, these groups can assume an authoritative role and exert considerable control over data and information management. This control, and its implicit coordinating ability, ensures a smooth transition to a data base environment.

Aside from their technical expertise, these groups traditionally have had an overview of all the firm's systems and can identify their points of commonality and integration. Through their architectural functions, they can create the models or blueprints for the integration of the firm's systems. These groups should focus the firm's development efforts and recommend the optimal scheduling of development plans to achieve the maximum overall benefit.

The Role of Data Administration

Within integrated data base and information environments, input data must be commonly defined and consistently organized. Transactions must be designed so that they enter the system once and update all of the requisite data base records. In addition, data such as part numbers and customer or employee identification codes must be standardized. This eliminates duplicate data storage and introduces data integration and integrity.

The management of data can be compared with the management of finances—as there is a controller to manage money, there must be an administrator to manage data. Further, the controller uses ledgers, balance sheets, statements, and journals to record and control financial items; the administrator correspondingly uses function maps, logical designs, data flow analysis, source and use analysis, documentation, and dictionaries to control and structure data items.

Because each element of data has a source, a custodian, and a user, the data administration function must deal with the following questions:
- If most DP systems serve the needs of operating supervisors, and if most

DATA BASE MANAGEMENT

information systems are designed to serve middle and senior management, how can operational and informational data bases be structured and integrated to satisfy the information needs of all organizational levels?
- Can a single data base be structured to meet the needs of multiple levels, or must different data bases be created for each horizontal level?
- Can different functional areas share a common data base?
- Can a single data base supply the information needed by managers with diverse functions, or must separate data bases be designed for each functional area?
- Should expensive external data be incorporated into the data base to satisfy upper-level management information needs?
- Can the completeness, timeliness, and accuracy of external data be ensured?
- Can suitable flexibility to meet varying data requirements be built into the logical data structures underlying the data base?

To address these and other questions, the various forms that a data base assumes in a specific firm must be defined along with the components that are developed (either for many different data bases, each one serving a particular functional unit, or for one data base serving all parts of the organization). In this context, the impact of each of these designs on the organization must be evaluated.

This design evaluation should not be performed from the perspective of the software that makes the data base implementation possible. Also, it should not deal with the hardware and personnel problems inherent in a data base environment; instead, the evaluation should focus on the following concerns:
- Defining the data base requirements
- Designing the structure
- Specifying the degree of sharing that will occur
- Protecting the data base.

DBMS SELECTION

Once the organization has determined which form of data base environment it will develop (operational, informational, administrative, or hybrid), the specifications should be developed. The determination is based largely on the age of the organization's current application systems and the extent of their development. For example, there is little need to replace, or refurbish, relatively new applications that use fourth-generation techniques.

Given the need for migration to a data base environment, however, it is advisable to select a DBMS (and its accompanying software) based on the functional needs of the environment rather than technical criteria.

The functional needs of a high-volume, transaction-oriented, and processing environment (operational) differ from those of a query-driven, ad hoc, and analytical environment (informational). Also, informational environments must be more user friendly than operational environments. Finally, the development time frames of each environment are decidedly different. While development cycles of operational systems, are usually preceded by extensive analysis, are well defined, and require complex procedural programming, informational systems are developed in short time frames (measured in weeks, days, or sometimes hours) and iterative in nature (the processes change until the desired results are achieved).

Each environment requires different tools for effective operation. DBMS selection should focus on the range, flexibility, and functionality of the tools available for each DBMS.

Although capacity and performance criteria must be examined by the technical staff, management must examine the impact other factors have on productivity. These factors include: ease of training the existing staff to use the new package; availability and cost of training; availability of specialized, highly trained technical personnel to support the software if needed; vendor support availability and reliability; frequency and impact of vendor software changes; availability and cost of staff replacements and additions; and, perhaps most important, amount of support for the selected DBMS available from additional vendors or other industry sources.

COST/BENEFIT ANALYSIS

The final issue for management to consider is cost. This analysis will consider cost trends, direct and indirect costs, and other cost/benefit relationships and considerations.

Cost Trends

Hardware costs, on the whole, have been decreasing, while personnel costs have been increasing. In addition, while software costs have been going up, productivity improvements obtained from using software have risen even more sharply.

A cursory analysis of these trends reveals that, for the foreseeable future, any effort to reduce people costs will provide overall organizational benefits. In addition, as more development is performed by the software, the overall cost of development will go down. The rising use of user-friendly software will reduce the need for costly development staff even further. It must be realized, however, that use of this new software, while slowing standard development cost increases, has a dramatic effect on the cost of the DRM and IRM specialist.

Direct and Indirect Costs

Although direct and indirect costs depend on the individual installation, the following generalizations can be made:
- Any program reducing ongoing or recurring costs should be considered.
- General and flexible software benefits the widest range of users and results in the lowest per-user cost.
- If most of the time spent completing a project is devoted to analysis rather than implementation, post-installation maintenance will be reduced substantially.
- The higher the level of data integration and commonality, the lower the overall cost of software and application development.

DATA BASE MANAGEMENT

Other Cost Considerations

Although the direct costs of any acquisition can be easily examined, other costs may be harder to identify and analyze. These include lost-productivity costs incurred during the start-up, learning, and training periods; conversion costs of modifying existing systems to operate from data bases; and lost-opportunity costs resulting when resources are diverted from new development into replacement, enhancement, and refurbishment.

Implicit in the development of common data sources and storage is the concept of sharing the costs of their definition, creation, development, and maintenance throughout the entire user community. Although the one-time cost of developing a common data base may be greater, it is shared among more users, will remain in place longer, and will result in lower per-unit costs for each user. In addition, the burden of file design and control shifts from the development staff to the DRM or IRM staff, allowing more analytical and development time to serve user needs.

ACTION PLAN

The acquisition and implementation of a data base or information base environment cannot be made solely on technical considerations; certain business trade-offs must be made. Management must understand the impact and implications of such a decision and make significant contributions to the decision process at all levels.

Reference

1. C.F. Gibson and R.L. Nolan, "Managing the Four Stages of EDP Growth," *Harvard Business Review*, 52 (January 1974): 483–500.

Bibliography

Davis, G. *Management Information Systems*. New York: McGraw-Hill, 1974.

Sanders, D.H. *Computers and Management in a Changing Society*, 2nd ed. New York: McGraw-Hill, 1974.

"Selection and Acquisition of Data Base Management Systems." A report prepared by the members of the CODASYL Systems Committee, New York: ACM, 1976.

Sibley, E.H. "The Development of Data Base Technology." *Computing Surveys* 8 (March 1976): 1–5.

VIII-2
Controlling the DB Environment
Ian A. Gilhooley

INTRODUCTION

Today's highly competitive business climate, characterized by more educated consumers and shorter product cycles, forces companies to be information driven. Corporate decision makers derive information by analyzing raw data—gathered internally or externally—in a particular business context. Therefore, to be successful, a company must ensure that this raw data is captured and readily available for analysis in various forms. If such data is not easily accessible, various levels of support must be built before meaningful information can be obtained.

Generally, a company's base of data remains relatively stable as long as the company remains in the same line of business. However, the type and volume of required information changes. Over time, decision makers may be able to discern trends in this information and reach the higher levels of data interpretation: knowledge and understanding. At the knowledge level of data interpretation, decision makers have enough information to observe trends. At the understanding level, decision makers have enough knowledge of predict trends with reasonable certainty and within acceptable margins of error. Figure 1 shows the various levels of data interpretation graphically.

Today's computer systems provide information, they do not make decisions. Human intervention is required for the user to attain the higher levels of data interpretation (i.e., knowledge and understanding) illustrated in Figure 1. Decision support systems and expert systems are an attempt to reach the knowledge level of data interpretation with minimal human intervention. The industry is many years away, however, from artificial intelligence systems that truly understand a particular situation. The data base manager (DBM) is responsible for managing corporate data resources so that they are easily accessible and provide accurate, timely information. This enables decision makers to reach the knowledge and understanding levels of data interpretation needed in today's competitive business environment. This article examines the management principles and practices that must be in place to facilitate this process.

DATA RESOURCE MANAGEMENT

Data resource management is the term used to describe the methods of

DATA BASE MANAGEMENT

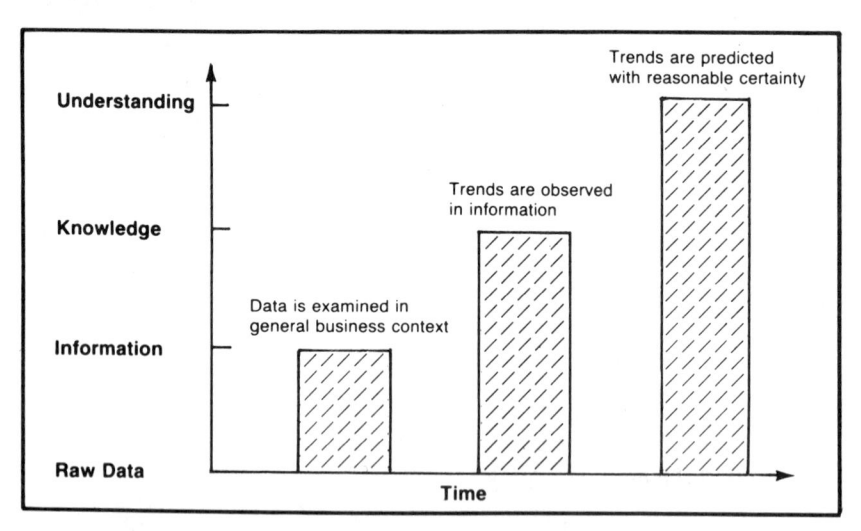

Figure 1. Levels of Data Interpretation

managing the corporate data resource so it provides the required information in the most effective manner. The three principles of effective data resource management are discussed in the following paragraphs.

Computer Systems Development Must Focus on the Data. The traditional approach to developing computer systems focuses on the processes to be performed, particularly with operational-type systems. However, process-oriented system designs generally do not fulfill subsequent tactical or strategic information needs. In many cases, information requests go unanswered because either the source data does not exist or custom building software that supports ad hoc inquiries is too costly and time-consuming. This inability to yield complete, timely, and accurate information is a major disadvantage of many conventional systems. The data resource management approach overcomes this limitation by focusing on data and information requirements during systems planning and building. Data items are incorporated into a corporate data model that is reflected—typically through an integrated data dictionary—in the application systems and inquiry routines written to convert this data into information.

Data Must be Separated From Its Uses. This principle extends the idea of focusing on the data rather than individual processes. Data base management systems (DBMSs) have always used data independence as a major selling point, but until recently, the data structures in many DBMSs were somewhat inflexible. However, emerging commercial relational and relational-like DBMSs show great promise in making data independence a reality.

Data Must Be Structured For Varied Access. Once the data is separated from specific applications, various applications can view the data base according to their specific needs. Therefore, the logical view of data as presented in the corporate data model and data dictionary can be quite different from the physical presentation and organization of the data on computer-readable media. Data access methods not only must be flexible but also must meet acceptable performance criteria.

MANAGING THE CORPORATE DATA BASE

Effective management of the corporate data base requires that the following activities be addressed consistently and logically:
- Planning—The corporate data base must be planned according to the specific needs of the company.
- Organization—A data driven company requires new organizational entities.
- Acquisition—Once the corporate data base has been planned, the needed data must be acquired.
- Maintenance and Control—The data in the corporate data base must be securely, accurately, and completely maintained. In addition, proper control must be exercised over access to the data base. Data ownership, use, and custodianship issues must also be addressed.
- Usage—The corporate data base must be available to all authorized users in the company.

These data management activities are discussed in the following sections.

Planning

The information used in a company generally falls into two categories—external and internal. Table 1 lists the types of information that typically constitute each category. Some of this information, particularly external information, cannot be computerized—at least not by traditional methods.

Table 1. Types of Information

External	Internal
Economic	Financial
Political	Products and Services
Social	Productivity Analysis
Market Condition	Precedents
Competitive	Interdepartmental Correspondence
Noncompetitive	
Fiscal	Customer
Technological	

The wide distribution of corporate data adds to the problem of managing it. End-user computing and the proliferation of microcomputers have spread corporate data across many different data bases, each with its own format, update rules, and state of completeness. Although end-user computing has many benefits and should be encouraged, it must also be controlled. Otherwise, any problems with data integrity, data duplication, data maintenance, and availability are compounded.

Planning entails the preparation of a corporate data model. This is best achieved through interviews with the department heads of each functional area in the company. These managers should be asked to determine what data influences their functional areas and what information is required to suc-

DATA BASE MANAGEMENT

cessfully operate and manage their departments. After all the interviews are completed, the collection of data items must be analyzed and distilled into a model that can be understood, presented, and accepted by corporate management. This analysis should include a determination of the source of the data as well as its characteristics and interrelationships with other data items. This corporate data model must then be compared with currently held and maintained data. The difference between what is currently available and what is ultimately required determines what data must be collected.

Organization

There are two distinct aspects of organizing the corporate data base. The first is the business aspect: identifying which data is relevant to the company, its source and method of capture, and the interrelationships among data items. The second is the technical aspect: storing data on computer-readable media in a form readily accessible by the corporate decision makers. The business tasks of organizing the corporate data base require the creation of two organizational entities: the relatively new chief information officer (CIO) position[1] and the more traditional data administration function.

The Chief Information Officer. The CIO is the executive in charge of the information systems department and is responsible for formulating an information strategy that includes all systems development, computer operations, and communications planning and operation. This individual must know the business and manage information technology in the best interests of the company. The CIO's title and reporting relationships (the CIO usually reports directly to the chief operating officer) emphasize the importance of delivering corporate information where needed and the data management activities required to produce this information.

The Data Administration Function. Data administration links computer systems and the business functions they are designed to serve. The group responsible for data administration builds and maintains the corporate data model. A properly constructed data model places the systems to be developed into a proper business perspective. This model is also instrumental in the preparation of the information systems department's strategic plan.

The technical tasks of managing the corporate data base are performed by the data base administration function. This group translates the logical view of the corporate data model (as developed by the data administrator) into a physical form on computer-readable media while still providing the required business functionality. The data base administration group is also concerned with the integrity of the data contained in the data base, performance issues relating to data access, and the various security issues associated with the data base, including backup and recovery.

The four organizational groups involved in the development of any computer system are:
- The data administration—Responsible for developing and maintaining the integrity of the logical view of the corporate data base and, typically, the custodianship of the data dictionary

- The systems development group—Responsible for developing the logic and building the system that turns data into information
- The data base administration—Responsible for the physical representation of the data base, the performance of the production data base, and data security
- Computer operations—Responsible for systems operations and monitoring

These responsibilities must be clearly understood by the four groups involved. The development methodology in use also must be modified to reflect these split responsibilities. The implications of data resource management on the traditional approach to systems development are not discussed in this article. However, Figure 2 presents an overview of the responsibilities and interactions of these groups during a data base development life cycle and its subsequent operation in a production environment.

Acquisition. In a data driven organization, information strategy is derived from the corporate data model. Systems planned for development should provide information or a level of service that was previously unavailable. In a typical systems development project, a major part of the effort is spent in acquiring and storing the data that is used to produce the required information.

Although data analysis and design is defined as a separate activity in the definition of data resource management, application programs to collect and validate data items and add them to the appropriate data base must still be written. The interactions among systems development, data administration, and data base administration must be in place to ensure that the corporate data base effectively acquires data.

Certain types of information are not usually derived from data bases and designed as input to application programs (for example, such external information as political and social climate). However, this textual information is no less important to the corporate data model than the factual information, which is the natural product of application systems. Therefore, this external information must be made available in a form readily accessible by the users. For example, electronic mail and corporate bulletin boards are used by many progressive companies to capture such information and deliver it throughout the organization. Through proper archival procedures, external information can be preserved indefinitely and can thus enable decision makers to perform trend and regression analyses.

Maintenance and Control

Maintenance tasks include making changes to the corporate data model, reflecting these changes in the data dictionary, and properly communicating changes to all users who must know the model's current status. Given the degree of data independence that can be achieved in today's DBMSs, changes to the data base should not necessitate changes to application programs. However, the addition of new data items and changes or deletions to existing data items must be controlled as rigorously as changes to application systems. That is, the change control principles applied to application pro-

DATA BASE MANAGEMENT

Development Phase	Phase Description	Interactions
System Definition	Preliminary identification of the systems to be developed. System definitions are produced as a result of developing the information strategy.	System definitions emanate from the development of an information strategy and corporate data model. This strategy is developed by the CIO in conjunction with the managers of system development and data administration.
Feasibility Study	Detailed study on the cost and benefits of developing the new system.	This development phase is carried out by the systems development group. Approval to proceed to the next phase must be obtained from the DP steering committee.
Detailed Design	Expansion of the general design to the point where programming and procedure development can begin.	Systems development manages this development phase. However, a data analyst is assigned from data administration for as much time as is necessary to define the data elements and structures and to modify and document the test version of the data dictionary and corporate data model. Approval of the detailed design must be received from data base administration, computer operations, and data administration before proceeding to the next phase.
Program and Procedure Development	Development and testing of all computer programs and manual procedures (i.e., develop the total system).	This phase belongs almost exclusively to systems development. However, there will probably be periodic interaction with the data analyst if changes to data definitions are required.
Acceptance Testing	Independent testing of the entire system to ensure that it is acceptable to the users and meets all operational requirements.	Data base administration, computer operations, and the users are involved in this phase. All parties must sign off before the introduction of the system into production.
Implementation	Controlled migration of the system from the test environment to the production environment.	The move from test to production involves computer operations and data administration. Computer operations moves all object and source code into production. Data administration updates the production data dictionary and corporate data model.

Figure 2. **Responsibilities and Interactions in a Data-Driven Development Environment**

grams—segregation of duties, proper testing and migration procedures, and a documented audit trail—must be applied to changes in data definitions used by these programs. Before the separation of programs and data, the data definitions were embedded in the programs, and controlling changes to the programs meant controlling changes to the data definitions. These control proce-

DB Environment

dures no longer apply because data definitions are maintained externally from individual application programs.

Data security issues (e.g., preventing accidental and intentional unauthorized disclosure, modification, or destruction of data) are critical in data driven organizations. The data is used and relied on by all corporate users, including high-level decision makers. Procedures must be established that define what level of access an individual should be granted (e.g., read-only, read and update, or delete authorization). Unauthorized access must be detected and reported. The cause of the infraction also must be determined, and action taken to prevent its reoccurrence.

The distinction must be made between data owners (i.e., those with update authority) and data users (i.e., those with read-only access or limited update authority). The computer operations group is the custodian of all data. This group must ensure that proper monitoring is performed and that backup and recovery procedures are in place and functioning. The data administrator should also have sufficient authority to arbitrate any ownership disputes between rival users.

Maintenance and control activities should also monitor system performance and the time required to access needed data items. The data base administration group should monitor system performance and take whatever corrective action is needed to provide an adequate level of response to users or systems requiring access to particular data items.

Usage

Procedures that clearly define how to use the data base must be established. First, potential users must know what data exists. Then, tools must be provided to enable users to easily access selected data items. For example, query languages that provide flexible data base access and allow what-if questions to be presented and answered are implemented in many companies. Another area of great potential is the ability to interface selected data items with business software tools (e.g., spreadsheet applications and trend analyzers). These interfaces provide users with more meaningful presentations of the extracted information.

The delivery vehicle used to bring the data to the users must also be considered. Many companies have established information centers to provide a user-friendly environment for data access. This access may be provided through interactive query languages that enable users to view results online or through batch report generators that enable users to obtain preformatted printed reports.

Downloading segments of the data base to a microcomputer is another method of information delivery that is becoming more common. The microcomputer environment typically provides the user with interactive access to the data as well as easy-to-use and powerful software. With the continuing emergence of local area networks (LANs), more and more data will be downloaded to microcomputers for use by the end-user community.

DATA BASE MANAGEMENT

ACTION PLAN

To improve the management of corporate information resources, the DBM and the organization as a whole should use the following guidelines:
1. A corporate data model should be prepared based on the information needs of the company's decision makers.
2. The data base function should be reorganized to facilitate its role of delivering corporate information as needed.
3. The data needed to provide decision-making information must be identified, captured, and made accessible to users.
4. Proper change control, data security, access control, and performance monitoring procedures should be established.
5. Users must be provided with tools for accessing corporate data such as query interface languages and business application software. Vehicles that deliver data to the user, such as information centers and LANs, should also be considered.

Reference

1. "The Chief Information Officer Role," *EDP Analyzer* 22 (November 1984): 1–12.

VIII-3
Centralized Versus Decentralized Data Bases
Martin E. Modell

INTRODUCTION

One of the first questions addressed during the planning and implementation phases of a migration to a data base environment is whether that environment will, or should be, centralized or decentralized. A clear and complete description and definition of each type of environment for the sake of comparison and analysis is necessary to answer this question. The planner needs the parameters of each to make an intelligent choice.

The determination depends on many factors; most important is the number of discrete data models that can be developed for the organization. Each data model reflects data entities and their relationships for the organization or a segment of it. Decentralization differs from distribution and distributed data. The key to the centralization/decentralization decision is found in the data modeling process.

This chapter defines, describes, and contrasts centralization and decentralization. The organization's environment and not the aggregate of the applications is the perspective presented. The data base is examined not as a file or even a set of files, but rather as that base of data the organization must use to service its various functioning units.

DEFINING CENTRALIZED AND DECENTRALIZED DATA BASES

A data base can be characterized as follows:
- It is an organized collection of data that services the firm or firm segment.
- It includes all entities and all relationships.
- It may be one file or multiple files.
- It is the common data repository.
- For each organization segment there is one data base. The number of data bases within the overall organization is determined by the number of distinct data models that can be developed for the organization.

Both centralized and decentralized data bases can be geographically dispersed or physically contiguous. When an organization maintains more than one data base, and those data bases are not linked in some manner, they are

DATA BASE MANAGEMENT

decentralized. When the corporate data base has multiple segments, and they are linked in some manner so that information passes between them or so that portions of the common data can be at each node, then they are centralized but distributed.

MANAGEMENT LEVELS

Robert Anthony describes three levels of management in his book *Planning and Control Systems: A Framework for Analysis.* They are:
- Strategic planning—Determines the objectives of the organization, changes these objectives, determines the resources needed to obtain these objectives, and determines the policies that are to govern the acquisition, use, and disposition of those resources.
- Management and control—Ensures that resources are obtained and used to effectively accomplish the organization's objectives.
- Operational control—Ensures that the specific tasks are executed effectively and efficiently.

Anthony represents these levels in a pyramid with operations at the base and strategy at the apex (see Figure 1). In the centralized organization, an interchange of data takes place between all units on each level and between levels. A homogeneous data model can be constructed to represent the uses, relationships, and flow of data within the organization. This model can be constructed regardless of the geographic location of the individual functional units.

In a decentralized environment, Anthony's model would appear differently (see Figure 2). Multiple discrete data models can be constructed, thus implying different sources, uses, descriptions, and flows of data. It also implies that different entities, relationships, or attributes of entities may exist in each model, or that the entities play a different role in the organizational segment on which the model is based.

All organizations exhibit aspects of centralized data usage, usually in the strategic or possibly senior managerial levels. Ultimately, all corporate data flows up to the senior levels for review, evaluation, and possibly corrective

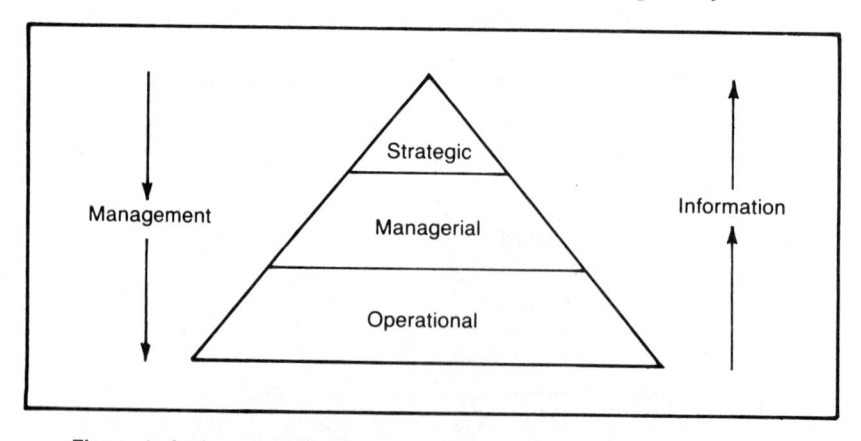

Figure 1. Anthony's Management Pyramid in a Centralized Environment

Centralized Versus Decentralized Data Bases

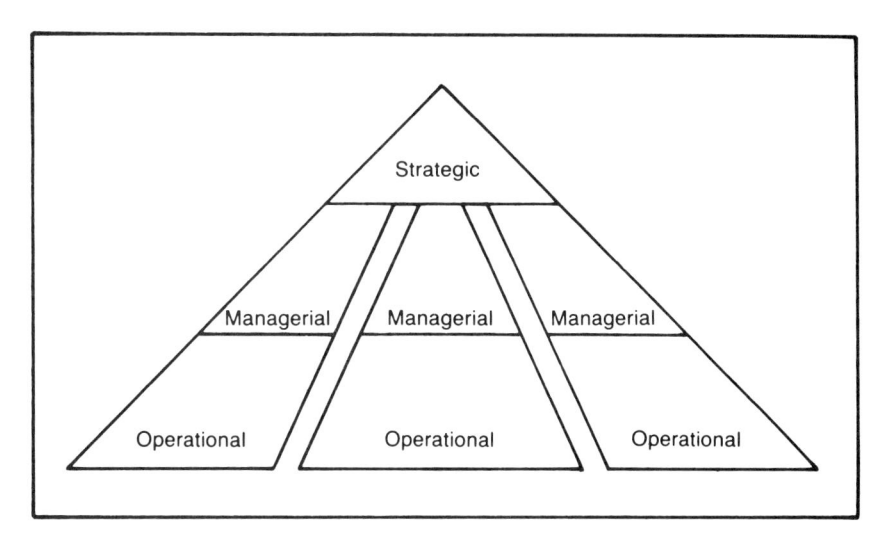

Figure 2. Anthony's Management Pyramid in a Decentralized Environment

action or modification. Thus, in the decentralized environment, some portion of a centralized data base is still needed. These centralized data bases in the decentralized environment usually support corporate internal—rather than external—functions (e.g., accounting, budgeting, personnel/payroll).

Another option is a completely decentralized environment consisting of multiple data bases constructed on the same data model and serving the same or very similar functions. A nationwide retail chain system, for example, has geographically separated stores, each supporting a complete but totally separate set of company functions. Although these data bases would have the same structure, because all stores handle the same products and provide the same functions, decentralization might be chosen. This is because each store is a self-contained unit with no need to use data from another store. In this case there is similarity, not commonality, of data usage. If this same chain had different products, different types of customers, and offered different services at each location, then a heterogeneous decentralized environment with dissimilarity of data and thus noncommonality of usage would exist.

The same concept would hold true if different divisions or operating companies were housed in the same plant or office building and each organization segment provided a completely distinct line of product or service to a completely distinct set of customers. Again, there would be no similarity of data or commonality of usage (see Figure 3).

REPLICATION OF DATA

In either the centralized or decentralized data base environment, replication of data is not only unavoidable but, in some cases, mandatory. The entities and their attributes and relationships appear in the data base as groups or collections of data elements. Individual data elements may appear in multiple attribute groupings to describe a particular aspect of the entity. Relationships by their nature describe the state or interaction of one entity vis-à-vis anoth-

DATA BASE MANAGEMENT

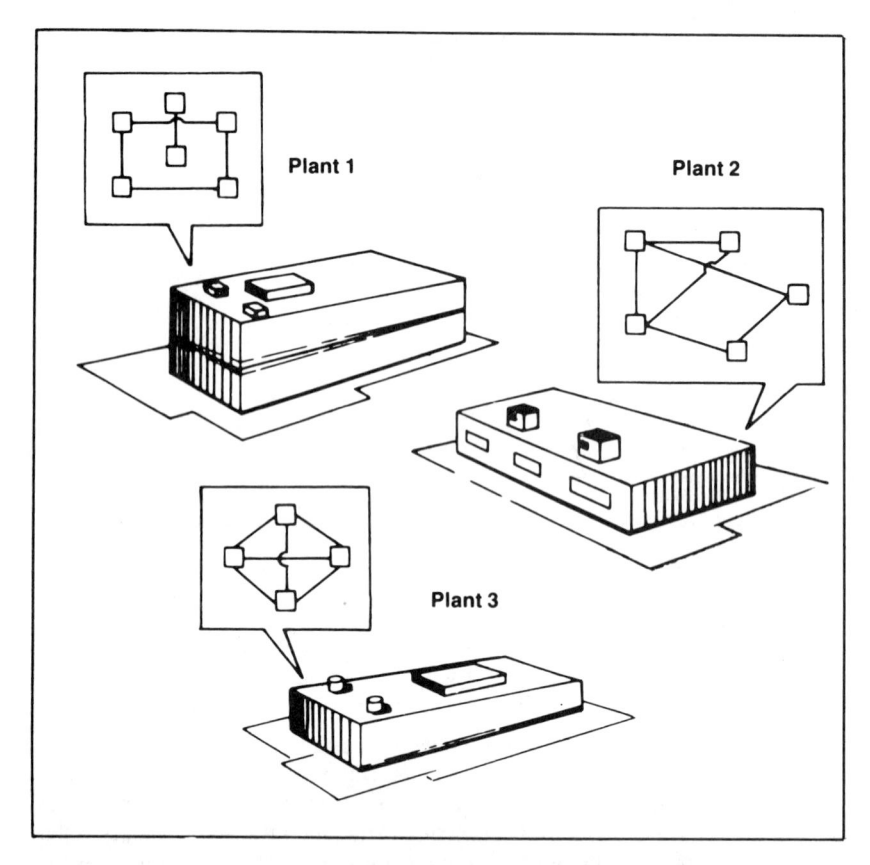

Figure 3. Multiple Information Models

er. Since the relationship can be viewed from either entity, some of the elements will necessarily be duplicated. In other instances, the data flow may indicate that processing efficiency would be substantially increased if certain data elements were carried in multiple locations.

In the decentralized environment, replication meets the specific needs of the organizational segment served. Because no connection exists between the decentralized data bases, it is valid to replicate certain data. Thus, when data is transferred between data bases (usually upward in the organization or possibly between locations), the target entity can be readily identified. Replication in a decentralized environment is mainly on selected key data that is needed to locate or associate entities outside the decentralized data base.

THE CENTRALIZED DATA BASE ENVIRONMENT

As is the case with any design decision, advantages and risks are associated with each choice. The centralized environment has the obvious advantage of consolidating and integrating data from all parts of the organization into one cohesive unit. This permits both management and operations personnel to obtain required information without regard to its origins, confident that the data thus obtained is accurate, consistent, and time concurrent. It also permits management to view the flow of data through the organization and to access the impact of its decisions. The common definition and single-source character of the centralized environment, coupled with standard names and common definitions, allow unambiguous data interpretation.

Data Integration. The logical, structured, controlled storage of data in a common pool allows management access from all parts of the organization and assures that all data reflects the same time value. Data files can thus be transformed from their normal passive role of providing historical support for forthcoming decisions to an active role of controlling (if desired) business operations. The recording of business transactions in files for reporting purposes is transformed into an interactive base, with random retrieval for management and operational decision making.

Management Awareness. Inasmuch as the data base is based on a data model of the organization, the analysis that precedes its definition and construction is useful to all levels of management and operations. The graphic definition of data interaction, flow, and usage provides a clearer framework for understanding how the various functions interact and affect the individual functional unit. The centralized environment by virtue of its shared data usage provides a freer interchange of information and greater cooperation among functional areas. This interchange and cooperation is almost mandatory in a centralized environment and is subject only to the constraints of any security and access restrictions imposed on the installation as a whole.

Privacy and Security. The consolidation and availability of data through a centralized data base requires a more precise definition of the data security profiles of each functional unit. In particular, the organization must define who, when, how, and under what circumstance data may be updated and accessed. The budgeting and forecasting functions illustrate this problem clearly. During the forecasting period, each unit determines its target for the coming periods, based on its estimates of its own activities and those of others such as sales and production. While it is to management's advantage to allow all units access to historical data for projection purposes, it is usually not advantageous to offer forecast data freely in case various units might be influenced by the overly optimistic or pessimistic estimates of others. As a check and balance mechanism, management usually reserves the right to access independent forecasts.

Error Proliferation. In the centralized data base environment, the effects of errors are greatly magnified. A single misstatement can cause misinformation to spread throughout the entire organization. This is mitigated if all data is scrutinized by more units than in the non-data-base or decentralized environment. This potential for error implies a greater need for editing and cross checking or validation. The converse of this problem, however, is that if data is lost, it is lost to the entire organization and not to just one or two functional units.

Organizational Impact of Change. The centralized data base reflects the

DATA BASE MANAGEMENT

data model of the organization, including all of its functions and current lines of business. Should a radical change take place in the business or the entities with which it deals, this impact now affects all areas because of their reliance on the central data pool. A shift in strategy, operational functions, management philosophy, or lines of business can cause a major change in the data model and thus in the central data base. Such a major change can even cause a shift from a centralized to a decentralized environment or vice versa.

Size and Volume. In a data base environment, economies of scale do not always apply. That is, it is more—not less—difficult to handle and control a large data base than a number of small ones. This difficulty is reflected not only in the sheer volume of data, but also in larger user population and the diversity of management levels, style, and functional requirements. The analytical process to develop the model and implement it requires a greater degree of planning and control than a more segmented approach.

THE DECENTRALIZED DATA BASE ENVIRONMENT

Whereas organizations utilizing the centralized data base approach are served by a single data base, the decentralized approach consists of multiple data bases each serving some segment. The usual environment for decentralization is one in which multiple independent or semi-independent organizational units are controlled or directed by a parent unit.

When referring to a decentralized data base, the distinction is made between it and a data base segment. A decentralized data base is a full and complete unit and the organizational unit or segment that it serves can satisfy all of its data needs from the data base.

Functional Specialization. The thrust toward decentralization is usually aimed at and best suited to functionally specialized organizations. There is no segment of an organization that is completely segregated from all other parts of the organization. At some point, either vertically (the usual manner) or horizontally, there is a data linkage. Therefore, decentralized data bases must provide for these linkages, however tenuous, to external data bases.

Local Differences. Because an organization's information needs reflect management's desires and decision-making processes, no two organizational models are exactly alike. These variations usually result in a customized data base for each unit in a decentralized data base environment. This occurs because opportunities for compromise are limited by diverse data requirements, usage, and definitions at the local level. In effect, each local unit is a separate organization with little in common with other units under the parent company other than that data is fed upwards to senior parent management.

In addition, there is less chance of ambiguity, because generalized data definitions are not required. The units that do share data in a decentralized environment are more homogeneous and can thus more easily derive locally standard definitions and relational structures.

Accounting Differences. Distinct differences in accounting practices can also make decentralization the correct choice. For example, even when producing the same items, an assembly line plant and job shop plant can require vastly different data. Although both plants may manufacture a defense-oriented product, one may be marketed domestically and the other overseas. Thus, the reporting and tracking requirements of the plants would differ, possibly to a degree that would make the accounting structures incompatible.

User Proximity. The decentralized data base is closer to the user, has a narrower audience, and tends to serve the individual user better than a centralized data base. Each data administrator within the constraints of the corporate parent's data requirements can organize the decentralized data base for individual needs. Definition and enforcement of corporate data requirements is a must, however, if the parent applications that span multiple divisions and their data bases are to be executed successfully and consolidated correctly.

The finer delineation and definition of data for the specific functional groups within the decentralized environment facilitates local access of data. The creation of overly complex access restriction procedures is usually unnecessary. By definition, nondivisional users have no access other than that closely defined and limited by the dictionary processing.

Ownership of data in the decentralized environment is clearly defined. The local data administrator has fewer variables to coordinate when assigning responsibility for and maintaining the quality of the data.

User Confidence. One advantage of decentralized data bases is not inherent in the data itself; rather, it concerns the confidence of the users. The data base becomes their data, and they are more likely to take an active interest in its protection and use. In addition, clarity of data ownership promotes increased data integrity. Any flaw in data base content can be readily traced to the group responsible. This tends to foster greater care in data entry.

Lack of Central Control. Decentralized data bases are the property of the decentralized, not corporate, management. They alone decide what form their data will take. This decision is based in part on the data entities and relationship with which they deal, and on what data about those entities and relationships decentralized management is interested in. Thus, the coordination of decentralized data bases and their interaction is a difficult task.

Corporate-Level Reporting. The main advantage of the centralized data base environment to upper management is the ability to obtain data related to planning, control, and decision making. Dispersion of data and local definitions in a decentralized environment makes aggregate, cross-unit reports more difficult to prepare.

Decentralized data base retrieval from a central location involves a multi-step process of message transmission, receipt, translation, and reduction to eliminate the effects of data dialects (see Figure 4). Obviously, more components involved means more operations are necessary to gather all required data.

DATA BASE MANAGEMENT

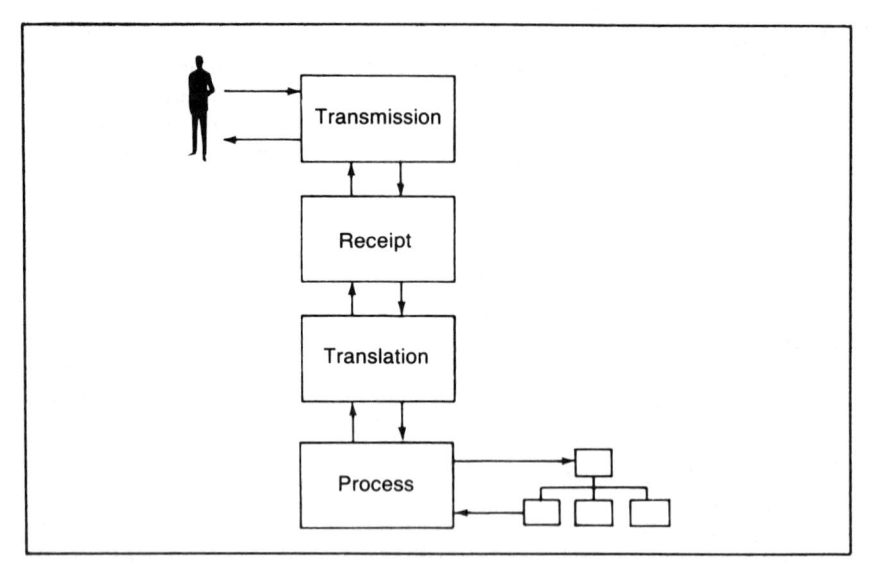

Figure 4. Decentralized Inquiry Flow

Time Differential. The relationships that protect against time differentials are strong within the local data base but very weak between local data bases. Each organizational unit operates at its own speed and according to its own time frame.

Although accounting periods usually coincide, the pace at which activity occurs and is recorded differs from unit to unit and site to site. These differences in time reference are transparent to the local users, yet they are detrimental to data that is synthesized centrally from data generated at multiple locations.

Data Redundancy. While redundancy is undesirable in a data base environment, communication between decentralized data bases requires duplication of certain data, thus creating the reference points for correlation. This redundancy reduces the prime advantage of the centralized data base approach: that all users use the same data rather than different, unsynchronized versions.

Each unit maintaining a local data base must either collect the inputs to update the redundant data itself or obtain input data from a central source. The former approach creates discrepancies and inaccuracies; the latter demands increased activity and requires additional management control.

The tendency toward the development or evolution of dialects within the local data definitions also diminishes the effectiveness of common data definition that would be available in the centralized environment.

Loss of Synergy. The synergistic quality of the centralized data base arises from the quantity of data stored and from the global structure used as a framework for the informational model. When this global model is fragmented—as it would be in a decentralized environment—the synergistic quality is lost.

THE ROLE OF THE DICTIONARY

A data base is the source of data for the organization or a segment of it. The dictionary is the source of data about data (i.e., metadata). The contents of the dictionary define the data, the owning units, the using units, and the relationship between data elements and entities. The importance of the dictionary both in the modeling and design phases and as an ongoing reference cannot be overemphasized.

Prior to the data base analysis, modeling, and design phases, a dictionary should be established to document the results of those processes. The dictionary is a design tool and a means of communicating definitions and usage patterns to the developers and the user community. It contains a narrative explanation of the meaning of each data element, its content, format, usage, names, and sources.

The gathering, analysis, and validation of the metadata in the dictionary is time-consuming and requires skilled data analysts who have clear understanding of the corporate functions being examined. Most of these tasks can be accomplished early on and the remainder as needed. It is from a comparison between and analysis of the dictionary's definitions that the analysts can make the first-cut determination as to whether centralized or decentralized data bases are called for in the organization.

In a decentralized data environment, the data dictionary serves as a translator of multiple dialects of a language. Each of the multiple definitions, pronunciations, and/or formats of an element located in the local data bases must be recorded in the dictionary. In contrast to the centralized environment, the decentralized mode requires that intersite communications be translated by mechanisms or routines that have access to other local dictionaries. This type of interchange is not unlike two people speaking through interpreters; much care must be exercised to ensure that the translation is correct (see Figure 5).

The dictionary also acts as a directory that is consulted every time data is accessed by an application program in a different or higher site. Decentralization does not always create a lack of conformity in the central definition; however, separating parts of the data base to serve the individual units creates a strong tendency in that direction just as separation and isolation lead to the development of dialects within a spoken language (see Figure 6).

DATA ADMINISTRATION IN THE DATA BASE ENVIRONMENT

Data analysts must confer with user department representatives at various levels of management to create common data definitions. This implies that there is agreement or, in the absence of agreement, an arbitration or deadlock resolution authority delegated to those analysts. Common usage of and reliance on commonly defined data elements implies a centralized function that coordinates and protects the common interest.

The need for arbitration and coordination of this type has caused the evolu-

DATA BASE MANAGEMENT

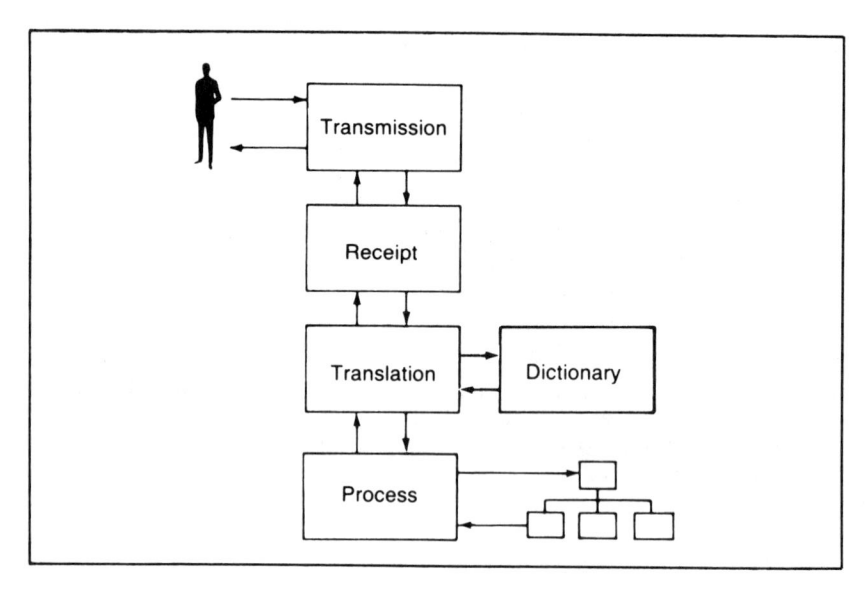

Figure 5. The Dictionary as a Translator

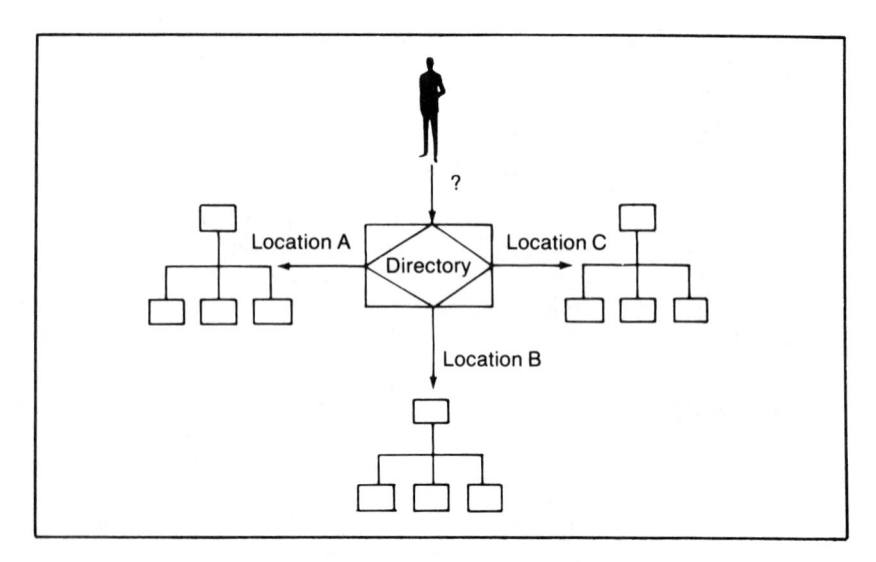

Figure 6. The Role of the Directory as Locator

tion of a new managerial function called data administration. A data administrator is responsible for conflict resolution, definition of data elements, and the conceptualization and practical implementation of the data base structure. The data administrator is also the guardian of the corporate data resource as it resides in the data base.

The most important function of the data administrator, however, is to act as the master architect of the design function. This entails defining on a corporate basis the information model and constructing one or more data bases to support that model.

Managerial Control

Data administration is really a special form of managerial control that includes authority over data as its primary function. Conceptually, the data administrator performs the same control function for the data resource that the comptroller performs for the financial resource; that is, he or she integrates and monitors the sources and uses of the data resource. The data administrator also chooses the tools and facilities for processing and controlling the data; the security structure is defined and implemented, and the dictionary is maintained by the data administration staff. By introducing a single authority and by analyzing information about the user community, the best data structure for all users can be defined. A strong data administration function is required to support either a centralized or decentralized data base environment.

DATA ENTRY

If the data base truly is intended to integrate and interface various functional areas while supporting corporate-level management, a certain degree of control must be placed over data entry. A large volume of data enters the data base from throughout the organization with each department or division providing information for storage and use by other parts of the company.

Because of the diversity of the data sources, many data forms typically occupy the input stream. Care must be exercised so that incoming data conforms to the predetermined definition of form and is stored according to precise rules. Data that does not match the definition or form must not be allowed to enter the data base.

ACTION PLAN

In the traditional non-data-base environment, the application and its files are closely wedded, and a change to one only affects the other. In a data base environment, the user community is large; an error, omission, or misspecification in the data base affects the entire community of users.

The analysis and design necessary to construct a data base environment must start with the information modeling process to permit selection of centralization or decentralization and determination of the model or models on which the centralized or decentralized data base is constructed. The analyst must understand and examine the organization at each level and from every aspect to make the proper decisions with respect to the organization's data needs.

The data base approach—whether centralized or decentralized—has the same form and definition. The decentralized form differs from the centralized in that it reflects the functional or physical divisions of the organization rather than the corporate whole. In addition, the data included in the local data base reflects local management rather than the compromise required to support the central organization.

DATA BASE MANAGEMENT

Local data bases are usually developed along the lines of the organization's functional segmentation. Because the data reflects local and not central needs, the ownership is more clearly defined, and the access and usage conflicts can be resolved more easily.

The diversity of information requirements within the organization is reflected in the difficulties of the modeling and design process. A thorough analysis of each organizational function is mandated in order to map the sources and uses of data. It is also mandatory that the data base be modeled on the one thing that is relatively impervious to change—the business itself. In other words, the players change but the game is less likely to. A model reflecting the real world objectives of the business in generic form is more likely to withstand the test of time than one reflecting processes or individual needs.

Bibliography

Anthony, Robert. *Planning and Control Systems: A Framework for Analysis.* Cambridge MA: Harvard Business Press, 1965.

Brown, R.R., and Ramey, T.L. "The Concept and Practice of ERA Information Modeling." *Entity-Relationship Approach to Systems Analysis and Design,* Edited by P.P. Chen. New York: North-Holland Publishing Co, 1980.

Canning, Richard G. "Data Security in the Corporate Data Base." *EDP Analyzer,* Vol. 8, No. 5, May 1970.

Chen, P.P. "The Entity-Relationship Model: Toward a Unified View of Data." *ACM Transactions of Database Systems,* Vol. 1, No. 1, June 1976.

Chen, P.P. *Entity-Relationship Approach to Logical Database Design.* Wellesley MA: Q.E.D. Information Sciences Inc, 1977.

Chen, P.P., ed. *Entity-Relationship Approach to Systems Analysis and Design.* New York: North-Holland Publishing Co, 1980.

CODASYL Systems Committee. *Selection and Acquisition of Data Base Management Systems.* New York: Association for Computing Machinery, 1976.

Date, C.J. *An Introduction to Database Systems,* 3rd ed. Reading MA: Addison-Wesley Publishing Co, 1981.

Davis, Gordon B. *Management Information Systems.* New York: McGraw-Hill, 1974.

Dearden, John. "MIS Is a Mirage." *Harvard Business Review,* January/February 1972.

Fry, James P. "Managing Data Is the Key to MIS." *Computer Decisions,* Vol. 3, No. 1, January 1971.

Gorry, Anthony G., and Morton, Michael S. "A Framework for Management Information Systems." *Sloan Management Review,* Vol. 13, No. 1, Fall 1971.

Joyce, James. "Principles of Data Base Management in a Distributed System." *Computer Communications,* Vol. 1, October 1978.

Luke, John W. "Data Base Systems: Putting Management Back in the Picture." *GSC Report,* Vol. 9, No. 1, May 1975.

Martin, J. *Computer Data Base Organization.* Englewood Cliffs NJ: Prentice-Hall, 1975.

Martin, J. *Security, Accuracy and Privacy in Computer Systems.* Englewood Cliffs NJ: Prentice-Hall, 1973.

Miller, Myron. "A Survey of Distributed Data Base Management." *Information and Management,* Vol. 1, December 1978.

Olle, William T. "The Large Data Base: Its Organization and User Interface—Transcription of a Panel Session Held at the 1968 ACM National Conference, Las Vegas, Nevada." *Data Base,* Vol. 1, No. 3, Fall 1969.

Sanders, D.H. *Computers and Management in a Changing Society,* 2nd ed. New York: McGraw-Hill, 1974.

Sibley, Edgar H. "The Development of Data Base Technology." *Computing Surveys,* Vol. 8, No. 2 (March 1976), p. 2.

VIII-4
Improving the Quality of Data
William R. Durell

INTRODUCTION

Improved corporate decision making depends on accurate data and translates directly into higher profits. This relationship is illustrated in Figure 1. An organization that makes sound business decisions can provide better products and services at a lower cost, thus increasing the company's competitive position. However, effective corporate decision making depends on the quality of the information available to make these decisions. In turn, the quality of information depends on its integrity—that is, its accuracy, reliability, timeliness, consistency, and standardization. This chapter discusses the impediments to data integrity—various forms of redundancies and inconsistencies—and reviews the software tools available to help the data administrator solve these problems.

DATA REDUNDANCY PROBLEMS

An overabundance of data within an enterprise is a symptom of improper data management. The average enterprise is drowning in data yet thirsty for information because of inadequate planning and coordination of information requirements. This situation is further complicated by the proliferation of inconsistent and redundant microcomputer-based data repositories within the user community. Thus, an inverse relationship exists between the quality of information and the quantity of data. By employing proper data management procedures, an organization can significantly reduce the quantity and complexity of its data. When data integrity is increased, the organization's return on investment from the information resource also increases.

Forms of Redundancy

The MIS manager must carefully examine the various forms of redundancy that can obscure the integrity of corporate data.

Storage Redundancy. Storage redundancy exists when the same data is stored in more than one data base, file, table, system, or location. In a distributed environment, data is often replicated from a host or central location to multiple, remote locations. When data is distributed from the host in a

DATA BASE MANAGEMENT

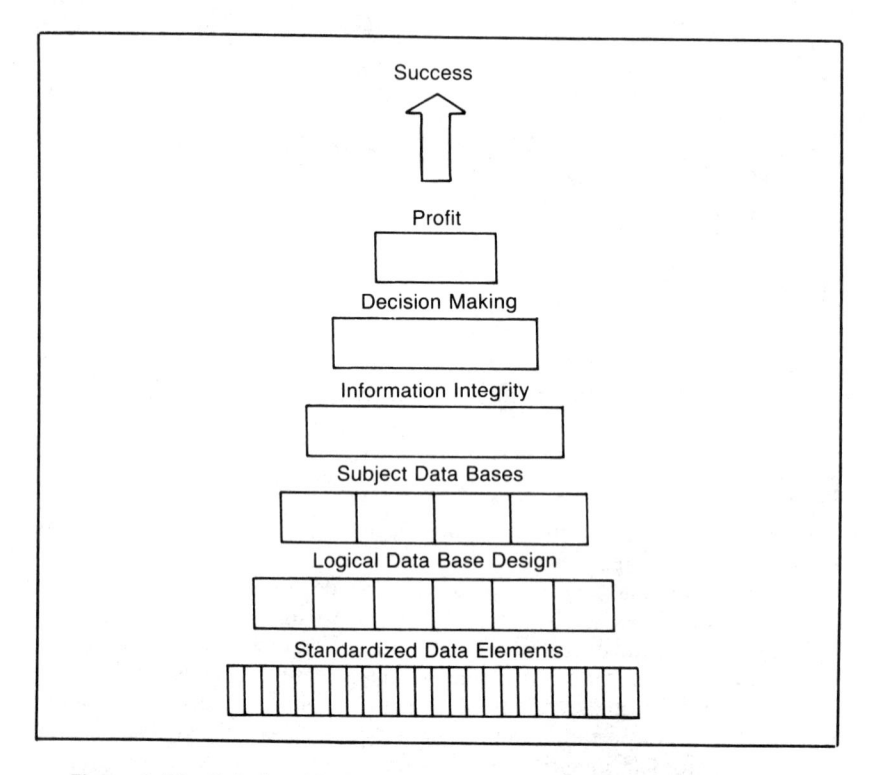

Figure 1. The Relationship Between Information Quality and Profitability

coordinated and timely manner, planned and controlled redundancy results. However, most storage redundancy results from the proliferation of inconsistent, nonstandardized data that is the direct result of inadequate data management, planning, and procedures.

Reference Redundancy. Reference redundancy exists when MIS personnel or users assign different labels to identical data. For example, typical examples of reference redundancy concerning SUPPLIER-NUMBER records are:

- SUPPLIER-NO
- NUMB-OF-SUPPLIER
- SUPPLIER-NBR
- SUPP-NO
- VENDOR-NUM
- VEND-NUMBER.

Definition Redundancy. Definition redundancy occurs when the same piece of data is used to represent multiple or overlapping facts. This situation is common in many DP systems that have been greatly modified or enhanced. Table 1 provides an example of a data element that has multiple meanings or purposes.

Quality of Data

Table 1. An Example of Definition Redundancy

DESTINATION-CODE

Definition:
    Information about the nature of the receiving location or status of the shipment.
Valid values:
    A = foreign
    B = domestic
    10–15 hazardous area—foreign
    16–20 friendly nation—status
    21–30 hazardous area—South America
    31–40 hazardous area—Southeast Asia

Subset Redundancy. Subset redundancy exists when a portion of the information contained in one piece of data is also represented by another unit of data. Table 2 shows an example of partial or subset redundancy within records containing part number and part-type–code information.

Table 2. An Example of Subset Redundancy

PART-NUMBER

Format: X-99999-YY
Valid Values:
    X: L = left-hand part
           R = right-hand part
           M = male part
           F = female part
    99999 = serialized part number
    YY: 00 = unit part
          01 = subassembly
          02 = assembly

PART-TYPE-CODE
Valid Values:
    L = left-hand part
    R = right-hand part

Attribute Redundancy. Attribute redundancy exists when two or more like data elements are designed with differing characteristics. Table 3 provides an example of like data items with inconsistent formats and lengths.

Table 3. An Example of Attribute Redundancy

Data Element Name	Length	Format
AGENT-LAST-NAME	30 characters	Alphanumeric
AGENT-L-NM	25 characters	Alphabetic
AGENT-LST-NM	25 characters	Alphanumeric

DATA BASE MANAGEMENT

DATA ADMINISTRATION INC
USE BY AGREEMENT ONLY

REPORT LINE NO.	KEYWORD	DATA ELEMENT NAME		KEYWORD LENGTH	NAME LENGTH	NO. WORDS IN NAME
1	ABILITY	ABILITY-RATING	ITEM	7	14	2
2	ACC	EMP-ACC-CANDIDATE-CODE	ITEM	3	22	4
3	ACCOUNT	ACCOUNT-NUMBER	GROUP	7	14	2
4	ACCOUNT	LABOR-ACCOUNT-NUMBER	GROUP	7	20	3
5	ACCR	VAC-ACCR-EXCESS-CODE	ITEM	4	20	4
6	ACCRUED	SICK-LEAVE-PAY-HOURS-ACCRUED	ITEM	7	28	5
7	ACCRUED	VACATION-PAY-HOURS-ACCRUED	ITEM	7	26	4
8	ACCT	EMP-PAY-BANK-ACCT-NBR	ITEM	4	21	5
9	ACCT	GENERAL-LEDGER-ACCT-NBR	ITEM	4	23	4
10	ACCT	LABOR-RECORD-ACCT-NBR	GROUP	4	21	4
11	ACCT	PROJECT-COST-ACCT-NBR	ITEM	4	21	4
12	ACCUM	ACCUM-TIMECARD-CD	ITEM	5	17	3
13	ACT	LAST-JOB-CHNG-ACT-CODE	ITEM	3	22	5
14	ACTION	LAST-PERS-ACTION	ITEM	6	16	3
15	ACTION	LAST-PERS-ACTION-DATE	GROUP	6	21	4
16	ACTION	LAST-PERS-ACTION-DT-DA	ITEM	6	22	5
17	ACTION	LAST-PERS-ACTION-DT-MO	ITEM	6	22	5
18	ACTION	LAST-PERS-ACTION-DT-YR	ITEM	6	22	5
19	ACTIV	LAST-BASE-RATE-CHNG-ACTIV-CODE	ITEM	5	30	6
20	ACTIVE	ACTIVE-MILITARY-DUTY-END-DATE	GROUP	6	29	5
21	ACTIVE	ACTIVE-MILITARY-DUTY-END-MO	ITEM	6	27	5
22	ACTIVE	ACTIVE-MILITARY-DUTY-END-YR	ITEM	6	27	5
23	ACTIVE	ACTIVE-MILITARY-DUTY-START-DATE	GROUP	6	31	5
24	ACTIVE	ACTIVE-MILITARY-DUTY-START-MO	ITEM	6	29	5
25	ACTIVE	ACTIVE-MILITARY-DUTY-START-YR	ITEM	6	29	5
26	ACTIVE	EMP-ACTIVE-CODE	ITEM	6	15	3
27	ACTIVITY	ACTIVITY-CODE	ITEM	8	13	2
28	ACTIVITY	LAST-ACTIVITY-DATE	GROUP	8	18	3
29	ACTIVITY	LAST-ACTIVITY-DATE-DA	ITEM	8	21	4
30	ACTIVITY	LAST-ACTIVITY-DATE-MO	ITEM	8	21	4
31	ACTIVITY	LAST-ACTIVITY-DATE-YR	ITEM	8	21	4
32	ACTIVITY	TIME-ACTIVITY-FILE	FILE	8	18	3
33	ACTIVITY	TIME-ACTIVITY-REC	GROUP	8	17	3
34	ACTUAL	ACTUAL-PAYROLL-EFFECTIVE-DA	ITEM	6	27	4

Figure 2. KWIC Statistics Report

Quality of Data

Value Redundancy. Two or more data elements exhibit value redundancy if they have the same definition and use, but their domain (i.e., valid values) differ. Table 4 provides an example of value redundancy.

Table 4. An Example of Value Redundancy

```
ACCOUNT-PAYABLE-STATUS
       01 = delinquent account
       02 = account in good standing
       03 = account turned over to collection agency
ACCT-PAYABLE-ST
       D = account 90 days overdue and delinquent
       G = good customer
       C = has been assigned to a 3rd-party collection agent
```

Quantifying Data Redundancy

Because of the inconsistent classification and identification of data, most organizations have trouble physically inventorying their information and thus cannot quantify data redundancy. However, the symptoms of data redundancy abound. According to a recent nationwide survey of MIS installations conducted by the author, the procurement of direct access storage devices is increasing at a rate of 40 percent per year. Various data administration studies also conducted by the author have revealed that, on the average, a 20:1 ratio exists between the total number of data names and the unique data elements within a single data processing system. These studies have also revealed a ratio as high as 200:1 for reference redundancy throughout an entire organization. The average large MIS organization examined in these studies had more than 800,000 data names in existing COBOL libraries; a medium-sized organization had approximately 50,000 data names. The vast majority of these data names were found to represent synonyms and homonyms of a relatively few data elements.

MINIMIZING DATA REDUNDANCY WITH SOFTWARE TOOLS

Data dictionaries alone cannot control all types of data redundancy. However, several software tools can significantly improve information consistency and minimize data redundancy. Keyword, or keyword-in-context (KWIC) lists aid in identifying and reducing data-naming variations. KWIC lists enable the data administrator to detect and identify superfluous data names based on their component parts. KWIC lists provide alphabetical listings of data element names based on their component words or character strings. Figures 2 and 3 provide examples of KWIC reports. Figure 2 shows the statistics provided by such a report; Figure 3 shows the similarities among keywords.

Other software tools automatically detect similarities among component or synonym words used in various data names. Table 5 provides an example of a report generated by such a tool.

DATA BASE MANAGEMENT

```
DATA ADMINISTRATION INC
USE BY AGREEMENT ONLY

DATA ELEMENT NAME

                    MANAGEMENT-JOB-LEVEL*CD
                     MULTI-MAIL-GEOG-LOC*CD
                 PAYCHECK-DELVR-ROUTING*CD
                          PAYROLL-OFFICE*CD
                      PREV-ST-WORKED-LIVED*CD
                  SALARY-RECLASSIFICATION*CD
                           SHIFT-WORKED*CD
                        TAXING-JURIS*CD-PREV1
                        TAXING-JURIS*CD-PREV2
                         TIMECARD-TYPE*CD
                    TRANSACTION-GROUP*CD
                               TUC-JOB*CD
                   WAGE-ATTACHMENT-CALC*CD
                   70200-TRANSACTION-TYPE*CD
                             RET*CERT-BARG-UNIT
                             RET*CERTIFICATE-NO
                       BASE-RATE*CHANGE-INC-DEC-AMT
                             HR-AREA*CHANGE
                    LAST-BASE-RATE*CHANGE-MO-YR
                    LAST-BASE-RATE*CHANGE-PERCENTAGE
                      LAST-JOB-CODE*CHANGE-DATE
                      LAST-JOB-CODE*CHANGE-DATE-DA
                      LAST-JOB-CODE*CHANGE-DATE-MO
                      LAST-JOB-CODE*CHANGE-DATE-YR
                         OLI-HR-AREA*CHANGE
                              LABOR*CHARGE
                              LABOR*CHARGE-NEXT
                              LABOR*CHARGE-PREV
                                  *CHECK-NUMBER
                                  *CHECK-TYPE
                              BENE*CHNG-DATE
                              BENE*CHNG-DATE-DA
                              BENE*CHNG-DATE-MO
                              BENE*CHNG-DATE-YR
```

Figure 3. KWIC Report Showing Similarities Among Keywords

Table 5. Report of Component or Synonym Words

Searching For: LAST-LABOR-ACCT-CHANGE-DATE

Suspected Redundant Data Names:

CHANGE-DATE-LABOR-ACCOUNT
DATE-LABOR-ACCT-CHANGE
ACCT-NBR-CHANGE-DATE
CHANGE-LABOR-DATE-INDICATOR
ACCOUNT-DATE
CHANGE-DATE
COMPANY-LABOR-ACCT
DATE-GENERAL-LEDGER-ACCT
DATE-OF-LAST-POSTING
LABOR-ACCT-NUMBER
LABOR-DATE
PAYROLL-CHANGE-DATE
RETRO-LABOR-ACCOUNT-NUMBER

Quality of Data

DATA ADMINISTRATION INC USE BY AGREEMENT ONLY NAME/WORD IN ERROR	ERROR CODE	ERROR MESSAGE	ERROR POSITION
ACCT-NO-DTE	075	THIS NAME DOES NOT CONTAIN A CLASS WORD	01
	050	THIS NAME DOES NOT CONTAIN A PRIME WORD	01
	950	NAME IS UNACCEPTABLE—WRITTEN TO INVALID OUT FILE	
AN-ILLEGAL-WORD			
AN	375	THIS WORD IS AN ILLEGAL WORD	01
	075	THIS NAME DOES NOT CONTAIN A CLASS WORD	01
	050	THIS NAME DOES NOT CONTAIN A PRIME WORD	01
	950	NAME IS UNACCEPTABLE—WRITTEN TO INVALID OUT FILE	
DT-COMPLETED	050	THIS NAME DOES NOT CONTAIN A PRIME WORD	01
	950	NAME IS UNACCEPTABLE—WRITTEN TO INVALID OUT FILE	
IN-DT-1 1	400	THIS WORD IS TOO SHORT—NUMBER OF CHARACTERS IS 1	07
	050	THIS NAME DOES NOT CONTAIN A PRIME WORD	01
	950	NAME IS UNACCEPTABLE—WRITTEN TO INVALID OUT FILE	
NBR-UNACCEPTABLE-ERRORS			
UNACCEPTABLE	425	THIS WORD IS TOO LONG—NUMBER OF CHARACTERS IS 12	05
	050	THIS NAME DOES NOT CONTAIN A PRIME WORD	01
	950	NAME IS UNACCEPTABLE—WRITTEN TO INVALID OUT FILE	
IN-1 1	400	THIS WORD IS TOO SHORT—NUMBER OF CHARACTERS IS 1	04
	100	THIS NAME IS TOO SHORT—LENGTH IN CHARACTERS IS 4	01
	075	THIS NAME DOES NOT CONTAIN A CLASS WORD	01
	050	THIS NAME DOES NOT INCLUDE A PRIME WORD	01
	950	NAME IS UNACCEPTABLE—WRITTEN TO INVALID OUT FILE	
EMPLOYEE-SOCIAL-SECURITY-NO	075	THIS NAME DOES NOT CONTAIN A CLASS WORD	01
	950	NAME IS UNACCEPTABLE—WRITTEN TO INVALID OUT FILE	
STATUS	150	THIS NAME HAS TOO FEW WORDS—NUMBER OF WORDS IS 1	01
	075	THIS NAME DOES NOT CONTAIN A CLASS WORD	01
	050	THIS NAME DOES NOT CONTAIN A PRIME WORD	01
	950	NAME IS UNACCEPTABLE—WRITTEN TO INVALID OUT FILE	
NBR-OF-WORDS-IN-A-DATA-NAME			
A	375	THIS WORD IS AN ILLEGAL WORD	17
A	400	THIS WORD IS TOO SHORT—NUMBER OF CHARACTERS IS 1	17
	175	THIS NAME HAS TOO MANY WORDS—NUMBER OF WORDS IS 7	01
	050	THIS NAME DOES NOT CONTAIN A PRIME WORD	01

Figure 4. Data Element Name Error Report

DATA BASE MANAGEMENT

THE NEED FOR CONSISTENT AND STANDARDIZED DATA

Unless data bases are constructed from a foundation of clear, concise, and standardized data, accurate or reliable information from such data cannot be compiled. Furthermore, data is of little value unless it can be combined, totaled, or compared with other data. Unless the component data parts are compatible, information synthesis cannot be performed. Therefore, the data within an organization must be standardized in order to increase the quality, value, and integrity of corporate information.

Data Identification, Classification, and Nomenclature Standards

Classification Words. Classification words should be a component part of every data name. Classification words enable accurate data labeling and improve the accuracy of information searches or queries. Commonly used classification words are AMOUNT, NAME, CODE, NUMBER, CONSTANT, PERCENT, COUNT, TEXT, DATE, and TIME.

Prime Words. Prime words should be used to accurately label data elements based on the major business uses of the corporate data. For example, prime words for an insurance company would be AGENT, CLAIM, POLICY, and SUBSCRIBER.

In addition, organizations should avoid the creation and use of synonym data names and the use of synonym words within data names. The data administrator should also create and maintain standardized lists of abbreviations and acronyms.

Data Attribute Standards

The data administrator should ensure that variations of data formats and length are minimized. Furthermore, the data administrator should standardize the attributes of data elements within common classification words. For example, all date fields can be defined with a standard format of YYYYMMDD (year, month, day).

Data Definition Standards

The definitions of data should be concise, clear, and accurate. The following guidelines should be employed when the definition or purpose of data is documented.
- The definition should describe the logical, not the physical, characteristics of data. In other words, the definition should explain the purpose of the data but not necessarily where the data is used (e.g., systems or programs), when it is used, or who uses it.
- The definition should describe the data's business relevance to the organization, rather than how the data is used within a particular DP system.
- The definition should be complete. For example, regarding a code-type data element, the definition should include an explanation for all permissible code values.

Quality of Data

IMPROVING DATA INTEGRITY WITH SOFTWARE TOOLS

Although a data dictionary can be a valuable and effective tool for storing information concerning DP systems, its ability to improve the quality or integrity of stored information is limited. Thus, KWIC tools are needed to complement the data dictionary. Certain software tools can verify whether the data elements entered into the dictionary match the corporate naming conventions. Figure 4 presents an example of an error report generated by such a software tool.

In addition, data base and information modeling tools can assist the data administrator with entity analysis and logical data base design.

ACTION PLAN

A data analyst (the complement of a data base analyst) should be assigned to every new systems development project. The data analyst should be responsible for information modeling, logical data base design, and data standardization. Assigning such a specialist to an application development project relieves the systems analyst from the burden of analyzing and designing the data structures. The systems analyst can then concentrate on process-related project activities that increase the quality of the data and process design.

Today's complex, high-volume, and highly integrated information systems require the data administration staff to use automated tools whenever possible to detect violations in standards and ensure compliance with corporate objectives. The data administrator's standards, procedures, and deliverables should be integrated throughout the systems development life cycle. The use of automated tools encourages compliance with standards and helps minimize the possibility of delays in the system development life cycle because of deviations from, or compliance with, data administration standards.

VIII-5
Introduction to Relational Data Bases

G. Sandberg

INTRODUCTION

During the past decade there has been continuously increasing interest in relational data base systems, most of which was initially created by university and research activities. Relational data base systems are now available for operational data processing installations. Examples of such systems are the IBM Query-By-Example[1] and IMPS.[2] Commercial availability of a number of other relational systems is expected within the next few years.[3] This chapter describes basic concepts of relational data base systems and identifies potential benefits of the relational data base approach, comparing relational implementation with present implementations and hierarchic and network data base systems.

WHAT IS A RELATIONAL DATA BASE SYSTEM?

The most fundamental property of a relational data base system is that data is presented to the user as tables instead of as networks or hierarchies. Thus, the data is structured in the form of *tables* consisting of *columns* and *rows*, with the rows corresponding to traditional data base records or segments and the columns representing fields within the records. Table 1 shows a relational data structure for employee information.

This table shows three facts about each employee—employee number, name, and department—each in a separate column of the table. The table has only five rows (records), one for each employee. Such a data base for a company large enough to require a data base would have many more rows.

The internal data storage format is not relevant to the relational view. This is not to say that internal access and storage techniques are unimportant; on the contrary, these techniques determine whether the data base system performance is acceptable. Performance implications, however, are not part of the definition of the relational view.

The important fact is that the relational view exists in terms of the way the user sees the data. The user may, for example, be a person sitting at a CRT and interacting with the system in a specialized query language or a programmer using conventional programming languages like COBOL or PL/1.

DATA BASE MANAGEMENT

Table 1. Relational Structure of Employee Records

		COLUMN OR FIELD		
		1 EMPLOYEE NUMBER	2 NAME	3 DEPARTMENT
ROW OR RECORD	1 2 3 4 5	61256 38972 09181 74245 22318	MYGIND CHEMNITZ BARCLAY SANDBERG PERSSON	NFSC NMC NFSC NFSC NMC

Any hierarchical or network data structure can be transformed into a set of relational tables. One technique is to convert each predefined access path in the network or hierarchy into a key field column in a relational table. All the fields from the hierarchy or network record can then be named explicitly in the relational table. For example, two tables can be substituted for a parent-child record structure in a hierarchy or for an owner-member set in a CODASYL network. The first table represents the parent record type, and the second is equivalent to the child record type but is expanded with the key field of the parent as an extra column. The transformation of a hierarchy of two record types into corresponding relational tables is shown in Figure 1.

If a relational data base view is simply a view of records with the same format, how does this view differ from program views of traditional flat files? The differences include specificity of rules. The following rules must be followed if the data base view is to qualify as a relational view:
- Each table contains only one record type.
- Each row (record) has a fixed number of fields, all of which are explicitly named.
- Fields are distinct (atomic) so that repeating groups are not allowed. (This is the only normalization requirement for a relational data base.)

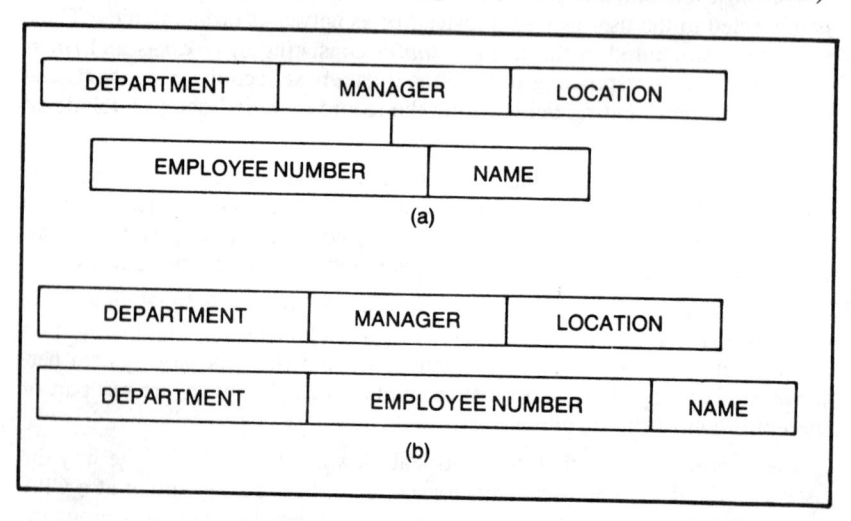

Figure 1. Transformation of (a) a Hierarchy of Two Record Types into (b) the Corresponding Relational Tables

- Each record is unique (i.e., duplicates are not allowed).
- Records can come in any order; there is no predetermined sequence.
- Fields take their values from a domain of possible field values.
- The same domain can be used for many different field types, thus becoming the source of field values in different columns in the same or different tables.
- New tables can be produced on the basis of a match of field values from the same domain in two existing tables.

The formation of new tables, which does not apply to access methods handling flat files, is a key to relational systems. The access methods are not designed to combine such files into new files, however; that is an application program responsibility.

NOTES ON RELATIONAL CONCEPTS

When relational data base systems are studied theoretically, terms are often found in the literature that are different from those used in business data processing environments. This disparity makes the subject appear unnecessarily complex and has contributed more than anything else to a misunderstanding of the concepts of tables.

The following list of terms presents the formal name (usually found in technical literature) followed by its everyday data processing equivalent.
- Relation—Table or record type
- Tuple—Row or record occurrence
- Attribute—Column name or field type
- Element—Field
- Degree—Number of columns in a table
- Cardinality—Number of rows in a table
- Binary relations—Table with two columns
- N-ary relations—Table with N columns
- N-tuple—A record from a table with N columns

There is no corresponding term for *domain,* but it has the following meaning: all values that may occur for a specific field type come from a domain of all the possible values of this type. Many different field types may use the same domain.

Even today, many authors of research articles use their own (and sometimes variant) definitions of relational terminology as a starting point for developing further ideas. This is a clear indication that relational theory is still evolving and currently may mean different things to different people.

TABLE OPERATIONS

One of the new operations available in relational systems is the capability of combining relational tables, which is called a *join*. Other relational operations are *selection*, which creates a subset of all the records in a table, and *projection,* which creates a subset of all the columns in a table. A key characteristic shared by all relational operations is that the results they produce are always new tables. This makes it possible to provide very powerful and concise languages for the manipulation of relational data structures.

DATA BASE MANAGEMENT

Selection. The simplest of these relational operations is selection, in which certain rows in a given table are selected and used to build a new table. A selection criterion may be, for example, that one or more fields has a specific value; all rows satisfying this condition are selected for the new table. Table 2 is an example of selection. Note that all rows of Table 2a in which the employee's department is NFSC are selected for the newly created Table 2b.

Table 2. Selection of Employees in (a) Who Are in Department NFSC for Inclusion in the New Table (b)

(a)

EMPLOYEE NUMBER	NAME	DEPARTMENT
61256	MYGIND	NFSC
38972	CHEMNITZ	NMC
09181	BARCLAY	NFSC
74245	SANDBERG	NFSC
22318	PERSSON	NMC

(b)

EMPLOYEE NUMBER	NAME	DEPARTMENT
61256	MYGIND	NFSC
09181	BARCLAY	NFSC
74245	SANDBERG	NFSC

Projection. With the projection operation, only certain columns in a given table are selected and used to build a new table with fewer columns. When the new table is complete, it may contain some rows that are identical, because values in the retained columns may be identical. Since duplicates are not allowed in a relational table, all but one of the duplicate rows are discarded. Projection is illustrated in Table 3; the operation is performed on the Name and the Department columns in Table 3a to form the resultant Table 3b. No duplicate rows are shown in this example.

Table 3. Projection Using the NAME and DEPARTMENT Column in (a) to Form the New Table (b)

(a)

EMPLOYEE NUMBER	NAME	DEPARTMENT
61256	MYGIND	NFSC
38972	CHEMNITZ	NMC
09181	BARCLAY	NFSC
74245	SANDBERG	NFSC
22318	PERSSON	NMC

(b)

NAME	DEPARTMENT
MYGIND	NFSC
CHEMNITZ	NMC
BARCLAY	NFSC
SANDBERG	NFSC
PERSSON	NMC

Relational Data Bases

Selection and Projection Combination. Quite often, selection and projection are combined into the same request. In such a case, the search criterion may be that a certain field must exceed a specified value and only certain named columns are of interest. The first operation selects the rows that satisfy the size condition, and the second operation projects the relevant columns.

Join. Join merges two tables based on values from one column in each table. (A join may also be performed on two columns in the same table as well as on multiple columns simultaneously.) The two tables are said to be joined over the two columns. In Table 4, the two tables (4a and 4b) are joined on the basis of the Department column in each. When this is done, the Manager and Location columns form the join on the Department column shown in Table 4c.

Table 4. Join on DEPARTMENT (c) Consists of MANAGER and LOCATION Information in (b) Combined with EMPLOYEE NUMBER and NAME in (a)

(a)

EMPLOYEE NUMBER	NAME	DEPARTMENT
61256	MYGIND	NFSC
38972	CHEMNITZ	NMC
09181	BARCLAY	NFSC
74245	SANDBERG	NFSC
22318	PERSSON	NMC

(b)

DEPARTMENT	MANAGER	LOCATION
NFSC	JARENO	STOCKHOLM
NMC	HOFFMAN	COPENHAGEN

(c)

EMPLOYEE NUMBER	NAME	DEPARTMENT	MANAGER	LOCATION
61256	MYGIND	NFSC	JARENO	STOCKHOLM
38972	CHEMNITZ	NMC	HOFFMAN	COPENHAGEN
09181	BARCLAY	NFSC	JARENO	STOCKHOLM
74245	SANDBERG	NFSC	JARENO	STOCKHOLM
22318	PERSSON	NMC	HOFFMAN	COPENHAGEN

For the join operation to make sense, the two columns must contain field values that are comparable, that is, that come from the same domain. If there is one domain of all possible dates and one domain of all possible prices, it is not reasonable to join two tables on the basis of dates in one and prices in the other. Relational implementations do not always check such conditions; rather, the user must determine that the operation is reasonable.

A criticism of relational systems is that the method of operation for a join is very time consuming and expensive if implemented directly as previously described. Improved query optimization and indexing techniques are being developed, however. Thus, in the join operation previously discussed, if there were an index on a column in the second table only the index might have to be searched. Moreover, for some rows in the first table, a search would not be necessary in the second table. Furthermore, if there were also an index on a column in the first table, the search for equal values could be

DATA BASE MANAGEMENT

performed entirely in the indexes. Alternatively, the data base system can keep statistics about actual or intended usage in order to optimize the search order internally. It seems that improved optimization methods are sufficiently developed to make large-scale relational testing possible.

ACCESS PATHS

Records in a relational data base system are accessed only through the matching of field values. There is no path-following mechanism in a relational system that is comparable to those in a hierarchic or network approach, where access paths are predefined in the data structure seen by the user. A programmer of a hierarchic data structure uses the implicit hierarchic structure to navigate through, for instance, an access path from a parent to a child segment type. However, any new access requirement that does not directly follow the predefined access paths in the data structure requires additional programming logic.

In the relational approach, no paths are predefined in the data structure seen by the user. Because all access is accomplished by the matching of field values, many potential paths exist. This means that the relational approach has considerable potential for extensions and restructuring and provides a very high level interface to the data structures as compared with data models that use predefined paths.

At the same time, there is increased risk of inefficient and costly data access. Since users do not see which access paths are internally favored, they cannot decide whether optimum paths are followed.

The essentials of relational operations and access paths are summarized as follows:
- Relational operations work on whole tables (i.e., sets of records).
- The result of each operation is a new table.
- Operations are based on field values in the tables as the one and only means of access.

The characteristics of today's network and hierarchical data structures follow:
- Network and hierarchical systems operate on individual records, one at a time. This is not an inherent necessity, however, since set operations on networks and hierarchies are also conceivable.
- The result of data access operations is normally a single record, since network and hierarchical systems work with individual records. (In the case of DL/I path calls, the result may be a few records along the hierarchical path instead of just one single record.)
- Operations are based mainly on predefined access paths in the data structures, and different access paths may require different coding techniques.

RELATIONAL LANGUAGES

The basic relational operations of selection, projection, and join have been discussed. The way in which these functions are provided to the user through relational language facilities is a very important aspect of relational systems.

Relational Data Bases

Even the form of the language is important in terms of the ease-of-use aspect of the relational approach.

Many different languages have been defined for use with relational data base structures. Most of them are query-type languages, but there are also languages of the traditional type intended for incorporation into such programming languages as COBOL and PL/1.

A language that explicitly provides select, project, and join is called a *relational algebraic language*. An example of an relational algebraic language is SQL. Relational algebraic languages work with sets of records; that is, they work on tables as a whole.

Other relational languages can be called *relational calculus languages* (e.g., ALPHA.)[4] This type of language is even less procedural than relational algebraic languages are. A very important characteristic of both algebraic and calculus languages is that any operation results in a new table. This means that composite expressions can be constructed in which the result of one operation becomes the operand of another.

A third class of relational languages includes *display-oriented languages*, for instance, Query-By-Example (QBE). With display-oriented relational languages, instead of the relational operations being specified in linear statement form directly as joins, selections, and projections, they are achieved by the manipulation of graphic symbols on a display screen.

A few examples of query languages are also based on network or hierarchical data models. Experience shows that these are most effective when the predefined access paths in the data structure are used directly, however. When indirect access paths must be used, the query logic specified by the user immediately becomes more complex although the query itself appears to be simple. Therefore, predefined access paths sometimes appear as asymmetry and complexity to the user.

RELATIONAL DESIGN CONCEPTS

As with many evolving concepts, the idea of relational data bases breaks down into several areas, some of which are different and independent. Preceding sections have discussed the tabular view of data, data access using such views, and languages that may be used. On this level, the relational approach is an alternative to a hierarchic or a network approach.

A quite different area of relational data base concepts deals with data base design theories, which cover the design of records. The theories are concerned with normalization and functional dependencies in record structures[5] and are often presented with much mathematical formalism.

The prime objective of these theories is to help define data record structures that remain stable as the data base grows. Well-defined record structures avoid unnecessary update problems and serve as a basis for future extensions. Existing record structures should not have to be restructured because of new application needs, although they may have to be extended and new record structures added. But existing structures should survive such evolution without need for rearrangement of fields in existing record structures.

DATA BASE MANAGEMENT

In this sense, design theories should apply to a number of data base management systems (DBMSs); a systematic design procedure is desirable regardless of whether the resulting records are grouped into tables, hierarchies, or networks. Normalization theory, for example, is not an issue in the realization of a set of record structures in certain DBMSs. Rather, the potential controversy lies in which data model is most suitable for the anticipated data access and for manipulation of the record structures. Thorough data base design is thus a valuable and desirable practice for all three data models. The penalty for bad design is loss of data independence, the implications of which are clear to experienced users of DBMSs.

With these basic concepts as background, one might ask what is so dramatically new and useful in the relational view of data. A major potential drawback should be clear—performance for table operations may not be acceptable. It is not that relational data base systems are inherently less efficient in handling data requests than hierarchical and network implementation. On the contrary, they can make use of improved techniques in indexing and access methods. The problem is that performance may be poor if the user is encouraged to do work that is as complex as that usually done with other data base systems, but he or she does not possess the same awareness of the required I/O operations and the like.

The relational external interface offers none of the predefined access paths that are found in the hierarchical and network approaches. This does not mean that optimized paths are precluded during a relational data base implementation; existing relational systems place emphasis on providing access path optimization internally, not visible to the user.

It is also possible that such developments in specialized hardware as associative processors or logic-per-track devices might be especially suitable for efficient relational data access[6] and might further improve the performance of relational data base operations. Specialized hardware, however, is not a practical or economical alternative.

EVALUATING THE RELATIONAL APPROACH

In this evaluation of the relational approach, the potential benefits are considered first; then the effect of the approach on different types of users is considered. Finally, situations in which a network or hierarchical data view is currently preferable to the relational view are considered.

The five major strengths of the relational view are discussed in the following sections.

Ease of Understanding

To some extent, complexity in such data base implementations as CODASYL or DL/I is caused by the multiplicity of different concepts and implementation constructs. This, in turn, depends on the asymmetrical ways of data access. Separate concepts are needed when predefined paths of different types are used. Examples are access to a hierarchy using a secondary index or access through a hierarchical path.

On the other hand, most people have a common and intuitive idea of what a table is; the basic concepts are easy to understand. The words common and intuitive indicate that the idea of a data base is potentially more easily available to many more users than those who understand a CODASYL set or a DL/I logical data base hierarchy.

Until now, there have been a limited number of relational data base implementations. It is possible that in future implementations the simplicity of the high-level relational approach to data base access may be compromised by implementation particularities; a large, shared data base with many complex relationships among data items may need specialized facilities for certain crucial operations. The relational concepts are by their nature straightforward and uncompromising in this respect. To a large extent, the simplicity inherent to data in existing systems is an important part of the relational discipline itself.

Increased Data Independence

The relational data base view deals directly and exclusively with rows and columns. All fields are explicitly known and seen by the user. Operations on tables do not depend on any predefined access paths that are implied in the data structure.

Relational data structures do not depend on physical attributes of storage structures because there is a distinct boundary between the external data base view and the internal storage of data.

This implied comparison with other implementations may not be realistic in the sense that it compares concepts of one with implementations of another. And practical implementations that must serve many different applications with a large, shared data base may require specialized language constructs for efficiency. Nevertheless, the relational approach provides a new chance to achieve a cleaner high-level interface.

Power and Ease of Use

A major reason why relational operations are powerful and easy to use is that they achieve set access in contrast to record-at-a-time access. As such, relational operations are less procedural than network or hierarchical data base operations; relational operators express more directly what the end result should be rather than describing how the end result should be produced. This permits the DBMS rather than the user to perform retrieval and update operations at the detailed level. Less procedurality is a big step toward increased productivity and high-level data base programming.

This characteristic becomes even more important in query applications where a user cannot be expected to specify in detail how a particular question should be answered. Consequently, query applications are seen as the first production environments for relational data base systems.

There is a parallel here involving comparisons of high-level programming languages such as COBOL and FORTRAN with more machine-oriented languages such as BAL and Autocoder. There is currently agreement on the benefits of high-level programming languages, and there well may be the same type of agreement on the set-wise approach to data base access as opposed to detailed record-at-a-time techniques.

DATA BASE MANAGEMENT

Theoretical Foundation

Research work on relational operations dates to the late sixties; thought continues to evolve in this area.[7] A barrier to early application, however, is that much of this work is presented with a lot of mathematical formalism. Practitioners are often skeptical of excessive formalism and mathematical notation. The theoretical foundation of relational systems, however, should not deter the practical and pragmatic MIS professional for it is the theoretical foundation that makes the results of relational operations predictable. This foundation is the basis for statements that relational operations always produce the answer in the form of a new table, for example.

In this regard, there is a clear distinction between relational systems and the more pragmatic DBMSs currently in use. Today's systems are the result of functions gradually extended or progressively improved with the increasing demand for additional or modified functions. Therefore, some functions in present implementation are ad hoc in nature and are not always compatible with previous concepts. In this regard, the relational view of data provides an opportunity for cleaner implementations of high-level data access.

Both users and implementors of DBMSs may benefit from this more theoretical approach to data base operations. For implementors, it means that a relational request may be more easily broken up into its component parts and rearranged, resequenced, and optimized. Intelligence may thus be transferred from individual program procedures to the DMBS.

With regard to data access, most emphasis has been placed on applications of retrieval theory; far less emphasis has been placed on the more complex data base update operations. Increasingly, however, updating operations through relational views is receiving the necessary theoretical attention.[8,9] Thus, because of their potential usefulness, theoretical studies should be appreciated and encouraged.

Table Operations and Data Definitions

The language of table operations used for data access may also be extended and generalized to data definition, thereby allowing for common interaction among data base administrators (DBAs), query users, and programmers. In contrast, different languages for data definition and for data manipulation are used in CODASYL and DL/1. This contributes to complexity and difficulty in communication among various user groups.

Even more important is the fact that the increased power and flexibility in data definition may also eliminate the need for some programming because the relational user view already expresses the data that is of particular interest to an application. As such, a more powerful data definition can replace some programming, thus diminishing the distinction between programming and data definition.

The programming effort may be further reduced because a relational data definition can allow one user's views to be expressed in terms of other users' views. Thus many levels of views-on-views are possible, such that a user view does not have to refer back to the stored data directly. This means that the underlying stored data can even change in structure, sometimes without affecting many existing user views. Instead, a previously stored structure is replaced by a mapping of a new user's view. That new view, in turn, refers back to the new stored structure.

The concept of many levels of views-on-views is particularly powerful and valuable in achieving increased data independence. In addition, the data base system becomes more forgiving in that a previous data base design can be more easily modified with new user views. The restructuring of a previous data base design is simplified because new structures can be expressed in terms of older ones and added to the system gradually. Many slightly different user views can all be present simultaneously, thereby reducing maintenance requirements.

CONCLUSION

It is often speculated that relational implementations will gradually replace network and hierarchic implementation. Such speculations seem too far-reaching. At the present time, certain applications seem to lend themselves to a solution that uses tables as a data structure, whereas many others are best served by data hierarchies or networks. The potential value of relational data bases will probably not be the same for all types of users. For some, the benefit will only be marginal, whereas for others it will be significant.

Users who are not MIS professionals (i.e., end users) may see the greatest value in the tabular view. Such people typically make unplanned query requests from data bases. Users sometimes find that present implementations are not completely successful in providing clear, precise, and simple language functions using hierarchies and networks. Similar queries must often be specified differently, depending on which predefined path in a hierarchy or network is used, because the query language is asymmetrical. The relational view is designed to provide a symmetrical, simple, high-level interface for the query specifier. At the present time, however, specialized skill is needed to properly specify queries.

For programmers, the value of relational systems strongly depends on the application. Often the same or a greater amount of programming logic is required when using a relational view than when the data base is seen as a hierarchy or network. This is particularly apparent when data has to be accessed one record at a time, for example, in a bill-of-material application where one has to follow the explosion/implosion loops individually. In other applications, a relational system may require many operations on multiple tables, whereas a hierarchical system could possibly produce the desired result with a few operations that make use of the implicit hierarchical structure of the underlying data.

In other applications, especially when set-oriented retrieval or updating is applied, a relational view may simplify the programming logic. In those cases, the simplification in logic makes the programs easier to understand and maintain and thus helps reduce maintenance costs. In set operations, for example, the same operation applied to a number of rows in a table could, for instance, increase all prices in a price table by a given percentage or change all old locations in an employee table to a new location. Common among such operations is their property of being fairly simple and straight-

DATA BASE MANAGEMENT

forward. Exceptions on an individual basis, however, cannot be handled; they require instead record-by-record processing.

On the other hand, in some applications, gains made in a relational system by reduced procedurality may be lost in other ways by the requirement to work with many variations of tables and with the multitude of implied relationships among them. Because access paths are predefined and explicitly shown, a hierarchical or network diagram may capture in one quick glance an immediate understanding of many complex interrelationships. In contrast, it may take greater time and effort to digest the same information using a large set of interrelated tables.

The programming of many applications should benefit from relational data definition capabilities because data needed for a particular application can be more directly and precisely expressed to the program. This should eliminate requirements for the program to deal with those parts of a data base that are not of direct interest to the particular application. This apparent ease of use may also, to some degree, depend on such things as earlier programming background, education, and programming style.

The problems of data base administrators are similar whether they use a relational, network, or hierarchical data base system. The administrator must still choose and define various storage operations, maintain operation procedures, and monitor performance. Backup and recovery procedures must be maintained, and storage utilization must be monitored. It is possible, however, that the number of options and alternatives can be reduced in a relational implementation. One reason is the simplicity of the interface between external and internal definitions, which can allow the DBMS to take over internally more and more of the functions handled by the DBA. This implies, however, that useful implementation alternatives may be sacrificed for the sake of simplicity.

The data base design effort is expected to depend highly on the comprehensiveness of the DBMS. The more a system can take over the maintaining, reorganizing, and optimizing of access paths to the stored data, the less effort is necessary to achieve thorough data base design. A relational system has great potential in this area because of the clean and simple interface to the user.

Flexibility in data definition is expected to considerably simplify the design effort to accommodate new or changed data requirements, especially in small, private data bases. In private data bases, the data is often isolated from application to application, and performance implications are less important. To some degree, flexibility in relational data definition may also simplify design of larger data bases that are to be shared among many applications and users.

When designing individual record structures, designers should not experience much difference among types of data bases. Good design practices, such as normalization and elimination of dependencies among field types, are desirable whether the resulting record structures are used in a network, hierarchical, or relational system.

References

1. *Query-By-Example Terminal Users Guide.* SH20-2078. IBM Corporation. Available through IBM branch offices.
2. *Interactive Management and Planning System: User Guide.* SB11-5220. IBM Corporation. Available through IBM branch offices.
3. Kim, W. "Relational Data Base Systems." *ACM Computing Surveys,* Vol. 11, No. 3 (September 1979), pp. 185-211.
4. Codd, E.F. "A Data Base Sublanguage Founded on the Relational Calculus." *ACM SIGFIDET Workshop on Data Description, Access, and Control.* San Diego, 1971, pp. 35-68.
5. Beeri, C., Bernstein, P.A., Goodman, N.A. "A Sophisticated Introduction to Data Base Normalization Theory." *Proceedings of the 4th International Conference on Very Large Data Bases,* West Berlin, West Germany, 1978. Available from the Association for Computing Machinery, 1133 Avenue of the Americas, New York NY 10036.
6. Langdon, G.G. "A Note on Associative Processors for Data Management." *ACM Transactions on Database Systems,* Vol. 3, No. 2 (June 1978), pp. 148-158.
7. Codd, E.F. "Extending the Data Base Relational Model to Capture More Meaning." *ACM Transactions on Database Systems,* Vol. 4, No. 4 (December 1979), pp. 397-434.
8. Bancilhon, F. "Supporting View Updates in Relational Data Bases." *Proceedings of the IFIP Working Conference on Data Base Architecture.* Venice, Italy, 1979. Amsterdam: North-Holland Publishing Company, 1979, pp. 213-234.
9. Dayal, U., and Bernstein, P.A. "On the Updatability of Relational Views." *Proceedings of the 4th International Conference on Very Large Data Bases.* West Berlin, West Germany, 1978. Available from the Association for Computing Machinery, 1133 Avenue of the Americas, New York NY 10036.

Bibliography

Date, C.J. *An Introduction to Database Systems.* Second Edition. Reading MA: Addison-Wesley Publishing Company, 1977.

Date, C.J., and Codd, E.F. "The Relational and Network Approaches: Comparison of the Application Programming Interface." *ACM SIGMOD Workshop on Data Description, Access, and Control.* Edited by R. Rustin. Ann Arbor MI, 1974, pp. 11-41.

Fry, J.P., and Sibley, E.H. "Evolution of Data Base Management Systems." *ACM Computing Surveys,* Vol. 8, No. 1 (March 1976), pp. 7-42.

Kent, W. *Data and Reality, Basic Assumptions in Data Processing Reconsidered.* Amsterdam: North-Holland Publishing Company, 1978.

Michaels, A.S., Mittman, B., and Carlson, C.R. "A Comparison of the Relational and CODASYL Approaches to Data Base Management." *ACM Computing Surveys,* Vol. 8, No. 1 (March 1976), pp. 125-150.

Senko, M.E. "Data Structures and Data Accessing in Data Base Systems Past, Present, Future." *IBM Systems Journal,* Vol. 16, No. 3 (1977), pp. 208-257.

Smith, D., and Smith, J. "Relational Data Base Machines." *Computer,* Vol. 12, No. 3 (March 1979), pp. 28-38.

Su, S. "Cellular-Logic Devices: Concepts and Applications." *Computer,* Vol. 12, No. 3 (March 1979), pp. 11-25.

1978 New Orleans Database Design Workshop Report. *Proceedings of the 5th International Conference on Very Large Data Bases.* Rio de Janeiro, Brazil, 1979. Available from the Association for Computing Machinery, 1133 Avenue of the Americas, New York NY 10036.

Section IX
Managing the Human Resource

We all know that the essence of success for an enterprise lies with people, but how often we forget that they are our most valuable resource. One of my earliest lessons in management, learned in the early 1960s and with me still, came from Douglas MacGregor's book, *The Human Side of Enterprise*. MacGregor, of course, developed Theory X, Theory Y, and his basic message is that if the manager clears away the impediments, the workers will do wonders. Many times since, I have seen proof of this classic theory, which is not at all theory, but fact. Properly guided, given goals they can identify with and believe in, and recognized for the work they do, well-trained and properly placed subordinates will consistently exceed management's expectations. This section is dedicated to reinforcing these aspects of managing the human resource: selection and placement, training, motivation, and rewarding. Successful managers know this method works; unsuccessful tyrants wonder why they fail.

Too often we assume that newly appointed supervisors intuitively know how to interview candidates, ensure a succession of qualified personnel, and motivate their employees. However, there is nothing intuitive about managing people: it takes training, coaching, practice, and guidance. This section of the handbook should be required reading for every supervisor and manager in MIS and should be studied very carefully by those who aspire to management.

IX-1
Human Resource Management
Janet Bensu

INTRODUCTION

This chapter discusses the tools and tasks involved in setting up a human resource management (HRM) system. An HRM system should address the following MIS problems:
- The enormous cost associated with recruitment, training, and poor performance
- The loss of qualified personnel because of the lack of career paths or opportunities for growth within the organization
- The inability to prepare the current staff for future needs because of poor planning
- Low productivity because employees lack the knowledge and skills needed to accomplish specific tasks.

Meeting the Training Challenge

Most MIS departments are faced with high turnover, shortages of qualified personnel, and inflationary salaries. Ensuring the professional growth of the organization's MIS people is one possible solution to these problems. To accomplish this, the MIS manager can:
- Creatively manage and protect the group's valuable human resources
- Hire and retain good employees by offering candidates job opportunities that meet their needs
- Prepare employees for future career opportunities, matching the needs of the organization with the abilities and career objectives of individuals
- Help individuals grow in their current jobs and reach their optimum level of productivity and effectiveness

An HRM system, implemented across the organization by the training function in conjunction with management, is designed to help managers realize these goals. This chapter highlights the HRM activities that can maximize the organization's return on its DP investment.

THE CHARACTERISTICS OF AN HRM SYSTEM

An HRM system comprises a comprehensive group of ongoing activities that help both the organization and the individual meet their objectives.

These activities must be based on the business plans, philosophy, and operating objectives of the organization, and must be interrelated to reinforce each other and to eliminate overlaps and contradictions in goals and procedures.

An IIRM system should be designed to meet the following goals:
- To provide training on a planned basis so employees continue to grow professionally and improve competency on current jobs as well as prepare for future career opportunities
- To ensure employee awareness of management's expectations and of how their skills and abilities are viewed
- To communicate advancement opportunities in the organization and the eligibility requirements
- To build an esprit de corps in the organization, giving employees a reason to stay.

Support for Managers

An HRM system provides managers with tools to help them fully utilize their staffs. These tools include procedures and guidelines for human resource activities, and forms and reports for organizing the HRM data collected. The resulting information can be used in formulating staffing plans that ensure the right people are available when and where they are needed.

Support for Employees

The HRM system gives employees a clear understanding of what is expected of them and feedback on job performance to help them know how they are doing. They will have visible career opportunities and identifiable entry points to new positions. They will also be aware of the skill requirements of these positions and will be able to prepare for them by participating in training for the skills they lack. Such an environment gives employees a reason for commitment to the organization and its goals.

HRM COMPONENTS

An HRM system is only as effective as the information it makes available. Therefore, the components of the system must not only provide data but convey it in a form that aids personnel management decisions. Table 1 lists the activities, input required, and resulting information in an HRM system.

Information about the organization provides the framework for an HRM system and should include:
- Position responsibilities for the tasks performed
- The skills needed to perform the tasks
- The structure of the organization
- Staffing requirements
- The technical environment
- Any existing human resource programs

Knowledge about the employees must include:
- Skill levels
- Weaknesses and strengths
- Career objectives
- Training

Human Resources Management

Table 1. HRM Activities

Activities	Input	Results
Skills assessment	Skills glossary Position description (skills list) Manager's modification	Individual's evaluation
Performance	Position description Standards of performance	Weaknesses and strengths
Job development/ career planning	Skills evaluation Weaknesses and strengths Position descriptions Skills-to-training list Training curricula Career objectives Staffing requirements	Development and training plan
Career counseling	Career pathing charts Position descriptions	Career objectives
Organizational needs analysis	Plans (human resources and other)	Training and staffing requirements
Training program	Organization's needs Individual's needs	Training

- Work experience
- Additional skills, training, and experience needed

Those responsible for training need information on:
- Employee training requirements
- Training needed to support the MIS department's plans
- Resources available to satisfy these needs

To manage their careers, employees need information on:
- Available opportunities
- Skill requirements for the positions
- Available training
- Career objectives
- Their own strengths and weaknesses
- Performance standards

The HRM system must efficiently maintain this data and produce reports that provide management with the information needed to make personnel planning decisions and to ensure the proper placement, evaluation, training, and development of all employees.

BUILDING THE SYSTEM

A solid foundation is needed to build a successful HRM system. Therefore, some tasks must be accomplished before the project can begin:
1. Gain senior management commitment to the system and the resources needed to develop, implement, and maintain it.
2. Establish a task force to review the project's progress.
3. Establish clear objectives and long-term goals for the system.
4. Define the system components and how they will interrelate.
5. Determine what tools should be developed.

MANAGING THE HUMAN RESOURCE

6. Define a recordkeeping system, preferably automated.
7. Define the required management reports.
8. Define the required data bases.
9. Determine who will maintain the system.
10. Determine who will monitor and control the system.
11. Establish criteria for evaluating the system and assign responsibility for evaluation.
12. Identify aspects of the system that are the responsibility of other functions in the organization and ensure their commitment and support for the HRM effort.

Once these tasks are completed, a project plan should be developed outlining each task to be performed with its subtasks and activities. Target dates should be established for each task. The plan should also specify who will be involved, whose approval is needed, and the deliverables for each activity. Figure 1 illustrates a sample segment of an HRM project plan. The plan should be circulated to all personnel involved in the project to inform them of their involvement, the amount of their time needed, and how their contribution fits into overall organizational goals. Maintaining good communication with the participants is critical. Project reviews should be scheduled and held regularly.

The following tasks should be included in the project plan:
1. Analyze the organizational structure. If it does not facilitate growth and mobility, propose an alternative structure.
2. Create career pathing charts (position networks).
3. Write or update position descriptions.
4. Develop task lists and descriptions for each position by job family.
5. Develop tasks-to-skill and skills-to-task lists.
6. Develop skills lists and descriptions for each position by job family.
7. Develop a skills glossary.

Task	Date	Responsibilities Key	Responsibilities Support	Deliverables
III. Develop skills matrix by job family				Skills-to-task list
				Tasks-to-skill list
A. Identify skills needed for each task	6/1	H. Williams	W. Johns	Skills glossary
				Skills list for position description
B. Get manager's input	8/1	E. Thomson		
C. Develop tasks-to-skill list	9/1	W. Johns	S. Lynne	
D. Manager review	9/15	E. Thomson		
E. Modify if necessary	9/30	H. Williams	W. Johns	
F. Develop matrix—indicate level required	11/1	H. Williams		

Figure 1. Sample Segment of HRM Project Plan

8. Determine the procedures and the tools required for each HRM activity.
   9. Write guidelines for using the tools.
   10. Develop procedures for maintaining the components, tools, and data bases.

Before the system can be implemented, two more important steps must be taken. First, the managers who will use the system must be trained in the skills needed to perform the activities. These include coaching and counseling, interpersonal, and communications skills. Second, the announcement of the system to the entire staff must be coordinated.

HRM TOOLS

The tools available to manage the HRM activities should provide the information necessary to make appropriate personnel management decisions. These tools include:
- Position descriptions
- Skills glossary
- Skills-to-training list
- Career pathing charts (position networks)
- Policies and procedures
- Management reports
- Data files

Managers must know what the tools are and how to use them. The tools must be readily available, up to date, and easy to use.

Position Descriptions

Position descriptions should be properly written and current since they are used as a guide in job interviews, performance appraisals, and career planning and development sessions. They should inform an employee what is expected of him or her. In career planning, position descriptions help employees determine suitable growth paths.

A good description indicates areas of responsibility and includes a task list. The tasks should be observable and measurable; each should be described as a series of steps or actions.

Positions should be grouped into job families, and the positions in each family should be designed to facilitate growth through increasing levels of responsibility. A matrix listing tasks on the vertical axis and positions on the horizontal axis can illustrate such growth within a family (see Figure 2).

The skills required to perform these tasks should also be analyzed. Skills should not be limited to technical proficiencies but should include management, business, and human relations skills. The list of skills should reflect the knowledge and actions needed to perform the job. More than one skill will probably be needed to perform a task, and more than one task will require the same skill. By developing skills-to-task and tasks-to-skill cross-reference listings, managers can determine what training is required or which skills have the greatest impact on overall performance (see Figures 3 and 4).

MANAGING THE HUMAN RESOURCE

	Tasks	P/A I	Positions P/A II	P/A III	Sr P/A
T25	Provide user liaison	—	A	P	S
T35	Prepare requirements definition	—	A	P	S
T40	Prepare for system testing	A	P	S	—
T60	Code programs	A	P	P	S

Legend
A Performs with assistance
P Performs alone
S Supervises
— Not applicable

Figure 2. Task Matrix for Programmer/Analysts

A skill should be defined in measurable terms, and different skill levels should be identified. These levels can be defined by examining the task matrix (see Figure 2). The level of responsibility a person is given should be related to the skill level required.

Skills Glossary

A glossary of skill definitions should be maintained, with the skills numbered for easy reference. A skill might be defined differently depending on its application, a problem that can be avoided by using different names or assigning each definition a different number. For example, leadership skills can be defined differently for a data center operations manager and a shift supervisor in operations.

The glossary must be kept up to date. As a task changes, the associated skills or the criteria for measuring them might change.

Task	Skills
T10 Develop and administer education activities	S15 Project management S18 Time management S20 Procedure writing S30 Interviewing S35 Interpersonal communication S40 Data gathering S58 Decision making

Figure 3. Skills-to-Task List

Skill	Tasks
S18 Time management	T10 Develop and administer education activities T12 Publish education newsletter T18 Develop courses T19 Develop education schedule T29 Manage programmer trainee program

Figure 4. Tasks-to-Skill List

Skills-to-Training List

The skill definitions can be used as a starting point for establishing objectives for training courses. A training curriculum can be developed by job family for each position in that family.

Career Pathing Charts (Position Networks)

Career pathing charts are an essential tool in planning short- and long-term goals for individual employees. The charts should show the interrelationships of job families. The ability to move to a position must be based on the skills required. Therefore, the next step for an employee might be down rather than up or across if the gap between the individual's skills and the new position's requirements is too wide. The skills required for the top position in one job family might be entry-level requirements for another family.

Policies and Procedures

Clearly defined policies and procedures are helpful to both the manager and the employee. Senior management must establish policies that reflect its philosophy regarding who has responsibility for HRM activities. Procedures should document each tool and activity, including who is involved, what input is needed, what results are produced, and what to do with them.

Management Reports

Management must be able to monitor the system to determine how well it is working. The system should also provide information that management can use in making human resources planning and other personnel decisions.

Data Files

Specifications for the data files of the HRM system should be established. Knowing how they will be accessed and for what purpose will help in determining what the files should contain. In addition to the documents discussed in this chapter, data files should include employee master files. Whether manual or automated, the procedures for maintaining the data files must be documented, and responsibility for this task must be assigned.

MAJOR ACTIVITIES

The major activities in the HRM system are skills assessment, performance appraisal, job development and career planning, career counseling, organizational needs analysis, and training program development. Of these, the only one that an employee's manager must initiate is the appraisal session. The training function is responsible for the needs analysis and the training program. The employee can be urged to assume responsibility for the skills assessment and for job development and career planning. It is the manager's responsibility, however, to assist the employee and to provide guidance and counseling when it is requested or needed.

Skills Assessment

A skills assessment should be performed by each employee. This activity requires two tools: the skills profile listing those needed in the position and the skills glossary defining those used throughout the MIS department. Not all jobs with the same title require the same skills. Job skills required of individual employees can vary within a title by the type of assignment, for example. Therefore, before the employee performs the skills assessment, the general skills profile for the position should be tailored to the individual.

The employee should assess his or her skills against this adapted skills profile, and the assessment should then be discussed with and approved by the employee's manager. During performance evaluation, the manager uses the assessment to determine how the employee has applied the skills in meeting his or her performance objectives.

The assessment should be compared with the skills profile to determine the employee's training needs. In addition, the skills assessment is used to determine the next career step for the employee. The assessment should be updated as the employee demonstrates that a new skill has been acquired.

Performance Appraisal

The evaluation of employee performance—how employees apply their skills to their jobs—is a key activity in the HRM system. Since the organization rewards performance, this activity must be carefully planned. The organization must know what human resources it has, how skilled they are, and how effectively they work. The individual needs to know how the manager views his or her work and what his or her strengths and weaknesses are.

Position descriptions should identify the employee's areas of responsibility. The manager must indicate what criteria will be used for evaluation in each area and review them with the employee in advance. During the performance evaluation, the manager should describe what the employee has accomplished and how well he or she has accomplished it. A brief explanation should describe the nature and quality of the performance. Frequently the difference between positions in a job family lies in the responsibility and skill levels required. Therefore, the appraisal should also evaluate each of these levels. It is important that the manager use relevant and specific examples to explain to the staff the performance criteria used in arriving at the ratings.

Job Development and Career Planning

The results of the performance review session should form the basis for establishing a job development and career plan. The career planning session should be separate from the review session. A performance review is initiated by the manager and focuses on past performance. The manager maintains the initiative and is in control. In addition, the review is tied to salary and can create a climate of anxiety. The focus of the planning session, on the other hand, is the future. It should be a two-way discussion between the employee and the manager. The employee can initiate the talk and can even maintain control.

The job development and career planning session serves two purposes. First, it provides the employee an opportunity to become competent and

Human Resources Management

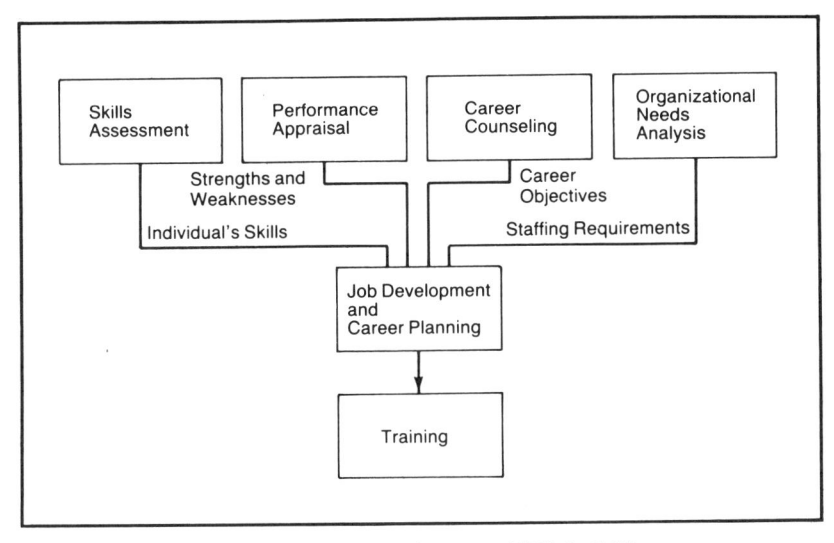

Figure 5. Relationships between HRM Activities

grow in his or her current position. Second, it prepares the individual to meet his or her career objectives.

Input to the session includes the weaknesses and strengths identified during the performance review, skills identified during the skills assessment, and the career objectives established during career counseling (see Figure 5). The objective of the session should be to develop a plan to build or strengthen the individual's skills through job experience or training, whether for improvement in the current position or in preparation for another position. By comparing the skills that the employee has with the skills that are needed, specific activities, assignments, and courses can be selected to fill the gap.

Also, by examining the task list for the position, the manager can determine whether the individual has performed all the tasks listed. If the employee has not performed some tasks, they should be assigned.

The position description for the next step in the employee's career path, with its related task and skills list, should be used to determine the plan the individual must follow in preparation for the move. A list of courses cross-referenced by skill is helpful when identifying training options.

This planning session is critical to the success of the HRM system. The manager must commit the time required and assist the employee in following the plan as long as it supports the organization's objectives. In addition, each employee is responsible for arranging and following through on the planning session. Since the MIS environment changes rapidly, the employee must be aware that adaptability is important in career planning.

A review of what was planned and what was accomplished should be part of the performance appraisal meeting or the next planning session. If training was scheduled, then the knowledge and skills learned should have been applied on the job. The session should evaluate the relevance of the course material and how well the employee adapted it to the work environment.

Career Counseling

To progress in the organization, individuals must establish career objectives. These objectives will change as the individual matures. The MIS department can provide a valuable service to the entire organization by conducting group and individual sessions on career opportunities. The group sessions could include talks by various members of the department on such topics as DP careers, project management, programming opportunities, or the responsibilities of a computer operator. These sessions can help make employees outside of data processing aware of the MIS department and its career opportunities and can realistically present the DP function, clearing away some of the mystery and misunderstanding surrounding computers. These sessions are very effective for filling entry-level positions with in-house personnel rather than recruiting new employees.

The individual sessions should focus on making employees aware of the skills they have used on the job as well as those that have not yet been used. If the employee wants to move to another discipline, the sessions should explain what is involved and what skills are needed. The employee should talk to those currently in the position and find out what the job is really like. It is up to the individual to obtain as much knowledge as possible before making a career decision and presenting that decision to the manager. Career pathing charts, together with the task and skills lists for the positions indicated on the charts, are important tools for this purpose. The manager must consider both the employee's and the organization's goals and objectives and must be realistic about what opportunities will be available. The results of these sessions are career objectives, which are used when developing the individual's training and development plans.

Organizational Needs Analysis

A needs analysis should establish a relationship between the requirements of the organization and the skills of the individual employees. The types of new skills and tasks that will be required should be determined by analyzing the organization's plans. These requirements should then be compared to the current staff's abilities. This assessment of the organization's requirements should form the basis of a plan to upgrade the skills of the current staff and to identify the criteria for recruiting and selecting personnel. When a specific need is identified, someone already qualified may be given the assignment or, if no one is available, training must be provided to bring an employee up to the minimum skill level.

Anticipated turnover, promotions, and transfers should be projected. This data will be used in the career counseling and career development planning sessions. The results of this analysis should be used to develop an effective job-related training program.

During the career counseling sessions, managers can provide the individual with pertinent, accurate information about the organization's plans. This provides the opportunity for employees to plan their growth in relation to that of the organization.

Training Program

It is the trainer's responsibility to locate the training resources needed and tailor them to the organization and the individual. General training curricula should be established using the data available in the skills lists for the job families. Using the organization's needs analysis and the training portion of the development plans, training can be closely tied to the goals and objectives of both the individual and the department. If all other HRM activities are carried out, DP training can provide training designed to develop the skills needed for the job tasks that must be performed. A training program focused on these skills can be cost-effective.

ACTION PLAN

To be successful the HRM system must have senior management support. Senior management must understand and approve the time, money, and people resources required and must ensure that line managers and subordinates are trained in HRM techniques. A staff function headed by a high-level manager should be created to develop and maintain the HRM system, and a good reporting system should be established to monitor the HRM system. Senior management must be willing to hold line managers accountable for results.

The system can only be effective if all parts are maintained; no portion should be allowed to become obsolete. The relationship between jobs and the various tasks needed to perform them must be constantly reviewed and updated. As the tasks change, the skills necessary to perform them also change. The lists of task and skill relationships must also be reviewed and updated.

The system should be integrated with associated programs or systems. For example, those in charge of such areas as compensation, employment, employee relations, and EEO must be aware of the HRM system. When integrating the HRM system with other systems, the objectives of both should be compared to determine if they coincide.

At the beginning of the project, management must be realistic in defining how it will evaluate the system. Often the greatest benefits, such as lower turnover, will not be realized for at least two years. It should take a year just for the system to go through a full cycle. A task force should be formed to evaluate the system and make recommendations for fine-tuning it. How well management communicates its expectations to the staff—and follows through on these expectations—will determine the system's success.

IX-2
Testing MIS Personnel

Larry Richman
Bruce Winrow

INTRODUCTION

Current turnover rates range from 20 to 35 percent for MIS personnel with at least two years of experience. Most organizations face continual pressure to find suitable replacements. In this competitive market, correct evaluation of MIS applicants is critical to success. Although recruiting techniques vary, most have one thing in common—they are expensive. Many companies use placement agencies that charge 20 to 30 percent of the candidate's first-year salary as a placement fee. Newspaper advertising is also expensive, especially considering the number of man-hours required to screen resumes and interview applicants. Successful candidate evaluation is often hindered by an unstructured interview process and poor execution and follow-up of the job offer.

This chapter discusses the need for planning the entire evaluation process, the value of testing as a selection tool, and some important criteria in test selection. In addition, the EEOC testing guidelines, their relevance to testing in the DP environment, and a general overview of the validation study process are provided.

THE HIRING AND EVALUATION PROCEDURE

The most important step in hiring and evaluating experienced MIS personnel is planning such matters as the recruitment method, associated costs, senior management approval, and training requirements. Evaluating the current method of staff selection and documenting its strengths and weaknesses are worthwhile planning exercises.

A Typical Applicant Screening Process

In many organizations, the hiring process goes as follows. An organization receives a requisition for new programming personnel. Since the personnel department lacks special talent to handle extensive screening, it screens resumes for buzz words used in the requisition, matches salary requests with the range for the job, and ensures that all periods of an applicant's career are accounted for on the resume. Personnel then interviews the applicant to determine whether his or her personality is likely to lead to success on the job.

Next, a senior-level technical manager arranges for further screening of candidates who pass the personnel department's review. This technical appraisal can be assigned to anyone from senior manager to staff programmer, depending on who is unavailable because of production cycles, technical problems, and crash projects. In most cases, the technical interviewer has little expertise in employment interviewing. Consequently, the applicant is evaluated on the basis of superficial shop talk and a camaraderie based on similar interests and personalities.

Because this screening process is largely based on subjective judgments, it provides little assurance that the candidate is truly qualified for the job and can meet the long-range needs of the MIS organization.

TESTING AS A SELECTION PROCEDURE

To help minimize the risk of a bad hire, MIS managers should consider using an objective test for evaluating applicants. Currently, several hundred testing tools are commercially available for screening employees and job candidates. Some excellent job-related aptitude tests are available to measure the likelihood of success in such DP positions as systems programmer, systems analyst, computer operator, and entry-level programmer. In addition, at least one testing organization produces generalized proficiency tests in such specific subject areas as COBOL, OS JCL, CICS/VS, and TSO/SPF. These tests yield detailed reports on the candidate's score, strengths, and weaknesses. They are particularly useful as an alternative to or a double check on the technical interview.

Once the test has been administered and scored, experienced nontechnical interviewers from the personnel department can continue the selection procedure more confidently.

In selecting a test, at least three factors should be considered:
- Relevance—A relevant test measures abilities that are critical to job success.
- Reliability—A reliable test should be shown to have predicted success on the job over a long period of time and in a wide range of applications.
- Predicting on-the-job success—Test scores should closely agree with supervisory ratings of performance on the job.

To optimize fairness, time-limited and multiple-choice tests should be avoided. In addition, physical security measures should be used during testing to ensure against cheating. During cost evaluation, a better test should not be rejected just because it is more expensive. The higher cost is justified if the test prevents hiring a poor candidate.

Prices can range from $5 to $250 per test (generally, the more discriminating the test and the more complex the job being tested for, the higher the cost). Many testing organizations provide volume discounts. Tests that provide written evaluations, conclusions, and recommendations are superior to those for which the organization has to draw its own conclusions.

When planning to incorporate testing into the personnel evaluation procedure, the MIS manager should contact several testing organizations for information and product samples with descriptions of the benefits of each. Tests that seem most applicable to the organization's needs for equipment, software, and skill levels of current and new employees should be administered to current employees. This will indicate the test quality and the relevance of each test section to installation needs. In addition, the validity of test results can be judged by comparing them with the job performance records of current personnel. In addition, by testing current employees, the organization can establish norms for future hiring. If cost considerations forbid testing these employees, the value of the selected tests should at least be verified by contacting other similar companies that have used them.

The organization should predetermine who should have access to the test results. The legal aspects of this question should be explored by the organization's counsel.

Figure 1 is a checklist that should be reviewed by employers who use or plan to use testing as part of their employee selection procedures. This checklist concerns the relationship between testing and fair employment practices.

EEOC GUIDELINES

The EEOC was created to enforce nondiscriminatory hiring guidelines defined by the Civil Rights Act of 1964. This act forbids discrimination based on race, color, sex, religion, or national origin in all employment practices. In 1978, the EEOC adopted a set of uniform guidelines for employee selection.

Because of the intense scrutiny to which aptitude tests have been subjected by the EEOC, many employers wonder whether they can legally use objective tests as part of their selection criteria. Employers should realize that testing is not illegal; it is not even disapproved of. Organizations are free to use any professionally developed aptitude test that is not discriminatory. They are also free to use a test that, in practice, screens out protected classes of individuals in disproportionate numbers, provided the test can be proved a valid indicator of on-the-job performance.

Public and private employers with 15 or more employees who work at least 20 weeks per year must comply with EEOC guidelines. The guidelines cover any procedure used to make an employment decision, including interviewing, reviewing of applications, work experience, oral and written tests, and physical requirements. The fundamental principle of the guidelines is that employer policies or practices having adverse impact—as determined by the 4/5 Rule illustrated in Table 1—on the employment opportunities of any race, sex, or ethnic group are not permissible unless justified by business necessity.

Employers who use a selection procedure that does not adversely affect a protected group may avoid application of the guidelines. Selection procedures that do have adverse impact should be validated to demonstrate the relationship between the procedure and on-the-job performance. In the case of testing, scores must predict performance on the job. If the employer has substantial evidence of a particular test's validity, it may be used in the selection procedure while data is collected for a local validation study. To deter-

MANAGING THE HUMAN RESOURCE

1. If an organization administers employment tests:
   - ☐ Does the test administrator always give the same instructions to each applicant?
   - ☐ Are these instructions clear to the applicants being tested?
   - ☐ Does the test administrator understand the test and the testing process well enough to answer questions clearly?
   - ☐ Can the test administrator speak and read effectively?
   - ☐ Is each applicant given the same amount of time to complete the test?
   - ☐ Is the test administrator sensitive to special problems (e.g., anxiety about tests, confusion about the use of IBM answers sheets, language problems) that some people, especially minorities, might have, and does he or she take steps to minimize these problems?

2. Are the testing facilities adequate with regard to:
   - ☐ Lighting?
   - ☐ Space?
   - ☐ Temperature?
   - ☐ Noise level?
   - ☐ Interruptions or distractions?

3. When testing is completed:
   - ☐ Are the answer sheets checked for scoring accuracy?
   - ☐ Is there a procedure whereby an applicant can learn how he or she performed on the test?
   - ☐ Is there a process by which an applicant can review the results of his or her employment test or request a retest?
   - ☐ Are scores and answer sheets retained for both successful and unsuccessful applicants for at least 15 months?
   - ☐ Are tests, answer sheets, test scores, and scoring keys available to authorized and trained personnel?

4. Are the tests constructed so that:
   - ☐ Instructions and questions are written at an appropriate language level for the applicant?
   - ☐ The mechanics of the test (e.g., mark-sense answer sheets) can be easily handled by all applicants, especially minorities?
   - ☐ The time limits are reasonable?
   - ☐ Success on the test is not highly influenced by previous testing experience (e.g., there are no clues in questions or format; one question does not answer another)?

5. When selecting for future success in training or task proficiency:
   - ☐ Is there a clear, specific description of the job?
   - ☐ Have the tests been proven to predict success by a statistical study showing a significant relationship between test scores and job proficiency (i.e., test validity) or do studies from other companies show test validity for similar jobs?
   - ☐ Do these studies show that the tests do not discriminate against minorities?

6. If the test measures skills (e.g., typing, keypunch, or stenography) that will be required immediately on a job, does the job description clearly indicate that the applicant will need these skills?

7. If asked to discuss the employment testing program, could the organization show:
   - ☐ A copy of the tests the organization uses?
   - ☐ A test manual or similar document giving general information and administrative and scoring instructions for each test?
   - ☐ The instructions given the examinee, time limits, scoring procedures, and how scores from tests and parts of tests are weighed when no manual exists?

8. Can the organization describe:
   - ☐ How the tests were administered?
   - ☐ How the tests were scored?
   - ☐ How the tests were used in the selection decision?

Figure 1. Checklist for Employers Who Test*

> 9. Does the validity studies' documentation show:
>   - [ ] When the studies were made?
>   - [ ] Which people were studied (the sample)?
>   - [ ] The sample size?
>   - [ ] The criterion for successful performance?
>   - [ ] The validity coefficients or other validity information?
>   - [ ] The minority groups studies and if their results were similar to those of the total sample?
> 10. In general:
>   - [ ] Are the same standards applied to everyone?
>   - [ ] What percentage of total applicants pass?
>   - [ ] What percentage of minority applicants pass?
>   - [ ] What percentage of applicants are screened out before tests are administered?
>   - [ ] What percentage of minority applicants are screened out before tests are administered?
>
> *This checklist was developed by the California Fair Employment Practices Commission.

Figure 1 (Cont)

mine substantial evidence, the abilities required for successful job performance should be established and these criteria compared to what is measured by the test. If the criteria in the job description and those in the test are very much the same and if the test has been validated elsewhere, the test can be used. It should be considered only one factor (less than 50 percent) in making the selection decision.

To perform a local validation study, a sample of at least 30 persons—either present employees (concurrent validation) or new hires (predictive validation)—must be measured over a period of time to determine whether there is a meaningful relationship (predictive validation coefficient) between on-the-job performance ratings and test predictions. The testing organization that markets the tests should gather the data for the employer, perform all necessary statistical work, and then write a detailed validation report showing the results of the study for the employer's organization. The results of a sample validation study are shown in Figure 2.

Three basic types of validation strategies are recognized by the EEOC guidelines:

- Content validity—established when a selection procedure consists of a representative sample of the exact kinds of tasks performed on the job
- Construct validity—established when measures of abilities, aptitudes, personality characteristics, and interests abstracted from the study of human behavior match the job requirements
- Criterion-related validity—established when there is a significant statistical relationship between selection procedure scores (predictors) and job performance (criterion)

Table 1. Determination of Adverse Impact (4/5 Rule)

Selection Procedure Administered to	Hired	% Selected	Hiring Ratio%
100 males	65 males	65	33/65 (50%)
60 females	20 females	33	

*In this example, the hiring ratio for females is less than 80% of that for males, indicating hiring practices adversely affect females. This means the selection procedure must be validated.

This validation study of a systems programming aptitude test (SPAT) demonstrates a significant relationship between test scores and supervisory performance ratings. This report, based on the findings at 18 client companies, was conducted by a prominent testing organization in the United States.

Purpose: The purpose of this study is to demonstrate the predictive validity of SPAT by comparing test scores to job performance, as measured by supervisory ratings.

Job Description: A systems programmer is responsible for programming modifications and development of computer operating systems, telecommunications programming, terminal support systems maintenance and development, data base programming, and programming relating to the functioning of the computer hardware.

Procedures and Population: Data was collected from 37 systems programming candidates at 18 client organizations of the test supplier. Among the sample candidates were 29 males and 8 females. Participating organizations included companies in the fields of banking, insurance, transportation, retail, aerospace, manufacturing, electric power, and MIS as well as government agencies.

Scores of the candidates ranged from 41 to 100 percent. The mean score was 86.6 percent, and the median score was 89.5 percent.

Supervisory ratings were described as:

Marginal	1
Acceptable	2
Good	3
Very Good	4
Excellent	5

The mean rating was 3.76 and the median rating 4.00, computed approximately six months after hiring.

A significant relationship exists between SPAT scores and supervisory job performance ratings. The correlation coefficient (r) was computed to be 0.33 at the 0.05 level of significance. This means that only five times out of 100 could this result occur by chance. Therefore, SPAT appears to predict on-the-job performance for systems programming candidates.

Job Traits Measured: SPAT measures the following job traits:
- Logical ability
- Accuracy
- Ability to reason with symbols, according to stated definitions
- Ability to understand highly complex relationships
- Ability to deduce generalizations from a series of specific cases
- Ability to interpret precisely intricate specifications and definitions
- Ability to analyze a problem that cannot be solved by trial and error alone
- Attention to detail

Test completion times ranged from 110 minutes to 420 minutes. The mean time was 206 minutes and the median time 180 minutes.

Results: The mean test scores for males and females were 85.5 and 90.4, respectively. The mean supervisory rating for males was 3.79; for females, it was 3.75. Although the sample is too small for appropriate statistical measures, the female candidates appear to have outperformed the males on the SPAT, suggesting that the test is not unfair to women. More data is needed, however, for a definitive opinion on this matter.

Summary of Results: Based on an interim validation study, SPAT appears to predict on-the-job success as measured by supervisory ratings.

Figure 2. Sample Validation Study

Criterion-related validation is the most practical and most often used validation strategy for testing.

The MIS manager should realize that EEOC guidelines apply not just to testing, but to all hiring procedures, including the interview process. In fact, the EEOC encourages the use of tests if they result in fairer hiring practices.

A study conducted by a large bank with 2,500 DP employees found that those who were tested as part of the selection procedure were rated 20 percent higher by their managers than those selected without having been tested. In addition, turnover was three percent lower among those who had been tested as part of the hiring process.

THE TESTING ENVIRONMENT

If testing is used as a tool for selection, the MIS manager should ensure that administrative details are taken care of first. This may include arranging for testing premises and ensuring that enough tests are on hand. Because potential employees will be taking the test, the company should give a professional first impression. There is no excuse for administrative foul-ups, considering the enormous value of hiring the best candidates. As many people as possible should be tested at one sitting, especially if the candidates are likely to know each other. Most good tests are designed with the assumption that the problems are new to the applicant. Scheduling as few testing sessions as possible greatly reduces the chances of one applicant coaching another.

The organization should remain in constant contact with the applicant at all stages of the selection process, especially if test results are delayed. This reduces the chance of surprise if a candidate accepts a position elsewhere and provides an opportunity to make a hiring decision without test results if the organization feels that a good candidate will be lost in the interim. It also improves the organization's professional image. An organization with a personal follow-up procedure has a competitive edge over those with shoddy hiring practices. Even if a candidate is turned down, he or she is in a position to refer future candidates; thus, the selection process should leave all candidates with a positive image of the organization.

ACTION PLAN

When hiring and evaluating experienced MIS personnel, the organization should:
- Plan the entire recruiting and evaluation process.
- Evaluate different selection tools and pursue those that are relevant to the organization.
- Contact several testing organizations to determine what support services they provide, if testing is used.
- Become familiar with the EEOC guidelines governing selection procedures.
- Establish competitive salary scales.
- Conduct planned and professional interviews with appropriate follow-up.
- Prepare a better job offer procedure than the competitors.

IX-3
Interviewing Techniques
Jerry Gitomer

INTRODUCTION

A common problem in hiring MIS personnel is that the senior staff members who make the final hiring decisions are not always qualified to hold effective interviews. Their strengths are in managing technology and implementing systems rather than in screening and interviewing job candidates. This lack of interviewing skill is one reason why senior staff members often pick former co-workers for a position rather than seeking new candidates.

This chapter provides the novice interviewer with sufficient information to conduct an interview with confidence and offers the veteran interviewer some tools and techniques to aid in securing the most promising employees. The nontechnical aspects of interviewing are emphasized for two reasons. First, most installations are already aware of the technical requirements for the positions they are trying to fill. Second, the rapidly changing environment in most organizations makes an ability to adjust to new conditions and problems more important than a thorough knowledge of a single technical environment.

GENERAL CONSIDERATIONS

It is essential that the interviewer have a general DP background, but an in-depth knowledge of the specialty for which the candidates are being sought is not necessary.

The personnel practices of the organization can have an effect on the quality of the candidates who are attracted. The personnel department must have a clear understanding of the type of applicants desired. An overzealous personnel manager lacking such understanding might have placed the following ad in a newspaper:

> MIS MANAGER — Full responsibility for systems analysis, programming, and operation of data center with 3 computers. Must be familiar with OS internals, ANS COBOL, and IMS.

Although a knowledge of these areas is desirable, these should not be the primary qualifications for the position. The requirements listed here could be met by a systems programmer. The manager responsible for an installation with three mainframes, however, should be an executive with strong skills in managing both personnel and systems. In addition to attracting candidates,

MANAGING THE HUMAN RESOURCE

the personnel department must perform screening, testing, background gathering, and a certain amount of pre-interviewing to determine which candidates should be rejected without an interview. An inadequate or overly restrictive screening process will be reflected in the quality or limited number of the candidates, and the MIS department should request modifications in the screening process.

Screening Applicants

Generally a personnel department or employment agency function, screening eliminates unsuitable candidates from consideration without expending the time and cost of a technical interview. In practice, interviewers should realize that poorly qualified candidates occasionally slip through and therefore not assume that all who are interviewed are qualified.

The first step in screening is a review of the candidate's resume or application form. A specialized employment agency is often more qualified for this task than an internal personnel department. Not being familiar with DP, the personnel staff cannot be expected to evaluate candidate experience effectively. For example, a member of the organization's personnel department cannot usually be expected to know that "DOS" and "disk operating system" are the same entity, that the same acronym may mean two different things on different systems, or that Basic Assembly Language is different from the BASIC language.

Some key points to consider when reviewing resumes or applications are:
- Amount of experience
- Applicability of experience
- Desired salary
- Relocation requirements
- Education

No single factor should be treated as an absolute requirement; the best candidate is sometimes deficient in one category. The manager responsible for the design and development of a very successful operating system for a major vendor does not have a college degree, and the chief programmer responsible for the design and development of an outstanding minicomputer FORTRAN majored in archaeology. Of course, if the candidate is deficient in two or more areas and there are no compensating strengths, the candidate should not be interviewed.

Testing. Many organizations use tests as the first step in screening, especially for trainee positions. Industry opinion on the effectiveness of testing ranges from one extreme to the other. Some find no value in testing, while others believe that properly constructed tests eliminate the need for interviews. Many installations rely on a combination of testing and interviewing. Most of the available tests are of little value for positions above entry level.

There are two important considerations when using tests. First, an unsuitable test will probably result in hiring the wrong candidate. The skills and aptitudes required of programmers, analysts, and computer operators are not at all similar. The most common test, The Programmer Aptitude Test, is therefore not helpful when hiring operators or analysts. Second, tests are designed to be given in an environment free of interruptions and distractions. Failure to provide such a testing environment can result in invalid scores and may eliminate desirable candidates.

Pre-interviewing. One excellent screening technique is to schedule a general pre-interview immediately before the technical interview. The pre-interview, which can be conducted by the personnel department, an administrative assistant, or a personnel agency, is intended to acquaint the candidate with the position and the organization, while enabling the organization to eliminate candidates deemed unsuitable on nontechnical grounds. The pre-interview should cover:
- The nature of the organization
- The structure of the organization and the DP installation
- Working hours, pay periods, and administrative details
- The benefits package
- Any unusual aspects of the job or organization

If the candidate does not pass the pre-interview or is uninterested in the job, the technical interview should be cancelled. It is good practice not to eliminate a candidate at this point unless two different interviewers agree that the candidate is unsuitable; this ensures that a personality clash with a single interviewer does not eliminate a suitable candidate.

Choosing Interviewers

If any manager or senior staff member has an outstanding record in selecting superior candidates, the choice of interviewer is easy. If no one on the staff has demonstrated such talent, however, the interview should be conducted by the manager to whom the candidate will report if hired.

In some organizations any candidate above the trainee level is subjected to three or more separate interviews. This practice can turn off the best candidate, since it leaves the impression that management is incapable of making a decision. A better practice is to schedule one interview with one member of management and have anyone else whose approval is required drop in and conduct a segment of the interview while the original interviewer remains in the room. Another approach is to conduct an information interview after hours with all of the involved managers.

One problem that is becoming more common is hiring specialists in areas unfamiliar to the present technical staff. Fortunately, even the most esoteric DP specialities are built on a foundation of familiar concepts. One useful technique is to ask the specialist candidate to explain his or her specialty in simplified terms. The field of candidates should be narrowed to include only those whose explanations are understandable. The final selection should be based on whatever objective qualities the interviewer is competent to evaluate. While this procedure may not favor the best specialist, it will usually result in the selection of the best candidate for the particular organization—the one who is best able to communicate with the rest of the staff.

Tailoring the Interview

The interview should be tailored to the candidate's level of experience.

Regardless of the type of job, there are common requirements based on the needed experience level.

Trainees know little or nothing about DP, having acquired at best some theoretical background during their education. Three key criteria in selecting trainees are intelligence, attitude, and aptitude. Intelligence and aptitude generally can be determined from well-constructed tests or inferred from the candidate's educational record. The technical interview should therefore focus on determining the attitude of the candidate.

Qualified junior level personnel have already been trained and have some experience, but cannot work without close supervision. An interview therefore should verify that the junior candidate has sufficient experience and knowledge to be placed at the junior level.

Qualified senior level personnel have sufficient experience and judgment to work with little supervision and to be given group leadership assignments. An interview for a senior level position should focus first on the experience level of the candidate and, if this is satisfactory, determine whether the candidate has sufficient maturity and judgment to be trusted with senior-level responsibilities.

Supervisory personnel should be selected primarily for their ability to manage the people who actually do the work, not for their ability to perform the work themselves. Highly skilled senior staff members often prove to be incompetent supervisors. Their most common failings are an inability to resist doing the work themselves and a lack of tolerance when dealing with employees with lesser technical ability. The interview for a supervisory position should establish that the candidate has sufficient technical knowledge to understand the senior staff members he or she will be responsible for; however, more emphasis should be placed on determining the candidate's ability to deal with subordinates, peers, and superiors.

PREPARING FOR THE INTERVIEW

A job interview is often a traumatic experience for the candidate, and sometimes for the interviewer as well. Each is tense because of the fear that he or she will not measure up in the eyes of the other. Each tries to make a good impression, while not painting too rosy a picture. Neither may know what to emphasize or omit in the interview.

The first step in preparing for an interview is to make it clear to the personnel department that qualified DP candidates are very scarce, and are sometimes a bit unusual. Courteous treatment of candidates is therefore necessary. A lack of common courtesy by the personnel department can counter the interviewer's efforts to make a good impression on the candidate.

When the appointment is set up the candidate should be briefed on what to expect: what forms must be filled out, who will conduct the prescreening and technical interviews, and how much time will be required. If the candidate is from out of town and the organization is paying for the transportation expenses, the candidate should also be told what receipts should be obtained, what limits to observe on expenses, and when reimbursement will be made.

Interviews should be held in a quiet setting where there will be no interruptions. If this is not possible, the interviewer should arrange for all telephone calls to be held and inform his staff that all questions should be delayed except in case of an emergency. The pre-interview screening usually varies in length; if it immediately precedes the interview, the interviewer should schedule short, easily interrupted tasks for himself for the morning or afternoon of the interview.

The interviewer should be familiar with the candidate's resume and/or application before the interview. The interviewer should be notified if the candidate passes the pre-interview screening process and the interviewer or the interviewer's secretary should escort the candidate to the interviewer's office. If the interview is being held elsewhere, the candidate should be escorted to the interview site and told that the site was chosen to minimize distractions and interruptions.

The Interviewing Site

The average office is a poor place to conduct an interview. The desk serves as a barrier and is frequently loaded with piles of papers and lamps that create visual and physical barriers. Even the chairs in the average office work against a good interview; the interviewer is able to lean back in a comfortable swivel chair while the candidate is stuck in an uncomfortable, upright side chair. When there is no alternative to the office, the office environment should be improved. Borrow a comfortable side chair and, if space permits, place it alongside the desk instead of on the other side of it. Clear the desktop so that the interviewer and the candidate can see each other without craning around stacks of paper and lamps.

If at all possible, however, the interview should be held in a setting other than an office. Schedule a conference room, or meet off-premises. The setting should encourage comfortable discussion, not an inquisition.

Finally, before conducting the interview the interviewer should establish specific objectives and a plan for attaining each objective. Some of the questions an effective interview should answer are:
- Does the candidate meet the technical standards of the organization for the job?
- Will the candidate fit into the organization?
- Does the candidate have strengths and capabilities beyond those required for the initial job?

CONDUCTING THE INTERVIEW

A sound rule is that all interviews for a position should be conducted by the same interviewer. This will help ensure that all candidates are evaluated similarly.

Strategies

The first step in conducting an interview is to put the candidate at ease and establish a rapport. The best interviews evolve into informal discussions. To get an interview rolling, the easiest approach is to find a common interest for discussion. The interviewer may notice something in the resume that is related to his own experience but not necessarily to the job at hand. For example, if the candidate has written a payroll program and the interviewer has in-depth knowledge of payroll, then, by all means, the interview should start off on this subject. This kind of opening usually relaxes both participants and gives the interviewer a chance to validate the information in the resume.

Programmers and operators are sometimes more difficult to interview than other candidates because they often lack skill in verbal communications. One way to overcome this problem is to begin by describing the duties and opportunities of the position and then ask the candidate for comments. It is important not to ask questions that can be answered briefly. If this is not possible, the interviewer should counter a terse response with a request for an explanation. For example, if a candidate responds, "I can handle the job," the interviewer should ask why the candidate believes this. Another technique that can help to get things rolling is to describe an actual problem and solicit the candidate's advice. The candidate can also be asked to evaluate and comment on practices and policies of the organization that differ from those he is accustomed to.

At the other extreme is the highly qualified senior analyst who is a better interviewer than the interviewer himself. When dealing with such articulate candidates the best approach is to ask the candidate to explain his or her approach to the job. The important consideration is not the specific approach selected, but the candidate's thought processes.

Another consideration when interviewing for high-level positions is to be wary of candidates who become too involved in low-level details. Programming managers are paid to manage programmers, not to write code. Analysts are paid to define problems and make general recommendations. Designers are paid to develop systems only to the point where the implementation team takes over. Senior level personnel and managers are paid to exercise their judgment and provide guidance to junior personnel, not to do the work of lower level employees.

Because the interview is not a normal work situation, the candidate's behavior is probably atypical. The interviewer should realize that the candidate is likely to be nervous and should concentrate on asking specific questions. One useful technique is to ask the candidate to describe his current job in general terms and to explain any specific practices the candidate feels are especially good or bad. The replies will not only give the interviewer an understanding of the candidate's experience, but will also reveal the candidate's attitudes, perceptions, and judgment. Another effective question is, "What would you do differently if you were your present manager?" The main purpose of this question is not to reveal the candidate's conception of his or her strengths and weaknesses, but to determine if the candidate's perception of roles is valid, and to see if the candidate might be a misfit in the organization.

Evaluating Experience

Interviewers should realize that all experience is not equally important. Many MIS personnel have several years of experience in a very limited area rather than several years of diverse experience. Sometimes this may not be a problem; for example, when hiring an analyst responsible for establishing and maintaining a complex inventory system, the ideal candidate may be one who has made a career working with similar inventory systems. The important task is to separate those candidates who work by rote from those who understand what they are doing. One way to do this is to ask the candidate to describe his most recent project, including the time the project took, the scope of the project, his or her responsibilities, which tasks the candidate is proud of, and which tasks the candidate would like to do differently if the project were repeated.

Another method of determining a candidate's skill enables the interviewer to compare the candidate with present staff members. This approach involves presenting a hypothetical problem to the staff members and to each job candidate. The candidates are asked how they would solve the problem, what techniques they would use, and why they did not select specific alternative methods.

Making Commitments

The interviewer should be cautious about making commitments during the interview. The candidate is naturally anxious about whether he will be selected, and about how much money will be offered. If many candidates are to be interviewed, tell the candidate that it may be some time before a decision is announced. Do not promise that the candidate will be notified in a few days when things simply cannot happen that fast.

Salary is a touchy interview problem. Generally no figure should be established during the interview, because it is mandatory to maintain a reasonable equity with present employees, and a review of the candidate's relationship to other employees must be made to fix the salary.

A candidate may ask if his salary requirement is in line with what is being considered for the position. If it is too high, say so. If it is too low, yet the candidate appears qualified, he may be told that salary is not likely to be a problem.

Often the salary is noted on a resume or application as "open." If the applicant indicates a current salary that is in line with the budget, then a salary negotiation may prove fruitful. A candidate often declares that salary is open when he is less concerned about money than other aspects of the job.

Body Language[1]

An interview may be a stressful situation. Questions are answered carefully, and the candidate may adjust his answers to fit what he thinks the interviewer wants to hear. The gestures that a candidate makes are important clues to what the candidate means and how he feels. Watching these nonverbal communication signals helps in judging a candidate and can give the interviewer more confidence in his final selection.

Eye Contact. Some people are more prone to eye contact than others. If a person seems normal in this regard yet averts his gaze when certain questions are asked, then those questions have made him feel uncomfortable or guilty.

Arms Crossed. When a candidate crosses his arms, he has become defensive or bored. If the interviewer has not been talking much, this gesture may mean that something just said troubles the candidate. Back up and try to find the trouble.

Locked Ankles. A candidate who sits with his ankles locked is somewhat apprehensive. Coupled with trembling (noticeable in the hands), the candidate may be communicating desperation for the job. Try to reassure him and get him to relax.

Steepling. The well-known gesture of putting the fingers of the two hands together to form a steeple indicates superiority. The steeple need not point up. A candidate may form a steeple while responding to some tough technical question. The steeple indicates his confidence in that area.

Talking Through the Hand. When a candidate answers a question while covering his mouth with his hand (or fingers), he is probably uncertain. Feel free to immediately respond to his answer with, "Are you certain about that?" His reaction to the follow-up question should clear any doubts the gesture gave with the first answer.

Raising the Hand (or Finger). Probably a holdover from raising a hand to ask a question in school, this gesture indicates the candidate has something to say and wants to interrupt you. Let him.

Reading the Signs. There are many gestures that are reliable indicators of what a person is thinking. Sometimes what is said and the accompanying gesture do not match. Practice reading these nonverbal signals in situations other than interviewing until you feel confident about spotting them and knowing what they mean.

If a person forms a steeple, move on to another topic, confident that he knows what is currently being discussed. If he talks through his hand or averts his gaze, then linger in that area for a while and see what you can find. If signs of nervousness are obvious, try to eliminate them before continuing.

THE TOUGHEST INTERVIEW

The toughest interview is one with a candidate whose salary is equal to or above that of the interviewer. In some professions, a manager may have a number of people reporting to him who make more money than he does. Examples are engineering, research, and sales. This situation is not common in the computer field, however.

When an interviewer is confronted by a candidate making nearly as much or more than he is, his usual sense of superiority and confidence may be badly shaken. The reasons for this are clear: the candidate must be considered a peer and dealt with as such, and the employment interview does not provide a good environment for a relationship of this type. The interviewer may also feel threatened; a ranking member of the staff is a competitor for future promotions.

Even the interviewer who is extremely secure will inevitably compare the candidate to himself. Should the candidate suffer from that comparison because of a loss of objectivity on the part of the interviewer, a good prospect may be missed. Indeed, the interviewer may reject all such persons, making it impossible to fill the position.

Unless the interviewer has demonstrated his effectiveness in handling this kind of interview, the interviewer's manager should take precautions to ensure selection of the best available candidate. Such precautions can include a manager's review of all applicants and of the interviewer's write-ups of the results of the interviews.

FOLLOW-UP

At the conclusion of an interview a summary of the results should be written down. This is vitally important when several people are being interviewed in succession. Names and faces quickly blur without written notes to refresh the memory. Even when only a few interviews are conducted, getting fresh impressions down on paper can help avoid a later mistake about which candidate had which skill. The summary should be considered part of the interview, and time should be allocated for writing the summary before starting something else. The sample interview results form shown in Figure 1 requires less than 10 minutes to complete in detail.

All papers related to an applicant should be filed together, and notes should be made on an appointment calendar if the interviewer has to call the applicant or be contacted by him. Give unsuccessful applicants the courtesy of a "no thank you" letter within a few days of the interview. An exception can be made for applicants supplied through an employment agency, in which case the agency should be contacted by phone and instructed to notify the applicant.

REFERENCE CHECKS

References should be checked for applicants who look promising. Two references should be checked, including a former supervisor if possible. A reference can be expected to be complimentary; for this reason references should be checked by telephone so that the interviewer can hear *how* the compliments are communicated. Hesitation or groping for words may indicate a weak knowledge of the candidate. Evasive answers or compliments with little enthusiasm may indicate a reluctance to give a wholehearted endorsement. What is hoped for in the reference check is that the reference will confirm the interviewer's opinion. If this objective is to be achieved, the reference must not be led or have words put into his mouth.

THE OFFER

After reviewing the notes, resumes, and applications of the top candidates, the interviewer should make a selection and decide on a salary offer (plus relocation expenses and any other money-related benefits) and a desired starting date. Management approval should be obtained, and the successful applicant should be called as soon as possible. A follow-up offer letter should then be sent. The phone call will reduce the chance that the candidate will accept a competitive offer, which he may have in hand already. When a

MANAGING THE HUMAN RESOURCE

INTERVIEW RESULTS

INTERVIEWER _____ DATE INTERVIEWED _____

CANDIDATE'S NAME _____

Complete the following at the conclusion of each interview. Attach completed form to resume:

1. Personal Attributes — Personality, Appearance, Motivation, Attitude

2. Experience—Comment on quantity and quality.

   Technical: Hardware, Software, Online, etc.

   Functional: Non-DP Understanding of Applications Areas

3. Responsibilities—Evaluate ability at highest responsibility level.

4. Communication—Ability to Listen, Oral, Written

5. Last/Current Job

   Accomplishments: Was a major accomplishment indicated?

   Dislikes: Management, Working Conditions, Level of Work, etc.

   Change: Why does candidate want to change jobs?

6. Salary: How much does candidate want?

   How much do you think we should offer?

7. Contribution to the Company

   Strengths: Expertise above Current Staff

   Weaknesses: Areas That Would Require Correction

8. Recommendations—Hire? _____ Salary? _____

   Comments: _____

Figure 1. Interview Results Form

lot of time and effort has been spent to get the best candidate, the interviewer should not rely on the mail to close the deal.

ACTION PLAN

As a starting point, the ideas presented in this chapter should be circulated to staff members who are or could be interviewers. Let it be known that a new or improved approach to interviewing prospective employees is to be instituted. This should be followed up with meetings to determine interviewing policies and designate interviewers.

The interviewing process is largely subjective; some staff members are more perceptive than others and make more successful interviewers. Give these individuals a trial, and encourage those who have had experience to hand out tips. It takes time to recognize successful interviewers; however, with patience and a watchful eye, the manager will assemble an effective interviewing team.

References

1. Much of the material in this section can be found in *How to Read a Person Like a Book*, Nierenberg and Calero, Pocket Books, 1973.

IX-4
Succession Planning and MIS—Structure from Chaos
Norman H. Carter

INTRODUCTION

Three major complaints heard from MIS managers are:
- "One of my managers is quitting, and I have no one to replace her."
- "We don't have time to train people. We're too busy getting the work out."
- "I don't spend much time on management development. I end up preparing good managers for other companies since my best people are the ones most likely to be stolen from me."

All three of these statements indicate the need to examine the organization's human resource planning and development posture and the need to establish a comprehensive program that would reduce turnover and provide a more consistent managing force.

Turnover is often blamed on the individual's quest for more money. Post-departure interviews, however, often reveal a different reason: "I left because I didn't know where I was going; the new company was able to tell me more about my career."

When this type of response comes from an employee on whom the organization has been relying, the damage to the organization can be severe. One way to reduce the problem, improve management planning, and show the most promising employees that they have a future in the organization is to provide a succession planning system.

A succession planning system provides a basis for:
- Communicating career plans to each individual
- Establishing development and training plans
- Establishing career paths and individual job moves
- Communicating upward and laterally concerning the MIS management organization
- Creating a more comprehensive human resources planning system

This chapter discusses a system that provides the MIS manager with planned continuity of management as well as an effective approach to meeting the business needs of the MIS department and the organization.

WHAT IS SUCCESSION PLANNING?

Succession planning is a means of:
- Identifying critical management positions, starting at the levels of project manager and supervisor and extending up to the highest position in the organization.
- Describing management positions to provide maximum flexibility in lateral management moves and to ensure that as individuals achieve greater seniority, their management skills will broaden and become more generalized in relation to total organizational objectives rather than to purely departmental objectives.

For example, if the organization plans to move an outstanding systems project manager into management of broad applications development, it may be of value to first identify one or more staff position moves that would broaden the individual's experience. Such moves might include:
- Manager of documentation and standards for a year, to become aware of the need for and value of these functions
- Manager of planning for one or two years, to develop an all-inclusive view the organization's plans and of their relationship to system designs

Of course, careful communication of these moves and their relevance to the individual's career are critical.

System Relationships in Succession Planning

Figure 1 illustrates the relationships that must exist for a succession planning system to be complete and integrated into the organization's human resource development systems. Four major areas involve:
- The individual planning process
- Organizational determinations
- Summaries for use internally and for communication with other managers
- Presentations of senior managerial candidates to divisional and organizational management.

THE INDIVIDUAL PLANNING PROCESS

The individual's entry into the management succession planning system begins with identification of the managerial position requirements, preferably stated in terms of critical success factors (CSFs) rather than narratives. CSFs can be measured, and their completion or progress reviewed, as part of an overall performance appraisal.

For example, the position description for programming manager should include CSFs similar to the following:
- Will maintain estimated schedule and budget on at least 80 percent of all jobs put into work.
- Will complete training of "X" number of people in technique "Y" each quarter of the forthcoming year.
- Will investigate the applicability of language "XYZ" to business systems problems at the company and will report findings to management by "Z" date. (If affirmative action is recommended, a plan for implementation must also be presented.)

Succession Planning

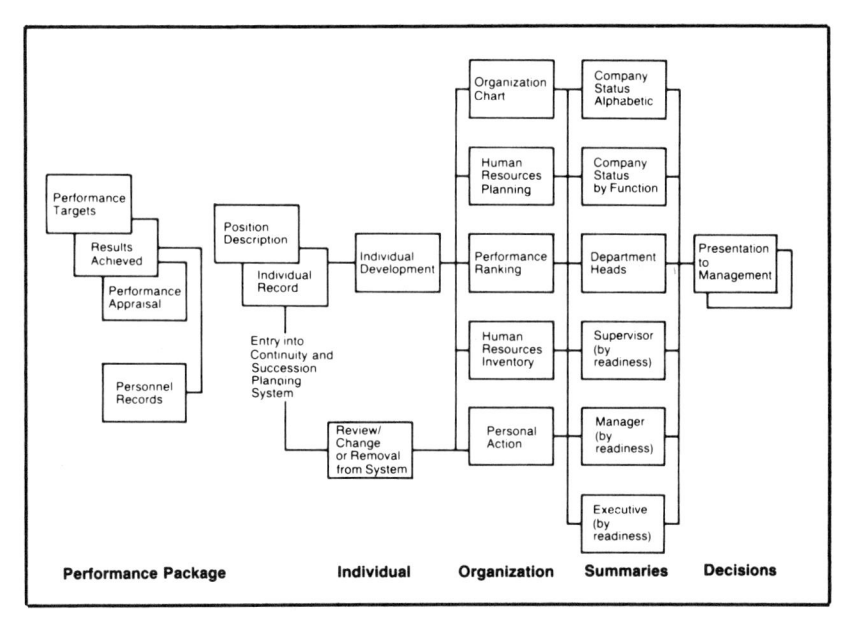

Figure 1. Management Continuity and Succession Planning System Relationships

A separate file must be established that will identify the following for each individual in the program:
- Performance targets and results achieved, for inclusion in performance appraisal and progress review sessions
- Background data and information about the individual, possibly selected from personnel records with his or her assistance and concurrence, integrated into an individual record for use in the program and updated at least annually
- An individual development plan

This separate file provides the MIS manager with a comprehensive overview of the needs, potentials, and strengths of his or her section managers; it can be reviewed to ensure that the goals for manager development are being met. Figure 2 presents a sample form used in a personal history and development plan.

CAREER PATH PLANS

Career path plans that define a succession of positions through which managers are likely to move as they progress are of obvious importance to both the individual's managerial development and human resource planning. For the individual, the career path plan defines a series of goals on which development efforts can be focused and by which development progress can be measured. For human resource planning, career paths identify future available positions and the managers who should be ready to fill them.

Career path plans should be developed for every manager included in the management continuity and succession plan. Because of the time and effort

MANAGEMENT CONTINUITY AND SUCCESSION PLANNING PERSONAL HISTORY SUMMARY	
CURRENT PHOTOGRAPH	Employee Name (Last, first, & initial)
	Date of Birth / Date Employed
	COLLEGE/UNIVERSITY Major
Nondegree Significant Education	
In-Company Management Education Programs Completed	
Out-Company Management Education Programs	
Company Experience (List earliest experience first) Division Position & Location Reporting to Date Assigned	
Significant Noncompany Experience:	

Figure 2. Personal History Summary

required to prepare them, however, these career path plans should initially identify only the next two positions through which the managers should progress.

Although developing a career path plan takes a good deal of time on the part of both superior and subordinate, this is not a valid reason for deferring career plan development. In fact, the in-depth and detailed discussion of the career development process contributes in itself to a manager's development.

What Goes into a Career Path Plan?

Every manager's career path plan will be different; however, they all

should contain the following:
- The next position, defined as specifically as possible, and the length of time to be spent in that position. Wherever possible, alternative positions should be specified.
- The purpose of moving into the next position. This should answer the question, "Why this position rather than another?"
- The requirements for moving up to the next position, specifying those abilities the individual must develop before being qualified to assume higher-level responsibility.

Career path plans should emphasize that the training and development activities necessary to develop the abilities required at the next higher level of management should occur before the individual is considered eligible for promotion. Every manager must understand that outstanding performance in a present position does not in itself indicate readiness for a higher position that may in fact require quite different managerial abilities.

Career Path Planning Guidelines

The following should be kept in mind in developing career path plans.

In the Early Stages of a Manager's Career, Broadening the Manager's Product and Technical Background Is of Primary Importance. This rationale influences most job rotation decisions. Job rotation in itself, however, does not develop an individual's ability to handle responsibilities involved at higher levels of management. What must be planned at this stage are training and development activities that will provide an individual with the abilities required by higher managerial positions (e.g., administrative and conceptual skills).

A Manager Should Be Exposed to Successively Greater Levels of Diversity and Complexity. Sometimes this can be accomplished by moving the manager from a small operation to a larger one. In making this kind of career plan decision, however, it must be recognized that size is not necessarily synonymous with diversity and complexity.

Recognition Must Be Given to the Critical Difference in Responsibilities as an Individual Moves from Functional Management into General Management. General management requires proven ability to view the business in its entirety and to make decisions and take actions while recognizing all factors that bear on the success of the total enterprise, whether that is a department, a group of departments, or the profit center as a whole.

Every High-Potential Manager Needs Exposure to Corporate Experience and Perspective. This exposure helps to familiarize the manager with staff responsibilities and provides on-the-job opportunity to develop the necessary range of skills and abilities.

ORGANIZATIONAL DETERMINATIONS

The employees and their career path plans form the management plan, which must be related to the organization's structure and plans.

MANAGING THE HUMAN RESOURCE

The management plan should be inventoried annually to list expected changes in the organization (see Figure 3). This inventory provides a basis for preparing for:
- Planned and unplanned retirements
- A normal rate of voluntary separations and involuntary retirements
- Position changes that will occur as a result of previous human resource planning or to fill positions outside the organization as part of overall development
- Changes that might result from moving the organization about during the forthcoming year.

The inventory should also include requirements for Affirmative Action and EEO targets, to fit into the MIS department's and organization's goals.

SUMMARIES AND PRESENTATION TO MANAGEMENT

Summaries are needed to display status of the MIS department's overall

	Confidential	Need and Availability by Position
		Organization _____ Prepared by _____ Date _____
Code: P Candidate in Profit Center C Candidate in Company 0 No Candidate	Positions	Total
If no change, check here.		

Retirement
  Early
  Regular		

Separation
  Voluntary
  Involuntary		

Position Change
  Promotion
  Transfer		

New Position
  Existing Organization
  Organizational Change		

Figure 3. Human Resources Inventory Form

management needs and the availability of candidates, listed according to managerial level. Figure 4 provides a chart for displaying such a summary. In addition, communication to senior management on the status and readiness of MIS management candidates is needed. This will provide a basis for integrating the MIS manager's employees and plans with general management needs of the organization.

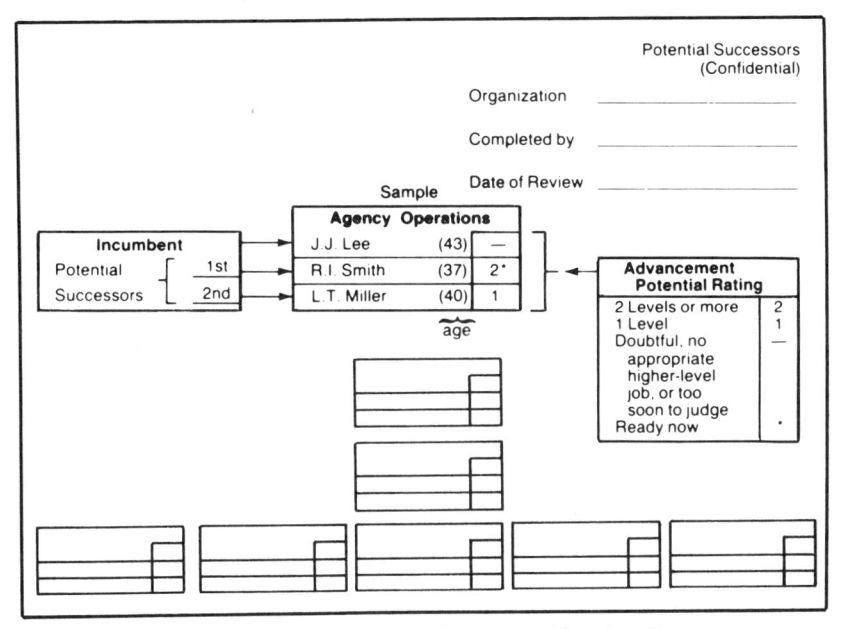

Figure 4. Manager Human Resources Planning Form

SOURCES OF HUMAN RESOURCE PLANNING INFORMATION

The sources from which the required needs and availability information can be derived are many and varied. Some information is readily available, such as who is going to reach age 65 and retire during the year. Information on early or late retirement is more difficult to obtain. As early as possible, efforts must be made to identify which managers are going to elect nonstandard retirement dates. Past data may be helpful.

Some information is not generally available because it is known only to those who will be involved in making key personnel decisions. Some information is confidential, such as which managers are not performing satisfactorily and may be demoted or dismissed. Some information on voluntary separations is impossible to obtain because such decisions are based on past events or circumstances known only to the individuals. MIS managers should have some idea of how many in their group are likely to leave voluntarily during the year. Prior experience in the organization may offer clues that can help an MIS manager predict, on a statistical basis, how many subordinates will be lost by this route.

Some information depends on the organization's business plans and strategies, from which the MIS manager should be able to forecast what new positions will need to be filled. In addition, some of the required information can be developed only after other personnel decisions have been made. This is true of openings that result from position changes, such as promotions or transfers.

Much of this information depends on the managers' judgment and on their intimate involvement with the people in their profit center. Information on management needs and availability must begin at the bottom, with each manager developing such information in his or her own division or department.

TRACKING THE PLAN—AND THE BUDGET

One of the values of formal succession planning is that it allows profit center managers to determine at any point whether the human resources aspects of the MIS center's plans are on target and what corrective action is indicated if there is a variance. Procedures for tracking the succession plan must therefore be established. Tracking becomes more essential when expenditures related to human resource planning are budgeted on the same basis as other divisional expenditures.

MIS managers should evaluate management training and development expenditures with a cost/benefit analysis approach such as the following.

When a training or development activity is being considered, specific objectives should be defined in writing to justify the time and money involved. For example, if a manager wants to take a particular course—or if a superior recommends that it be taken—these two questions should be answered:
- Do the defined objectives represent the top improvement or development priorities of this individual?
- If the objectives do represent the manager's top improvement or development priorities, is this the best course to attain these objectives, or are there more logical alternatives?

After any training or development activity has been completed, the individual should be required to report how effectively it achieved the objectives for which it was undertaken and what on-the-job actions are being planned to use the knowledge.

A system must be developed for monitoring expenditures related to human resource planning, including those associated with performance improvement and manager development. An analysis should be made to determine how much has been and will be spent by each division on human-resource-related activities during the current fiscal year. This analysis makes it possible to compare the training and development activities of each division and, based on that comparison, to determine an appropriate level of human-resource-related activities for inclusion in the budget for the next year's plan.

KEY PROCEDURES AND FORMS

Initial Presentation to Managers

All managers must understand the program when it is implemented. An in-depth briefing should:
- Identify the need for and the value of a succession planning program.

Succession Planning

- Identify the expectations and reservations each participating manager has about such a system.
- Conduct a walkthrough of the functional descriptions and key elements that compose the system.
- Have each manager complete a series of entries on the key forms to ensure that they understand the forms.
- Present summary documents with typical entries to show the managers how they are to be used to supplement organizational information on individuals.
- Set schedules for managerial actions and identify points of contact for additional data or support in completing the forms.
- Respond to each expectation or reservation expressed at the beginning of the session.

Approximately three hours will be needed for an effective presentation.

Management Human Resources Inventory

This inventory provides each manager with a consistent method for forecasting management needs and for reporting the performance and potential of his or her managers and supervisors. The human resources inventory chart (Figure 3) is a means of identifying changes created by planned retirements, separations, position changes, or new positions; it serves as a basis for predicting turnover. This first check is completed by position title with the intent of identifying presence or absence of candidates.

The configuration of the human resources inventory organization chart (see Figure 5) suggests that it be used to represent the supervisor or manager reporting to each individual manager. The top square represents the Director; the next, any managers reporting to him or her; and the other squares, the supervisors reporting to that manager. There should be one sheet for each manager. Table 1 presents the key for filling out the form.

Management/Executive Resources Individual Development Plan

Figure 6 provides a form for use by the manager of each individual in the program and by the manager's superior to periodically review and document the management/executive resources of each division within the organization. It consistently and comprehensively presents the position of each individual in the program as viewed by the immediate superior manager. The superior manager can discuss these plans with the next level of management prior to promoting the individual.

Using a form ensures that the needs of all management individuals will be considered consistently. The form should be prepared annually, prior to performance appraisal. When approved, this form should be discussed with the individual and should become part of the individual's management continuity and succession planning record. Since these individual development plans are filed, new managers are able to quickly review commitments, discuss them with the individual, and thereby ensure that a continuity of development is provided for each individual and for the organization. Thus commitments need not fall through, as they often do when managers are changed. Table 2 outlines the major steps in the plan.

MANAGING THE HUMAN RESOURCE

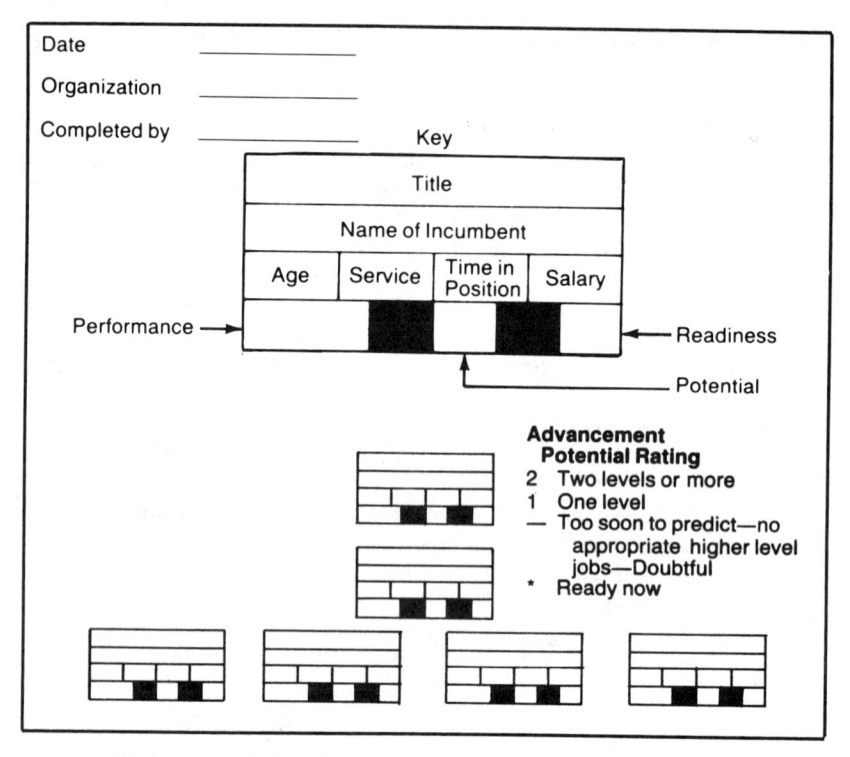

Figure 5. Management Human Resources Inventory by Organization

Management Scope Potential

The purpose of the individual development plan is to identify management scope of individuals in the system so that a reasonable balance is maintained between general managers with broad experience and those with technical management skill only. Company managers of three types or categories are required. Not all managers are capable of being wide-range managers; it is not necessarily advantageous if they all are. The detailed managing required by certain technical specialties (e.g., actuarial) is best performed by managers with high technical skills and closely directed management capabilities.

The organization should be able to observe how many candidates of each type exist in the top three levels of management. The following paragraphs define the three categories of management scope.

Wide-Range Broad Management. This type of manager is capable of the broadest form of general management, regarding the company as it is and as it is to be developed in response to strategic goals, government and public requirements, and market considerations. Candidates normally include the organization's 8 to 10 senior officers.

Broad Management—Specific Area. This type of manager is capable of managing a division or product line of the organization but is less comfortable with the complexities of interdivisional management. He or she pos-

Succession Planning

Table 1. Management Human Resources Inventory Definitions

Performance Rating	Definition
X	New—In position less than three months. Not evaluated.
1	Unsatisfactory results and performance.
2	Marginal—Does not meet requirements of position (with learning discounted). Attitude and/or initiative not acceptable. Remedial action indicated.
3	Satisfactory—Generally meets job requirements but room for improvement. If in a major learning phase, considerable room for improvement.
4	Above average—Surpasses overall job requirements but lacks strength in some areas.
5	Superior—Some elements of performance may rate as exceptional, but overall performance falls below an exceptional rating.
6	Exceptional—General all-around excellence in quality/quantity of work, initiative, self development, new ideas, and attitude. Rapid learner.

Potential	
A	Outstanding—Can advance two levels above present position.
B	Considerable—Can advance at least one level above present position and/or assume substantial added responsibility at present level.
C	Some—Can assume added responsibilities at present level.
D	Limited—At or near capacity in present position.
E	Key capability in current position—Vital technical knowledge precludes movement.
X	New—In position less than three months. Not evaluated.

Readiness	
R/O	Qualified to move now.
R1	Within one to two years.
R2	Within two to four years.
N/A	Current level appropriate.

Table 2. Succession Plan Responsibilities

	Responsibility	Objective
Manager	Reviews files and performance	Draft individual development plan
	Discusses plan with immediate supervisor/manager	Gain consensus and obtain plans for all reporting managers
	Discusses plan with individual in program	Obtain agreement of negotiation changes
	Reviews with immediate superior manager	Gain consensus if change is required
	Budgets for activities	Ensure plan can be executed
Individual	Reviews and discusses plan with manager	Ensure these activities are consistent with individual's reviews and requirements and ensure that any pertinent facts and data have been considered
Immediate Superior Manager	Reviews and discusses plans with manager	Give commitment and support to proposed activities and decisions

MANAGING THE HUMAN RESOURCE

MANAGEMENT/EXECUTIVE RESOURCES: INDIVIDUAL DEVELOPMENT PLAN

Employee Name	Performance Eval	Date of Evaluation
Position	Position Level	Month/Year Assigned

Current Assignment (refer to Management Position Description)

Employee Strengths (personal attributes and management abilities; give examples)

Recent Development Actions Accomplished (indicate when completed)

Development Needs (e.g., on-the-job, cross-function experience, management development, out-company training)

NEEDS	PLANS	DATE

Possible Future Assignments within Next 4 Years (project when ready for each)

Employee's Preference for Future Positions/Locations (include interest in other functions/divisions)

Ultimate Potential (highest position individual may attain based on current capability)

Prepared by:	Date:	Reviewed by:	Date:

Figure 6. Individual Development Plan Form

sesses direct knowledge of products and specifics related to that one department rather than to other parts of the organization.

Limited Management—Technical Area. This type of manager is capable of managing a major specialized function within a profit center where high technical skill or knowledge of a professional skill is constantly exercised (e.g., systems management).

The development plan form should identify individuals capable of both broad and technical management and those who have limitations in one or both areas.

Summary of Actions Required

This summary provides a brief description of actions, responsibilities, and timing for the system's key activities. At least 12 significant actions must be completed during the year if the system is to present to company officers a complete, timely picture of management availability. Table 3 describes what action is to be taken, by whom, and when to ensure availability of the necessary information.

Annual Presentation of Status to Executive and Profit Center Management

Summaries of the profit centers' management needs and availabilities should be presented annually at a succession planning review meeting. Several objectives of this presentation are:

- To present in concise form the status of all management positions in the organization so that the strengths, weaknesses, excesses, and shortages of management personnel will be known.
- To identify the effects of change (as presented in the organizational strategy and business plans) on the supply or availability of managers.
- To summarize the amount and cost of training that is required to continually enhance the quality of management.
- To present the status and plans for each candidate expected to enter executive and senior profit center positions within a two- to four-year time frame, as a means of involving current senior management in these individuals' development.
- To permit executive and profit center management to ask questions and receive answers related to all levels of the organization's management.

MANAGEMENT SKILL CATEGORIES

As an aid to succession planning, the MIS manager should review individuals and their career path plans, to ensure that all three of the following management skill categories are developing.

Functional Skills

Functional skills and abilities reflect specialized expertise and experience related to a specific function (e.g., sales, engineering, accounting). "Knowledge of present job" and "attitude toward job assignments" are examples of how to judge performance in this category.

MANAGING THE HUMAN RESOURCE

Table 3. Actions Required in the Succession Plan

What Is Done	By Whom	When
1. Establishment and maintenance of manager inventory file.	Human resource function or designee of profit center management.	Continuing.
2. Development of position.	Each manager for his own and subordinate positions. Human resource function should assist in preparation and audit for compliance.	Continuing—reviewed twice a year.
3. Personnel change notice.	Manager initiating action. Assistance provided by human resource function.	As required.
4. Performance appraisal.	Each manager with each subordinate, in accordance with established procedures.	Annually. Greater frequency recommended for high-potential and new employees.
5. Performance improvement and development needs analysis worksheet.	Same as above.	Within one month of completing performance appraisal.
6. Career path plan.	Same as above.	Same as above.
7. Preliminary manpower planning.	Every manager in profit center.	One month prior to strategy review date.
8. Final human resource planning.	Same as above.	Two months prior to annual plan review date.
9. Divisional worksheet summaries.	Human resources department.	Two months prior to annual plan review date.
10. Final review worksheet summary.	Profit center executive and human resources department.	One month prior to annual plan review date.
11. Human resource planning.	Profit center manager and division department managers with human resources assistance.	Quarterly update.
12. High-potential and officer candidate list.	Profit center executives.	One month prior to annual plan review date.

Administrative Skills

Administrative skills and abilities involve organizing people and work, delegating responsibility, and tracking performance, and includes the ability to work effectively with one's peers and superiors. Also important in this category are skills in interpersonal relationships, notably training and communication skills. Skills in motivating others, which are included among the skills and abilities listed in the performance appraisal form, belong in this category.

Conceptual Skills

Conceptual skills and abilities reflect the fact that a manager must be able to perceive an area of responsibility as a whole, whether that area of responsibility is one product or project, an entire department or division, or the whole company. This category includes the ability to make judgments that take into account complex interrelationships between a wide range of tasks and people.

More broadly, this category includes the ability to identify and assess competitive factors as well as the impact of economic, governmental, technological, and environmental influences. Most important, it involves thinking innovatively about alternatives, assessing profitability and risk, and taking decisive action. Specifically, it includes the ability to make sound business strategy and policy decisions as well as decisions concerning product or asset management.

All three categories of skills are required in some measure at every level of management included in the management continuity and succession planning program. In addition, the relative importance of these three categories of skills changes significantly as an individual moves up in management. At the lower levels of management, technical and functional abilities are of greater importance to a manager's performance. At the intermediate levels, supervisory and administrative skills have an increasing impact on a manager's performance since responsibilities broaden to include a wider range of work and people. At the divisional level or above, highly developed conceptual and creative abilities are most closely associated with outstanding performance.

For human resource planning in the MIS department, this analysis of the changing mix of skills is of prime importance. It helps to:
- Identify the training and development activities that the organization must plan for to improve the performance of its present managers.
- Define the skills and abilities that a manager must develop to become a candidate for promotion.
- Determine whether, and when, a manager is ready to be promoted.
- Determine a manager's potential. How many levels an individual can rise to depends on the extent to which the mix of abilities required at each successive level of management has been developed.

CONCLUSION

In addition to the contributions that succession planning makes to human resource planning and management development, it answers the following questions that talented managers ask of top management:
- Where am I going?
- How and when am I going to get there?
- How is the company going to help me achieve my career objectives?

By implementing a succession planning system such as the one described in this chapter, an MIS manager can take an active role in retaining his or her best managers, preparing for inevitable succession, and improving the quality of the MIS department staff.

IX-5
Personnel Motivation: Benefits and Techniques

Frank J. Stanley

INTRODUCTION

If MIS managers want to motivate employees toward successful goal achievement, they must understand the answers to the following questions:
- Why motivate people? What are the specific purposes of motivation and what benefits can be anticipated?
- How are people motivated? What are the basics of motivation? A fundamental knowledge of the basics of motivation theory will provide the starting point from which each manager can develop his or her own unique style.
- How is the data processing industry unique? What peculiarities of the DP profession call for special motivational techniques? Can these techniques be implemented? A knowledge of the "DP personality" and various DP positions will help guide the manager's efforts.

Motivation is a highly subjective matter touching on the realm of psychology, but its application is of primary importance in today's highly competitive business world. This chapter provides MIS managers with some motivation basics as well as ideas on how motivation can be applied in their organizations.

THE IMPORTANCE OF MOTIVATION

Many business, psychology, and management texts include a section or article on how to motivate employees. The daily business mail usually contains enticing offers for books, tapes, and seminars guaranteed to provide the keys to motivating people. Motivation is a big business, a popular topic, and a word revered by management, yet few managers are able to specifically define what motivation is, how it is accomplished, or how its effects are measured. Seldom are the "whys" of motivation discussed, since the answers appear to be obvious. Motivation techniques can be effective when applied properly, but they require more than just a passing effort. An understanding of the payoff that can be expected for the effort encourages managers to take a serious look at motivational techniques and to expend the effort necessary to apply them.

What Is Motivation?

Motivation consists of those factors that cause an individual or group to perform at a level higher than that which is necessary to maintain their jobs. Motivation is a cause-and-effect phenomenon in which higher productivity can be traced to causes, or motivating factors. Motivating factors have varied sources and effects; a factor that increases one person's effort may have little or no effect on another. Motivation can come from within a person, from a person's peers or superiors, or from someone or something external to the organization. This difficulty in pinpointing the origins of motivation has made it a difficult concept for many managers to grasp, resulting in haphazard application of techniques. Realizing that people have different needs and are motivated by different factors is essential to motivation.

Benefits of Motivation

Assessing the benefits that can be obtained by motivating employees will help illustrate just how important a management tool motivation can be.

Increased Productivity. Most managers will cite increased productivity as the main benefit of motivation, but few realize just how great an increase can be expected. While conducting research on motivation, William James of Harvard found that although employees paid by the hour could maintain their jobs by working at only 20 to 30 percent of their capability, they would work at 80 to 90 percent of their capacity if highly motivated. The difference in productivity between an employee just getting by and one who is motivated is too dramatic to ignore; this added capacity can and should be tapped. Other studies draw similar conclusions; productivity is related more to motivation than to skills; a highly motivated worker with low or average skills can outperform a highly skilled worker who is poorly motivated.

Employee Turnover. Motivation can dramatically reduce employee attrition. In data processing, turnover is usually related to employee desires to grow technically, remain challenged, and gain satisfaction from their accomplishments; salary is seldom the primary reason for turnover. Motivated employees generally find most needs that lead to job changes satisfied and therefore remain with the organization. Several benefits result:
- Retention of employees who know the organization's systems, programs, organization, and business
- Savings of considerable time, money, and effort that would have been spent in recruiting new employees
- Elimination of training periods for new employees.

Higher-Quality Work. A motivated employee not only gets more work done but the work is often more thorough and accurate. Employees who receive positive feedback and feel good about their efforts tend to develop a professional attitude and strive to make their work reflect this attitude. As a result, the amount of supervision necessary to ensure proper completion of tasks can be significantly reduced.

Improvement in Morale and Image. Many organizations use the MIS department as the scapegoat when things go wrong. If management appears to tacitly accept this, employees can become frustrated or even embarrassed to be associated with the department, and they will have little confidence in the success of their efforts. Using motivation techniques from the managerial level on down can significantly improve employee morale and self-image, which, again, reflects in their attitude and work. As a result, the department may be perceived more positively within the organization.

MOTIVATION HISTORY AND THEORY

Motivational theories have developed along with American industry and the work place. This century has witnessed a proliferation of information about motivation: Theory X and Theory Y, Taylor's scientific management theory, the Hawthorne studies, and Herzberg's work are but a few of the major efforts.

The work of Frederick Taylor, the "father of scientific management," was the first widely publicized theory on motivation in industrial society. Taylor's theory states that money and fear are the prime motivators and that the promise of increased rewards results in additional productivity. For the worker in the early 1900s who was struggling for existence, this may have been true. The Hawthorne studies by Mayo, directly linking more abstract factors (e.g., achievement, participation, and a sense of belonging) to productivity, mark the beginnings of the human relations movement. Douglas McGregor's Theory X and Theory Y, which are essentially restatements and formulations of these earlier theories, have come to be accepted as standards. Theory X is based on the premise that humans are lazy by nature and have to be coerced to work. Theory Y, on the other hand, views workers as having a psychological need for work, responsibility, and a sense of achievement.

Needs Hierarchy

Dr. Abraham Maslow has made a significant contribution to the study of motivation with his hierarchy of human needs. This hierarchy describes various levels of human needs:
- Level 1—Physiological needs (i.e., food, water, clothing, shelter, sleep, and sexual satisfaction)
- Level 2—Safety needs (i.e., economic security and protection from harm, disease, and violence)
- Level 3—Social needs (i.e., love, sense of belonging, togetherness, approval, and group membership)
- Level 4—Esteem needs (i.e., prestige, power, reputation, the respect of others, recognition)
- Level 5—Self actualization (varies among individuals but is usually associated with competence, achievement, confidence, and self-esteem)

According to Maslow, humans direct all their energies to meeting level 1 needs first. Once those needs are satisfied, people direct their efforts toward level 2 needs. This step-by-step approach is followed through level 5. If given sufficient impetus, people will reverse direction; for example, if a financially secure individual faces a severe financial problem, he or she may start looking at financial rewards alone in order to meet level 1 and level 2 needs.

MANAGING THE HUMAN RESOURCE

Although much has been learned about what motivates humans, much undoubtedly remains to be realized. Modern managers who want to motivate employees must sort through an abundance of human-motivation research and choose approaches compatible with their management styles and environments.

BASIC MOTIVATION

Psychological studies of employees have shown that a composite psychological profile can usually be drawn for individuals within a particular profession or occupation. Although the features of this profile influence worker motivation, certain fundamental principles cross occupational boundaries and can be used as effective motivators by almost any manager.

Needs

The following list is a hierarchy of needs that are most frequently experienced by employees in today's working environment:
1. Achievement
2. Recognition
3. Work itself
4. Responsibility
5. Opportunity for advancement
6. Growth
7. Salary
8. Relationships
9. Status
10. Company policies
11. Working conditions
12. Personal needs
13. Security

This list, a composite of several research studies, is not all-inclusive nor will its order agree with all other sources. It is intended to help managers recognize and give priority to the various human needs that they must strive to fulfill when developing a motivation plan. Most of these needs are related to levels four and five of Maslow's hierarchy, an interesting indication that physiological, safety, and social needs are largely taken for granted in developed countries today.

Meeting Needs. Meeting needs is what motivation is all about; a thorough motivation plan addresses the most serious needs of all individuals. By getting to know the employees a manager can identify their needs and tailor motivational practices to each individual. These practices include the following:

Being a Good Leader. Managers' attitudes tend to affect employees' attitudes. A strong, confident leader provides employees with a feeling of security and an example that they can follow; a manager who expresses doubt and demonstrates a weak will can only generate uncertainty. All motivation techniques could fail if employees do not perceive their manager as a competent, worthy leader.

Acknowledging Noteworthy Performance. Recognition of effort makes employees feel that their work is important and worthwhile. An employee will never mistake lack of criticism for recognition. Credit or recognition can be a simple pat on the back or a promotion, letter of recognition, salary increase, or public (organizational) acknowledgment. Recognition should always be an exceptional gesture made specifically because of performance, a fact that should be made clear to the individual. When used as a method of motivation, recognition often becomes a standard by which employees gauge their performance. If recognition is inconsistently applied or abruptly withheld, employees may end up confused and anxious instead of motivated.

Delegating Authority and Maintaining Control. Nothing fosters employee self-confidence better than properly delegated responsibility. It gives individuals a chance to learn and grow and makes them feel like contributors; it can turn mediocre performers into stars. Authority must be delegated carefully so that employees know what management's expectations are. Performance should be monitored closely at first in order to correct errors and recognize successes.

Getting to Know Employees. People respond positively to those who take a sincere, personal interest in them. By discovering employees' personal interests, finding the time to chat occasionally, or reviewing employees' professional aspirations with them and giving advice, a manager can motivate while building close relationships and loyalty.

Letting People Grow. Although managers must always provide guidance, they should encourage employees who know the objectives and can figure out methods for attaining them to do so. This involvement gives employees a personal interest in their jobs, the competence to grow into more responsible jobs, and the ability to react practically when abnormal situations occur.

Practicing Participative Management. Employees quickly develop a personal interest in their jobs and in the organization when asked to participate in such traditionally managerial functions as setting standards or solving problems. This participation can result in much readier acceptance of change and also gives employees a sense of importance and belonging. To properly implement participative management, managers must solicit ideas, thoughts, and opinions from the employees. The idea exchange can be achieved through a formal suggestion system, but it will be more effective if it is made personally. Once information is solicited, the employee should be apprised of what action has been taken and how his or her input was utilized. Even if employee ideas cannot be put into effect, the fact that ideas are considered can be a powerful motivating force.

Providing Challenging Work. Employees should be constantly challenged; they should be hired so that they can grow into their positions and, eventually, into positions with more responsibility. Most employees want to advance and will see a challenge as an opportunity to do so. If work is dull, challenge can be introduced by delegating more responsibility to employees, eliciting ideas for innovative methods, setting higher standards, and offering promotional opportunities both within and outside the department whenever possible.

Communicating. Managers should invest in a book, course, or seminar that covers such topics as effective listening and verbal and nonverbal communication. Effective communication can increase a manager's perception and greatly enhance his or her ability to successfully implement motivational practices. Communication skills used in career counseling, performance appraisals, interviews, and employee-problem situations can be greatly improved through training and will result in a more meaningful and useful dialogue between management and employees.

These methods of motivation can be supplemented by others found in books and publications on the subject. It is important that managers adopt the methods with which they are comfortable because employees will recognize insincere or strained efforts. Once begun, a motivation effort must become an intrinsic part of daily routine; it should not necessarily consist of planned events but instead should become part of the manager's natural leadership style.

MIS PERSONNEL CHARACTERISTICS

Studies have characterized MIS personnel as creative people with a preference for working alone who are motivated by growth, achievement, and recognition. Motivation techniques for MIS people should therefore emphasize those areas.

Growth

MIS personnel thrive on professional growth, one measure of which is the number of software acronyms, programming languages, applications areas, and types of hardware with which an employee has experience. Too often, however, MIS managers stifle the career growth of their people by putting them into dead-end niches, or specialities. By adhering to the following guidelines, managers can protect their people from monotony.

Avoiding Task Specialization. For example, maintenance programming may be a good way to develop the skills of a junior programmer, but it should not become someone's sole job function. Maintenance should be performed by both junior and senior programmers, depending on the complexity and immediacy of the task.

Avoiding Application Specialization. Many managers foster specialization by consistently assigning work in the same or similar application areas to persons who have some familiarity with the problems of the area. Although this policy has merit, it concentrates all knowledge of an area in a small number of individuals. Furthermore, this policy limits the employees' scope of knowledge, which eventually leads to a lack of motivation and increases the possibility that the employees will leave, thus jeopardizing the organization. Cross-application work not only provides employees with fresh areas of interest but provides valuable cross-training to safeguard the organization.

Providing Training. Training is usually given a great deal of lip service but low priority in most organizations. It can, however, provide a number of valuable benefits: it expands a person's skills, motivates by fostering a desire to use those skills, and serves as a form of recognition. Training, which can include seminars, classes, audio or video cassettes, and/or a well-stocked technical library (and the time to use it), should always be related to skills that the employee can actually use on the job. Training and cross-training are especially valuable in operations, where skills are unique and a high degree of familiarity is required for proficiency. Since operations has less growth potential for individuals, training can provide motivation that would otherwise be missing.

Providing a Career Path. Career paths exist in all organizations, but many employees are not aware of the opportunities available. Career planning should be part of an employee's performance evaluation or should be reviewed at the employee's request. The employee should be made aware of the types of positions that may be open to him or her (both in the near and distant future) and the requirements of those positions. Such documents as job descriptions and career planning charts should be made available to employees. Personal guidance and advice from one's superior is usually sought during this type of review and can achieve a lasting motivational effect. The manager should be careful not to make promises that cannot be kept during these sessions.

Recognition

Recognition provides great possibilities for motivating the MIS professional but is often overlooked. MIS employees need to know that their efforts are needed and appreciated. While salary increases may serve as an annual reward, they do not take the place of regular, ongoing forms of recognition. Recognition can be done simply or in a formal manner as the following suggestions illustrate:

- If periodic meetings are held to review progress and work schedules, an individual's accomplishments can be mentioned. Recognition in the presence of the achiever's peers is very effective.
- When others comment favorably on an individual's performance, they should be encouraged to put their remarks in a letter. Commendations can be placed in personnel files or temporarily displayed in the office area.
- Upon completion of a major effort, company officials should be encouraged to recognize the efforts of those involved. Although the officials will probably be glad to do so, they may not think of it without a reminder.
- If individuals are asked or expected to perform difficult or extraordinary tasks (e.g., periods of overtime or shift work), some form of recognition is imperative. Treating them to lunch or giving them an afternoon off serve as both recognition and reward for extra effort.
- Project reviews with either the individuals or the groups involved should be held at milestones of any undertaking. These meetings should focus on what has been done, how well it has been done, and where improve-

ments can be made. In addition to giving employees recognition, managers should use these meetings to solicit ideas from employees for improving productivity and efficiency.

Achievement

Achievement can usually be used as a motivator by providing tasks that are interesting, challenging, and demanding. Efforts that require employees to perform to the utmost of their abilities provide them with a sense of personal satisfaction and make them feel their contributions have real value. Since the type of work and level of complexity varies considerably from one MIS shop to another, the manager must maintain a staff mix that fits the work load. Certain procedures, moreover, can ensure that personnel are used as effectively as possible:

- Maintaining a proper mix of people. The types of work performed should be reviewed, and open positions should be filled by those with appropriate skill levels. A systems and programming department that performs 50 percent routine maintenance obviously should not have a majority of senior-level analysts.
- Providing opportunities for responsibility. Since it is impossible to always assign challenging work to all employees, additional duties can be provided that add challenges and opportunities for growth to routine tasks. Temporary responsibilities such as project leader, the pressure of tighter time constraints, or the use of a new technique or methodology can provide additional incentive to excel.
- Recognizing individual differences. Some employees may be eager to take on responsibility, pressure, and new tasks at a moment's notice, while others may prefer to move more slowly and cautiously. To an eager programmer, learning CICS on the job may be challenging; to a more cautious programmer, however, a course in CICS may be challenging, but a direct, on-the-job experience may be frustrating and demoralizing. Knowing the levels at which employees are comfortable, challenged, or overwhelmed is invaluable to a manager who wants to provide the opportunity to achieve.

RESULTS

The application of motivational methods should not be expected to produce dramatic results immediately. Changes in attitudes and work habits will occur gradually and may be difficult to detect unless a monitoring or measurement system is in place. In the long run, however, properly applied motivation techniques can result in a well-organized, cooperative group of employees who perform in a productive, professional manner. When a manager believes in the potential of motivation and expends the effort necessary to incorporate motivational practices into his or her everyday routine, the benefits will far exceed the effort.

ACTION PLAN

A commitment to motivation is the first and most vital step. A manager must believe in his or her ability to motivate, understand what motivation is and how it works, and be willing to take the time and effort necessary to

pursue the effort. MIS managers should take the following actions:
1. Determine where better motivation is needed and what methods will be used to measure the effectiveness of the effort.
2. Prepare a checklist for each employee and review his or her skills, abilities, likes, dislikes, and personal interests. Identify the needs most important to each individual.
3. Determine what motivational practices are already used, which needs are being met, and which needs require attention.
4. Decide what motivational techniques will have a positive effect in the organization. Can they be carried out individually, or do they require support and assistance from others (i.e., increased training, restructuring of work roles and assignments)?
5. Prepare a plan for improving motivation to ensure a written commitment and provide a reference point for review. The plan can be prepared on an individual employee level, if necessary, or it can deal with functional areas or larger groups.
6. Apply motivational techniques consistently and fairly, avoiding any appearances of favoritism.

With personnel costs representing an ever-increasing portion of the MIS budget, every MIS manager should strive to help the MIS staff perform to the best of their abilities. A persistent effort by management can turn motivation from a meaningless buzzword into a valuable tool for improving productivity and reducing turnover.

Bibliography

Cougar, J. Daniel, and Zawacki, Robert A. "What Motivates DP Professionals." *Datamation*, Vol. 24, No. 9 (September 1978), 116–123.

Drucker, Peter F. *Management: Tasks, Responsibilities, Practices.* New York: Harper & Row, 1974.

Fried, L., and Umbaugh, R.E. "Developing Personal Management Skills." **Data Processing Management.** Pennsauken, NJ: Auerbach Publishers Inc.

Hersey, Paul, and Blanchard, Kenneth. *Management of Organizational Behavior.* Englewood Cliffs NJ: Prentice-Hall, 1977.

James, William. *The Principles of Psychology—Volume 1.* London: MacMillan and Co Ltd, 1890.

Kerzner, Harold. *Project Management: A Systems Approach to Planning, Scheduling and Controlling.* New York: Van Nostrand Reinhold, 1979.

Terry, George R. *Principles of Management.* Homewood IL: Richard D. Irwin Inc, 1968.

Umbaugh, R.E. and Fried, L., "Developing Personal Management Skills." *Auerbach Data Processing Management,* vol. 11, no. 4. Pennsauken, NJ: Auerbach Publishers Inc, 1983.

Section X
MIS Security

MIS Security is a lot like life insurance: few are really enthusiastic about it until it's too late. However, MIS security is a lot harder to get than life insurance, and the sicker you are, the harder it is to get. The secret is to build security while healthy and then stay that way.

The complexity of today's business computing systems and the potential for misuse of information contained in them require an organizationwide program to preserve and protect the organization's information resources. The basis for such a program is a well-defined classification system that identifies the sensitivity and importance of various types of information. Chapter X-1, "Protecting Information Resources," outlines such a classification system and discusses its use in developing an information preservation and protection program.

As in nearly every other aspect of information management, people are the key to a successful security program. Security measures can be undermined by employees who do not understand the need for control. A security awareness program for all employees can reduce the possibility of a breach in security caused by employee carelessness. While educating employees on the importance of security controls, the MIS manager can also encourage employees to participate in the security program by asking them to identify exposures and recommend methods of reducing them. Chapter X-2, "People: The Key to Security," presents guidelines for establishing a successful security awareness program for your employees.

Physical security, protecting the tangible assets of the organization, is that area of security most often addressed first by MIS management. Chapter X-3, "Physical Security Measures," helps the MIS manager focus his or her effort in establishing a solid physical security program. It addresses site selection, protective strategies, access control, security decision making, fire protection, environmental controls, and water damage protection.

A less tangible asset, data, also deserves substantial consideration in developing a security program. Chapter X-4, "Managing Data Security," recommends the appointment of an individual with specific responsibility for data security and outlines steps to take when establishing a data security program.

To be effective, a security program must be perceived by employees as integral to a company's business operations. Publishing a data security manual that delineates corporate security policy, security standards, and guidelines for their implementation establishes the ground rules for such a program. Chapter X-5, "Data Security Standards," discusses the standards and guidelines necessary to educate managers, define base security controls, provide auditors with a document against which systems and departments can be audited, and put senior management on record regarding the level of security it will support.

Related to physical security and data security are those steps that should be taken to provide an appropriate level of security in a network environment. Dial-up networks present special problems because of the almost unlimited number of access points into such systems. Chapter X-6, "Open Network Security," proposes steps that can be taken to minimize the risks associated with open access networks.

X-1
Protecting Information Resources

Richard C. Koenig

INTRODUCTION

For years the public paid scant attention to the MIS industry. Then they slowly discovered that the data being processed was really *information*. Much of their education came from news stories and articles about computer abuses. The public learned that information is a valuable commodity and that possession of information is power. They became very concerned when they realized that some of the data out there was about them—and that they had little or no control of its use or misuse.

The transition from data processing to the information processing environment in which computer abuse has become a major social issue occurred slowly. Most of those in the data processing industry were not totally aware of the potential problems that were arising. This is unfortunate, because if those concerns had been expressed, an information management capability might have been developed in concert with the technology. Now MIS professionals must step back, analyze the existing and potential problems, and retrofit information management solutions.

PRESERVING AND PROTECTING INFORMATION

To understand the nature of the problems, it is useful to define the overall goals of a computer security program. The two primary information processing security goals can be defined as follows:
- To preserve the continuity of computing service to the organization
- To protect organizational assets that the information processing function owns or has custodial responsibility for

The two key terms in these definitions should be clarified. The term "preserve" refers to avoiding or minimizing hazards to information processing assets which, if physically damaged or destroyed, would cause a significant interruption in computing service. Typical measures employed to preserve information processing assets are physical access controls, fire prevention systems, and backup and recovery practices.

The term "protect" refers to preventing the misuse, theft, or (in the case of information itself) improper disclosure of information processing assets.

MIS SECURITY

Typical protective measures include data access controls, administrative and personnel procedures, and system design and control criteria.

Preservation measures are used for assets required to continue providing critical computing services to the organization; protection measures are used for valuable, confidential, and/or sensitive assets. Thus the two issues that must be addressed are the criticality and confidentiality of information assets. These issues are important because a number of exposures are unique to the computing environment and merit special consideration:
- The computing environment results in a tremendous concentration of information. This concentration increases the potential exposures.
- The data stored on computing and communications equipment is usually the largest single aggregation of current information in the organization. Yet its real value in terms of replacement cost or business interruption is rarely well defined and sometimes not even recognized.
- Computerized information is unique in that it can be accessed from remote terminals; thus theft or disclosure can be accomplished without physical access and without altering the information.
- At present there is no cost-effective foolproof way for a computer system to positively identify an individual or a terminal. Thus, access can be gained by masquerading as an authorized individual or a legitimate terminal. (This situation is complicated even further because computing or terminal equipment can be used to access systems belonging to other companies.)
- An accomplished individual can circumvent software controls and avoid leaving an audit trail so that there is no evidence or record of unauthorized activity.
- Because computer crimes are a relatively recent development, there are few pertinent laws and legal precedents. In addition, most of those involved with the administration of justice do not understand the complex technology or techniques involved; thus, the traditional legal deterrents are almost completely ineffective against computer crime.

CLASSIFYING INFORMATION ASSETS

The first step in addressing these problems is for the organization to recognize that information is an asset with quantifiable value sufficient to warrant protective measures. The next step is to integrate computer security analysis and planning activities with day-to-day security efforts, because the problems are not unique to the computing environment. In fact, the basic problems have always existed—they have only been emphasized by computers. Thus the solutions must be generic and address all information security needs, not only those associated with computers.

To be cost-effective, protective measures must be applied selectively. To do this the organization must identify the information to be preserved from loss and protected from misuse. Establishing the criticality and the confidentiality of information, therefore, requires two formalized classification processes.

Reasons for Classification

In addition to the most considerations, classification is necessary for several other reasons:

Technical Exposures. A number of technical exposures are increased in the automated, non-office environment. A uniform, formal classification approach is necessary to ensure effective protection against these exposures.

Human Variances. One person's response may differ from another's, based on his or her background, environment, and other variables. In addition, an individual's responses may vary over time, particularly if there is no way to gauge what is expected or what is proper. If employees are not informed of management expectations in this area, they cannot be expected to behave consistently. Fraudulent activities often start out as minor variations in behavior that can easily be controlled if they are defined as unacceptable and if prompt corrective action is taken.

Internal/External Influences. Even in the absence of a formal classification process, a variety of existing requirements (some internal and some external) establish special classification criteria and require protective measures. These include:
- Government retention requirements for tax, earnings, and other financial information
- Securities Exchange Commission and federal securities laws or regulations regarding disclosure of certain information
- Trade secret and proprietary information conventions
- Traditional protection for salary and other personnel information
- The control provisions of the Foreign Corrupt Practices Act

In the past, the preservation needs addressed by most organizations were those caused by a geographic location vulnerable to natural disasters (e.g., hurricanes, floods, earthquakes) or by proximity to a probable military target in the event of a nuclear war. Efforts variously known as "records retention" or "vital records" programs were put in place to guarantee the survival of an organization under the worst possible conditions. The primary purpose of these programs is to ensure the continued existence of essential records through geographic dispersion of copies or through storage of backup copies at a special location. These programs usually predated the use of computers and were routinely extended to computer files as they replaced paper records; thus any concerns about preserving vital information have already been addressed in some organizations.

In many cases, however, these preservation needs were not frequently recognized or formally addressed. The government, some financial and credit institutions, and a few high technology industries exhibited concern; however, this concern was usually very selective and did not result in a uniform policy.

ORGANIZATION-WIDE CLASSIFICATION PROGRAM

Increasingly, organizations are recognizing the need for both preservation

MIS SECURITY

and protection measures, and for the classification process that serves as the basis for a cost-effective information security program. Combining the two classification processes into a single organization-wide program enables a single review effort to satisfy both needs. The following sections define classification terms that are often used informally (and inaccurately) and provide a formal structure for meeting the organization's information security needs.

Preservation Considerations

The preservation goal can be illustrated by relating it to a specific protective measure—disaster recovery planning. The four major elements of a complete disaster recovery plan are:
- Off-site storage program
- Alternate site recovery procedures
- Disaster site restoration procedures
- Disaster site restart procedures

(These steps assume that an alternate recovery location is available. If not, recovery must occur at the disaster site, and the third step—restoring the disaster site—must precede the actual recovery effort.)

Off-Site Storage Program. This program involves setting up a remote storage facility as a backup tape library. The facility must be physically secure, must have environmental control equipment and a fire detection system, and should be monitored to ensure that no unknown problems occur. The type of information that should be stored in this facility is the critical issue for the classification program.

Alternate Site Recovery Procedures. These procedures specify which applications must be run at the alternate processing location, how to transport the files and other needed resources, what must be done to get those applications up and running on the alternate computing equipment, how to get the input from the alternate location and the output back to the users, and who is responsible for each of the many tasks involved.

Disaster Site Restoration Procedures. These procedures include a complete current equipment inventory, a list of facility requirements, where to obtain everything needed, and who is responsible for tasks ranging from assessing the damage and meeting legal and insurance requirements to installing and checking out the new equipment.

Disaster Site Restart Procedures. These procedures explain how to transfer applications from the alternate location and how to start up and catch up on all of the jobs that were not transferred to the alternate site. These restart procedures rank lowest on the list because the necessary time and manpower should be available while the site restoration activities are taking place.

After defining the elements of a disaster recovery plan, it is still necessary to determine which information and which systems warrant the ongoing effort and expense involved in backing up files and ensuring that applications can be transferred. By examining the total collection of information stored (including both raw and refined data), computer programs, system controls, and software, it is usually fairly easy to distinguish a small group of resources that are essential to the existence of the organization. This group is normally comprised of such files as stockholder records, current accounts receivable and payroll masters, and such other substantial accounting records as operating and revenue statements, property records, and so on. This subset is probably already backed up and securely stored to comply with an existing vital records program.

At the other end of the scale are files and programs that the users or operations department have informally backed up for a variety of reasons. Files or programs may be backed up to placate an overly concerned user or someone sensitive to the work involved in recreating a particular file; they may also be backed up because of concern based on prior bad experience. These types of judgments are too difficult and expensive to define and cannot easily be formalized. The information assets involved may be significant to an individual or group, but their significance to the whole organization may not be great. On the other hand, due to human nature, these backups cannot be eliminated without even more effort; they should therefore be recognized as discretionary and be given a common category (e.g., "valued").

Defining Organizational Purpose. Ensuring backup for vital files and programs and providing backup for valued resources on a discretionary basis is not enough to minimize losses in the event of a major disaster to a key computing facility. The next area of concern in classifying information resources involves the purpose of the organization. For many organizations, this is simply profit; for government, it could be national defense. The purpose must be identified, and those functions crucial to the purpose must be singled out—particularly functions that must be performed in a timely manner.

In most businesses, the crucial functions are those that affect the bottom line, either by producing income or avoiding costs. Once these functions have been identified (or criteria have been established to identify them), requirements for protective measures can be established. If we call these functions "critical" to the organization, then critical functions that are computerized are "critical systems" or "critical applications." It is important to recognize that these *functions* are critical to the organization whether or not they are being performed by computer-based systems.

Preservation Program

Three cumulative preservation categories have been defined (see Figure 1):
- Vital—essential to the organization's existence
- Critical—crucial to the organization's purpose
- Valued—of recognizable value to the individuals or segments of the organization

These three categories permit the criticality issue to be dealt with through a policy and program. Organizational policy can specify that:
- The vital category preservation requirements must be met without exception.

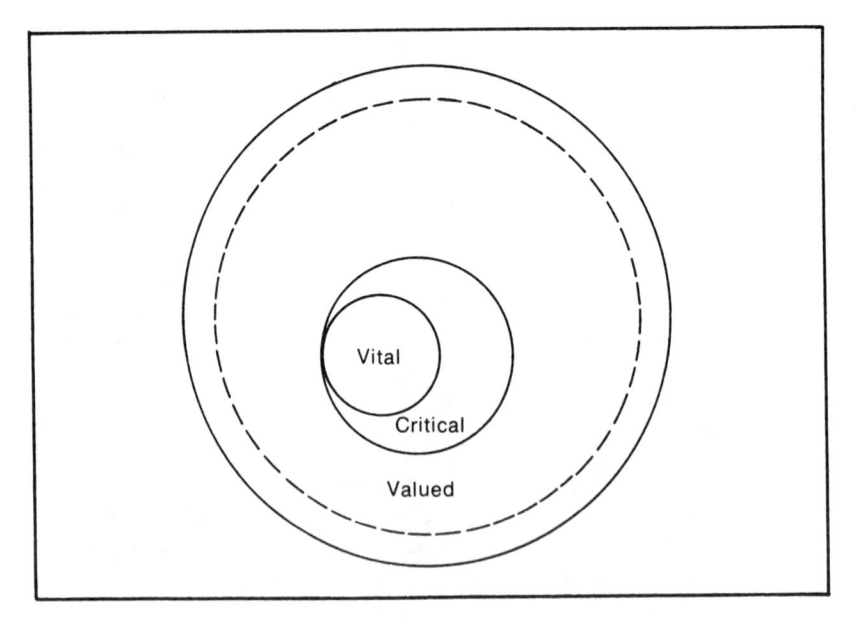

Figure 1. Information Categories for Preservation Purposes

- The critical category requirements must be met unless an exception can be justified.
- The valued category has no formal requirements, and preservation measures will only be employed if they can be cost justified.

Using such a policy, a preservation program for the computing environment can be implemented. The basic criterion for vital resources is very straightforward: If a computer file exists in only one version, it must be copied and sent to the remote storage location. The criterion for valued resources is also simple: If the user's concern can be expressed in financial or other terms that justify the expense involved, then the information, system, or function should be backed up and included in the off-site storage program.

The only really difficult decisions involve the critical category. First, realistic criteria must be established. They should be broad enough to include all truly crucial resources or functions and yet narrow enough to ensure that the backup costs are tolerable to the organization.

The cost-effectiveness of the alternatives must be carefully examined:
- Should the function have all of the necessary resources backed up in the off-site storage program, be designated as a critical system, and be included in the alternate site recovery procedure?
- Should the function have manual backup procedures that are the responsibility of the system "owner" rather than the information processing group?
- Can hybrid backup procedures (part manual, part computerized) be developed?

The central issue is not how the requirements are met, but which information, systems, or functions must be preserved—and the classification criteria are the keys to an effective disaster recovery planning effort.

Protection Considerations

Information protection goals can also be discussed in terms of the organization's needs and then implemented in a protection program. The portion of the total collection of stored information that is of quantifiable value outside of the organization can be identified. This smaller subset requires measures to restrict it to internal use and to protect it from theft, misuse, or unauthorized disclosure. This subset can be called "restricted."

It is fairly easy to distinguish a small group within the valuable subset that is highly sensitive or confidential and that if lost, misused, or improperly disclosed could have a substantial negative impact on the organization. Most of this information either is time sensitive, with a significant financial or emotional impact, or deals with highly valuable technology. Preannouncement information concerning major reorganizations or personnel changes, acquisitions, divestitures, earnings, and dividends or information about long-range marketing and product plans or high-value proprietary processes would fall in this category. This "highly confidential" subset is probably already being protected to some degree even if the organization lacks a formal protection program.

The next subset of information that requires protection is also sensitive and/or confidential, but the consequences of its theft, misuse, or improper disclosure would be far less serious. This category can be called "confidential." The types of information in this category could include personnel and medical records, salary and promotion plans, all types of financial information, and low- to moderate-value technological and trade secret information. The range of sensitivity or confidentiality in this grouping can be considerable, so it may be appropriate to consider the use of more than one category to cover this spectrum.

Subcategories. More than three categories can be useful if the types of information belonging to each can be specifically defined and if the protection requirements can be logically specified. Most organizations that have more than three categories use subcategories such as:
- Business confidential—for administrative and financial matters not related to employees
- Personal (or personal and confidential)—for all administrative, financial, medical, and other employee-related records
- Proprietary (or technical confidential)—for trade secret and technical information

The protection requirements that differ for each subcategory are usually procedural in nature and involve limiting the distribution of the information to certain groups of employees (e.g., technical versus administrative or staff) or to certain levels in the organization (e.g., management positions versus supervisory positions). They may also be useful for indicating that an envelope or package should only be opened by the addressee.

Limiting the number of categories to three, however, has two advantages.

MIS SECURITY

First, it simplifies the protection program and the program requirements. Second, labeling information simply "confidential" or "business confidential" does not indicate the nature of the information; this provides a measure of protection. (Restrictions on copying and distributing information or on opening envelopes and packages can be communicated by optional, supplementary labeling such as "restricted distribution," "do not copy," or "to be opened by addressee only." Three categories should satisfy most organizations' needs, and in many organizations the confidential category might encompass 20 to 30 percent of the valuable set.

The protective measures for the three protection categories (highly confidential, confidential, and restricted) illustrated in Figure 2 become more stringent as the confidentiality of the information increases. The measures specified should depend on the type of organization and the type of information being protected as well as on the protection needs caused by the potential exposures in the organization's environment. In general, however, the restricted category should have very few requirements, and the highly confidential category should have strict requirements that establish accountability and provide a continuous audit trail. The restricted category is primarily intended to reinforce the concept that all information is classified and of value to the organization.

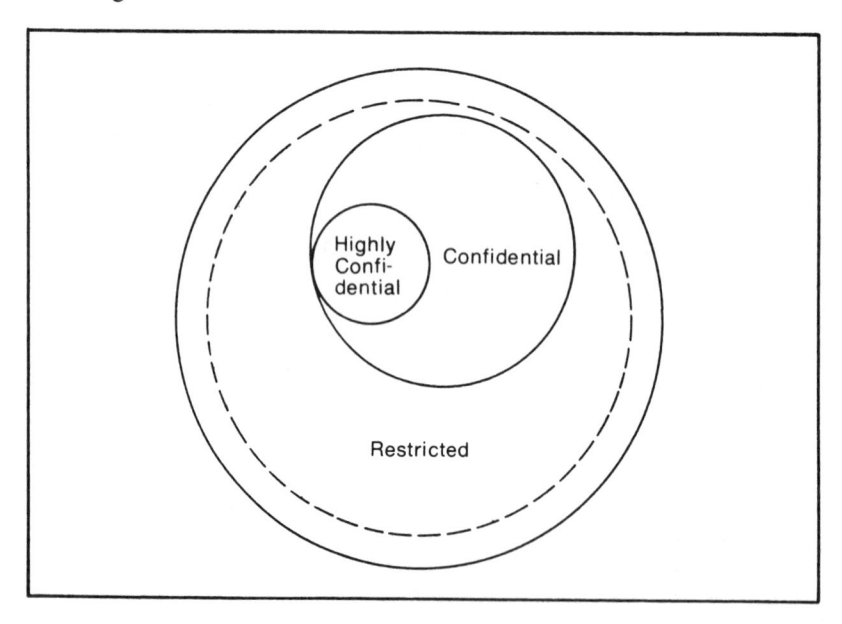

Figure 2. Information Categories for Protection Purposes

To clarify the relationship between the preservation and protection categories, it should be pointed out that there is no parallel between the two classification groups (e.g., vital is not equivalent to highly confidential). The two classification processes are independent of one another. Information that is identified as essential to the existence of the organization (vital) may or may not be sensitive or confidential; it should be evaluated separately for protec-

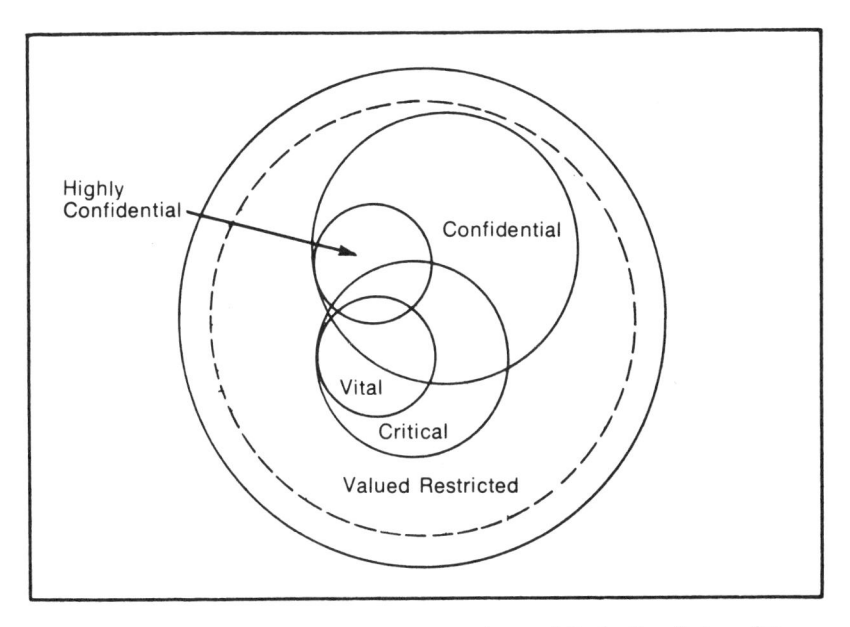

Figure 3. Relationship between Preservation and Protection Categories

tion purposes, based on the type of information involved. Figure 3 illustrates the relationship between the preservation and protection categories.

A MODEL PROTECTION PROGRAM

The preceding sections provide the information needed as the basis for an information protection program. This section defines the structure of such a program and the specific requirements for each element.

Information Protection Policy

The following tenets should be included in a policy that serves as the foundation for a new program:
- Information should be formally established as an asset that is the property of the organization and is not to be used or disclosed outside of the organization without prior management approval.
- Information that has not been specifically classified by organizational policy should be classified by the originator, because he or she should be best able to make the classification decision.
- Information should be disseminated within the organization only on a need-to-know basis.

Policy should also establish that information an employee develops in the course of his or her work is a product as real as the products of a manufacturing operation and as such is the property of the organization.

Elements of the Program

The major elements of an information protection program might include the regulations that follow. These regulations should be published and distributed to all appropriate employees.

MIS SECURITY

Classification and Labeling Regulations. This section establishes and defines the classification categories, provides examples for each category, and specifies the labeling requirements and standards for confidential information.

General Regulations. This section lists the program requirements that are common to all categories of information so that the distinctions between the categories can be made clearer. Regulations that can usually be generalized include:
- Responsibility for the security of information rests with the individuals having possession or knowledge of the information.
- Transferring custody of information when an employee leaves or transfers is the responsibility of the individual's supervisor, who should collect all confidential information and either transfer it to the employee's successor or destroy it, as appropriate.
- Information can only be reclassified by the originator or his or her superiors, and any recipients of the information must be notified of the change.
- Information disclosure to outsiders must be approved and should be in writing; if the information is confidential, a secrecy agreement is required.
- Enforcing the program is necessary to protect the organization's legal rights.
- Program infractions must be formally reported and reviewed to determine what remedial action should be taken.
- Exceptions to the program requirements must be referred to the appropriate authority for resolution.

Specific Regulations. These apply to the two confidential categories of information and describe specific protection requirements and/or standards as well as the responsibilities involved for the following activities:
- Preparation and handling—who is permitted to prepare confidential information and how workpapers, drafts and scrap materials are protected or destroyed
- Labeling—what labels are available, how they are used, and when usage is mandatory or optional
- Reproduction—who may copy confidential information
- Distribution—who determines the distribution of the information, both for the original and any subsequent distribution
- Transfer—how to transfer confidential information properly whether by physical, verbal, or electronic means (e.g., teletype, facsimile, computing equipment)
- Storage—how confidential information is to be securely stored
- Loss—how losses are to be reported and followed up.
- Destruction—how to properly dispose of confidential information

Special Regulations. Specialized requirements can be grouped in this section. For example, controlling distribution, storage and destruction of information for computing and word processing systems presents unique problems and requires such special considerations as password protection and/or encryption of confidential information to control access and copying, and erasing or overwriting regulations (instead of physical destruction regulations).

In order to avoid redundancy and unnecessary detail, most specific regulations should be worded to apply without being reworded in this section. Compliance should be required, but discretion should be permitted to simplify the program.

An information protection program structured with only the four major elements described can be kept relatively simple and tailored to the particular needs of the organization. An overly detailed program, or one that is specifically directed to a specialized environment—such as the information processing department—is far less likely to be understood or followed. Again, as with the preservation program, proper classification is the key.

ACTION PLAN

The criticality and the confidentiality of information are related issues linked by the information preservation and protection goals of the organization. Information security needs are most effectively addressed through proper classification and application of the appropriate preservation and protection measures. A classification program should be directed at the nonautomated environment in order to be effective and understandable.

X-2
People: The Key to Security
Leslie C. Chalmers

INTRODUCTION

Good security programs depend on attention to detail. Sensitive reports should be shredded before they are discarded, passwords should be both long and obscure enough to prevent successful guesswork, and the specifics of how a control procedure works should not be disclosed to those who do not need to know. Every employee has the potential to undermine a security program if he or she does not observe such precautions.

A few years ago, a telephone company lost more than $1 million to a man who penetrated the company's computerized ordering system and diverted expensive telephone equipment for his own use. He reported that he had obtained the necessary information by delving into the trash containers behind a company facility and by talking to "helpful" employees. If the employees had been trained to shred sensitive documents before disposing of them and to refrain from discussing details of company procedures with outsiders, the fraud probably would not have occurred.

In another fraud involving a large bank, a guard admitted the perpetrator to the wire transfer room, not realizing he was no longer associated with the bank. Once inside the wire transfer room, the trespasser found the necessary test key (a kind of password) taped to the wall next to a terminal. Again, attention to detail could have prevented this fraud.

Department or branch employees can be one of the first lines of defense against internal fraud and embezzlement if they know what to look for. An MIS manager or auditor is unlikely to see all the shortcuts or laxities in following procedures during an annual or biennial visit, because most employees are on their best behavior under such circumstances. If employees understand the need for controls, however, they will be less likely to circumvent them and more likely to encourage their co-workers to comply.

Recently, another large bank lost several million dollars in a scheme requiring the perpetrator to carry out certain transactions every Friday. If his co-workers had known the importance of the company policy requiring each employee to take a vacation, someone might have reported that the perpetrator was not complying with the mandatory policy. The fraud might have been uncovered many months and millions of dollars sooner.

Each of these frauds could have been prevented if employees had been

MIS SECURITY

more alert to the need for effective security controls. An MIS manager can improve the effectiveness of the security program if he or she undertakes to educate all employees about their role in making the program work. Management must also be involved in ongoing security education and must hold employees accountable for compliance with security controls. This chapter discusses the elements of a security awareness program that can help ensure that controls are each employee's responsibility and concern.

WHAT MUST BE TAUGHT

The MIS manager setting up a security awareness program should tailor its content to the organization. A general security awareness program should focus on items common to most or all employees. Specific programs for key areas (e.g., the wire transfer room of a bank) should focus on details that affect only that area. In general, the awareness programs should teach:
- What should be protected
- What employee actions are required
- What employees should do if a problem is found.

What Should Be Protected

The first priority is to explain to employees what information needs protection. This varies from organization to organization; for example, bank and insurance company employees must be aware of issues related to customer privacy, manufacturers must protect trade secrets, and oil companies need to secure information about explorations. Every organization must protect employee information (particularly payroll data), long-term business and marketing strategies, and supply and inventory information.

Classification System. One security method used by the military has been adopted by some businesses: classifying information. A classification system makes employees aware of which information is sensitive. Documenting sensitive information is of limited usefulness; clearly labeling a report, tape, or word-processing diskette to identify the sensitivity of the contents is much more effective. A classification label will also alert all employees that the information requires special handling during distribution, storage, and disposal. Mail clerks, for example, cannot be expected to provide special handling for sensitive documents unless they know which envelopes contain sensitive materials.

What Employee Actions Are Required

All employees must understand their part in improving security. How the expected actions will protect security should be reinforced by examples. For instance, if employees are asked not to disclose passwords, the aforementioned bank wire transfer fraud could be used as an example of what can happen when password secrecy is compromised. If employees understand the consequences of failure to comply with a control, they will be more likely to abide by it.

The MIS manager should remember that what seems obvious to a security expert may not be obvious to a clerk. Most security managers know the importance of locking up confidential reports at night, but a clerk may not understand this. Although employees may follow instructions, they are more likely to forget them if they do not comprehend the reasons behind them.

What to Include in a Security Awareness Program. Although the topics to be covered in a security awareness program vary with the organization, the following general topics should be included:
- Password management—procedures for password selection and change, rules against sharing passwords, password holder's accountability for its use
- Physical access controls—keeping keys under control, not allowing piggybacking into restricted areas unless authorized, escorting visitors, wearing badges
- Environmental controls—fire prevention and suppression, use of plastic sheeting to protect equipment from water leaks
- Information storage—locking up sensitive information when it is not in use, protecting essential information from destruction
- Information distribution—packaging sensitive information for mailing, using special messengers or couriers, verifying caller identity before revealing information over the telephone
- Information disposal—shredder location and use, using special locked containers for sensitive trash, enforcing classified waste disposal program
- Authorization—who should authorize transactions and when, the importance of verifying authorization signatures
- Errors—error prevention, detection, and correction; use of balancing reports or control totals; what to do if an error cannot be corrected using standard procedures
- "Loose lips sink ships"—the importance of not discussing the controlled information or the methods used to control it
- Disaster recovery—each employee's responsibilities in an emergency, special recovery teams' responsibilities, who is in charge of those teams

It is important to emphasize the practical steps that each person can follow to promote security both in his or her daily routine and in emergency situations.

What Employees Should Do If a Problem Is Found

Alert employees who understand the need for security and the principles behind the controls can help detect internal fraud and other problems. If employees are asked to respond to a suspected fraud, they must know what action to take. The MIS manager does not want to create an environment in which every employee feels watched by others; however, he or she does not want employees to ignore problems simply because they do not know how to respond. This is especially important if an employee feels that his or her supervisor may be part of the problem. For example, the bank employee who took no vacation was a branch manager. The only employees who could have noticed and then reported his failure to comply with bank policy were his subordinates. Even if a branch employee had noticed that the manager did not take a vacation, he or she might have hesitated to report him if there was no established mechanism for doing so.

MIS SECURITY

Reporting Security Problems. Each employee should know who is responsible for security investigations and should understand the role of internal auditors, the security manager, and anyone else involved in investigating a security problem. An employee could report a problem to an employee representative, such as someone in the personnel department. There may be false alarms, or disgruntled employees may try to use the problem-reporting system to make trouble for their supervisors or fellow employees. An employee representative should be skilled at weeding out such cases from the legitimate problems.

Telephone numbers for physical security personnel should be published. Everyone should know where to report a fire or other environmental hazard or a suspicious person lurking outside the building. This emergency telephone list should also include the number to call in a medical emergency.

Employees Can Improve the System. Controlling routine problems can be just as important as handling suspected frauds and emergencies in ensuring secure and effective operations. An employee who understands the need for security may devise a way to improve controls within his or her department. An employee suggestion system is an excellent vehicle for collecting such ideas. Anyone discovering a new or better way to control information should receive recognition or perhaps a cash reward from management. Publicizing the suggestions of one employee may encourage others to offer ideas.

A WORD OF CAUTION

Thorough employee security education must not turn into detailed instruction on how to commit a fraud. Knowing that a company lost money to someone who searched the trash is sufficient information to stress the need for control; a detailed description of how that information was used is unnecessary. A manufacturer of silicon chips can emphasize the impact of the loss of chips on the company without mentioning how much a competitor would pay to obtain those chips. An insurance company can stress the importance of accurate posting of premium payments without discussing ways in which the payment processing system could be used for embezzling. Training material should be general enough to make the point without suggesting how an employee could profit from a security weakness.

The MIS manager should resist the temptation to drive home a point by citing an example from the company's history. Although this would certainly convince employees that it *can* happen here, it could also encourage someone to try the same ploy. There is also the risk of inadvertently disclosing information never reported to the police or the media. This could embarrass the company and damage the security program.

SECURITY TRAINING METHODS

Teaching usually connotes lecturing a group of people and then answering questions. If a company employs more than several hundred people, it is probably too large for this teaching method to work. On some occasions a presentation is helpful, but the MIS manager cannot expect to reach every employee in this way. Many less time-consuming methods can deliver the security message effectively.

Publications

Newsletter Articles. Internal publications are an excellent means of reaching every employee. The security manager could write a series of articles for the company newsletter covering basic security concepts. Examples of other organizations' security mishaps and how they could have been prevented should be included. These articles should always end with a list of actions that each reader can implement.

The articles must be simple and clear. Someone representing the target audience who knows little or nothing about security or controls should be selected to read and comment on the articles; if they are unclear to that person, they will not effectively promote security.

Security Booklets. Another means of publicizing the security program is a booklet summarizing general points that affect every employee. Too often, security requirements are published only in a management manual that few employees see. Detailed standards for certain audiences, such as computer programmers, can be published selectively; however, general security guidelines belong in a manual or booklet distributed to all employees.

The security booklet may be combined with an emergency response manual. A combined manual is more cost-effective, and the inclusion of all material in one booklet may ensure publication of the security material. A major drawback, however, is that too many guidelines merged in one book may confuse the reader.

If the organization employs many non-English-speaking people, a foreign language version should be published. The personnel department should be able to provide guidance in this area; if internal material routinely appears in more than one language, so should the security booklet.

Presentations

Formal presentations are sometimes useful with certain groups. For example, when a new badge access control system is being introduced, it might be advantageous to give a presentation for employees in the affected building. Those affected by the installation of a Halon system in the computer room should be given a presentation detailing the new system's operation. Ideally, the vendor who sold the system will send someone to make the presentation; this arrangement is most desirable since the vendor presumably knows more about the system than the MIS manager, and the presentation will not take up the MIS manager's time.

Informal security presentations should be considered. Some organizations offer lunchtime lectures on a variety of subjects; security topics could occasionally be included. Since attending such lectures is voluntary, care should be taken to make them entertaining as well as informative. A film or videotape could be obtained from a vendor or perhaps from a television station.

MIS SECURITY

For example, a 1981 program in the PBS series "Nova" provided a good overview of the privacy issue and explained some of the technology (e.g., public key encryption) currently being developed to protect the privacy of computer records. A videotape of that program can be rented or purchased. Security equipment manufacturers and computer vendors may also have informative films. The MIS manager or security manager should prescreen any film to make sure it is appropriate for the intended audience.

New Employee Training

Security awareness must be a part of newly hired employees' orientation. Each new employee should be required to sign an agreement to abide by the organization's policies and rules. Some organizations also have their professional staff sign nondisclosure or noncompetition agreements when they are hired. Although this is useful, it does not commit employees to shredding sensitive trash or refraining from disclosing passwords. In addition, such statements often are not required of nonexempt employees. A general compliance statement for *all* employees alerts them to the importance of policies and rules, including those for security.

Each new employee should receive a copy of the general security rules and the specific rules that apply to his or her work area. If the organization has a security booklet, it should be included in the orientation packet along with insurance enrollment forms, the employee handbook, and other literature. This will help to impress the importance of security on each new employee.

A short talk on security should be given during the orientation program. This talk should include the reasons for the organization's need for security, some general points about security measures that affect all employees (e.g., the use of badges to control access to company buildings), and references to publications (e.g., the security booklet or specific manuals) where they can obtain more information. The MIS manager and security manager should work with the personnel department to develop the material to be covered and to train the speakers in answering questions on what may be a new subject for them.

New Systems

When a new computerized system is introduced, employees who will be working with the system should be instructed in the security controls that will be used. For example, when installing an electronic funds transfer system, each user of the system must be instructed on the use and control of test keys. If a new accounting system depends on certain control totals to detect erroneous or fraudulent data, those responsible for balancing the totals must be aware of their importance and what steps must be taken if an out-of-balance condition is detected.

The user guide for the system must clearly explain the controls and procedures to be used in protecting the system. As with other training material, the instructions must be general enough so that employees do not learn ways to circumvent the controls. It is sufficient to tell employees that they will be held accountable for every transaction entered with their ID and password; it is not necessary to point out all the transactions that might be used to defraud the organization with a compromised password.

An employee who is issued a user ID and password for a computer system should sign an acknowledgment stating that he or she has received the password, promises to use it only for its intended purpose, and will promptly report any suspicions that the password has been compromised. This should be an ongoing procedure for new users of the system as well as for the original users.

MAINTAINING SECURITY AWARENESS

Any training is likely to be forgotten over time. Groups as diverse as lawyers, teachers, and paramedics are required to take periodic refresher courses and, in some cases, to pass a test every few years to maintain their certification or credentials. The same principle must apply to security training. Most people eventually relax some of their diligence in following procedures, particularly those procedures that are not directly responsible for getting the job done. If they are under pressure to meet high productivity standards, they may begin to look for shortcuts. Security controls may be perceived as a time-consuming impediment to productivity and thus bypassed. The security awareness program must be an ongoing effort to remind employees of their part in the total security program.

General Reminders

The security manager should continue to publish articles in the company newpaper. Subjects covered more than a year before should be reviewed and brought up to date or discussed from a different perspective. It is also helpful to include any changes relevant to the topic of the article. For example, if the organization has implemented an access control software package since the last article on password controls was written, the article should be updated.

Notices or posters reminding employees of security should be placed in areas where sensitive information is handled. Some posters are commercially available, or the organization's art department could produce them.

Some organizations require officers or managers to sign an annual acknowledgment or statement that they have reread the policies. This could be extended to other employees, especially those who work in sensitive areas.

Security Objectives

The performance appraisal of each employee might include an assessment of how well he or she has maintained security and a review of security procedures and controls. Certain jobs could have a procedures and controls checklist to be discussed with the employee being reviewed. Each point and how well the employee has complied with it should be examined. Where appropriate, objectives related to security should be included in the goals for the next performance appraisal.

MANAGEMENT RESPONSIBILITIES

Every manager or supervisor is ultimately responsible for compliance with security within his or her unit. Some of the suggestions in this article for increasing and maintaining security awareness can be carried out only by the line managers. Every manager, therefore, should be involved in the security awareness program. Managers should participate by promoting security awareness among their staff and by enforcing procedures and controls.

Promoting Security Awareness

Managers should be responsible for training their staffs. In addition to the general security presentation given at orientation, specific training should be provided for new employees by their supervisors. Mangers should also hold periodic refresher discussions on these controls with all employees. For example, the data center manager should review the fire suppression system with all data center personnel at least once a year. The office manager should review which documents and materials are to be locked up at night, and the marketing manager should discuss with his or her staff the confidentiality of strategic plans.

Consistent Enforcement

In training managers to promote security, it is important to emphasize that even small deviations from security controls can cause an indifferent attitude among employees. Managers must insist on full compliance. If a manager of an area with badge-reader-controlled access occasionally allows employees to piggyback others when he or she is present, they will be likely to continue the practice when the manager is absent. Each manager must assume responsibility for enforcing security controls. If the manager of the wire transfer room in the aforementioned bank fraud had recognized the importance of securing test keys, he or she would have controlled them more carefully within the room.

Managers must also realize that they set the example for their employees. If the data center manager smokes in a no smoking area, everyone else will also ignore the signs. If the manager is careful to extinguish a cigarette before entering the room, the employees also will exercise more care.

Security Violations. Managers are also responsible for following up on any violation or attempted violation of security procedures. For example, if a manager discovers that someone has left a terminal logged on, the matter should be discussed immediately with the person involved. If the violation is not dealt with promptly, the employee will believe that it is unimportant and probably will not hesitate to repeat the act. Employees must be able to see that their managers are committed to supporting the security controls if they are to have any respect for these rules.

Senior Management Role

Senior management must also play a role in a security awareness program. In addition to encouraging the managers who report to them to support the program, senior management must set clear policies regarding enforcement of the security controls. Senior management should also set a policy that protects anyone reporting a problem with controls or their enforcement. An employee who discovers that a control is being ignored or circumvented should be protected from reprisals by his or her supervisor or fellow employees. It should be possible for an employee to remain anonymous. For example, the employee could report a problem to an employee relations representative, who would forward the information without revealing its source. Employees who desire recognition for reporting problems should receive it.

CONCLUSION

An organization-wide security awareness program will do much to improve security. The goals of the program are to educate all employees about the importance of security and to encourage them to participate by complying with controls, identifying problems, and suggesting new ways to improve controls. The MIS manager, security manager, line managers, and senior managers must all be involved in setting policies and objectives, providing continuing training, and enforcing security procedures. Employees who understand the need for security and know what they must do to promote it are the best protection against the kinds of fraud described in the beginning of this article. Only security-aware employees can provide the attention to detail vital to a successful security program.

X-3
Physical Security Measures

Gerald I. Isaacson

INTRODUCTION

Physical security is an important facet of a comprehensive security program. Too often, physical security problems are considered solved by the acquisition of an access control system or are delegated to an existing corporate protection department that may not understand the requirements of an MIS operation. Physical security, however, should always be the first line of defense in protecting data processing resources.

THE VULNERABILITY SURVEY

The MIS manager should conduct a vulnerability survey to identify the weakest areas of physical security as the first step in protecting data processing resources. The resulting data can be used in requesting the necessary resources from management. The following areas should be included in a vulnerability survey:
- Location and construction of the data processing facility
- Access control
- Fire protection
- Electrical power
- Environmental systems
- Water protection

Pragmatically, the real vulnerabilities faced are in the accidental or malicious loss of support systems.

The vulnerability survey, for the most part, can be performed by conducting a walkthrough of these areas, looking for weaknesses from the viewpoint of someone or something trying to penetrate and/or damage the data processing capability. A checklist can aid in this process; however, it must be recognized that checklists are only starting points. They are written without concern for a particular environment. For example, until recently, very few checklists included volcanic ash as a potential problem.

Following the traditional view of physical security as being built upon increasingly strengthened rings of defense, a vulnerability survey could begin by reviewing access control from the perimeter of the organization. If the organization owns the entire facility, the survey should start outside the property and work into the data center and the critical functional areas, looking for ways an outsider or, as is usually the case, an unauthorized insider can

MIS SECURITY

access unprotected areas. This review should highlight both physical and procedural weaknesses, the latter being more prevalent. Procedural weaknesses are usually lapses in policies that can be corrected without any capital outlays. If serious threats of any kind are uncovered, they should be immediately addressed.

When reviewing the problems of fire and water detection, fire suppression, electrical power requirements, and air conditioning, it may be necessary to consult specialists. Any qualified corporate staff or outside vendors can provide the necessary expertise.

Once the survey is completed and the vulnerabilities are identified, the next step is to evaluate appropriate safeguards or countermeasures. A basic consideration in any safeguard evaluation is that the cost and complexity of protective measures increase as maintenance requirements, training, and operational complexity increases. A relatively low portion of the security budget provides a relatively high level of protection; however, any recommended additional protection could be very expensive.

Concepts used in the developing of an effective physical data security program include:
- Diversification—using distributed data processing or alternate facilities
- Avoidance—locating data resources away from hazards
- Hardening—physically securing the site
- Closure—restricting access to sensitive resources

Protective strategies used in conjunction with these concepts appear in Table 1. Table 2 provides a matrix of countermeasures effective against MIS

Table 1. Protective Strategies

Strategy	Object	Effect	Type of Countermeasure
Containment	Control access	Reduce probability	Affect environment Reduce target attractiveness
	Isolate assets	Reduce probability	Control access to target Plug holes in defense Remove target from threat
Deterrance	Deter motives	Reduce probability	Advertise punishment Increase chances of being caught
	Prevent threats Detect results	Reduce probability Reduce loss	Detect early Thwart attack Detect all activity Review audit trails
Obfuscation	Conceal assets	Reduce probability	Cryptography Hide physical assets Control proprietary information
	Disperse assets	Reduce loss	Backup and recovery Alternative processing Multiple locations Isolation (barriers)
Recovery	Replace assets	Use other resources	Emergency procedures Backup and recovery Contingency planning
	Transfer loss	Absorb prior loss	Insurance

Physical Security

Table 2. Matrix of Common Threat Classes

Threat Classes \ Countermeasures	Physical Protection	Physical Access Controls	Backup Procedures	Operating Procedures	Personnel, Motivation, Screening, and Control	File Privacy Transformations	Threat Monitoring	Auditing Procedures	Terminal Access Controls	File Access Controls	Hardware Access Controls	Communications Privacy Transformations
Natural Risks (fire, earthquake, power failure, and air-conditioning failure)	X		X	X								
Accidental (human error)			X	X			X	X	X			
Sabotage	X	X	X	X	X							
Theft		X	X	X	X							
Copying		X		X	X	X	X		X	X		X
Tampering (modification of software)		X	X	X	X	X	X	X	X	X	X	
Masquerading (use of someone else's password)							X		X	X		
Browsing/Snooping (wiretapping, looking in ashcans)						X	X		X	X		X

threats. Finally, Figure 1 presents a total expected cost model for developing an overall framework for a cost-effective physical aspect of a data security program.

Facility Site Selection and Construction

Creating an environment to protect the computer facility begins with the judicious selection of site. The MIS manager and data security staff should play a key role in selecting the location.

When selecting a site, avoid locations prone to natural disasters such as floods, earthquakes, tornadoes, or hurricanes. To lessen the possible damaging effects of a disaster, backup/contingency security planning should be an essential part of the site planning.

The ideal facility to house a data center is a standalone building. In a multistory building, physical security problems increase. If the organization is not the sole tenant of a multistory building, operations could potentially be affected by another organization's problems.

Locating the data center in the basement makes access control easier but involves a higher risk of water damage in the event of a fire or plumbing problems. Locating the data center on one of the lower (first five) floors, however, provides easy access for fire fighting and still permits an adequate level of access control.

Proposed construction or reconstruction of a facility should completely isolate the data center and its supporting utilities from the rest of the building, thereby developing a totally separate environment in terms of access control and support systems. The data center should be separated from the rest of the building by true floor to true ceiling construction and not, as in some cases, construction that only connects a raised floor to a dropped ceiling. The data center should have no windows. Doorway windows should be limited in size and constructed of heat resistant, wired glass. Controlled access to the facili-

MIS SECURITY

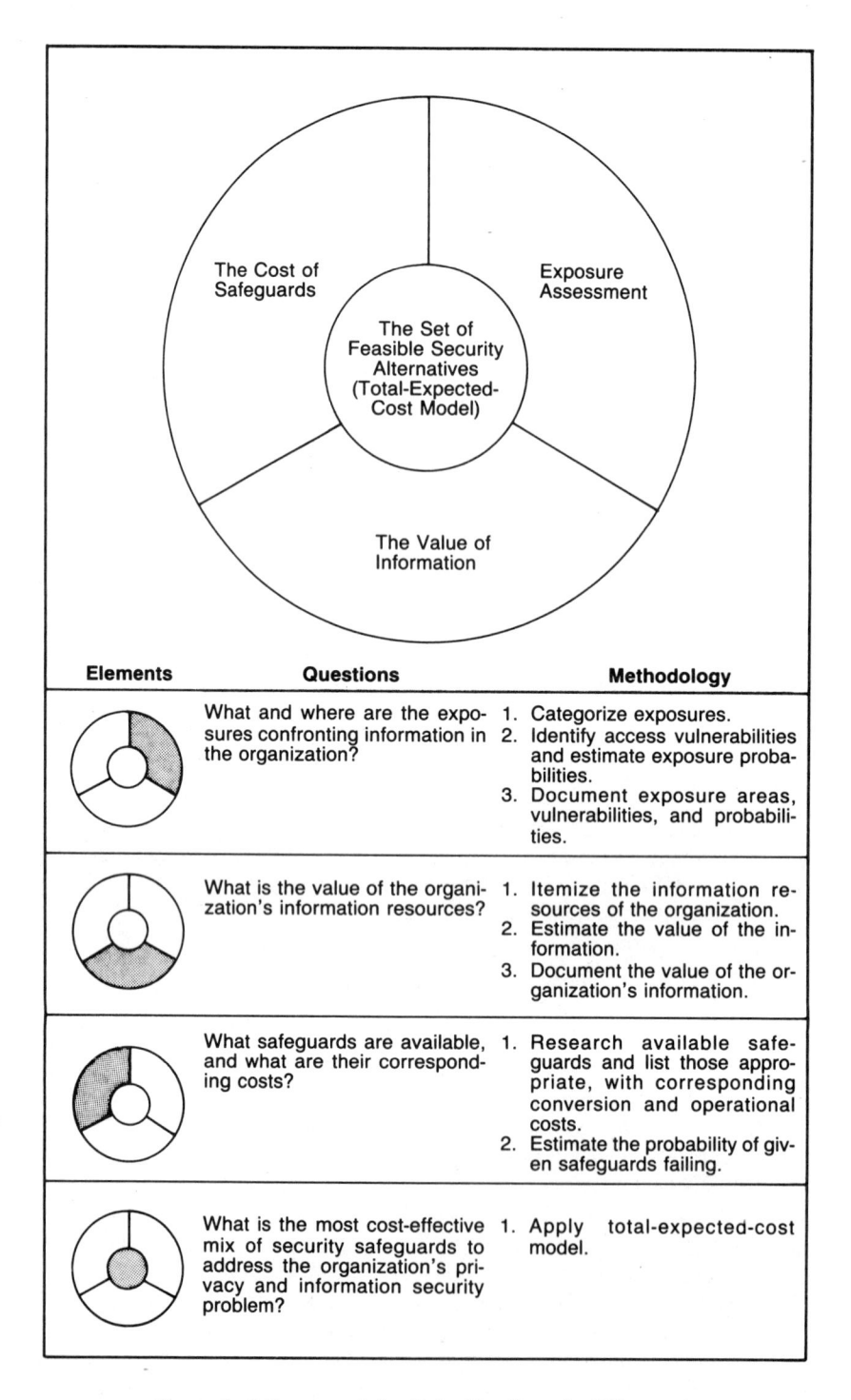

Elements	Questions	Methodology
	What and where are the exposures confronting information in the organization?	1. Categorize exposures. 2. Identify access vulnerabilities and estimate exposure probabilities. 3. Document exposure areas, vulnerabilities, and probabilities.
	What is the value of the organization's information resources?	1. Itemize the information resources of the organization. 2. Estimate the value of the information. 3. Document the value of the organization's information.
	What safeguards are available, and what are their corresponding costs?	1. Research available safeguards and list those appropriate, with corresponding conversion and operational costs. 2. Estimate the probability of given safeguards failing.
	What is the most cost-effective mix of security safeguards to address the organization's privacy and information security problem?	1. Apply total-expected-cost model.

Figure 1. A Framework for Selecting Security Safeguards

ty should apply to personnel and materials. Fire exits, as required by local fire codes, should be equipped with panic bars and alarms.

Architects should consider security when designing data centers. If the architects used do not have the appropriate security background or training, security consultants should review the site plans prior to construction. Some do's and don'ts of site selection and construction are found in Table 3.

Table 3. Do's and Don'ts of Site Selection

DO	DON'T
Locate the data center in a separate area	Publicly advertise the location of the facility
Separate the data center from the rest of the building	Locate the facility near an area with a high volume of traffic
Provide separate air conditioning	Connect data center to building air conditioning
Limit the number of entrances	Locate the data center in a basement
Alarm all exits	Ignore normal patterns of employee movement to areas such as rest rooms or lounge areas
Provide a separate access to media libraries	Locate the DP manager in the data center

Access Control

Access control techniques are built on three basic principles:
- Access control—prohibiting unauthorized access to data processing resources
- Use control—prohibiting unauthorized use of data processing resources
- Threat monitoring—recording unauthorized use of data processing resources

The goals of the potential attacker are:
- Denial of service
- Unauthorized modification
- Unauthorized disclosure
- Unauthorized use

Many areas inside and outside of the data center require physical access control. These areas include:
- Computer room
- DP users' offices
- Elevators (passengers and freight) within the data center
- Media library
- Programmers' areas
- Off-site storage
- Terminal and RJE rooms
- Rest rooms within the data center
- Telephone panels and rooms
- Janitor closets adjacent to the data center
- Air shafts coming into the data center
- Roof above the data center

MIS SECURITY

- Mechanical equipment rooms
- Electrical panels and rooms
- Engineer's office (building plans)
- Boiler rooms
- Basement areas
- Entrances and exits
- Utility sources (gas, water, electrical, and telephone)
- Building exterior and parking lots

In more general terms, protecting the above areas means protection for:
- Personnel
- Computer hardware
- Word processing equipment
- Office equipment
- Telephones
- Environmental equipment
- Security equipment

Access control techniques are designed to limit access to particular areas only to users with a legitimate need. Access control techniques are categorized as:
- Animate transportable characteristics (lock and key system)
- Inanimate transportable characteristics (password)
- Nontransferrable characteristics (fingerprints)

The most widespread means of access control is a lock and key. All data resource areas should be locked, particularly when unoccupied. While a lock does not provide a very high level of protection, it does raise the level of deterrence. Lock and key or card access systems are relatively inexpensive, easily installed, and readily accepted by users.

The weakness of these access control systems is that keys and cards can be lost or given away (transported). To improve the operation of these access control systems:
- Do not identify the organization on the card. Use a post office box for the return of lost cards.
- Use photo ID cards, which have a higher deterrent value than ID cards without photos.
- Use online computerized access systems to facilitate removing access rights for lost cards; to allow higher resolution control by area and time of day; to provide anti-passback control (preventing someone from passing a card to someone behind him); and to permit a printed audit trail of access through any and all doorways.
- Issue a complete new set of cards when 10 percent of the original set has been lost.

Other transportable characteristics are key combinations, standard combination locks, push buttons, rocker keys, and other similar systems. Their security can be increased by:
- Changing combinations frequently
- Using nontrivial combinations
- Imposing stringent penalties for disclosing or writing a password in observable areas

Table 4. Combustibility of Records

Records	Description	Storage	Burning Characteristics
Magnetic tapes	Made of polyester, PVC, or cellulose triacetate, with an iron oxide coating, and wound on metal or plastic spools	Stored in metal or plastic drums	Polyesters are easily ignited, burn slowly, but can be made self-extinguishing. PVC and cellulose triacetate are difficult to ignite. PVC is self-extinguishing, but if large quantities are ignited in a confined space, combustion may be sustained and accompanied by the production of corrosive fumes.
Magnetic sheets	Two types: 1. A kind of flexible paper card 2. Polyester, with one side magnetizable	Both types are usually kept in metal trays	Both types are easily ignited and the card type burns readily.
Magnetic disks	Two types: 1. Plastic-covered aluminium on an iron frame 2. All metal with a magnetic deposit, such as cobolt-nickel	Type 1 kept in removable polystyrene envelopes Type 2 kept permanently on the machines	Polystyrene is easily ignited and burns readily.
Punched cards	Made of paper	When punched, cards are kept in metal trays or drawers.	Readily combustible
Punched tape	Rolls of paper	Discarded after use	Readily combustible

- Overprinting a password area prior to its printing on a hard-copy terminal
- Blanking a video terminal to avoid displaying a password on a CRT terminal

Nontransferrable characteristics are generally referred to as biometric devices and are designed to measure or identify an individual by a personal trait. Among the traits currently used are:
- Hand geometry
- Signature dynamics
- Fingerprint analysis
- Palmprint analysis
- Signature verification
- Voice recognition
- Retinal pattern identification

Theoretically, these characteristics are unique to the individual and so differentiate between people with access rights and people without access rights. Nontransportable biometric access control devices provide a high degree of data security. On the other hand, these devices are expensive, require longer installation time, and are relatively new on the access control scene. If a higher degree of security is required for sensitive areas and the number of people with access to the area is low, the additional cost of installation and maintenance may be justified. In the future, as these devices become more widespread, their cost decreases, and reliability increases, they will take a more prominent place in the access control device market.

Fire Protection

Fire is the single most feared physical hazard to the data processing environment. A data center can be threatened by fire originating in the data center or spreading from elsewhere in the building. There are three phases of fire protection. The first is prevention: doing everything possible to prevent fires from occurring. Prevention begins by constructing the facility with fire resistant materials and by building floor-to-ceiling fire resistant barriers to separate the data center from the remainder of the building. All material inside the data center, such as furniture, decorations, and interior construction material, should be fire retardant. The amount of combustible materials brought into the facility should be limited. These materials include not only paper and card stock but also magnetic tapes, cleaning fluids, and service manuals. Table 4 gives a detailed analysis of the combustibility of common computer supplies.

Smoking in the computer room must be prohibited. A smoking lounge in the data center must be separated by fire-resistant barriers. Prevention also includes general cleanliness of the data center, cleaning under the floor at least quarterly, and use of Underwriter Laboratories (UL) approved fire-retardant waste recepticles

If a fire does start in the data center, early detection (the second phase) helps reduce the total damaging effect. Figure 2 shows the full development of a fire. Detection identifies a fire through ionization and smoke. Detectors should be located in the normal air flow (on the ceiling, above a dropped

Physical Security

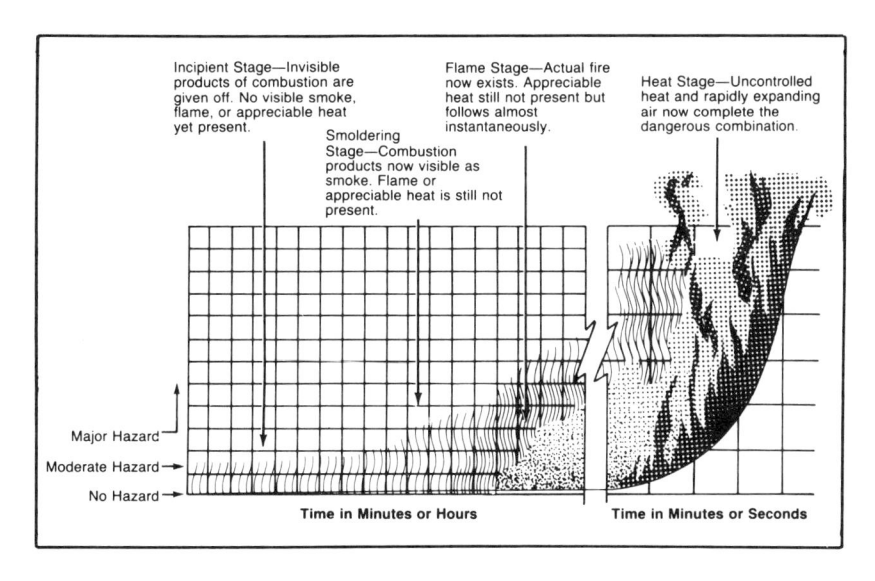

Figure 2. The Four Stages of a Fire

ceiling, in air-conditioning ducts, and below a raised floor), not in dead air pockets or in an area of rapid air flow; detectors will not operate under the latter circumstances.

Detectors should tie into central alarm stations, set off local alarms, and notify the local fire department. They are generally cross zoned, so that the first detector sounds the alarm while the second activates all fire suppression systems.

The final phase is extinguishing a fire. The three most widely used agents for fire suppression are carbon dioxide (CO_2), inert gases called halogen compounds, and water from sprinkler systems. Carbon dioxide is available in either handheld extinguishers or full-flooding systems. Full-flooding CO_2 systems are being replaced, however, because of the hazards to room occupants.

Halogen compounds are generally known by their Dupont trademarks, HALON 1301 for full-flooding and HALON 1211 for handheld extinguishers. HALON systems use inert gas that spreads rapidly throughout the installation under intense pressure. HALON extinguishes fires by interrupting the oxidation chain reaction. Since burning (i.e., the oxidation process) stops eventually, the fire source cools to a point below the combustion level and the fire danger ends. To accomplish this a sufficient supply of HALON must continue the process until this point. Since HALON is pressurized, unless the fire area is airtight, the level of available gas tends to dissipate until the gas is ineffective and a fire can reflash or reignite. A 5 to 7 percent HALON mixture with air must be maintained to be effective and still remain a minimal threat to human life. All duct work, doors, windows, and any other air passages must be sealed. If a fire burns its way into the data center, the HALON will escape through the entrance opened by the fire. The relatively high cost of the gas itself often mandates that organizations have only a single set of

MIS SECURITY

tanks. If these do not extinguish a fire, the danger of recurrence becomes a serious problem.

A water sprinkler system is the least expensive method of fire suppression. Sprinklers, however, do not save burning computer equipment. By the time the temperature-activated sprinkler heads open, the equipment on fire is probably beyond repair. The computer room and other equipment in the area, however, may be salvaged. Problems include cleanup; the time required to pump out water and dry equipment; and the difficulty in reaching fires under raised floors. Dry, pressurized systems do not retain water and have reduced some inherent sprinkler problems, such as corrosion or accidental release of water by knocking a sprinkler head off.

Current designers of data centers are leaning toward a two-fold approach. Many data centers are now equipped with dry, pressurized sprinkler systems and under-floor gas systems. The heavier-than-air characteristic of extinguishing gases provides concentration and rapid spreading of gas under raised floors.

Electrical Power

A data center requires sufficient consistent electrical power to run. Providing this power is a matter of improving the power supplied by the utility if their power output is not satisfactory.

Electrical problems vary from season to season and area to area. Insufficient electricity results in brownouts, blackouts, and other electrical disturbances. Power-correcting equipment ranges from inexpensive voltage regulators to motor generators with heavy flywheels or rotors (to maintain consistent voltage through brief interruptions) and to uninterruptible power supplies (UPS). A UPS provides consistent power through a set of batteries charged by the utility power. If the utility power dies, the batteries provide from 15 minutes to one hour of reserve power so the system can be shut down without damage. If constant power is required, the time can be used to start up diesel or gas turbine generators.

Environmental Systems

Computers require clean, filtered air at a specified temperature and humidity. Figure 3 shows the normal distance between the disk drive head and a magnetic disk compared with the size of some common contaminants found in a computer room. The potential for damage to disk surfaces or heads is obvious. Air conditioning in a computer room is process cooling not standard office cooling. A smaller amount, about 15 percent, of fresh air is used. The air flow starts from the air-conditioning unit, goes under the floor, through the equipment and returns to the air-conditioning unit. Data center air-conditioning units should be modular to preclude complete outages if one unit fails and should be separate from building air conditioning.

Air-conditioning systems, particularly heat exchanges, located outside the facility also require protection. Air intake vents should be equipped with dampers to shut off polluted outside air. If air vents are not located out of human reach, harmful elements can be sprayed into the vents and damage the

Physical Security

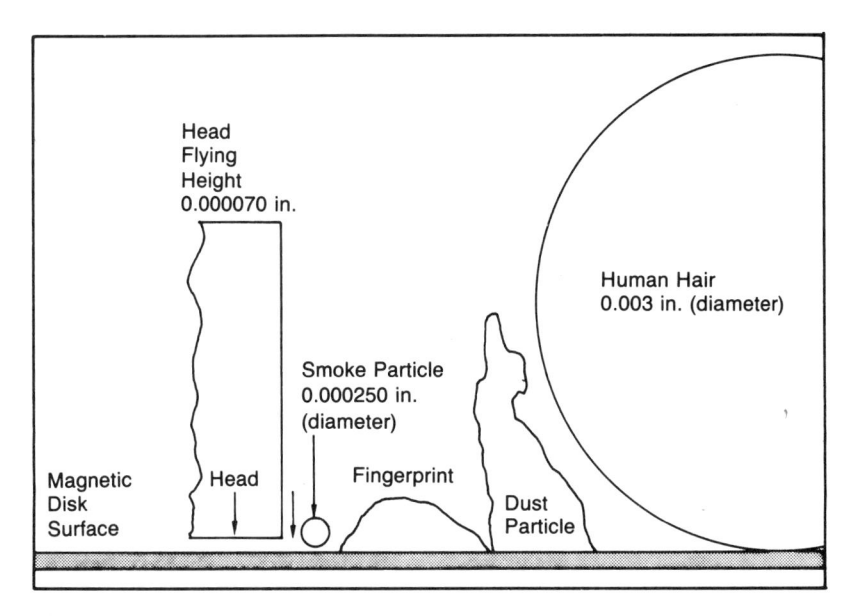

Figure 3. Comparison of Head Flying Height and Common Computer Room Contaminants

facility. Also, the facility's exhaust system should seal the room during a fire but ventilate the room following a fire.

Water Protection

The best defense against water damage is to locate the facility away from potentially hazardous areas, such as flood plains and underground springs. Locating the data center above basements, under rest rooms, or near cafeterias should be avoided. The ceiling should be watertight, with seals installed at all openings. The floor should have adequate drainage to prevent flood backup.

Even with these precautions, water leaks can still occur from air conditioning, coolers, fire-fighting methods, and leaking pipes elsewhere in the building. A variety of water leakage detection devices are available.

CONCLUSION

The value of a physical security program for a data center exceeds the protection of the individual devices. The key element of the program is a vulnerability survey that determines physical security needs. The care and attentiveness of MIS management in securing the data center is rewarded in the form of more secure operating procedures and minimal security problems.

X-4
Managing Data Security
Sandra M. Mann

INTRODUCTION

The primary purpose of computer systems is to process data. Traditionally, only secondary consideration is given to security capabilities because computers were designed to operate in a benign environment.

Most security capabilities in existing systems are based on private knowledge, keys, or badges, none of which ensures security. This can only be ensured by positive identification of individuals—identification based on something not transferable between individuals (e.g., fingerprint, voiceprint, signature). This type of identification is not widely used commercially because of high cost and implementation problems.

Since no hardware manufacturer can guarantee data security, the primary responsibility falls on the user.

In many organizations, management resists improvement in data security for several reasons. First, because many MIS professionals are still unfamiliar with security concepts, they assume that MIS exists in a benign environment. The belief that security problems will not strike them is common. The security professional, on the other hand, sees MIS operating in a potentially hostile environment. Second, while many information technologies continue to increase in capability and decrease in cost, effective security solutions remain expensive and sometimes elusive. It is difficult for management to quantify risk exposures in order to justify the "hard" costs of implementing security measures. Third, security measures sometimes reduce productivity. The bottom line is that everyone may want security, but no one is willing to pay for it. Management must realize that the cost of security measures is part of the cost of doing business.

DEVELOPING SECURITY TACTICS

In light of the issues and attitudes previously mentioned, today's challenge is to develop tactics for effectively managing the data security function. These tactics may be divided into two basic categories: managerial and operational.

MANAGERIAL TACTICS

The primary managerial tactics for an effective data security program are:

MIS SECURITY

- Obtain top management commitment
- Appoint body/committee responsible for security policy
- Form data security division
- Define responsibilities/standards

These tactics are discussed in the following paragraphs.

Top Management Commitment

Management recognition of the data security problem is essential. It can be obtained through a top management policy statement that security is a corporate problem, not merely an MIS problem, and that management is committed to implementing reasonable security measures by appropriating staff and funds. Specifically, senior management should publicize and support the initiation of a corporate security program; the greater the fanfare the better. Ideally, the president should issue a memo to all staff members explaining how critical security is to the organization's existence, stating his or her support and exhorting the staff to be equally cooperative.

Security Policy Definition

Management should appoint a body responsible for defining security policy. In a small company, this task can be performed by one individual, the DSO. In a major corporation, an MIS security committee may address security policy. The membership of this committee should be limited to seven senior managers in such areas as security, operations, programming, data communications, and EDP auditing, thus providing a global perspective. The chairman of this group should be the corporate DSO reporting to the company president or board of directors.

In addition to defining policy, the DSO or MIS security committee may be responsible for setting priorities and justifying the budget for security measures. Even in small companies where only one individual makes security decisions, senior management should review policy recommendations.

At one major bank, the MIS security committee is chartered as a standing committee. It meets once a month, unless an emergency meeting is required. The agenda is prepared two weeks in advance and is sent out with all necessary documentation. This enables the committee members to read the material, speak with their staff to review potential operational impact, resolve ambiguities or inconsistencies, and reach an informed conclusion. The committee is useful as a body initiating policy directives and as a high-level body formally concurring with and supporting a position recommended by the data security division. During the past few years, this committee has dealt with such items as encryption, physical security at MIS facilities, acquiring a software security package, and resolving issues raised in internal EDP audit reports.

The Data Security Division

The third managerial tactic is to establish a data security division and develop a formal charter, including a basic mission statement, a breakdown of the major organizational units, and an outline of the group's primary responsibilities. In small companies, one or two people may be responsible for most security tasks; in companies with large MIS facilities, it is usually more efficient and cost-effective to divide the security division into specialized areas. The following sections might be created.

Software. This section supports all the software security subsystems that are common to more than one application, such as program library products, access control software, and file encryption software. It is staffed by systems programmers who implement all security software and handle any security incidents or analyses concerning the operating systems.

Internal Security Consulting. This section advises the applications development, data communications, and MIS facilities staffs on such matters as data and network security, risk management, encryption utilization, security products, and physical security. It is staffed by security specialists with such diverse backgrounds as EDP auditing, operations, and network design.

Contingency Planning. This section oversees the development, testing, and maintenance of the contingency plan for the MIS facility.

The Data Security Manual

The responsibilities for security throughout the organization and the standards, guidelines, and parameters for security measures can be communicated to the organization in a security manual. This manual should provide guidance in physical security, data and software security, personnel security, contingency planning, external MIS security services, and insurance. These directives can be prepared internally by the security staff or with the assistance of external security consulting firms. After publication, a data security manual should be modified frequently as the environment changes.

The table of contents from one large corporation's MIS security manual appears in Figure 1. The first chapter is very general: it discusses the reasons for implementing a security program, delineates the scope of the program, and summarizes one or two key points from each of the following chapters. The second chapter details the responsibilities for security throughout the company, including those of the MIS manager, other department managers, and line managers. The third chapter states the intent of the risk management program and explains the basic philosophy and method of risk analysis. Chapters 4 through 9 are devoted to standards in the security areas previously mentioned. The final chapter is a glossary.

Before the company published the MIS security manual, the chapters were revised many times. Since some responsibilities were assigned to the personnel, legal, insurance, and auditing departments, interdepartmental coordination and review were required. The security division staff divided the text into manageable portions that were then individually reviewed by the MIS security committee members. The staff reassigned some responsibilities when they determined that a particular task could be accomplished more effectively by a department other than the one originally designated. Terms were clarified and the text developed in more detail. After all members contributed their ideas, they revised each chapter, which the committee then reviewed once more.

MIS SECURITY

Chapter 1. Purpose, Objectives, and Policies
  A. Purpose
  B. Objectives
  C. Scope and Applicability
  D. General Policy

Chapter 2. The Data Processing Security Program and Management Responsibilities
  A. Purpose
  B. Responsibilities
  C. Program Implementation in MIS Group Departments
  D. Program Implementation in All Other Corporate Groups, Departments, and Divisions
  E. Building- or Facility-Level Implementations
  F. Data Processing Installation Implementation

Chapter 3. The Data Processing Security Risk Management Program
  A. Purpose
  B. Objective
  C. Roles and Responsibilities
  D. Risk Management Policy
  E. Basic Elements of Risk Management

Chapter 4. Data Processing Personnel Security
  A. Importance of Personnel to MIS Security
  B. Basic Policies
  C. Responsibilities
  D. Sensitive Data Processing Positions
  E. Personnel Practices
  F. Security Education and Training
  G. Contractor Personnel

Chapter 5. DP Physical Security
  A. General
  B. Access Control
  C. Environmental Controls
  D. Distributed Processing
  E. Data Storage, Marking, and Media Protection
  F. Security of Documentation, Blank Instrument Stocks, and Other Sensitive Forms
  G. Facility Design and Construction Considerations
  H. Summary of Minimum Physical Security Standards

Chapter 6. Data and Software Security
  A. Purpose
  B. Background
  C. Resources to Be Protected
  D. Ownership
  E. Custodianship
  F. Authorization and Change Control
  G. Access Control
  H. Logging and Audit Trails
  I. Violation Reporting and Follow-up
  J. Encryption

Chapter 7. DP Contingency Planning
  A. Background
  B. Purpose
  C. Objectives of Contingency Planning
  D. Responsibilities
  E. Management Considerations
  F. Requirements Definition
  G. Preparation Activities
  H. Maintenance Activities
  I. Implementation and Recovery Activities

Chapter 8. Computer Insurance
  A. Background
  B. Purpose
  C. Objectives of a Computer Insurance Program

Figure 1. MIS Security Manual Table of Contents

Managing Data Security

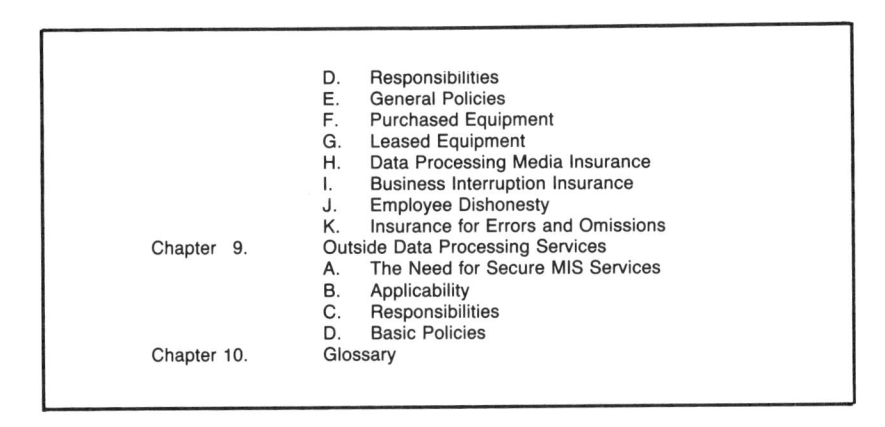

```
                     D.   Responsibilities
                     E.   General Policies
                     F.   Purchased Equipment
                     G.   Leased Equipment
                     H.   Data Processing Media Insurance
                     I.   Business Interruption Insurance
                     J.   Employee Dishonesty
                     K.   Insurance for Errors and Omissions
      Chapter 9.     Outside Data Processing Services
                     A.   The Need for Secure MIS Services
                     B.   Applicability
                     C.   Responsibilities
                     D.   Basic Policies
      Chapter 10.    Glossary
```

Figure 1. (cont)

OPERATIONAL TACTICS

Obtaining management commitment to the security effort using these management tactics provides a framework within which operational data security tactics can be applied. The following tactics are discussed:

- Utilize available audit trails
- Develop security incident report procedure
- Maintain site files
- Centralize all security consulting
- Establish security involvement in the system development life cycle
- Install security software
- Develop and implement encryption policy
- Maintain security systems library
- Stay visible.

Audit Trails

The audit trail is a straightforward security tool that is useful even in a small DP shop. The data that is collected by the operating system, software packages, or application programs should be examined. This examination may reveal that some available security options (e.g., a log of the execution of sensitive utilities), as well as valuable audit data that could be easily captured by writing an extract program, are being overlooked. In general, available audit trails should be used to monitor compliance with the standards documented in the security manual.

Incident Reporting

A formal security incident report procedure should be implemented. Loosely defined, a security incident is an action or situation that could indicate a security violation. For example, an incident may be the disappearance of a company confidential document from a work area or the disappearance of a data set from a time-sharing user's disk area.

MIS SECURITY

Not all incidents are violations, however. In the first example, an authorized staff member may have borrowed the document and forgotten to leave a note saying so. In the second example, unless the user deleted his or her own file, data confidentiality may have been violated.

In any case, security incidents should be documented in a predefined format and forwarded to the security division for investigation. The security incident report alerts management to problem areas or trends requiring policy and/or procedure definition. The security division's follow-up visibly reinforces the corporate commitment to a viable security program.

Site Files

The third organizational tactic is to establish and maintain site files. For a multilocation firm, one file should be set up for each MIS facility. A one-location firm should use one comprehensive file or a separate file for each functional area. Each file should contain all documentation relating to the area (e.g., a list of the current hardware, operating system software, and application systems, risk analyses, security incident reports, EDP audit reports). Site files provide a management tool to analyze and establish security systems for each area. They are also useful in quickly bringing new security staff up to speed in the DP environment.

Security Consulting

The security division should be the center for all security consulting in any area (e.g., physical, data, or network security problems) where a department within the organization may need help. From fairly simple physical security problems to very complex data communications problems, the security division should be responsible for determining whether in-house expertise is adequate or whether an outside consultant can handle the situation more efficiently.

A file should be maintained on outside security consultants. If assistance is requested in an area where internal expertise is insufficient or the needed resources cannot be allocated in the desired time frame, the security division can send a request for proposal to the appropriate consultants. The security division should evaluate the proposals, recommend the selection, assist the user in securing budget approval, and coordinate and monitor the consultant's work.

Systems Development Life Cycle

The security division should be established as part of the systems development life cycle in those companies that develop or modify application systems. Whether a formal or informal systems development methodology is used, one or more security checkpoints should be established at certain life-cycle milestones. This practice can help ensure implementation of the best possible system. More specifically, it helps ensure that major security problems are identified and corrected before they interrupt or delay system implementation.

A good working relationship with the internal EDP auditors is important.

The auditors can be sources of informal information outside the normal communications channels (especially in large organizations) and supportive allies when controls are particularly lacking.

Security Software

Security software should be purchased and installed within a reasonable time frame. Rapid technological advances can make packages sitting on the shelf obsolete. Therefore, if several security software packages are needed, they should not be purchased all at once unless a large installation staff is available. Risk vulnerabilities and the implementation of the necessary packages should be ranked by priority and scheduled accordingly.

Commercially available packages designed for access control (e.g., ACF2, RACF, SAC, TOP SECRET, SECURE) offer various capabilities, ranging from password protection of data sets and audit trails of access attempts to more sophisticated capabilities, such as IMS security, enforced password changing, terminal and TSO command security, and tape volume security. Other software packages, such as PANVALET and ADR/LIBRARIAN, provide source and executable program library control. The cost of these packages must be justified by the organization's environment and needs. Although these packages are not foolproof, they can significantly decrease the probability of security breaches.

Encryption Policy

If justifiable through cost/benefit analysis, an encryption policy should be developed and implemented. Encryption is not a panacea, nor is it effective in every environment; however, wherever reasonable, sensitive data stored on files or transmitted over communications links should be encrypted.

Depending on the sensitivity of the data, differing levels of encryption may be desired. Anyone considering encryption should design and conduct a pilot project since little is published on commercial encryption application.

One major corporation's MIS security committee formed an encryption steering committee that was chartered and funded to develop an encryption policy, conduct pilot projects, and develop an implementation strategy. Pilot projects in file and link encryption were conducted using several vendors' products. The results were evaluated from technological and organizational aspects. The security committee reviewed and approved the encryption policy and included it in the security manual.

Security Systems Library

One of the most valuable qualities of a security division is the ability to react quickly to industry changes. This is best accomplished through developing and maintaining a security systems library. In this one instance junk mail should be welcomed. The security division should be on the mailing lists of every security system manufacturer, vendor, and consultant and should subscribe to various security publications. Universities usually offer information on their security systems at no cost. Not all information must be carefully read. Rather, a file or catalog should be maintained on all the various hardware and software systems and articles of interest sorted by applica-

MIS SECURITY

tion. For example, one file may contain information about physical access systems (e.g., badge readers, locks). Other files may contain literature on fire detection and suppression systems, computer crime, or software security packages. The following is a sample file subject list:

- Audit techniques
- Hardware
- Software
- Minicomputers
- Data communications
- Distributed data processing
- Data base
- Project management
- Systems development life cycle
- Statistical sampling
- Legislation
- Industry (specific)
- Management
- Miscellaneous data processing
- Access control
- Fire detection/protection
- Security systems
- Computer crime
- Security

Library resources can be used to effectively track the state of the art and to campaign for security measures necessary for the organization's MIS environment. For example, circulating an article about a breach of ABC Company's system is a good way of alerting the upper management of the DSO's organization to its own risk exposure. In organizations with a formal security committee, the DSO should periodically prepare a simple state-of-the-art bulletin for the committee. The better informed the data security committee is, the more readily it will endorse the security division's ideas, give a positive response, and justify security program costs. Because changes in the environment may require quick security changes, the committee should be kept up to date. Thus, when the organization needs a new security system, the security committee will not have to be taught the basics of the system before giving approval.

CONCLUSION

Data security is as important to organizational survival and integrity for a small company with a single minicomputer as for an international corporation with a multimillion-dollar data center. In any organization, every manager is vying for funds, and the DSO must devise methods to obtain budget recognition for security programs.

Therefore, the final tactic for effective data security management is to *stay visible,* because the security division's visibility will make people *think security*. Managerial talent is needed to increase security awareness and to motivate line management to accept security responsibility. The more the data security function is seen and heard, the more everyone in the organization will realize that security is here to stay and the easier it will be to obtain support for security projects.

X-5
Data Security Standards
Leslie S. Chalmers

INTRODUCTION

Few MIS personnel and even fewer users understand the need for security. Those who do often do not know how to establish effective controls for the data they work with daily. Line managers of departments that use MIS services through either online terminals or batch systems may not even realize their vital role in a security program. Without standards, systems and procedures could undermine even the most carefully designed security software.

Data security professionals know that every user of an online system should have a unique user identification code with some form of authentication (e.g., password or fingerprint record); yet systems are still developed that do not even require the user to sign on. Passwords must be carefully chosen, protected from disclosure, and changed frequently; yet systems are developed without mechanisms for enforcing passwords with a minimum length, that store passwords without encryption to prevent browsing the password file, and whose passwords either cannot be changed or only with great difficulty.

Even if the data security officer (DSO), or MIS manager, persuades a software development team that certain controls are necessary, other project teams may not be so easily convinced. Lacking a standard requiring software developers to include certain controls, the DSO may spend a great deal of time explaining or arguing for the same controls with one team after another. For example, every decision to implement password controls in an online system might have to be justified separately for each new application. The DSO will be much more effective if his or her role involves assisting teams to meet published standards rather than debating the merits of unpublished controls.

In organizations with many systems and departments, the MIS manager may find it impossible to spend time with every manager in order to identify critical or sensitive data and to establish procedures for protecting that data. A standard that requires all managers to ensure that passwords are changed every two or three months will reach every manager even if the DSO cannot. The DSO will not need to convince every manager of the value of this practice; instead, it will be a standard that must be followed.

MIS SECURITY

PUBLISHING DATA SECURITY STANDARDS

Publishing data security policy and standards in a manual distributed to all affected managers ensures that the data security program will be perceived as an important part of the way the company conducts business. The cost of preparing, distributing, and maintaining a separate manual, however, may be prohibitive for some organizations.

Deciding to publish standards means taking into consideration their distribution to those responsible for making them work. Some standards affect every employee (e.g., a classified waste disposal program), some affect programmers (e.g., designing good controls into a system), and some affect only managers (e.g., procedures to be followed when an employee is terminated).

Among the justifications for including data security standards in an organization's publications are:
- A central data security manual could contain all corporate standards.
- A programmer's manual could incorporate all the data security standards that apply to program design and coding.
- A personnel manual could incorporate those standards that apply to personnel procedures (e.g., required vacations, screening new hires, dealing with violations of standards).
- A manager's manual could restate the standards for managers enforcing and supporting the data security program.

It may be advisable for all employees to receive a booklet that discusses the importance of securing information and states those standards that affect a wide range of employees.

Since each organization may choose to publish data security standards in any one or more of these ways, this chapter discusses the development of security standards without reference to their published form. The MIS manager should carefully consider how the standards can best be communicated to managers, programmers, operators, and other employees.

GUIDELINES VERSUS STANDARDS

A standard is a statement by management that a rule must be followed; it is binding on all MIS personnel and users. A guideline, however, lacks force and authority, and too often managers or programmers decide that a guideline is too much trouble to follow. Guidelines do have a use, however, in support of standards.

The Role of Guidelines

Certain controls are practical only for data of the greatest sensitivity or with the highest probability of being compromised. If data security standards do not address such controls, they will not be implemented, even if they are appropriate. A possible control for telecommunications transmissions, for example, is to encrypt those transmissions. Very few organizations can afford the luxury of encrypting all their data; a standard requiring encryption across the board therefore is probably unworkable. Some suggested controls, or guidelines, that include the encrypting of transmissions, however, could support a standard requiring control of access to computer systems. The guideline brings encryption to the attention of telecommunications systems developers so that it can be considered for the most sensitive applications without being imposed on systems where it cannot be cost-justified.

DETERMINING THE SCOPE OF STANDARDS

Good security is not confined to the computer room. An elaborate system to protect the payroll files is useless if the payroll department leaves reports from those files in unlocked desks that could be accessed after business hours. In an organization with strict standards for systems design, the legal department manager may acquire a microcomputer and process highly confidential information on it without ever involving the MIS department. The marketing department may prepare reports about future marketing strategies without ever involving a computer, yet those reports are just as sensitive as the most highly protected computer files.

Data security standards should be broad enough to protect information in any form, regardless of department, and should not be limited to protecting information under the control of the central MIS facility. Figure 1 shows an outline of sample security standards.

I. Data Security Policy Statement

II. Statement of Responsibilities
    A. Owner Responsibilities
    B. Custodian Responsibilities
    C. User Responsibilities

III. Information Classification

IV. Standards for Information in Hard-Copy Format
    A. Labeling Information
    B. Distributing Information
    C. Storing Information
    D. Discarding Information
    E. Backing Up Essential Information
    F. Accountability

V. Standards for the Control of Computers
    A. Use of Company Equipment
    B. Ownership of Software
    C. User Identification
    D. Password Controls
    E. Testing
    F. Software Access Controls
    G. Backing Up Computer Processing and Computer Files

VI. Physical Security for Computers
    A. Fire
    B. Water
    C. Physical Access Controls
    D. Environmental Controls

VII. Data Entry

Figure 1. Outline of Sample Data Security Standards

MIS SECURITY

Management Support

Occasionally an organization will develop data security standards in response to a directive from senior management. In most cases, however, the MIS manager, DSO, or the auditors—internal, external, or both—initiate the development of standards. Top management support and involvement are required in any case to ensure the success of the program.

Standards should not be published for those areas in which management support is lacking. If no management support exists for data security standards outside the MIS department, security standards should be limited to those areas over which MIS has control (e.g., program design, use of the computer, operational procedures). It is better to publish standards that are limited but enforceable than to publish an unenforceable standard, since it may undermine the credibility of the entire data security program.

DEVELOPING SECURITY STANDARDS

Once the support has been obtained for generating standards, they can be developed in various ways.

Senior Management Approval. The DSO may develop standards and submit them directly to senior management for approval, a straightforward approach that could take as little as one month to complete. There is a risk, however, that the standards will be perceived by others in the organization as too stringent or arbitrary (a serious problem if the DSO has been recently appointed). Often when a company decides a data security program is needed, the newly hired or transferred DSO launches a standards program before sufficient time has elapsed to gain the respect of co-workers.

Committee Approval. Submitting standards to a committee for comments and approval as the DSO drafts them is a second approach. Its advantages include support from the committee members before the standards are published and elimination or modification of standards that committee members consider unworkable. A variation, having the same advantages, is to create a task force to draft the standards. The disadvantage, however, is that it is difficult and time-consuming to obtain a consensus on the contents and even the wording of the standards. The resulting standards may be too general because of the need to satisfy all committee members.

Use of a committee or task force can overcome the problem of a DSO working in the MIS department rather than at a corporate level. If the committee members represent each major department, the scope of the standards can be broadened to include the entire organization. Each committee member should keep his or her managers informed of committee work and help win their approval of the standards.

Project Team Approval. A third approach is to organize a project team and assign sections of the standards to members. If the project team is drawn from several departments in order to obtain broad-based support, some members will probably lack expertise in data security principles and practices. If so, the DSO should take time to educate them accordingly.

CONTENTS OF A DATA SECURITY STANDARDS PUBLICATION

As a first step in the development of standards, the DSO should obtain copies of published standards from other organizations. These models will illustrate the form and content of the standards. Such standards can be obtained from the following sources:
- Some are in the public domain.
- IBM has published its standards in a manual.
- The federal government has published a number of standards for its MIS centers. (These are available through the National Technical Information Service, U.S. Department of Commerce, Springfield VA 22161.)
- Vendors may be able to recommend DSOs at other organizations who are willing and able to share their standards.
- Data security classes and conferences may introduce the DSO to people who can provide copies of standards.

Another approach is to select from a book on controls those that should be standards. One possibility is *Internal Controls for Computerized Systems* by Jerry Fitzgerald.[1]

Implementation Considerations

Throughout the development process, the MIS manager and DSO should consider how the standards will be implemented. If a standard seems necessary but is impractical in the organization's environment, it should be rejected. Controls that could work but that cannot be strictly enforced should be downgraded to guidelines.

Topics for Security Standards

The DSO faces many considerations in developing a set of standards: for example, the sensitivity of the organization's business, the amount of money that can reasonably be spent, and the size of the staff available to implement the standards. The following topics are suggested areas of coverage for security standards; not all are appropriate for every organization.

A survey of company publications may uncover many topics that are already addressed in some other manual. If the material already published is sufficient, the DSO may omit the topic.

Policy Statement. A statement of policy sets the general tone of the standards program and also defines its scope. It says, in effect, that data security is a serious concern and that corporate policy dictates the protection of data. One possible wording in which the DSO has sufficient support to develop standards for the entire operation is: "Information is an asset of the organization and, as such, steps will be taken to protect it from unauthorized modification, destruction, or disclosure, whether accidental or intentional."

Some policy statements elaborate, for example, that the amount of money spent on protection will not exceed the value of the information being protected and its annualized risk exposure. This restriction is useful in reassuring managers that the security standards will not place unreasonable demands on them.

MIS SECURITY

Information Classification. A standard or guideline should state which information is to be protected. Two factors can lead to data requiring protection: sensitivity to disclosure and sensitivity to modification and destruction. Information that is not secret may still be absolutely essential to company operations (e.g., the computer operating system, unless a licensing agreement commits the company to nondisclosure of information about the operating system). Other information must be kept secret but need not be protected from destruction (e.g., an outdated marketing report on corporate strategy). Some information is sensitive to both types of threats (e.g., the master payroll file).

A classification standard requires that information be assigned a level of sensitivity based on its importance to the organization. The standard should cover who is responsible for assigning a classification and some examples of how information should be classified. The levels of information classification should be named and defined. One company, for example, may term the levels *public, confidential,* and *top secret;* another may title them *unclassified* and *classified.* Two scales of classification may be used (e.g., public/noncritical, secret/noncritical, public/critical, and secret/critical) or only a single scale, with a requirement that information be classified above the lowest level if it is sensitive to either of the two types of threats.

Information outside the Computer. An organization should consider developing standards for information in hard-copy form. Such standards could require that papers be locked in a drawer when not in use, sent through interoffice mail in a sealed envelope, and shredded before discarded. Classified information should be labeled. Some experts believe that labeling a report draws unnecessary attention to it. Others argue that a label assists employees in locating sensitive information requiring special protection.

Access to Computers through Online Terminals. Every online system should have a sign-on procedure combining an identification code (user ID) with some form of verification (e.g., a password). Since passwords are the most common form of authentication, publishing standards or guidelines for password management is important. These standards should cover such topics as requiring that a password be given before access is granted, that it be stored in an encrypted format, that it be changed every 30, 60, or 90 days, and that it have a minimum length.

Other standards for online systems may include controlling dial-up terminals (or prohibiting their use entirely), requiring that terminals be automatically logged off after five or ten minutes of inactivity, and requiring that the user provide a reauthentication code after five or ten minutes of inactivity. If the organization does extensive sensitive telecommunications work, encrypting the transmissions could be in order; it might then be necessary to set a standard for the method of encryption to be used (e.g., the Data Encryption Standard).

Access to Computer Areas. Access to computer rooms or buildings housing computers is an important topic in most organizations. Restricting physical access to computers to only those with a need for that access is essential. Most organizations began to control access to their computers more than a decade ago with the realization that even visitors could accidentally damage equipment. Restricting access to equipment also helped protect the data stored on the equipment.

In today's distributed environments characterized by reliable hardware, managers with little or no MIS background may be acquiring and installing computers lacking the physical protection common to large mainframe installations. The standards should state the physical protection requirements for all computers, not just the central mainframes.

Environmental Controls. In addition to affording protection from intruders, the standards could also cover environmental hazards. Most computers should be protected from fire, flood, water leaks, overheating, and particulate matter (e.g., dust, smoke). The standards should define the requirements for engineering a computer installation to reduce the risks from such hazards. For example, computers should be installed above the flood level but below the fifth or sixth floor so that they can be reached by firefighters. The standards may also require that air-conditioning equipment incorporate automatic shutoff to prevent spreading smoke or that every computer room have plastic sheeting available to protect the equipment from water leaks.

Emergencies. Despite careful planning and installation of the most sophisticated environmental controls, hazardous situations may still arise. When they do, the initial responses of personnel in the immediate area will determine whether or not the situation escalates to a full-scale disaster. To avoid this, the standards could spell out the training requirements for computer room personnel or contain instructions on how to respond to common emergencies. Possible topics include how to extinguish fires, how to use plastic sheeting, what to do if an intruder bypasses the access controls, and what information to write down if a bomb threat is received. If the data security publication does cover emergency responses, it should also include information on how to handle noncomputer-related emergencies (e.g., medical emergencies).

Restrictions for Authentic Users. Controlling who can use the computer is in itself an insufficient restriction. A user should also be limited in what he or she can do while using the computer. Standards should spell out the requirements for protecting the information on the computer from users who do not have a need for that information. Topics include instituting software access controls (e.g., passwords protecting sensitive files, using an access control software package), requiring that all changes to production programs be made by a change control group, and limiting programmers to testing with test files rather than live production files. A standard should also be devised for the separation of duties (e.g., programmers should not have access to the production environment, computer operators should be separate from systems programmers).

Program Controls. A programmer can undermine even the best system controls if he or she does not include controls for application programs in

MIS SECURITY

program design. Poorly designed programs and documentation also pose a threat to the organization. The data security standards should spell out the design requirements for programs and documentation. For example, a standard could be devised for the type of audit trail that must be maintained by an application program, particularly for online applications. Other standards may require that all information be backed up on tape and stored off-site or require documenting how a system should be run in a disaster recovery situation.

If there is no existing MIS manual for programmers, the DSO may want to include such topics as standard programming language and structured programming. It should be noted that the organization could have its MIS capability impaired if a programmer leaves and no one else can decipher and maintain a critical program.

Disaster Recovery. Every organization dependent on its computers for smooth operations must have a disaster recovery plan. The plan itself deserves a separate manual, but the data security standards should carefully define who is responsible for developing and maintaining the plan, particularly if the company has several DP sites. In addition to requiring that each site develop a plan, the standards may outline the plan's contents. For example, the standard could include the names and telephone numbers of every participant in a recovery operation. Standards could be implemented for testing disaster recovery plans (e.g., methods for testing) and for reviewing all changes that might affect the plans.

Enforcement. The standards must define who is responsible for their enforcement and how that enforcement is to work. For example, if the standards require that passwords be changed every three months, the manager of password holders must ensure that they change their passwords, if the system allows them to do so, or that the application programmers design a method for automatically forcing users to change their passwords. One excellent standard for enforcing program design standards is to require all system designs to be approved by the DSO or auditing (or both) before coding begins.

Many organizations define the responsibilities of owners, custodians, and users of information. A standard may require that all information have an identified owner who is the only individual authorized to approve access to the information. Custodians are responsible for implementing the controls specified by the owner (e.g., making backup copies of critical files). Users must comply with the requirements of the data security standards and any others imposed by the owner.

Personnel Controls. Standards should exist for screening new employees and dealing with those who have been terminated, particularly if they work in sensitive areas. In addition, some companies require their employees to be out of the office for five or ten consecutive business days. If personnel procedures do not cover such circumstances, the DSO may wish to incorporate them in the data security standards.

Miscellaneous Controls. Another standard should state that company computers are to be used only for company business. Without such a standard, it may be difficult to discipline an employee who misuses the computer. It should be clearly stated that the programs developed by an employee while working for the organization belong to the organization. This is often handled with an agreement that all employees must sign when hired; otherwise it could be included in the data security standards.

SELLING THE STANDARDS TO MANAGEMENT

The most carefully written standards are worthless unless management is committed to making them work. As previously mentioned, the DSO should elicit management support before drafting the standards. The scope of the standards should be determined by the breadth of management support.

Justifying the Impact

Once standards have been drafted, the DSO must be prepared to pitch them to management. The most important step for the DSO is understanding the impact of the standards. Management will not approve standards, particularly those that mandate spending money, unless the changes and their cost are itemized and justified. One way to lessen the impact of new standards is to apply them only to new systems as they are developed; systems that are already running or are nearing implementation need not comply with the standards. While it may help to convince management that the cost of the standards will not be excessive (it costs considerably less to design in good security than to modify an existing system), such a strategy does weaken the organization's overall security. But it is better to have standards only for future systems than none at all; if the company is not prepared for the expense of incorporating standards into old systems, this may be the only means of getting the standards approved.

Receiving Key Department Approval

A second step that the DSO should take to ensure management's confidence in the standards is to submit them to key departments for comment and approval. Certain departments should be involved regardless of the organization's structure: legal, auditing, personnel, and MIS. Other groups selected depend on the organization. If any of these reviewers have reservations regarding the standards, either the standards should be revised or the DSO should meet with the dissenting reviewers to make sure that they understand the need for the standards.

Once the DSO has garnered the support of the key departments and is prepared to discuss and justify the implementation of the standards, he or she should submit them to management for approval. This approval, if possible, should come from the organization's CEO, ensuring the standards immediate visibility and support. If unable to present the standards to the CEO for approval, the DSO should take them to the highest level possible. At the very least, the MIS manager should approve them. Any lower-level manager will not be able to guarantee the support and enforcement of the standards.

AVOIDING THE PITFALLS

Some companies have found that publishing data security standards does not have the desired impact. One major problem is that no one is responsible for implementing or monitoring the standards. The responsibilities of every group involved in the implementation should be clearly defined. The DSO should also plan to devote considerable effort to meeting with various groups to explain the standards and to discuss their role in the implementation.

In some companies, the DSO does not have sufficient staff or budget to oversee the implementation. This problem should be addressed in one of two ways: either the responsibility for implementing the standards should be decentralized or the DSO should seek approval of staff and budget along with the standards. Senior management should understand that resources are necessary to make the standards work, particularly if the DSO is responsible for their implementation.

The DSO can avoid misinterpretation by submitting standards to others for review. The standards may also contain examples to illustrate them. Although this clarifies controls, it may cause problems if the examples are misconstrued as standards in their own right. Examples, therefore, must be carefully chosen.

It is possible for the standards to require controls that cannot be implemented for various reasons. The DSO may not catch all of these details unless assisted by a task force or committee. The DSO should also consider a provision for waiving standards under certain circumstances. For example, if the developer of a new system can demonstrate through risk analysis methodology that the cost of complying with a particular standard cannot be justified because the risks are too low, a mechanism for submitting this risk analysis and a request for a waiver to an individual or group for approval should be in place.

Little or no compliance with standards can be avoided by planning for implementation before standards are published. The DSO must continue to urge managers to carry out their responsibilities. In addition, the auditors should include the standards in their checklists when they audit any department that should be complying with the standards. If this is not possible, departments should have plans to achieve compliance that include deadlines and resource commitments.

CONCLUSION

A set of data security standards and guidelines will aid the DSO by clearly establishing organization-wide rules for data security. By obtaining management approval for standards, the DSO gains support for the entire data security program. Numerous methods are available for developing standards on many possible topics. The DSO should select the methods and topics that are best suited to his or her organization and that management will support, thus ensuring the best chance for success.

Reference

1. Fitzgerald, Jerry. *Internal Controls for Computerized Systems.* Redwood City CA: FitzGerald and Associates, 1978.

X-6
Open Network Security
Alan Berman

INTRODUCTION

Although no single measure provides universal protection of computer resources and data from unauthorized dial-up users, several measures aid in this effort. Managers who recognize the security risks inherent in the dial-up environment can implement some or all of these measures to increase computer and data security.

This chapter discusses many products and services currently available. Which types of protection are most appropriate depends on what the financial and other results of a security breach would have on an organization. This chapter addresses security risks and describes ways of minimizing the possibility that a system may be compromised by an intruder using the dial-up facility.

BACKGROUND

In the 1960s, the large central-site mainframe computer established its presence as the technological wave of the future. It permitted large amounts of data previously stored on paper to be stored electronically. The computer-stored information was retrievable through various means in detail as well as summary forms.

This new technology had a major drawback: it was very expensive. Few companies could afford to purchase their own machines. In addition, highly trained technicians and programmers required large amounts of time and computer system resources to develop specific programs for individual scientific and commercial applications.

Time-sharing. The advent of computerization and its attendant problems spawned the time-sharing industry, wherein companies purchased computers for the sole purpose of selling time on the machine to other companies that either could not afford their own machines or elected not to use their own computers for costly program development work. Time-sharing required users to access the computer from outside the building in which it was housed. Standard telephone lines served as the medium through which remote users could dial up, or communicate with, the central computer site.

While this innovative means of computer use grew, protecting the data stored in the shared computer was rarely considered by either time-sharing

MIS SECURITY

suppliers or users. Time-sharing suppliers provided customers with an access code and sometimes even a password, but these were used primarily by the suppliers for billing information. Little or no protection was provided for the programs that were retrievable by the mainframe. Typically, protection was provided only by program developers to safeguard their creations.

During this early stage of dial-up access, it was not uncommon for a programmer to access the system and remotely print out the source code of programs developed by others. If programmers saw some interesting code applicable to other projects, they could simply appropriate it or copy it into a private library. It was not unusual for programmers from competing firms to compare programs without the consent or knowledge of their companies.

Dial-up Software. As data processing moved into the 1970s, so did the use of dial-up terminal access. Time-sharing was still used by program developers, but the service was being marketed as a means by which end users could avail themselves of software supplied by time-sharing companies. The initial offerings consisted of payroll and personnel systems and accounts payable and receivable systems. In addition, many corporate data centers began providing dial-up service for their customers. Customers were provided access to information concerning order delivery schedules, personnel files, cash balances, and other information that was previously available only by calling a customer service representative. These inquiry-only application systems gave birth to the data entry systems that soon became commonplace.

Electronic Funds Transfer. During the late 1970s and early 1980s, facilities were introduced that allowed for electronic funds transfer initiated from terminals located throughout the world. Retailers and wholesalers could place orders with distributors to expedite the movement of merchandise. Brokers who had portable dial-up terminals could trade securities without being present at the stock exchange. Travel agents could make airline bookings without contacting a reservation clerk. Salespersons could demonstrate services or products and establish accounts or place orders from the customer's office.

Passwords and IDs. While technology was extending the dial-up service facility during the early 1970s, very little was being done to enhance security. Passwords for entry to dial-up computer systems were offered to customers, and some facilities offered multiple user IDs and passwords that permitted only specified employees to access certain files or programs; however, no extensive protection was provided to track unauthorized access to computer files or verify data integrity. Neither suppliers nor users of shared computers were sufficiently aware of the dangers of such laxity to clamor for adequate protection.

This situation began to change in the late 1970s as the following factors introduced a major emphasis upon security:
- General industry concern for computer security as a result of incidents of computer fraud
- Evidence that "hackers" (generally students and home computer buffs) were able to breach the security of major commercial, government, and

public-service data centers and gain access to data through dial-up facilities
- The issuance of third-party computer fraud insurance by major insurance corporations, and their requirements for stronger computer security before granting insurance
- The awareness that suppliers of packet network switches were unable (and in some cases, unwilling) to provide adequate security
- Media attention that focused on the problems and consequences of inadequate computer security and raised alarms on the part of both the general public and computer users in business and government

These factors evidenced and accelerated a new demand, one that suppliers were quick to try to fill.

TYPES OF DIAL-UP ACCESS

Unlike leased lines, which are always connected to a computer system through communications controllers, dial-up capability uses a standard telephone and telephone line, which can be used for voice communications as well as data transmission. An interface device called a modem is required to use the telephone to transmit and receive data. A modem is a modulator/demodulator unit that translates a digital data stream into an analog signal. The modem at the user's site converts computer data coded in binary bits into an analog (audible) signal and sends that signal over a telephone line to the computer site. The modem at the computer site translates the analog signal back to binary-coded data for automated processing. The procedure is reversed to send data from the computer site to the user site.

There are two methods by which users can be supplied with dial-up capability: standard telephone company direct-dial service, and packet-switching networks.

Direct Dial. A direct-dial facility is exactly what its name implies. A user is provided with a telephone number that connects the originating device to the host computer. The computer site maintains a dedicated modem and communications port to handle the telephone line.

The cost of standard dial-up lines can be inordinately expensive, especially if the transmission involves anything other than a local call. For example, a customer in California who needs access to a brokerage or bank service in New York would find the cost of doing business over a standard telephone company dial-up line prohibitive for daily or even weekly access and two-way transmission.

Packet Switching. Packet-switching networks provide a solution to the prohibitive telephone costs of long-distance dial-up service. The California user, for example, only need install the same type of telephone and modem used on a direct dial-up system. But instead of dialing a number with a New York telephone area code, the user dials a local telephone number that establishes a connection to the switching node within the local area.

Internally, packet-switching data transmission is handled differently than direct dial-up message transmission. Rather than forming a direct connection

MIS SECURITY

and sending and receiving streams of data to and from the host computer, packet-switching networks receive several messages at a node. Messages are then grouped into data packets. Each packet has a size limitation, and messages that exceed this size are segmented into several packets. Packets are passed from node to node within the network until the assigned destination is reached. To indicate the destination of the message, the user enters an assigned ID code and a password. The entered codes correlate to authorization codes and specify the central computer site. For the user's purposes, the connection to the host computer is the same as if a direct dial-up line had been used, but the cost of the telephone call is drastically reduced.

In both dial-up service and packet-switching networks, the host site is responsible for protecting access to data stored in the computer. Because packet-switching networks require a user ID and password to connect to a node, they would appear to provide an extra measure of security; however, this is often not the case.

Unmonitored Access. For some time, users of certain vendors' packet-switching network facilities have known that it is possible to bypass the user ID and password check. Many users discovered that, with very little experimentation, anyone could gain access to various dial-up computer sites in the U.S. and Canada. This unmonitored access is possible because the address codes of these computer site communications ports are prefaced with the three digits of the respective telephone network area codes. The remainder of the computer address consists of three numeric characters and one alphabetic character. Thus, rather than determine a dial-up number comprised of ten digits (including area code), a hacker must simply determine the proper alphanumeric code sequence identifier. The alphabetic character search is simplified or eliminated by assuming that the first address within the numeric set uses the letter A, the second B, and so on sequentially through the alphabet until the correct code is entered. Accessing a computer site requires only a local node number, and these numbers are commonly posted in packet-switching networks sites. Use of the local node number also substantially reduces dial-up access line costs for the unauthorized user.

TYPES OF RISKS

To protect against the risks associated with unauthorized dial-up users penetrating a computer system, it is important to understand what damage such penetration can cause to an organization.

Four types of acts are connected with unauthorized access to a computer facility:
- Data destruction
- Data modification
- Data theft
- Computer time theft

The first three acts are concerned with manipulation and removal of data. The fourth is often overlooked or dismissed as the least harmful, but it may result in the most damage.

Modification of Data

Unauthorized data modification is potentially the most damaging type of computer crime. Such alteration is the basis for manipulating funds, inventing nonexistent corporations and generating false invoices for the purpose of stealing merchandise, changing names and addresses on accounts so that deliveries will be made to someone other than the actual customer, and similar frauds.

Targeted Penetration. Unlike the case in which a stranger randomly tries to dial into any computer facility, this type of penetration is specifically targeted. Someone has set out to penetrate the system, modify specific records, commit a theft, restore records to their original form, and leave no trace of the incursion. After penetrating the system security screen, the intruder could wait weeks or months before committing a crime, particularly if he or she is from outside the victimized organization. During this period, the intruder can dissect record structures, examine program run procedures, and study various programs. However, if the dial-up perpetrator is knowledgeable about the data processing information and procedures, data modification can be consummated in a few days.

Destruction of Data

Hackers who penetrate someone else's computer system may only be participating in an intellectual exercise to prove their superiority over the security system. They may accidentally discover a data site by randomly dialing phone numbers or randomly selecting packet-switching network addresses. Once a hacker has gained access, a cat-and-mouse game usually ensues, and to win, the hacker must notify the loser—the computer owner. The simplest way of leaving a mark is to delete a data set (or sets). Such a meaningless act of vandalism can cause extensive damage to the victimized organization, depending on how vital the files are and how well the company can recover from the destruction. Such vandalism often goes undiscovered for a long time; sometimes an entire data set must be regenerated. Some organizations without complete documentation (and there are many) must recreate an entire program or set of programs to fill the gap caused by such destruction.

Personal Reprisals. Although the threat of a hacker leaving a calling card should not be taken lightly, it is minor compared to the damage done by unauthorized dial-up users bent upon destroying data for personal reasons. Such a person may be a current or past employee who is disgruntled with the organization or one of its members. It may be a competitor who believes that destroying key files will reduce a rival's ability to complete or put the competitor out of business. It may even be someone who has embezzled money, stolen inventory, or committed other more obvious crimes and is trying to cover up those thefts. The opportunity to appropriate large sums of money or great stores of merchandise can be too big a temptation even for the casual hacker. A growing number of cases are being uncovered wherein a casual hacker finds little risk in appropriating equipment or funds. What starts out as intellectual amusement can quickly turn into felony.

MIS SECURITY

Theft of Data

The risks associated with data theft are often overlooked. Even though no data is destroyed and no information is manipulated, such theft represents a potential for substantial damage.

Computer Espionage. Although it is difficult to quantify such theft, organizations that rely on such information as customer lists or clients' financial transaction histories should realize the value of this data and the ramifications accompanying its loss. For example, if a competitor acquires specific information regarding the net worth, financial goals, and credit ratings of an organization's clients, the data thief can concentrate on those clients who represent substantial income to the organization and convince them to move their accounts to the competitor's firm. Such computer espionage is more insidious than a physical break-in because there is no physical evidence to alert security forces that a theft has occurred.

Even more damaging may be the public disclosure of government activities. In recent years, information concerning foreign governments' investments in U.S. corporations has proven so embarrassing that these governments have discontinued doing business with certain major U.S. trust banks, especially after copies of their portfolios were prominently reproduced in newspapers.

Theft of Computer Time

Theft of computer time and services is often viewed as relatively harmless. The unauthorized user may initially appropriate computer time for such activities as developing game software, doing homework, or trying out new programming techniques. However, once the system is penetrated, the unauthorized user can create operating system and application programs and store them in the system library. The stored programs can be executed simply by dialing up the system.

The "Trojan Horse". A greater threat to the security of computer time and resources is the unauthorized user who sets up programs that are activated at a later time. This type of software code, commonly called a "Trojan horse", allows the user to destroy, modify, or steal data without the risk of accessing the computer a second time. A Trojan horse code can be used to bring down the system at a particular moment, thus depriving an organization and its customers of valuable information and services.

MINIMIZING RISKS

Two general types of precautions can be implemented to thwart the unauthorized dial-up user from damaging a computer system: positive identification of users at the time of access, and data protection if an unauthorized user penetrates the system.

Identification

Making a positive identification of the dial-up user is essential for restricting access to a system. Passwords and physical devices are the primary ways to identify users. Whether to employ one or both of these identification methods depends on the level of security needed.

Unfortunately, many attempts at identification security have been ineffectual against hackers and other system intruders. This ineffectiveness is usually attributable to ignorance of successful identification products and methodologies; a lack of trained security personnel; the ingenuity of those attempting to gain entry; or giving responsibility for system security to already overloaded software personnel.

Passwords. Passwords are the most widely employed method of authenticating the identity of a computer system user. Passwords are easy to design, require no additional hardware, and can be implemented very quickly. When the proper methodology is used, password security provides a significant deterrent to unauthorized system access without major expenditure.

Certain rules should be followed to make password identification and authentication an effective security tool:
- Passwords should be of sufficient length to prevent their discovery by manual or automated systematic attack or pure guesswork.
- Password length should not be so great that it is difficult to commit to memory and is likely to be written down.
- Passwords should be derived by algorithm or stored on a one-way encrypted file.
- Password assignment should be random; users should never be allowed to choose their own password.
- Passwords should be distributed under tight controls, preferably online.
- An audit trail of previously issued passwords should be established.
- Individual passwords should be private.

If sufficient time is not available for an in-depth study of password identification methodology, a basically sound password structure can be created by using a six-character alphabetic password that has been randomly selected and stored on an encrypted file. Such a procedure provides some measure of security, but time should be taken to design and implement a more substantial methodology.

Physical Devices. Whereas passwords are a relatively inexpensive means of providing identification and authentication security in the dial-up environment, physical devices involve capital expenditure. The cost depends on the intricacy of the device. Determining which device is best suited to a particular environment requires careful analysis of the consequences of dial-up penetration.

Precoded Terminals. Perhaps the least expensive physical device employed to improve dial-up user identification is a programmable read-only memory (PROM) microchip installed by the supplier when a terminal is purchased. The PROM contains a precoded identifier affixed to all messages sent from the dial-up terminal to the host computer. If the identifier code is valid at the time of connection, the host computer completes the connection and allows additional transmission. If the identifier code is not valid, the connection is not completed and the call is terminated.

MIS SECURITY

Precoded IDs provide an excellent means of security for portable terminals that use any telephone to dial into a central computer site. The unique identifiers permit positive identification of each user's terminal. However, with the advent of larger, more powerful desktop or personal microcomputers equipped with specific dial-up communications software, PROMs are no longer as effective for identification security. A microcomputer can be programmed to simulate either a single identifier or a series of identifiers until it finds one that is valid for a particular installation.

Dial-up/Call-back Systems. To protect against the kind of system penetration possible when only precoded identifiers are used, manufacturers have developed dial-up/call-back systems. With this technique, two telephone calls must be completed before access is granted.

After dialing up the host computer, the user must enter a valid password. Upon receipt of the password, the host computer terminates the connection and automatically places a call to the telephone number associated with the password. If an authorized terminal is being used, the connection is established and the user can proceed as though working at a direct-connect terminal. Some dial-up/call-back systems place the return call through least-cost routing on local lines, WATS lines, and other common carrier facilities, thereby reducing the cost of the call-back procedure.

One problem associated with dial-up/call-back systems is that the authorized caller is restricted to a single predetermined location. This restriction prohibits the use of portable terminals for travel assignments.

Interceptors. Many of the problems associated with precoded identifiers and dial-up/call-back systems can be resolved through the use of an interceptor, a hardware device attached to the modem of a computer's communications controller. When a user accesses the system, the interceptor requests (usually by digitized voice) an identifier code. If the identifier code is valid, the interceptor completes the connection; if the identifier code is invalid, the interceptor either disconnects the user or diverts the call to a selected alternate extension phone, which alerts a security officer to the attempted unauthorized use. The security officer can either trace the call or turn off the interceptor and modem, thereby rendering that particular access route inoperable.

Interceptors provide substantial protection against random callers as well as attacks directed at a particular computer site. Although not as secure as dial-up/call-back systems, interceptors do not restrict authorized users to a single, predetermined call-back location. Interceptors can cost less to use than dial-up/call-back systems, depending on the number of modems that must be protected.

The decision to purchase any of these devices depends on such factors as cost of installation and cost of manpower to monitor the hardware.

Encryption

If an unauthorized dial-up user penetrates the identification and authentication defenses of a computer system, encryption can forestall if not prevent data modification and theft. Messages are encrypted at the point of transmission and can only be decrypted at a terminal supplied with the key used in the encryption process.

DES. Various encryption algorithms are available, and the complexity of the algorithm should depend on the value of the data being protected. In 1977, the National Bureau of Standards approved the Data Encryption Standard (DES) as the only encryption method to be used by civilian agencies of the federal government. DES is widely used and is highly resistant to automated attack.

File Encryption. Although encryption and decryption is primarily used in data transmission, it can also protect key files and programs from external threat. Encrypting data and program source code makes it very difficult for an unauthorized user to determine what information or code is contained in a particular file. Encrypting files also protects file relationships that can be determined by reading the source code of programs that use such files. For the intruder unfamiliar with an organization's data components and flow, such an obstacle can discourage any further unauthorized activity. Even for authorized users, encrypted files bear no relationship to the information the users are accustomed to seeing. In addition, if used only for key files and programs, encryption does not involve significant memory use.

CONCLUSION

The security method chosen to protect central data sources will have great impact on an organization's resources and procedures. Initial costs, implementation time, client reaction, and related factors can only be addressed by performing a thorough risk analysis that examines current as well as future needs. The measures described in this chapter should not be interpreted as an isolated set of precautions, but rather as components of an overall security umbrella designed to protect the organization from all threats, internal and external. The first step will provide the basis for establishing an organizational awareness that will lead to a more secure environment for dealing with all dial-up users.

Section XI
EDP Auditing

Recent, highly publicized cases of computer-based fraud and embezzlement have reminded management of the need for tighter security and control of business information systems. MIS departments have often neglected or downplayed these functions and have not conducted an unbiased review of them when they are performed. Organizations are therefore turning to EDP auditing to review and help control those systems that handle the major share of corporate assets.

The chapter titled "Do You Need an EDP Auditor?" describes the advantages of an independent review of MIS activities. MIS management should regard the auditor as a management tool and not as a threat. The job of the auditor is to impartially assess the strengths and weaknesses of systems and operations and to make recommendations for correcting deficiencies. Any prudent manager should welcome such input.

Chapter XI-2, "An Audit Plan for MIS," points out that the EDP audit planning function first decides which audits should be performed by assigning priorities to each area and then schedules the audits. When developing an audit plan for the MIS function, the audit manager must provide for audits of the organization; the reliability and integrity of computer systems; and MIS finances, administration, and personnel. This chapter discusses these audits, their objectives, and the method for selecting and scheduling individual audits.

The concentration of corporate resources in many data centers may sometimes be likened to "putting all the eggs in one basket." Not only is there a concentration of hardware and software resources; many organizations also depend heavily on system availability for daily operation. Management must appreciate the consequences of losing this resource and carefully perform an effective review of data center security. The EDP auditor, whether internal or external, can be very helpful to management in conducting this review. Chapter XI-3, "Auditing the Security of Your Data Center," contains useful checklists and forms for use in reviewing your DP operations center. Even if you do not have access to EDP auditors, you can use these techniques to review your center. The checklist can also be used by MIS management in preparation for a review by external auditors or consultants.

While conducting an audit, the EDP auditor attempts to explain the EDP auditing process to auditees and encourages their participation and support.

MIS personnel react in different ways, however, and their attitudes toward the auditors and the audit process can affect the audit's success. When auditors understand how MIS personnel react to the EDP audit process, they are better prepared to work with them and with management. Chapter XI-4, "Taking Full Advantage of EDP Auditors," explains how auditors are used and misused and points out how they can improve relationships with MIS management. This chapter also can help MIS management and supervisors understand the role that the auditor plays and the sensitivity of the auditing process.

XI-1

Do You Need an EDP Auditor?

William E. Perry

INTRODUCTION

The daily operation of an economic organization (e.g., country, state, province, or industrial unit) is highly dependent on the communication of financial data through a series of statements and reports, which illustrate the overall financial health of the organization. These reports may describe the results of an operation; the current budget; the current status of assets, liabilities, and stockholders' equity; and information for government agencies.

Individuals rely on reports when they buy stock, financial institutions use them when they arrange loans, and government units assess taxes on the basis of such statements. Because of their importance, the validity of these financial statements must be guaranteed.

The accepted method for ensuring the validity of these reports is to have a third party examine them and render a professional judgment regarding their accuracy. This individual is the auditor, who may work for the organization in question, for a government unit, or as an independent agent.

IMPACT OF THE COMPUTER ON AUDITING

The independent verification capability—auditing—has gained greater importance with the advent of the computer. The proper functioning of the many accounting and procedure-related DP systems cannot be ensured until the results have been subjected to time-honored independent verification tests. Although it is essential that guidelines and principles concerning documentation, audit trails, and controls be prescribed for the construction of such systems, the independent verification of results remains the final qualitative measure of system performance. Until a system is tested, any evaluation of its performance consists largely of theory.

Although some organizations are considerably more advanced than others in auditing and controlling data processing, it is generally conceded that the existing capability for independently verifying a DP system is inadequate. Audit findings and experience to date emphasize the seriousness of this shortcoming. Problems and deficiencies uncovered as a result of a small amount of effort in auditing DP systems indicate a need for substantially extending this activity.

EDP AUDITING

Most systems are developed and operated by competent technical personnel who have relatively little background in accounting practices and procedures. Conversely, those with accounting knowledge and a background of organizational policy and operations have generally been involved to a limited extent in systems development. This undesirable situation is not unusual and is therefore a matter of concern throughout the DP systems world.

Independent verification is the process of comparing results produced by the system, as preserved in the audit trail, with the requirements imposed on the system. Although this is done by individuals not associated with the implementation and operation of the system, each step of the process depends almost entirely on knowledge of the system and its requirements. Such knowledge can be gained only from system documentation.

Despite the guidelines and principles for system documentation, auditors often find the documentation inadequate for their purposes. Although documentation designed to meet the needs of operating personnel is generally good, documentation written at the summary level is often deficient or even nonexistent.

Many control and auditing problems experienced by auditors and management result from their inability to understand and evaluate DP systems. As an extension of management, auditors merely reflect the same problems and concerns that management has experienced for several years. The difference, however, is that auditors can devote their time and expertise to working with MIS personnel in order to evaluate and supplement the MIS controls, audit tools, and techniques.

AUDITING CONCERNS

Auditors involved in reviewing a DP system should focus their concerns on the system's control aspects.

Auditors must look at the total systems environment—not just the computerized segment. This requires their involvement from the time a transaction occurs until it is posted to the organization's general ledger. Specifically, auditors must ensure that provisions are made for:
- An adequate audit trail so that transactions can be traced forward and backward through the system
- Controls over accounting for all input and controls to ensure the integrity of those transactions throughout the computerized segment of the system
- Handling exceptions and rejections from the computer system
- Testing to ascertain whether the systems perform as stated
- Control over changes to the computer system to determine that the proper authorization has been given
- Authorization procedures for system overrides
- Determining that organizational and governmental policies and procedures are adhered to in system implementation
- Training user personnel in the operation of the system
- Developing detailed evaluation criteria so that it is possible to determine whether the implemented system has met predetermined specifications

- Adequate controls between interconnected computer systems
- Adequate security procedures to protect the user's data

This list affirms that the auditor is primarily concerned with adequate controls to safeguard the organization's assets.

TYPES OF AUDITORS

Although this chapter deals primarily with EDP auditing, the auditing field comprises many specialized groups, including independent auditors (public accounting firms), internal auditors, and special interest auditors.

Independent Auditors

The job of the independent auditor is to comment on the impartiality of financial statements reporting the financial position, results of operations, and changes in financial position of the organization under study. In the report, the auditor states whether the examination has been made in accordance with generally accepted auditing standards. These standards require auditors to state whether they believe the financial statements examined conform with generally accepted accounting principles. The auditor must also determine whether such principles have been applied consistently in the preparation of current financial statements in relation to those of the preceding period.[1]

Internal Auditors

Internal auditing is an independent appraisal of operations within an organization. It is a managerial control function that measures and evaluates the effectiveness of other controls.

The objective of internal auditing is to help all members of management effectively execute their responsibilities. Internal auditors furnish management with analyses, appraisals, and recommendations on the activities reviewed. This often involves research beyond accounting and financial records to fully understand the operations under review. Attaining this overall objective involves such activities as:

- Reviewing and appraising the soundness, adequacy, and application of accounting, financial, and other operating controls and promoting effective control at reasonable cost
- Determining the extent of compliance with established policies, plans, and procedures
- Ascertaining the extent to which company assets are accounted for and safeguarded from all losses
- Checking the reliability of management data developed within the organization
- Appraising the quality of performance in carrying out assigned responsibilities
- Recommending operating improvements

The responsibilities of internal auditors should be clearly established by management policy. The related authority should provide the internal auditor full access to all relevant organizational records, properties, and personnel. The internal auditor should be free to review and appraise policies, plans, procedures, and records.

EDP AUDITING

The internal auditor's responsibilities should be:
- To inform and advise management in a manner consistent with the *Standards for the Professional Practice of Internal Auditing* of the Institute of Internal Auditors, 1978
- To coordinate audit activities with those of other personnel to achieve the audit objectives and the goals of the organization

In performing these functions, an internal auditor has no direct responsibility or authority over any activities reviewed. Therefore, the internal audit review and appraisal does not relieve other personnel in the organization of their responsibilities.

Independence is essential to the effectiveness of internal auditing. This independence is obtained primarily through organizational status and objectivity.

The organizational status of the internal auditing function and its support from management are major determinants of its scope and value. The head of the internal auditing function should report to an officer who has the authority to ensure a broad range of audit coverage and the adequate consideration of and effective action on audit findings and recommendations.

Objectivity is essential to the audit function. An internal auditor should not develop and install procedures, prepare records, or engage in any other activity that would normally be reviewed and appraised. The auditor's objectivity need not be adversely affected, however, by the fact that the standards of control recommended may be applied in the development of systems and procedures under review.

Special Interest Auditors

The independent auditor is contracted to assess the impartiality of the reported financial position of an enterprise. The internal auditor is an employee of the organization for which the audit reports are issued. Special interest auditors, on the other hand, usually work either for a government organization or for an organization doing business with the group being audited.

Special interest auditors may work with the following:
- Internal Revenue Service
- State sales tax
- Defense contract audit agencies
- Renegotiation boards
- Occupational Safety and Health
- Major suppliers or customers when a contractual agreement exists between the organizations (e.g., licenses and royalty agreements).

APPROACH TO EDP AUDITING

The audit methods that were effective for manual audits proved ineffective in many EDP audits because of the following factors:
- Electronic evidence—The evidence needed by the auditor was not physically retrievable by most people, nor was it readable by people in its original electronic form.
- Terminology—The tools and techniques used in automated applications

are described in terms difficult for non-EDP auditors to understand.
- Automated processes—The methods of processing are automated rather than manual, making it difficult for the non-EDP auditor to comprehend processing concepts and the logic of these concepts.
- New risks and controls—Threats to computer systems and the countermeasures to those threats (i.e., controls) are new to non-EDP auditors, and the magnitude of the risks and the effectiveness of the controls are not understood.
- Reliance on controls—In manual systems, the auditor can place some reliance on hard-copy evidence regardless of the adequacy of the controls, whereas in automated systems the electronic evidence is only as valid as the adequacy of controls.

Because the rate of these changes varies among systems in organizations, the methods and approaches of auditing automated applications differ among applications and organizations. For example, some organizations still rely heavily on hard-copy evidence while others have eliminated much of it.

Two questions have been argued about EDP auditing since the early 1960s. Should EDP auditors come from an auditing or a data processing discipline? Should EDP auditing be a specialty or should all auditors audit DP?

Appropriate EDP Audit Background

The debate continues regarding whether it is better to train an auditor in DP or to train a DP professional in auditing. When many auditing departments began to audit DP, they did the latter. It is now generally agreed, however, that the better route is to train auditors in DP. A major research project funded by the IBM Corporation concluded in 1977 that, of the companies surveyed, auditors trained in DP were more effective.[2]

Generalist versus Specialist

Organizations began computerizing applications during the late 1950s. At that point, most of the audit work load involved manual systems, so it seemed reasonable to include specialists on the staff to audit computerized applications.

As more and more of the organization's information processing became automated, the size of the specialist groups increased. It soon became apparent that most audits involved DP. Because EDP auditors were in short supply, alternative approaches were explored. Many organizations conducted audits using a team composed of financial and EDP auditors. Others used EDP auditors to support the financial staff by writing audit software and performing control reviews.

Now, more than 25 years after organizations began automating their systems, few audits do not include some responsibility for DP. This means that all auditors have some DP responsibility, making the average internal auditor the equivalent of the EDP audit specialist of 10 years ago. This is still a transition period, however, and extensive training is needed to upgrade the EDP audit skills of many auditors.

The trend for the future seems clear: all auditors will be required to have a

EDP AUDITING

basic knowledge of DP. This will not eliminate the need for audit specialists. The EDP auditor of the future will be more concerned with the operating environment as opposed to application systems. This environment includes the operating, communications, and security systems, program libraries, and data base management systems, plus other support packages available to individual locations.

THE ROLE OF THE EDP AUDITOR

The auditor evaluating today's complex systems must have highly developed technical skills in order to understand the constantly evolving methods of information processing. Contemporary systems carry such risks as system backup, information security, and contingencies, which were minor concerns in earlier, less sophisticated environments.

Auditing the processing environment is divided into two parts. The first and most technical part of the audit is evaluating the operating environment —major software packages (e.g., the operating and security systems) representing the general or environmental controls in the automated processing environment—and this is usually done by the EDP audit specialist. The second part is the automated application, which is audited by the general auditor who possesses some DP skills.

As the use of DP in organizations continues to grow, auditing DP must be accomplished without many of the guidelines established for traditional auditing effort. In addition, the new uses of DP introduce new risks, which in turn require new controls. EDP auditors in their role as counselors influence the development of standards that will enable the enterprise to perform in a controlled environment. EDP auditors are also in a unique position to evaluate the relevance of a particular system to the enterprise as a whole. Because of this, the EDP auditor often plays a role in upper-management decision making.

The EDP Auditor as Skilled Technician. The traditional methods of auditing "around the computer" are rapidly becoming obsolete because of technological trends that make operations and data "invisible." The separation of operational duties, which formerly could be observed in manual or batch-oriented systems, is lost in integrated online or real-time systems. Source data formerly contained in hard-copy audit trails becomes less visible with increased use of online entry.

In addition, the automated processing of information introduces many new risks. The concentration of information that results from DP technology raises such issues as contingency, reconstruction of data, physical security, and theft of services or data. These issues are relatively new, and final resolution is not yet clear. Although the detection of fraud was not always considered an internal audit responsibility, today there is an increasing tendency to view it as such.

All of these issues require the auditor to "get inside the computer." To do this effectively, the EDP auditor must have some degree of expertise in programming languages, computer operations, hardware, software, and systems analysis. The auditor must be thoroughly capable of preparing programs or using audit software packages to evaluate the operation of a system.

The EDP Auditor as Counselor. Historically, users have abdicated responsibility for controlling DP systems, mostly because of the psychological barriers that have surrounded the computer. As a result, there are few checks and balances, except for the EDP auditor. Auditors, therefore, must take an active role in developing policies on auditability, control, testing, and standards. They must also persuade users and MIS personnel of the need for a controlled DP environment.

An EDP audit staff in a large corporation can make a major contribution to DP system control by persuading user groups to insist on a policy of comprehensive testing for all new systems and all changes to existing systems. By reviewing "base case" results, user groups can control the accuracy of new or changed systems—actually performing a complete control function.

Control of DP can also be enhanced by insisting that all new systems be reviewed at predefined checkpoints throughout the systems development life cycle. The prospect of audit review should prompt both user and systems groups to define their objectives and assumptions more carefully; here, too, EDP auditors can subtly extend their influence.

The EDP Auditor as Partner of Senior Management. Although the EDP auditor's roles of counselor and skilled technician are vital to successful company operation, they may be irrelevant if the auditor fails to view auditing in relation to the organization as a whole. A system that appears well controlled may be inconsistent with the operation of a business.

Decisions concerning the need for a system traditionally belonged to senior management, but because of a combination of factors (mostly the complex technology of the computer), this function has not been successfully performed. When allocating funds for new systems, management has had to rely on the judgment of MIS personnel. Although their choices of new and more effective DP systems cannot be faulted, MIS personnel have often failed to meet the true business needs of the organization.

Management needs the support of a skilled MIS staff that understands the needs of the organization, and EDP auditors are in such a position. They can provide management with an independent assessment of the impact of MIS decisions on the business. In addition, the auditor can verify that all alternatives for a given project have been considered, that all risks have been accurately assessed, that the technical hardware and software solutions are correct, that business needs will be satisfied, and that costs are reasonable.

Other Contributions. To maximize the use of DP resources, the EDP auditor can examine the productivity of persons interacting with the computer or the productivity of the computer itself. The auditor can compare a system's predicted benefits against the actual gains. The EDP auditor can also examine the computerized planning models used by the organization to assure management that the assumptions and techniques are correct and that the

EDP AUDITING

system's data is reliable. The auditor's expanded role will prove beneficial to both the organization and the MIS department.

As auditors become more involved in the design phase of computer activities, it may be advantageous to have them review the system during its development.

Each application system is unique and must be evaluated according to its own characteristics. Figure 1 illustrates a method systems managers can use to determine whether to involve the auditor in the systems development phase. The matrix allows consideration of the following questions for each application system:
- Is the application system a financial system in that the results developed will be posted to the organization's financial records?
- Is it a high-risk system involving such negotiable assets as cash, accounts receivable, inventory, or securities?
- Is the system expensive to implement in relation to other computer systems being developed by the organization?
- Are the results of the computer system being used by outsiders to the organization for billing systems and stockholder record systems?
- Is the user involved in the development of the system and, if so, to what extent?
- Are multiple users involved in systems development? (For example, a

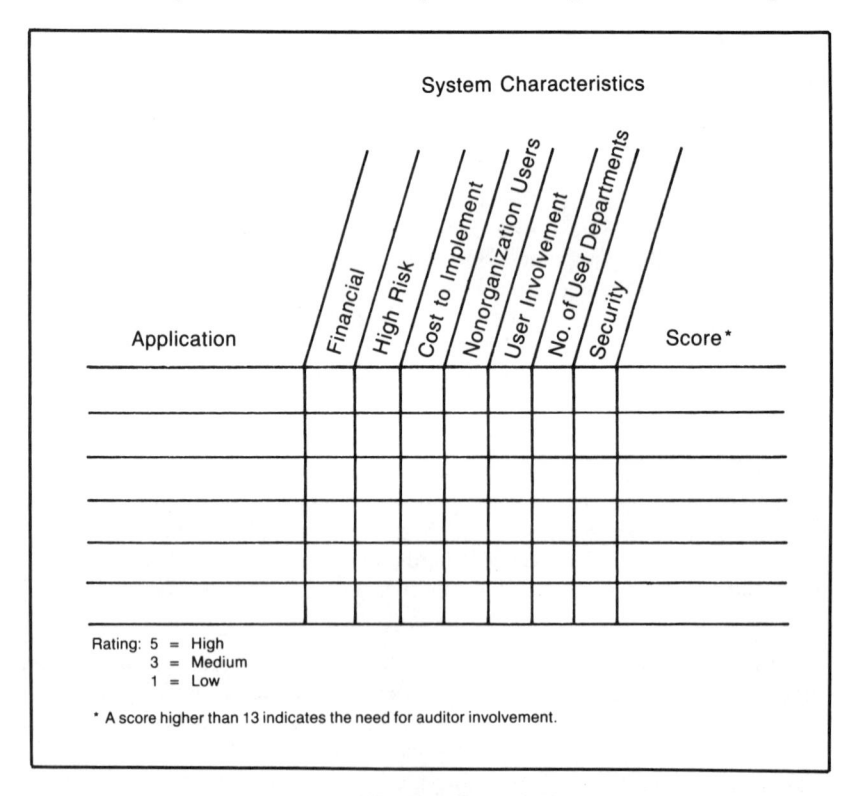

Figure 1. Auditor Involvement Matrix

Rating: 5 = High
3 = Medium
1 = Low

* A score higher than 13 indicates the need for auditor involvement.

combined billing/accounts receivable/inventory system may involve three or more departments within an organization.)
- Does the application system involve security of confidential or sensitive business/customer information and if so, to what extent?

The systems manager should rate each application being considered by assigning a score to each of the preceding characteristics. These relative characteristics are evaluated by selecting a 5 (high), 3 (medium), or 1 (low) and entering the number into the matrix. If the total score exceeds 13, it is recommended that the auditors become involved in systems development.

TRENDS IN EDP AUDITING

Data processing's impact on most organizations is increasing dramatically. Many experts predict that the effect of moving to a total organizational data base will have a greater impact on business than the movement from punched-card sorting equipment to computers. The auditor's future role in data processing depends, to a large degree, on the evolution of data processing systems.

Although predicting future trends is always problematic, some developments seem likely:
- Systems will involve less hard copy and more electronic transfer of information.
- Users will have more direct access to the computer.
- More work standards will be developed in the MIS department, and management will have to ensure their use.
- The MIS department will be run like a production job shop, and management will have standards to measure performance.
- Management will only approve funds for new projects after a detailed financial analysis.
- The use of microcomputers in user areas will grow as an alternative to centralized processing.
- More applications will be purchased and fewer applications developed in-house, including audit software.
- The use of communications facilities will increase, providing greater interaction between people and computers.
- More sophisticated auditing techniques will emerge, permitting the auditor to make more use of the computer in auditing the computer.

If most of these predictions are accurate, then auditors, as representatives of management, will become more involved in the daily operations of the MIS department. To build controls into DP systems, auditors must develop a high degree of competence in data processing and become involved in the complete life cycle of DP systems.

CONCLUSION

MIS management has assumed major responsibilities in implementing systems. As the systems become more complex, organizations begin to rely more heavily on them. At the same time, many of the checks and balances that existed in manual systems have been replaced by computer techniques.

EDP AUDITING

The roles of the auditor and the MIS organization are changing. The MIS department no longer needs to promote the use of data processing; instead it can concentrate on the technical aspects of implementing and operating applications. Similarly, the auditor must be more involved with DP systems as their part in the financial aspects of an organization's operation increases. Because both groups are destined to work in the same area, MIS personnel and the company's auditors should develop cooperative working relationships.

References

1. *Codification of Statement on Auditing Standards.* New York: AICPA, 1981, paragraph 110.01
2. *Systems Auditability and Control.* Altamonte Springs FL: Institute of Internal AUDITORs, 1977.

XI-2
An Audit Plan for MIS
Ian A. Gilhooley

INTRODUCTION

The objectives of auditing an MIS organization are to ensure that the MIS department functions according to corporate goals and that it segregates incompatible staff responsibilities—for example, the developer of an application system should not control its operation.

To satisfy the first objective, the auditor must ensure that the MIS plan matches the goals and objectives of the overall corporate plan. In addition, the auditor must confirm that the steering committee directs the MIS department in application systems development and other hardware, software, and telecommunications capabilities. Compliance to the MIS plan and the effectiveness of the steering committee can be verified during other audits, primarily those of application development and the data center. (These audits are discussed in later sections.)

To satisfy the second objective, the auditor can review the MIS organizational chart and job descriptions to determine whether MIS staff functions are adequately segregated. The auditor can further verify that this objective is being met through the data center, change-control, data security, financial, administrative, and personnel audits.

Audit Frequency

The MIS plan, organizational chart, and job descriptions should be reviewed at the start of each fiscal year and whenever a substantial change occurs. At the end of each fiscal year, the degree of compliance with these documents, as verified by the various audits, should be reported to management.

RELIABILITY AND INTEGRITY OF COMPUTER SYSTEMS

Reliability and integrity of computer systems depend on several factors:
- Data center operations—The data center converts user data into information that satisfies an organization's business and financial requirements.
- Change-control procedures—A comprehensive system for controlling changes to software, hardware, and telecommunications equipment ensures a stable processing environment within the data center.
- Data security—A data security program includes standards and proce-

EDP AUDITING

dures that protect data against any unauthorized disclosure, modification, or destruction.
- Computer application controls—The design and development of any application must incorporate sufficient controls to ensure accurate, complete, and timely processing of user data.
- User control procedures—System users must have effective controls to ensure that input is authorized and that output is verified and used to meet the business and financial needs for which it was designed.

Because system integrity and reliability depend on balancing these components, the audit plan must address each factor satisfactorily if senior management is to be provided with a comprehensive report on the adequacy of the MIS function.

Environmental versus Application Audits

The MIS function must develop, maintain, and operate numerous computer systems. Three of the factors that ensure system reliability and integrity—data center operations, change-control procedures, and data security—are common to all systems and form the environment in which they run. The other components—computer application controls and user control procedures—are usually unique to each application system. A single environment, therefore, supports multiple application systems.

The audit plan can be modeled on the division between environmental and individual applications. Environmental audits identify interface control points between the environment and applications. If an application complies with these control points, the auditor can verify a secure operating environment with minimal testing and can concentrate on identifying and testing controls pertinent to individual applications (i.e., those at the user level and relative to the application programs).

Environmental Audits

To assess the adequacy of environmental controls, the auditor can test three interrelated areas: the data center, the change-control system, and the data security program.

Data Center Audit. This compliance audit is based on the policies, practices, and procedures established in the data center manual. Its purpose is to determine whether the data center is providing adequate service—that is, timely, secure, and reliable data processing. The data center audit allows the auditor to verify that the control points highlighted in other environmental and application audits have actually been established and are enforced.

The objectives of the data center audit are to ensure that:
- Staff duties are adequately segregated within the organizational structure of the data center.
- Physical security measures guarantee continuous processing.
- The MIS department complies with established change-control procedures for hardware, software, and telecommunications equipment.
- The data center provides timely, complete, and accurate data processing.

- The MIS department complies with established data security policy and procedures.
- Management is provided with sufficient information to manage the data center effectively.

Change-Control Audit. Change represents potential exposure to an internal control system. Environmental stability and reliability is directly related to the adequacy of change-control procedures. The first step in auditing this environment effectively is to review current change-control procedures and to identify any omissions or vulnerable areas. These procedures should specify that changes in hardware, software, and telecommunications can be implemented only after proper testing and management approval. Once an application system has been implemented, it is subject to the change-control procedures.

After this initial audit, the auditor must assess the ongoing adequacy of the change-control procedures and the impact of change on internal control. This assessment can be made as a change occurs. Any change affecting the internal control of the environment should be monitored from initiation to implementation. Standard procedure should require that the MIS department promptly notify the audit department of significant changes in the environment, including those in the production versions of application systems.

This assessment can also be made as part of an ongoing application system audit. The auditor must ensure that changes to an application system are handled according to established procedures. In addition, the auditor must assess the impact of previously unexamined changes on the internal control of the application system.

A third opportunity for this assessment occurs during the data center audit. The auditor should compare the current environment with that documented during the last data center audit. Sample testing of hardware, software, and telecommunications changes identifies the degree to which changes are processed according to defined procedures.

The report to management on the adequacy of change-control procedures should be updated annually, or as appropriate, based on the results of the compliance audits.

Data Security Audit. A data security audit assesses the adequacy of the standards and procedures designed and implemented to protect data against any unauthorized disclosure, modification, or destruction. Data is classified into three categories: business, system, and administrative. Business data is maintained on or printed from computer-readable media to support an organization's business requirements. System data is vendor-supplied software (e.g., operating systems, utilities, compilers, and sorts) and application programs purchased or developed to process raw business data into the information needed to meet business requirements. Administrative data is maintained by the data center to support computer processing (e.g., password data sets, data dictionaries, and data base definition tables). Because these various types of data are interrelated (e.g., administrative data establishes the business data that a user accesses by using system data), each category of data must be audited.

The initial data security audit determines whether the MIS department's approach to establishing data security is appropriate. This approach must be flexible enough to allow the organization to adjust to changes in applications and environment. The first step in this approach is to assess what the organization must protect; that is, existing controls must be documented, and additional controls must be determined and justified in terms of cost versus necessity of protection.

As with change control, the data security audit (after the initial audit) is ongoing and can be executed at various levels. For example, the audit can be conducted during the review of the implementation of new data security software. Auditors should treat the introduction of proprietary software packages as they would in-house application systems development. The purchase and implementation of proprietary software packages should be modeled on the development methodology applied to application systems (i.e., analysis/feasibility, design, and implementation). The design phase for proprietary software involves tailoring the packages to the specific organizational needs. The auditor should be involved at the same review points that have been established in the development methodology for application systems. The auditor must ensure that the selected package is properly justified in terms of cost and organizational needs, is approved by management, is fully tested, and is integrated into production in a controlled manner.

The data security audit also can be included in an audit of an ongoing application. One objective of an application audit is to ensure the reliability and integrity of data processed by the application system. In addition, when performing the data center audit, the auditor tests to ensure that the physical and administrative aspects of the data security system comply with defined policy. The auditor also tests data security software to ensure that proper protection is afforded to the organization's business, system, and administrative data.

Application Audits

An application audit is performed either during application systems development or as an audit of an application's ongoing operation.

Application Development Audit. Based on an organization's current development methodology, this compliance audit assures management that the application is being developed on time and within budget, meets the defined and approved user needs, and contains sufficient controls over input, processing, and output.

Auditors must be involved in application systems development if they are to verify the adequacy of system control. Contemporary systems are too complex for auditors to comprehend within the limited time allowed for an operational audit of a system in production. Therefore, as part of the auditor's review of systems development, a permanent file should define the following: location of the control points within the system, reliance of the control points, and possible control testing methods. The auditor also should highlight system vulnerabilities, define the extent of each weakness, and describe compensating controls.

Audit Plan for MIS

Two other important advantages of auditor involvement in application development are the development of audit subsystems and the prompt correction of system errors. If auditors define their own requirements for the system as it is being developed, an audit subsystem that continuously audits the system can be formed. For example, an audit file containing information on exception conditions can be accessed and authenticated by the auditor at any time. When the only review of a system occurs immediately before (or after) implementation, correction of control weaknesses within the system is more difficult.

From a planning standpoint, several front-end activities must be completed before the auditor reviews an application under development. For example, the auditor should review the MIS organization's current methodology for developing application systems and should notify management of weaknesses or omissions. This step is necessary because the auditor subsequently relies on compliance with this methodology as a measure of effective and efficient application systems development.

The auditor should develop a checklist of the audit department's activities, requirements, and output for each stage of development defined by the methodology. This document should be presented to the MIS department, which should establish a protocol for communicating significant events in new application development to the audit department.

In addition, the auditor should establish criteria for determining which applications should be reviewed during development. Because most auditors cannot review all applications under development, the number of applications to be reviewed varies, depending on the ratio of auditors to development staff. Selection must therefore be based on such factors as budget allocations, the application's criticality to daily operations, and its corporate, financial reporting, and legal aspects.

Ongoing Application Audits. Typical objectives of an ongoing application audit include determining whether:
- The general accounting principles incorporated into the application are consistent with accepted accounting practices, organizational policy, and all legal requirements.
- Incompatible staff responsibilities within the application under audit are adequately segregated.
- The degree of user participation in the design, development, and testing of application system changes is sufficient.
- Data transmitted and captured by the application system is authorized, complete, and accurate.
- Material calculation routines are correct and calculated amounts are applied correctly.
- The application system detects and reports all errors and provides an adequate audit trail for posted or applied transactions.
- The reporting mechanism within the application system provides information that is accurate, complete, timely, and relevant to user needs.
- Contingency plans for prolonged hardware, software, or telecommunications downtime are adequate.

- The application system documentation is sufficient to facilitate successful and continued operation.

The first step in an ongoing application system audit is documenting the locations of controls within the system. Auditors' involvement in systems development ensures a place for this information in the permanent file; otherwise, the auditor must search existing documentation (e.g., data control and user manuals) to establish control documentation. After control documentation is completed and verified, the auditor should judge the overall adequacy of the intended level of system control and should plan the extent and type of testing for the next audit phase. Test results and recommendations should be reported to management.

Because a typical organization has many application systems, an annual audit of each system is usually infeasible and unnecessary. In deciding which applications must be audited, the auditor should consider:
- The importance of the application to daily operations—An organization may depend so heavily on certain applications that its ability to function effectively and efficiently would be seriously damaged if the integrity of these applications were compromised or computer facilities were unavailable.
- The sensitivity of the application—An application's sensitivity may be determined by the importance of its output from a standpoint of public visibility (e.g., a finance company's credit card billing system). Sensitivity is also a factor if unauthorized disclosure of data processed or produced by the application could cause a competitive disadvantage, public embarrassment, or employee dissatisfaction.
- Organizational and legal policies—The auditor may need to audit certain applications because of their organizational or legal implications. Examples include applications that formulate the pricing structure of manufactured goods (organizational implication) or produce reports to be sent to the government as official returns (legal implication).
- Financial statements—The auditor must verify the fairness and accuracy of financial statements and must be satisfied with the integrity of application systems that contribute data to those statements.

Figure 1 shows the relationships between the various audits and components that ensure system reliability and integrity.

Audit Frequency

Audit planning must make optimum use of the limited resources available to audit management. Several points should be considered during audit planning. First, the auditor should remember that the data center exists to provide services to the organization. A data center audit, therefore, should be conducted on a regular basis (at least annually) to ensure operational efficiency and to uncover actual or potential deterioration in service levels, which then can be promptly reported to management. This audit also provides valuable input to other audit activities. Second, the auditor must verify the reliability and integrity of the processing environment before reviewing individual applications. If this is not done, or if change-control or data security systems

Audit Plan for MIS

Audits / Components	Environmental			Application	
	Data Center	Change Control	Data Security	Application under Development	Ongoing Application
Data Center Operations	X	X	X	X	X
Change-Control Procedures	X	X	X		X
Data Security	X		X	X	X
Computer Application Controls	X	X	X	X	X
User Control Procedures	X	X		X	X

Figure 1. Matrix of Relationships between Audits and Components for Ensuring System Reliability and Integrity

have been altered, audits of these areas should be scheduled before application audits. Finally, selection criteria for scheduling audits must be defined.

Advanced Audit Techniques

User departments are generally audited on a regular basis (e.g., annually). Because an ongoing application audit is performed less frequently, the auditor must continuously monitor the application and understand the relationship between application and user controls so that management is provided with an accurate report of system reliability and integrity.

Because of time constraints, the auditor must use advanced audit techniques, which require use of a computer, to perform an in-depth audit efficiently and effectively. Examples of advanced audit techniques and their applications are discussed in the following sections.

Regression Testing Facility. A regression testing facility requires the establishment of a test master file and transaction file that contain all known conditions. Each record is documented with a statement of its content and use during the test run. Documentation for the transaction file should also include the expected results of the transaction's application. Because these files are used to run the tests, the tests can be rerun when the system is changed or audited, and the two sets of output (i.e., the output before and after the change was made) can be compared. Unexpected discrepancies must be followed by the auditor who conducts the test. Output can be compared either visually (which can be time-consuming, tedious, and error-prone) or by an automated file-compare facility.

A regression testing facility requires much documentation as well as a commitment to maintaining documentation and file currency. For example, the testing files and documentation must be updated to incorporate a new condition. The improved auditing that results, however, renders the additional effort worthwhile.

EDP AUDITING

Integrated Test Facility. An integrated test facility (ITF) incorporates certain test records into the live master file for testing. These records can be amended, deleted, or expanded, depending on the test requirements. Auditors can submit transactions for processing within the system's production environment without disrupting the run. Care must be taken, however, to ensure that the ITF records are not confused with live data or used in reporting actual results.

Audit Subsystem. An audit subsystem designed into the user's system provides the auditor with output for use in future system audits.

Parallel Simulation. In parallel simulation, the auditor writes a program that simulates the live system functions requiring testing (e.g., calculation routines or complex logic conditions). The auditor then verifies the accuracy of the live system's output by running the simulated system with the live system's input.

FINANCIAL, ADMINISTRATIVE, AND PERSONNEL AUDITS

A financial audit ensures adherence to organizational policies for expense management and reporting, inventory control, and budget planning and control. The administrative audit ensures that controls have been established for the costs of developing, maintaining, and operating systems and that a method of providing management with sufficient information to facilitate proper organizational planning has been defined. Personnel audits ensure adherence to organizational policies for hiring practices, staff appraisals, termination practices, vacation management, and salary administration.

Because these MIS functions should be governed by the same rules and procedures that govern other departments, financial, administrative, and personnel audits should be included in the overall schedule for departmental audits. Specific DP knowledge is unnecessary for these audits, because they involve the same procedures as other similar departmental audits.

Audit Frequency

These audits should be conducted annually and, depending on the size of the MIS department and corresponding amount of auditing involved, they should be performed simultaneously.

CONCLUSION

The audit department must provide management with an assessment of the adequacy and effectiveness of the internal control system and of ongoing operations. The scope of any departmental audit should match that of the functional areas within that department. For the MIS function, the audit department must prepare an audit plan that addresses the organization, system reliability and integrity, and financial, administrative, and personnel concerns.

By following the principles described in this chapter, the audit department can, at the end of each fiscal year, issue a report to management that indicates whether the internal control and operation within the MIS function are satisfactory.

XI-3
Auditing the Security of Your Data Center
Robert W. Klenk, Jr.

INTRODUCTION

Hardly a week passes without at least one article in the computer trade press (and sometimes the national press) about a significant loss to a company through the use of its computer. Losses have resulted from errors, omissions, fraud, or destruction of the data center, or a combination thereof. Although the computer itself is an asset, the data and software it contains may be even more valuable to the organization, depending on the complexity of the system.

Companies with a data processing facility depend on it to conduct daily operations. For example, an airline reservation system must be continually available in order to accurately process changing schedules, cancellations, and other transactions. Organizations must establish and maintain a data center security plan to help ensure continued operation of computer facilities.

In addition, an organization's proprietary software and data must be secure. Recreating lost or destroyed data is often costly, sometimes impossible. In some cases, the disclosure of data or programs can reveal trade secrets or new product development. In a recent case a programmer used programs he had stolen from his former employer to start his own business, undercutting the prices charged by the former employer. It has been debated whether a company is responsible for nondisclosure of software that is protected by copyright. This is a new area of concern for MIS management, especially in shops that depend on purchased software packages rather than on software developed in-house. Although improved data center security cannot completely insure against such losses, it is an important part of the overall internal control of the organization.

Interference with normal DP activities usually has an undesirable impact on the organization. The causes of interference are defined as intentional or unintentional:
- Intentional damage is destruction, sabotage, or fraud by dishonest employees, terrorists, and criminals. DP resources are a common target for these activities because of their widespread impact on the organization and the potential value of proprietary data.
- Unintentional damage is a result of environmental disasters (e.g., fire, flood), carelessness, and negligence.

EDP AUDITING

Because of DP's importance, a data center security plan should be established. The objective of such a plan is to provide reasonable and adequate security measures that protect the data center by allowing it to perform its stated purpose without disruption and/or disclosure of proprietary information. The specific steps required in developing a data center security plan addressed in this chapter are summarized as follows:
- Developing a data center security auditing program
- Performing the security audit
- Analyzing reasonable and adequate security measures.

DEVELOPING A SECURITY AUDIT PROGRAM

To determine reasonable and adequate data center security measures, an audit—an independent and objective examination of data center security—is performed to determine whether adequate protection against intentional and unintentional damage is present. This audit must be performed by individuals independent of the MIS department to provide impartial findings, and the EDP auditor should be responsible for the evaluation. The audit encompasses a review of all security policies and procedures as well as compliance testing of these procedures to determine if they are currently being followed and if they conform to government, industry, and organization standards.

The first step in planning the data center security audit is an analysis of DP's role in the organization. DP activities and importance vary among organizations, and the security measures used should be tailored to that particular environment. For example, a data center using a highly sophisticated teleprocessing network for an online/real-time inventory control system would require greater overall security measures than a batch-oriented minicomputer dedicated to research and development applications. In the online/real-time situation, the impact on the organization would be greater if the application processing was disrupted.

The assessment of DP activities should correspond to the security philosophy based on the company's individual goals and systems. Senior management commitment is necessary to ensure that actions called for by a data center security plan will be implemented. With such commitment, MIS managers are more aware that data center security is considered a priority and that their actions will receive support.

The assessment of MIS activities should be performed jointly by the EDP auditor, MIS personnel, and user-department representatives. Figure 1 is a suggested format for assessment. The following information is required:
- Major system—identification of each major application system
- Processing mode—primary processing approach, for example, online/real-time, online batch, or offline/batch
- Criticality of system—evaluation of each system, specifying the effect of downtime and disclosure of data to the organization as either high, medium, or low
- Impact—effect of downtime or disclosure of data and the reasons determining the criticality rating
- Current backup procedure—the ability of the system to recover from a loss of computer processing

Auditing Data Center Security

Major System	Processing Mode	Criticality of System					Impact	Current Backup Procedure
		Effect of Downtime	High	Med	Low		
Accounting	Online/Batch	1 day			x	If necessary, applications could be processed manually	Manual
		1 week			x		Manual
		1 month		x			Manual (if possible)
		Indefinite	x				Manual (if possible)
		Disclosure		x		Moderate	
Inventory/Order Entry	Online/Real Time	1 day		x		Inconvenience	Manual
		1 week	x			Lost sales	Use backup sets
		1 month	x			Out of business	
		Indefinite	x			Out of business	
		Disclosure			x	Minimal	
Research and Development	Offline Batch	1 day			x	Inconvenience	None
		1 week			x	Inconvenience	None
		1 month			x	Inconvenience	Use data service bureau
		Indefinite	x			Reduced operating efficiencies	
		Disclosure	x			Hindrance to future growth	

Figure 1. Analysis of DP Systems

EDP AUDITING

The impact of downtime and loss of proprietary data vary with the application and processing mode. The research and development batch system is least critical with regard to downtime but most critical with respect to the loss of confidential data; the converse is true for the inventory/order entry system. Generally, highly sophisticated processing modes and operational systems have greater security implications for the organization than administration-oriented systems.

After the assessment is completed, the data center security audit program should be formulated. How critical the systems are determines the amount of security necessary. The scope and depth of the audit should therefore be adapted to the specific organization. It is possible to define different auditing programs for the same organization at two independent data centers where each center processes applications of differing importance.

Defining the scope of the audit should begin with a review of the criticality of the systems. Second, data center security auditing objectives specified in this chapter should be evaluated (see Figure 2). These objectives were developed for data center processing systems of varying criticality and are recommended for use with large data center security audits. Objectives for smaller data centers and those processing less critical systems need not be as comprehensive.

If it is important that the computer operate continuously, the EDP auditor should discover whether every method to achieve this end has been considered. One method of minimizing downtime is the use of redundant systems. In these systems, the hardware and/or software may be duplicated in order to switch from a malfunctioning component to a working one without interrupting processing. Currently, only a few computer manufacturers are producing redundant systems, but it has been estimated that within the next five years all major computer manufacturers will offer some type of redundant processing. The assessment of the criticality of continuous computer uptime determines whether the organization should consider redundant systems as an option.

After the auditing program objectives are defined, auditing program steps and procedures must be specified. The recommended techniques to perform the audit include:
- Checklists—detailed questions relating to specified auditing objectives. This facilitates an evaluation of data center policies and procedures.
- Compliance testing and observation—to verify that the stated policies and procedures currently exist and that individuals using these controls understand and execute them correctly. In addition, this would include verifying the procedures to determine conformance with government, industry, and organization policies.

Compliance testing is necessary to identify which procedures must be followed without deviation (e.g., a master file backup). A recent case demonstrates the need for compliance. On the day when routine file backup procedures were mistakenly not followed, the data center for a city blood bank burned down, and irreplaceable data files were lost.

The actual auditing program steps and procedures to be followed relate to the criticality of data center systems, the specified auditing objectives, and

Auditing Data Center Security

A. Fire Exposure
1. Examine building construction and contents regarding fire protection.
2. Review the adequacy of fire protection planning and prevention measures.
3. Review the adequacy of:
   (a) Detection devices
   (b) Alarms and power shutoff
   (c) Extinguishing equipment
   (d) Emergency lighting.

B. Water Damage Exposure
1. Review measures to prevent and reduce water damage.
2. Locate all plumbing and determine its age and serviceability.

C. Air Conditioning (Temperature, Filtration, and Humidity)
1. Assess the adequacy of the air conditioning system, taking into consideration:
   (a) Temperature
   (b) Ventilation
   (c) Filtration
   (d) Humidity
   (e) Protection
   (f) Backup

D. Electricity
1. Determine the quality of the primary power supply.
2. Determine the necessity and type of uninterruptible power supply and review tests of the same.
3. Review for compliance with local electrical wiring codes.

E. Natural Disaster
1. Determine whether the data center facility is reasonably protected against natural disasters.

F. Access Controls
1. Review appropriate security procedures and locking devices to prevent unauthorized access.
2. Determine whether doors and windows are adequately constructed.
3. Identify the minimum number of necessary doors and windows.

G. Housekeeping
1. Determine whether housekeeping procedures minimize risks associated with:
   (a) Combustible materials
   (b) Dust and other contamination
   (c) Static

H. General Concerns
1. Review and assess organizational security planning.

I. Personnel Policies
1. Review hiring policies to assure background checks have been performed on all MIS personnel.
2. Review education and training policies for adequacy.
3. Review termination policies and protection procedures against damage by disgruntled employees.

J. Contingency Plan
1. Review or aid development of a complete backup and contingency plan.

K. Backup Procedures
1. Review backup hardware and its security.
2. Review formal agreement and test results of alternative processing site.
3. Determine adequacy of hardware and servicing backup.
4. Assure adequate backup of:
   (a) Data and files
   (b) Programs and software
   (c) Documentation and run instructions

L. Insurance
1. Review coverage for adequate protection against a variety of disasters:
   (a) All risks
   (b) Extra expenses
   (c) Business interruption loss.

Figure 2. Data Center Auditing Program Objectives

EDP AUDITING

the scope of the review. The Data Center Security Checklist provided at the end of this chapter satisfies the cited objectives for a sophisticated high-criticality data center. A small data center would require a less comprehensive checklist.

The checklist parallels the auditing objectives. Verification of the responses should be performed by compliance testing or observation. It is the EDP auditor's responsibility to determine the appropriate verification procedure for each question, taking into consideration the unique environment of the data center. Space provided on the checklist allows the auditor to indicate how each question was verified.

PERFORMING THE SECURITY AUDIT

The data center audit should be performed through initial use of the checklist to interview MIS senior management. It may be necessary to interview several individuals to complete the questionnaire. The responses to the questions should be classified as "yes" or "no," accompanied by clarifying comments as necessary. The answers should be verified either by compliance testing or by observation.

Adequate security for a data center depends on many factors unique to that installation. Even though data centers are rarely identical in their security needs, there is a standard approach for determining the appropriate security measures. The first step requires identifying security weaknesses determined by the security audit. For each weakness, the probable impact on the data center must be specified.

Figure 3 presents a chart that can be used in this evaluation. When the chart is completed, the probability of the security threat to each classification of DP assets should be assessed. The probability of each security threat is to be specified as high, medium, low, or negligible.

Figure 3 requires the following information:
- Destruction—the probability of total loss of any DP asset by intentional or unintentional causes, such as fire, explosion, water, natural disaster, malicious mischief, sabotage, riot, or vandalism.
- Fraud/theft—the probability of manipulation of an asset for personal financial gain.
- Human error—the probability of loss resulting from carelessness or indifference on the part of an employee causing loss.
- Disclosure—the probability of loss of proprietary data or release of an asset to persons lacking authorization for such information. An example would be the delivery of proprietary data to a competitor.
- Equipment failure—the probability of loss (or distortion in the case of data) from electronic or mechanical failure of DP or environmental equipment.

In order to interpret Figure 3, the value of the DP assets must be determined. In addition, if an asset is destroyed or damaged, an analysis is required to determine any anticipated extra expense and business interruption loss that will be incurred until the data center is functioning normally. This information is requested in the Cost Evaluation Checklist at the end of this chapter and is summarized in Figure 4. Figure 4 requires MIS personnel to

Auditing Data Center Security

DP Assets/Risks	Destruction	Fraud/Theft	Human Error	Disclosure	Equipment Failure
DP Equipment					
Data Center Facility					
Data/Files					
Software					
Documentation					

Probability of Occurence:
High 75%
Medium 50%
Low 25%
Negligible 5%

Definition of Terms
DP Equipment—all equipment, including mainframes, peripherals, data entry
Data Center Facility—total installation other than DP equipment as defined, including rooms, lighting, air conditioning, furniture, fixtures
Data/Files—all data files and magnetic media
Software—all application and operating system programs
Documentation—all system and program documentation and user guides

Figure 3. Probability Analysis of Security Threats

determine the replacement or recreation cost for each asset and the extra expense that would be incurred to process normally if an asset were destroyed. Business interruption loss should be determined by the operating user departments and by referencing the systems' criticality and impact of downtime as reported on Figure 1. The Data Center Security Checklist also provides the organization's insurance manager with detailed information regarding the risk exposure of DP activities.

The organization should have a written recovery plan in effect. Recovery includes backup, for a short term interruption of business, and disaster, for loss of the entire computer installation.

A minimum written plan should cover the following areas:
- Staffing requirements
- Equipment requirements
- Operational procedures
- Application software, systems software, and documentation
- Production files
- Transportation
- Supplies

Figure 4 requires the following information:
- Replacement/recreation cost—current acquisition cost of DP equipment and the data center facility should be specified from the Cost Evaluation Checklist. The recreation cost for the data/files, software, and documentation should also be specified, based on the utilization of off-site backup.
- Days required to replace/recreate—estimated time required to replace/recreate a destroyed asset to its former operational level. If the data/

… EDP AUDITING

Asset	Replacement/ Recreation Cost	Days Required to Replace/ Recreate	Estimated Downtime Loss							
			1 Day		1 Week		1 Month		Indefinitely	
			EE	BIL	EE	BIL	EE	BIL	EE	BIL
Equipment										
Data Center Facility										
Data/Files										
Software										
Documentation										

EE = Extra expense
BIL = Business interruption loss

Figure 4. Security Risk Exposure

files, software, or documentation is stored in an off-site backup location, only the reconstruction time should be specified, based on past MIS department experience.
- Estimated downtime loss/extra expense—costs required to conduct a business during the specified downtime of an asset (e.g., the additional clerical salaries and overtime to manipulate data the computer would normally process).
- Estimated downtime loss/business interruption loss—lost revenue to the organization if an asset were unavailable for the specified time (e.g., lost sales to an airline unable to confirm reservations).

Once the figures have been determined, the organization's data center security risks and its financial exposure can be evaluated. For example, if the probability of DP equipment destruction is high as determined by the security audit and indicated on Figure 3, and if the replacement cost exceeds $1 million as indicated on Figure 4, the risk exposure to the company is probably unacceptable and requires the implementation of additional security measures.

For the organization to determine reasonable and adequate security measures, a cost/benefit/risk analysis must be performed. The analysis at this point only addresses the organization's potential security risk and financial impact based on the probability of occurrence. The cost of additional security measures that would reduce the financial exposure must be determined to balance the cost/benefit equation. In most cases, the benefits of reduced security threats must exceed the cost of the security measure if management is to be expected to approve the additional expenditure. Figure 5 focuses on this issue and should be completed for each major category of security threat. Potential security measures to be evaluated are included in the Data Center Security Checklist. Figure 5 requires the following information:
- Security threat/DP asset—identifying security risks and DP assets.
- Probability of occurrence—see Figure 3.
- Alternative security measures
  —Description. Identifying security measures for fire, water damage, air conditioning, electricity, natural disaster, access controls, housekeeping, general concerns, personnel policies, contingency planning, backup procedures, and insurance.
  —Initial cost. One-time cost of the security measure.
  —Annual maintenance cost. Annual upkeep and maintenance expense.

Auditing Data Center Security

Security Threat/ DP Assets	Probability of Occurrences (before)	Alternative Security Measures				Revised Probability of Occurrence (after)
		Description	Initial Cost	Annual Maintenance Cost	
Destruction DP Equipment Data Center Facility Data/Files Software Documentation					
Fraud/Theft DP Equipment Data Center Facility Data/Files Software Documentation					
Human Error DP Equipment Data Center Facility Data/Files Software Documentation					
Disclosure DP Equipment Data Center Facility Data/Files Software Documentation					
Equipment Failure DP Equipment Data Center Facility Data/Files Software Documentation					

Figure 5. Alternative Data Center Security Measures

—Revised probability of occurrence. Reduced risk as a result of this proposed security measure.

The completion of Figures 3, 4, and 5 facilitates performing the cost/benefit/risk analysis shown in Figure 6. Figure 6 compares the cost of additional security measures to the organization's financial exposure. This allows the EDP auditor and management to plan and select security measures consistent with the organization's general policies to gain the greatest benefit in reducing the probability of risk for the least cost. Figure 6 requires the following information.
- Security threat/DP asset—identifying security risks and DP assets.
- Probability of occurrence—See Figure 3.
- Maximum financial exposure
  —Replacement/recreation cost. See Figure 4.
  —Days to replace/recreate. See Figure 4.
  —Estimated downtime loss

EDP AUDITING

Security Threat/ DP Assets	Probability of Occurrence (before)	Maximum Financial Exposure					Alternative Security Measures				Comments
		Replacement/ Recreation Cost	Days to Replace/ Recreate	Est Downtime Loss		Description	Initial Cost	Annual Maintenance Cost	Revised Probability of Occurrence (after)	
				Extra Expense	Business Interruption Loss					
Destruction DP Equipment Data Center Facility Data/Files Software Documentation										
Fraud/Theft DP Equipment Data Center Facility Data/Files Software Documentation										
Human Error DP Equipment Data Center Facility Data/Files Software Documentation										
Disclosure DP Equipment Data Center Facility Data/Files Software Documentation										
Equipment Failure DP Equipment Data Center Facility Data/Files Software Documentation										

Figure 6. Determination of Data Center Security Measures

- Extra expense—All extra expenses to be incurred by the organization until an unusable asset can be replaced or recreated.
- Business interruption loss—The business interruption loss to be incurred by the organization until an unusable asset can be replaced or recreated.
- Alternative security measures
  —Description. Identifying the security measure.
  —Initial cost. See Figure 5.
  —Annual maintenance cost. See Figure 5.
  —Revised probability of occurrence. See Figure 5.

Figure 6 is intended as a guide for determining reasonable and adequate security measures; interpretations deriving from it will focus attention on high-risk/high-financial-exposure items and implementation of additional security measures to reduce the risk. There are occasions, however, when additional security measures are not cost justified but required just the same. Protection against the disclosure of proprietary information would fall into this category. As a result, the cost/benefit/risk analysis approach to data center security is not the only method of determining security, but the first step in the area of data center security planning. This approach should be modified and adapted to meet each organization's requirements.

CONCLUSION

The results of the data center security audit may be classified as an appraisal of current security measures versus the ideal "standard." It is important to realize that few installations will be completely protected against all potential security threats. In some cases, security costs exceed protection costs. In others, it is impractical to implement security measures—for example, limited access to the computer if the machine is located in an open office. Security audit results should therefore be evaluated as compared to the ideal "standard" and to the results of previous audits.

It is not always feasible to implement many new security measures simultaneously, and the data center audit report should therefore address both security needs and security performance based on prior audits.

Although no security system is perfect, the audit report gives management a tool to help make the computer system as secure as possible.

This chapter provides a framework for conducting a security audit and an approach to effectively plan for reasonable and adequate security measures. The security audit should be a part of a total EDP auditing program to protect the assets of the organization and to provide the assurance of uninterrupted data processing.

EDP AUDITING

DATA CENTER SECURITY CHECKLIST
(Adapted from "Federal Information Processing Standards Publication: Guidelines for Automatic Data Processing Security and Risk Management," June 1974)

	Yes	No	Comments	Verification Method

A. Fire Exposure
1. Is the data center housed in a building that is fire resistant or fireproof?
2. Is the computer room separated from adjacent areas by noncombustible or fire-resistant partitions, walls, floors, and doors and isolated from hazardous materials?
3. Are raised floors and hung ceilings (including support hardware and insulation) noncombustible?
4. Are carpets, furniture, and window coverings noncombustible?
5. Are paper and other combustible supplies stored outside the computer area?
6. Is smoking restricted in the data center?
7. Are operations personnel trained in fire-fighting techniques and assigned individual responsibilities in case of fire?
8. Is the data center protected by automatic extinguishing systems using:
    (a) Water?
        (1) If so, does activation sound an alarm and delay the release of water?
    (b) Halon?
    (c) Carbon dioxide?
        (1) Have personnel been given proper safety precautions?
9. Are portable fire extinguishers placed strategically around the data center with location markers visible?
10. Are emergency power shutdown controls easily accessible at exits?
11. Does emergency power shutoff control heating, ventilation, and air conditioning?
12. Is a shutdown checklist used?
13. Are smoke and ionization detectors installed in:
    (a) Various data center zones?
    (b) Ceilings?
    (c) Raised floors?
    (d) Return air ducts?
14. Does smoke/ionization detection activate emergency power shutoff?
15. Are detectors regularly tested?
16. Are fire drills conducted regularly?
17. Is water available for fire fighting?
18. Are there enough fire alarm boxes throughout the data center?
19. Does the activation of the fire alarm sound:
    (a) Locally?
    (b) At guard/security location?
    (c) Central fire alarm station?
    (d) Fire department?

Auditing Data Center Security

	Yes	No	Comments	Verification Method

20. Is the rating given to the local fire fighting force by the American Insurance Association's Standard Fire Defense Rating Schedule known?
21. Are flammable materials used in computer maintenance? (If so, they should be used in small quantities and stored in approved containers.)
22. Can emergency crews gain access to the data center without delay?
23. Is there an adequate supply of emergency lighting throughout the data center? Is it regularly tested?

B. Water Damage Exposure
1. Are computers and related equipment located above grade?
2. Are overhead water and steam pipes excluded from the computer room except for sprinklers?
3. Is adequate drainage provided under raised floors and in other areas of the data center?
4. Is there adequate drainage on the floor above to prevent ceiling water leakage?
5. Is adequate drainage provided in areas adjacent to the data center?
6. Are all electrical junction boxes under raised floors held off the slab to prevent water damage?
7. Are exterior doors and windows watertight?
8. Is protection provided against accumulated rainwater or leaks in the roof and rooftop cooling towers?
9. Are plumbing diagrams available for reference on construction projects?
10. Are periodic checks conducted to ensure the integrity of the plumbing?
11. Are there sufficient covers for all equipment to protect against water damage and are they checked for rips and tears?

C. Air Conditioning (Temperature, Filtration, and Humidity)
1. Is the system exclusively used for the data center?
2. Are duct linings and filters noncombustible?
3. Are fire dampers provided?
4. Is the compressor remote from the data center?
5. Is the cooling tower adequately protected?
6. Is backup air conditioning capacity available?
7. Are air intakes:
    (a) Covered with protective screening?
    (b) Located above street level?
    (c) Located to prevent intake of pollutants or other debris?

EDP AUDITING

                       Verification
               Yes No Comments Method

D. Electricity
1. Is the local power supply reliable?
2. Is the line voltage recorded with a voltmeter that displays transients?
3. If the line voltage is unreliable, have alternative measures been investigated?
4. If the criticality of the systems processed at the data center is high, have uninterruptible power supplies been investigated?
5. Does all wiring in the computer center conform to generally accepted local electrical codes?

E. Natural Disaster Exposure
1. Is the data center building structurally sound and protected against:
 (a) Hurricanes and wind?
 (b) Flood damage?
 (c) Earthquakes?
2. Are the building and equipment properly grounded for lightning protection?

F. Access Controls
1. Is the data center an unlikely target for vandals?
2. Are guards stationed at all data center entrances?
3. Does entrance to the data center require positive identification (e.g., a photo badge system)?
4. Is access to the data center restricted to authorized individuals whose job performance requires their presence?
5. Is limited access to the data center adequate on a 24-hour basis?
6. Are keys, cipher locks, badge readers, or other security devices used to control access?
7. Are personnel trained to challenge improperly identified visitors?
8. Are controls adequate for data center visitors?
9. Is advertising the data center location discouraged?
10. Is each entrance to the data center necessary?
11. Are data center doors that are necessary to provide ventilation and light protected by a gate or screen when open?
12. Are fire doors protected by exit alarms?
13. Are doors, locks, bolts, hinges, frames, and other building apparatus constructed to reduce the probability of unauthorized entry?
14. If access to the data center is electrically controlled, is standby battery power available during power failures?

Auditing Data Center Security

	Yes	No	Comments	Verification Method

G. Housekeeping
1. Is trash accumulation prevented in the data center?
2. Are equipment and work surfaces regularly cleaned?
3. Are floors washed regularly?
4. Are the surfaces beneath the raised floors cleaned regularly?
5. Are wastebaskets emptied outside the data center to reduce dust discharge?
6. Are the carpeting and floor wax antistatic?
7. Is eating in the computer room discouraged?
8. Are low-fire-hazard waste containers used in the data center?
9. Is smoking prohibited or restricted in the computer room?
10. Are maintenance areas kept clean and orderly?

H. General Concerns
1. Are security and operations personnel briefed on how to react to civil disturbances?
2. Are personnel trained to handle bomb threats?
3. Does a liaison program exist with local law enforcement agencies?

I. Personnel Policies
1. Are background checks performed on all new employees?
2. Are employee backgrounds rechecked periodically?
3. Are employees cross-trained?
4. Is management informed of disgruntled employees?
5. Are policies established for containing dismissed employees who may constitute a threat to the data center?
6. Does a continuing education program exist on security measures?

J. Contingency Plans
1. Does a written contingency plan exist? If so, are the following items included:
   (a) Identification of minimal necessary equipment configurations:
      (1) Machine type and model?
      (2) Core sizes?
      (3) Peripheral quantities, types, and models?
   (b) Specification of operating system, JCL, and other system software?
   (c) Identification of responsible individuals by functional area?
   (d) Detailed notification procedure for implementation of the plans specifying who calls:
      (1) Management?

EDP AUDITING

	Yes	No	Comments	Verification Method

   (2) Emergency crews?
   (3) User department?
   (4) Backup facilities?
   (5) DP vendor personnel?
   (6) Service personnel?
   (7) Others as necessary?
  (e) Criteria for determining the extent of disruption?
  (f) Responsibility for retaining source documents and data/files for each application?
  (g) Identification of individuals responsible for the decision to utilize backup facility and to plan for permanent resolution for disruption?
 2. Does a contingency training program exist for all MIS personnel?

K. Backup Procedures
 1. Backup facility:
  (a) Are backup computers available?
   (1) Is the computer located:
    —Within the data center?
    —Within the building?
    —Off-site?
   (2) Do backup computers have available capacity to process critical applications?
  (b) If access is available to another computer:
   (1) Is a contractual agreement in effect?
   (2) Is testing performed regularly?
   (3) Are security measures adequate at the backup facility?
   (4) Has the backup site been approved by security personnel?
   (5) Is capacity available to process critical applications?
  (c) Has a backup implementation plan been developed?
   (1) Is the plan reviewed and tested regularly?
  (d) Does the DP service vendor stock spare parts locally?
  (e) Does a regular preventive maintenance program exist?
 2. Backup of data/files and software
  (a) Are procedures established for determining records retention and backup policies?
   (1) Are these policies tested and reviewed regularly?
  (b) Where are critical backup data/files and software stored?
   (1) On-site, locked in fireproof location?
   (2) Off-site, locked in fireproof location?
   (3) Has the off-site storage location been evaluated for adequate security?

Auditing Data Center Security

	Yes	No	Comments	Verification Method

    (c) Are all data/files and software stored in the data center in fireproof containers?
    (d) Are dry runs periodically performed utilizing backup data/files and software from both on- and off-site locations?
    (e) Are data/files and software backup generated at regular intervals?
    (f) Is documentation backup consistent with data/files and software backup procedures?

L. Insurance
1. Are the following included in the property insurance:
   (a) Fire?
   (b) Water damage?
   (c) Civil disorder?
   (d) Vandalism?
   (e) Natural disaster?
      (1) Lightning?
      (2) Hurricanes?
      (3) Earthquakes?
   (f) Structural collapse?
   (g) Aircraft?
   (h) Air conditioning failure?
   (i) Explosions:
      (1) Gas?
      (2) Boiler?
   (j) Damage to organizational property?
   (k) Blanket crime?
   (l) Fraud?
   (m) Power failure?
   (n) Extra expense?
   (o) Product warranty?
   (p) Business interruption loss?
   (q) Loss of proprietary data or trade secrets?
2. Is specific coverage available for:
   (a) DP equipment?
   (b) Storage media?
   (c) Extra expense?
   (d) Business interruption loss?
   (e) Software and documentation?
3. Is valuable paper insurance available for computer media loss:
   (a) Accounts receivable records?
   (b) Other records?

EDP AUDITING

COST EVALUATION CHECKLIST

                                                                                              Replacement/
                                                                                              Recreation
                                                                                                Cost

A. Replacement/Recreation Cost
   1. DP Equipment
      (a) Mainframe
      (b) Peripherals
      (c) Data entry
      (d) Communications
      (e) Storage media
          (1) Disk packs
          (2) Tapes
      (f) Supplies
      (g) Other _____
      (h) Other _____
          Total

   2. Data center facility
      (a) Site preparation
      (b) Construction
      (c) Heating, ventilation, and air conditioning
      (d) Electrical
      (e) Plumbing
      (f) Fire prevention and detection
      (g) Office furnishings and fixtures
          (e.g., desks, chairs, storage units)
      (h) Other _____
      (i) Other _____
          Total

   3. Data/files
      (a) Recreation cost if off-site backup does not exist
          (1) Data entry (source documents)
              —Labor
              —Outside services
              —Out-of-pocket expenses
              —Materials
              —Other _____
              —Other _____
              Total

      (b) Recreation cost if backup exists
          (1) Restoration of files
              —Computer rental
              —Labor
              —Out-of-pocket expenses
              —Materials
              —Other _____
              —Other _____
          (2) Data entry information not available through backup
              —Labor
              —Outside services
              —Out-of-pocket expenses
              —Materials
              —Other _____
              —Other _____
              Total

Auditing Data Center Security

                    **Replacement/
Recreation
Cost**

4. Software
   - (a) Recreation of all programs if off-site backup does not exist
     - (1) Outside services
       - —Program packages
       - —DP consulting services
     - (2) Modification of existing operating procedures
     - (3) In-house analysis and programming
       - —Labor
       - —Out-of-pocket expenses
       - —Materials
     - (4) Other _____
     - (5) Other _____
       - Total
   - (b) Recreation of all programs if backup exists
     - (1) Restoration of files
       - —Computer rental
       - —Labor
       - —Out-of-pocket expenses
       - —Materials
       - —Other _____
       - —Other _____
       - Total

5. Documentation
   - (a) Recreation of documentation if off-site backup does not exist
     - (1) Labor
     - (2) Reproduction expense
     - (3) Out-of-pocket expenses
     - (4) Other _____
     - (5) Other _____
       - Total
   - (b) Recreation of documentation if backup exists
     - (1) Labor
     - (2) Reproduction expense
     - (3) Out-of-pocket expenses
     - (4) Other _____
     - (5) Other _____
       - Total

B. Extra Expense Required to Process Normally if DP Asset Is Destroyed
1. DP equipment
   - (a) Purchased computer time
   - (b) Data entry expense
   - (c) Other purchased services _____
   - (d) Labor (DP and/or clerical)
   - (e) Out-of-pocket expenses
   - (f) Materials
   - (g) Other _____
   - (h) Other _____
     - Total
2. Data center facility
   - (a) Purchased computer time
   - (b) Data entry expense
   - (c) Other purchased services _____
   - (d) Labor (DP and/or clerical)

EDP AUDITING

                                                                      Replacement/ Recreation Cost

    (e) Out-of-pocket expenses
    (f) Materials
    (g) Other _____
    (h) Other _____
        Total

3. Data/files
    (a) Labor (manual operations)
    (b) Out-of-pocket expenses
    (c) Other _____
    (d) Other _____
        Total

4. Software
    (a) Labor
    (b) Out-of-pocket expenses
    (c) Other _____
    (d) Other _____
        Total

5. Documentation
    (a) Labor
    (b) Reproduction
    (c) Out-of-pocket expenses
    (d) Other _____
    (e) Other _____
        Total

C. Business Interruption Loss

Estimate lost revenue resulting from inability to normally process (include the effect of all processed applications)
1. Downtime
    (a) 1 day
    (b) 1 week
    (c) 1 month
    (d) Indefinitely
        Total

XI-4
Taking Full Advantage of EDP Auditors
William E. Perry

INTRODUCTION

Financial areas of an organization have always been audited. For employees who work in those departments, audits are an integral part of the job. Although they may not like this situation, it is expected and accepted.

For many years, MIS departments were not audited, nor were they involved in the audits of financial areas. The organization's computer was often an adjunct of the financial department and simply provided printed evidence for auditors.

The increasing complexity and integration of computer systems as well as the decreasing amount of hard-copy evidence, however, forced auditors to become more involved in data processing. The EDP audit profession was established as a result of the 1973 Equity Funding fraud and the issuance of SAS 3 by the American Institute of Certified Public Accountants (an auditing standard describing the CPA's computer audit responsibilities).

Because most major financial applications were computerized, it was difficult to conduct any audit without involving data processing. In addition, the MIS department itself was audited, because many of the organization's general controls were now automated and under that department's control.

Many MIS personnel were unfamiliar with the audit process. Some did not understand the difference between an internal and external auditor. Others were uncertain to whom auditors reported and who received copies of audit reports.

In some organizations, EDP auditors actually worked in the MIS department, and many MIS professionals thought the auditors were part of those departments. When the audit reports were issued, however, many MIS personnel were shocked into an enduring prejudice against the audit function.

Complicating the auditor-auditee relationship was the fact that many EDP auditors were themselves MIS professionals, who often had no auditing experience or training. Hostile attitudes were a surprise to many of these individuals, who understood neither the reaction nor how to cope with it.

EDP AUDITING

Auditor-Auditee Relationship

Practical experience by thousands of auditors supports the thesis that there is a natural resentment to being audited. Although people can intellectually understand the need for audits, emotionally they feel they are being evaluated. The negative tone of most audit reports reinforces this feeling. When reports intentionally list only problems, the auditee soon realizes that even at best the audit report notes a few minor flaws and that the worst case could negatively affect someone's job with the organization.

Auditors must understand how auditees react so they can take appropriate countermeasures. Sometimes the reaction is positive, and auditee personnel are supportive of the audit process. At other times they react negatively to auditors, which can affect audit efficiency, audit findings, or both. The auditees may use audit findings to their own advantage, or they may use auditors to champion a cause for which they do not want or cannot gain appropriate management support.

Auditors are not beyond being manipulated. Clever auditees can shape audit findings and recommendations to their advantage; they can also conceal problems or make it difficult for the auditors to perform their function. Auditors can be used to champion an auditee cause, require adherence to an unpopular procedure, or interpret organizational policies and procedures in the auditee's favor. Auditees can also misuse the auditor by leading the auditor to a questionable finding to justify a pet project, undermining the acceptance of valid audit findings and recommendations, or holding back information until after the report is issued to discredit the auditor.

Attitude Adjustment

The audit process is enhanced when the auditor understands auditee attitudes and attempts to change negative concepts about the process. This is possible if the auditor can identify auditee attitude types and has a positive desire to change those opinions. The recommended attitude-adjustment process is:
- Categorizing auditee attitude—The auditor must be alert to the type of attitude expressed before taking appropriate action.
- Identifying attitude attributes—The behavioral attributes resulting from the auditee attitude must be identified.
- Initiating countermeasures—Once the situation has been analyzed, the auditor can institute countermeasures to adjust or reduce negative effects of these attitudes on EDP auditors or the audit process.

This process is not formal (as a diagnostic audit is), but it is a process in the sense that the auditor must perform an analysis and base action on that analysis. It is an important adjunct to the audit itself and one that helps create a favorable atmosphere.

CATEGORIZING AUDITEE ATTITUDES

Every audit area is different, and auditees and their reactions are even more varied. Evaluating the auditee as a person is an important first step in the audit process.

An audit may involve many individuals in key positions, and not all auditees exhibit identical attitudes toward auditors. There may be more similarities than differences, however, among individuals working in the same area. Experience shows that auditees generally fall into one of the following three categories:

Hostile Auditees. Hostile auditees do not like auditors or the audit process. They often perceive the auditor as a management spy looking for evidence to use against them. The auditor becomes a symbol of the poor practices of senior management. Hostile auditees do not trust the auditor to place much value on the auditor's ability to find anything meaningful or to help the organization in any way. These auditees are usually not difficult to identify, because they often openly disparage the audit process.

Defensive Auditees. Defensive auditees feel responsible for the proper functioning of the area under audit. Problems discovered by the auditor, therefore, reflect directly on their inability to manage the area properly. Some findings may be embarrassing and might cause auditees to become concerned about their jobs. The auditee therefore disputes all audit findings and recommendations, believing that if the findings and recommendations were worthwhile they would have been previously integrated into the auditee's procedures.

Friendly Auditees. Friendly auditees may openly encourage their staffs to support auditors. This type of auditee knows how to use the auditor to get things done. The friendly auditee often understands the audit process and may, in fact, have once been an auditor. This individual can manipulate audit findings and recommendations to personal advantage. The auditor should be warned, however, that the friendly auditee may be setting a trap by withholding information until after the audit report is issued.

During the initial conference and/or early meetings with the auditee, auditors should recognize the type of auditee they will be dealing with. Categorizing auditees in this manner may be difficult, but it is important in selecting the appropriate strategy for dealing with adverse attitudes.

IDENTIFYING ATTITUDE ATTRIBUTES

After the auditee is categorized, the behavior resulting from that attitude should be identified. It may not be possible to change an auditee's attitude, but the behavior is alterable. To do this, the auditor must be aware of the most likely outcome of the auditee attitude.

Auditee behavior in response to auditors and the audit process can be expressed in terms of both reactions and results. Reactions are how auditees express their attitudes regarding auditors. The results of that expression are of primary concern to the auditor, because they may require countermeasures. The following sections identify the most common reactions to an audit. Identifying auditee behavior should be done early in the audit, and the necessary countermeasures should be initiated promptly.

EDP AUDITING

Hostile Auditee Behavior

The auditee reaction and results for the hostile auditee are listed in Table 1 and briefly described in the following sections.

The Auditee as Victim. "Why me?" is a question asked by many auditees. This is particularly true of data processing areas that have never been audited before. They are suspicious of why auditors choose to audit one area rather than another, or why they spend more time auditing a particular area. Project leaders and other members of MIS management may misread the audit selection process. In addition, if one area is audited constantly (e.g., computer operations) while other areas receive few or no audits, the feeling of being persecuted may increase. This reaction normally results in the auditee fighting the audit process, sometimes complaining to senior management about unnecessary audits.

Table 1. Hostile Auditee Behavior

Auditee Reaction	Result
Auditee as victim.	Auditee fights back by complaining to management.
Auditor as management spy.	Auditee sends messages (through auditor) to management about overworked, understaffed conditions.
No-win situation.	Auditee volunteers nothing and says as little as possible.
Auditor is incompetent.	Auditee lets the auditor sink; may ignore, mislead, or withhold information.
Auditee is not trusted.	Auditee exhibits an attitude of "good luck if you can find anything wrong here."

The Auditor as Management Spy. Auditors may be viewed as special representatives of management assigned to gather evidence about auditee misdeeds. Auditors are perceived as going through wastebaskets and performing special computer analyses to detect improper acts for the purpose of punishing employees. The very presence of auditors creates negative feelings when they are viewed as spies. This results in the auditors being closely watched; some areas even maintain records of when the auditors enter and leave. Viewing auditors as management spies results in the auditee giving auditors messages to take back to management. Obviously, the messages are always positive about auditee practices.

No-Win Situation. Some auditees believe that auditors are out to get them, and that nothing can be done to prevent a bad audit report. If the auditees are cooperative, the information volunteered will be used against them; if the auditees are resentful, that too will be reported. In this situation, the most common reaction is not to volunteer anything. Although auditees recognize that this tactic will not help, they also believe it cannot hurt—why help the enemy?

Auditor Is Incompetent. A common data processing attitude is that the auditors lack the technical skills needed to adequately understand the area under audit. Although auditing standards require that auditors be competent in that area, auditees may establish unrealistic technical standards for them. The result of this attitude is to let the auditors sink. Believing the auditors to be incompetent, the auditees may withhold information, ignore the auditors, or mislead them into proposing improper or unreasonable findings and recommendations.

Auditee Is Not Trusted. A variation of the management-spy attitude is one in which the auditees believe management does not trust them to safeguard assets or to do an acceptable job unless they are continually reviewed and evaluated. Of course, the auditees feel that they should be trusted; they also normally feel that their area is doing a good job. This belief results in a smug, "good-luck" attitude toward the auditors as the auditees believe nothing of any consequence will be found.

Any form of hostile behavior is harmful to the audit. Knowing that such an attitude exists, however, provides the auditor with an opportunity to take positive steps to improve the situation. Failure to recognize a hostile attitude may result in ineffective EDP auditing.

Defensive Auditee Behavior

The defensive auditee fights the auditors from the start of the audit. This characteristic is most frequently exhibited by individuals who have never been audited before or who have received unfavorable evaluations in previous audits. Individuals who are concerned about the performance of their departments and suspect they may receive an unfavorable audit report may also be defensive.

The most common defensive auditee reactions and their results are listed in Table 2 and described in the following paragraphs.

Table 2. Defensive Auditee Behavior

Auditee Reaction	Result
Auditee is embarrassed by findings.	Auditee wants to water down findings to save face.
Auditee honestly disagrees with auditor.	Auditee explains in detail the auditee position.
Auditee is uncertain findings are correct.	Auditee tests how thoroughly auditor has developed and supported findings.
Auditee believes findings are insignificant.	Auditee agrees with situation but argues about significance.
Auditee believes findings are irrelevant.	Auditee argues that findings do not relate to auditee role and responsibility being reviewed.
Auditee believes findings are taken out of context.	Auditee argues that auditor does not know all the facts.

EDP AUDITING

Auditee Is Embarrassed by Findings. Facts discovered during the audit may be an embarrassment to the auditee. The findings may indicate that the organization's policies and procedures have not been followed, that a series of errors have occurred, or that resources have been lost as a result of mismanagement. These may be conditions that have existed for months or years but that were not previously noted by the user. Because defensive auditees generally feel responsible for all events in the area under audit, they normally want to eliminate or water down the findings. Although the defensive auditee may not argue about the correctness of the findings, the wording of the report may be extremely important, because the defensive auditee wants to save face in management's eyes.

Auditee Honestly Disagrees with Findings. It is possible, although rare, that the auditee really disagrees with the auditor about the validity of the findings. For example, the auditor may feel that the auditee has not complied with policy, but the auditee disagrees with the auditor's interpretation and feels that a different perspective would reveal no problem. This normally results in a detailed explanation to the auditor of why the auditee disagrees with the findings.

Auditee Is Uncertain Findings Are Correct. Auditors occasionally find conditions that the auditee is not aware of. These conditions may surprise the auditee, who may therefore dispute the validity of the finding. For example, the auditor may question the performance of personnel in the auditee area or compliance with organization policy. Auditee management discovers that if the findings are correct, they must take a position against their own personnel. The result is that auditee management wants to test how thoroughly the auditors have developed and supported their findings. Auditee management will challenge the facts, the completeness of the process, or the reasonableness of the conclusions, so as to discredit the audit findings.

Auditee Believes Findings Are Insignificant. The MIS personnel may agree that the findings are correct but consider them not worthy of inclusion in the audit report. The auditee is often right; it is generally better not to include minor problems in audit reports. For example, the auditor may note that a naming convention was not complied with in a program, but that the net result of noncompliance has had little effect on the organization. Although it is worth noting to the project personnel and worth correcting, it may not be important enough to include in the audit report.

Auditee Believes Findings Are Irrelevant. Irrelevance is a point often debated during discussions about the type of documentation required for computer applications. Auditors want to see separate control documentation. Systems analysts argue that it is irrelevant whether the documentation for controls is separate or integrated with the regular system documentation, as long as it does exist; project leaders may argue that it is not their responsibility to provide separate control documentation. The defensive auditee agrees that the findings are correct but argues that they do not relate to the roles and responsibilities under review.

Auditee Believes Findings Are Taken Out of Context. In the course of day-to-day work, auditee personnel must handle a variety of situations. Some of these may result in the deviation from normal procedures to deal with a specific situation. For example, customers may not be allowed cash refunds after 30 days, but such a refund may be authorized to keep the good will of a high-volume customer. If the auditors note that the policy has been violated, the auditee would argue that the finding is taken out of context and that the auditor does not know all the facts. The auditee normally explains the situation and expects the auditor to understand that certain occasions dictate that normal procedures be violated.

Auditors usually know where they stand with a defensive auditee. The individual is concerned about audit findings and continually interacts with the auditor to ensure that the auditor understands the situation from the auditee's perspective. Obviously, the auditor is obligated to learn all the facts and then present the situation so that the action the auditor believes is preferable is taken.

Friendly Auditee Behavior

A friendly auditee makes the audit function more enjoyable and makes auditors feel their services are appreciated. On the other hand, this type of auditee is also the one who may use audit findings for personal benefit. The more common reactions of the friendly auditee to an audit are listed in Table 3 and described in the following sections.

Table 3. Friendly Auditee Behavior

Auditee Reaction	Result
Auditee believes auditor can implement unpopular procedures already desired by auditee management.	Auditee uses auditors as excuse for unpopular changes.
Auditee agrees with findings.	Auditee makes auditors feel good.
Auditee wants predecessor to look bad (occurs when manager is new in position).	Auditor attributes problems to past actions.
Auditee wants to circumvent supervisor.	Auditee uses auditors to sell ideas previously rejected by supervisor.
Auditee wants vague general comments for later use.	Auditee wants to use audit report as reason to install a new procedure or policy.
Auditee wants supervisor to look bad.	Auditee identifies cause of any problem as a direct order from supervisor.
Auditee wants auditors to look bad.	Auditee waits until audit report is issued to undermine credibility with withheld information.

Auditor Can Implement Unpopular Control. The friendly auditee sees the auditor as the way to implement an unpopular policy or procedure. For example, an MIS manager does not want computer operators to smoke in the computer room but has been hesitant to say so. When the auditors bring up the subject, the MIS manager is enthusiastic because the auditors are now the reason for implementing a policy that was desired but never executed. The

EDP AUDITING

typical result is to strongly support the auditors and to use them as an excuse to make an unpopular change.

Auditee Agrees with Findings. Occasionally, the auditee states that the findings are correct, relevant, and will be implemented. It is these moments that make auditors feel that their job has been well done.

Auditee Wants Predecessor to Look Bad. This occurs most frequently when the auditee manager is new in the position. Anything that has occurred in the past that makes the predecessor look bad provides an opportunity for the current manager to look good. Some new managers will go out of their way to identify problems for the auditors so that they can present the area as being in the worst possible condition, which they can then correct—and take credit for the improvement. Auditee management wants to ensure that the auditors know the problems are attributable to the previous management.

Auditee Wants to Circumvent Supervisors. Not all recommendations made by MIS personnel are accepted. Requests for new personnel are refused, items included within the budget are rejected, and proposed projects are turned down. If the auditors make a recommendation that was previously rejected, it must be reconsidered not only by the next level of management but also, frequently, by much higher levels. For this reason, the friendly auditee attempts to manipulate the auditors to make recommendations to add resources or personnel for functions they particularly desire (e.g., the acquisition of a data dictionary to document organizational data). The auditors are used to sell an idea previously rejected by the auditee's supervisor. In some cases, auditees may introduce the auditor to a fact or recommendations that they hope will appear in the audit report.

Auditee Wants Vague General Comments for Later Use. Many actions are based on comments, findings, and recommendations that appear in audit reports. The action, however, may not always be that intended by the auditors. Friendly auditees can use audit reports as a basis for justifying all sorts of changes in the data processing area. The more generally worded the audit report, the more opportunity the auditee has to interpret those comments in a favorable manner. The auditor may therefore be requested to include a certain phrase or wording in the audit report that will enable the auditee to use that report as a reason to install a new procedure or policy.

Auditee Wants Supervisor to Look Bad. Although employees do not always agree with their supervisors' orders, they are obligated to carry them out. When auditors indicate that the action resulting from certain orders may be improper, employees may see that as an opportunity to make their supervisors look bad. To identify the supervisor as the cause of the problem, such employees will strongly support the inclusion in the audit report of any problem resulting from a direct order with which they did not agree.

Auditee Wants Auditors to Look Bad. Improper or unsupported findings included in audit reports degrade the credibility of the auditors. Friendly auditees may be aware that a finding is incorrect but may not reveal that fact until after the report is issued. Because the auditee appears friendly, the auditor believes that the auditee is being supportive. The auditee is able to undermine the auditor's credibility after the audit report is issued by introducing information not known or overlooked by the auditor. This type of auditee is, in fact, a hostile auditee masquerading as a friendly one.

There is nothing wrong with an auditee's use of auditors to implement a positive change, and if the auditors can contribute to its implementation, they should not mind being used in such a manner. Auditors should be aware, however, that they may be used to implement policies and procedures that they did not recommend and may not believe are in the best interest of the organization.

INITIATING COUNTERMEASURES

All three types of auditees pose a challenge to the auditor. Although the friendly auditee is the most desirable, countermeasures are required against all adverse reactions to the audit function. Without countermeasures, the auditors may be used in a manner they do not desire. Many auditors are oblivious to the fact that they are being used during the audit process. An awareness of the auditee attitude coupled with the appropriate countermeasure can put the audit process back on track.

The following four countermeasures are most commonly used by EDP auditors to counteract unfavorable reactions to EDP auditors and the audit process.

EDP Audit Education. Auditees are less afraid of something they understand. EDP auditing is new to many MIS professionals, and the time and effort taken to explain the role and responsibility of the EDP auditor can help gain acceptance and support of the EDP audit function. Among the methods used to provide this education are:
- Formal presentation to the MIS department
- Distribution of EDP audit work programs
- Report explaining EDP auditing.

Strong EDP Audit Image. A strong, respected EDP audit image gains the type of support needed to make the function effective. Image is enhanced through the following practices:
- Timely and well-developed audit reports
- Audit reports concentrating on key issues
- Well-structured audits
- Professional attitude by the audit staff.

Interaction with Auditees. The auditor must continually read the auditee reaction and respond immediately. When auditors believe the auditee is concerned about their actions, the process should be explained. This countermeasure uses public relations practices to encourage support. The practices that are helpful include:
- Entrance and exit conferences
- Explanations of what the auditors will do during the audit
- Issuance of interim oral or written reports.

EDP AUDITING

Strong Management Support. Nothing helps the audit process more than strong management support, which not only builds the confidence of auditors but also encourages auditee cooperation. Strong management support can be indicated by:
- Initiation of each audit by letter or personal visit
- Involvement if auditee replies are late or unrealistic
- Comments to auditee about the audit findings and recommendations

Most people do not want to be audited. When new areas are subject to audit for the first time, this normal resentment may erupt into open hostility. The EDP auditor must understand how this hostility can be interpreted and then do what is necessary to reduce or counteract any unfavorable reaction to the audit process.

Section XII
Quality Enhancement

Organizations today are preoccupied with improving the quality of their products. At Ford Motor Company, "Quality is Job Number One," and Lee Iacocca, in his autobiography, describes the extraordinary efforts expended by Chrysler Corporation to improve the quality of its products.

We in data processing have been concerned for years with the quality of our products and services, although few of us have initiated a formal program directed at improving quality. Quality circles have been seized on as a technique to improve quality, but they usually have proved fully effective only as part of an overall quality enhancement program.

The systems development life cycle should be a key focus of any quality enhancement program. Quality control can reduce systems development costs by helping management and supervisors detect errors early in the development process. Such techniques as design walkthroughs, work breakdown structures, comprehensive testing, software configuration management, and change management can help. Making use of the systems auditor can also help. Chapter XII-1, "Systems Development and Quality Control," describes these techniques and presents forms that can prove useful in documenting the QA process.

A program of software quality assurance is designed to ensure that software products and related documentation are reliable and maintainable. The program involves the review of software and documents for completeness, correctness, consistency, readability, and conformance to applicable standards and conventions. The two chapters titled "Software QA" and "Verification and Validation of Software" present a comprehensive approach to quality assurance. Depending on the size of the DP operation, the MIS manager may either draw on specific techniques discussed in this approach or use it as a model for developing a complete QA program.

XII-1
Systems Development and Quality Control
Richard Cotter

INTRODUCTION

The cost of fixing a defect during the requirements definition phase increases 10 times by the design phase, 1000 times by system acceptance, and 3000 times by actual system production (see Figure 1). Project managers, project team members, quality assurance analysts, and EDP auditors can correct potential defects as early as possible when they apply quality controls throughout the systems development life cycle.

Systems development is affected by four factors, which can be emphasized variedly throughout the life cycle: cost, schedule, requirements, and quality. For example, system cost can be reduced by eliminating a low-priority requirement or a schedule can be maintained by providing less documentation or testing.

Cost, schedule, and requirements are well understood by project managers and users and are therefore typically used to measure progress in the life cycle. Quality, an abstract concept little understood by many users and systems developers, usually suffers at the expense of adjusting the other three factors. It is imperative, however, that project managers and users understand quality as a measurable factor in systems development; it is an important and verifiable element of a successful system.

Definitions of Quality and Quality Control

Quality is conformance to requirements, including documented user requirements and the organization's requirements regarding development methodologies and security. Quality control is the process by which quality is measured.[1] A defect is the failure of system content, functionality, or performance to conform to the documented requirements.

QUALITY CONTROL TECHNIQUES

Five basic techniques are recommended to ensure system quality: a work breakdown structure, testing, walkthroughs, discrepancy/change management, and software configuration management. These techniques are described individually in the subsequent sections. Recommendations for draft-

QUALITY ENHANCEMENT

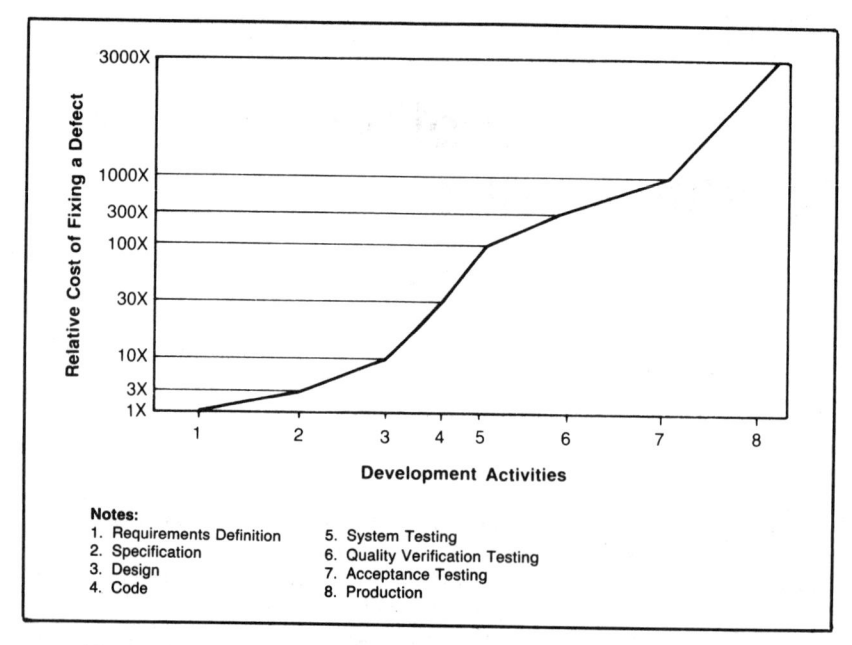

Figure 1. Cost Comparison by Development Phase of Fixing a Defect

Notes:
1. Requirements Definition
2. Specification
3. Design
4. Code
5. System Testing
6. Quality Verification Testing
7. Acceptance Testing
8. Production

ing a quality management plan that incorporates all or a combination of these techniques follow.

The Work Breakdown Structure

The work breakdown structure lists the project tasks, detailing what needs to be done and by whom, the start and completion dates, and the task prerequisites. Figure 2 shows a typical form for the work breakdown structure (sometimes called the project management system or project control system).

Testing

Because testing is such a vast and technically demanding area of quality control, it cannot be covered adequately in the scope of this chapter. The reader is therefore referred to the bibliography at the end of this chapter for further investigation.

Walkthroughs

Walkthroughs are semiformal meetings of technical personnel to identify system defects in an atmosphere of professional cooperation.[2] Defects are documented for later evaluation and correction on a walkthrough action list (see Figure 3). Management should not attend the walkthrough, recognizing it as a gathering of technical personnel with knowledge and interest related to the system at hand.

A walkthrough should be limited to four to seven persons and should include representatives from the development, user, and operations departments. The attendees register on a walkthrough sign-off form (see Figure 4).

WORK BREAKDOWN STRUCTURE

Project Name ____________________
Originator's Name ____________________
Originator's Dept ____________________

Project Acronym ____________________
Page ___ of ___
Date ____________________
Revision No. ____________________

Activity Network			Description	WBS Ref. No.	Responsibility		Worker-days			Start Date		Completion Date		
Current Action No.	Req'd by	Depends on			Name	Dept.	Est.	Act.	Diff.	Est.	Act.	Est.	Rev.	Act.

Figure 2. Work Breakdown Structure Form

QUALITY ENHANCEMENT

```
                    WALKTHROUGH ACTION LIST

  Discrepancy/Change Management No. (if applicable) _____
  Date of Walkthrough _____        Page _____ of _____
  Start Time _____ End Time _____ Location of Walkthrough _____
  Project Name _____ Acronym _____

  Identification of
  Walkthrough Material:
  Originator's Name:

  | No. |           ACTION ITEMS                    |
  |-----|-------------------------------------------|
  |     |                                           |
```

Figure 3. Walkthrough Action List

The group reviews a self-contained logical subset of the full system (e.g., edited input data code or test cases); the material should be limited to that which can be covered in a few hours.

When the walkthrough should be conducted depends on how the system is developed. Structured development provides logical units at regular intervals throughout the life cycle:

- Specification walkthroughs reveal errors, omissions, and ambiguities in the specifications for the system.
- Design walkthroughs uncover errors, omissions, and ambiguities in the design products.
- Code walkthroughs pinpoint errors in the code, complex coding that could affect maintenance, and coding that does not reflect design specifications.
- Test walkthroughs examine test cases (not test results) to ensure that they cover all conditions and logic paths.

```
┌─────────────────────────────────────────────────────────────┐
│                    WALKTHROUGH SIGNOFF                      │
│   Date of Walkthrough _____ Page ____ of ____   │
│   Start Time _____ End Time _____ Location of Walkthrough ____ │
│   Project Name _____ Acronym _____      │
├─────────────────────────────────────────────────────────────┤
│  Identification of                                          │
│  Walkthrough Material:                                      │
├─────────────────────────────────────────────────────────────┤
│  Originator's Name:                                         │
├──────────────────────┬──────────────────┬───────────────────┤
│   Names of Attendees │                  │                   │
│     (please print)   │    Signature     │    Department     │
├──────────────────────┴──────────────────┴───────────────────┤
│                                                             │
│                                                             │
│                                                             │
│                                                             │
│                                                             │
├─────────────────────────────────────────────────────────────┤
│  Individual or Group Comments:                              │
│                                                             │
├─────────────────────────────────────────────────────────────┤
│  Group Decision (one of the following):                     │
│                                                             │
│       Another Walkthrough Required _____ Accepted _____  │
└─────────────────────────────────────────────────────────────┘
```

Figure 4. Walkthrough Sign-Off Form

A coordinator should be designated to make arrangements for the room, distribute the material with sufficient lead time for review, see that order is maintained at the meeting, and record items noted as potential defects. An originator should be designated to prepare the material to be walked through; sufficient time should be allotted to send the material out for review by the other participants. The originator gives an overview of the material and then initiates a detailed discussion, addressing ambiguities, complex conditions, deviations from standards, omissions, and incomplete information. The discussion must be constructive and must center on the material under review, not on the originator.

At the end of the walkthrough, the coordinator asks the attendees whether they accept the material or require another walkthrough. Acceptance means that the attendees are either satisfied with the material or have minor reservations. Findings are documented on the walkthrough sign-off form, and the changes generate change request forms. The comments section of this form is for participants to document their impressions of the walkthrough.

QUALITY ENHANCEMENT

Discrepancy/Change Management

Discrepancy/change management comprises the procedures, policies, and personnel used to enhance the system or correct a defect at any point in the system development life cycle. This management system records the proposed change, tracks its evolution, and documents its final disposition; it interacts with software configuration management by authorizing software changes under its control. (Software configuration management is used to report the status of the change to discrepancy/change management.)

Forms and Log. Discrepancy/change management forms document requests to enhance or correct the software (see Figure 5). They should describe the need for the correction and the results of the discrepancy/change management assessment, assign an executor, and list the authorizing personnel as well as report the approved changes. The log records the number from each request form (see Figure 6); the status of each request is identified (e.g., received, under evaluation, being changed, or accepted or rejected).

Software Configuration Management

Software configuration management comprises the procedures, policies, personnel, and technical tools that enable an organization to control systems development. It identifies software components, controls the software changes, and details executed software changes and project status (see bibliography).

Identification. Software configuration management identifies the components of the applications software and assigns each a unique name in the development process. It also distinguishes between different versions of each component under development.

Controls. Software configuration management controls software changes during systems development and production by accepting only authorized requests with the necessary documentation and by ensuring that authorized changes are implemented in logical order. Although it rejects unauthorized change requests, it should log them.

Status Accounting. Software configuration management accounts for the status of each software component and version and lists past changes.

QUALITY MANAGEMENT PLAN

The quality management plan defines the user requirements in terms of quality rather than in terms of the functions that the new system is to provide. This plan emphasizes what the users expect from the system and how users and developers can determine when their expectations have been met.

The plan includes a statement of the quality attribute expected for each requirement, how the developers will achieve it, and the measures used to determine when that attribute has been achieved. The following 11 quality attributes are represented in every well-designed system:
- Correctness—The extent to which a system satisfies its specifications and fulfills user requirements

Systems Development Quality Control

```
┌─────────────────────────────────────────────────────────────────┐
│               DISCREPANCY/CHANGE MANAGEMENT FORM                │
│  Discrepancy/Change                                             │
│  Management No. _____                                       │
│  Originator's Name _____ Title _____ Dept ____  │
│  Project Name _____ Acronym _____ Date _____   │
│  Change is to                    Change is to CORRECT           │
│  ENHANCE the system _____      AN EXISTING PROBLEM _____   │
├─────────────────────────────────┬───────────────────────────────┤
│                                 │ Impact of Problem:            │
│  Failure: in Production _____  │ Immediate _____ $____  Loss  │
│           in Development _____  │ Potential _____ $____  in    │
│                                 │ Long-Range _____ $____ Assets │
├─────────────────────────────────┴───────────────────────────────┤
│  Severity of Failure/Discrepancy:                               │
│  Terminal ____ Severe ____ Moderate ____ Minimal ____ Trivial __│
├─────────────────────────────────────────────────────────────────┤
│  Describe the Enhancement or Correction:                        │
│                                                                 │
│                                                                 │
│                                                                 │
├─────────────────────────────────────────────────────────────────┤
│  Disposition of Discrepancy/Change Management Form              │
│  (from systems developer):                                      │
│                                                                 │
│                                                                 │
│                                                                 │
│  Requires                                                       │
│  Changes to:                                                    │
│  Documentation _____ Software _____ JCL _____ Data Base _____ Other _____│
├─────────────────────────────────────────────────────────────────┤
│  Responsibility          Approximate Date of Implementation ____│
│  Name_____ Title _____ Dept _____ │
├─────────────────────────────────────────────────────────────────┤
│  Authorizing Signatures                                         │
│    Systems: _____ Title _____ Dept _____ │
│    User: _____ Title _____ Dept _____ │
└─────────────────────────────────────────────────────────────────┘
```

Figure 5. Discrepancy/Change Management Form

- Reliability—The extent to which a system is expected to perform its intended function with required precision on a consistent basis
- Efficiency—The amount of computer resources and code required by a system to perform a function
- Integrity—The extent to which access to software or data by unauthor-

QUALITY ENHANCEMENT

DISCREPANCY/CHANGE MANAGEMENT LOG

Project Name _____ Project Acronym _____
Originator's Name _____ Originator's Dept _____

Discrepancy/Change Management No.	Originator	Originating Dept	Date Received	Person Responsible	Status	Disposition of Form	Disposition Date	Total Days with Project

Figure 6. Discrepancy/Change Management Log

ized persons can be controlled
- Usability—The effort required to learn, operate, and prepare input to and interpret output of a system
- Maintainability—The effort required to test a system to ensure that it performs its intended functions
- Testability—The effort required to locate and fix a system error
- Flexibility—The effort required to modify the system
- Portability—The effort required to transfer a system from one hardware or software configuration or environment to another
- Reusability—The extent to which a system or its parts can be used in other applications
- Interoperability—The effort required to couple one system with another

Users and developers must work together to determine the attributes that best suit the specified business requirement. One attribute may satisfy several requirements. Conversely, several conflicting attributes (e.g., maintainability and efficiency) may fit one requirement; in this case, priorities must be assigned to each attribute.

The developers should review the quality attributes and determine the best techniques for attaining them. For example, maintainability might require writing structured program modules with comments built into the code. The selected techniques are documented in the second part of the quality management plan.

The plan also provides measurements for each quality attribute. For example, maintainability could be defined as fewer than 300 statements per module or as a mean time to fix of two days maximum for each module; reliability could be defined as a mean time between failures of 20 days. The quality management plan documents quality requirements, techniques, and measurements in a concise and accessible format.

AUDITOR INVOLVEMENT IN QUALITY CONTROL

Data processing is integral to the success of most organizations. Management therefore recognizes its significance and seeks assurance that systems are adequately designed, tested, implemented, and controlled. Although auditors are often called on to satisfy this function, quality assurance groups are gaining prominence. The quality analyst is equipped with specialized tools, techniques, technical jargon, and development methodologies that require in-depth DP expertise in assessing the adequacy of quality control in the systems development environment.

EDP audit and quality assurance should work together to ensure that the audit and quality review plans do not duplicate effort and that an assessment of every type of control has been addressed by one of the two groups. The quality analyst and the auditor use many of the same practices in performing their respective functions. By cooperating, the quality analyst gains a better perspective on internal controls and the auditor becomes more aware of the problems of systems development, thus obtaining the insight to recommend reasonable and workable systems criteria.

When an auditor determines that quality control is lacking, management should be made aware of the potential benefits of its implementation. The

QUALITY ENHANCEMENT

recommendations to implement quality control may be directed to other DP groups as well as senior management. For example, recommendations should be presented to the standards group, documenting the quality control methods in the DP development methodology. DP training might be informed of what the quality control processes are, how they work, how they benefit the company, and when they should be invoked.

The EDP auditor could also recommend that a quality assurance group be formed to review the quality control processes used by the systems developers and the adequacy and effectiveness of systems controls. Quality assurance would also promote awareness of quality in the systems development and user communities.

Notes

1. P.B. Crosby, *Quality is Free* (New York: New American Library, 1979); J.M. Juran, *Quality Control Handbook* (New York: McGraw-Hill, 1974).
2. G.M. Weinberg, *The Psychology of Computer Programming* (New York: Van Nostrand Reinhold, 1971).

Bibliography

Bersoff, E.H., et al. *Software Configuration Management, An Investment in Product Integrity.* Englewood Cliffs NJ: Prentice-Hall, 1980.

Cooper, J.D., and Fisher, M.J., eds. *Software Quality Management.* New York: Petrocelli Books, 1979.

Perry, W.E. *Effective Methods of EDP Quality Assurance.* Wellesley MA: Q.E.D. Information Sciences, 1977.

Freedman, D.P., and Weinberg, G.M. *Handbook of Walkthroughs, Inspections, and Technical Reviews.* Wellesley MA: Q.E.D. Information Sciences, 1982.

Yourdon, E. *Managing the Structured Techniques.* New York: Yourdon Press, 1979.

XII-2
Software QA
Lynda E. Edwards

INTRODUCTION

The past decade has been marked by numerous breakthroughs in improved systems design, development, and maintenance. Their application alone, however, guarantees neither the efficiency nor the effectiveness of DP activities.

Many DP operations are growing rapidly as more functions are automated and more complex systems are built. Even well-organized, disciplined operations are reexperiencing traditional DP problems, such as frequent delays in schedule, cost overruns, inadequate or unreliable software, and an apparent lack of acceptable developmental and operational standards and guidelines. These problems are partly caused by accelerated growth, which, along with dramatic staff growth and increased technological and organizational complexity, severely strains MIS management.

In this environment, an effective Quality Assurance (QA) function can enhance MIS management and operations. It establishes a quality-oriented environment with reduced crisis management through problem avoidance. Consistent rules and methods are also established for a disciplined development process that ensures the integrity of product development and production systems. In addition, the level of productivity and productivity improvement awareness increases. The key to gaining these advantages is the successful standardization and institutionalization of many MIS management and technical functions and the consistent application of resultant standards and guidelines. Software QA must play a leading role in the management of data processing and must have processes and checkpoints that permit the identification of problems before they occur. A quality assurance staff should be able to identify and understand technical issues while applying management judgment to formulate recommended solutions.

QUALITY ASSURANCE PLANNING

As with other project functions, successful implementation of a QA program depends heavily on QA planning during the early phases of the software development life cycle (SDLC). To accomplish this, the designated QA manager should completely review early project documentation (e.g., system specifications and the project plan). The review culminates in tailoring QA procedures to standardize QA functions, tasks, and responsibilities and to

QUALITY ENHANCEMENT

identify the QA tools needed to ensure sufficient software quality. Software quality is measured by accountability and reliability as well as by the ability to be tested, used, and maintained. The resulting QA manual or plan is then reviewed by functional members of the development staff and approved by the systems development manager. After QA procedures approval, QA tasks are assigned. These assignments are usually based on level of effort and must remain flexible to adapt to the needs of the current phase in the SDLC, shifts in areas needing attention, and unscheduled demands placed on QA by the systems development manager.

The systems development manager ensures that the QA manager and staff know exactly what tasks are to be done and the time frame for completion. The QA manager must ensure that task descriptions, technical responsibilities of QA personnel, staffing requirements, and communication and approval routes are executed correctly.

QA Tasks

The systems development manager, the QA manager, and the intended user group must set realistic milestones for accomplishing the following QA tasks:

- Establishing standards and conventions for design, coding, testing, and documentation
- Preparing forms and procedures for each review task
- Reviewing design and related documentation at specified points during the course of software development
- Reviewing code listings
- Reviewing test plans and procedures for conformance to established standards and conventions
- Reviewing all other documentation (including user and maintenance manuals)
- Participating in formal configuration audits
- Conducting informal audits of the configuration management (CM) function
- Planning for the transfer of QA responsibilities to operations personnel

Methods for accomplishing these tasks are described later. The QA manager's function includes reviewing and evaluating systems development performance. This implies at least limited participation by the QA manager in one or more of the tasks listed.

Technical Responsibilities

Because the technical responsibilities of the QA staff involve the enforcement of standards and conventions to be used in the design, coding, and testing of software and in the preparation of related documentation, a thorough understanding of good software practices is necessary. Standards and conventions must be explicitly described in a QA plan or manual to avoid ambiguity and misunderstanding. It is not sufficient for a manual merely to recommend that good software practices be followed.

Although the QA staff is not directly responsible for the technical validity of software standards and conventions, it must still understand some techni-

Software QA

cal issues. This knowledge prevents the staff from enforcing impractical or infeasible standards. The QA manager should ensure that an adequate QA program is formulated and that the applicable standards and conventions are established and enforced. In addition, the manager must be able to distinguish between actual and apparent adherence to standards. The ability to make such a distinction requires a thorough understanding of the required standards and a solid background in the use of software development tools and techniques.

Although some of these activities may be carried out by the use of automated tools, QA personnel must still choose the proper tool and apply it correctly. Several types of automated programming standards enforcers are available. Most are language or machine specific and therefore not applicable to all projects. In addition, the standards enforcer selected must check for violations of the appropriate standards. For example, some standards enforcers do not check for parameter passing conventions and permissible construct utilization.

Staffing Requirements

QA personnel must have some technical expertise and knowledge of effective software and QA practices to enforce established standards and conventions.

A member of the organization's operations staff should be represented in the design/development effort early in the SDLC. This representative may assist the systems development manager in choosing a QA manager and staff.

The systems development manager may also employ a consulting service if system size or complexity, time, or staffing constraints warrant it. In such a case, the systems development manager must at least designate a QA monitor to oversee the QA activities of the contractor. (In extremely large, complex development efforts, the QA monitor should be assisted by appropriate staff.)

The QA staff must be independent of actual development activities, with the QA manager reporting directly to the systems development manager. Such factors as staff size, estimated work load, and personnel skills must be considered when choosing the organizational structure of the QA staff. Several options follow:

- Each staff member performs one QA task for all software products; for example, one member is responsible for evaluating all documentation.
- Each staff member performs all QA tasks associated with a particular software product; for example, one member monitors and reviews all design, coding, testing, and documentation procedures for one program.
- The QA organization is a team in which all members perform the QA tasks. Team leadership might rotate depending on specific personnel skills.

The QA staff should examine the output of the program development staff for conformance of deliverable software and related documentation to QA specifications. Although the QA manager and the representative of the opera-

QUALITY ENHANCEMENT

tions staff must be aware of all QA functions throughout the SDLC, the QA staff actually performs the QA activities.

Communication/Approval Routes

During program initiation, the systems development manager should establish communication routes and encourage communication between the QA manager and development personnel. It also must be determined whether this communication should be carried on interactively or in the form of after-the-fact approval. An open working relationship should be established between the two groups. A QA organization viewed by development as an adversary threatens the success of the project. The QA manager should work directly with the development staff to resolve all questions, with final sign-off being the responsibility of the systems development manager.

QA SUPPORT DURING DEVELOPMENT

The QA staff should prepare forms and procedures to be used for reviews at each stage of development (i.e., design, coding, testing, and final auditing). These should be prepared well in advance of the actual reviews. A sample general nonconformance report is illustrated in Figure 1. Although specialized forms may be developed for each development phase, all nonconformance reports should include the information contained in the sample.

When an irregularity or deficiency is identified and reported to the development staff, the QA staff must formally handle the nonconformance report to ensure that the problem is corrected. Depending on the type of problem, a second review may be necessary after the problem has been corrected. The review and approval cycle of each report must include a review by the QA manager. The verification and validation (V&V) manager should also participate when any substantial changes to test plans or procedures are necessary. Final QA approval should not be given until all corrections have been made and approved. The QA manager signs off on the report upon successful completion of the correction cycle.

Design Reviews

The four major design reviews in the typical software life cycle are system requirements review, preliminary design review, system design review, and critical design review. The QA organization participates in these formal reviews and possibly in other informal reviews. The QA role throughout this process is to ensure adherence to design and documentation standards and conventions by identifying, reporting, and ensuring correction of deficiencies.

Method. Material is reviewed for adherence to format standards, clarity of objectives, acceptable writing style, and consistency of cross-references. Technical content is examined for inclusion of:
- Software development plans
- Task assignment and authorization procedures
- Configuration management plans

Software QA

```
                                        No. _____
                                        Priority _____
                   Nonconformance Report (NR)

Project Name _____
Nonconforming Area _____
                    (e.g., design modularity, unstructured code)
Associated NR _____
Item Involved _____
                (e.g., module name, test ID, subprogram, line no.)
Originated by _____ Date _____
Validated by _____ Date _____
              (QA manager)
───────────────────────────────────────────────────────────
Description of Nonconformance:
(detailed description of problem)


───────────────────────────────────────────────────────────
Assigned to _____ Date _____
───────────────────────────────────────────────────────────
Description of Corrective Action Required:
(specific changes required)


Review of Correction Needed?    Yes _____    No _____
───────────────────────────────────────────────────────────
Approvals:

_____  _____
Responsible Manager      Date   QA Manager               Date

                                _____
                                QA Monitor (if applicable) Date
```

Figure 1. Sample Nonconformance Report

- Requirements specifications
- Design documents
- Interface design specification
- Design implementation plans
- Software standards
- Test plans and procedures
- Acceptance test plans
- User manuals

Not all of these items will be available at the same review, but they should be examined at some time during the life cycle for conformance to standards and conventions. For example, during preliminary design review, computer program functional flow descriptions are checked for conformance to design conventions as required by established standards. The structure and organiza-

QUALITY ENHANCEMENT

tion of data bases are examined for the correct identification and characterization of all data types and for the proper form of the structure layout. Functional interfaces, as described in the interface design specification, are checked for correct message formats and word lengths. Test documentation is reviewed for compatibility with program objectives and adequacy.

The following documents, more detailed than those presented at preliminary design review, should be examined in the same manner during critical design review:
- Program description document, with program design language
- Storage allocation charts
- Test documentation
- Test requirements
- Detailed interface design specification.

Problem Identification. The QA staff checks specific design criteria at the design review. This checking can be done manually by carefully examining all design documentation, including software development plans, for conformance to applicable standards and conventions. The use of requirements specification languages and program design languages facilitates the review process and allows the use of automated tools for analysis, including automated standards checkers and automated design language verifiers. Examples of these languages are Gypsy, developed by the University of Texas at Austin, and SPECIAL, developed by SRI International. Sample questions regarding established design standards and conventions are listed in Table 1.

Table 1. Design Criteria

Modularity
Does each component have a single entry point and a single exit point?
Is each component restricted to one function?
Do components have a high degree of strength?
Are components loosely coupled?
Are components predictable?
Is each component small enough to be readily comprehended?

Hierarchical Top-Down Design
Is the design hierarchical?
Do levels of the hierarchy correspond to levels of program control?
Is each level small enough to be viewed and accomplished within a reasonable time?
Are functional flow diagrams comprehensible?
Do these functional flow diagrams show the hierarchical nature of the design?
Does the topmost level include the basic control functions?
Has the topmost level been specified first?
Has each succeeding level been specified in order?

System Interfaces
Have all interfaces with other systems/subsystems been specified?
Does the design take into account the purpose of each interface and the data to be exchanged?
Is the interface design understandable?

Data Base Structure
Are common data items identified and described?
Does the terminology in the data base description document conform to that in the program design specification?
Is the structure understandable?
Has the particular application (e.g., funds transfer) been adequately addressed in the design?

Software QA

A design review may reveal some deficiencies in the design and its related documentation. Some of these may indicate noncompliance with format standards and conventions and should be easily corrected. Other deficiencies may violate modularity or hierarchical, top-down design standards and require a costly redesign effort. Many of the graver problems can be prevented by a more active QA role during the design phase of software development.

The QA responsibility is to confirm that the design criteria are satisfied. Correction of noncompliance may be the responsibility of V&V or configuration management. If the design is not technically correct, the V&V staff takes action. If the documentation is incomplete or does not correspond to current design, the CM staff is responsible for correcting it.

Code Reviews

Each program listing should be reviewed for substance and style. The review of the technical correctness of the program, its completeness, and its correspondence to the design is a V&V function. The initial review of all program source listings for adherence to coding standards and conventions should occur as soon as possible after each component is first entered in the program support library so that violations of the established standards can be corrected promptly. Because program components usually change, however, each listing should be periodically reviewed for possible violations made after the initial review. In particular, QA should again review all program source listings before the physical configuration audit. This audit is the formal comparison of the "as-built" configuration of a unit of programs or modules with its technical documentation to establish the unit's initial product configuration identification. The configuration identification provides a means of traceability and accountability for that unit as it progresses through the development cycle.

Method. Manual or automated techniques may be used for code review; the choice depends on the number and size of the listings to be reviewed and the availability of automated tools to review code written in the particular programming language(s).

Problem Identification. The QA staff should look for such problems as:
- Use of unauthorized programming languages
- Use of unstructured code where not permitted
- Violation of naming conventions (e.g., data base, program, symbol, or statement)
- Improper column alignment
- Violation of convention for use of embedded blanks or leading zeros
- Incorrect form of diagnostic messages
- Incomplete or improper initialization of memory
- Use of prohibited I/O techniques
- Insufficient comment statements

V&V, rather than the QA staff, is responsible for detecting such problems as incorrect program logic, inefficient programming techniques, unreachable code and nonterminating loops, and lack of correspondence between code and detailed design.

QUALITY ENHANCEMENT

Testing Reviews

The QA staff should review all integration plans, including test plans, procedures, and reports, to verify that they adhere to the established testing standards. Testing documents must be reviewed manually because no automated tools for analysis of test plans and procedures are currently available. In addition to examining test-related documentation, QA witnesses the execution of all tests to verify conformance to established procedures.

The QA staff should search for violations of approved standards of program integration and testing. Examples of possible violations are use of bottom-up integration methods, integration in advance of unit testing, and omission of regression testing when a major module is added to a system. The QA staff should identify all instances of nonconformance to procedures during execution and should examine all reports to ensure that results are accurately recorded. It must also verify that all required tests are executed and reported. The V&V manager should be informed of these testing reviews in case substantial changes to test plans or procedures are necessary.

Documentation Reviews

All software-related documentation is read and reviewed by the QA staff for conformance to the established standards and conventions. These documents include the system specification, software configuration management plan, software quality assurance plan, software development plan, program performance specification, program design specification, interface design specification, program listings, test plans/specifications, test procedures/reports, program maintenance manuals, user manuals, and the program description document.

Method. The QA staff should review each document in its three stages:
- Draft—First typed version
- Preliminary—Version to be printed
- Final—Version to be delivered

A sample checklist for the documentation review is given in Figure 2.

A QA review cycle for such informal documents as monthly progress reports is also desirable, but it should be shorter than for formal ones.

Problem Identification. The QA staff should search for errors in format, spelling, and grammar, violation of documentation standards and conventions, obscure style, typographical mistakes, sections or pages out of order, and missing or duplicate sections or pages. Readability should not be sacrificed to technical sophistication. For example, all abbreviations and acronyms should be spelled out the first time they are mentioned. Whenever possible, examples, figures, tables, and graphs should be used to clarify content.

Different types of documents require different emphasis in the review. The QA staff must take these differences into account when examining the documents for acceptable style. Specifications should be checked for completeness and to ensure that program organization is described in sufficient detail. Superfluous and esoteric language should not be permitted. User manuals and other operational support documents should be clearly written, with many examples and step-by-step procedures.

Software QA

Document Title _____		Version Number _____
Item	OK	Unacceptable–Recommendation
Proofreading Complete		
Pagination		
Paragraphing		
Figure/Table Sequence		
Margins		
Heads and Feet		
Spacing		
Type/Line Density		
Symbols		
Abbreviations		
Titles, Legends Match Text References		
Line Weights and Lettering Sizes Consistent throughout Publication		
Reviewed by _____ Initial Approval _____ Final Approval _____		Date _____ Date _____ Date _____

Figure 2. QA Checklist for Documentation

Configuration Audits

The QA staff performs two functions during configuration audits. It supports the CM staff, which has primary responsibility for these audits, and it performs its usual function of checking for adherence to established standards and conventions, using comment forms and discrepancy notices. A comment form explains, illustrates, or criticizes the meaning of the text. The QA staff should investigate these comments, but corrective action is not necessary to successfully complete the audit. A discrepancy notice indicates items that are inadequately identified or that do not comply with established standards and conventions. It should clearly note the difference between actual and desired conditions. These discrepancies must be corrected in order to successfully complete the audit. In support of CM, the QA staff should monitor the processing of nonconformance reports, discrepancy notices, and other CM action items.

Two formal configuration audits occur near the end of the software development phase, prior to the operation/maintenance phase of the life cycle.

QUALITY ENHANCEMENT

These are the functional configuration audit, to verify that configuration items perform as specified, and the physical configuration audit, a formal examination of the code against its technical documentation. The QA activities for each of these audits are similar, although different items are audited.

Functional Configuration Audit. Before this audit, the development staff should supply a list of items to be audited. At the time of the audit, this list is checked to verify that all items are available, complete, and current. The QA staff also checks the list of current documentation, including user manuals, to ensure that it is complete, and it prepares a list of the documentation and computer programs that should be available at the physical configuration audit.

Physical Configuration Audit. The QA staff should confirm that current listings are correctly identified and available for each computer program component. Supporting data is reviewed to ensure that it is the correct type and quantity. The following items should be checked for proper entries and format:
- Program design specifications
- Computer program component descriptions and interface requirements (e.g., interface design specifications)
- Functional flow diagrams
- Data base descriptions
- Storage allocation charts
- Handbooks and manuals
- Program description document.

Informal Audits. In addition to the two formal configuration audits, frequent informal audits should be conducted to monitor all project activities. The scheduling of these informal audits should be a part of the QA plan. The QA staff thus monitors the preparation of all project documentation and identifies any nonconforming areas before the document is finalized. Any problems discovered during these informal audits should be formally reported and their correction validated.

QA SUPPORT DURING OPERATION AND MAINTENANCE

Although QA participation is reduced during the operation/maintenance phase of the SDLC, the QA staff must review new or updated software products and documentation.

New requirements generated during operation and maintenance and correction of system errors usually necessitate a design change. The QA staff must verify that all design modifications are implemented and documented according to applicable standards and conventions.

The QA staff must review all code modifications and additions and all new or revised documentation to verify conformance to applicable standards and conventions. Verification of the technical correctness, accuracy, and completeness of the updates is a V&V function. The QA staff should, however, review any new or altered test plans or procedures for conformance to the testing standards.

QA is responsible for making and enforcing revisions to standards and conventions. The standards and conventions manual may need revision after formal system acceptance. Changes in accepted programming techniques, the emergence of a better programming language, or the addition of a new functional requirement for which the previously authorized languages are not well suited may necessitate revisions.

CONCLUSION

QA includes developing project standards and monitoring technical audits of software products and processes. The application of prescribed QA procedures, tools, and techniques during the SDLC ensures that the software product meets or exceeds specified standards, or, if such standards do not exist, that the software is of acceptable quality.

Software QA is designed to provide accurate and sufficient planning, controlling, and reporting to ensure the development of software products that meet user requirements. With its independent, projectwide visibility, the QA organization is uniquely situated to anticipate and identify problems. QA must actively participate in the decision-making process of the MIS organization and should be in a position to influence direction and strategy if management wants to realize the maximum benefit.

Bibliography

1. Bryan, William L. "The Practical Application of Software Product Assurance." ACM/NBS. *19th Annual Technical Symposium,* 1980, pp. 131–135.
2. Edwards, Lynda E. "Software Verification and Validation." *Data Processing Management.* Pennsauken NJ: AUERBACH Publishers Inc, Portfolio 4-04-05.
3. Myers, Glenford J. *Software Reliability.* New York: John Wiley and Sons, 1976.
4. Parnas, David L. "On the Criteria to Be Used in Decomposing Systems into Modules." *Communications of the ACM,* Vol. 15, No. 12 (December 1972), 1,053–1,058.

XII-3
Verification and Validation of Software
Lynda E. Edwards

INTRODUCTION

Software verification and validation (V&V) is the process of confirming that system requirements are accurately stated, that the software is being developed in accordance with the stated specifications, and that in the operational environment it satisfactorily performs the functions for which it was designed. Verification substantiates that the requirements, design, and code are complete and consistent with each other. It involves the review of all software documents at each stage of the software life cycle to ensure that they conform to earlier documents and ultimately to the requirements.

Validation confirms the feasibility and testability of requirements and the correctness of design and code. It involves exercising and analyzing the software to ensure its performance according to specifications and to discover latent errors. The validation effort further guarantees a correct system by comparing expected results with actual performance when the system is extensively exercised.

V&V PLANNING

To achieve maximum benefits, an organization should establish a V&V program at project initiation (or at contract award if all or part of the development is being contracted for). However, it can also be initiated during a later phase of projects already in development. The following sections describe the steps necessary for planning an adequate V&V program.

Scope of V&V Effort

Because V&V covers a broad spectrum of possible activities, the project manager must tailor the scope of the V&V effort to each particular project. A full-scale V&V effort includes:
- Verification and validation of requirements and design
- Preparation and review of system performance test requirements, specifications, and procedures
- Verification and validation of such documents as user manual, operator manual, and program description document

QUALITY ENHANCEMENT

- Verification and validation of source code
- Integration, system, and acceptance testing
- Review of test plans, procedures, specifications, and reports
- Participation in all reviews and audits
- Planning for transition of V&V responsibilities to the operation/maintenance (O/M) staff

Such comprehensive V&V activity is appropriate to large, highly critical projects where system reliability is particularly essential. Minimal V&V activity, on the other hand, might only involve verification of the project documentation, approval of the criteria for acceptance testing, and witnessing the software system and acceptance testing. Such a scaled-down effort is appropriate only to a small, well-defined project with minimal interfacing between a few nearly independent software modules in a noncritical application.

Table 1 lists criteria to be considered in determining project complexity. A value should be assigned to each factor based on its complexity. The sum of the individual factor values indicates overall complexity. No hard-and-fast rules can be made relating a given complexity total to a certain level of V&V effort, although obviously very complex projects (e.g., total complexity value between 35 and 45) require a comprehensive effort. The program or the MIS manager must decide how much effort to expend.

Verification and validation should be performed at every stage of the software life cycle. This approach is called constructive V&V and requires the active participation of V&V personnel throughout each phase. When this commitment is impossible (e.g., for programs in later stages of development), evaluative V&V can still be performed. This technique involves retroactively verifying the completeness and consistency of documentation and validating the correct operation of the software.

Although more difficult to manage, an ongoing V&V effort is more valuable than one performed when development is complete. The V&V activities are repeated during O/M whenever changes requiring new development are implemented. Therefore, the V&V effort spans the entire software life cycle, and all V&V activities must be carefully planned so that they are synchronized with the traditional software development process. Whenever a software product is produced, the V&V personnel who will review it should be trained and ready to perform their functions. If the software development has been contracted out, the project manager's V&V monitor works with and oversees the contractor's V&V personnel throughout the entire effort.

Independent V&V

To provide an unbiased evaluation of the software, the project manager should have an independent V&V group. The systems development manager has a vested interest in software development and, because errors reflect poorly on the project, is unlikely to insist on a thorough V&V effort. The independent V&V manager has no such conflict of interest and is free to devote every resource to the effort.

The complexity and criticality of the project determines the degree of independence necessary. For small, well-defined, noncritical projects, an inde-

Software Verification and Validation

Table 1. Level of Project Complexity

Factors \ Complexity	1	2	3	4	5	Value
1. Originality Required	None, Reprogram on Different Equipment	Minimum, More Stringent Requirements	Limited, More Environment, New Interfaces	Considerable, Apply Existing State of the Art to Environment	Extensive, Requires Advance in State of the Art	
2. Degree of Generality	Highly Restricted, Single Purpose	Restricted, Parameterized for a Range of Capacities	Limited Flexibility, Allows Some Change in Format	Multipurpose, Flexible Format, Range of Applications	Very Flexible, Able to Handle a Broad Range of Applications on Different Equipment	
3. Change in Scope and Objective	None	Infrequent	Occasional	Frequent	Continuous	
4. Equipment Complexity	Single Machine, Routine Processing	Single Machine, Routine Processing, Extended Peripheral System	Multicomputer, Standard Peripheral System	Multicomputer, Advanced Programming, Complex Peripheral System	Master Control System, Multicomputer, Auto I/O and Display Equipment	
5. Personnel Assigned	1-2	3-5	5-10	10-18	18 and over	
6. Developmental Cost	$1,000–$12,000	$12,000–$60,000	$60,000–$250,000	$250,000–$600,000	More than $600,000	
7. Criticality	Data Processing	Routine Operations	Personnel Safety	Operational Accomplishment	Operational Survival	
8. Average Response Time to Program Changes	2 or More Weeks	1-2 Weeks	3-7 Days	1-3 Days	1-24 Hours	
9. Average Response Time to Data Input	2 or More Weeks	1-2 Weeks	1-7 Days	1-24 Hours	0-60 Minutes	
					Total	

QUALITY ENHANCEMENT

pendent group within the MIS organization may be used. Members may also belong to the organization's independent test group. An independent contractor may be employed on large or critical projects to allow even greater separation of responsibility between the development and V&V groups.

Regardless of the approach used, the V&V group must be established early. Management must address the issue of independent V&V during the project initiation phase. If a separate V&V contractor is not employed, the systems development manager must submit a V&V plan to ensure the necessary degree of independence of the V&V staff. Since contractors in any contract environment may be hesitant to allow a competitor access to their software development process without a formal agreement, the development contract should specify the documents required and the degree of participation by an independent V&V contractor.

Staffing Requirements

A member of the project manager's staff should be selected to manage the organization's V&V group or to monitor the independent V&V contractor. This individual should be familiar with modern software development practices and knowledgeable about V&V. The V&V staff should understand the concept of V&V as presented in this chapter; problems can arise if V&V is viewed as merely testing. The V&V manager or monitor should also work with a representative of the O/M staff so that the V&V effort continues throughout the entire software life cycle.

Communication/Approval Routes

The project manager should establish communication/approval routes at project initiation. Reports are submitted directly to the project manager. The V&V manager is then responsible for informing the development staff or contractor of any deficiencies in the software. If a development contractor provides an independent V&V group, communication must be independent of the software development group. Final approval and notification of completed V&V activities is the responsibility of the project manager with the support of the V&V manager or monitor.

Reporting Problems

The V&V group should prepare forms for reporting and tracking all problems discovered during the systems development life cycle. These forms should list the following information:
- Identification of deficient document
- Location of deficiency within document
- Precise nature of deficiency
- Person reporting deficiency
- Report date
- V&V manager or monitor's signature and date
- Person assigned responsibility for correcting deficiency
- Deadline for correcting deficiency
- Priority of this effort (optional)
- Brief description of method of correction
- V&V manager or monitor's signature after verifying correction and date

Software Verification and Validation

A review and approval cycle for problem reports should also be established. Every report should be reviewed by the V&V manager or monitor who should sign off upon correction of each reported deficiency.

A general form can be used for all problem reporting, or special forms can be designed for each aspect of V&V. Figure 1 shows a sample form for reporting a software discrepancy discovered during code analysis.

Software Discrepancy Report			
Module Name: Source Listing/ID/Page:		Routine Name: Entry Point: Line Numbers:	
Analysis:	Date:	Priority:	
Correction:	Date:	Approval:	Date:
Impact:	The routine will not work correctly. The routine is inefficient. The routine is not easily maintainable. Other.		_____ _____ _____ _____
Description:			
Comments:			
Suggestions:			

Figure 1. Sample Software Discrepancy Report

REQUIREMENTS ANALYSIS

As mentioned, V&V activities must be initiated early in the software life cycle to achieve maximum benefits. The first phase of the software life cycle requiring V&V activity is the requirements analysis. Methods for performing this analysis follow.

Evaluation of Requirements

System requirements, which should be defined in terms of user needs, include functional specifications, performance requirements, design constraints, and context analysis.

Functional specifications should state the function to be performed by the system, how it will interface with the user, and why it should function this way. The required response time, timing requirements, and required system throughput should be noted in the performance requirements. Whether the system will be dedicated or shared is also specified. Design constraints should include the hardware configuration, the system's requirement for de-

QUALITY ENHANCEMENT

velopment of new hardware, and the system's availability and data capacity. The primary and secondary memory storage requirements and alternative design approaches should also be provided. In a context analysis, the external system interfaces and the physical environment are defined.

Studying the software requirements document to verify that these specifications are adequately stated is a V&V function. Requirements analysis is traditionally performed with the aid of checklists that describe general attributes of acceptable requirements. Several attributes are:

- Consistency—Each requirement should contain uniform notation, terminology, and symbology within the requirements document.
- Necessity—Each requirement should be essential for achieving the goals of the system.
- Sufficiency—The requirements document should be examined for missing or incomplete requirements.
- Feasibility—Requirements should be analyzed to determine whether they can be implemented using existing hardware and technology.
- Testability—It should be possible to construct tests to determine if a requirement has been satisfied.
- Traceability—It should be possible to verify that each software requirement has its origin in the system requirements or user needs.
- Clarity—Each requirement should be written so that it is readily understood.

Analytic Methods

Methods for analyzing requirements include comparisons with related project documentation, existing systems, and standard references; simulation and analytic modeling; and timing analysis.

Because software requirements are almost always expressed in natural-language text, automated tools are rarely used in requirements analysis.

DESIGN ANALYSIS

Each element in a software design can be analyzed according to its ability to meet the desirable properties of the final product. These properties and the methods for analyzing them are discussed in the following paragraphs.

Design Evaluation

During the preliminary design stage of full-scale development, the software requirements are translated into a software system design, or the program performance specification. The major subsystems of the software architecture are described, the modules that comprise them are defined, and the functional capabilities of the total system are allocated among these subsystems and modules. Specific algorithms to be used in each module are selected, and each module is allocated its timing and sizing requirements. High-level internal and external system interfaces are defined, and the general flow of control and data through these interfaces is specified. The design of each module is completed later during the detailed design stage, based on the program performance specification.

Software Verification and Validation

The following elements can be part of a software design:
- Mathematical equations
- Mathematical or logical algorithms
- Module descriptions (input/process/output)
- Module interfaces
- External system interfaces
- Data flow diagrams
- Descriptions of and references to data structures

These elements can be analyzed by using informal checklists similar to those used for requirements analysis. Some important properties of a design are:[1]
- Consistency—Module interfaces should be consistent. Data base formats should be compared to input data formats.
- Traceability—Each design element should be traceable to a requirement.
- Sufficiency—Each requirement should be implemented by one or more design elements.
- Correctness—The correctness of mathematical equations and computational algorithms should be checked. The correctness of control logic in the design should be analyzed.

Analytic Methods

Several methods can be used to analyze the design properties. Cross-referencing design elements and requirements can verify both the necessity and sufficiency of the design elements. Comparing common parts of different design elements can help ensure the consistency of interfaces. Control logic can be checked by analyzing each logical path through the top levels of a top-down design to confirm that different logical paths correspond to different classes of data. Analytical models that represent the system mathematically can be used to evaluate algorithms and equations during the design stages. These models improve reliability by ensuring that the chosen algorithms meet specified accuracy and performance requirements.

Computational algorithms can be verified by functional analysis. This involves examining the actions taken for different classes of input data to verify that they result in different types of output. Mathematical equations can be verified by comparing them with independently derived equations and standard references. Unit analysis is also useful in verifying the correctness of equations by analyzing the physical units (e.g., time, mass, distance) of each term in the equation and checking that the units on both sides of the equation correspond. Design inspections and structured walkthroughs are also frequently used methods of design analysis.

Several manual and automated tools can facilitate software design analysis. The U.S. Army Ballistic Missile Defense Advanced Technology Center uses a process design methodology to develop system designs from performance requirements. The use of a programming design language is an essential part of this methodology. Computer Science Corporation, TRW, and RCA all use Threads, a vehicle for representing input/processing/output at successively lower levels of detail, to trace requirements through detailed design.

Requirements specification languages, such as SPECIAL (Stanford Research Institute) and GYPSY (University of Texas at Austin), are being used

QUALITY ENHANCEMENT

to state design specifications for several projects. They present the design specifications in nearly machine-readable form. Research on these languages may result in the automated implementation of the design. The languages are intended to state specifications in a way that will facilitate verification of design to requirements. This verification may also be automated in the future.

The increasing awareness of the importance of modularity in the design process has resulted in the construction of tools to formally verify the consistency of module interfaces. Users of TRW's Design Analysis Consistency Checker formally state properties of the input and output variables for system modules in the form of input and output assertions that describe the names, units, types, and coordinate systems and dimensions of individual variables or data structures. This tool then checks the module connections for consistency of related input and output assertions. It can also handle some completeness checks.

V&V Participation in Design Reviews

The V&V staff should be continually involved in informal reviews of the work in progress. It should study all software specifications and design documents as they are being prepared, looking for evident or potential problem areas. A representative of the V&V staff can participate in all design inspections to provide feedback early in the design process. The V&V staff should also perform independent validation of critical algorithms, equations, or sophisticated techniques being considered for the design when necessary. Independent derivation, analysis, and simulation are appropriate methods for this validation.

Either the contractor's V&V staff or the independent V&V group should participate in all formal design reviews with the V&V manager or monitor. These V&V responsibilities are summarized in Table 2.

CODE ANALYSIS

During the coding stage, the detailed design is translated into source code and all compilation or assembly errors are removed. Unit testing of each program component in isolation is then performed, usually by the programmer, to remove all obvious errors before integration into the rest of the program. Identifying subtle but critical errors in the unit-tested source code is a V&V function. The V&V group should not wait until unit testing of a program component is complete before studying it and planning the V&V approach.

Verification

Verification of the code is a manual process of reviewing the source listings, correlating them with the detailed design, and establishing the traceability of each section of code back to the requirements.

Code analysts examine both the program source language and the compiled, or assembled, object code. The program's equations and logic are reconstructed either manually or by using automated aids and are compared to those specified in the design; this process identifies errors made in translating

Table 2. V&V Functions in Design Reviews

Review/Audit	Documents to Be Reviewed	V&V Functions
System Requirements Review	System Requirements Specification	Analyze Requirements for Validity, Completeness, Mutual Consistency, and Testability
System Design Review	Functional Concept/Design Approach	Determine Techniques and Economic Feasibility
	Acceptance Test Requirements	Evaluate Acceptance Test Requirements
Preliminary Design Review	Program Performance Specification—(includes functional descriptions of all configuration items and computer program configuration items)	Analyze Preliminary Design for Validity, Consistency with System Requirements Specification, Completeness, Testability, and Reliability
	Interface Design Specification	Analyze Interface Design Specification for Clarity, Completeness, and Feasibility of Proposed Interfaces
	Acceptance Test Plan	Determine Sufficiency of Acceptance Test Plan
	Integration Test Requirements	Evaluate Proposed Software Integration Approach
Critical Design Review	Program Design Specification—(includes detailed design of all configuration items and computer program configuration items)	Analyze Detailed Design for Validity, Consistency with Program Performance Specification, Completeness, Testability, and Reliability
	Detailed Interface Design Specification	Analyze Detailed Interface Specs for Completeness, Feasibility, and Consistency with the Design
	Integration Test Plan	Determine Adequacy and Completeness of Integration Test Plan

QUALITY ENHANCEMENT

the design into the programming language. Data structures and all addressing techniques used to reference them are checked for conformance to design. Specialized language or machine features, such as conditional assembly, partial-word addressing, special-purpose registers, and reserved memory cells, are identified and analyzed for correctness. Real-time programs are examined for proper interrupt enabling and disabling and for potential conflicts in the use of machine or program resources.

In addition to revealing programming errors, code analysis detects such poor programming practices as taking advantage of a system quirk, use of an instruction for other than its intended purpose, tricky programming, and violation of programming standards. These are noted for action by the Quality Assurance staff.

Validation

Validation involves exercising and analyzing the software to ensure its performance according to specifications and to discover latent errors. The two types of validation are static and dynamic analysis.

Static Analysis. Static analysis has traditionally referred to program analysis methods that assist the user in analyzing the program while not requiring its execution. Static analysis includes techniques that either produce general information about a program (e.g., cross-reference tables) or search for particular errors (e.g., uninitialized variables). Three classes of static analysis are discussed in the following paragraphs.

Logic Structure Analysis. Although limited for V&V purposes, logic structure analysis is useful for clarifying the internal logic structure of a program. However, it does not identify specific errors in the code. This class includes such traditional programming tools as symbol table generators, subprogram dependency (call-graph) analyzers, generation of external references with cross-reference table generators, and automatic flowcharting routines.

Static Error Analysis. This is used to identify dangerous constructs or errors in a program (e.g., uninitialized variables; violations of specified programming standards and conventions; inescapable, unreachable, or unexecutable code). Automated tools can often be used to find a particular kind of error. Programming standards enforcers check for violations of specified programming standards and conventions. Program structure analyzers perform loop analyses and identify inescapable, unreachable, or unexecutable code. Individual logic paths in a program component can be identified through the use of path analyzers. Most compilers, which perform substantial error checking and diagnostics, are also useful for static error analysis.

Symbolic Execution. This technique is used to validate the correctness of computational algorithms and logic. Numeric variables are allowed to take on both symbolic and numeric values. A symbolic value is an algebraic expression or a text string used by the programmer to stand for the value of a variable (often a variable name).

When a programmer symbolically executes a program, he or she chooses the paths to analyze and assigns values to input variables. The symbolic execution of a path is then carried out by symbolically evaluating the sequence of assignment statements occurring in the path. An arithmetic or logical expression is symbolically evaluated by substituting the symbolic values of the variables in the expression for the actual variables.

Dynamic Analysis. Dynamic analysis involves instrumentation of the source code so that the program provides internal information concerning its behavior while it is executing. Dynamic analysis tools can be used with most compilers. A typical execution analyzer first preprocesses the source code to analyze source statement characteristics and to insert appropriate code for gathering run-time statistics. The modified program containing both the original and the inserted source code is produced for compilation/assembly and execution. Run-time statistics may be retrieved at program termination or while under user control. Reports based on these statistics are then generated by a postprocessor or a standard statistical package. The analyzer thus generates a profile of the execution of a program by altering the source code to add certain tracing features (e.g., counters or selective output) to determine, for example, what statements and subroutines in the code have been executed and how often and the range of values the variables have assumed. This profile aids error location and helps measure test effectiveness.

TESTING

Role of V&V in Testing

Testing can detect many errors not detected by previous verification activities. Two aspects of V&V relate to testing. The first, which is the essence of the traditional V&V function, is the independent planning, conduct, analysis, and reporting of the testing itself. Its objective is to exercise the capabilities of the evolving software system. The second is monitoring and reviewing the progress of the testing effort. The V&V staff should determine how the testing is progressing, how thoroughly the evolving software is being exercised, whether the test results are being properly interpreted and are conclusive, and whether the test reports thoroughly and accurately reflect the test results. The V&V functions associated with testing include:

- Verifying that the system meets all stated requirements and specifications.
- Demonstrating that the user system interface meets expectations. Valid input should produce the required output, and illegal input should be handled in a prescribed manner without causing system failure.
- Producing feedback at each stage of development sufficient to prevent major design changes in the final stages of implementation.
- Verifying modules, data bases, and interfaces during all stages of system integration.
- Validating test drivers and/or stubs.
- Preparing for all aspects of acceptance testing, including scripts or scenarios, report documentation, and selection and preparation of supporting test equipment.

QUALITY ENHANCEMENT

An independent V&V group is particularly important for testing and evaluation. Although programmers generally scrutinize their design or code to discover errors or inefficiencies, they often test superficially and move on to the next program.

Levels and Types of Testing

Because testing must span several phases of the software life cycle, it is generally broken down into several levels.

In unit/module testing, individual units or modules are debugged in isolation. This is generally performed by the module developer; V&V staff participation is minimal.

Subprogram testing involves integrating the individual modules into subprograms, or computer program configurations, demonstrating major functions within the computer program configuration item (CPCI). Integration and testing should be performed by the development staff in coordination with the testing and V&V groups.

During CPCI performance testing, the entire CPCI is validated against the requirements in the program performance specification. The test is conducted by the independent test team and monitored by the V&V staff. Successful completion of the CPCI performance test should ensure that a majority of programming errors have been eliminated and that the software is ready for system integration.

System integration testing entails verifying system integration of computer programs with equipment, other systems, and man-machine interfaces and demonstrating functional completeness and satisfaction of performance requirements. The V&V staff is responsible for planning, performing, analyzing, reporting, and monitoring the system test effort.

Comprehensive testing of the entire system in its operational environment against the system specification constitutes acceptance, or system performance/quality testing. This test demonstrates readiness for operation. An independent test group should perform this test when time and budget permit. Although acceptance testing comes at the end of the software development cycle, the project manager must begin planning for it during requirements analysis. The V&V staff should determine that the requirements are testable. If the acceptance test requirements, plan, and procedures have been properly generated, the actual conduct of the tests should involve following the prescribed test procedures and recording the appropriate system responses.

The type of testing most useful at each level may vary. The two basic types are branch testing, in which the program structure is closely examined and every instruction or branch tested at least once, and functional testing, in which the program is treated as a black box and tested directly against the system requirements.

Branch and functional testing complement each other well. Branch testing forces the programmer to examine the code structure and thus is useful for unit and early integration testing. Because it addresses the program as it actually exists and not as it was intended to function, functional testing of the

Software Verification and Validation

total system is also essential. Functional testing is appropriate to the latter stages of integration testing and is the only adequate way to perform system and acceptance testing. It may occasionally be necessary, however, to test a particular branch within the program during system testing.

OPERATION/MAINTENANCE

The need for V&V continues into the O/M phase of the software life cycle. V&V serves the same purpose of confirming that the delivered (and accepted) software system conforms to stated specifications and satisfactorily performs the functions for which it was designed. However, the level of V&V activity changes during O/M. Rather than addressing a continuous activity, the V&V effort is concerned with two activities occurring at different points. The first involves identifying errors and verifying their correction. The second involves verifying and validating changes made to the software. Staffing requirements during this phase reflect the discrete nature of the V&V activities. Although a V&V staff does not have to work full time throughout O/M, it should be on call. Members of the O/M staff can be used or an independent contractor can be employed on a task-order basis. Although the need for V&V during O/M arises from two separate sources, the functions are similar to each other and to V&V activities that occur throughout the software development cycle.

Operational use of the software often uncovers errors that were not discovered prior to acceptance, partly because complete testing is virtually impossible. Inadequate or inaccurate documentation is also a source of errors because the software does not operate as the documentation implies it should.

When an error is discovered, a software trouble report is filed for action. The V&V group is often responsible for identifying the error's cause, but the O/M staff (or maintenance contractor) is usually responsible for correcting the error. After the error has been corrected, the V&V group should test the corrected portion of the software and conduct regression testing to ensure that the software system as a whole performs as described.

The discovery of an error sometimes leads to major changes in the system because the error cannot be corrected without modifying the system. Changes may also be desired to enhance performance or to eliminate a source of errors. Proposals that involve both hardware and software changes include software enhancement, software change, and engineering change proposals. The V&V group reviews the impact analysis of the proposed change before approving it. If the change is to be implemented, V&V is involved in verifying that the design conforms to the change specifications and that the implementation correctly reflects the design. V&V is involved in planning for testing, performing the tests for the changed portion of the software, and performing regression testing of the system. It is also responsible for certifying the software change and ensuring that the documentation reflects all changes.

CONCLUSION

Although V&V activity overlaps the Quality Assurance function, the emphasis in V&V is on technical accuracy rather than conformance to standards

QUALITY ENHANCEMENT

and conventions. When properly applied, software V&V should determine that the requirements for a given system are accurately stated, that the software is being developed in accordance with specifications, and that it satisfactorily performs the functions for which it was designed.

Reference

1. Bell, Thomas E., Bixler, David C., and Dyer, Margaret E. "An Extendable Approach to Computer-Aided Software Requirements Engineering." *IEEE Transactions on Software Engineering* (January 1977), pp. 49–60.

Bibliography

Boehm, B.W., McClean, R.K., and Urfrig, D.B. "Some Experience with Automated Aids to the Design of Large-Scale Reliable Software." *IEEE Transactions on Software Engineering*. Vol. SE-1, 1975, pp. 125–133.

Fujii, Marilyn S. "Independent Verification of Highly Reliable Programs." *Proceedings of COMPSAC 77*. Chicago: IEEE, 1977, pp. 38–44.

Howden, William E. "A Survey of Static Analysis Methods" in *Software Testing and Validation Techniques*, W.E. Howden and E. Miller. New York: IEEE Computer Society, 1978, pp. 82–96.

Section XIII
Productivity Improvement

Choosing the right product, paying attention to quality, and caring about customers—this is a certain recipe for success in any business. And why shouldn't MIS be treated like business? Some MIS departments today are losing business as their customers (i.e., users) turn elsewhere, often to personal computers, to satisfy their needs. More effective management of MIS can recapture those customers to the benefit of the entire organization. Chapter XIII-1, "Running MIS Like a Business," will help you get a handle on some of the key problems facing MIS management today and lead the way to a more effective, more productive organization.

In Chapter XIII-2, "Improving MIS Productivity," we offer more than 50 ideas you can adopt or adapt to make your MIS department more productive. These ideas touch on almost every facet of MIS management and apply to small as well as large DP installations.

Forging a link between office technology and white-collar productivity is not always easy. Chapter XIII-3, "Office Technology Brings Higher White-Collar Productivity," addresses this issue and explores several aspects of the office automation related to demonstrating benefit for the investment involved.

Another major area of investment for many MIS departments is in data management. With the advent of end-user computing, the productive management of data becomes even more important. A data dictionary is one means of more effectively controlling this often costly effort. A data dictionary system is a software package that captures data and data relationships. Its effective use requires the establshment of data management disciplines and procedures for all application project teams. Unfortunately, most application teams do not eagerly embrace new standards and procedures; one method of changing this attitude is to create a data management environment that supports the data dictionary system as a useful productivity tool. Chapter XIII-4, "A Path to Improved Productivity—Effective Data Management," details such a method to help the MIS manager achieve optimal benefits from data dictionary use.

XIII-1
Running MIS Like a Business

Kenneth L. Dunn
Dennis R. Schuster

INTRODUCTION

A company's MIS organization offers one major product—information—and one major service—easy, reliable, and timely delivery—to its users, or customers. If customers are dissatisfied, they will go elsewhere for the products and services they need.

The major problem is that the MIS function has not been treated as a business. Corporate management has tended to ignore essential elements of successful business practices, such as implementing market analysis and product planning; employing modern equipment, methods, and procedures; and establishing quality control. As a result, the MIS department as a business has had difficulty satisfying customer needs, and the customers have been going elsewhere. The explosive growth of personal computer use in the offices of MIS customers is, in part, testimony to the customers' dissatisfaction with the company's MIS department.

Once the technical mystique that surrounds it is penetrated, the MIS business is essentially no different from any other. Thus, to function successfully, the MIS department must be viewed and run by company management as a business. Management could adopt a more businesslike approach by implementing the following recommendations:
- Identify customers and their needs
- Completely retool, bringing in modern data bases, communications networks, and productivity tools to increase productivity and cut costs
- Establish an adequate quality control function.

IDENTIFYING CUSTOMERS AND THEIR NEEDS

One of the biggest problems facing the MIS business is the fragmentation of the customer market. Each market segment needs different kinds of information. Companies must constantly examine the target market to determine who the customers are and what products and services they need and are willing to buy. After the examination, the company should investigate what the MIS business currently has to offer or could create to satisfy each particular need.

PRODUCTIVITY IMPROVEMENT

Market Segments

An MIS market segment is a group of customers that needs or reacts to a particular product or service (in this case, information) in the same way. The same group of customers can be segmented several different ways, and depending on his or her needs at a given time, a customer can move from one segment to another.

The MIS market can be divided into four segments:
- Dependent decision makers—These customers make decisions based on information others gather for them. They have no detailed knowledge of how the information was gathered. This market segment includes executives and officers, general managers, secretaries, clerks, and hourly employees.
- Independent decision makers—These customers make decisions based on information they gather for themselves. They can create their own products (though simple and limited) by using the services provided by an MIS business. This group includes middle managers, supervisors, and staff professionals.
- Support staff for decision makers—These customers have the functional knowledge and skill to develop application-specific information products for their own departments by using the services provided by an MIS business.
- Staff professionals—These customers are systems professionals who create or supply the products and services that are sold. This market segment includes systems designers and analysts, program analysts, and programmers.

Another method of segmenting the information systems market is by the skill level of the customer. This is not a separate market but a further refining of the four segments. For example, help screens might be provided for dependent decision makers, but command languages might be appropriate for staff professionals.

After the marketing and planning departments have identified and segmented the customer market, they must determine what products and services can be sold to each segment. The MIS groups that are akin to a business's product design and engineering department and manufacturing department must then make or buy the products and services.

Unless the MIS business can accurately determine what customers need to build systems and then supply them with the best products and services available, it will fail to meet customer expectations and suffer the consequences just as any other business.

The Make-versus-Buy Decision

How does an MIS business design and build the products and services its customers need? In many cases, it doesn't. With today's information systems technology, an MIS business can often buy products or services from manufacturers who specialize in the particular product or service needed and then sell them to customers.

Digital Equipment Corporation's Datatrieve, Information Builders Inc's

Running MIS Like a Business

FOCUS, and Lotus Development Corporation's Lotus 1-2-3 are typical of such products. Instead of developing its own products, an MIS business can buy Datatrieve and FOCUS, implement them, and then sell them to customers in less time and at a much lower cost (but not at a lower profit). In the case of Lotus 1-2-3, the customer buys the package, and the MIS business offers complementary services, such as advanced support and training.

Make-versus-buy decisions should be frequent exercises. The following are reasons to buy rather than make:
- Basic business functions (e.g., accounts payable, accounts receivable, inventory control) are essentially the same from company to company. Standard packages that deal with these functions can be bought and used by many companies interested in saving the time and cost of developing their own packages.
- Because development costs for companies that build packages for sale to other businesses are distributed over hundreds of sales, these companies can sell packages for much less than it would cost a single company to develop its own.
- Because of the specialized nature of their work, software houses are generally able to attract and employ the most talented systems designers and programmers.
- A package that has been on the market for a year or so and is sold by a company with a good reputation will have been sufficiently debugged and thus will be more likely to work right the first time.
- Even if a customer has unique requirements, it is usually faster and less costly to purchase a package that satisfies the vast majority of needs and then custom build the unique parts. In some cases, the customer may wish to consider modifying the business. In the DP profession, the rule of thumb is: Find a package that satisfies 80 percent of your needs, buy it, and then build the rest or modify the business.

An MIS business can be successful by selling and supporting personal computers, query language packages, integrated packages, spreadsheet packages, report writing packages, graphics packages, and large application-specific packages. However, one very important caution must be noted: although buying the right package will save considerable time and money, buying the wrong package can be more costly and time-consuming than custom building. An MIS business must perform a complete, detailed, and thoroughly professional analysis of the customers' needs and a product's functionality. In addition, an MIS business must ask application developers for assistance in integrating independently purchased systems.

BUILDING SHARED DATA BASES

In many cases, satisfactory packages are not available, and the information systems business must help customers build needed application systems. To provide this service, the business must have shared data bases and other modern tools.

Shared data bases support particular business entities (e.g., customers, products, orders); traditional application-specific data bases support particular applications (e.g., accounts payable, shop floor control, and sales re-

PRODUCTIVITY IMPROVEMENT

turns). A data base built for a business function can be shared by many customers through the use of application generators, report writers, and fourth-generation query languages. Customers can thus access business-entity data bases with minimal effort, cost, and development time.

If an MIS business replaces its application-specific data bases with application-independent data bases, it can sell customers the products and services they need to get their jobs done. Moreover, the business can reassign people working on application development to data base, telecommunications, and end-user support activities. This reallocation can greatly improve the productivity of the MIS business and its customers.

IMPLEMENTING MODERN TOOLS

Modern technology has given MIS businesses new machinery with which to create shared data bases and, if need be, to build highly complex systems for customers. Using these new tools, businesses can get jobs done faster and less expensively.

More Cost-Effective Computers

Computer hardware is becoming better, faster, and less expensive. For example, a company can almost double the performance of an IBM mainframe by investing an amount equal to approximately 33 percent of the original purchase cost into hardware upgrades. Such technological improvements enable an MIS business to provide many products and services with significantly increased performance at a relatively small cost to customers.

More Cost-Effective Tools

Many, if not most, MIS businesses are still using slow, outdated compilation tools. These should be replaced by more cost-effective tools, which can almost double productivity. These tools are described in the following paragraphs.

Application Prototyping. With prototyping, screens and data flow specifications can be created "on the fly," with both the systems professional and the customer online together.

Application or Program Generators. These generators enable the professional to produce full-blown application programs with only a few lines of generator code. The use of application generators has been shown to increase productivity by 600 percent.

Very High-Level Languages. COBOL and FORTRAN, still used by many MIS businesses, can and probably should be replaced by FOCUS, APL, NOMAD, MARK IV or V, or any of a host of other fourth-generation languages, all of which are faster, easier, and far more maintainable than the older languages. In some cases, approximately 60 lines of COBOL can be replaced by one line of APL, NOMAD, or ADS/O. Using such languages, an MIS business can improve output without increasing costs and can deliver higher-quality products far more quickly and at a lower cost.

Revising Blocks of Reusable Code. If marketing and engineering wanted to make 50 new products, each with completely different materials and parts, someone would surely get upset and try to establish common materials and parts. The same is true for programming. Instead of reinventing the wheel, programmers should electronically copy large blocks of common code. In most modern DP shops, very few programmers write virgin code.

If an MIS business is to develop competitive products, it must bring its manufacturing techniques up to date and train MIS personnel in the use of these new products.

QUALITY CONTROL

Any business that manufactures a product or offers a service has a quality control function to make sure that the customer gets a product that conforms to standards. Until a few years ago, however, most MIS departments did not have a quality control function (usually called quality assurance) to check the work and create and enforce standards. Instead, manufacturing supervisors checked their own work. Such a practice is akin to letting employees approve their own expense accounts or customers prepare their own bills. Furthermore, it indicates that until recently, corporate management did not consider MIS a business that produced a product for sale to customers—a product that required a quality control check.

The lack of quality assurance standards and a quality assurance function to enforce them has been a major factor in the inadequate applications generated by MIS businesses and the poor customer relations that have frequently resulted. To sell high-quality, low-cost products successfully, an MIS business must mirror standard business practice and provide a separate quality assurance function to enforce standards.

CONCLUSION

A company's MIS organization can be extremely successful if management perceives it as a business and treats it like one. An MIS business must be equipped with application-independent data bases, communications networks, and fourth-generation productivity tools. The staff must be able to provide expert advice on whether packages should be purchased or systems should be custom built. A quality assurance function must be established to ensure that MIS customers get high-quality, dependable products. The creation of a permanent customer analysis and product planning function is another step toward success. However, the key strategy can be summed up as the application of solid business skills to MIS decisions.

XIII-2
Improving MIS Productivity
Robert E. Umbaugh

INTRODUCTION

Improving the productivity of the information processing function is important because of rapidly increasing DP costs and because of the extent to which all areas of today's organizations depend on the MIS department to increase their efficiency.

Improving productivity does not necessarily mean cutting costs. It does, however, mean increasing and/or improving output for a given level of input. Quality circles, suggestion systems, rewards, recognition, and improved work methods are potential means of improving the level and quality of output. Although some organizations have capitalized on one or two of these techniques, improved productivity demands a total management commitment in which such techniques are adapted to the organization and to the changing conditions in which it operates.

Unacceptably low levels of productivity can stem from many causes, but primary among them is management indifference. To counter this attitude and begin to improve productivity, a formal program must be established with the full and active support of management, preferably of senior management. A formal program provides the umbrella under which small, specific steps are carried out. Formality focuses attention on the need and desire for more efficient use of resources; however, the specific daily actions of line management and supervision provide the results.

This chapter is designed to help MIS management initiate a productivity improvement program. It details steps that have been implemented in some installations and can probably be adopted in most information systems organizations. These steps also serve as examples of what can be done in specific parts of the organization and thus should stimulate the thinking of MIS management and lead to other steps that can improve productivity.

The potential benefit of improved productivity is significant; however, a program designed to improve productivity should be approached like any other program: with a plan, a schedule, and someone assigned the responsibility for seeing that it gets done. The ideas discussed in this chapter are grouped into eight broad categories to help structure the program and to facilitate assigning responsibility for carrying out the program. The eight categories are:

PRODUCTIVITY IMPROVEMENT

- Resource planning and control
- Product refinement
- Standards and standardization
- Systems design and implementation
- Data communications facilities
- Staff management
- Organizational productivity
- Management innovation.

RESOURCE PLANNING AND CONTROL

A major portion of the MIS department budget is expended on hardware. All steps in the forecasting, planning, procurement, and operation of computer hardware should therefore be reviewed to identify opportunities to improve the productivity of the process and the use of hardware resources. The following paragraphs describe specific steps that can be taken in resource planning and control.

1. *Use purchase credits to buy a CPU and/or peripherals and then resell during an upgrade.* Often overlooked in a mainframe vendor's lease is the purchase credit clause, which allows a percentage of the monthly lease payment to be applied toward the purchase of a CPU or peripherals. The cost of buying the equipment and its market resale value can quickly be determined. Tens of thousands of dollars of profit can be generated by this little-used technique.

2. *Consider alternate vendors.* A typical saving from contracting with plug-compatible or third-party vendors ranges from 25 to 35 percent. Add-on main memory, tape and disk drives, channels, and other peripherals are natural candidates for procurement from plug-compatible vendors. Before this step is taken, however, several factors should be considered. The availability of service, parts, and bundled software as well as the willingness of the primary vendor to continue supporting installed equipment, for example, may outweigh any cost benefit gained by switching to a third party. Mainframe vendors have a service organization of trained technicians who most likely are stationed nearby and can respond quickly to service needs. Because many third-party vendors contract for maintenance from yet another firm, service may be unacceptable. Customers of third-party vendors under consideration should be contacted, and the local service level confirmed. The adequacy of local parts for the equipment being considered should be checked, as should the procedure for obtaining parts or specialized technical support from another city, state, or country.

3. *Review equipment utilization to eliminate components or to downgrade.* Particular attention should be paid to the utilization of low-speed devices (e.g., card readers, card punches, printers). Most operating systems can build spool files for these devices so that schedules can be met with slower equipment. It may be possible to eliminate some tape drives or to trade in all tape drives for slower, less expensive models without affecting throughput.

When an inadequate number of tape drives limits scheduling optimization, the bottleneck can be remedied by adding lower-speed devices. The MIS manager should determine in this case whether some CPU memory can be returned or whether the installation can trade down to the next smaller (i.e., slower) CPU without significantly degrading service.

4. *Use hardware monitors to determine true utilization.* One major problem MIS managers face is the difficulty, if not impossibility, of determining by simple observation whether hardware is being used effectively. A hardware monitor can help to accurately determine utilization as well as help to identify bottlenecks caused by insufficient capacity and highlight excess capacity. Before ordering new equipment, a hardware- or software-based monitor should be used to ensure proper utilization of current equipment.

5. *Delay hardware expansion.* Frequently, upgrading to a more expensive configuration can be delayed for a considerable period by adding a third shift to an operation, by adding a weekend shift, or buying time from an outside source to handle peak loads. As long as these measures cost less than the proposed hardware, money can be saved by deferring the upgrade.

    Another course of action that can delay the need for new hardware is improving the quality of operations. If reruns account for more than 5 percent of production time, for example, improving operations should become a priority. MIS management should set a specific objective for the reduction of reruns and check each week to ensure that progress is being made toward the objective. The causes of reruns should be identified, and corrective action taken. In this case, knowledge plus action equals improved productivity.

6. *Replace the current CPU with a larger, older, less expensive model.* Mainframe vendors frequently announce new products within existing product lines, an action that often depresses prices of established models, particularly on the resale market. Because the technical (i.e., useful) life of CPUs far exceeds their usual economic life, substantial bargains can be found.

7. *Anticipate hardware planning for personal computers.* If planning for hardware upgrades is difficult in a centralized DP shop with only one or two installed mainframes, the complexity of planning personal computer upgrades will be considerable. Upgrades of PCs will almost certainly become common, and, as long as users stay within the same product line, there will be upward compatibility. Major problems will arise when a vendor other than the one providing the installed equipment offers a product that is too good to resist. The DP shops will have to become involved at this point in order to advise users on how to shift data from one format to another. Complicating the matter will be the necessity of incorporating upgraded PCs into the data communications network.

8. *Purchase hardware time from a service bureau to process a varied work load.* In a sense, the only difference between an equipment ven-

PRODUCTIVITY IMPROVEMENT

dor and a service bureau is that the former sells computer time by the month and the latter by the hour. Although outside hourly rates are generally higher per unit, the purchase of some outside time may prove less expensive than paying overtime, running extra shifts, adding specialized equipment, or upgrading components within the hardware or software configuration.

9. *Periodically reevaluate hardware and software features and eliminate from vendor invoices those that are unneeded.* The needs of an installation change over time. Even if the total work load remains within the limits of the present system, the configuration requirements should periodically be analyzed in detail. A special hardware or software feature occasionally is installed to meet a short-term need and then overlooked when no longer required. Invoices should be checked carefully for unused features, which should then be removed promptly. This task should be assigned to one person (e.g., the hardware coordinator) and reviewed to verify that it is being done.

PRODUCT REFINEMENT

The primary product of the information systems organization is service to the user of DP resources. This service takes many forms, such as reports, online systems, consulting, and time-sharing support. MIS management should review its product offerings to increase their cost-effectiveness for the user and to improve the efficiency of their production. The following ideas present some approaches to product refinement. The MIS manager should treat the review of the DP product mix as a manufacturer would and try to create the best product for the resources invested.

1. *Conduct a survey to eliminate unused reports.* MIS management can eliminate runs that are not essential to business operations, reduce the number of reports and/or copies, or change the type of report to "action" or "exception" to reduce volume. From the standpoint of the DP installation, the best report is the one that does not have to be run; logically, reports that are not used should be identified and eliminated. This approach reduces forms costs, computer usage, and direct labor without reducing the effectiveness of user service.

    A reduction in the number of required copies of a report also benefits the installation. In many cases, two or more recipients of a report can share one copy. For example, if several merchandise buyers are usually each given a full inventory and movement report, one copy can be divided into sections that are then distributed to each buyer according to product.

    In some cases, two users in the same department may use a report differently. For example, the manager may review the report and make notes before discarding it, while a clerk in the same department may work from a second copy for a week or longer. In this situation, it may prove cost-effective for the manager and clerk to use the same copy; the manager can pass the report to the clerk instead of discarding it.

    One way to discover who really does not need a copy of a report is a "trash-can survey"—that is, searching trash cans to determine who discarded reports the day they were run. The assumption is that the recipient either does not require the report or needs only to glance at it. In the first case, the report can be eliminated; in the second, arrangements can be made for the recipient to review someone else's copy.

2. *Eliminate preprinted forms.* Although insignificant compared to total DP costs, the cost of custom-printed forms can be considerable during the course of a year. In addition to the cost of printing and inventory, a less obvious cost associated with custom forms is the idle time resulting from operator setup when changing forms in the printer.

   One disadvantage to eliminating preprinted forms, however, is that all existing computer programs that currently output to custom forms may have to be modified to print the required page and column headings. Programs requiring this change can be modified by a single heading routine, which should be identical for all programs except for the value of the literals printed as titles.

3. *Reduce the frequency of reports.* Many reports must be produced at a specified frequency (e.g., weekly paychecks, monthly statements). Some reports, however, are not directly related to frequency intervals dictated by external sources. If a report is run on the 10th, 20th, and 30th of each month instead of every week, paper costs for that report can be cut by more than 25 percent.

4. *Reduce paper volume by redesigning forms.* From an aesthetic point of view, wide margins at the sides, top, and bottom of a page are appealing. This format, however, can prove expensive in terms of paper usage. Another waste of paper is caused by unneeded double and triple spacing between heads and the body of a report. In many installations, a 10 percent reduction in forms usage can be realized by redesigning formats and rethinking the way in which forms are used. Care must be taken, however, not to make the reports so dense and cluttered that user or report productivity is lost. In this, as in many productivity improvement steps, balance is the key to success.

5. *Use micrographics.* Although computer output microform (COM) is a proven means of cost reduction, relatively few installations have converted a substantial amount of their printer output to this medium. The substitution of a microform for hard copy of program dumps has proven highly productive. Online, dry-process COM replaced 15 million printed pages per month in one large installation to produce a monthly saving of $80,000.

6. *Replace printed user reports with microfilm.* Installations that use COM maintain that their users prefer microfilm to paper reports and that their output costs have been reduced. With storage space at a premium and users increasingly willing to accept the use of a new technology, aperture cards, microfiche, and roll microfilm often can be substituted for hard-copy reports. MIS managers should survey user departments to determine their preferences and to identify strong candidates for conversion.

PRODUCTIVITY IMPROVEMENT

High-quality microfilm is now accepted by government agencies to satisfy archival records with long retention periods. Files needed to meet the retention requirements of the IRS, SEC, and other federal agencies can now be stored on microfilm, and permanent hard-copy files can be destroyed in many cases.

STANDARDS AND STANDARDIZATION

Although most DP installations have written standards, not all regard standards as vehicles for productivity improvement; some standards are even counterproductive. MIS management should not only review existing standards to determine which impede productivity but should consider taking steps to build improved productivity into new standards. Part of that productivity improvement results from standardization. The following paragraphs present examples of this approach.

1. *Standardize equipment.* MIS management can standardize equipment at the home office and plants, sign national contracts with certain vendors, ensure that all expansions meet corporate standards, and exercise central control over user requests. As hardware costs decrease and the popularity of personal computers grows, more users are purchasing their own equipment. Managers who recognize that such growth can be counterproductive are trying to control it through standardization of equipment and procedures. A single set of documentation standards for all sites will bring long-term benefits, and supporting equipment from a small number of vendors generally is less expensive than trying to satisfy everyone.

2. *Negotiate volume supply contracts and require full-year, fixed-price bids.* Supplies can often cost 15 percent of the annual hardware budget. Obtaining bids on an annual basis with a guaranteed price or buying in sufficient volume to obtain large discounts reduces supply costs. If unfamiliar with product standards for various supplies, the MIS manager should request standards from three or four vendors of quality products. Standards common to three of the four vendors can be considered sufficiently universal to incorporate in bid requests. Including such standards helps guard against vendors of inferior products.

3. *Adopt a standard shop programming language.* Advocates of the "one computer, one language" approach maintain that optimizing the use of people is more important than optimizing the use of hardware. Advantages of the single-language shop include increased proficiency in that language, improved programmer productivity, increased likelihood of programmers understanding one another's work, and greater uniformity among the installation's programs.

4. *Form a joint committee with other MIS managers for volume purchasing.* How an organization buys can sometimes be more important than from whom it buys. A purchasing co-op may prove productive for a group of small DP installations. MIS management should take a creative approach to material and equipment acquisition.

5. *Implement a change control management process.* Engineering organizations use a formal process to control changes to drawings and systems. A change control process is important in this environment because engineering projects and their documentation are large and complex. The same holds true for most DP activities. Increased productivity, in the form of a reduction of wasted effort, results from designing and adopting a change control process for the organization.

As the volume of backlogged changes to a hardware or software system grows, a ranking process is needed to determine which changes must be installed, which can be deferred or cancelled, and which can be combined for installation. A change control system helps pinpoint conflicting changes and highlights components that require immediate corrective action. A documented change control system provides a historical record that can identify hardware or software components requiring repeated changes in order to be maintained at peak operating levels.

SYSTEMS DESIGN AND IMPLEMENTATION

The ideas presented in this section are intended to stimulate MIS management to consider specific steps that can be taken to improve ongoing operations in the systems design and programming environment.

1. *Use a common architecture to achieve more productive systems.* When the major activity in an environment is the development of online systems, the evaluation of a generalized architecture to handle edits, screen formats, and transaction protocols is worthwhile. Many DP installations are using a generalized architecture to improve the productivity of online systems programmers. In many cases, thousands of lines of code can be replaced by a few hundred generalized statements and entries to table processors.

2. *Improve programming productivity; have all programming done in a team environment using structured analysis, design, and coding techniques.* The prudent use of structured techniques can substantially decrease the number of logic errors in new systems, reduce the number of bugs in new code (thereby limiting call-outs), and improve the quality of the documentation produced during systems development. Once systems analysts and programmers become proficient in using the newer structured techniques, management should see improved staff productivity, improved quality of the delivered product, higher employee morale, and greater user satisfaction.

Although giving programmers their own online terminal may seem expensive, productivity improvements on the order of eight to one compared to batch methods for program check-out are reported. Adding online terminals can aggravate the prime-shift work load problem in many shops; however, the fact that most systems and programming departments are overloaded and backlogs continue to grow justifies investigating any means of improving programming productivity. Some DP shops have a goal of achieving one terminal per programmer in the near future.

PRODUCTIVITY IMPROVEMENT

3. *Assign specific responsibility; use a limited number of employees for program maintenance.* Responsibility for application maintenance should be assigned to a specific programmer or team of programmers. As the programmers become intimately familiar with the application, maintenance becomes more efficient.

    Some companies have reduced the cost of modifying existing systems and increased the funds available for new development by limiting the size of the maintenance staff. Experience shows that most companies get greater return from new applications than from minor refinements to existing systems.

4. *Provide user-oriented software.* MIS management should consider purchasing user-oriented report generators, spreadsheet systems, models, and other commercial software to minimize programmer support of the user. User involvement in some aspects of processing can conserve scarce and valuable programming time. The ready availability and wide acceptance of user-friendly software offers the MIS manager an opportunity to reduce the large backlog of application systems work. If these products are carefully selected and implemented, the productivity of the MIS department and users can be improved. However, some user-friendly products use an inordinate amount of CPU power, and their imprudent use can literally swamp existing work. Balance is the key to implementing user-oriented software successfully.

5. *Give users a personal computer.* To reduce the backlog in the systems and programming shop, MIS management should consider allowing users to acquire personal computers or even using MIS finances to supply PCs. When benefits and other overhead are considered, the cost of a PC probably would not exceed one month of a senior analyst's labor costs. Although many PCs are justified by the argument that work can be offloaded from the main computer, studies show that 85 percent of the work done on a PC was never done before on any computer. The PC, however, can start to reduce the large backlog in most DP shops. Thus, the need to integrate the PC into the overall information processing scheme of the organization cannot be ignored.

    An organization should also consider the feasibility of using a PC for standalone or geographically remote applications. In addition, by giving a PC to a troublesome user, the MIS manager can concentrate on productive work in other areas.

6. *Examine the benefits of purchasing software packages.* Every software decision involves two options: make or buy. The best alternative for a particular application is dictated by the quality of the staff and the availability of commercial software. Unique requirements are seldom met by package vendors; however, the relatively common applications—even those that are complex—generally are available. Preprogrammed applications have been available for more than 15 years, although their acceptance was limited until the advent of popular PC software.

    Experience with applications software for PCs has proved that pre-

Improving MIS Productivity

programmed applications can be used profitably if organizations are willing to adjust their needs to fit the limitations of the software rather than trying to modify the software to fulfill every requirement. Large central-site installations often have rejected packages out of hand. Although this attitude is tolerable during times of high budgets and excess staff, today the prudent MIS manager will insist that serious consideration be given to purchasing software packages. Users can have most, if not all, of their needs satisfied earlier, the MIS staff can be assigned tasks that are not addressed by preprogrammed packages, and costs can be more effectively controlled.

7. *Contract carefully; use software contracts that enforce performance standards and penalty clauses.* Although frequently used in other agreements, penalty clauses seldom are found in software services contracts. To persuade the vendor to include such clauses, the buyer may have to write more detailed specifications; subsequent changes to these specifications may require renegotiation. All deliverables, including documentation and test systems that may be required for future maintenance or modification of the software, should be specified.

8. *Use outside contracting for the skeletal system; the vendor writes the system except for the reports, which are preprogrammed in-house.* The effectiveness of this arrangement depends on several factors. If the number of reports required for an application is high in relation to the number of processing programs and a good report generator is available, the technique can result in a substantial saving.

9. *Use outside programming for small, specialized tasks.* In most small and medium-sized computer installations, the in-house staff does not have sufficient expertise in all aspects of the programming required by the organization. As a result, considerable time can be spent researching unusual problems and developing specialized solutions. MIS management may save money by contracting these jobs with an outside group with experience in handling specialized tasks. Full documentation, however, must be provided in a form that the MIS staff can understand and use to maintain the delivered programs.

10. *Use scanning for input when feasible.* Scanning is an underutilized medium in data processing. The only special requirements in the field are a sharp pencil and a user with minimal training. Extensive experience with scanning demonstrates that the accuracy and quality of the input are improved when the user fills in a mark rather than when the user enters figures on paper that are subsequently keyed into the system. Scanning is especially well suited for such applications as meter reading, reporting labor costs on service calls, and entering merchandise orders.

11. *Use the project librarian concept.* A project librarian is responsible for documentation maintenance on large development projects. This approach helps to reduce the amount of time that highly trained programmers and systems analysts spend on menial tasks and provides a good training ground for future programmers. The librarian can coor-

PRODUCTIVITY IMPROVEMENT

     dinate test runs, learn JCL, maintain the central project documentation file, and perform other administrative tasks for project members.

12. *Use online training.* Powerful computer-assisted training models are available to instruct users in the operation of new systems and to train new users of existing systems. The Interactive Instruction System (IIS) from IBM is one example of this type of product. Users learn at their own pace, and the need for intensive face-to-face training is reduced (though not eliminated).

13. *Use flex time to improve response time.* Flexible work hours for programmers and analysts using online systems for the development and checkout of programs can actually help reduce the heavy load on time-sharing systems during the prime work hours, thereby potentially improving response time for other users who must work a strict eight-to-five day. In many large shops, response time is remarkably good before 8:00 A.M. and after 5:00 P.M.

DATA COMMUNICATIONS FACILITIES

One portion of the MIS budget that should be watched in the future is the cost of data communications. Some MIS managers do not yet fully appreciate the impact of increased costs in this area. Four trends should contribute to the substantial increases expected in data communications costs:

- An ever-increasing number of systems are going online, even such traditional batch applications as accounting.
- PCs are being installed in the workplace at a rapid pace and will increasingly incorporate a data communications capability, including SNA compatibility.
- The growth of office systems is particularly important as these systems become further integrated into the general information processing scheme of an organization and the demarcation between traditional DP systems and office systems diminishes.
- The availability of remote information services (i.e., transaction-based inquiry services) that are designed specifically for business applications (e.g., The Source from Reader's Digest) is increasing.

These four trends, along with the growth of distributed data processing for remote organization support or to provide some element of security, will result in an ever-greater percentage of the MIS budget being spent on data communications.

MIS management can take several specific steps to improve the productivity of the data communications function, as detailed in the following paragraphs.

1. *Use network modeling techniques.* Sophisticated network modeling techniques largely based on queueing theory are now available to facilitate the complex task of designing and tuning communications networks. The alternative to using a network model is to over-engineer the network, incurring needless costs.

2. *Check line speeds; use dial-up lines for low-volume batch transmissions between field terminals.* Ten years ago, transmissions faster than

Improving MIS Productivity

1,800 baud required dedicated lines in many parts of the U.S. The Bell companies, independent telephone companies, and private carriers have since invested heavily in upgrading long-distance and local service facilities. As a result, many sites that formerly required dedicated lines can now use dial-up lines. Low-speed devices on dedicated lines should be investigated to determine whether dial-up lines are feasible and economical based on traffic loads and patterns.

3. *Highlight user costs; reduce the number of terminals by charging terminal costs to user budgets.* One advantage of a chargeback system is that the user realizes the cost of MIS services. This important concept in improving productivity can encourage more efficient use of resources by putting the responsibility for controlling costs on the primary users.

4. *Employ improved technology; reduce line costs by using minicomputers for terminal concentration for some communications, thereby decreasing the bandwidth required to support terminal clusters.* Communications costs are generally reported to be declining at an annual rate of 11 percent. The fact that new technology must be adopted to realize the savings, however, often is overlooked.

   The cost-effectiveness of each link in a network should be evaluated independently. Although switching from dial-up to microwave transmission may reduce costs, for example, switching only some of the lines may produce an even greater cost saving.

5. *Perform periodic checkups of communications facilities.* The MIS manager may elect, for example, to implement an autodial capability on the local RJE station to reduce the level of operator intervention required in sign-on/sign-off procedures and to shift telecommunications traffic to nighttime operation. In addition, the management of existing telecommunications facilities can often be improved by reviewing the system after more capable terminals are added. An ongoing traffic analysis program can determine where economies can be realized while service level is maintained or even improved.

STAFF MANAGEMENT

Effective personnel management often is the key to a successful productivity improvement program. An initial investment in training is returned many times, if the staff is retained. Work force balance and work load scheduling are also critical to getting the most from personnel dollars. Some specific steps to improve the productivity of MIS personnel follow.

1. *Reward employees for recruiting new hires.* From a morale standpoint, it is far better for an organization to reward an employee for recommending a new hire than to pay an employment agency fee. A further advantage of this approach is that employees rarely recommend marginally qualified people. As a result, the quality of the new employee may be higher than that of a person hired through an agency.

PRODUCTIVITY IMPROVEMENT

2. *Pay data entry operators incentive rates.* Because most current data entry equipment can optionally collect statistical information on operator performance, MIS management should establish piecework standards—that is, pay some base minimum with a bonus or increment based on productivity. This system must also include a provision stipulating that the operator loses bonuses or incremental pay for errors; otherwise, a fast but careless operator can earn more money than one who is slightly slower but more accurate.

3. *Attract highly qualified personnel by paying slightly more than the market rate.* Organizations that maintain salaries slightly above the prevailing rate can be more selective in hiring. Although salary must be accompanied by other job benefits, a higher pay rate can reduce long-term costs by lowering turnover. Money alone probably will not motivate employees over the long term; a reputation for paying less than the market rate, however, can discourage qualified candidates from considering employment and may encourage key people to seek employment elsewhere.

4. *Implement rotating shifts to increase coverage.* To ensure effective staffing of computer operations that must maintain 24-hour-a-day, 7-day-a-week coverage, DP operations managers should consider implementing work schedules that deviate from the traditional 8-hour-a-day, 5-day-a-week format. Four or five shifts of 10-hour-a-day, 4-day-a-week workers can often be utilized effectively. Flexible work hours have also proved highly productive for certain classes of employees, particularly those in data entry, distribution, and peripheral operations. Although the original version of flex time, which generally allows employees to set their work hours, may not prove feasible, certain core hours of coverage can be established, with employees given the option of how to structure their work day around those hours.

5. *Cross-train employees to broaden their career paths; train personnel in several areas for backup.* Career paths exist within the MIS department as well as in other departments. Cross-training provides employees with an understanding of other jobs in the installation. The benefits for management are twofold: more trained people are available to substitute absent employees, and employees who are suitable for transfers and promotions can be identified.

6. *Investigate partial staffing to lower costs.* Because work loads in data entry shops fluctuate, some MIS managers are staffing the data entry function to perform 80 percent of the expected work load and using data entry vendors to complete the remaining 20 percent. These vendors usually are able to pay a lower wage rate than most large corporations and rely heavily on part-time and intermittent personnel. Reportedly, the quality of work is high, schedules are met, and overall vendor performance is very good. As much as a 10 percent reduction in data entry costs is achievable using this technique.

ORGANIZATIONAL PRODUCTIVITY

Organizational structure varies; one large bank may be decentralized,

Improving MIS Productivity

while another exhibits a classic central bureaucracy. Organizational balance can prove an important tool in improving productivity. The ideas presented in the following paragraphs should assist the DP manager in effectively organizing the MIS department.

1. *Centralize computer authority; control resource application and personnel and the corporate data base.* It is not uncommon for larger organizations to have several computer installations, each operating independently. Frequently, these installations perform the same work but in incompatible ways and duplicate systems development efforts. Another result of this fragmentation of MIS authority is that incompatible formats prohibit the development of a consolidated corporate data base.

   A decentralized operation also has common DP problems that are best resolved by one group, which should incorporate the requirements of all operating groups in its design and implementation solutions. Because the resulting systems are applicable to the entire organization, redundant development efforts are eliminated.

   The establishment of a central authority is strongly recommended, even in decentralized operations. At a minimum, the central authority should have the power to prevent redundant software development efforts; establish uniform hiring, promotion, and compensation standards; specify design, documentation, and operations standards; and ensure that communications networks and devices are compatible throughout the organization.

2. *Transfer functions; eliminate the entire data entry department and have users perform this task.* Data entry departments often enter data that has been preprocessed by the user department. With the growth of distributed systems, transferring the entire data entry function to users often is cost-effective.

3. *Distribute or redistribute the processing load.* MIS management, for example, could install a minicomputer in a field office instead of adding load to the host telecommunications system, institute local billing processing to eliminate postal delays, and install a key-to-disk system with remote key stations and printers, removing the burden from the mainframe and postponing a mainframe upgrade.

   Distributed processing may, in some cases, be better termed redistributed processing, because processing loads are assigned to the most effective location based on the needs of the organization. The location of a processing function should be considered from both a technical and productivity point of view. For example, processing delays in billing can be costly because of the time value of money. A single approach to the distribution of processing power may be inappropriate. In the long run, the technique that best suits a particular environment is usually the least expensive alternative.

4. *Develop policies to standardize the use of word and data processing.* Many DP installations ignore word processing and office systems or consider them a threat. MIS management must recognize this function as a legitimate organizational element and work with word processing

PRODUCTIVITY IMPROVEMENT

users to integrate them into the overall MIS plan.

5. *Improve budgetary control.* Many managers do not understand how to use budgets to monitor and control an organization. As a result, budgets are viewed as a document to be prepared annually and then forgotten until next year. An effective cost-accounting system includes a budget that forms the basis of a monitoring and control system. The use of standard costs and the apportionment of overheads in cost accounting are based on budget figures. Deviations from standard are based on comparing actual results to budgeted expectation. Use of the budget as the foundation for a cost-accounting system is self-feeding because the system results provide the initial input for subsequent budgets.

MANAGERIAL INNOVATION

Innovative management is the star that guides the MIS productivity program. Developing a creative idea or refining a borrowed one can help the MIS manager and the organization remain competitive. The following ideas meet these criteria.

1. *Avoid excess inventory.* The MIS manager should know how much of the organization's money is tied up in MIS department inventory, which includes paper, forms, cards, tapes, and other unused or unapplied material. The Japanese system of Kanban, or just-in-time inventory, can help reduce the organization's cost by decreasing the inventory. This technique requires closer coordination with suppliers and occasionally involves modest risks; however, properly managed Kanban can reduce inventory costs. One way of improving Kanban is to pool supplies among data centers that are within a company or across company lines but within a small geographic territory.

2. *Implement a trouble desk.* As a single point of contact for user problems, a trouble desk can be an important element in quality assurance and productivity improvement programs. A central collection point for problems helps MIS management control problem tracking and resolution and minimizes interruption to data center employees. If users can be trained to contact a trouble desk when they experience difficulties (e.g., a misrouted report, a failing terminal, poor response time), the person best suited to correct the problem can be alerted more quickly. The MIS manager can also obtain more accurate information regarding the nature of the problems and the time required to fix them.

3. *Market in-house software or sign a marketing agreement with the hardware vendor.* There is a major difference between software written for internal use and that developed for sale. Of particular importance are the quality of the documentation and the reliability of the code. In addition, little quirks that can be tolerated in an in-house application system are unacceptable in a package. If the MIS department has extremely high systems development standards for documentation, systems design, and programming and the organization is prepared to guarantee the product and provide after-the-sale service (i.e., debugging and updating), marketing in-house software may prove feasible.

Improving MIS Productivity

4. *Use the junk-yard technique; remove older CRTs from service and use their spare parts to keep other CRTs functioning; drop the maintenance agreement.* This step is feasible only in organizations with available trained personnel. Unlike mainframes, CRTs have very high voltages and working on them can be dangerous.

5. *Recycle dormant tapes.* Many MIS managers overlook the fact that money is tied up in dormant tapes that could be recertified and recycled if users release them. A concerted effort to release tapes from vaults can pay large dividends for most shops.

6. *Use students part-time for some remedial tasks.* Managers of university MIS departments are aware of the large and low-priced student labor pool. Managers of DP installations located near a college or secondary school with a strong DP or computer science program should also recognize that students can be a source of high-quality personnel. Although students may need some initial training, they are often extremely enthusiastic and eager to demonstrate that they can do a good job.

7. *Use internal auditors as a management tool.* Most MIS managers avoid auditors as much as possible. The most effective managers, however, welcome auditors and use them to augment their management abilities. Auditors can help identify functions that are candidates for improvement and then annually assess the progress of the MIS productivity improvement program. Specifically, auditors can review rerun levels in computer operations, establish performance standards for data entry operations, review the extent to which documentation standards are met, and consult on the effectiveness of the change control process.

CONCLUSION

The ideas in this chapter can be used to initiate a formal program of productivity improvement in the MIS department. The MIS manager should start by identifying the areas of greatest potential and then decide how to measure progress. Employees should be informed that high-quality work and improved productivity are central to MIS objectives and to their jobs. Those who contribute to the program should be rewarded, and a concerted effort should be made to involve all employees in the search for ideas to improve all areas of the MIS operation. The leverage that MIS offers the entire organization can also be applied to its own functions if MIS management is willing to invest the time and effort in developing a productivity improvement program. Although the format and content of the program will vary according to organizational needs, its effect can be universal.

XIII-3
Office Technology Brings Higher White-Collar Productivity

Jacob Nussbaum

INTRODUCTION

The current debate over stagnant office productivity has focused sharply on white-collar workers, who have become the target of consultants and equipment vendors, all seemingly dedicated to improving productivity. Behind this apparent self-serving promotion, however, is the conviction that some combination of technology, organizational changes, and motivational programs can significantly increase white-collar productivity.

Unfortunately, there is little agreement on how to implement such improvements. Suggestions include:
- Following a slow-paced and controlled approach
- Using anxiety-reducing schemes to ease user resistance
- Modifying job and organizational structures to maximize the use of equipment and system capabilities

It is also argued that increased white-collar productivity is a result of the proper application of behavioral science and that technology's contribution occurs only after the appropriate organizational changes have been implemented.

Despite determined attempts to carry out these ideas and despite the aggressive marketing of electronic products, the automated office is still resisted. Vendors and consultants attribute such opposition to the inability of most organizations to measure office-worker productivity. As a result, they cannot determine what benefits to expect from office automation.

Increased productivity should not be the only justification for investing in office technology, for two reasons. First, white-collar productivity would have to be measured at each job skill level—an impossible task. Second, by concentrating on increasing efficiency, an organization overlooks office automation's other benefits.

Office technology investments should be evaluated on the same comprehensive basis used by most managers to judge the long-term value of other capital investments. The standard cost/benefit analysis is especially applicable to office technology as its originally discrete capabilities become integrated and geographically linked through telecommunications.

In addition, technologically enhanced white-collar productivity depends on a thorough understanding of how industry and organizational differences influence automation requirements. The technology-versus-psychology debate has contributed little to the real problem—increasing office productivity. Although behavioral science can make an important contribution to a productivity program, the experience of many service industries suggests that greater office efficiency primarily results from a strong managerial commitment to office automation.

The decision to invest in any technology is usually based on a comparison of project expenditures and reduced labor costs. This singular emphasis on office productivity, however, applies only to clerical and other manual processing activities. Another drawback is that such an analysis biases technology decisions toward short-term investments, excluding projects that have long-term benefits but an inconsequential—or even negative—initial impact on productivity. A third disadvantage of the project-by-project investment philosophy is that performance improvement becomes a departmental responsibility that, at best, only vaguely relates to organizational goals.

How can managers overcome this decision-making myopia? One solution is to base technology decisions on a capital-investment policy that incorporates overall business strategy; operationally, this means linking technology and corporate planning. Since most technology investments both improve organizational performance in general and increase productivity in specific activities, managerial efficiency concerns are the focus of corporate decision making. How to measure the benefits of technology, however, remains unresolved.

The concept of office automation must be clarified before its benefits for white-collar workers can be examined. Office-based technology can aid the performance of both line and staff functions. Securities salespeople retrieving quotations and account data while buying or selling stock and the traders of financial instruments who use terminal-based access to financial market data and message transmission systems are examples of automated line activities. (The application of automation to staff functions is now so common that it need not be discussed in detail.)

The use of office technology is clearly gaining momentum; its benefits, however, are difficult to identify and measure because white-collar functions are service oriented and produce little tangible output. Nevertheless, several benefits are obvious, including:
- Savings on resource input (primarily reduced clerical and professional labor)
- Output improvements, which may translate into market share growth, higher product prices, and/or greater profitability
- Strategic business planning support (e.g., decision support systems or the application of technology in new product development)

Assigning values to such benefits is the most difficult part of measuring office technology use. Although direct labor savings can be easily calculated, it is almost impossible to affix a value to technologically produced information. Whether it is necessary to do so, however, is questionable. When a manufacturing company develops a technologically advanced production process, the expected benefits are usually lower unit production costs, an enhanced product, and/or expanded capacity for capturing an increased market share. In the evaluation of manufacturing projects, financial data, market, and other projection analyses, as well as sound judgment, are translated into incremental benefit and cost dollars. Similar analyses can be applied to potential office automation investments.

BENEFITS OF INFORMATION SYSTEMS

This section describes an approach for identifying and measuring the benefits of office information systems on organizational performance, productivity, and business strategy. This conceptual framework is based on the premise that the resources used in information systems development must produce measurable benefits.

Organizational Performance. Organizational performance concerns corporate goals that address return on investment, market share growth, new product success, and market positioning. The value of achieving such goals can be estimated even in the absence of accounting data. Senior marketing managers, for example, can easily place a value on market share increases.

Information systems can affect these goals in two ways. First, such systems can effectively support activities that are critical to the attainment of organizational goals.[1] For example, critical activities for a supermarket operation include product mix, shelf space management, pricing, and promotion. Second, when an information system is the key ingredient of a product or service, it can directly increase organizational performance. In banking, for example, computers and telecommunications are crucial to cash management services. Regardless of whether technology supports critical activities or contributes directly to products and services, its cost is known. Since achieved goals have a recognized value, information systems costs and benefits to performance can be identified and measured.

Productivity. Productivity involves an organization's use of resources—money, staff, and materials—in the production process. Productivity therefore improves when resource use is economized. Productivity increases, however, cannot always be distinguished from improvements in organizational performance. For example, when products or services are primarily undifferentiated commodities and competition is based on price, an organization's productivity improvements also have a strategic value. In such industries, because productivity increases mean that products and/or services can be offered at a lower price, an organization can undersell its competition and obtain a larger share of the market. Regardless of whether information systems improve productivity, enhance organizational performance, or do both, these benefits can be identified and their value quantified.

PRODUCTIVITY IMPROVEMENT

Business Strategy. Business strategy benefits—technological improvements to the development of new products, services, and/or businesses—are easier to measure than those of organizational performance and productivity. Because any initial development activity requires an organization's commitment of capital funds, investments (including those in technology) are made only when an adequate return on investment is forecast. Technology improvements in business strategy or initial systems development are therefore quantifiable.

INDUSTRY-SPECIFIC TECHNOLOGY REQUIREMENTS

Despite vendor efforts to provide user-friendly products and tailor systems to user needs, the most distinguishing characteristics of industries are seldom addressed by office automation configurations. Because technology is now aimed toward professional and managerial activities, these deficiencies have a significant impact. For example, depending on the industry, market, competition, and other factors, managerial styles and technology needs can differ substantially.

Although the difficulty in meeting these needs has a limited impact on hardware characteristics (e.g., the functional capabilities of workstations and terminals), the variety and dynamic nature of business requirements are affected. For example, the information needs of newly established, small to medium-sized organizations operating in a competitive environment differ from those of larger, more mature organizations with control over their markets. In addition, industry planning horizons vary for service industries with rapidly changing products (e.g., banking) and heavy manufacturing organizations whose products have long gestation periods (e.g., steel). Although decision support systems are beginning to focus on these differences, adequate support for professionals and managers is not imminent.

Industry differences further highlight the shortcomings of using only increased productivity to justify the cost of technology projects. A low market share or inadequate capacity use can negate the value of improved productivity if additional capital investments merely make a slow growth company more capital intensive. The broad cost/benefit framework presented in this report, however, can limit such misjudgments. The consideration of such factors as changing markets and the need for product innovation can lead to a new rationale for technology investment.

The demographic composition of office workers, presence or absence of unions, turnover, and absenteeism also affect the success of office automation projects within various industries.

All these factors suggest that the probability of success (or failure) for office automation projects can differ substantially among industries and organizations. Another dimension of that risk concerns how technology projects affect other capital investments. An office automation program that seems to be a financial risk may be advantageous if it can reduce the overall uncertainty of an organization's mix of capital investments.

An investment in a new technology can be a hedge against existing systems or operating capacity reaching economic obsolescence earlier than expected. For example, the banking industry has invested in automated teller machines (ATMs) on the assumption that traditional branch offices will become economically obsolete. Although to date ATMs have not been profitable, this new technology and alternative systems for delivering retail banking services should soon be productive. These and other decisions can be easily evaluated within the proposed cost/benefit framework.

TECHNOLOGY AND PSYCHOLOGY

The debate over whether technology or psychology is more important in increasing productivity continues to gain momentum. At one extreme, vendors, automation designers, and consultants argue that only additional capital investment in technology will improve white-collar productivity. The proponents of this argument claim that capital investment comparisons between office, manufacturing, and agricultural environments suggest that differences in investment are the primary causes for variations in productivity growth among these functions. These individuals also reason that, in addition to capital investment, individual positions and organizational structures must be modified to maximize the use of available equipment and systems. Anxiety-reducing programs are recommended for easing user resistance to automation.

For various reasons, including the perceived inability to measure white-collar productivity, organizations often question technology's ability to increase office efficiency. Although they accept automation as a key element in a long-term productivity solution, users are also examining other approaches.

The major alternative to automation is a motivational program that includes participatory management, job enrichment, and salary incentives. Behavioral specialists contend that these techniques can achieve the highest possible white-collar productivity gains and that automation permits additional improvements only after such programs are implemented. It is also suggested that automation be introduced into the office only to the extent that it can be comfortably accepted by workers. A major drawback of psychologically based productivity improvement efforts is that many dramatic productivity increases are temporary. Several studies of the links between motivation and productivity indicate that one-time, all-purpose motivational programs cannot provide continuous white-collar productivity improvements.

Where then can users find guidance in implementing productivity programs? Is there a systematic record of experience that is relevant to the office?

Researchers at the Work in America Institute, Scarsdale, New York—an organization specializing in productivity-related research—as well as other analysts stress that productivity improves more from managerial innovation than worker motivation or conscientiousness. Studies by the Strategic Planning Institute, Boston, suggest that automation clearly increases productivity but that careful analysis is required to identify the organizations that would benefit from such technology. It is also commonly accepted that, like manufacturing organizations, service industries can benefit from capital investment. The application of technology to services is described as industrialization; that is, services produced from combining preplanned systems with people and equipment are substituted for services that were previously supplied on an individual basis.[2] This infusion of technology into services also describes the automation of the office—the center of most service activities.

Technology, therefore, is central to any strategy to improve office efficiency. Furthermore, the declining price/performance ratio of electronic technology mandates its substitution for expensive labor; this cost saving, however, should not be the only consideration in automating office functions. Because technology is increasingly used as the basis of service delivery systems (important marketing tools in a growing competitive business environment), its application in terms of revenue is also justified. The infusion of technology into the office is therefore influenced by the conditions and requirements of specific industries and organizations.

Although behavioral science still plays an important role in improving office efficiency, its application must be tailored to business requirements. Organizational changes must satisfy an organization's internal requirements and be responsive to external competitive pressures. The use of behavioral techniques, therefore, must be based on specific industry and organizational needs. The administrators of productivity programs must also remember that worker efficiency depends on many factors—not simply one or two elements.

CONCLUSION

White-collar productivity and office technology are closely linked. If office technology is to succeed, automation designers must be more sensitive to the user needs of particular industries and maximize the value of motivational programs as an adjunct of broadly based productivity efforts. Accordingly, productivity increases result from management's commitment to and careful implementation of technology and the use of human resources; quick-fix schemes are not the answer to improving white-collar efficiency.

References

1. Rockart, John. "Chief Executives Define Their Own Data Needs." *Harvard Business Review,* March–April 1979.
2. Levitt, Theodore, "Industrialization of Service." *Harvard Business Review,* September–October 1976.

Bibliography

Umbaugh, R.E. and Juliff, R.J. "Office Technology, Paperwork, and Productivity," *National Productivity Review,* Summer 1982, 250–269.

XIII-4
A Path to Improved Productivity—Effective Data Management

Richard J. Nauer

INTRODUCTION

Simplification of input procedures for the information captured in a data dictionary system (DDS) is the first step in controlling data management. The need for naming standards that will easily gain acceptance is fundamental to these procedures. In addition, user-friendly data-entry screens must be developed to aid data collection. Despite the "selling" of data resource management to MIS and user departments, data collection remains a problem. It has a tangible cost and is considered a clerical function. Although all computer applications must pass through a data collection phase, this function is usually performed in a less than structured manner.

A preprocessor (i.e., a program or set of programs that feeds the data dictionary system and is custom fitted to the front end of the DDS) is also essential to the success of the data dictionary system. The preprocessor captures raw data and applies editing and transaction generation functions that ensure the compliance of the captured data to data management standards.

Efforts must be directed at generating reports that are meaningful and acceptable to end users and management. A major problem with the data collection effort is that it is often perceived as one-sided; that is, much effort is directed at collecting data and entering it into the dictionary, but meaningful results are not immediately apparent.

The introduction of a DDS as the major tool for data collection may be met unenthusiastically by the person assigned as data dictionary coordinator when:
- The user who is required to input data to the dictionary believes that he or she will be reviewed and critiqued by others. The user is concerned that the data element definition may be incomplete or incorrect, or that the grammar and style of writing may be thought unprofessional.
- Data dictionary users believe they will be required to follow data management disciplines, specifically data management standards and naming conventions. Standards are often resisted in the hope of maintaining

PRODUCTIVITY IMPROVEMENT

individual creativity. Unfortunately, this is a major obstacle to creating a viable data dictionary environment.

This chapter addresses the latter concern and proposes an approach to overcoming resistance to data dictionary use and creating an environment in which the data dictionary is perceived as a productivity tool.

SIMPLIFYING INPUT PROCEDURES

The first step in creating an environment conducive to data dictionary use is to simplify input procedures. This can be accomplished through the following four activities.

Adopting Easy-To-Use Naming Conventions

The problem of establishing simple naming conventions must be addressed when the data dictionary is considered for the data collection process. Esoteric naming conventions require a trained professional to encode and retrieve the data. Most organizations, however, do not have a trained librarian who can perform the name assignment and must rely instead on the application and end-user staff to perform the data collection function. Naming conventions therefore must be simple to avoid a significant training and time commitment.

The easiest naming convention to adopt allows acceptance of the end user's name tag as the dictionary name. If, for example, the end user refers to an item as *account distribution code*, the data dictionary could also input this item as such. Retaining in the dictionary the name the end-user community uses to refer to a data item is acceptable; however, problems may arise when the end-user community refers to the item with redundant adjectives that relate a nature of ownership. For example, if this item is also identified as *payroll account distribution code*, *personnel account distribution code*, or *marketing account distribution code*, then the problem of identifying the generic term must be addressed. The adjective preceding the generic name usually may be removed; the more difficult problem is getting the various functions to agree on a common definition for the data item.

Once the generic name has been identified, it may be used as the official data item name. Most commercially available dictionary packages limit the dictionary name field to approximately 30 characters but, not surprisingly, many names of end-user data items are much longer. One solution is to adopt standard abbreviations. For example, the name *account distribution code* could be abbreviated *ACCT-DIST-CD* (the dashes would be included for readability and compatibility with procedural languages). Such standard abbreviations generally are easy to interpret. For additional clarity, the first line of the description category in the data dictionary could be used to spell out the full DDS name, thus providing complete documentation. Assigning a standard location for providing this information name enables the system to generate the full name in dictionary reports.

In addition, the standard abbreviations used to compose the name are themselves valuable pieces of data for future searches. In the previous example, the assigned dictionary name indicates that this data item deals with account, distribution, and code. This information also helps in answering such ad hoc requests as what account or distribution codes are in the dictionary. Entering this information into the dictionary is often referred to as classifying the data or assigning keywords.

Facilitating Use of Naming Standards

Ease of use facilitates user acceptance of the naming standards adopted. The individual responsible for data collection is usually the person who assigns the dictionary names. Typically, in concert with the end-user community, the applications development staff performs the data collection activity and therefore applies the naming standards. Consequently, the names assigned to the dictionary are the end-user community's assigned names, but without personalized adjectives.

Creating the initial inventory of standard abbreviations becomes the responsibility of the data administration function. In lieu of such an official function, responsibility falls to the individual who assigns the standards for the dictionary.

Literature is currently available that lists names and suggested abbreviations. These books must be used judiciously, because most organizations already have a commonly accepted and used set of abbreviations. These abbreviations should be used first with additional ones then assigned as needed. Outside information sources can then be used as guides to determine appropriate abbreviations. Once standard abbreviations have been assigned, they should be accepted, and development of multiple versions should be avoided.

The first project to use standard abbreviations will take the most time because the inventory of abbreviations must be developed from scratch. The need for the same names will arise quickly, especially for applications from the same functional area. Applications introduced from new functional areas create a need for new names. The effort involved quickly reaches a point of maturity, and though never completely fulfilled, the need for new abbreviations reaches a plateau.

Limiting Information for Capture

The strength of the data dictionary is its data relationship power and flexibility. The application development staff often misuses the data dictionary by entering too much information. During the initial stage of data collection, the application project team has access to large quantities of data, which they feel obligated to document. Two problems result: extra time is required to code and enter this information into the dictionary, and unless the project team plans to maintain this information, it quickly becomes obsolete and unused.

In addition, the dictionary may acquire a negative reputation if management believes that too much time was spent on the data dictionary, only to have the data become obsolete and unused. This reputation discourages future users before they even know what the dictionary is or can do for them. Thus, the application development staff should be dissuaded from introducing additional information into the dictionary that they do not plan to maintain.

PRODUCTIVITY IMPROVEMENT

Which information should be captured in the dictionary depends on the environment in which it is used. The dictionary is typically used to support project development. Data items are established with descriptions and technical parameters, and data relationships are provided that relate groups, records, segments, files, and data bases. When this information is documented and subsequently maintained, the dictionary becomes an excellent tool for developing a formalized change control system.

Many organizations also use the dictionary to perform such functions as functional analysis, data modeling, data flow diagrams, data base design interfaces, and front-end business system planning. When the dictionary is perceived as a viable means of supporting these efforts, the specific data required for such support must be addressed.

Creating User-Friendly Data-Capture Screens

Once the amount of information for the dictionary has been decided, the approach to data capture (i.e., use of batch-coded forms, worksheets, or data entry screens) must be determined. Before data collection begins, a decision must be made regarding how to treat captured data. This information must be coded into the data dictionary; however, filling out coding forms is cumbersome, especially when compared with today's online data entry systems. Therefore, easy-to-use data entry screens must be developed that are simple and straightforward, with facilities for easy change and correction.

The number and type of screens developed for data entry depend on the dictionary's planned used. Special data entry screens should be developed for each intended use of the dictionary (e.g., business system planning, data flow diagrams, functional analysis). Usually, screens developed for typical dictionary use can be separated into stages. The end user should use one set of screens to support the basic assignment of dictionary names and data descriptions, and the application development staff should use another set to input technical attributes relating to records, segments, and data bases.

THE NEED FOR A PREPROCESSOR

A preprocessor facilitates dictionary use for the project development team and end user. Each preprocessor may be customized to meet an organization's established data management disciplines. The amount of editing and the ease-of-use capability built into the preprocessor are a function of the resources readily available for establishing such a facility.

Items for consideration in preprocessor planning are discussed in the following sections.

Automatic Assignment of Dictionary Name

A preprocessor that can generate data dictionary names is desirable. Regardless of the simplicity of the naming standards developed, the end-user or project development team must translate user names according to established naming standards. One solution is to develop an online data entry screen that allows the user to enter the full data item name and the preprocessor to assign the dictionary name. If, for example, standard abbreviations are used to establish the dictionary name, as suggested in this chapter, a program can be written to automatically look up and assign the appropriate abbreviations. Such a program is more sophisticated than it seems. For example, if the name assigned to the dictionary is a compound word, a search for the complete words must be conducted before each separate word is examined and abbreviations are assigned separately.

A major advantage of the preprocessor approach to assigning dictionary names is that it does so more reliably and consistently than manual assignment, especially when more than one person is involved. Subsequent audits of the manual approach usually reveal inconsistencies in the name assignments.

Automatic Assignment of Classification Categories

Another major advantage of using a preprocessor is that the keywords, or classification categories, can automatically be assigned (e.g., from physical or logical terminal, user identification, or department number) during dictionary name creation. Therefore, by simply introducing the data name on the screen, the user can automatically generate the assigned dictionary name and the appropriate keyword classifiers that form the name.

Automatic Assignment of Computer Program Names

Once the data dictionary name has been assigned, extending the naming standardization to the names used in programs should be considered. One suggestion is to assign the COBOL and PL/1 data names the same name as the dictionary name; extending the preprocessor to assign the program's data name automatically is then easy.

Use of Dictionary Generation Facilities

The data dictionary can also automatically generate many other features. For example, the COBOL and PL/1 data statements, including the file definition and record layout, may be automatically assigned and all technical data base interface controls generated. The major advantage to data dictionary generation of this information is consistency and integrity of data.

Although members of the application development team could create their own data base control blocks and COBOL data division entries for a DBMS, the high frequency of change in these areas decreases the probability for correct timely documentation when left to manual individual discipline.

The dictionary may be thought to slow a project because making a change requires the project development team to first update the dictionary—an extra step. This situation demands strong management backing: the enforcement of standards and procedures must be mandated and supported by project and top management. Otherwise, as data becomes obsolete, the initial efforts of entering information into the dictionary will have been in vain. If only one project team member circumvents the dictionary update step, the dictionary entry could quickly be perceived by others as obsolete, thus eliminating any impetus to use it.

A positive benefit of the dictionary is its use as support in generating

PRODUCTIVITY IMPROVEMENT

record layouts. In the early stages of application development during the business system design, often the best efforts are made in documenting the record layout. This layout is usually neatly typed and the documentation perceived as complete. Dynamic applications may require many changes to the record layout. Late into the project life cycle, however, the chance of generating timely and typewritten updates to the record layout is slight. Thus, the programmer often writes programs from an incorrect, outdated record layout.

DATA DICTIONARY REPORTS

Regardless of the DDS package used, providing useful dictionary reports to the end-user community, project development team, and general management is essential. Because management typically prefers, or is accustomed to, reading typed pages, the dictionary reports should appear typewritten; many managers have an aversion to printouts that resemble computer dumps.

Management Reports

A management report summarizing information contained in the dictionary should be generated. The information should be presented in a format that enables an end user to easily read the data description inventory. A management glossary report that lists all data items by function is also useful and can be easily accessed by end users if printed alphabetically.

Management reports should provide various levels of detail. A detailed report of use should furnish information for each specific data dictionary entry by displaying all the data relationships in which this data item is involved.

Application Development Reports

The application project team has access to all management reports as well as more detailed reports. A data element entry, for example, might be used in two groups, four records, three files, a data base, a program, and a system. Each of these entries should be printed in turn until the where-used chain is complete. These types of reports are generally built from the bottom up. Conversely, a report providing a data structure from the top down should be available. For example, a file may use two records, three groups, and twenty elements; each entry would be printed in turn until the last element is completed.

Relationship Reports. A relationship report that provides comprehensive cross-referencing of data dictionary entries should also be available. Each selected dictionary item and its related entries should be identified, including upward relationships detailing where the entry is used and downward relationships listing which other elements reference it. Cross-references should be obtained for any standard data dictionary name. If a data item entered into the dictionary during the business design has not been assigned to a record, file, report, or other category, it should be flagged as not referenced. Thus, a relationship report can also serve as a fail-safe mechanism.

Name Analysis Report. A name analysis report that provides the facility to analyze data dictionary names should also be available. The report should expand the compound names (i.e., the string of standard abbreviations that constitute the name) into their components and then cluster identical components. This report is useful in finding dictionary redundancies that may not be immediately obvious.

Graphic Reports. Graphic reports should provide detailed record and field layouts and identify the data items that compose the record and file structures. These reports should be easy to read, with narrative descriptions identifying the data items by order sequence and related picture clauses. The format should be readily usable by a programmer to initiate programming activities.

End-User Reports

Data element and group definitions and descriptions, particularly for those data elements used in reports, can help the user interpret the information presented in reports and used by the project development group. The end user can be given a total inventory of data items that relates to the data items within the application systems, which is valuable in monitoring data description changes. For example, if a business tax law is changed or a government regulation revised, the end user can use the dictionary to reflect these changes. The systems analyst may then evaluate these changes for the computer programs that may need revision.

The business needs of the application system, along with embedded data relationships, may also be documented in the dictionary. The data dictionary provides the facilities to document detailed business needs and their descriptions, requests, and respective frequency of occurrences. Once this information has been recorded, appropriate reports that summarize and detail this information should be made readily available.

INTEGRATION OF INFORMATION

The data dictionary is a valuable tool during the analysis, design, development, and implementation of an application system. At each project phase, the dictionary may be used to capture and retrieve timely information relating to specific data descriptions and technical attributes.

Feasibility Study Phase

The feasibility of a new application system or proposed enhancement to an existing one must be evaluated. The data dictionary can determine the current level of data information, the levels of business needs that must be changed, and the information needs that must be added to the dictionary.

Without a dictionary, documentation for existing applications will likely be obsolete, fragmented, or even nonexistent. The dictionary provides a central up-to-date source for identifying modifications in progress and the documentation currently available.

By using dictionary reports, an analyst can quickly determine the effect of proposed business changes on segments and programs. This can help the analyst prepare more accurate estimates of the costs and time required to implement proposed modifications.

PRODUCTIVITY IMPROVEMENT

Business System Design Phase

During the business system design phase, business needs are documented and data items are identified, described, and assigned dictionary names (assuming the data had not been previously recorded in the dictionary). The data items can subsequently be connected into meaningful groups, segments, data bases, reports, forms, programs, and other classifications. Data descriptions can be added, deleted, or revised as needed until the definitions are agreed to and finalized. Intermediate and final dictionary reports detailing and summarizing this dictionary information should be readily available both online and with hard-copy backup. The dictionary reports become the permanent documentation for this development phase and serve as input to the computer system design phase, which can build on and revise these data descriptions if necessary.

Use of the data dictionary in the business systems design phase also directs attention to planned changes to existing data descriptions at an early stage in the project development. This helps stimulate appropriate planning throughout the project development and helps encourage more integrated planning when changes of business needs are proposed for other application areas. When data descriptions are found incomplete or incorrect, dictionary maintenance corrects them immediately and preserves the integrity of data descriptions by means of permanent documentation. The problems of correcting previously distributed documentation and releasing piecemeal corrections are avoided.

Computer System Design Phase

During the computer system design phase, data elements and groups defined in the previous phase should be grouped into segments and data bases, along with narrative descriptions and technical attributes. Graphic reports detailing record and file layouts with appropriate picture clauses can be produced, and different views of record and file layouts should be easily generated. Interim and final working documentation may be provided with many detailed and management-oriented dictionary reports. These documents should be available to other members of the project development team to support the application activity.

Programming Phase

During the programming phase, the descriptions and the processing options for each program are entered into the data dictionary. Data base control blocks may be generated, depicting data base call structures as viewed by the program. The dictionary's technical information can be reviewed to detect errors and omissions prior to computer compilation or testing and before they extend into the program code. During the actual programming phase, COBOL source statements defining segment I/O areas and the appropriate control blocks may be generated by the data dictionary and transferred to a copy member library. The automatic generation of required data base control block information reduces the coding and debugging effort and the need for training most programmers in related formats and rules.

Implementation Phase

The data dictionary should provide an orderly process of application implementation through controlled use of the production information it contains. This wealth of information provides a valuable documentation resource; documentation charts can be generated from the dictionary, revealing a top-down documentation description from the system to the program modules and data elements.

CONCLUSION

The data dictionary is the focal point for establishing and maintaining a controlled data management environment. Unless the data administration function has sufficient staff to assign each project team the roles of both data analyst and data collector, it is necessary to motivate the application project team to use the data dictionary.

The best incentive is a management directive that insists on data dictionary use and the creation of an environment in which the dictionary is perceived as a productivity tool. This perception results from the development of simplified input procedures, creation of a preprocessor to the dictionary, and generation of a set of extensive, management-oriented dictionary reports, as discussed in this chapter. Education and training should be periodically scheduled to promote and reinforce dictionary use to management, the end-user community, and the application development project teams.

Section XIV
New Directions in Technology

In the introduction to this handbook, we discussed the need to balance management responsibilities with an understanding of technology. Keeping abreast of the new developments in products and technologies in a rapidly changing environment is a key challenge. The purpose of this final section is to shed light on some of these technologies and to provide MIS management a source of guidance on their application. One of the most promising applications that combines computer-controlled hardware and sensor-based recognition technology is in the field of robotics.

Robotics, as an industry, has progressed from isolated programmable devices capable of performing specific tasks to an integral systems approach in which robotics is only part of a totally computer-integrated manufacturing system. Considered by many to be an integration of artificial intelligence concepts with mechanical and manufacturing technology, this interdisciplinary field is now expanding beyond manufacturing applications. Chapter XIV-1, "Robotics and Robotics Software," outlines recent progress in robotics and considers the current and future issues affecting robot integration. It highlights current robotic capabilities and dicusses the advances needed to make the field of robotics even more appealing.

Another area of considerable interest is high-speed, high-volume data transmission. The proliferation of computerized business applications has created a steadily growing need for massive data communications. Originally, organizations had only two methods of electrically interfacing data communications equipment: twisted-pair wiring and coaxial cable. Fiber-optic cable can now provide a more cost-effective method of making these connections. Chapter XIV-2, "Advances in Fiber Optics," examines fiber-optics technology and discusses promising applications for fiber-optic systems.

Not only must we transmit huge amounts of data, we must also store it. Designing systems that economically and efficiently store and retrieve documents containing graphs, drawings, signatures, and other forms of optical input is a continuing challenge for MIS management. Central to that challenge is the need to create integrated systems that combine rapid access to document images with fast retrieval of associated data files. Chapter XIV-3, "Optical Disk Technology," describes this emerging technology, which allows integrated storage and retrieval of these files and represents one key component in a potential long-term systems solution.

The combination of high-volume, high-speed data transmission and high-volume, cost-effective data storage has also given rise to wider use of computer graphics. No longer a technological curiosity understood and used by a select few, computer graphics is moving into the mainstream of data processing. This change is resulting from implementation of the Information Center as well as from developments in graphics software and the expanding use of microcomputers in user departments. Chapter XIV-4, "Graphics Terminal Technology," provides the information needed by MIS executives and end-user management to keep current with developments in three key areas: hardware, with emphasis on microcomputers; graphics software; and effective methods of implementing and supporting computer graphics.

Another technology that has taken advantage of greater data communications and data storage capabilities is speech recognition and voice response. As noted in Chapter XIV-5, "Speech Recognition and Voice Response Technology," speech I/O technology is becoming increasingly feasible as research results are incorporated into practical products. Voice response provides intelligible synthetic speech at low bit rates for economical automation of information-reporting functions in a variety of applications. By offering a convenient means of data entry and control, speech recognition is increasing both accuracy and productivity for a growing number of military, scientific, and industrial applications. Speaker verification, an adjunct of speech recognition technology, provides accurate, cost-effective verification of speaker identity for secure access control. As these techniques are incorporated into widely available hardware, MIS managers will find many ways to apply them in their installations.

Perhaps the culmination of the integration of all these technologies comes in the promise of expert systems or, as some call it, knowledge-based systems. Expert systems, a form of artificial intelligence (AI), are emerging as a more intensive yet practical use of computers in a range of applications. The use of AI potentially can improve the accuracy, timeliness, and quality of decision making in those jobs that are performed by several persons, that involve repetitive tasks requiring human judgment, and that can be done best by access to expert guidance. Like any tool, however, expert systems have limitations that must be considered before a project is undertaken. Chapter XIV-6, "Expert Systems and Artificial Intelligence," reviews developments in this rapidly growing, high-potential field, noting the progress of Japan's Fifth-Generation Computer project.

XIV-1
Robotics and Robotics Software

Roger N. Nagel
Nicholas G. Odrey

INTRODUCTION

World competition for sales of new products has led to the formulation of production systems with the flexibility to meet the demands of the new marketplace. Product life cycles have shortened, and designs have proliferated and become more complex. The advent of the flexible manufacturing system can be traced to the development of the mircoprocessor and its utilization in providing the intelligence necessary on the factory floor.

Concurrent with the growth of the flexible manufacturing concept has been the introduction and development of the robot. Flexible manufacturing has a noted superiority over "hard" automation because its automation resides in the software and is not built into the hardware of the machine. Robotics has become an integral part of flexible manufacturing systems and has been progressing from simple pick-and-place mechanisms to more complex mechanisms with increased intelligence.

This chapter reviews the state of the art of robotics hardware and software and discusses the integration of robotics within what is termed the factory of the future. The architectures, programming environments, and control structures of the automated factory will continue to have considerable impact on data processing, and the management of such complex integrated systems will require a high degree of planning for proper execution.

Not only must data processing capabilities be extended to the robot programming environment, but links must be established to the various functions that make up a production environment. These functions consist, in part, of material requirements planning, inventory control, production control, and scheduling. Synergism of such functions with the more production-oriented elements, such as computer-aided design (CAD), computer-aided manufacturing (CAM), group technology, and their associated data bases, will lead to the fully automated unmanned factory. (Group technology, a methodology that includes the coding and classification of parts with similar design or production attributes into groups, enables the creation of a more useful data base for management.) Networking of the distributed computer systems that constitute the automated factory will require considerable investment in software, communications capability, and maintenance staff.

ROBOTICS STATE OF THE ART: HARDWARE

Industrial Robots—Background and Definition

The word *robot* entered the English language in 1923 when Karel Capek's play *R.U.R (Rossum's Universal Robot)* was translated. Although the term *robot* suggests the C3PO or R2D2 robots of *Star Wars* fame, in reality the modern robot is far removed from such science fiction figures.

The first technically realizable robot can be traced to George C. Devol's patent for "Programmed Article Transfer" in 1956. It was at a chance meeting at a cocktail party that Devol and Joseph P. Engleberger met and the modern robotics industry was born. The first industrial robot was installed in 1961 and was limited to the unloading of a die-casting machine. Such a task was ideal for a first application because it was uncomplicated and met the criteria of relieving workers from dangerous, debilitating, and repetitive tasks. From such simple early endeavors, robots have been developed into more complex mechanisms, and synergistic combinations of robots and industrial equipment have been formed to perform more complex tasks.

Many attempts have been made to define the term *robot*. In lay terms, a robot would be called a mechanical arm or a device possessing certain anthropomorphic characteristics. Such a definition, however, could include almost all automation devices with a moving lever. The Robot Institute of America (RIA) has adopted the following working definition:

> A robot is a programmable multifunctional device designed to move material, parts, tools, or specialized devices through variable programmed motions for the performance of a variety of tasks.

The key words in the definition are programmable and multifunctional. It is the programmability of a robot that gives it the flexibility to perform various tasks.

Currently, robots can be configured into four structural types, as depicted in Figure 1. Each type is distinguished by the coordinate system applicable to the arm. These configurations are:
- Cartesian coordinate configuration—A robot of this configuration consists of three orthogonal slides that provide an x, y, and z motion commensurate with the axes of Cartesian coordinate space. Such a robot is capable of moving its arm to any point in a three-dimensional rectangular work volume.
- Cylindrical coordinate configuration—In this configuration, the robot body has vertical motion (z axis) and swivels (θ degrees) about the vertical axis. In addition, the arm can move in and out perpendicular to the vertical axis (r axis). The work volume describes a cylinder in space.
- Spherical (polar) coordinate configuration—In this configuration, the work space within which the arm moves forms a partial sphere. The

Robotics

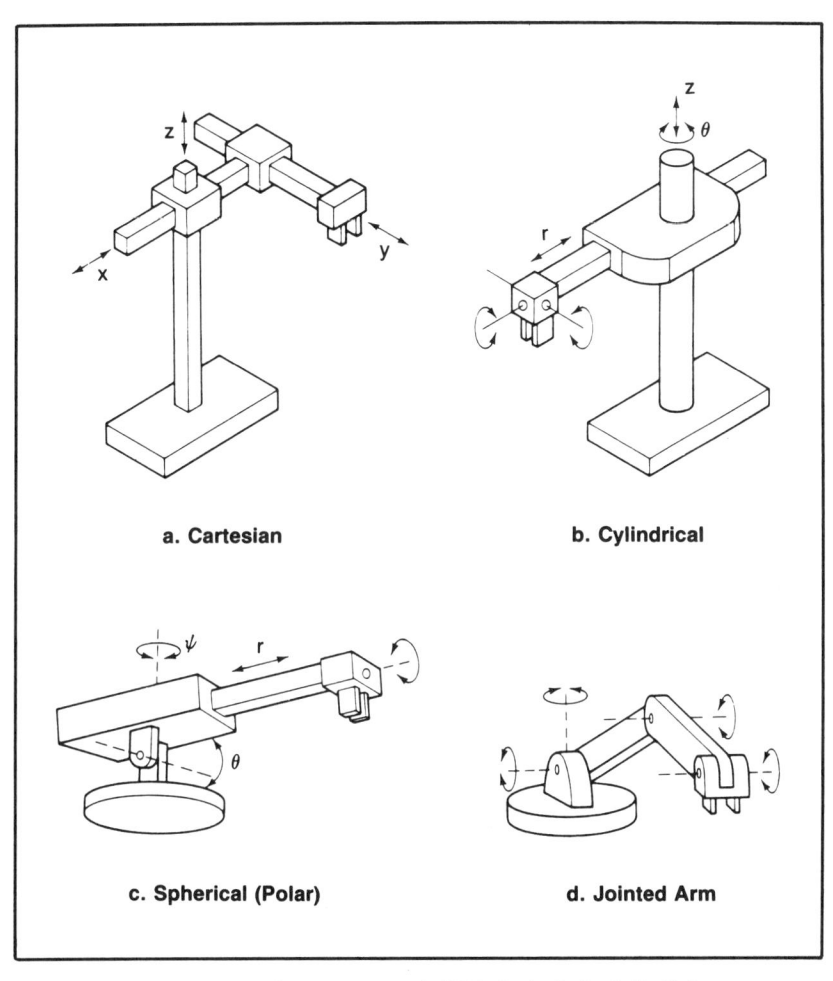

Figure 1. The Four Most Common Robot Configurations

a. Cartesian b. Cylindrical c. Spherical (Polar) d. Jointed Arm

Reprinted with permission from Toepperwein, L.L., et al. ICAM Robotics Application Guide. *Air Force Wright Aeronautical Labs Technical Report No. AFWAL-TR-80-4042*, Vol. 2, April 1980.

coordinates (r, ψ, θ) describe, respectively, a telescoping arm (r), a rotation about a vertical axis (ψ), and a pivoting (θ) about the axis perpendicular to the base vertical axis that can raise or lower the arm.
- Jointed arm configuration—Also known as articulated or revolute arm, this configuration consists of elements connected at joints that are analogous to the human wrist, elbow, and shoulder. The robot is rotatable about a base, which enables it to reach points in a quasi-spherical space.

A mechanical manipulator of an industrial robot of any of the preceding configurations consists of a set of three axes (either rotary or slide) that position the end of the wrist in space. These three axes determine the work volume, or envelope, in space. For full flexibility, a gripper, or hand, can be attached to the wrist of a robot. The gripper introduces three additional axes that specify the orientation of the hand. (Not all robots have six axes to specify position and orientation.) The motion provided by these axes is referred to as the degrees of freedom of the robot. It is important to note that the gripper or tool attached to the wrist is not considered part of a general-purpose industrial robot. Rather, it is a special-purpose device attached to the wrist for use in one or more applications.

Robot Components

The three main components of an industrial robot are the mechanical manipulator, the actuation mechanism, and the controller. The actuation mechanism is typically hydraulic, pneumatic, or electric. Hydraulic and pneumatic mechanisms transmit power to the joints as pressure. Although pneumatic actuators are simpler and less expensive to operate, they cannot handle the heavy loads and high speeds of the hydraulic units. Pneumatic actuators typically are used for small, inexpensive pick-and-place robots. Electric actuators do not have the payload capability of hydraulic actuators; however, they do have advantages in that there is no contamination of the work area (as could occur with hydraulic system leaks) and noise level is considerably lower during operation.

Most electrically actuated robots have servomotors or stepping motors. Stepping motors are common to small robots (e.g., desktop instructional robots) in which the payloads are small. Servomotors typically run on DC, but many AC servos are making inroads as a result of the efforts of Japanese manufacturers. Electric servomotors are more accurate than hydraulic systems. Servo mechanisms are feedback controlled (i.e., closed-loop systems) to correct mechanical position. Conversely, nonservo open-loop systems do not have position and rate-of-change sensors on each axis; thus, the position of the robot is not known as it moves from one point to another. Positioning accuracy is attained in nonservo systems through the use of limiting techniques at each extreme of manipulator travel. Such limits could be as simple as a switch to indicate to the controller when a certain limit position has been reached.

The controller is the device that stores the program for the industrial robot and communicates with the actuation mechanism to control the manipulator. The controller architecture for robot servo feedback systems includes a central processing unit, memory, I/O devices (such as a keyboard terminal, serial I/O devices, disk drives, and a teach pendant), and an axes actuator capability and axes feedback signal converters to indicate position and velocity feedback signals.

The controller's function is to provide coordinated motion along or around several axes simultaneously. In a servo controller robot with feedback capability, the controller monitors the position and velocity of the manipulator trajectory and compares it with an ideal trajectory stored in memory. A control algorithm minimizes positional and velocity differences either along the complete trajectory or at the end points. The exactness of the task is a function of the complexity of the control algorithm. Minimization of differences in position and velocity at the end points of a trajectory is sufficient for such tasks as pick and place or machine loading and unloading. Complex tasks, such as arc welding, require control at various points along a preplanned trajectory.

Controllers have undergone the most extensive evolution of all the components of an industrial robot. This evolution has occurred not only in the hardware but, for the most part, in the software complexity allowed and the method of programming (i.e., the human interface). The past few years have seen a trend toward computer control of industrial robots, as opposed to plug-board and special-purpose devices (e.g., mechanical stops).

Mechanical designers are currently working on the kinematics of design, models of dynamic behavior, end effectors, and alternate design structures for industrial robot manipulators. These efforts are leading to highly accurate manipulators. In the U.S., much of this work is being done at university laboratories, such as those at MIT, Carnegie-Mellon, Lehigh, and Stanford. This research should affect future industrial robots in the following ways:
- Robots will have access to models that predict behavior under load, thereby allowing for corrective programming.
- Use of robots to apply measured force and torque will be possible.
- Greater accuracy and compliance to expected performance will be available.
- End effectors will be developed that improve dexterity, and quick-change hands will enable a robot to handle a variety of objects.

Many of these research areas concern increasing the accuracy and dynamic performance of robots. Accuracy is one of the fundamental problems in robotics. To be programmed offline, a robot must go to a commanded coordinate point. Current industrial robots do not have adequate absolute positioning accuracy; thus, they cannot be programmed from an external data base. In addition, it is not currently possible to transfer programs between robots. The need for accuracy has led to very rigid mechanical structures in current industrial robots. Improvement is needed in advanced control systems that enable the robot to adapt to changing inertial loads when in motion and to the difference in payload that it must transport. This would lead to improvements in robotic design, an increase in the strength-to-weight ratio of the robot, and the capability to take advantage of lighter-weight, more-flexible structures.

Robotic Systems

Systems Integration Considerations. The integration of robotics on the factory floor implies the establishment of not only communication links but also the physical layout of the robot and associated equipment into a functioning work cell. Engleberger notes that the work cell can be configured in several ways. These configurations include:
- Cell is centered on the robot—The work is arranged around a robot. Earlier installations were of this nature since such a layout involved the least amount of effort and commitment.
- Work is brought to the robot—A typical example would be the assembly line, in which work is conveyed to the robot, the robot performs its tasks, and the work is forwarded to the next station.
- Work travels past the robot—The robot performs its tasks as the work moves past. This requires more sophisticated control algorithms. Two

variations are moving-base line tracking and stationary-base line tracking. In moving-base line tracking, the robot is mounted on a transport mechanism and moves in conjunction with the line. The stationary-base line method involves coordination of the motion of the robot with a moving part.
- Robot is mobile—A robot is mounted on tracks and travels to different machine tools or is mounted on an overhead gantry system.

The configuration chosen is dependent on the work system strategy employed and the economics of implementation.

Fundamental to robotic systems integration is the computer command and control structure employed. Current activities are directed toward the establishment of hierarchical control methodologies. Such an approach is considered the most workable for resolving the intricacies of large, complex industrial systems. One such hierarchical approach is that taken by the National Bureau of Standards (NBS) in the development of the Automated Manufacturing Research Facility (AMRF).

In the AMRF, the command and control structure has goals or tasks at higher levels broken down into sequences of subtasks that are passed down the hierarchy (and further broken down) until a sequence of primitive tasks is generated that can be executed with single actions. At the factory floor level, a robot, a machine tool, an automatically guided vehicle, conveying capability, and associated smart sensors would constitute a workstation. Tasks within a workstation would be coordinated by a workstation controller.

Computational modules at all levels of such a hierarchy would affect the processing involved as well as the data management. Real-time processing demands at the low levels (e.g., vision systems) would be considerable, resulting in a need for algorithm development and faster processing capabilities. At the higher levels is the need for further development of expert systems. Links must be established not only with CAD data bases to facilitate robot programming development but also with the informational data bases needed to manage the overall system.

Foreseeable within the next five to ten years are the start of developments in natural language data bases, the connection of expert systems to natural language systems, automated design assistance for the building and upgrading of expert systems, hierarchical task-oriented interface languages designed for process planners, and interfaces to nonhomogeneous computers. The advent of the robot has led to a flexibility in manufacturing that, in turn, is spurring the development of today's computer-integrated manufacturing systems and automated factories.

Toward Higher Intelligence. From a hardware perspective, higher intelligence implies the development of improved sensors. Robotics research is concerned primarily with the development of vision and tactile proximity sensors. Although the Defense Advanced Research Projects Agency (DARPA) has sponsored research in speech sensors, this work has not been extensively applied to robotics. Other human senses (i.e., smell and taste) have been ignored in robot research to date.

A robot without sensors would severely limit the tasks that could be performed and would make the cost of fixturing (i.e., precisely locating parts to be manipulated) extremely high. The purpose of sensors is to give the robot the capability of adaptive behavior—that is, the ability to adapt to a changing environment. Sensor research for robotics can be grouped into (1) sensor physics and data reduction, which produce meaningful information and (2) the application of artificial intelligence techniques, which make more intelligent use of sensory data.

Vision sensors have been the most active research issue, and several robot vision systems are on the market. Commercial vision systems currently available can handle subsets of the following tasks (in order of increasing complexity):

1. Identification (or verification) of objects or of which stable state an object is in
2. Location and orientation of objects
3. Simple inspection tasks

More complex tasks being researched include:
- Visual servoing for robot guidance
- Navigation and scene analysis
- Complex inspection

With visual servoing, a vision system is incorporated into the feedback loop of the robot control system in order to improve the accuracy and guidance capability of the robot. Vision systems digitize an image obtained from a video camera and then "threshold" the digitized image. A digitized image consists of several gray levels (i.e., levels of intensity as in black-and-white television). To reduce the data-handling requirements for real-time operation, it is common practice to segment the image into a smaller number of gray levels by choosing thresholds within which only specified gray levels are transmitted. In the simplest case, thresholding can convert the number of gray levels in an image into a black-and-white binary image.

Vision systems operate by measuring a set of features on known objects during a training session and, when shown an unknown object, matching the same feature set to identify the object. Objects having more than one stable state are labeled separately. Such techniques, developed at Stanford Research Institute, have been successful but are limited in their ability to handle overlapping objects. Research is underway at, for example, the University of Rhode Island to develop techniques and algorithms for handling overlapping objects and picking randomly oriented parts from a bin.

Not all commercial vision systems employ the Stanford techniques, and various laboratories are involved in vision research and development. For example, Robot Vision Inc has made a commercial product for robot guidance. Others, such as AT&T-Bell Laboratories, MIT, and the Jet Propulsion Laboratory in Pasadena, CA, are developing algorithms and chips for faster and more economical vision computation. Vision research is a maturing field with many topics of interest, including the speed of algorithms, parallel processing, handling of incomplete data, and the application of artificial intelligence techniques.

Vision research can be classified into two general areas:

- Low-level vision—A term applied to aspects of a system that involve operations that are not knowledge based. Such operations involve the extraction and measurement of various shapes and other features from the images. These operations are currently being reduced to the hardware level.
- High-level vision—A term applied to a vision system that exhibits the use of a cognitive processor, geometric models, goals, and plans. High-level vision is concerned with identifying a manageable goal (i.e., isolating an information processing problem) and finding a method for meeting the goal (i.e., resolving the problem). High-level vision essentially devises computational theories and proofs dealing with the problems of a task. Such systems could combine knowledge about objects (e.g., features, shapes, relationship) with expectations about the image and involve processes to aid in interpretation of the image.

Vision research is related to, and dependent on, the results of very large scale integration (VLSI) and artificial intelligence (AI) research. Although considerable research activity is underway, it is difficult to fully predict results. Some of the problems currently being addressed by AI include:
- Knowledge-based representation of objects and their relationships
- The interaction between low-level information and high-level representation
- Interpretation of stereo (three-dimensional) images

The other major aspect of sensor research in robotics is the use of tactile sensors. The use of these devices in an industrial setting is still primitive. With the expected growth of robotics in such application areas as assembly, touch sensor technology is moving from the research laboratory to the factory floor. Most industrial robots today are limited to contact detection between the robot and an object by varying versions of the limit switch concept. Few robots operating on the factory floor have force or tactile sensors. One notable exception is the IBM RS1 robot, which incorporates strain gauges and a light-emitting diode in its gripper to give proximity and force feedback.

General needs for sensing in manipulator control are proximity, touch/slip, and force/torque. The most advanced force/torque sensors for industrial robots have been developed at Draper Laboratories in Cambridge MA. In addition, the remote center of compliance (RCC) developed at Draper has allowed passive compliance in the robot's behavior during assembly. The RCC is mounted between the gripper and the robot tool plate or wrist. Its function is to allow part movement for the purpose of alignment between mating parts. In the past few years, instrumentation has been added to the RCC to provide active feedback. Such instrumented versions represent the state of the art in compliant devices.

Slip sensing is essential to meeting of performance requirements in many manipulation tasks. In contacting, grasping, or manipulating an object, adjustments to gripping forces are necessary to avoid force overloads or slippage of the object. Requirements for touch/slip sensing have resulted in new developments in gripper design. Such developments have included the advent of fingered grippers embedded with artificial skin that could yield tactile information of a complexity comparable to that yielded by the human sense of touch. This has led to further research in conductive materials and arrays produced with conductive polymers and rubbers.

A 1983 study published by the Manufacturing Studies Board of the National Research Council predicted that within five years, force-sensing wrists and techniques for programming and controlling force will be available in the commercial market. In addition, end effectors will be able to handle a variety of objects, and multifingered hands capable of grasping a variety of three-dimensional shapes will have emerged from the laboratories. Regarding vision sensors, the next five years should see the implementation of VLSI devices that will facilitate the development of fuller feature sets. Three-dimensional vision systems, structural light, and stereo approaches will enter the market, enabling the containment of depth maps and three-dimensional surface inspection.

ROBOTICS STATE OF THE ART: SOFTWARE
Methods of Programming Robots

Programming methods can be classified according to level of user interaction during the programming process. These methods can be divided into four categories (based on increasing interaction):

1. Joint control languages
2. Primitive motion languages
3. Structured programming languages
4. Task-oriented languages

The first level requires that the user program in joint space. In this method, the programmer specifies joint angles (revolute) or positions (prismatic) for each axis to obtain a programmed end-effector position. This type of language is found most frequently on small educational robots, such as those manufactured by Microbot or Rhino (the language ARMBASIC and RASP, respectively). Such languages are atypical of large industrial robots.

Most industrial robots of the past two decades have used point-to-point primitive motion languages. Programming this type of robot controller involves storing, or teaching, a series of points corresponding to the path that the robot end effector is to follow. Such teaching by example can be subdivided into two distinct methods: the walkthrough method and the leadthrough method.

The walkthrough method is one in which the programmer physically moves the robot's end effector and arm through the motion sequence of the work cycle. Movements are recorded into memory and can be played back for the actual production cycle. The method has been used in paint spraying and arc welding applications. The leadthrough method uses a teach pendant terminal or joystick to control the robot's movements. Programmers generate program points by driving the robot to a point to be programmed with, for example, the teach pendant and storing the point by depressing a program switch on the pendant. Such a programming method is used by the Cincinnati Millacron T3 robot, the IBM motionlevel language EMILY, and the Unimation language VAL. Such primitive motion languages provide program editing capability, simple subroutines and branching, interfacing with external equipment, and the capability of programming in different coordinate systems. The largest disadvantage of such methods is the loss of production while the robot is being programmed. This has generated considerable interest in offline programming languages. Offline programming can be accomplished while the robot is still in production on the preceding job.

Offline programming has proved more feasible if structured programming techniques are used. Examples of robot programming languages using this technique are the IBM AML (A Manufacturing Language), the McDonnell Douglas MCL (Manufacturing Control Language), and the General Electric Help. Structured programming language characteristics offer a major improvement compared with primitive motion languages. Such characteristics include:
- Use of structured control constructs
- State-variable concepts
- Extensive use of coordinate transformation and frames
- Improved use of sensor commands and parallel processing capability
- Extensive branching and subroutine capability

The primary advantage of structured programming approaches has also proved to be its major impediment in implementation. The advantage is the use of coordinate transformations to specifically describe tasks as they would occur in complex assembly operations. The disadvantage is the educational burden placed on the programmer by the mathematics of the coordinate transformations, which must be coded in a structured format.

Nevertheless, second-generation language capability allows programming statements for control of the manipulator and provides the ability to extend the language in a hierarchical fashion. It affords the opportunity to build intelligent robots by providing the necessary controller language modules.

Task-oriented languages enable the user to work in the domain of the manufacturing problem without having to know the detailed mathematics of the coordinate transformations. Low-level aids, such as sensing and branching, are also transparent. A user need only specify a task in a natural language. For example, a command could be simply INSERT PIN A IN HOLE B. Task-oriented languages are currently being studied by various research organizations. The most notable accomplishment is the Autopass language developed by IBM.

Software of commercially available robot systems performs a variety of functions. Such functions include trajectory calculation, kinematic translation, interpretation of sensory data and conditional execution, and some rudimentary adaptive control. There is a commercial need for expanded interfaces to data bases of geometric models. The Manufacturing Studies Board of the National Research Council has predicted that within the next five years the following progress should occur:
- The ability to graphically lay out robotic cells will be commercialized. One current example is the Unigraphics PLACE package.
- Programming languages will take advantage of CAD systems to interact with geometric information stored in the CAD data base and aid in the process of generating robot motion.
- Robot operating systems will do more for users who use sensors to permit task orientation.

- Data bases from CAD, CAM, and other sources will be incorporated into the language and control structure.
- Artificial intelligence will play a larger role. Expert systems, natural-language front ends, and knowledge representation will become more prevalent.
- Hierarchical task-oriented interface languages based on current structural languages (e.g., AML, RAIL) will be developed. This will allow process planners to program applications.

Robot Programming Environment

As previously mentioned, second-generation robot programming languages are currently available. Programming robot systems with such languages is similar to programming mainframe computers in assembly language before the development of operating systems. What is needed are robot operating systems that do for robot users what current computer operating systems do for computer users in areas such as graphics and input and output.

A robot operating system would serve as a major step toward implicit languages. An implicit language can be defined as one in which the commands correspond to the task at hand, for example, INSERT PIN IN HOLE. Use of such an implicit language is further complicated by the fact that robots perform families of tasks. As mentioned, the Autopass system developed by IBM comes closest to an implicit language, but more research is needed in this area.

Other concerns related to the robot programming environment are data base issues and graphical robot programming and simulation. As robot programming moves from simple teach-pendant programming to that of a textual language, several new demands for data arise. Of great interest is access to the data bases of CAD/CAM systems. Such access would give the geometry and physical properties of the parts to be manipulated and the data concerning the machine tools and fixtures with which a robot interacts. Unified data bases that describe the physical and volumetric properties of objects would prove very beneficial in offline programming and in simulation of a robot in a work cell. Computer-assisted robot programming (CARP) arises from the belief that graphics is a good mechanism for describing robot motion. Companies such as Computervision and Automatix are conducting research in this area. CARP would be done at interactive graphics terminals, and the robot motions necessary to manipulate parts would be similar to graphic numerical control (NC) programming for machine tools.

Robot graphic simulation is motivated not only by the need for offline programming languages but also by the need for debugging languages. Other benefits derived from graphic simulation are robot cell layout, training mechanisms, and the ability of the robot to stay in production while new programs are being developed. Simulation is important for solving implementation, optimization, and collision problems that might arise. Real-time simulation is not yet available in standard systems but would be beneficial to users in understanding the dynamic and real-time problems in robotics. Work on robot simulation is hindered by the lack of standards, but progress is being made at IBM for AML, McDonnell Douglas for VAL, and at various universities.

NEW DIRECTIONS IN TECHNOLOGY

Sophisticated simulation, which would require simulation of sensor systems for sensor-based robots, is a subject that has not yet received much attention.

As robot programming evolves, robots will become an integral part of the total computer-integrated manufacturing scene. As such, robots would report to shop-floor control systems, report up in a hierarchy to work-cell controllers, and upgrade process planning inventory control systems and the various factory control, management, and planning systems that are in place or under development. In such an integrated approach, robot controllers must access various data bases and have established communications with other factory systems.

ACTION PLAN

Robotics is a young industry with many potential applications. The introduction of robots in factories has spurred the development of flexible manufacturing systems and totally integrated factory information systems. As it evaluates the applications and implications of robotic technology, management should observe the following guidelines:

- Match the application to current or projected need. This involves detailed homework. For example, a spherically configured robot may be more suitable for a particular series of tasks than a Cartesian configured robot.
- Consider the cost/benefit ratio before installing a robotic system. Carefully evaluate the potential benefits before making a decision.
- Consider alternatives. A complete robotic system with sensor capability can involve an investment of more than $100,000.
- Recognize that training is essential. Short courses and seminars are available through various trade organizations. Consider establishing ties with a local university.
- Pursue offline programming for robots. This will save considerable downtime and improve overall productivity. If a vendor-specific package is chosen for implementation, it should be compatible with existing hardware and software.
- Participate in major standards-generating organizations, not only to contribute to standards development but to monitor existing and proposed developments.
- Design robotic application programs that are modular and extensible, with a well-defined programming structure.
- Make plans for developing computer-generated robotic programs using CAD systems. Particular attention should be paid to data base management systems, which can contribute significantly to CAD system improvement and robot program generation.

Bibliography

Bonner, S., and Shin, K.G. "A Comparative Study of Robot Languages," *Computer* (December 1982): 82–96.

Engelberger, J.F. "Robotics in Practice: Management and Applications of Industrial Robots," *aMa COM* (a division of American Management Association) 1983.

Nagel, R.N. "State of the Art and Predictions for Artificial Intelligence and Robotics." *Robotics and Artificial Intelligence.* Edited by M. Brady et al. NATO ASI Series: Springer-Verlag, 1984.

Simpson, J.A.; Hocken, R.J.; and Albus, J.S. "The Automated Manufacturing Research Facility of the National Bureau of Standards." *Journal of Manufacturing Systems* 1 (November 1982): 17–32.

XIV-2
Advances in Fiber Optics

Richard McCaskill
Otto Szentesi

INTRODUCTION

Fiber optics is a communications technique that transmits light through a hair-thin fiber of plastic or glass rather than electrical currents through conventional copper wire. In this process, electrical energy from a computer interface is converted to light energy by a light source, typically LEDs or lasers. There are two types of LEDs: the visible, which transmits in the red light spectrum, and the invisible, which transmits in the infrared light spectrum. A laser converts electrical energy into more intense light than do LEDs.

Once emitted from the light source, light is coupled into the optical fiber, which guides the lightwave. The center element of the optical fiber is called the core, and the outer structure, the cladding (see Figure 1). The light beam is transmitted through the cable because the refractive index of the core exceeds that of the cladding.

Three types of fiber are commonly used: step index multimode, graded index multimode, and single mode (see Figure 2).

In step index multimode fiber, the refractive index changes abruptly at the interface between the core and the cladding. Light is guided through the fiber in multiple paths, or modes. As the light beam approaches the cladding, the cladding acts as a mirror and reflects the light back into the core. Light rays traveling at different angles to the fiber axis travel effective path lengths in traversing a finite length of fiber. This causes the signal to spread out along the fiber and limits the bandwidth in step index multimode fibers to about 25MHz-km (MHz-km is the product of bandwidth multiplied by distance).

In graded index fibers, the refractive index of the core decreases toward the core-to-cladding interface. Through tailoring of the index profile, all modes can have virtually the same net velocity along the fiber. The bandwidths of graded index fibers can exceed 1GHz-km.

In single-mode fibers, the core size is small, as is the difference between the core and cladding, and only one mode is allowed to propagate. The bandwidths of such fibers can exceed 10GHz-km.

Light exiting the fiber is projected onto a light-deflecting device, which

NEW DIRECTIONS IN TECHNOLOGY

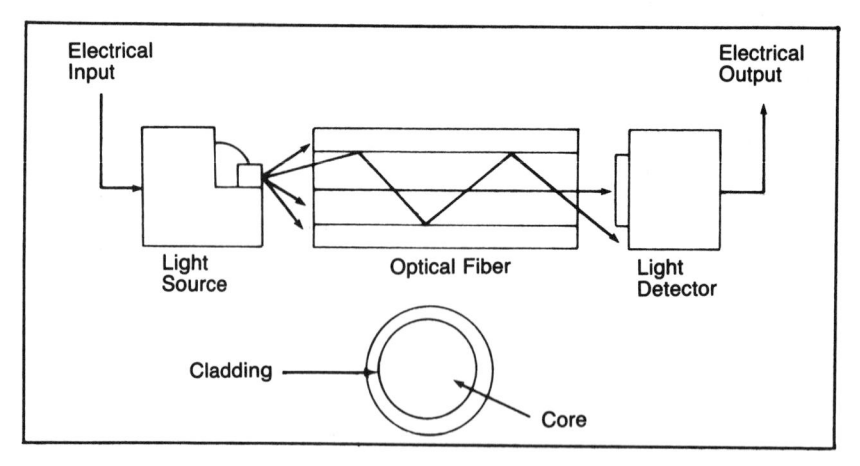

Figure 1. Fiber-Optic Communications

produces an electrical current. Light-deflecting devices are either P Insulated N-channel (PIN) diodes or Avalanche Photodiodes (APDs). The PIN diode produces electrical current in proportion to the amount of light energy projected onto it. The APD is a more complex device that amplifies light energy while converting it to electrical energy. This amplification process is important in a system that spans long distances between amplifying stages.

BENEFITS

As with other newer technologies, a fiber-optic system must be carefully examined for its cost-effectiveness in typical installations. Nevertheless, the fiber-optic cables provide unique performance capabilities in many applica-

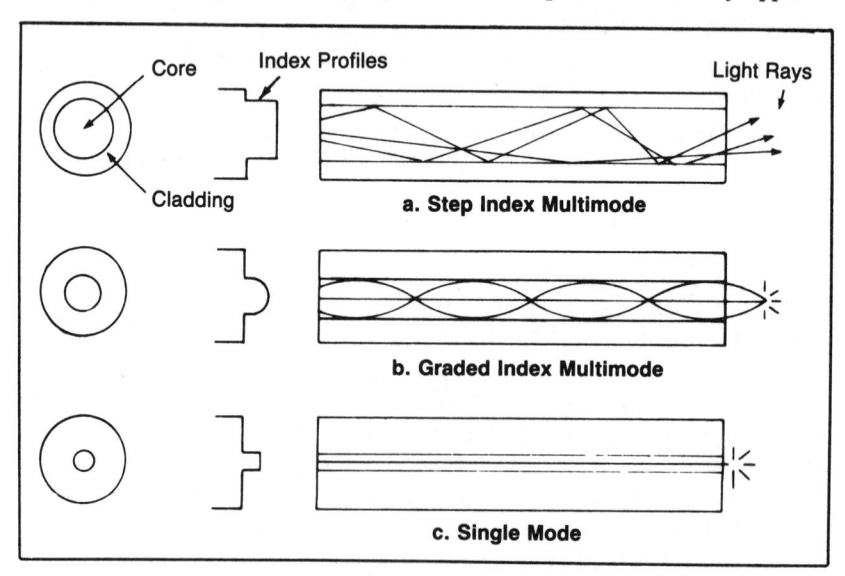

Figure 2. Common Types of Fiber-Optic Cable

tions. Fiber-optic cables offer features superior to those of twisted-pair wires or coaxial cables. Several of those features and their advantages are:
- Wide bandwidth—Increased data carrying capability, future expansion capability, and low cost per channel
- Immunity to electrically generated noise—Reliability and a lower bit-error rate; no crosstalk
- Resistance to taps—System security
- Total electrical isolation—Elimination of ground loops
- Compactness—Space and weight savings and lower installation costs
- Environmental stability—High resistance to environmental factors, such as fire or corrosion.

Bandwidth

The greatest advantage of fiber-optic cable is its wide bandwidth. Its information carrying capacity increases directly with frequency, and the availability of laser-driven fiber-optic links allows data transmission at speeds up to 10^{14} bits per second. Thus, the use of lasers has opened up a portion of the electromagnetic spectrum in which frequencies are 10,000 times greater than the upper ranges of radio frequency bands. This is possible because lasers can emit a nearly monochromatic beam of intense light in the infrared regions of that spectrum. Rapid advances in multi- and single-mode optical fibers have provided a transmission medium for harnessing the capabilities of lasers. Fiber-optic systems can transmit data at rates in excess of 1GHz to 3GHz. Such large-bandwidth performance allows both high-speed data transfer between processors and the multiplexing of several low-speed channels for subsequent transmission over a fiber-optic medium.

Whereas the limited bandwidths of twisted-pair wiring and coaxial cable forced networks into parallel transmission to obtain a desirable throughput rate, the larger bandwidth of fiber-optic cable enabled them to transfer data serially by multiplexing a 16-bit data bus onto one cable. This reduces connector hardware and wiring requirements. The bandwidth capabilities of fiber-optic cable far outstrip those of twisted-pair wiring and exceed those of even the most expensive coaxial cable. The most publicized applications using this bandwidth capability are the telephone company installations, which use fiber-optic cabling techniques that allow the multiplexing of 6,000 voice-grade channels on a single optical fiber.

As shown in Figure 3, signal attenuation in a fiber-optic cable is relatively independent of frequency when compared with signal attenuation in a copper-wire system. Signal attenuation in coaxial cable, even for the highest grade, increases rapidly with frequency. By contrast, attenuation in the optical waveguide is flat over a range exceeding 1GHz in some cases. Fiber-optic cables containing graded index fibers are currently being manufactured and used with bandwidths in excess of 1GHz-km, and single-mode cables are available with bandwidths greater than 10GHz-km.

Noise Immunity

Fiber-optic cables are essentially immune to electrically generated noise; radio interference from electric motors, relays, power cables, or other induc-

NEW DIRECTIONS IN TECHNOLOGY

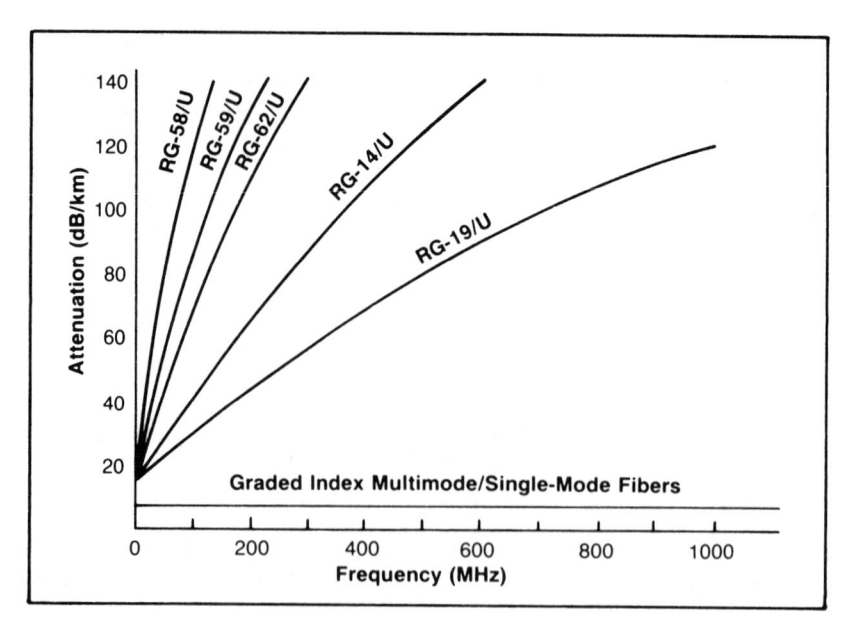

Figure 3. Comparison of the Bandwidths and Attenuation of Coaxial Cable and Optical Waveguide

tive fields; and radio or radar transmission sources. Such immunities are significant because they reduce bit-error rates. A typical system using fiber-optic cables has a bit-error rate exceeding 10^{-9} as compared with the 10^{-6} bit-error rate usually found in metallic connectors. Electromagnetic noise does not affect the fiber-optic cable; therefore, its bit-error rate depends only on the signal-to-noise ratio within the fiber-optic system. In addition, because of the higher noise immunity, a system designed with fiber-optic cables does not require as many error checks as a wire system. Not only are overall data transfer rates increased by slashing error-checking overhead, but overall system performance is improved by reducing retransmission.

Fiber-optic cables do not aggravate the electromagnetic environment in which they are installed—a factor that can help simplify system design. The nonradiation features of fiber-optic cable enhance system reliability by virtually eliminating crosstalk and thus reducing the bit-error rate. Innerchannel isolation of 90 decibels or more is readily attainable in a multifiber optic cable. This feature becomes cost-effective for applications used, for example, in train depots where the electronic monitoring of trains is momentarily interrupted by electrical or diesel electrical generations and in manufacturing plants that have equipment driven by electrical motors or arcing equipment in the processing plant.

Security

Security is an important consideration. Copper wire can be tapped by directly connecting to the wire or wrapping a coil around the wire. An optical link, however, can be tapped only by directly accessing the fiber, and this is difficult to accomplish. If a readable amount of light is removed from a fiber, a power loss in the fiber-optic system occurs and can be easily detected.

In addition, because the fiber-optic cable is nonconductive, signals and electromagnetic noise do not radiate from it and the cable resists conventional tapping techniques, reducing its potential as a security problem. These security features become cost-effective in government, military, banking, and commercial applications that require secure data transmissions.

Isolation

Fiber-optic cables isolate transmitters and receivers, eliminating the need for a common ground. The nonconductive qualities of fiber-optic cables benefit data communications systems because the equipment is totally isolated from one point to another. Because the cable is made of glass or plastic, electrical isolation problems, such as ground loops in an installation, are eliminated, and the amount of noise in the electronic system is decreased.

Moreover, because the nonconductive qualities of fiber-optic cables prevent such dangers as a short circuit or spark, these cables are suitable for systems installed in dangerous gas atmospheres, such as petroleum refineries or chemical processing plants. A copper-wire connection between remote pieces of equipment (e.g., an electronic-based test station or recording instrument and a central processor), on the other hand, increases the danger of a spark causing an explosion or fire.

Size and Weight

The size of optical fibers is typically designated, in microns, by the core diameter followed by the outside diameter of the cladding. For example, 8/125 indicates a single-mode fiber with a core diameter of 8 microns (0.0003 inches) and an outside diameter of 125 microns. Common multimode fiber sizes are 50/125, 63/125, 85/125, and 100/140 microns. Typically, the smaller the core size, the higher the available bandwidth, the larger the core size, the more easily light passes into a fiber. These fibers are then coated with plastic and cabled. The small diameters of fiber-optic cables offer substantial size and weight advantages over metallic cables of equivalent bandwidths.

The respective tensile strengths of available single-fiber cable, an RG-58/U coaxial cable, and a twisted-pair cable are 90, 60, and 40 pounds. The small size and light weight of the fiber-optic cable facilitate shipping, handling, and storage and solve the problem of pulling cable through crowded ducts. Weight and size criteria are important in aircraft applications, for example, in which lighter weight and smaller size can increase the overall operating range or payload of the aircraft. Fiber-optic cable usually can be installed with little or no difficulty in applications whose crowded conduits prevent installation of bulkier metallic cables. (A 10-fiber cable has less than a 3/8-inch diameter.)

Environmental Factors

The use of fiber-optic cable is generally less restricted by harsh environments than that of its metallic counterparts, and it is not as fragile or brittle as might be expected. Fiber-optic cables usually can be protected by proper jacketing of the signal-carrying glass or plastic member. For example, high tensile strength can be provided by the strengthening members surrounding the fiber and within an outer protective jacket. Fiber-optic cable can be manufactured to solve most cabling problems, including those in aerial, burial, underwater, or duct applications.

Fiber-optic cable is more corrosion resistant than copper wire because it contains no metallic conductors. Hydrofluoric acid is the only chemical that affects optical fiber. Corrosion resistance is a particular concern at splicing locations, where complete protection from the environment is impossible. In addition, optical fiber can withstand greater temperatures than copper wire can. Even when fire melts the outside jacket of the surrounding fiber, a fiber-optic system usually can still operate.

TYPICAL APPLICATIONS

To understand when fiber-optic cabling is best used, data communication link applications must be explained. Although the following discussion covers only intra- and interbuilding applications (computer-to-computer and computer-to-peripheral connections), fiber-optic local area networks are also available.

Computer-to-peripheral connections in an intrabuilding application are either local or remote. Local-grouped peripherals include card readers, memory disks, and high-speed, parallel-driven printers, which are usually configured within 50 feet of the computer room. Because local-grouped devices are usually located in controlled environments and the distance from the computer to the peripheral is short, cable interference problems often can be solved with metallic cable. Remote-grouped peripherals on a local data network, however, can be located hundreds of thousands of feet from a central processor and usually are not housed in a special environment. Terminals in this category can be used for applications ranging from low-speed RJE to interactive graphics. Data rates for these terminals are usually as high as 19.2K bits per second, newer terminals operating at 56K bits per second or faster. As a result, the interference problems associated with remote terminals are more difficult to solve.

The three methods used to connect remote terminals are direct connection by ordinary copper cable, the use of line drivers and cables, and the use of limited-distance modems (LDMs) and cables. Generally, the greater the distance, the more sophisticated the interface and the higher the price.

If cost is a major consideration in choosing twisted-pair wiring, coaxial cable, or fiber-optic cable, standard RS-232C equipment should be used. The only hardware required for any direct RS-232C connection (typically less than 50 feet) is a modem cable with a 25-pin connector at each end and a cable containing 3 to 25 wires. In the least expensive configuration, in which modem control signals are not required, such cables can cost $38 for 25 feet. Additional cable without connectors costs approximately 50¢ per running foot. If all modem control signals in the RS-232C specification are required, a 25-pin conductor cable is necessary. With a typical cable, such as Digital

Equipment Corporation's BC05D, a 50-foot link costs approximately $136; the cable costs approximately $1.50 per running foot. If the data rates and separation distance are within RS-232C specifications, a less expensive interface cannot be found. In this simple type of installation, fiber-optic data links would be more expensive and not recommended unless the physical and electromagnetic environments necessitate them. In hostile electromagnetic environments, where it is necessary to protect against radio frequency signal propagation, shielded cable not exceeding 100 feet should be used in remote terminals. Shielded cable for 12 pairs costs approximately $1.40 per running foot.

For applications requiring high data rates or greater shielding, coaxial cables are usually used. Coaxial cables cost approximately 15¢ per foot (for RG-62A/U), based on attenuation, bandwidth, and shielding. For better performance, a user can turn to fiber-optic cable.

Fiber-optic cable, such as the Siecor #104 single-core fiber cable with a loss of six decibels per kilometer and a bandwidth of 400 MHz, costs approximately 35¢ per foot. For duplex transmission (twin-core cable), the cost of two fiber cables ranges from 60¢ to 90¢ per foot, depending on performance.

PERFORMANCE ADVANTAGE

A useful formula for calculating the performance capabilities of twisted-pair wiring and coaxial and fiber-optic cables is the product of the bandwidth multiplied by the distance. The standard bandwidth/distance parameters are 1MHz-km for common twisted-pair wiring, 20MHz-km for coaxial cable, and 400MHz-km for fiber-optic cable; 36-Hz fiber-optic cables and higher-frequency coaxial cables are also available. A general cost/performance factor can be computed by taking the average cable cost (10¢ per foot for twisted-pair wiring, $3 per foot for coaxial cable, and 75¢ per foot for fiber-optic cable) and dividing the bandwidth/distance parameter into the cost per kilometer. The following relationship between the cost per MHz and the bandwidth for a kilometer shows that the fiber-optic cable has a definite cost/performance advantage over its metallic counterparts:
- Twisted-pair wiring—$300 per MHz per kilometer
- Coaxial cable—$450 per MHz per kilometer
- Fiber-optic cable—$5 per MHz per kilometer

The cost of a typical installation of line drivers or LDMs can also be compared to that of a fiber-optic installation. For applications requiring distances greater than the RS-232C, 50-foot-limit line drivers are usually used. Line drivers are required to overcome the signal distortion that limits the distance and speed attainable with cable. Extended-distance transmission produces pulse-rounding—a condition in which the edges of a square wave pulse are distorted because the high-frequency element is lost. In addition, transmission over extended distances increases signal attenuation, resulting in marginal reception and lost or erroneous bits. These adverse effects may be partially overcome by upgrading from twisted-pair wiring to coaxial cable. Cost/performance trade-offs can result in the selection of line drivers for each end of the interface to improve system performance. Line drivers usual-

NEW DIRECTIONS IN TECHNOLOGY

ly operate at speeds up to 19.2K bits per second. Special units that operate at data rates up to 1.5M bits per second are also available; distance may range from 100 feet to several miles.

If line drivers cannot be used to solve a communications problem, LDM is a less expensive and simpler alternative to a conventional telephone modem. The cost advantage of LDMs increases with the data rate because the three major functions performed by conventional modems can be relaxed. At low data rates, the cost difference is not great; however, at high speeds, the cost difference between an LDM and a telephone modem can be thousands of dollars. LDMs operating in a full-duplex mode require four-wire systems. Most LDMs use twisted-pair wiring; however, some transmitting at higher data rates (from 19.2K to 1M bits per second) use coaxial cables.

When customer-owned cable is used within a link interfacing an LDM, either twisted-pair wiring or coaxial cable can be used. Selecting the cabling technique to use with LDMs is a cost/performance trade-off.

When data rates of more than 19.2K bits per second are required, a coaxial system is usually incorporated in the network to eliminate crosstalk and electromagnetic interference. LDMs are priced from approximately $200 to $800 each.

In addition to direct connection, line drivers, and LDMs, new interfacing techniques that use fiber-optic cables are available. Some companies are producing RS-232C–compatible standard links for interfacing DP equipment to data terminals. The fiber-optic data link converts an RS-232C standard signal to optical-encoded information, which is then transmitted over a fiber-optic cable and reconverted from optical data back to the RS-232C standard data format. The RS-232C fiber-optic links available are plug-compatible with the RS-232C standard interfaces and cost from $250 to $650.

COST ANALYSIS

The figures cited can be used to analyze the connection of a remote terminal to a CPU. The remote terminal is a CRT terminal operating at speeds of 9.6K bits per second for 1,000 feet. Table 1 classifies the components and relative cost of each type of interface capable of performing in this installation.

Fiber-optic data links are less expensive than drivers and LDMs and outweigh them in performance. When a remote terminal is required to operate at higher data rates (e.g., 19.2K bits per second), a fiber-optic data link system has the expansion capability to meet this requirement. For the line driver and LDM, however, end modules must be replaced with a higher-performance device. In addition, the twisted-pair wiring cannot usually provide the perfor-

Table 1. Cost of Typical Link Installation

Link Type	Speed (K bps)	Distance (ft)	Ends $	Cable $	Total $
Line Driver	9.6	1,000	1,600	1,200	2,800
LDM	9.6	1,000	1,600	1,200	2,800
Fiber Optics	9.6	1,000	1,200	750	1,950

Advances in Fiber Optics

mance capability necessary to transmit at these higher data rates. Therefore, along with replacing the end links, the user must upgrade from twisted-pair wiring to coaxial cable.

PLANNING FOR A FIBER-OPTIC SYSTEM

With the increasing use of data communications and accelerating communications speeds, fiber-optics technology can be cost-effective in many applications. Although a fiber-optic system may be slightly more expensive to install than a wire-based system, its expansion capability justifies its application.

MIS management must consider the following variables when planning for a fiber-optic system.

Future Bandwidth

The bandwidth of the fiber-optic cable is superior to that of copper wire. Fiber-optic cable can vary in bandwidth from 25MHz-km to the GHz-km range. If the planner requires low-frequency communication, a step index cable with a bandwidth of 25MHz-km is an acceptable choice. If future requirements include such items as video communications or high-speed multiplexed data in the 50M-bit-per-second range, a graded index cable should be considered. The cost of the step or graded index cable is the same; however, the optical fiber used in a graded index cable is a little smaller and thus more difficult to couple light into. In addition, the interfacing equipment is slightly more expensive. If a high-speed communications system is a future requirement, a graded index cable with at least 200MHz-km bandwidth should be installed.

Cable Construction

Cable construction and environment—whether the cable will be installed in a duct or in an aerial, burial, or underwater installation—must be determined. Any type of cable construction using the copper-wire method can be applied to optical fibers. Cables have been used for aerial, burial, and underwater applications as well as in direct plow-in applications in which rodent-proofing was required. Fiber-optic cables can also have tensile load strengths of more than 6,000 pounds as well as a fire-retardant capability.

Number of Fibers

During cable selection, the number of fibers required must be determined. Multifiber cables containing two, six, and ten fibers are common; cables with as many as 144 fibers have been constructed. The first consideration should be the future expansion capability and the number of channels of information that will be used with fiber optics. The number of fibers to be installed in the cable can then be specified.

Repeaters

Although the fiber-optic cabling methods have less data loss than copper-wire techniques, repeater or amplification stages are required to span long distances. Most fiber-optic communications equipment can easily communicate up to one kilometer (3,000 feet) or more. Many long-distance communications (i.e., from 30 to 50 kilometers) are possible without any repeater or amplification stages, but special interfacing equipment is needed to transmit over these long distances. Usually, when fiber-optic communication equipment is being used, a repeater for approximately every one to one and a half kilometers should be considered if high-performance equipment is not being used.

Splicing

The planner should consider where to splice fiber-optic cable. The average fiber-optic cable is two kilometers long; however, finite-length cables are available. For telecommunications applications, cables approaching five kilometers in length have been made without any splicing required. If the spans are greater than two kilometers, accessible splicing locations should be provided. Mechanical epoxy splices and fusion are used in splicing.

Connectors

A variety of field-installable fiber-optic connectors is available. Prices range from about $6 to $40 each, depending on performance. Because field installation requires training and specialized tool kits, it is often convenient to install preconnectorized cables. Many fiber-optic connectors are small enough to be preinstalled and still be pulled through the conduit ducts.

Communications Equipment

The last item to consider is the type of optical communications equipment required in the installation. The planner has two choices: a fiber-optic modem for use in conventional modem applications running to the 56K-baud range or high-speed multiplexed trunk lines that use high-speed fiber-optic multiplexing techniques. These multiplexing techniques allow many communications channels to operate on one or two fiber-optic lines. The distance span requirements should be considered in the selection of an optical interface. This can help determine the total cost of the optical system. The cost of the equipment is higher when long distances must be spanned without repeaters. The equipment cost will also be higher when the frequency of the communications system is high.

CONCLUSION

Fiber optics is no longer a laboratory curiosity but a proven communications medium. The use of fiber-optic cabling techniques can increase performance by offering increased bandwidth, enhanced security, and freedom from electrically generated noise. Equally important is the improved cost/performance ratio that fiber optics will bring to future applications when long-haul communications is finally based on fiber-optic cabling techniques.

XIV-3
Optical Disk Technology

John A. Lacy
Raymond J. Wulf

INTRODUCTION

Although most businesses and government agencies need tailored document-based systems, many organizations have not yet taken advantage of recent advances in technology or begun planning for new integrated system possibilities. Progress has been impeded by divided information system responsibility and limited awareness of integrated technology advances. Two additional problems are the absence of a document image transmission link for computer micrographics systems and the delayed availability of optical disk technology because of difficulties with its commercialization.

Managers of document-based systems who have remained familiar with technology have been keenly aware of the inability of computer micrographics systems to electronically transmit microimages to remote locations. But a solution to this problem is imminent as companies develop technologies to electronically scan, digitize, and transmit microfilmed images.

Although optical disk systems hold great promise for document-based applications, their developers have encountered several commercialization hurdles. These include the selection and refinement of mass production techniques to yield high-quality disks at low cost and a disk design requirement to minimize serious image and data retrieval problems resulting from dust particles in a user environment. However, solutions to these and other optical disk problems seem close at hand.

Understanding this technology and its strengths and weaknesses will help MIS managers develop and implement systems that yield immediate gains in productivity and efficiency and that offer optical disk migration options.

DEMAND FOR DOCUMENT-BASED SYSTEMS

Efficient document-based systems are important to many organizations. Insurance companies must be able to retrieve policies signed by customers. Banks need access to loan agreements. Most manufacturing facilities need to be able to look up shipping and receiving documentation. Sales organizations require instant access to purchase orders and customer correspondence. Corporate offices must maintain personnel, legal, and patent files. Hospitals often must retain patient records, such as X rays, for decades. The archiving of

NEW DIRECTIONS IN TECHNOLOGY

deeds and birth, marriage, and death certificates is just the tip of the government application iceberg.

These and other applications have three common requirements: facsimile reproduction capabilities, retrieval reliability and speed, and overall system efficiency.

Facsimile reproduction is the duplication of graphics contained in an original document. For banks, insurance companies, and sales organizations, examples of facsimile requirements are customer-signed copies of loans, insurance policies, and purchase agreements. Generally, a computer printout of information extracted from an original document would not provide adequate transaction verification because it would not include the customer's signature.

Retrieval reliability and speed relate to the need of organizations to avoid losing documents and to respond quickly to information requests from customers as well as from within the organization.

Overall system efficiency must be maximized to ensure cost-effective and productive handling of information management activities, ranging from document capture to retrieval.

THE DATA PROCESSING–MICROGRAPHICS GAP

Until optical disk technology is refined and some obstacles to its widespread commercial application are overcome, MIS managers can implement advanced computer micrographics systems, which are reliable, cost-effective vehicles for storing and retrieving documents and related data.

If such systems are developed with care, they can offer compatibility to both existing document image files and future optical disk systems. Furthermore, MIS managers may find key applications, such as archival storage of information, for computer micrographics systems long after optical disk commercialization.

Microfilm has been a mainstay in the storage and retrieval of document-based information. In fact, many organizations' micrographics departments predate their MIS departments. These central micrographics units frequently are managed by specialists who are well versed in silver halide imaging technology but lack data processing background. Thus, these managers seldom are fully aware of the potential that data processing advances hold for micrographics systems. On the other hand, MIS managers who work hard to keep pace with new data system and application demands often lack the time to keep abreast of computer micrographics developments.

Increasingly, however, MIS managers are assigning combined responsibilities for data processing and document control systems to reap the benefits of both computer and micrographics technologies. These benefits have never been more apparent. In new systems, reliance on computer-assisted retrieval (CAR) techniques to provide rapid access to microfilmed document images is the rule rather than the exception.

OPTICAL DISK TECHNOLOGY: THE STATE OF THE ART

Many MIS managers are intrigued by the optical disk's potential to offer

Optical Disk Technology

unmatched data compaction capabilities. Current research indicates that optical disks can store 60 to 100 times more data than magnetic disks of the same size. For instance, a 14-inch-diameter optical disk can store the contents of about 100,000 8-1/2-by-11-inch business documents, the equivalent of about 4,000 megabytes of information. This amount approximates the storage capacity of 2,000 diskettes or 50 magnetic tapes.

Paired with this storage density is the ability to provide high-speed, random-access retrieval of information. Here, the rotating memory configuration gives optical disk systems an important edge over serial storage media, such as tape and microfilm, which require forward and backward searches.

Several demonstration optical disk systems are being introduced. Because these systems feature permanent, write-once media, they are most attractive for storing historical information and other types of data unlikely to require updates. However, if the cost of mass-produced optical disks drops sufficiently, users may find it cost-effective to use write-once optical disks for some applications in which working files are consolidated or merged. Optical media research is an active field in many laboratories, along with advanced magnetic recording techniques.

Because manufacturers can ensure a minimum media life span of only 10 years, archival data perhaps should not be stored on optical disks. In 50 to 100 years, readout devices for today's machine-readable data may not exist outside a museum; therefore, valuable archival information should be committed to a silver-base microimage.

Operation

Data and images are recorded on an optical disk as marks on a recording surface. The recording surface, which is sensitive to a specified laser light wavelength, absorbs the writing laser's focused light, creating microscopic pits, bubbles, or density marks, depending on the medium used in the recording layer. On Kodak's dye polymer recording layer, the writing laser can create a well-defined pit in 50 nanoseconds. The duration of each laser pulse determines the length of the individual pits to correspond to the digital bit stream. Marks on the disk surface are approximately one micron in size (approximately 1/40 the thickness of a human hair), and tracks are spaced at about 1.6 micron intervals.

Configurations

Optical disk technology poses many design and manufacturing challenges. Sensitivity, stability, and cleanliness requirements are extraordinary. For example, the odds that a surface imperfection will appear in a recording window should be about a million to one, and reference recording plane stability (flatness) of about 5 micrometers, or 0.0002 inches, is essential for critical focusing.

Recording layer materials must be sensitive enough to be marked during a 50-nanosecond laser light exposure yet immune to degradation if laser light of the same wavelength is used millions of times to read stored data.

For data storage applications, optical disks yielding raw bit error rates of

NEW DIRECTIONS IN TECHNOLOGY

10^{-5} or less should offer corrected bit error rates of 10^{-12} or less through the application of error detection and correction circuits. Superior signal-to-noise capability allows the system to record images containing many levels of gray.

Finally, the disk's recording surface must have a high degree of protection from microscopic dust particles. A 5-micron dust speck can easily hide 10 to 20 bits of stored data.

The manufacturing techniques employed to produce disks meeting these exacting standards must be economical enough to permit realistic pricing. To market high-performance optical disks at a reasonable cost, manufacturers are experimenting with various recording layer materials, manufacturing techniques, and disk configurations.

Candidates for sensitive recording layers range from tellurium alloys to organic dye polymer materials. Tellurium alloys absorb in infrared, show reasonably good sensitivity, and are compatible with plastic disk technology. Dye polymer materials are promising because they are capable of high resolution, can be tuned to receive various laser wavelengths, and may be coated in several ways.

The ability to tune recording materials to different laser wavelengths is significant because laser choice can affect system cost and performance. For example, small infrared diode lasers are easily mounted on drive heads for recording and are projected to be relatively inexpensive, while shorter-wavelength gas lasers may increase data compaction in certain recording systems.

For certain dye polymer laser write and read materials, the recording layer is coupled with layers that provide reflective and smoothing qualities and dust protection. This stack of coatings can be applied to an aluminum computer disk, a rigid plastic substrate, or even directly to a flexible film base that in turn can be laminated to a rigid substrate.

Manufacturing cost considerations at different production volumes may influence decisions on the support base and manufacturing method. Spin coating, for example, may be the most cost-effective manufacturing method for low-volume production, whereas web manufacturing technology, like that used to coat emulsions on photographic films, may offer savings in high-volume, mass production environments. In addition, it is theoretically possible to make double-sided optical disks using a laminated disk configuration.

Because a chief disk configuration criterion is dust protection, the disk should be packaged so that it can perform reliably without requiring special precautions in an office environment.

Optical disks can be designed with one of three dust controls: a thick protective overcoat in direct contact with the disk's recording surface, a permanent or semipermanent protective cartridge from which a disk is extracted only when it is inside the disk drive, or an offset cover sheet suspended above the recording surface.

The cover sheet approach offers users certain advantages because the disk housing resembles a miniature clean room that provides extra dirt protection during shipping, storage, handling, and disk drive operation. A special transmissive polymeric sheet stretched above the recording layer and secured to the inner core and outer diameter prevents dirt from entering the air space between recording layer and cover sheet. The cover sheet is positioned far enough above the recording surface to make even a soot-sized, 40-micron dust particle on its surface unnoticeable. Though larger dirt particles might impede recording or playback, they can be purged or filtered fairly easily from the cover sheet surface.

Recording, Storage, and Retrieval Options

Optical disk technology, when used to store images, requires a scanner to transform optical information into a digital bit stream. Images to be digitized can be from paper documents or microimages.

Either one- or two-wavelength systems can be used for disk readout. With one-wavelength systems, the same type of laser is used for reading and writing on the optical disk. In the read mode, the laser's power is cut to a fraction of its writing intensity to reduce the possibility of accidentally marking the disk during repeated reads. The reading light reflected by the disk's surface travels through an optical system that uses one or more photodetectors to sense the differences between light reflected from marked and unmarked portions of the recording medium. Because one-wavelength laser systems require the installation of only one laser in a disk drive, their economic appeal is strong.

Some manufacturers may instead introduce dual-laser systems with optical disk readback performed at a second wavelength. This technique may involve phase interference readout techniques similar to those used in biological microscopes. When the reading laser's light is reflected by the recording layer, the layer's refractive properties alter the light's velocity and optical path.

Because phase interference readout permits the use of more light than single-laser systems do, this approach can improve focusing and tracking and reduce noise.

In addition to alternative readout modes, there are different optical disk equipment options for accessing data. These include players, recorder-players, and multidisk autoloaders. The choice and mix of these devices depends in large part on application or system volume. For example, if optical disk technology is used to store a small amount of critical, frequently accessed information, a single-platter, online device may offer the fastest document access. When larger amounts of stored data must be accessed infrequently, a unit resembling a jukebox may be used to provide access to any of millions of documents stored on one of several optical disks.

Another configuration possibility is to couple local optical disk memory with an image-capable workstation for high-activity tasks. Of course, such an optical subsystem would have to be compact and low priced to suit such a distributed processing system.

NEW DIRECTIONS IN TECHNOLOGY

Limitations and Capabilities

Many current limitations on optical disk technology have already been discussed in this chapter. These include:
- A media life span of approximately 10 years
- Initial availability of only permanent, write-once disks
- The impact of production volumes and manufacturing techniques on media cost
- Stringent cleanliness requirements

Two more concerns should be added to this list. One is the absence of industry standards for disk configurations, lasers, or interfaces between disks and drives or between drives and computers. Because a new document storage system may not prove superior in use for some time, MIS managers should choose system vendors who are expected to remain in the market.

The other concern relates to the cost of systems integration, which will be discussed in greater detail later in this chapter. The cost of incorporating an optical disk subsystem into a total information system will depend in part on the ability of MIS managers to find and use technology bridges. These bridges should create forward and backward compatibility so that existing magnetic and microfilm data bases do not become obsolete.

Despite some technological constraints, the capabilities of this emerging technology clearly outweigh its limitations. High-speed random access, data density compaction capabilities 60 times those of magnetic storage, and the ability to remove the memory cartridge from equipment are key technological advantages. Another potential benefit is the corollary of a concern just cited. If managers carefully build document-based systems, optical disk technology can be phased into the systems as an enhancement. Existing systems thus will be enriched, not replaced.

Future optical disk advances are inevitable, too. Because many companies are researching erasable materials, erasable as well as write-once disks will eventually be available. Permanent disks, however, will probably offer performance advantages that will preserve their market niche.

Need for Networks

One certainty about the future of optical disks is that many configurations will be needed to optimize performance for organizations of varying sizes with unique document-based information requirements.

However, every potential system configuration, whether it relies on jukebox players that access multiple disks or pairs local disk memory with a workstation, assumes the existence of electronic networking capabilities.

At least a local area network (LAN) will be required to link high-resolution display terminals with the optical disk player. For maximum system efficiency, more elaborate systems featuring gateways to link individual LANs and to provide an interface to larger high-speed networks eventually may be needed. Such requirements make network architecture and the development and application of suitable software integration a focal point in forging total information systems.

Optical Disk Technology

COMPUTER MICROGRAPHICS ADVANCES

To build sturdy foundations for future systems, MIS managers can use several new computer micrographics building blocks.

Micrographics and CAR

Computer-assisted retrieval of information stored on microfilm is one such electronic micrographics system keystone. In CAR systems, the accuracy, economy, convenience, file integrity, and space savings of microfilm meld with the data organization, manipulation, and retrieval powers of computers.

In these electronic filing systems, such source documents as invoices and customer orders are microfilmed in random order on high-speed microfilmers. This permits fast and economical capture of a wealth of detailed information. (Only about 5 percent of source document data is estimated to be entered into a computer system.)

Data abstracted from the source documents is entered into a mainframe or minicomputer to create indexes for automating later retrieval of microimages. In addition, the indexes themselves may be accessed to answer simple queries.

Although computer-controlled microimage terminals can be interfaced directly with mainframe computers, many organizations are choosing stand-alone CAR systems that feature dedicated minicomputers. With this dedicated approach, turnkey systems can link proven micrographics hardware, powerful minicomputers, and specially designed software, thus reducing in-house DP programming requirements.

Microimage Transmission

CAR systems soon will become even more flexible system components through the addition of microfilm scanning, digitizing, and microimage transmission capabilities.

Microimage transmission enables individuals at remote workstations to access document images maintained in central micrographics files, eliminating the need for duplicate rolls of microfilm at remote locations. This new, more capable type of CAR system will offer other benefits, as the following brief overview of its architecture and operation reveals.

After microfilming and computer-indexing steps are completed, microimages are stored in a computer-controlled file on a network. When a document image is requested, the computer directs a film autoloader with built-in robotics to select the needed film magazine and image. The autoloader eliminates manual retrieval of microfilm, thus increasing retrieval speed and user productivity.

Next, a digital scanner using a charge-coupled device converts the microfilmed image to an electronic bit stream. If the terminal operator asks for several images, the resulting bit streams can be temporarily stored in a local buffer. This storage option allows the operator of the online display terminal to scan several images.

NEW DIRECTIONS IN TECHNOLOGY

Once the image is an electronic bit stream, it can be manipulated by the system user. This expands system functionality in several ways. For example, high-resolution terminals with windowing capabilities allow users to simultaneously view images associated with alphanumeric data stored on both optical disks and magnetic media.

Such multifunction workstations eliminate the need for separate CRT and microimage terminals. In addition, they offer productivity and ease-of-use benefits to individuals who command access to data and image bases that previously could be tapped only with multiple devices.

Image manipulation possibilities also expand. New options include enlarging and reducing images, screening out unwanted detail, and selecting portions of images for printout at workstations or laser printers within the local area network.

In addition, users may change or add to associated data files, which are windowed on the screen with images. A user can thus take action on a late accounts payable document, make a notation to the data file, and dump the screen to paper to create a new document combining original image and notes for customer documentation. With such processing options, microfilm is transformed into a dynamic storage medium.

An LAN will be the initial device linkage vehicle. Although cable limitations may pose some geographic constraints, LAN gateways will permit data exchange with other LANs. When fiber optics and satellite transmission advances usher in very high speed communications networks, these gateways will permit the interconnection for microimage transmission across the U.S. and around the world.

Once an organization has a document-based information system with LAN architecture and microimage transmission capabilities, it has a clear migration path to optical disk technology.

Microimage transmission is the bridge that can unite microfilm-based CAR systems and data bases with optical disk systems. Because microimages can be digitized, data stored in microfilm format can be interactive with images and data stored on optical disks. The optical disk player, in essence, becomes just one more mass storage device on the LAN that multipurpose workstations can access. At the same time, microimage transmission provides compatibility with existing microfilm files, eliminating the need to maintain dual document-based systems in order to reference historical data.

SYSTEM DESIGN AND PLANNING

A needs analysis is the starting point in designing a document-based system, just as it is for any information management system.

Current users of source documents should be surveyed to determine their information requirements and the volume of documents received, filed, and retrieved on a daily basis. Key research factors should include document retention requirements, acceptable retrieval response time, and file volatility. A paper flow diagram also may help to identify work stream problems and bottlenecks. The gathering of historical trend figures and information regarding proposed organizational or business climate changes is essential for clarifying future system requirements.

In addition to investigating paper-source document applications, MIS managers may explore the potential use of document-based systems to aid individuals who create documents electronically. For example, word processing centers often create extra printouts of correspondence documents simply to provide originators with paper copies for files. Several organizations are already experimenting with the use of computer output microfilm (COM) as an alternative to word processing output. Because new COM peripherals can create indexed 16 mm roll microfilm as well as microfiche, COM can become an input medium for a microimage transmission system. This would allow authors to access document files electronically. In addition, the ability to reconvert a microimage to a data bit stream might eliminate the need for disk or diskette storage of all word processing center documents as insurance against revision requests.

Once a needs analysis is complete, the MIS manager will understand current and future system requirements. In larger applications, the results may indicate a need for immediate implementation of a microimage transmission system; an application that is relatively small but growing might require a CAR system upgradable to incorporate microimage transmission.

Regardless of the entry-level system configuration, the MIS manager should attempt to install system components that offer maximum flexibility. For example, while film-based systems offer the most cost-effective means of capturing and storing vital document-based information, the components of such systems may affect future development efforts. Organizations installing state-of-the-art CAR systems probably will find the transition to microimage transmission a smooth one; those opting for bargain micrographics equipment that delivers inferior image quality may be less fortunate because rolls of film that are poorly exposed, incorrectly coded, or contain overlapping images will be more difficult to scan, transmit, and reconstruct.

CONCLUSION

Optical disk technology has potential for tremendous long-term benefits in the integrated mass storage of images and data. A multitude of optical disk components and configurations are envisioned to satisfy the unique requirements of organizations of varying sizes with individual document-based applications.

To design document-based systems that can immediately boost productivity and efficiency, MIS managers should conduct a thorough needs analysis that examines application growth and other factors that affect future system requirements. State-of-the-art computer micrographics systems offer one of the most cost-effective ways to fulfill most document-based information requirements. However, to incorporate emerging optical disk technology into existing systems with minimal dislocation, MIS managers must address the need for interfacing existing data bases and new technology. Interactive use of multiple technologies will be the hallmark of successful, versatile systems.

XIV-4
Graphics Terminal Technology
Alan Paller

INTRODUCTION

MIS departments can now offer online, one-button graphic information retrieval to managers and executives. Graphics terminals deliver charts to the executive's desk, and laser printers, plotters, ink-jet printers, and 35mm film recorders deliver hard copies in the form of paper, overhead transparencies, and 35mm slides. In addition, personal computers can be linked with departmental and central host computers and transformed into intelligent graphics workstations to offer the benefits of graphics without the usual limitations of standalone personal computers.

This chapter provides the information MIS executives and end-user management need to transform computer graphics from its current status as a frill into a strategic resource that will improve bottom-line profitability and forge new relationships between MIS and senior management. It focuses on developments in four key areas:
- Hard-copy graphics hardware, with emphasis on higher-resolution, higher-speed equipment
- Personal computers, particularly their role in integrated systems as a complement to their standalone graphics role
- Graphics software, including software needed to provide one-button access to visual summaries
- Strategies for effective support and management of end-user graphics.

HARD-COPY GRAPHICS DEVELOPMENTS

Developments in three major areas have set new standards for hard-copy graphics. The following paragraphs review the most important new developments and show how they will influence the future of computer graphics.

Black-and-White Hard Copy

Laser printers have redefined graphics throughput and quality. These machines produce charts with 6 million pixels, 100 times the resolution of a personal computer screen. In addition, lasers print 10 times faster than the popular dot matrix printers and digital plotters. The price of graphics laser printers recently fell below $10,000. At this price, laser printers can be afforded by both MIS and end-user departments. They are often justified as auxiliary printers (printing 600 to 1,500 lines per minute in crisp text on standard paper), but they can be used for graphics as well. These laser printers enable end users to integrate diagrams and charts with words or data listings on a printed page.

At least one vendor of laser printers, QMS Inc, offers an option that enables its laser printer to emulate an IBM 3287 printer so that it is compatible with an IBM operating environment. The Apple Computer Inc Laserwriter is another example of the trend toward full graphics on laser printers. At a price of $7,000, it sets a new standard for personal computer hard copy that Hewlett-Packard and Japanese vendors will no doubt quickly match.

Color Hard Copy

Low-cost ink-jet printers have made color hard copy affordable for all sizes of corporations. Resolution has increased to 150 dots per inch as prices have plummeted to below $1,000. New transparent paper and fast-drying inks enable ink-jet printers to create full-color overhead transparencies. Digital plotters have also gained improved resolution at much lower costs, and manufacturers of digital plotters are trying to hold on to a 50 percent market share for color hard copy. But the market is clearly leaning toward ink-jets and another newer technology—color thermal printers.

Ink-jet and color thermal printers are beginning to erode the market share of digital plotters primarily because they offer solid-color background and area fills at higher printing speeds than plotters. Color thermal printing features will soon include a resolution of 400 dots per inch (4,000 dots across a 10-inch page) and a throughput of more than one page per minute.

35mm Slides

Computers were used to produce 11 million original 35mm slides for business applications in 1983 and 20 million in 1984, and they will produce still more in 1985. Most of these were created on expensive systems designed for visual artists. However, computer-based 35mm film recorders are now being attached to general-purpose computers. Film recorders are too expensive to be locked into a single-user system, such as a personal computer, unless the system is to be used in a graphic arts department. Therefore, a large proportion of the high-quality computer-based film recorders (those with a resolution of more than 2,000 lines across the terminal screen) are networked to mainframe and superminicomputers so that they can be shared by all users with terminals or personal computers.

The falling costs of film recorders have persuaded MIS departments at more than 100 companies to make 35mm slides a standard offering of their mainframe computers. One of the most important influences on this decision was the price erosion in 2,000- and 4,000-line-resolution film recorders in 1984. 2,000-line film recorders fell below $10,000, while 4,000-line recorders dropped from $30,000 to less than $20,000.

PERSONAL COMPUTER GRAPHICS

Applications of Personal Computer Graphics

Recent studies on the growth of personal computer graphics have revealed that there were more than 1 million personal computer graphics users in 1984 and have estimated that there will be 10 million users by 1990. The three principal applications that have fueled the proliferation of personal computer graphics are discussed in the following paragraphs.

Immediate Visual Display of Spreadsheet Data. The most common form of personal computer graphics is the visual display of spreadsheet data from such software packages as Lotus 1-2-3. Users can view charts on the screen and produce hard copy on inexpensive dot matrix printers. Very few Lotus 1-2-3 users print the charts on plotters because the results are often ineffective in presentations.

Ad Hoc Charting. There are at least 190 products available for the IBM Personal Computer that can be used alone or in combination with other products to provide users with ad hoc paper and overhead transparencies for word, line, pie, and bar charts.

Integrating Text and Diagrams. The integration of diagrams with text in memos and other documents was first made popular by the Apple Macintosh. The output was dubbed MacMemos. The same capability is becoming available on the IBM Personal Computer as popular word processing packages are upgraded to allow diagrams, charts, and graphs to be embedded in text.

Problems with Personal Computer Graphics

The popular personal computer applications discussed in the preceding section, along with the zealous promotion personal computer graphics have received in larger organizations, have hidden three problems causing concern among MIS and end-user managers.

Data Entry. Much of the data that must be charted in repetitive applications already resides on a host computer. Although micro-mainframe links exist, a substantial number of personal computer graphics users find these links tedious and confusing. These users must read data from host computer printouts and type it back in to the personal computer—a time-consuming process prone to data entry errors. However, personal computers are used to produce a relatively small number of charts, so the occasional typing involved is seldom overwhelming.

Software Constraints. Each of the approximately 190 graphics packages for the IBM Personal Computer produces some charts, but about 80 percent of the packages fail to meet demands when the famous words, "I like it. Can we just add a table beside the chart?" are voiced. Many of the remainder fail when other requests, such as to place 12 charts on a page, are made. Software constraints can cause frustration when users must produce a chart and

NEW DIRECTIONS IN TECHNOLOGY

then manually add a table with a typewriter. Again, however, personal computers are used to produce so few charts that the cut-and-paste effort is not too burdensome.

Operator-Required Hardware. The problem of operator-required hardware generates such anger and frustration that it often causes personal computer graphics users to give up. The most commonly used hard-copy graphics devices for the IBM Personal Computer are two- or six-pen plotters into which users must constantly feed paper and new pens. Converting highly paid professionals into plotter operators is a waste of resources, and lower-level personnel either are unwilling to spend the necessary overtime or do not have the knowledge or expertise to supervise last minute changes.

Personal computers require plotter operators because most personal computer owners will not spend more than 40 percent of the computer's price on any peripheral. The only plotters that can be acquired at that price require users to manually feed in paper. This problem becomes critical when charts are needed immediately, requiring highly paid professionals to spend nights and weekends feeding pens and paper to the plotter.

The special applications and problems of personal computers lead to a clear conclusion: personal computers are outstanding for producing low-volume, simple, ad hoc charts but are inappropriate for repetitive, higher-volume applications. However, all high-payoff graphics applications require large numbers of charts, multiple charts per page, and repetitive production. None of these applications is feasible with most of today's personal computers.

There is a solution on the horizon, however, called cooperative processing. In cooperative processing, the personal computer is converted into an intelligent graphics workstation. Personal computer users preview charts locally and then send the charts through the network to a departmental or central host computer. At the host computer, the charts are automatically enhanced through more powerful software, and dozens or hundreds of charts are produced on high-speed shared hard-copy graphics equipment. Prototype graphics workstation products are already in use in many organizations. The coming year will bring more functions and more effective micro-mainframe solutions.

GRAPHICS SOFTWARE DEVELOPMENTS

Three trends in graphics software are changing the way MIS departments offer and support computer graphics:
- Microcomputer graphics users are adopting Lotus 1-2-3 and such paint programs Apple MacPaint as standards.
- Mainframe and superminicomputer users are increasingly adopting the ISSCO TELL-A-GRAF for end users, the SAS Institute Inc SAS/GRAPH for SAS programmers, and the ISSCO DISSPLA for general, scientific, and engineering programmers.
- Management users are awakening to the lure of one-button, online access to visual summaries (visual early warning systems).

Graphics Terminal

Lotus 1-2-3

Most organizations large enough to have an MIS department have chosen one standard spreadsheet program, usually Lotus 1-2-3. Lotus 1-2-3 offers built-in graphics that some users call unacceptable and others consider adequate. Regardless of their value, Lotus 1-2-3 graphics are already there and have therefore caused many organizations to ignore the 190 other graphics software packages available for the IBM Personal Computer. The trend toward Lotus 1-2-3 as a standard will expand greatly when links are created between Lotus-1-2-3 and mainframe and minicomputer packages, such as TELL-A-GRAF, enabling users to use Lotus 1-2-3 for instant previewing and then use the mainframe package to transform charts into high-quality versions without tying up user workstations.

MacPaint and programs for the IBM Personal Computer that operate like MacPaint are creating a second standard for today's personal computers. Drawing software like MacPaint or the Lifeboat Associates Dr. Halo enables users to add diagrams to memos.

TELL-A-GRAF on Mainframes and Departmental Minicomputers

TELL-A-GRAF is one of the most widely used graphics software packages on mainframes and minicomputers. In addition to TELL-A-GRAF, many MIS departments offer IBM graphics software, data base management graphics (Focus Graphics from Information Builders Inc or SAS/GRAPH), and DISSPLA for programmers. DISSPLA is especially popular in scientific and engineering environments, where it is used by engineers and system builders to create graphics applications for analysis and computer-aided design. Its popularity has expanded with the newly announced addition of graphical kernal system standards and interactive graphics input.

Visual Early Warning Systems

No application of computers is more appealing to top management than one-button access to visual summaries, now called visual early warning systems (VEWSs). If used effectively, VEWSs can make the value of information systems more apparent to top executives.

Newly developed software offers the three key features needed for success in these systems:

- One-button user interface in which users do not need to memorize commands
- Chart display in three to ten seconds from chart libraries of more than 1,000 charts
- Very high resolution hard copy in black and white or color, on paper or slides

MIS departments have long recognized that they must someday offer visual information systems with online graphics access to data. Articles in *Business Week* and other popular magazines describing one-button systems have increased the priority given to visual information systems. Now that off-the-shelf software is available to help MIS construct visual information systems, many organizations are planning or building these systems for managers throughout the organization.

IMPROVING END-USER ACCESS TO COMPUTER GRAPHICS

Although high-quality graphics hardware and the right graphics software are obvious requirements for widespread use of computer graphics, experienced users have found that hardware and software alone are not sufficient for achieving full productivity. A third requirement is an effective implementation strategy that provides maximum access for end users. Several pioneering users have found four effective techniques for managing computer graphics. Their innovative methods, outlined in the following paragraphs, are now being adopted by others.

Providing Wide Access

Companies such as 3M and Sikorsky Aircraft (a division of United Technologies Corporation) have made computer graphics available to every user of every terminal and communicating personal computer connected to the host computer, even if the terminal does not have its own graphics capability. This has been accomplished with device-independent graphics chart books and software and shared hard-copy graphics equipment. The software allows users to request a chart from a booklet of predesigned charts, view the chart at the terminal, and send it to a shared graphics device. Similar to printers, the graphics devices are set up for spooled output. The impact of such systems is illustrated at 3M, where more than 1,500 employees, or one of every ten white-collar workers, are now regular users of computer graphics.

Improving Productivity with Hard-Copy Chart Books

An overriding concern among graphics end users is designing the most effective chart. The more flexible the software, the more difficult it is to choose from among the many potential designs. Some organizations have solved this problem by using chart books designed by software vendors or the company's own graphics designers. Before signing on to the computer, users can look at a booklet or poster that shows the available designs. After selecting a chart, the user answers several prompts concerning the location of data and specific titles, and the computer produces the charts.

Chart books also allow substantial cost and time savings for users. They can improve productivity at computer graphics facilities up to threefold by alleviating most preview requirements. Because users no longer need to preview charts at a terminal, they can select and request charts from alphanumeric terminals, avoiding the need for graphics terminals for occasional users.

Avoiding the Closed Shop

Most organizations initially implement computer graphics facilities in a central location staffed by a technical assistance group whose members make charts for users. This approach has little chance of success in the long run (i.e., more than six months). If the service is good, demand will overwhelm the service center, and as users are turned away, they are also turned off. If the service is weak, no one will use it.

In most organizations, the chart-making support staff's time is booked up before even 5 percent of the potential high-payoff graphics applications is implemented. The solution is to offer technical assistance to help users make their own charts from their own terminals.

Integrating Graphics with the Information Center

Information centers make a good home for computer graphics. At initial installation, information centers usually offer graphics only on dot matrix color printers or plotters; 35mm slides, transparencies, and high-quality black-and-white charts are not available. But most users eventually need at least one of these high-resolution display formats. After a year or two of limited service, information centers in many large organizations have begun to include additional capabilities, including high-quality, device-independent software, links to 35mm slide services, and shared digital plotters.

ACTION PLAN

The growth of computer graphics has been a boon to many MIS departments. It has increased end-user involvement in computing without placing undue strain on hardware or personnel resources. More important, computer graphics have permitted MIS departments to respond directly to the daily information needs of, for example, senior executives, scientists, and marketing and financial managers. The productivity improvements associated with computer graphics are well documented.[1]

To realize these benefits, an organization can establish a productive visual information system by:
- Providing users with shared plotters and slide-making services that are accessible from alphanumeric terminals as well as from graphics terminals. Most companies accomplish this by acquiring one or two plotters to be shared by all terminals through a spooling system. More plotters and laser printers are acquired as demand grows. Some organizations make slides with digital film recorders; others create tape or disk files and transfer them to high-resolution slide-making service bureaus.
- Connecting personal computers to the mainframe as graphics terminals. Graphics terminals are valuable for previewing and for quick access to graphics data summaries. Personal computers can be converted to graphics terminals with software or combinations of hardware and software. This should be done only after shared plotters, laser printers, or slide-making systems have been installed.
- Following the advice of James Martin. This widely respected DP authority has stated. "Graphics is a particularly powerful way to communicate business information and understand the effects of what-if questions. Some information centers have emphasized the use of graphics. This has had a particular appeal to the user community. Graphics software differs greatly in quality. It pays to select the best in order to sell the information center capabilities to senior management and users."[2] In other words, skimping on graphics software reduces the value of graph-

ics and reduces the perceived value of the entire information system to upper and middle management.
- Providing a technical assistance and training service that will help new users get started in graphics. The technical assistants should not become a service bureau, making charts for all users; rather, their objective should be to make users self-sufficient as quickly as possible. The information center is an effective home for this type of service, especially as graphics tend to be a highlight of information centers.
- Searching for strategic, repetitive applications in the areas of sales and marketing, cost control, project management, quality and performance monitoring, and executive chart books. Too much emphasis on ad hoc presentation charts makes computer graphics an overhead item rather than a profit generator.
- Setting up one-button VEWSs for senior managers. There is no better way, in the opinion of the author, to improve the bottom-line profits of the organization and strengthen the relationship between MIS and senior management.

References

1. See, for example, "Wharton Business School Study: Graphics Influences Business Meeting Outcome," *Computer Graphics News* (April 1982). The report showed that graphics cut the time spent in business meetings by 28 percent and improved the competitiveness and effectiveness of speakers.
2. J. Martin, *Application Development Without Programmers* (Englewood Cliffs NJ: Prentice-Hall, 1982), 323.

XIV-5
Speech Recognition and Voice Response Technology
Raymond Watrous

INTRODUCTION

Speech recognition is the automatic translation of spoken words into machine-readable form. This translation can result in orthographic representations (i.e., correct, as opposed to phonetic, spellings) of natural-language utterances or machine language–encoded command and data sequences.

Voice response is the automatic production of artificial speech. The converse of speech recognition, it might be more accurately called speech generation or speech production. Voice response systems can generate spoken words from a fixed vocabulary or any combination of sentences in a particular language.

Speaker verification, an adjunct of speech recognition technology, is a means of accurately verifying a speaker's identity by analyzing voice characteristics that are nearly impossible to imitate. Speaker verification is distinct from speaker identification, which uses voice patterns to establish a speaker's identity rather than to confirm or reject a claimed identity.

Advantages

The advantage of speech recognition and voice response technology is that it allows human beings and machines to communicate through spoken language. Because people communicate through speech, automatic speech recognition and generation provide an interface that accommodates machine users rather than forcing them to conform to the computer's communication constraints.

Speech recognition and generation can provide the link that satisfies the character-by-character requirement of machine I/O and still conform to the typical human communication units of words, phrases, and sentences. The human-to-machine interface can thus be made very flexible without loss of precision. Consequently, people can use computers equipped with speech I/O technology without undergoing extensive training in artificial machine languages.

The advantages of speech recognition and voice response can be extended by natural-language processing to achieve a highly adapted human-to-

NEW DIRECTIONS IN TECHNOLOGY

machine interface. Speech recognition is often considered a preprocessor to a natural-language interface. The advantages of a completely natural spoken language interface generally can be realized only in a fully integrated interface in which syntax, semantics, and pragmatics (i.e., the ability of native speakers to infer implied meaning) are combined with phonetics and phonology to achieve true speech understanding.

Use of this technology also increases throughput speed and accuracy and user mobility. Speech provides a parallel data entry path that can be used in conjunction with eyes and hands to achieve increased, more accurate data throughput. The ability to enter data by voice while handling or inspecting objects eliminates the need to interrupt one task to accomplish another. In this way, both speed and accuracy can improve. Because speech recognition eliminates the need for direct physical contact with a data entry device, user mobility increases. In addition, voice can provide a communications channel where other channels are impractical, as in a totally darkened room.

For people with certain physical handicaps, speech I/O can provide a means of communication and control that reduces the degree of assistance they require from other people, thus enhancing their sense of freedom.

The advantage of speaker verification over other methods of identity confirmation is that it is biometric; that is, a person's speech characteristics are always present and are extremely difficult, if not impossible, to modify. Verification by speech can be done quickly, safely, and reliably.

STATUS OF THE TECHNOLOGY

Speech Recognition

Speech recognition is a complex process involving many variables, such as a speaker's language, dialect, speaking rate and volume, age, sex, health, degree of fatigue, vocal tract configuration, and emotional state as well as the level and type of background noise and the type of speech transducer used.

The three basic parameters used to classify speech recognizers are discussed in the following sections.

Speech Connectivity. Computer identification of word boundaries in natural speech is a difficult problem and a significant source of recognition error. Therefore, some systems employ *isolated speech,* which requires the user to self-consciously introduce short pauses between each spoken word. This provides increased accuracy at the cost of some inconvenience to the user. In some systems, this interword pause can be made so short that the data entry speed approaches that of natural speech. (This method, patented by Threshold Technology, is called QUIKTALK.)

The term *connected speech* refers to carefully spoken phrases without interword pauses. Some manufacturers claim to provide a connected speech capability but limit the number of words that can be spoken without a pause. Unfortunately, this term also has been applied to isolated speech with arbitrarily short interword pauses. Use of this term therefore should be carefully interpreted.

Continuous speech refers to unconstrained spoken sentences of unlimited length. This term also implies the use of a more flexible syntax that approximates the freedom of natural language.

Speaker Dependence. This is a measure of the amount of speech information each user of the speech recognition device must provide to obtain favorable results. Speaker-dependent systems generally require the user to train the recognizer by repeating each word in the vocabulary several times, usually between one and ten. (The recognition accuracy generally increases with each training repetition, up to about five.) Such systems then form word templates from these training utterances. Speaker-independent systems attempt to accommodate the speech of a large class of users, without a training process. Both approaches may also include an adaptive mechanism that updates the template data base as recognition proceeds in order to achieve better performance and dynamic characteristics. Some speaker-independent systems may require several sample sentences from the user to initially align certain recognition parameters.

In general, the performance of speaker-dependent systems is superior to that of speaker-independent systems. In addition, speaker-dependent recognizers can usually accommodate a much wider range of language and dialect than their speaker-independent counterparts. The obvious disadvantage of speaker-dependent systems is the inconvenience of repeating each word in the vocabulary several times.

Vocabulary Size. The size of the application vocabulary affects recognizer performance. As the vocabulary expands, the probability of acoustic error increases and the recognition accuracy decreases. In addition, the recognition processing time generally rises with increasing vocabulary size because the recognizer must consider more possibilities. These effects can be partially controlled by dividing the application vocabulary into smaller subvocabularies, which can be in effect at different points in the application task. Obviously, the vocabulary size for speaker-dependent recognizers is limited by the need to repeat each word. However, a surprising number of practical applications can be automated with small vocabularies, often containing only 50 to 250 words.

Other Considerations. Finally, the type of speech input device usually required for excellent recognition performance is a head-mounted, noise-canceling microphone. Hand-held or desk-mounted microphones are more likely to pick up background noise, which interferes with accurate performance. In addition, the bandwidth restrictions and channel noise of dial-up telephone lines have thus far limited the usefulness of speech recognition over the telephone.

Voice Response

There is a fundamental distinction between speech coding and speech synthesis. Speech coding is a means of efficiently storing spoken words in digital form, from which the original speech can be re-created. The speech signal is digitized and then encoded according to one of various algorithms to achieve differing degrees of data reduction. This data compression increases the number of words that can be stored in memory and reduces the serial bit rate for transmission over serial lines. The loss of speech quality and intelligibility is proportional to the degree of data reduction, with slight variations depending on the encoding technique. Speech synthesis operates by combining small units of speech, modified as necessary by certain sequence rules, into a string of spoken words. An input of phoneme strings or natural-language text produces the desired speech output. Devices performing this task are called text-to-speech synthesizers. Synthesizers vary in how natural the speech they produce is; this is generally related to the extent to which natural-speech production is modeled by the synthesizer. Natural variations, such as pitch, intonation, and cadence, require more sophisticated algorithms.

Speech coding, then, can provide voice response for a preselected vocabulary, whereas speech synthesis can produce speech output from an open vocabulary. Speech coding produces speech output derived from natural speech, whereas speech synthesizers produce speech artificially. These differences affect the cost, performance, and suitability of voice response applications.

Speaker Verification

Speaker verification uses speaker-dependent voice characteristics to verify speaker identity. Currently, this technology is probably more feasible than speech recognition, although it has not received as much attention. Because the task is much less complex, its performance is better; thus, the opportunity for successful application is greater. In addition, speaker verification is usually necessary only at the start of a transaction; this makes integrating speaker verification into existing tasks significantly easier than integrating speech recognition.

Hardware Availability and Performance

Speech I/O technology is currently available in products ranging from integrated circuits to fully integrated systems, including board-level products, personal computer peripherals, turnkey voice terminals, and application development systems. The cost of the technology ranges from less than $50 for recognition and synthesis chips to more than $50,000 for full systems.

The performance of this technology, however, is more difficult to specify. Vendors of speech recognizers typically claim better than 99 percent recognition accuracy. Hidden by this claim are variables affecting recognition accuracy, such as vocabulary size and acoustic complexity, the extent of syntactic constraints, type and level of background noise, operator experience, motivation and fatigue, and microphone type and placement. For speech synthesis the situation is similar, but the variables affect human perception rather than machine recognition of speech.

For these technologies, the performance must be evaluated in terms of the consequences of loss of performance. For recognizers, lower performance results in increased recognition errors, which require operator correction. For voice response devices, lower performance may result in less intelligible speech, greater monotony, and increased errors. For speaker verification, lower performance may admit impostors or deny access to authorized persons.

APPLICATIONS

Current applications of speech I/O technology, as well as several applications as yet not implemented, are discussed in the following sections.

Quality Control and Inspection. Quality control and inspection are manual and visual tasks that have been expedited through voice I/O. Meat grading, automobile assembly line inspection, and aluminum can lid quality control are examples of operations that have used voice recognition to eliminate task interruptions and two-stage data entry. In many instances, a wireless link is used to give the inspector complete freedom of movement.

In material handling applications, voice data entry and control have assisted in such tasks as airport baggage handling and postal package routing. Speech recognition has been used to streamline routing tasks, reduce errors, and simplify job training.

Computer-Aided Design and Engineering. In these visual applications, voice I/O technology can provide interactive control that enhances concentration on the complex design process. In cartographic data entry, a user can vocally identify map features while focusing on the map image. Voice response may also be used to confirm voice data entry.

Automatic Banking. Automatic teller machines, which are becoming exceedingly numerous, could be designed to support voice interaction. Banks currently appear to have little motivation to do this, as data entry by keyboard is adequate for brief transactions. However, speaker verification would greatly increase the level of security for banking and credit-charging transactions. The resulting cost benefit of protection against theft and fraud would be enormous. Some banks have taken advantage of these speaker verification capabilities to protect internal transfers of large sums.

Banking by telephone is another ideal candidate for voice interaction. Voice output is already in use, but the simplicity of the transactions would not appear to justify the expense of voice input. However, speaker verification would provide an additional level of security.

Office Automation. The speech typewriter for automated dictation has long been an attractive goal for automatic speech recognition. Its potential contribution to office automation is widely recognized, but progress toward this end has not yet resulted in practical products. However, voice input as a concurrent channel to keyboard input, has been demonstrated to increase speed, accuracy, and convenience for word processing tasks. Voice I/O is currently offered in desktop systems in which it is integrated with other voice-related functions, such as telephone dialing and voice mail.

Data Base Retrieval. Retrieving information from a large data base by using voice technology could provide user access for telephone inquiries and support information retrieval when the spelling of keywords was uncertain. Speaker verification could be used to control access to sensitive data.

Obvious examples of this application are telephone directory assistance services and information and reservation systems. The directory assistance service currently uses voice response to report telephone numbers. Fully automated interaction will probably be available in several years.

Military Applications. Military applications considered for voice technology have mainly included cockpit instrumentation and navigational support. Because of the number of instruments requiring the pilot's attention and the limited space for new indicators, voice I/O appears to be a good alternative for reporting aircraft conditions. However, the need for extreme reliability in such an application, coupled with the problem of the noise level in the environment, has limited this application to developmental studies. Voice response is now being used to perform similar functions in commercial automobiles.

Securing access to military installations is an obvious application of speaker verification technology. Communication security is another example of applied speech technology; linear predictive coding algorithms have been combined with encryption techniques to provide safe radiotelephone links.

Human Resources. Speech technology can aid people with physical handicaps that restrict communication and mobility. One of the earliest examples of such assistance is the Kurzweil reading machine for the sight-impaired; others include voice-controlled wheelchairs and environmental control units.

Despite government funding for research in these areas, market conditions have not yet encouraged significant product development efforts. Consequently, most advances in this field are being made by concerned individuals using speech recognizers linked to personal computers. The productivity potential of a large population of handicapped persons, the current expense of routine care, and the possibility of increased independence of handicapped citizens make this an impelling opportunity for speech technology.

Other Functions. Other application examples are voice programming of numeric control machines, medical report generation from radiographic and ultrasound analyses, and navigational assistance for tugboat pilots. Speech I/O technology is also being used for speech therapy and computer-aided instruction for children, for which reading and typing ability are not presupposed.

TECHNICAL AND ORGANIZATIONAL CHALLENGES

Human speech is a complex and subtle process, as research in linguistics, psychology, biophysics, and physiology has shown. Attempts to reproduce this process using machines have revealed the marvelous precision and flexibility of human language processing capabilities. These abilities create expectations of the artificial implementation that have yet to be met.

Robustness, a consistent level of reliability under various signal conditions, is one challenge affecting current recognizers. Dynamic range and accurate performance in different noise levels and types must be increased. A related problem is the use of noise-canceling, head-mounted microphones. This is often viewed as an inconvenience whose elimination should be required for robust performance. Similarly, the problems of bandwidth limitation introduced by switched telephone networks have not been entirely solved.

Speaker-independent recognition for unrestricted vocabularies is still a goal that must be reached for the full realization of office automation. There is general agreement that the results of careful research on the acoustic and phonetic properties of speech must be incorporated into the next generation of speech recognizers. Research in human auditory processing has suggested intriguing possible future directions that need evaluation. Current advances in artificial intelligence and computational linguistics must be integrated with acoustic processing to achieve natural speech recognition.

The primary challenge in speaker verification is product development. Some research is needed to further exploit speaker-dependent voice characteristics to improve discrimination, but the more pressing need is for inexpensive and practical implementations of existing technology.

Increasing the naturalness and intelligibility of synthetic speech must remain goals for voice response. This may involve more accurate modeling of the human speech production process at both the physiological and psychological levels.

The costs of production and ownership of these technologies must be reduced to make their benefits widely available. Advances in hardware architecture may be necessary, especially where cognitive modeling is employed. The reliability and robustness, particularly of speech recognizers, must be increased so that people who are not speech experts can use these devices with confidence. Improved software packages are needed to better support application development.

The most significant organizational challenge is, of course, economic. The decision to purchase speech I/O devices is based on increased productivity and the consequent payback period.

Another challenge is acceptance by individual users. The general resistance to new technology must be overcome as well as the specific problem of using a head-mounted microphone. This requirement has produced some resistance to using speech. Operator acceptance is also affected by device reliability, recognition robustness, and naturalness of synthesized speech. Advances are expected to address these problems so that use of speech I/O will become increasingly comfortable.

FUTURE OF SPEECH I/O TECHNOLOGY

The outlook for speech I/O technology is excellent. The benefits of the technology are clear, and a growing base of installed systems is providing practical experience in using speech for actual applications. An increasing number of publications, conferences, and trade shows demonstrate speech I/O capabilities and educate potential users.

NEW DIRECTIONS IN TECHNOLOGY

As a research area, speech is attracting an increasing number of scientists and engineers, as evidenced by the significant growth in attendance at professional conferences such as the meeting of the Acoustics, Speech and Signal Processing Society of the IEEE. The availability and quality of research tools for speech analysis are also increasing. The efficiency of these tools is important because of the quantity of data that must be studied. Because of the consensus that current developments have reached a plateau, there is a readiness among researchers to consider new directions. New research may take several promising approaches, some of which are based on earlier attempts that can now be renewed with greater resources.

Research conducted in the mid-1970s under the sponsorship of the Advanced Research Projects Agency of the Defense Department, as well as more recent work in computational linguistics, has increased knowledge of the contribution to language understanding made by various levels of linguistic processing. This knowledge will be the basis for systems that permit natural-language speech interaction between human beings and machines.

The Ministry of International Trade and Industry of Japan has set a series of ambitious goals defining the specifications for fifth-generation computers. These machines are to be able to perform millions of powerful logical inferencing operations per second and use natural-language speech I/O. A group of universities and industrial companies are cooperating to pursue these goals. The challenge to other countries is how they will respond to the Japanese initiative.

CONCLUSION

Organizations interested in using speech I/O should consider existing data entry tasks or human-to-machine interfaces that might be improved by its advantages. These potential applications should be discussed with several vendors having extensive application experience in order to assess the possibility of productivity increase and to make cost/benefit analyses. Finally, product selection should be based on documented and demonstrated performance on standard tests and a thorough understanding of the effort required to implement the application, especially when voice will modify a previous task format.

Readers interested in more information about speech I/O technology should consult recent issues of *Speech Technology* magazine (published by Media Dimensions, New York) for application reports, technical articles, and selection guides that provide vendor lists. For a detailed account of one company's experience with a voice data entry system, readers should see "Voice Data Entry for Assembly Operations: Lockheed Case Study," article 3.2.4 S4 in Auerbach's *Computers In Manufacturing: Execution and Control Systems.*[1]

Speech technology provides the great opportunity to accommodate the computer to the attributes of the human user of information processing systems. This development would make computational resources accessible to the widest group of people.

References

1. *Computers in Manufacturing: Execution and Control Systems,* Auerbach Publishers Inc, 6560 North Park Drive, Pennsauken NJ, (609) 662-2070, (800) 257-8162.

XIV-6
Expert Systems and Artificial Intelligence

Richard P. Ten Dyke

INTRODUCTION

Artificial intelligence (AI) has the potential to affect many aspects of life, including business, education, health care, and entertainment. Although current applications are limited, growing expertise and technical capability promise significant achievements in this area. This chapter reviews current research and identifies future trends.

WHAT IS AI?

AI is the use of the computer to perform tasks that currently require human intelligence. AI is not a computerized re-creation of thought. This distinction between thinking like a human and performing tasks like a human is the key to understanding AI's future opportunities and limitations. By analogy, in the past people wanted to fly like a bird; today they fly, though not like a bird. Philosophical debates about whether a computer can think are of limited value. The meaningful question is: Are there new ways that computers can be applied to accomplish useful work?

HISTORICAL PERSPECTIVE

AI actually predates the computer. George Boole, the founder of Boolean logic, on which AI is based, published his seminal works in the mid-19th century. In 1937, Claud Shannon pointed out in his MIT master's thesis that "(1) there is an algebra that applies to switching circuits, and (2) it is the algebra of [Boolean] logic."[1] The ENIAC, developed during the 1940s at the University of Pennsylvania and regarded by many as the first stored-program digital computer, was designed as a calculator using Boolean logic. John von Neumann later suggested that by using the same logic, calculators could modify their own instructions as if they were data. This modification initiated the large-scale development of the computer. The computer, therefore, can be considered an outgrowth of work on AI.

Because the stored-program computer was based on logical decision making, attempting to solve complex problems that required human intelligence was a natural next step. Early applications included theorem proving, language translation, and games like checkers and chess. Despite early successes with theorem proving and checkers, problems with more complex applications forestalled further achievement. In the 25 years since these early applications were developed, no one has written a chess program that consistently wins against top players. In addition, theorem-proving programs can prove many mathematical theorems, but they have uncovered no new ones. Language translation remains an unsolved problem.

The difficulty of extending early successes to more complex applications forced AI researchers to rethink their goals and methods. They began to realize that it might be helpful to set aside the notion that AI involves a re-creation of thought and to concentrate instead on specific tasks. Despite this change in emphasis, it is still useful to try to understand how people solve problems and attempt to automate those problem-solving activities that the computer can perform well. Furthermore, understanding how a computer solves problems can lead to useful observations about human thought patterns.

STATE OF THE ART

In Japan, research in AI is currently under way, the goal being to make future computers easier to use. This effort, known as the Fifth Generation project, is also concerned with the application of expert systems. Although much has been written about the potential impact of the Japanese effort, few results have been reported. Without results, it is difficult to assess the likelihood of achieving Fifth Generation goals.

AI today is at a crossroads, with some recent successes and several major unsolved problems. Certain applications of expert systems have been commercially successful. The unsolved problems concern computer creativity and learning. The remainder of this chapter focuses on these two areas as they apply to the development of expert systems.

EXPERT SYSTEMS

Expert systems are computer programs that act as expert consultants to users. For example, an expert system in the field of internal medicine could help a doctor diagnose a patient's illness and prescribe treatment. Another expert system might assist a computer salesperson in interpreting a customer's needs and designing a complete computer system, including cabling and physical configuration. A third expert system might help a geologist interpret information gathered from instrumentation in the search for mineral deposits.

An expert system consists of three components: a knowledge base supplied by an expert in the field, a set of facts supplied by the user, and an inference engine supplied by the program. In addition, the system includes a mechanism that interviews the user to determine the facts relating to the user's specific problem. An expert system can also describe how it is proceeding with its analysis.

Expert systems have been designed and proved feasible in the field. Digital Equipment Corporation, for example, is using such a system to help computer salespersons improve the accuracy and reduce the cost of ordering equipment. The internist expert system developed at the University of Pittsburgh has been used as a prototype, though improvements are needed before it can be used widely. The expert system designed to assist in the search for mineral deposits is undergoing a field evaluation.

There is potentially no limit to the problems that expert systems can help solve. They can be used to interpret photographic information, direct robots, assist a football coach in calling plays, pilot an airplane, and buy and sell commodities. Nevertheless, current expert systems are limited in their usefulness. Before discussing these limitations, however, this chapter will examine how an expert system is put together.

If-Then Rules

Expert systems are based on the premise that experts can describe how they solve problems by using rules of inference. These rules, which are closely related to Boolean logic, take an if-then form, *if* referring to statements and *then* referring to an action or conclusion. For example: *if* the car will not start *and* the engine turns over, *then* determine the status of the fuel gauge. It is possible that the car will not start because it is out of fuel. As many items as necessary can follow the *if* expression, and they can be combined by *and* or *or*. The set of if-then rules is combined with the user-provided facts, using the rules of formal (Boolean) logic, in order to draw conclusions from the facts.

Knowledge Engineering

The introduction of the if-then rules into a computer data base is accomplished through the cooperation of an expert in the field of study and a knowledge engineer conversant with expert systems. Because the field is new and available training is minimal, formal qualifications for the knowledge engineer have not been determined. It has been recommended that he or she combine the skills of a systems analyst, psychologist, linguist, logician, and philosopher. The partnership between the expert and the knowledge engineer is a critical and time-consuming phase in expert systems development. One practitioner estimates that developing a basic system takes a minimum of six months.

Using the System

Once the knowledge base is constructed, the system can be applied to specific problems. An expert-system user is generally familiar with the subject area, though not to the extent of the expert. To initiate the problem-solving process, the user enters the basic facts in a standard format, thus defining the structure of the problem. The system then queries the user in order to complete any necessary details. At this stage, the user may have to gather additional data. Some systems are designed so that the user can ask the computer why the additional information is required. The system then responds by printing out its logical path and indicating how the information will be used. When the system determines that it has sufficient information, it prints out its recommendation.

NEW DIRECTIONS IN TECHNOLOGY

The Inference Engine

The expert system reaches a conclusion by combining the user-provided facts and the knowledge base through the use of an inference engine. This part of the program examines the facts and the knowledge base in an attempt to draw useful, valid conclusions. If it cannot proceed because of a lack of information, the system will request additional data. If in response the user keys in "unknown," the inference engine will attempt to substitute other available information. The inference engine may also reach a conclusion based on available information but qualify the recommendation with a greater than usual degree of uncertainty. If more than one conclusion is possible, the inference engine may rank the choices; for example, "The treatment is based on the conclusion that the illness is probably x but possibly y."

The inference engine is designed with the knowledge base and is therefore tuned to the specific subject. A general-purpose inference engine that would apply to several fields eventually may emerge from current research.

Limitations

The following sections discuss the limitations of expert systems.

Restricted to Using One Expert. Expert systems cannot tolerate contradictions. Imagine that one party in a legal dispute hires two experts in the same field to support its case. The opposing attorney has each expert comment on the other's testimony, successfully casting doubt on the accuracy of both and thereby negating the value of the testimony.

An expert system operates as an attorney would, logically assembling facts in order to derive a conclusion. Formal logic is based on rigorous concepts of truth: a statement is either true or not true, with no middle ground. Therefore, when if-then rules contain hidden contradictions, the system becomes trapped in its own logic. Using more than one expert increases the likelihood of contradictions. With a single expert, such contradictions can be uncovered and resolved more easily. Finding and resolving contradictions is a time-consuming but essential part of the knowledge-engineering process.

The single-expert rule does not apply when the areas of expertise are dissimilar and complement rather than overlap one another. However, the development of the system is more difficult in these cases.

Unable to Learn from Mistakes. Ideally, an expert system should adjust itself when in error to avoid repeating mistakes. Unfortunately, this is not the case. Designers have not yet developed a system that improves the knowledge base through experience. To correct an error, the expert must locate and change the faulty rule.

Restricted to Narrow Domains. An expert system's area of expertise is its domain. Current systems are successful only when the domain is narrow and well defined.

Inefficient in Its Thinking Patterns. Although an expert may describe the solution to a problem in the form of rules, he or she will not necessarily use

Expert Systems and Artificial Intelligence

the same technique to solve the problem. Use of the internal medicine expert system has demonstrated that experts can piece together a full picture, or gestalt, of the problem based on incomplete information and then skillfully focus attention on the facts most relevant to the analysis. Computers have been unable to reproduce this gestalt technique and consequently follow lines of reasoning that an expert would ignore. The next version of the internal medicine system will attempt to introduce the gestalt concept into the program.

Inaccurate Regarding User Facts. The user may not know all the facts accurately (e.g., how many ounces of alcohol did you drink last week?). Because the set of facts may contain inaccurate data, the system may follow invalid lines of reasoning. An expert can assess which facts are questionable and either discard or investigate them.

Need for Adaptable Problem Solving

Expert systems are clearly feasible in well-defined applications for which an expert can describe how decisions should be made. Additional applications should be forthcoming, and certain earlier applications, such as chess, will be recast into an expert-system framework. Nevertheless, where the expert is an adaptable problem solver, the expert system is brittle and narrow. Although this may change with time, anyone considering installing an expert system should take these limitations into account.

Expert systems may provide the mechanism for solving various problems that have troubled AI researchers for years. For example, language translation is being considered as an expert-system application, as is "machine understanding"—the ability of a computer program to operate as though it understood the data being input. This ability may prove essential to language translation and natural language processors.

Clearly, progress in AI applications hinges on whether the computer can become an adaptable problem solver. This in turn suggests the need for new approaches to computer creativity and learning.

COMPUTERS AND CREATIVITY

Some argue that because the computer operates with rules, it is incapable of creativity. The argument is that although the development of rules may be creative, anything that follows from those rules is not.

If whatever the computer did could be predicted by following its rules to their logical conclusion, the computer could not be considered a creative machine. Programmed with rules, however, the computer can produce results that cannot be determined in advance and that have never been derived before.

The following paragraphs explore the creative process as it relates to the computer. The computer clearly can perform all of the tasks necessary to arrive at a creative solution; the difficulty lies in tying these elements together within the framework of a single problem.

NEW DIRECTIONS IN TECHNOLOGY

The Creative Process

The creative process, as it applies to computers, can be defined as the act of developing something that is new or an improvement. In terms of expert systems, this process can be divided into four major components:
- The knowledge base—Contains facts and rules that are useful and relevant to a set of problems
- Option generation—Uses these facts and rules to create options
- Option evaluation—Tests options using information in the knowledge base
- The environment, or user—Provides the final test of the option

These components must be able to communicate with each other; a control process determines the activities of each component and when those activities take place.

The Knowledge Base. The knowledge base provides the necessary information for option generation and evaluation. The information consists of strings of symbols that are assembled in a sometimes meaningful and useful way. The computer, however, does not need to know what is meaningful or useful to assemble an option.

A simple problem illustrates this process. A mathematician wishes to determine the next number in the sequence 1, 4, 9, 7, 7, 9, 13, 10, ___.[2] Although there may be more than one correct answer, a mathematical algorithm may exist to explain the eight numbers shown and predict the ninth. To solve this problem, a knowledge base would have to contain the concept of addition as well as that of assembling numbers into a computable form, that is, an algorithm.

The knowledge base must also contain rules and data to aid the evaluation process. The rule for solving the problem might be that any algorithm that can predict the sixth, seventh, and eighth numbers in the sequence can be used to predict the ninth.

The value of the knowledge base depends on the breadth and accuracy of its information and on whether it can locate needed information in a timely manner.

Option Generation. The option generator assembles information from the knowledge base to create an option, or idea. In the preceding problem, the option generator could assemble an algorithm to predict the nth number in a sequence, given several preceding numbers.

A good option generator develops options that are relevant to the problem to be solved, and that are new. In addition, the options ideally are generated quickly.

It is easy to generate options that are likely to work simply by repeating what has worked before. Such options may be relevant, but they are not new. It is also easy to find options that are new but do not work. It may appear that newness and relevance tend to be mutually exclusive. (This is statistically true; a new idea is less likely to work than an old one.) They are not logical opposites, however, and creative options should possess both characteristics.

Expert Systems and Artificial Intelligence

To achieve newness and unpredictability, designers must inject some randomness into the option-generating process. Too much randomness, however, will overwhelm the process and result in meaningless data; too little will cause the option generator to become a mere rule follower, incapable of generating a creative solution.

Systems designers and programmers make every effort to eliminate randomness from a system. From their perspective; a program should do the same thing every time it runs the same data. Deliberately introducing randomness into a system runs contrary to the principles of traditional systems design. The human mind, however, does in fact operate randomly. If a person is asked the same question twice, he or she will often respond with similar but different answers. Furthermore, when working on a problem, an individual is simultaneously confronted with myriad unrelated input. One of these random observations can result in a creative solution. The random element in the creative process may be the most important concept to AI researchers in their efforts to achieve higher levels of creativity.

The importance of randomness in the creative process is apparent in biological evolution. The sperm and egg both contain in their genetic code the human "knowledge base" developed over several centuries. Creating a new person through the combination of sperm and egg involves a tightly controlled degree of randomness that is essential to the survival of the species. As a result, children are similar to their parents but not identical. By virtue of that genetic similarity, each child has a high probability of survival. By not producing identical offspring, the species achieves the variability needed to adapt to a changing environment.

Option Evaluation. For each option, the option evaluation component calculates a value on which it bases a decision to recommend the option or create a new one. Using models and rules to simulate real-world conditions, the evaluation process tests each option for its ability to meet user requirements.

The test is imperfect because the evaluator can make two kinds of mistakes. It can accept options that have serious flaws, and it can reject options that are acceptable solutions. A measure of the quality of the option evaluation process is the degree to which it avoids these errors.

Another measure of quality is the speed/cost of option evaluation. Because a realistic option evaluation includes not one but a series of tests, the evaluation process can be shortened if these tests are efficiently sequenced. The first tests should be the least expensive and time-consuming and should have the highest probability of finding any flaws. The most effective tests, however, are often the most expensive and time-consuming. Sequencing tests is itself a complex problem requiring creative solutions.

A vital function of option evaluation is informing the knowledge base of results. If an option fails, the knowledge base should avoid re-creating the same option. A sophisticated program could indicate unsatisfactory characteristics of the option so that they could be avoided in future options.

The Environment. The user is considered the environment of the generated option. User input to the knowledge base regarding the success or failure of generated options is important to system effectiveness.

Toward Full Creativity

Although all the creative work discussed in the preceding paragraphs has been performed by computers, these tasks have not been integrated in a single working system; a system that is effective for one aspect of the creative process is generally not effective for others. For example, although computers can simulate an airplane in flight and provide essential performance data, human judgment is required to create the model of the airplane to be tested. Computers can generate art, music, and poetry but lack aesthetic values to evaluate what has been created.

A convergence of the concepts of creativity and learning and rule-based expert systems is the most likely development. Such a blend could offer formidable problem-solving capabilities.

AI TOOLS

AI programs can be created using standard computer programming tools. These programs, however, present two problems: they must be able to handle the creation and analysis of text information and to develop logical inference techniques, which include the searching of large, nonnumeric data structures.

LISP. The first problem is handled by LISP, AI's programming language for almost 30 years (developed in the 1950s by John McCarthy of MIT). LISP's popularity is based on its adeptness in handling strings of words. LISP, an acronym for LISt Processor, contains instructions for adding and deleting words, similar to the way in which a person adds or deletes words in a sentence. The language also enables program control and branching based on the content of the word strings.

LISP is distinguished from most languages by the programmer's ability to write subroutines that later can be used as instructions as if they were part of the original language. (A language with this capability is called recursive.) Users can also modify the program with string instructions during program execution. LISP performs arithmetic and algebraic calculations that can be intermixed with string operations. The language is implemented as an interpreter that speeds the programmer's ability to write and text programs.

LISP is so well adapted to the AI developer's needs that special-purpose computers are sold to implement it. The use of LISP has been so pervasive in the AI community that one reporter wrote that AI was "a program written in LISP." A measure of the language's flexibility is its ability to develop new languages that can run on a LISP machine.

PROLOG. The language PROLOG is becoming widely accepted for expert-systems applications. Designed specifically for expert systems, PROLOG contains direct mechanisms for implementing an inference engine as well as developing search techniques. Japan has selected PROLOG as the language for its Fifth Generation programs.

CONCLUSION

Although AI has been developing for years, it is still new from the standpoint of commercial applications. Most applications will be derived from the use of expert systems, but these must be approached with caution. The following course is suggested:
1. Do not expect the first attempt at AI to work more efficiently than a human problem solver. Experience shows that two or three iterations are often required before a useful system results.
2. Make sure that the application is well defined and limited in scope. Unless the organization has experience in the development of expert systems, the project should be designed to achieve limited, well-defined objectives.
3. Ensure that all necessary people are available and involved. Experienced expert-systems developers recommend a team of three to six members. The team must include an expert who is available to develop the knowledge base as well as a knowledge engineer trained in expert-systems development. (A few companies now offer this training for a fee.)
4. Remember that the user will need training.
5. Evaluate the potential benefits before initiating an expert system. Expert systems can help with tasks that are somewhat repetitive and that require judgment, as long as an expert is available. If improvements in accuracy, timeliness, or quality of decision making have measurable value within a company, an expert system will probably have real benefit.
6. Visit an AI professional conference. Attending such a conference is a quick way to become more knowledgeable about expert systems. The American Association for Artificial Intelligence offers tutorial sessions for novices along with its regular meetings.

References

1. Berkeley, Edmund C. *Giant Brains*. New York: John Wiley & Sons, 1949.
2. One possible answer is 9. The series can be generated by squaring sequential integers and adding the digits when the square is more than nine (e.g., $1^2 = 1$, $2^2 = 4$, $3^2 = 9$, $4^2 = 16$ and $1 + 6 = 7, \ldots$). Of course, the objective is not to manually find the correct answer or the algorithm that provides the answer but to develop the computer program that determines the algorithm.

Epilogue—A Parting Note

Compiling and editing a handbook of this scope in a field that's changing so rapidly is no easy task, but it's one that I eagerly accepted. I did so because I firmly believe that there are insufficient sources to which beleaguered MIS managers can turn in order to find useful—and I emphasize useful—advice. Many are quick to condemn when our efforts do not produce perfection. To them I would commend the admonishment: Let he among you without sin cast the first stone.

I have found that it is far easier to be a critic than an author. Critics need not be creative, nor need they be farsighted. Their only task is to look back, and, with the benefit of 20/20 hindsight, comment on our efforts. I don't mean that all critics are categorically destructive in their observations; rather, that there are some among them who are quick to criticize and slow to help.

It is my hope that this handbook will counterbalance those who are slow to help by offering some of that often-needed help. I fully recognize that not all the topics we, as MIS managers, have an interest in are included. Nor could coverage of each topic addressed be comprehensive enough to exhaust it. I believe, however, that if this handbook is viewed as a source, a stimulator of ideas, it will fulfill its intent. Its success will depend on how well you use it and how imaginative you are in molding the many ideas it contains to your use. If there are future editions of this handbook, it will be because you—the practitioners, educators, and managers—saw value in its pages.

The handbook is structured so that it can be particularly useful in training tomorrow's group of MIS supervisors and managers. It is organized in a way that makes it easy to read, and each chapter offers at least one lesson to be learned—most offer many. Groups of aspiring managers or supervisors could structure discussion groups around each chapter, or one could be assigned a chapter to read, summarize, and present to the group with a tutor or more experienced manager offering comments and different perspectives on each topic. To my knowledge, no other source offers as broad a coverage of such a wide range of subjects.

I am indebted to the many authors whose hard work and vast knowledge are captured in this book. I also thank Jim Gish of Auerbach, for whose diligence and inspiration I owe a week's vacation at the Southampton Princess in Bermuda.

Robert E. Umbaugh

Index

A

Access control
   corporate policies 46–47
   dial-up lines 639–647
   techniques 613–616
Application systems planning
   cost/benefit analysis 249–255
   definition 151–152
   establishing priorities 161–172
   input 154–156
   integration 159–160
   limitations 154
   maintenance 159
   objectives 152–154
   steps 156–159
Applications
   auditing 664–666
   centralization vs decentralization 118, 120
Artificial intelligence 827–835
Auditing
   application 664–666
   corporate policies 45–46
   data center 662–663
   data center security 669–688
   environmental 662–664
   frequency 666–667
   planning 661–668
   role of EDP auditor 651–660
   techniques 667–668
   use of EDP auditor 689–698

C

Career planning
   for data center personnel 421–430
   succession planning 559–573
CEO
   role in information technology 73–78
Change control
   auditing 663
Chargeback
   approaches 99–102
   definition 99
   implementation 105–112
   objectives 104–105
   rate changes 112–113
Checklists
   counseling interview 87
   data center design 455–467
   data center cost evaluation 686–688
   data center security 680–685
   design standards 716
   DP organization 128
   managing by objectives 85
   network planning issues 366
   quality of documentation 719
   testing MIS personnel 542–543
Chief executive officer (*see* CEO)
Chief information officer
   and corporate data base 484
Competition 15–21
Computer graphics
   end-user issues 816–817
   for personal computers 813–814
   hard-copy graphics 811–812
   software 814–816
Computer literacy
   personal computers 295–302
   program implementation 300–301
Conferencing 145–146
Controls
   corporate data base 481–488
   EDP auditing 651–660
   network processing 364
   personal computing 303–309
Corporate data base
   control 481–488
   management 483–488
Corporate information policies
   access control 46–47
   auditing 45–46
   cost allocation 46

Index-1

issues 41–43
MIS charter 44–45
MIS steering committee charter 45
policy statements 43–44
Cost/benefit analysis
    performing 257–269
    planning 249–255
Cost control
    centralization vs decentralization 119, 121
CPM
    project scheduling techniques 271–281
Critical success factors
    use in information management 19–20

D

Data administration
    centralization vs decentralization 497–499
    corporate data base 484–485
Data base management
    centralization vs decentralization 489–500
    control 481–488
    corporate information system model 476–477
    cost considerations 479–480
    data administration 477–478
    data consistency 508
    data integrity 509
    data redundancy 501–507
    organizational issues 471–475
    quality of data 501–509
    relational data bases 511–523
    selection criteria 478–479
Data bases
    centralization vs decentralization 489–500
    control 481–488
    corporate 483–488
    data dictionary 497–498
    development 483–488
    relational 511–523
Data center
    auditing 662–663
    career planning 421–430

design checklist 455–467
security audit 669–688
standards manual 409–414
work scheduling alternatives 431–435
Data communications
    communications lines 348–349
    fiber optics 791–800
    front ends 353–354
    line configurations 347
    integrating with voice 369–382
    line-sharing devices 351–353
    local area networks 399–405
    modems 349–350
    needs assessment 384–389
    network planning 354–355, 357–367, 383–384
    network security 639–647
    productivity improvements 754–755
    software 353–354
    terminals 350–351
    transmission modes 347–348
Data dictionary system
    planning 768–770
    reports 772–773
    use of preprocessor 770–772
    use in systems development 773–775
Data security *(see also Security)*
    auditing 663–664
    management tactics 621–624
    operational tactics 625–628
    standards 629–638
Data/voice integration
    advantages and disadvantages 371–374
    equipment 380–382
    implementation 376–380
    planning 370–371, 376
Decision support systems
    acquisitions 314–315
    administration 315–316
    applications 312–313
    characteristics 311–312
    development 313–314
Dial-up lines
    access control 639–647
Distributed processing
    network planning 357–367

DP operations *(see also Data center)*
   centralization vs decentralization 124–125

E

EDP auditor
   in quality assurance 709–710
   role of 651–660
   use of 689–698
End user computing *(see Personal computing)*
End users *(see Users)*
Ergonomics
   in office automation 325–331
Expert systems 828–831

F

Fiber optics
   applications 796–797
   benefits 792–796
   cost analysis 798
   definition 791–792
   performance 797–798
   system planning 799–800

G

Graphics *(see Computer graphics)*

H

Hardware
   from multiple vendors 415–420
   resource planning 23–39
HRM systems 527–537
Human resource management systems *(see HRM systems)*
Human resources *(see Personnel)*

I

Information center
   benefits 287
   definition 285
   establishing 290–294
   keys to success 289–291
   impact on MIS organization 294
   MIS and user responsibilities 285–287
   risks 290
Information retrieval
   in office environment 144–145
Information technology
   role of CEO 73–78
Information transfer
   in office environment 145
Interviews
   techniques 547–557

L

Local area networks
   environmental control 405
   identification/authentication control 339
   keys 400–403
   passwords 400
   security 399–405
   security devices 403–405

M

Management by objectives
   action plan 82–85
   concepts 79–82
   counseling and coaching 86–88
   management contracts 82–85
   reasons for failure 88–90
Management techniques
   management by objectives 79–90
   productivity improvements 758–759
Manuals
   data center standards 409–414
   MIS procedures 49–70
Microcomputers *(see Personal computing)*
Micrographics 807–808
MIS charter 44–45
MIS organization
   audit of 661–668
   business considerations 739–743

centralization vs decentralization 117–129
impact on information center 294
integrating data/voice communications 378–379
integrating information technologies 146–147
network planning and control 359
procedures 49–70
productivity improvements 756–758
project management 131–140
steering committees 91–98
succession planning 559–573
MIS steering committees 91–98
  charter 45
  permanent 92–97
  project 97–98
Motivational techniques 575–583
  management by objectives 79–90

N

Network planning 354–355
  issues 389–397
  steps 383–384
Network processing
  implementation 363–365
  management perspective 359
  planning 360–362
  reasons for implementation 357–359

O

Office automation
  ergonomics 325–331
  growth stages 335–336
  integration with DP 141–148
  management strategies 319–323, 343
  organizational placement 337–338
  planning 333–344
  productivity improvements 761–768
  research study on 334–340
  staffing 338
  tactics 338–339
  tools 333–334

P

Passwords
  for local area networks 400
Personal computing
  computer literacy 295–302
  control issues 303–309
  decision support systems 311–317
  graphics 812–814
  information center 285–294
  training 295–302
Personnel
  career counseling 563
  career planning 534–535, 561–563
  data center careers 421–430
  data center staffing 431–435
  EEOC guidelines 541–545
  evaluation 539–540
  interviewing 547–557
  introducing policies and procedures 53–54
  management 527–537
  management by objectives 79–90
  management skill categories 571–573
  motivation 575–583
  new employee handbook 63–65
  organizational needs analysis 536
  performance appraisal 534
  position descriptions 531–532
  productivity improvements 755–756
  security awareness program 599–607
  skills assessment 533–534
  skills definitions 532–533
  succession planning 559–573
  testing 539–545
  training program 537

PERT
    project scheduling techniques 271-281
Physical security
    vulnerability survey 609-619
Planning
    application systems 151-160
    centralization vs decentralization 117-129
    centralized vs decentralized data bases 489-500
    chargeback systems 99-113
    competitive use of information 15-21
    corporate information policies 41-48
    cost/benefit analysis 249-255, 257-270
    data center design 455-467
    data center security 669-688
    data dictionary system 768-770
    data security 621-628
    improving MIS productivity 745-759
    integrating data/voice communications 374-376
    integrating information techniques 141-148
    integrating multiple vendors 415-420
    MIS steering committees 91-98
    network processing 357-367
    office automation 333-344
    policies and procedures 49-70
    quality assurance 711-714
    quality management 706-709
    resource 23-39
    strategic 3-14
    succession 559-573
Policies
    corporate information 41-48
    introducing 53-54
Power *(see Uninterruptible power supply)*
Procedures
    administration 51-52
    corporate information 47
    developing 54-57
    interpreting 52-53
    introducing 53-54
    manuals 60-70
    sample 57-60
Procedures manuals
    developing 54-57
    guidelines 60-65
    new employee handbook 63-65
    sample table of contents 66-70
Productivity
    MIS as a business 739-743
    recommended MIS practices 745-759
    use of office technology 761-766
Project management
    advantages and disadvantages 135-136
    definition 131-132
    office automation 319-323
    organization and staffing 136-138
    PERT/CPM techniques 271-281
    software engineering techniques 219-247
    verification & validation 232-236, 723-736
Project scheduling techniques PERT/CPM 271-281
Prototyping
    systems implementation 185-187

Q

Quality assurance
    during operation/maintenance 720-721
    in systems development 701-710
    planning 711-714
    procedures 714-720
    staffing 713-714
    tasks 712
    technical responsibilities 712-713

R

Redundancy
    forms of 501-505

minimizing 505–507
quantifying 505
Relational data base systems
    benefits 518–521
    capabilities 513–516
    concepts 513, 518
    definition 511–513
    languages 516–517
Reprographics 144
Resource planning and control
    load duration analysis 24–32
    need projection 32–34
    peak load management 32
    productivity improvements 746–748
Robotics 779–790

S

Security *(see also Data security)*
    classifying information assets 588–595
    data center 669–688
    for local area networks 399–405
    in dial-up environment 639–647
    management responsibilities 605–607
    MIS role in 587–588
    overview 587–591
    personnel issues 599–607
    physical 609–619
    protection program 595–597
    training methods 602–605
    vulnerability survey 609–619
Software
    performance measurement 239–240
    quality assurance 711–721
    verification & validation 232–236, 723–736
Software engineering
    management techniques 225–239
    performance measurement 239–240
    programming techniques 236–239

software life cycle 220–225
system specifications 240–241
use of personal workstations 241–242
verification & validation 232–236, 723–736
Speech recognition technology 819–826
Standards
    data center 409–414
    data security 629–638
    improving 750–751
Strategic planning 3–14
    advantages 6–7
    centralization vs decentralization 117–129
    CEO role in information technology 73–78
    competitive use of information 15–21
    corporate information policies 41–48
    guidelines 10–13
    MIS steering committees 91–98
    planning process 7–10
Structured analysis 199–204
Structured design 204–207
Structured programming 209–212
Structured techniques
    analysis 199–204
    benefits 194–197
    design 204–207
    effect on software life cycle 192–193
    generalized system architecture 182–183
    methodology 189–198
    programming 209–212
    reasons for 190–192
    systems reviews 214–216
    testing 212–214
Structured testing 212–214
Succession planning 559–573
System reviews 214–216
Systems design and implementation
    productivity improvements 751–754

Systems development
    application priorities 161–172
    application systems planning 151–160
    audit of 664–665
    centralization vs decentralization 118–119, 121, 126–127
    corporate information policy 42–43
    cost/benefit analysis 249–255, 257–270
    data dictionary system 773–775
    generalized architecture 182–183
    implementation 173–187
    life cycle 174–180, 220–225
    management techniques 225
    office automation 319–323
    productivity improvements 751–754
    programming techniques 236–239
    prototypes 185–187
    quality assurance 701–710, 711–721
    software engineering 219–247
    software performance measures 239–240
    structured analysis and design 199–208
    structured methodology 189–198
    structured programming & testing 209–217
    transition systems 184–185
    user involvement 180–182
    verification & validation 232–236, 723–736

T

Technology
    artificial intelligence 827–835
    computer graphics 811–818
    fiber optics 791–800
    micrographics 807–808
    optical disk 801–809
    robotics 779–790
    speech recognition and voice response 819–826
Terminals
    data communications 350–351
Testing
    of MIS personnel 539–545
Training
    network processing 364–365
    personal computers 295–302
    security awareness program 602–605
Transition systems 184–185

U

Uninterruptible power supply (UPS)
    definition 437
    evaluation 438–440
    functions 437–438
    glossary 449–453
    installation 445–449
    selection 440–445
Users
    as customers 739–741
    improving service 648–750
    involvement in systems development 180–182

V

Value
    of information 249–253
    of information systems 17–18
    of information technology 74–76
Vendors
    multiple 415–420
Voice communications
    integrating with data 369–382
Voice response technology 819–826
Vulnerability survey 609–619

W

Word processing
    applications 142–146
    integration with DP 141–148

The Handbook of MIS Management